THE IMPOSSIBLE H. L. MENCKEN

Dedicated to the working journalist

Contents

CONTENTS

THOUGHTS ON EATING

MUSIC

THE AMERICAN LANGUAGE

THE NATIONAL LETTERS

ON LITERARY GENTS

CONTENTS

Foreword

GORE VIDAL

After politics, journalism has always been the preferred career of the ambitious but lazy second-rater. American exceptions to mediocrity's leaden mean: From column A, there was Franklin D. Roosevelt. From column B, H. L. Mencken.

Although Henry Louis Mencken was a magazine editor (*The Smart Set, The American Mercury*), a literary critic, an expositor of Nietzsche, and a school of Samuel Johnson compiler of *The American Language*, he never ceased to be a journalist for the *Sunpapers* in his hometown of Baltimore, where he was born in 1880 and where he died in 1956. From 1906 to 1948, he was connected with the Baltimore *Sun*, as a columnist, feature writer, editor. He was the most influential journalist of his day; he was also the wittiest.

As a working journalist, Mencken took as his lifelong subject nothing less than Freedom's land and Bravery's home, the (not so very) United States, where flourished such gorgeous clowns as Calvin Coolidge; "The Great Croon of Croons," Franklin D. Roosevelt; the not-so-great Great Commoner, William Jennings Bryan; and many, many others. But if only God could have invented such a cast, it was Mencken who proved to be God's most attentive and appreciative drama critic. It was Mencken who described the show. He reveled in absurdity; found no bonnet entirely bee-less. He loved the national bores for their own sweet sake.

As he contemplated the meager lives of our dull presidents, he wrote: "There comes a day of public ceremonial, and a chance to make a speech. . . . A million voters with IQs below 60 have their ears glued to the radio. It takes four days' hard work to concoct a speech without a sensible word in it. Next a dam must be opened somewhere. Four dry Senators get drunk and make a painful scene. The Presidential automobile runs over a dog. It rains."

American journalism's golden (a kinder adjective than "yellow") age coincided with Mencken's career; that is, from century's turn to mid-century's television. During this period, there was still a public educational system and although Mencken often laughs at the boobs out there, the average person could probably get through a newspaper without numb lips. Today, half the American population no longer reads newspapers: plainly, they are the clever half.

For Mencken, the old-time journalist, or "newsie," was a combination of François Villon and Shane. He was "wild-cattish." He was free-lance, a knight for hire. In 1927, Mencken was already looking back nostalgically to the time when a journalist "used to make as much as a bartender or a police sergeant"; now "he makes as much as the average doctor or lawyer, and his wife, if he has one, maybe has social ambitions." Today, of course, the "journalist" is often paid movie-star prices for movie-star appearances on television or along the lecture circuit, and he needs no wife to inspire him to a cozy lunch *à deux* with Nancy Reagan or Barbara Bush.

Mencken did acknowledge that, even then, some journalists liked to mingle with the wealthy and the powerful but, for him, there was always a greater fascination in those lower depths where dwell bartenders and police sergeants.

Mencken's ideal popular paper for that vast public which "gets all its news by listening" (today one would change "listening" to "staring"—at television) would be "printed throughout, as First Readers are printed, in words of one syllable. It should avoid every idea beyond the understanding of a boy of ten" on the ground that "all ideas are beyond them. They can grasp only events." But they will heed only those events that are presented as drama in "the form of combat, and it must be a very simple combat with one side clearly right and the other clearly wrong. They can no more imagine neutrality than they can imagine the fourth dimension." Thus, Mencken anticipated not only the television news program but the television political campaign with its combative thirty-second spot commercials and sound-bites. Movies were already showing the way, and Mencken acknowledged the wisdom of the early movie magnates whose simpleminded screened *agons* had made them rich. Unfortunately, once rich, they pined for culture, against which Mencken sternly warns with his famous injunction: "No one in this world, so far as I know—and I have researched the records for years, and employed agents to help me —has ever lost money by underestimating the intelligence of the great masses of the plain people. Nor has anyone ever lost public office thereby."

Today, Mencken's boisterous style and deadpan hyperboles are very difficult even for "educated" Americans to deal with, and Sanskrit to the generality. Although every American has a sense of humor—it is his birthright and encoded somewhere in the Constitution—few Americans have ever been able to cope with wit or irony, and even the simplest jokes often cause unease, especially today, when every phrase must be examined for covert sexism, racism, ageism.

American character (which does and does not exist) fascinated Mencken, who observed, in 1918, that the universal image of Uncle Sam the money-grubber was mistaken. "The character that actually marks off the American is not money-hunger at all; it is what might be called, at the risk of misunderstanding, social aspiration." For the American, money plays only a part in moving upward "to break down some barrier of caste, to secure the acceptance of his betters." Unlike Europe, "no one has a station" (so far as he knows, of course: class is a national dirty secret) "unless he makes it for himself." Of course Mencken lived in simpler times. For the American of 1918, "there is always something just behind him and tantalizing him, menacing him and causing him to sweat."

Mencken quotes Wendell Phillips. "More than any other people, we Americans are afraid of one another." Mencken acknowledges this truth, and he puts it down to the desire to conform, which means howling with the rest of the mindless pack as it careens from nowhere to nowhere in pursuit of such instant enemies of the week as Qaddafi, Noriega, Saddam, put in place by our packmeisters, successively, like that mechanical rabbit used to keep racing dogs on course. For this sense of collective security, the individual must sacrifice himself in order "to belong to something larger and safer than he is," and he can "work off his steam within prudent limits. Beyond lie the national taboos. Beyond lie true independence and the heavy penalties that go therewith."

A century earlier, that shrewd passerby Tocqueville also noted the force of the majority on the individual to conform. But Mencken was obliged to live a lifetime in such a society and so, unlike the French penologist, he could present data from inside the slammer: "The taboos that I have mentioned are extraordinarily harsh and numerous. They stand around nearly every subject that is genuinely important to man: they hedge in free opinion and experimentation on all sides. Consider, for example, the matter of religion. It is debated freely and furiously in almost every country in the world save the United States," but here the critic is silenced. "The result is that all religions are equally safeguarded against criticism, and that all of them lose vitality. We protect the status quo, and so make steady war upon revision and improvement."

In August 1925, Mencken meditated on how Europeans view Americans, and how they noted "our growing impatience with the free play of ideas, our increasing tendency to reduce all virtues to the single one of conformity, our relentless and all pervading standardization. . . . Europe doesn't fear our military or economic prowess, rather it is Henry Ford that gives them the shivers. . . . By Americanization it means Fordization—and not only in industry but also in politics, art and even religion." Nor is this simply the spontaneous power of public opinion; it is the deliberate power of the state brought into play. "No other nation of today is so rigorously policed. The lust to standardize and regulate extends to the most trivial minutia of private life."

At the time that Mencken wrote this, alcohol had been prohibited by law to the American people, as well as almost every form of sex, disturbing reading matter, and so on. Mencken also adverted to the Scopes Trial of that year, whose verdict forbade the teaching of Darwin's theory of evolution in the schools of Christian Tennessee. This trial convinced thoughtful Europeans that Americanism was "a conspiracy of dull and unimaginative men, fortuitously made powerful, against all the ideas and ideals that

BOOKS BY MARION ELIZABETH RODGERS

Mencken and Sara: A Life in Letters
The Impossible H. L. Mencken

seem sound to their betters," leading the Europeans to suspect "that a nation cherishing such notions and feelings, and with the money and the men to enforce them, deserved to be watched very carefully."

As a first-generation American, Mencken liked playing the vaudeville German, with a passion for beer, Brahms, German culture. "My grandfather made a mistake when he came to America, and I have always lived in the wrong country." Like so many echt Americans, Mencken deeply resented the British. Not only did he share in the tribal dislike of Teuton for Anglo but he resented the ease with which the Brits manipulated American politics in their favor at the time of the two World Wars. During the First World War, Mencken's pro-Germanism got him banned from the *Sun*. But despite Mencken's somewhat stagy dislike of Brits, socialism, radicals, the "Anglo-maniacal" Woodrow Wilson, and the reformers Franklin and Eleanor Roosevelt, he tended to make very good *patriotic* sense of American politics.

Mencken notes that from the start of the republic, "setting aside religion, [politics] was literally the only concern of the people. All men of ability and ambition turned to it for self-expression." This is wondrously wise and an echo of Pericles' comment that the man who thinks politics not his business has no business. In the eighteenth and early nineteenth centuries, politics drew "the best literary talent into its service—Franklin, Jefferson and Lincoln may well stand as examples—it left the cultivation of belles lettres to women and second-rate men." Now, of course, the second-raters have taken over politics. As for beautiful letters . . .

Mencken's alarm at our system's degradation was in no way based upon a starry-eyed notion of the revered but always circumvented Constitution. Although that long-ignored primer says that only Congress may declare war, President Bush has only recently confided to us that "we have fought 204 wars of which only five were declared," so put that in your peace pipe and smoke it! Mencken would not have been startled. For him, "all government, in its essence, is organized exploitation, and in virtually all of its existing forms it is the implacable enemy of every industrious and well-disposed man." This must have got a good chuckle from the Baltimore burgher over his breakfast of chipped beef and scrapple.

Mencken continues. Government "invades his liberty and collars his money in order to protect him, but in actuality, it always makes a stiff profit on the exchange. This profit represents the income of the professional politicians, nine-tenths of whom are professional rogues." That was then. The rogues are smoother now and often endearing on television. They are also no longer paid for by such chicken feed as kickbacks on city contracts. Rather, they are the proud employees of the bankers and the military industrial procurers who have bought them their offices, both square and oval. But though we are worse off than in Mencken's day, he was at least able to give one cheer for the Constitution, or at least for the idea of such a document, as a kind of stoplight: "So far you may go, but no further. No matter what excuse or provocation, you may not invade certain rights, or pass certain kinds of laws."

Inevitably, Mencken's journalism is filled with stories of how our enumerated rights are constantly being evaded or struck down because it is the reflexive tactic of the politicians "to invade the Constitution stealthily, and then wait to see what happens. If nothing happens they go on more boldly; if there is a protest they reply hotly that the Constitution is worn out and absurd, and that progress is impossible under the dead hand. This is the time to watch them especially."

Mencken also notes that in the first decade of this century there was "a sudden change. . . . Holes began to be punched in the Bill of Rights, and new laws of strange and often fantastic shape began to slip through them. The hysteria of the late war completed the process. The espionage act enlarged the holes to great fissures. Citizens began to be pursued into their houses, arrested without warrants, and jailed without any form of trial. The ancient writ of habeas corpus was suspended: the Bill of Rights was boldly thrown overboard."

Although the extent of the decadence of the democratic process at our end of the century was unknown, if not unsuspected, to Mencken, he knew enough of history and its engine, entropy, to declare that "no government, of its own motion, will increase its own weakness, for that would mean to acquiesce in its own destruction . . . governments, whatever their pretensions otherwise, try to preserve themselves by holding the individual down. . . . Government itself, indeed, may be reasonably defined as a conspiracy against him. Its one permanent aim, whatever its form, is to hobble him sufficiently to maintain itself." As a self-styled "Presbyterian Tory" (with Manichean tendencies),

Mencken regarded attempts at reform as doomed, while the thought of any Utopian system bettering things caused him deep distress because to create Utopia you would have to enslave more and more people in order to better—while worsening—their lot.

Curiously enough, of all those good and bad Americans who shuddered at the sudden sharp wind from the east known as communism, Mencken, as early as 1930, figured that there was no way that communism could ever set up shop within our alabaster cities much less take sickle to our fruited plains. Mencken's reasoning is exquisitely sound: "That Americans, in the mass, have anything properly describable as keen wits is surely far from self-evident. On the contrary, it seems likely that, if anything, they lie below the civilized norm." Incidentally, for several decades I have been trying to convince Europeans that Americans are not innately stupid but merely ignorant and that with a proper educational system, et cetera. But the more one reads Mencken, the more one eyes suspiciously the knuckles of his countrymen, looking to see callouses from too constant a contact with the greensward.

Mencken believes Americans to be more gullible than most people, dwelling as we do in "the home of freak economic schemes" (often, alas, contagious) and "the happy hunting ground of the most blatant and absurd sort of charlatans in politics." From this intimate knowledge of the American "mind," Mencken thinks that Americans, as lovers of "the bizarre and the irrational would embrace communism with joy, just as multitudes of them, in a previous age, embraced free silver. But, as everyone knows, they will have none of it." Mencken concedes the attraction of Utopias to the foreign-born and educated Americans, but "two-thirds of the native-born Communists that I have encountered are so plainly *mashuggah* that it would be flattery to call them stupid."

Mencken gives two reasons for the failure of communism/socialism to take root in the United States. The first is that Americans had long since been vaccinated by the likes of Bryan and Theodore Roosevelt against this sort of virus: in effect, the folks had been there before and they were aware of so "gross" a social and economic solution. Mencken's second reason strikes me as not only true but inspired. Americans were more sensitive to "the concrete debacle in Russia" because "they probably felt themselves, in a subtle and unconscious way, to be nearer to the Russians than any Europeans. Russia was not like Europe, but it was strangely like America. In the same way the Russians were like

Americans. They, too, were naturally religious and confiding; they, too, were below the civilized average in intelligence; and they, too, believed in democracy, and were trying to give it a trial."

For Mencken, communist literature was "as childish as the literature of Christian Science," while communism itself "will probably disappear altogether when the Russian experiment comes to a climax, and Bolshevism either converts itself into a sickly imitation of capitalism or blows up with a bang. The former issue seems more likely." This is not bad for 1930.

As Mencken thought all government bad, it follows that he was a Jeffersonian who believed that the least we had of a bad thing the better. As "an incurable Tory in politics," he was congenitally antiliberal, though "I always give heed to them politely, for they are at least free men." Surprisingly, he has respectful words for Emma Goldman and Alexander Berkman, victims of federal persecution (it is not taught in our schools that once upon a time, at the behest of the Secretary of Labor, foreign-born Americans could be deported, without due process). Mencken finds the two radicals "extremely intelligent—[and] once their aberrant political ideals are set aside they are seen to be very sharp wits. They think clearly, unsentimentally and even a bit brilliantly. They write simple, glowing and excellent English." Mencken confesses that he cannot understand how they can believe so childishly in the proletariat, but "the fact that a human brain of high amperage, otherwise highly efficient, may have a hole in it is surely not a secret. All of us, in our several ways, are illogical, irrational, almost insane." Mencken's tolerance for the bees aswarm in the bonnets of others was very great if the swarm be honest and its honey pure.

The state as hostile tropism is Mencken's central philosophic notion as a journalist. Whether the state is used to deport or imprison people for their ideas or the color of their skin (as in the case of the Nisei) or simply to harass citizens who drink whisky, he was that malevolent state's hard critic. He illuminates our marvelous Bill of Rights, no sooner promulgated than struck with the first of those sets of alien and sedition acts that continue, in one form or another, to this day. He is very funny about the Noble Experiment to prohibit alcohol (1913–33), which made the United States the world's joke-nation, a title still unceded.

As for America's once triumphant mass-production of the automobile, he notes that this achievement promptly became a pretext for the persecution of the citizenry by creating "a body of laws which fills two courtrooms to suffocation every day (in Baltimore), and keeps three judges leaping and tugging like fire-engine horses. The situation is made more intoxicating by the fact that nine-tenths of the criminals are persons who would not otherwise fall into their toils—that the traffic regulations tap whole new categories of victims. . . . The ideal of the *Polizei*, at all times and everywhere, is to get their hands upon every citizen at least once a day." Today the tobacco smoker is at risk. Tomorrow, who knows who will fall victim to the state's endless sense of fun.

Like all good writers, Mencken is a dramatist, at his best when he shows us the ship of state in motion on high seas while his character studies of the crew of this ship of fools still give delight, though every last one now lies full fathom five. Ding dong dell.

As a reporter, Mencken covered many political conventions from 1904 to 1948. As a Baltimore *Sun* columnist, he wrote about national politics whenever the spirit moved or, indeed, shoved him. In 1925 he was amused, as always, by the collapse yet again of the Liberals and their journals: "*The Nation* gradually abandons Liberalism for libertarianism. *The New Republic* hangs on, but is obviously not as vigorous and confident as it used to be." Mencken delighted in "Dr. Coolidge," Liberalism's natural enemy. But then "a politician has no actual principles. He is in favor of whatever seems to him to be popular at the moment." Even so, Coolidge "believes naturally in Law Enforcement—by lawful means if possible: if not, by any means at hand, lawful or lawless . . . he actually got his first considerable office . . . by posturing as a fascist of the most advanced type." This was in 1919 when Governor Coolidge of Massachusetts broke the Boston police strike and became famous.

But Coolidge is only an engaging character actor in a drama whose star throughout is William Jennings Bryan (Democratic candidate for President 1896, 1900, 1908—spokesman or -person for free silver and the common person—or man). Bryan had become famous and popular and dangerous to the status quo when he put together a huge coalition of poor farmers and poorer laborers and, in their interest, spoke against the rich and their gold standard. Bryan gave the country's ownership its first big scare since the rebellion of Daniel Shays. Alas, Mencken was not at the convention in '96, when with a single speech ("You shall not crucify mankind upon a cross of gold!") Bryan got the nomination at the age of thirty-six. As his friend and ally, my grandfather, used to say, "He never learned anything else ever again in his life."

As much as Mencken despised Bryan, the demagogue, he is moderately touched by Bryan's appearance at the 1904 convention "in his familiar alpaca coat and his old white string tie," looking "weak and haggard" (he was suffering from pneumonia) until he started to speak and brought down the house, yet again. Four years later he would be the doomed nominee: four years after that, Wilson made him his Secretary of State, a post he resigned when he saw that the Administration was moving toward war, an act of principle that Mencken rather meanly does not credit in a man he calls "the magnificent job-seeker."

At the end, Mencken was present in Dayton, Tennessee for the Scopes Trial, where the old man seemed "maleficent" to Mencken when he spoke for superstition and the literal interpretation of the Bible. Bryan and the Bible won the day, but Bryan himself was dead a few weeks later, killed, my grandmother always said, by an ungovernable passion for "chicken and rice and gravy."

For Mencken, Bryan is the *id*—to use Freudian jargon—of American politics: the ignorant, religious, underclass leader whose fateful and dramatic climax came in the trial to determine whether or not we are descended from monkeys. Herbert Hoover is the *ego*; he also represents the British interest, forever trying to draw the great stupid republic into their wars and combinations. Calvin Coolidge is a near-fascist clown whose career is "as appalling and as fascinating as a two-headed boy." Warren G. Harding is the master of a glorious near-English in which "the relations between word and meaning have long since escaped him." Harding's style "reminds me of a string of wet sponges; it reminds me of tattered washing on the line; it reminds me of stale bean soup, of college yells, of dogs barking idiotically through endless nights. It is so bad that a sort of grandeur creeps into it." Mencken's descriptions of these wondrous clowns are still a delight because, though the originals are long since erased from the collective "memory" of the United States of Amnesia, the types persist. "I am not not," Mencken observes demurely at one point, when blood is on the walls, "a constructive critic."

For Mencken, "the best of [politicians] seem to be almost as bad as the worst. As private citizens they are often highly intelligent and realistic men, and admirable in every way." But because of the superstitious mass, they are not allowed to make sense. "When they accomplish anything, it is usually by accident." Even of his sometime hero, Al Smith, he deplored his speeches but then, "like all habitual orators, he plainly likes to make speeches, no matter how dull the subject or hot the hall."

Mencken is quite aware that behind the diverting spectacle of our politics stands the ownership of the country, Business. He understands the general preference of the Business-boss for the Lawyer-employee in politics. Partly it is because "a lawyer practising his craft under Anglo-Saxon jurisprudence becomes a pedant almost inevitably. The system he follows is expressly designed to shut out common sense," which is just as well because "Big Business, in America, is almost wholly devoid of anything even poetically describable as public spirit. It is frankly on the make. . . . Big Business was in favor of Prohibition, believing that a sober workman would made a better slave than one with a few drinks in him. It was in favor of all the gross robberies and extortions that went on in the [First] war," and profited by the curtailment of civil liberties and so on. Coolidge was their man; so was Herbert Hoover, "the perfect self-seeker. . . . His principles are so vague that even his intimates seem unable to put them into words. . . . He knows who his masters are, and he will serve them."

Mencken is also aware that there is a small but constant resistance to the "masters," but he gives the resistance little aid or comfort. Essentially, he is on the side of Business if not Businessmen because "business is the natural art of the American people." He pities those with "believing minds" who would follow this or that demagogue, and he lived long enough to attend the 1948 convention of the Progressive Party, where Henry Wallace picked up the banner marked Nay; but Mencken was put off not so much by the poignant, plaintive "nay" as he was by the coloring of the letters, red.

Even so, the Tory Mencken understands the roots of radicalism. Although "it is assumed that men become radicals because they are naturally criminal, or because they have been bribed by Russian gold," what actually moves them "is simply the conviction that the Government they suffer under is unbearably and incurably corrupt. . . . The notion that a radical is one who hates his country is naive and usually idiotic. He is, more likely, one who likes his country more than the rest of us, and is thus more disturbed than the rest of us when he sees it debauched. He is not a bad citizen turning to crime; he is a good citizen driven to despair." But Mencken himself is no radical because "I believe that all government is evil, and that trying to improve it is largely a waste of time. But that is certainly not the common American view. . . . When they see an evil they try to remedy it—by peaceful means if possible, and if not, then by force." Yet, paradoxically, Mencken can also write that "history . . . is the upward struggle of man, out of darkness and into light," presumably a struggle with ooze alone.

Eventually, Franklin Delano Roosevelt would appear to be the answer to the radicals' dream and Mencken regarded him, at the beginning, with a cold but not disapproving eye as FDR metamorphosed from a John the Baptist for Al Smith to the Christ himself, or the national *super-ego*. With some pleasure, Mencken described the Democratic convention that nominated FDR for Vice President, largely because he bore the name of a famous Republican President. Also, he was chosen to "perfume the ticket." As "leader of the anti-Tammany Democrats in New York," he could be counted on "to exorcise the Tammany split from the party." Finally, "he is a civilized man and safely wet."

When FDR's turn came at Chicago in 1932, Mencken wrote, "I can recall no candidate of like importance who ever had so few fanatics whooping for him." But Mencken allowed that FDR was good on radio, and he smiled a lot. By the 1940 convention, Mencken was hostile not only to the New Deal but to the approaching war. To Mencken, 1940 looked like a rerun of 1916, when Wilson had campaigned as "the man who kept us out of war." Politics being nothing if not imitative of what has worked before, he glumly observed that "Roosevelt himself has promised categorically, on at least a dozen occasions, to keep out of the war, and with the most pious and eye-rolling solemnity" even though "his foreign policy . . . has been unbrokenly devious, dishonest and dishonorable. Claiming all the immunities of a neutral, he has misled the country into countless acts of war, and there is scarcely an article of international law that he has not violated." But Roosevelt won the election. And the war came.

Roosevelt's opponent in the election of 1940 was Wendell Willkie, an eloquent "barefoot boy," as they called him, "from Wall Street," with a Hoosier accent and considerable demagogic skills. Just before he was nominated, I shook his limp hand, and he glared at me with blind eyes in a white sweating face and croaked, "Ah'd be a lah-er if ah said ah diduhn wanna be Prez Nigh Stays." The only occasion where I gazed as Mencken gazed upon the same political spectacle was the Republican convention at Philadelphia where Willkie was nominated. This was in June 1940 and I was guide to my blind grandfather, former Senator T. P. Gore. A Democrat, TPG was not about to miss any convention that might be fun. On a hot evening, we rode to the convention hall in a streetcar with former Vice President Charles G. Dawes, a bright, crickety little man, wearing a white straw hat. At the hall, the heat was dreadful. Young women gave out palmetto fans with "Fan for Van" written on them; thus, the great moose of Michigan, Senator Arthur H. Vandenberg, majestically hurled himself into the ring. Senator Robert A. Taft was also a candidate. He was, even then, known as "Mr. Conservative." Twelve years later, when he was denied the nomination in favor of D. D. Eisenhower, he let slip a terrible truth that no Republican can be nominated for President without the permission of the Chase Manhattan Bank.

We sat in the bleachers to stage left of the podium, where stood the former President, Herbert Hoover, face like a rosy marshmallow. Carefully, I described the scene for my blind grandfather; he had entered political history not only as the first senator from the new state of Oklahoma but as the orator who had started the longest demonstration ever recorded at any convention (for Bryan, at Denver, 1908). TPG was one of the few speakers that Mencken could endure, noting that in 1928, when he "rose to second the nomination of his old friend, Senator Reed, there was humor in his brief speech, and also a very impressive earnestness. He won the crowd instantly and got a great round of applause. No other rhetorician came near his mark."

Hoover "stood before the mike like a schoolboy reciting a piece, and seldom varied his intonation or made a gesture." Mencken brings it all alive to me a half-century later, though he finds Hoover paler than I did but then I had never seen the President before —or since. I was deeply impressed by Hoover's rigid gravitas. But my grandfather, whose wit and politics were not unlike Mencken's, after listening to the ovation for the ex-President, said, "Hoover's the only man here who doesn't know that he's finished."

As the galleries chanted, "We want Willkie," I became addicted to the convention as then practiced and it is ironic that in 1968,

THE IMPOSSIBLE H. L. MENCKEN

thanks to some television "debates" with a right-wing publicist, I should have helped preside over the transformation of the party conventions from the comings-together of the nation's tribes to a series of low-rated TV specials. No one can now say, with Mencken, "Me, I like [conventions] because they amuse me. I never get tired of the show . . . so unimaginably exhilarating and preposterous that one lives a gorgeous year in an hour."

Currently, any use of the word "race" in the United States is considered an *a priori* proof of the user's racism. Abstract nouns are now subject to close scrutiny to make sure that the noun's deployer is not a racist or sexist or ageist or bigot. Meanwhile, any word or phrase that might cause distress must undergo erasure while euphemism (the E-—or is it U- or Eu-—word?) is the order of the day, as "body bag" suddenly becomes, in Pentagonese, "human remains pouch" since "pouch" is a resolutely cheery word, suggesting cute marsupials Down Under, while "bag" is a downer, as in "bag lady," Munich, appeasement, Hitler. A babble of words that no one understands now fills the airwaves, and language loses all meaning as we sink slowly, mindlessly, into herstory rather than history because most rapists are men, aren't they?

Mencken is a nice antidote. Politically, he is often right but seldom correct by today's stern standards. In a cheery way, he dislikes most minorities and if he ever had a good word to say about the majority of his countrymen, I have yet to come across it. Recently, when his letters were published, it was discovered that He Did Not Like the Jews, and that he had said unpleasant things about them not only as individuals but In General, plainly the sign of a Hitler-Holocaust enthusiast. So shocked was everyone that even the *New York Review of Books'* unofficial de-anti-Semitiser, Garry Wills (he salvaged Dickens, barely), has yet to come to his aid with An Explanation. But in Mencken's private correspondence, he also snarls at black Americans, Orientals, Britons, women, and WASPs, particularly the clay-eating Appalachians, whom he regarded as subhuman. But private irritability is of no consequence when compared to what really matters, public action.

Far from being an anti-Semite, Mencken was one of the first journalists to denounce the persecution of the Jews in Germany at a time when the New York *Times*, say, was notoriously reticent. On November 27, 1938, Mencken writes (Baltimore *Sun*), "It is to be hoped that the poor Jews now being robbed and mauled in

Germany will not take too seriously the plans of various politicians to rescue them." He then reviews the various schemes to "rescue" the Jews from the Nazis, who had not yet announced their own final solution.

To the British proposal that the Jews be admitted to British Guiana, Teutonophile Mencken thinks that the *Ostjuden might* hack it in British Guiana but not the German Jews, as "they constitute an undoubtedly superior group. . . . Try to imagine a German-Jewish lawyer or insurance man, or merchant, or schoolmaster [in] a place where the climate is that of a Turkish bath. . . ." Tanganyika he thought marginally better but still pretty bad, at least "as good as the worst parts of Mexico." He then suggests that Canada could "absorb 100,000 or even 200,000 with ease, and they would be useful acquisitions, especially in the western prairie populations, which are dominated today by a low-grade of farmers, without any adequate counterbalance of a competent middle class." Today Mencken could not write this because the Farmers Anti-Defamation League of Saskatchewan would be offended, and his column banned in Canada. "Australia, now almost as exclusive as Sing Sing, which it somewhat resembles in population, could use quite as many [Jews] as Canada and New Zealand." The Australian Government would, today, file a protest; and Mencken's column would be banned.

Then Mencken gets down to business: "The American plan for helping the refugees is less openly brutal than the British plan, but almost as insulting to them, and even more futile." After many official and unofficial condemnations of Germany, including "the Hon. Mr. Roosevelt's" declaration that "he could scarcely believe that such things could occur in a Twentieth Century civilization," the President is still not willing to relax the immigration laws or do anything "that might cause him political inconvenience." Mencken finds such "pecksniffery . . . gross and disgusting . . . and I hope that American Jews will not be fetched by it." Mencken also notes how the "Aframerican press" found amazing Roosevelt's solicitousness for German Jews, so unlike his complaisance to the ongoing crimes against black Americans.

Mencken concludes: "There is only one way to help the refugees, and that is to find places for them in a country in which they can really live. Why shouldn't the United States take in a couple of hundred thousand of them, or even all of them?" He notes two popular objections. One, there is already a lot of unemployment in the United States, to which he responds that it is unlikely the Jewish immigrants will either loaf or be incompetent. Two, there is anti-Semitism of the sort then being fanned by the Ku Klux Klan but, as he observes, "not many Jews are likely to go to Mississippi or Arkansas."

I am certain that those who wish to will be able to find anti-Semitism in Mencken's proposal to admit all Jewish refugees. Certainly he *generalizes* about Jews. (How does he know that they don't *all* want to go to Mississippi?) But then perhaps the whole message is code; certainly the remark about Jewish "efficiency" is a classic blood libel.

As of 1934, Mencken was moderately impressed by Eretz Israel and agreeably condescending to the Arabs, who "breed like flies but die in the same way." Mencken was generally approving of the European Jewish settlers, though he predictably cast a cold eye on the collectivist farms and kibbutzim. Of one of them, he wrote, presciently, "It was founded in 1921, and is still in the first flush of its success. Will it last? Probably not. As soon as its present kindergarteners grow up they will begin to marry outside, and then there will be quarrels over shares, and it will no doubt go the way of Brook Farm, Aman and all the other predecessors." Mencken thought that there was only a fifty-fifty chance of the Jewish plantation in Palestine enduring. "On the one hand (Er-e[t]z Israel) is being planted intelligently and shows every sign of developing in a healthy manner. But on the other hand there are the Arabs—and across the Jordan there is a vast reservoir of them, all hungry, all full of enlightened self-interest. Let some catastrophe in world politics take the British cops away, and the Jews who now fatten on so many lovely farms will have to fight desperately for their property and their lives." The catastrophe came right on schedule in the form of Hitler and of such professional Jewish terrorists as Begin and Shamir.

One of the few groups that Americans are fairly free to denounce, after the Arabs, are the Japanese. Mencken was most alert to "the yellow peril." (I used quotes to forestall the usual letters accusing me of hating all Orientals along with Mencken, when neither did nor does.) In 1939, Mencken was thinking seriously about Japan. As there is no public memory in the United States, let me remind the reader that since the Japanese victory over Russia in 1905, the United States had been preparing for a war with

Japan in order to establish who would be *numero uno* not only in
the Pacific but in Asia.

By 1939, Japan was busy conquering China, having acquired Korea and Manchuria, and the Nipponese imperial eye was set on
the Southeast Asian oil fields, at that time in the hands of two local
Asiatic powers, the British and the Dutch.

As a "racist," Mencken blithely generalized about race, a real
no-no in today's world, where each and every one of the five bil-
lion people on our common crowded planet is a treasured and
unique creation, sharing nothing at all with anyone else except,
maybe, the Big Fella in the Sky. But generalize he did, something
no longer allowed in freedom's land. Mencken wrote: "The Japanese, judged by Western eyes, are an extremely homely people,
and no doubt the fact has a good deal to do with their general
unpopularity." Mencken thought that they look both "sinister and
ludicrous," not an encouraging or likable combination. "They
look, talking one with another, like Boy Scouts with buck teeth,
wearing horn-rimmed spectacles. . . . I have never met a Caucasian who professed any affection for the Japs, though there are not
a few white fans for the scenery," etc. Already guilty of Racist
Generalizing, Mencken proceeded, sickeningly, to grade *all* Japanese: "They are a people of very considerable talents, and will
have to be reckoned with in the future history of the human race.
They have long since got past the stage of sitting respectfully at
the feet of the West. . . . In all the fields of human endeavor save
theology, politics and swine justice they are showing the way to
their ofay mentors. They have made important and durable contributions to knowledge in each and every one of the exact sciences, and they have taken such a lead in trade and industry that
the only way left to beat them is to murder them." But even this
solution, particularly favored by England, won't be easy because
they have "a considerable knack for war."

As "nearly all white men dislike the Japs and like the Chinese,"
Mencken tried to give an accurate impression of our soon-to-be
great adversary and, as I gaze out over the Hollywood Hills toward Japanese Universal Pictures, our eventual conquerors. But
accuracy in reporting on Pacific matters is always difficult because
the American press have always given us a view of the Japanese
that "is seldom accurate and not always honest," to say the least.
As of 1939, China and Chiang Kai-shek were, as always, on the
brink of victory; but, somehow, Japan always won and, as

Mencken remarked, "The Japs, in truth, had as sound a mandate to clean up China as the United States have had to clean up Cuba." Or Mexico, Nicaragua, Salvador, Panama, Grenada, not to mention Korea, Cambodia, Iran, and Iraq.

Three years later, the Japs, heavily provoked, sank the American fleet at Pearl Harbor and the great race war was on, with Round One (with guns) going to the white race (1945) and Round Two (with computers) going to the yellow race (1990). Mencken was particularly good—that is, prophetic—on American skullduggeries south of the border, where he often visited and duly noted our eerie inability to do anything honest or even intelligent, whether in Cuba or Haiti or in dealing with Nicaragua's Sandino.

Like Puck, Mencken found most mortals fools. He showed us odd glimpses of the vacuous Duke of Windsor and his Baltimore lady as well as of Rudolph Valentino, whom he once entertained in what must have been an unusually alcoholic session for a young Italian. Mencken commiserated with the assault by the press on the lad's manhood and he shed a public tear at the beauty's demise not long after.

In literary matters, Mencken was a shield to the meat and potatoes of naturalism-realism, a sounder diet than one of, shall we say, frozen fish? He was a champion of Dreiser; a foe of censorship. He was good on Conrad but at sea with James and insensitive to Wharton. He knew cooking and provided a sound recipe for "shore soup," the crab-based glory of the eastern shore of Maryland. He was passionate about music. Disliked jazz but admired "Aframerican" musicians. Interested in architecture, he was appalled by the ugliness of American cities except for San Francisco, where "there is nothing European about the way life is lived; the color is all Asiatic" because it is so happily cut off from "the rest of the dun and dour Republic." He described the average person's way of life in New York as that of a "sardine in a can," while "the grass in the so-called parks looks like embalmed sauerkraut." He hated chiropractors. He was amazed, as an editor, to find that graduates of West Point wrote the best English. He took a bitter pride in "the love of ugliness [that] is apparently inherent in the American people. They cherish and venerate the unspeakable."

Matthew Arnold wrote that a "style is the saying in the best way what you have to say. The what you have to say depends on your age." Mencken certainly said what he had to say about the age that he had been assigned to. When asked why, if he could find nothing to "revere" in the United States, he lived there, he replied, "Why do men go to zoos?"

Religion as generally practiced by the Americans of his day, he saw as a Great Wall of China designed to keep civilization out while barbarism might flourish within the gates. He himself was a resolute breacher of the Great Wall, and to the extent that some civilization has got through, he is one of the few Americans that we can thank. Plainly, so clear and hard a writer would not be allowed in the mainstream press of today, and those who think that they would like him back would be the first to censor and censure him.

As for Mencken himself, he wrote his own epitaph in 1921 for *The Smart Set*: "If, after I depart this vale, you ever remember me and have thought to please my ghost, forgive some sinner and wink your eye at some homely girl." I realize that he has, viciously, used the G-word and, even worse, the long-since-banned H-word. But there he is. And there we are, lucky we.

Introduction

"I am at my best in articles," H. L. Mencken once wrote, "written in heat and printed at once."[1] From 1899 to 1948, excepting two breaks during the two World Wars, Mencken reported on such diverse topics as the Scopes Trial, politicians, Prohibition, free speech, literature and language, and in the process, with his exuberant descriptions and outrageous opinions, helped shape our view of the American scene.

Of the approximately three thousand articles Mencken wrote for several major papers, "the stuff I wrote for the *Evening Sun* . . . included some of my best," he said, "and yet most of it is buried in their files."[2] The collection presented here consists of nearly two hundred articles taken from those files, primarily from the Baltimore *Evening Sun*, but also from the Baltimore *Sun*, the Chicago *Sunday Tribune*, the New York *Evening Mail*, and the New York *American*. The immediacy of the events he describes, couched in a distinctly American cadence reminiscent of Mark Twain, retains its appeal and humor even though these articles were published over sixty years ago.

Perhaps what will surprise many readers is the prescience of Mencken's assertions. As Stalin tightened his grip on the Soviet empire, Mencken predicted the collapse of communism. At a time when the logo "Made in Japan" was an object of derision, Mencken warned an overconfident America that mercantile Japan would be a force to be reckoned with in the near future. The new scheme of federal deposit insurance of banks, stated Mencken, worked only because "there have been very few bank failures. The next time we have a pestilence of them it will come to grief quickly enough, only because the taxpayer foots the bill."[3] In Palestine in 1934, where he observed Jewish immigrants cultivating the desert, he noted increasing resentment on the part of the Arabs: Jews "will have to fight for their property and their lives" if they are to stay, he warned.[4] Mencken told of the confusion between the sexes with the advent of feminism and the reordering of old codes of behavior. His observations reveal a native shrewdness and common sense. One day, Mencken predicted confidently, people would see that he was right.

* *

Henry Louis Mencken was born in Baltimore on September 12, 1880, the eldest son of August Mencken, a successful businessman of German descent who owned a thriving tobacco business, and in whose footsteps the young boy was expected to follow. A summer spent at neighboring Ellicott City put an end to such aspirations. The countryside did more for Mencken than introduce him to blackberries and dewberries, dogwood and chestnut, chiggers and poison oak: "it also determined the whole course of my life. For it was by gaping into the window of the old Ellicott City *Times* office that I got my first itch for journalism, and to that sad, but gaudy trade all my days have been devoted."[5]

There, he met his first hero. In the gloomy *Times* office he watched, entranced, while Josh Lynch, the stout pressman, hollered curses and rolled papers off the press. Lynch hardly noticed the thin, staring boy, whose bare legs were crisscrossed with bramble scratches, except to give him a glance now and then while he halted the press and took a chew of tobacco. Years later, he would be the assistant foreman of the Baltimore *Herald*'s composing room, and Mencken would be his managing editor.

The following Christmas the boy received a printing press, and spent the morning reproducing cards with his new pen name, "H. L. Mencken." Filching wrapping paper from the kitchen drawer, he printed his own weekly newspaper in imitation of the Ellicott City *Times*. At age sixteen, after the handpress had been relegated to a corner of the closet, he spent an afternoon in the bleachers of a stadium, scratching out a play-by-play report of a game between the Baltimore Orioles and the New York Giants. Afterward, while reading a late edition of the Baltimore *News*, he experienced the thrill of discovering its account of the game matched his own.

In 1896 he graduated from the Baltimore Polytechnic with the highest marks ever achieved by any pupil in the history of the school. His dreams to become a reporter for the Baltimore *Herald* were thwarted by August Mencken, who told him he would now be working at the family cigar business. His duties at "Aug. Mencken & Bro." were as an office boy and assistant bookkeeper, but after he broke the screw press he was ordered to sell cigars to tobacco and grocery stores. It is not difficult to see why it would be a depressing experience for him. There were salesmen at the factory who managed to sell up to $1,005 worth of cigars in four weeks, but in his first six months Mencken squeezed out only $171 in business; during the entire month of August he made only one sale, for a grand total of $3.50.[6] "In the end," he wrote, "it became apparent, even to my father, that I was hopeless as a salesman."[7] He was banished back to the office, where the mystifying tasks of running a business made him feel as if he knew next to nothing. When he went to the bank to make deposits he made mistakes; when he made out the bills he made even worse ones. Moreover, he was still required to sell cigars.

His evenings, however, were his own. After a brief walk from the factory to the house, he spent his time reading the classics as well as *Steps into Journalism: Helps and Hints for Young Writers* by Edwin L. Shuman of the Chicago *Journal*. He applied to a correspondence course with the Associated Newspaper School of Journalism in New York, and wrote on the application form of his hopes to "begin as a reporter and after that trust to hard work and luck for something better."[8] One teacher returned his stories, praising his work for being "written with a good deal of life and humor" yet advising Mencken not to use "long and pompous words in funny passages."[9] Whenever Mencken mentioned his ambitions to his father there was such an uproar the topic was dropped, and for two years the young boy continued his melancholy routine of working at the cigar factory by day, reading and writing by night, and, in darker moments, contemplating suicide.[10]

On December 31, 1898, August Mencken, Sr., suddenly collapsed in the living room with a kidney infection. As Henry ran in the cold and blustery night to fetch a doctor, past homes where happier families were celebrating New Year's Eve, the boy suddenly realized the full meaning of his father's illness. Panting his way through drifts of snow, he kept repeating to himself: "If my father dies, I'll be free at last."[11] Two weeks later, Henry Mencken became head of the household, grieved but determined to enter "the maddest, gladdest, damndest existence ever enjoyed by mortal youth."[12]

Almost immediately he applied for a job at the *Morning Herald*, only to be told there was not any position. Undeterred, he continued working at the cigar factory by day and showed up at the *Herald* office every night for six weeks, until finally Max Ways, its editor, assigned him a few stories. Toward the end of June Mencken was officially hired: he was introduced to his new co-workers as "Macon." Jubilant, he plunged into the job at $7.00 a week, heedless of his aunt Pauline's warnings (which nonetheless alarmed his mother) that all newspapermen were enormous boozers, and that large numbers of them died in the gutter.

His dream in those days was to write in the same manner as Edward P. Mitchell of the New York *Sun*. During the 1890s journalists were influenced by the nineteenth-century movement toward realism in art and literature, and rescued American prose from its old formalism and hollowness. Mitchell's articles described the daily life of the American people in a vivid, intimate, and humorous style, and Mencken tried to follow his example.[13]

The speed of his ascent was extraordinary. Two years after going to work for the *Herald* he was editor of its Sunday edition, writing articles, editorials, and editing the theater page. In 1903, he became editor of the morning paper, and then city editor of the evening paper in 1904, covering the great Baltimore fire. When the *Herald* folded, he joined the Baltimore *Evening News* but four weeks later transferred to the *Sunpapers*, becoming editor of the Baltimore *Sunday Sun*. In 1910, he became editor of the newly established Baltimore *Evening Sun*, and the following year was invited to write a signed column. "The Free Lance" addressed subjects of interest to Baltimoreans, becoming the most controversial local column in memory. It was suspended in 1915, as the United States headed into World War I and Mencken's pro-German sympathies became more defiant. When some of his war dispatches from Germany and his notes on the revolution in Cuba were censored in 1917, Mencken left the *Sunpapers*, writing instead for the New York *Evening Mail*. Within two years the publisher was arrested for allegedly being pro-German; Mencken lost his job. His newspaper career, he thought, was over.

During this period he completed four books, among them *In Defense of Women, Prejudices: First Series,* and the first edition of *The American Language,* which attracted the serious attention of scholars, always a butt of Mencken's satire. Since 1914, together with George Jean Nathan, he had been editing *The Smart Set,* a literary magazine that waged wars against bluenoses who supported Prohibition, demagogues of patriotism, and prudes who set themselves in opposition to culture, such as Anthony Comstock's New York Society for the Suppression of Vice. Mencken's reviews, along with the drama criticism of George Jean Nathan, gave *The Smart Set* a prestige that other and more established periodicals envied.

At the beginning of 1920, Paul Patterson became publisher of the Baltimore *Sunpapers* and urged Mencken to rejoin its staff. Together, H. L. Mencken and Harry Black, a prominent stockholder of the paper, wrote a document outlining the goals for making the *Sunpapers* "a nationally distinctive newspaper," claiming as one of its principles to be "absolutely free" from "any steady fidelity to either political party."[14] The memorandum became known in the *Sun* offices as "The White Paper." From 1920 to 1938 Mencken contributed a weekly article to the *Evening Sun* as well as reports on subjects of his choice; the "Monday Articles" and Patterson's reorganization of the paper helped give the *Evening Sun* national renown. For three and a half months in 1938, Mencken was temporary editor of the *Evening Sun,* and would continue to write for the *Sunpapers* until 1941, when he withdrew from the paper because of its war policy and what he saw as the abandonment of the principles stated in "The White Paper." His work on other newspapers included articles for the Chicago *Sunday Tribune* from 1924 to 1928, where he reworked his "Monday Articles" for a wider audience, and his articles on language, published by the New York *American* from 1934 to 1935.

Mencken's writing achieved national prominence when, after relinquishing *The Smart Set* in 1923, he founded *The American Mercury* in 1924 with George Jean Nathan, and continued editing that magazine until 1933. *The American Mercury* established itself as one of the leading intellectual magazines of the day. Although Mencken thought it only a sideline in his career, it was an important national forum for his social and literary criticism, and served as new ground for emerging authors.

Among his books were *George Bernard Shaw: His Plays*, published in 1905, the first book to examine the work of the playwright printed in the United States; *The Philosophy of Friedrich Nietzsche*; a volume of literary criticism (*A Book of Prefaces*); his studies of religion (*Treatise on the Gods*), ethics (*Treatise on Right and Wrong*), and political theory (*Notes on Democracy*); *A New Dictionary of Quotations*; and the four editions and two supplements to *The American Language*. These, along with his six volumes of *Prejudices*, three volumes of autobiography, and countless contributions to other volumes, established him as a major force in literary and social criticism, so that his reputation extended to Europe and, to a lesser degree, to Latin America.

Directly and indirectly, through his newspaper articles, magazines, and books, he helped the careers of F. Scott Fitzgerald, Sinclair Lewis, Theodore Dreiser, Joseph Conrad, and many other writers. He regularly included the work of black authors in the pages of *The American Mercury*, and persuaded publisher Alfred Knopf to publish many of their books, thus influencing the careers of those associated with the Harlem Renaissance. "In the South," Mencken wrote to a fellow journalist in 1948, "I am looked on as a bitter enemy of the local *Kultur*. But no man ever spent more time and energy than I did trying to hearten the microscopic minority of civilized Southerners."[15] His essay "The Sahara of the Bozart," published in the New York *Evening Mail* in 1917, infuriated many Southerners, who labeled Mencken variously as "a cockroach" and "a jackass." The intended and ultimate effect of his attacks on Southern literature was to spur Southern writers and journalists to reexamine their approach to Southern problems and mores; by the mid-1920s many Southerners began to hail Mencken as the principal instigator of the revival of Southern literature.

Considering the breadth of H. L. Mencken's interests it is futile to attempt to classify him at all. He himself, when the occasion arose, considered himself a journalist. Pecking out an autobiographical statement on his Corona in 1936, he wrote, in the third person: "Despite his books and his magazine editing, he always thought of himself as a newspaperman first of all, and the Baltimore *Sunpapers* dominated all of his other enterprises."[16] Alfred Knopf, who published his books and admired Mencken as a powerful force in literary criticism, acknowledged that the *Sunpapers* were the core of his life.[17] It was an opinion shared by Mencken's younger brother August, who knew him best: "In my brother's life," he said simply, "the *Sun* came first."[18]

* *

His boss Max Ways at the *Herald* gave Mencken advice at the beginning of his career. "I don't expect you," Ways told him, "to beat the *Sun* boys at getting the bald news. . . . But if you can't beat them *writing* the news after you have got it, then all I can say is you are a ——— ——— ——— ——— ———."[19] The newspaper articles Mencken wrote for the *Herald* are not in the style of the mature Mencken, but they were vividly written. Nonetheless, he depreciated his early writing as "pretty bad," stating that his own style did not come to fruition until 1906.

"The Free Lance" column in the *Evening Sun*, however, which he wrote almost daily from May 1911 to October 1915, is still not characteristic, with its self-conscious attempts to shock and horrify. Years later, when approached with the idea that "The Free Lance" columns could be microfilmed for posterity, he replied he did not see any reason why they should be kept at all.[20]

It was not until 1920, with his "Monday Articles," that he achieved the mastery of style that would continue for the remainder of his professional career. "A Carnival of Buncombe," the first of the "Monday Articles," discussed the presidential candidates for the upcoming election. After reading that all of them were "more or less palpable frauds . . . General Wood is a simpleminded old dodo with a delusion of persecution; Palmer is a political mountebank of the first water; Harding is a second-rate provincial; . . . Gerard and the rest are simply bad jokes," Paul Patterson told Mencken, "That's a fine piece of murder. I enjoyed it hugely."[21] The style intoxicated many of those writers who had previously been contemptuous of Mencken during World War I; for some, their own writing would never be the same.

The mature Mencken did not have to strain for effect. This ease is all the more incredible when one remembers that reporters working against a deadline have little opportunity to devise the unexpected; more often than not, as Mencken pointed out, their sentences fall back on a store of stale clichés a reporter acquires almost as soon as he learns how to make out an expense account: "*dash for freedom*"; "*blood streaming*" from wounds; news which "*spreads like wildfire.*" Somehow, Mencken seems to have survived what he called "the crippling strain of the city room" and even "the bellicose imbecility of the copyreaders" so that he achieved an originality of thought and a genuine distinction of style.[22]

Mencken had an ear for what he called "verbal delicacies"; he was "the man who searches painfully for the perfect word . . . there is in writing the constant joy of sudden discovery, of happy accident."[23] Although certain words and phrases were used again and again (*palpable, puerile, puissant, mountebank, hon. gentleman*) he attempted, nonetheless, to minimize repetition: after submitting one of his "Monday Articles" to editor Hamilton Owens, he advised him to change "*mountebank*" to "*quacksalver*" ("a good word, and too little used").[24] There were those words he invented and used frequently: "*Booboisie*" is perhaps the most famous; the one of which he was most proud was "*Bible Belt*" (which, he noted, was being repeated among Southerners, "although if they knew of its origin they'd probably be shy of it").[25]

He was able to dispose of something or somebody in a phrase. Washington, D.C., was "a hundred thousand miserable botches of ninth-rate clerks"; store-bought bread is "the tasteless, gassy white sponge that all Americans now eat"; sparkling wines were similarly dismissed: "Americans like such rubbish because, after a few glasses, they begin to imagine they are making whoopee in a bordello."[26] Warren G. Harding's prose style reminds him of "stale bean-soup, of college yells, of dogs barking idiotically through endless nights."[27]

Part of his vigor as a prose stylist was due to his humorous exaggeration of similes and metaphors: he was anything but a linguistic purist, making use of the neologisms that were fertilizing American English and borrowing from a wide range of languages. During World War I, he confessed, "I got a lot of fun out of using German words and phrases, for they infuriated the German-ophobes. Not infrequently they howled their loudest against what was really a Yiddish term."[28] For the humorist S. J. Perelman, H. L. Mencken was "the ultimate firework. He loosened up journalism. With his use of the colloquial and the dynamic, the foreign reference, and the bizarre word like *Sitzfleisch*, he brought adrenalin into the gray and pulpy style of the day."[29]

Despite his liking for the picturesque he felt a firm prejudice against sloppy inattention to the basic rules of language. He complained that all young reporters were imitating the "obscene example of *Time*," which had been "slaughtering" English grammar for years.[30] To Hamilton Owens he ranted against the "atrocious" usage of a capital letter after a colon; to the copy editors he left instructions to ensure his *abysm* wasn't changed to *abyss*. ("It is a quotation from the late William Shakespeare. Incidentally . . . if anyone complains about it ask them with my compliments to go to hell.")[31] To Paul Patterson he sent a clipping from the *Sun* to demonstrate how certain German words had been misspelled. "I hate to seem to be harassing the copy-desk," he apologized, but "even under the severest pressure . . . it is just as easy to be right as wrong."[32] So frequent were his complaints that in 1944 he devised a stylebook for the *Sunpapers*, advising against the use of "banal counterwords" and "clumsy forms" apparent in the other papers: "A good newspaperman does not ape bad models."[33]

Pounding out his articles on his Corona (later, an Underwood), he never graduated beyond the "one-finger school," striking the keys so hard and hitting the space bar with such force his thumb actually left an indentation. ("If I had to write a whole article by hand it would half kill me.")[34] The reports were, more often than not, composed under great difficulties and to his own extreme discomfort. Traveling from Germany in 1917, he banged out his stories with his typewriter balanced precariously on top of a suit-case. He reported Franklin Roosevelt's famous speech in darkness at Franklin Field on a wet typewriter while he sat in a flimsy press stand under the open sky after a day of rain: "While I was at work my soggy typewriter was bucking under my hands, and not infrequently I was barely able to see its keys."[35] Four years later he baked in the heat in an open field along with his "red-hot" typewriter so that he could report how Father Charles E. Coughlin fainted under the broiling sun.[36] His coverage was tireless. During the 1948 convention, the London *Spectator* reported the air-conditioned pressroom was mobbed with reporters drinking beer, "and even the sight of H. L. Mencken seated on the burning deck whence nearly all but he had fled did not shame any of his colleagues to returning to the field of action where the temperatures, hot air, television and miscellaneous noise made reporting harder."[37] To be a reporter meant one enjoyed such hardships, or so he always felt: to his surprise and dismay, younger reporters seemed to spend most of their time complaining about their work, quitting their craft early in the day in order to play golf.[38] Amazingly, the stories needed little or no revision; the carbons in his scrapbooks attest to the fact that what Mencken wrote the first time would be the printed copy.

Through the years, his articles lit up the pages of the *Evening Sun*, dazzling readers with their "brilliant style, incomparable humor, and virtuosity of language" that caused one reader to "grope for a dictionary" while "tears of laughter" streamed down his face.[39] Reactions differed. There were those who immediately turned to Mencken's column once the *Evening Sun* thumped against their doorstep: "Mencken was great tonight!" they would announce to their families as they approached the dinner table; others slammed their fist against the furniture, cursing "that goddamned Dutchman!"[40] Whether readers found him to be "a public nuisance" or agreed with Walter Lippmann that he was "the most powerful personal influence on this whole generation of educated people," invariably "What do you think of Mencken?" was the phrase of the day.[41] He stood out among journalists, according to one colleague, because "honesty and courage were what made him great."[42]

The newspaper articles accomplished an important purpose for Mencken: they provided him with a platform from which to launch his ideas. Some of these, in turn, were rewritten for *The Smart Set* and *The American Mercury*, but the germ for many of his *Prejudices* essays and later books came from his newspaper stories. *The American Language* began its majestic career with a series of articles, "The Two Englishes" being the first to appear, in 1910; *A New Dictionary of Quotations*, published in 1942, originated in "On Quotations" written in 1911. Most of his enduring prose was written for the New York *Evening Mail*, and when he wrote *In Defense of Women* and later, his *Prejudices* series, he repeatedly returned to the *Evening Mail* material to select his best out-of-print writing. The first publication of some of the material used in *Happy Days* originated in "Forty Years of Baltimore," published in the *Evening Sun* on March 19, 1923.[43]

One of Mencken's most appealing qualities is the exuberance and delight he found in everything around him, which is reflected in the breadth of topics on which he wrote. The charm of Baltimore is described along with the best method for preparing (and eating) crabs; the pure notes of a song by Brahms are enjoyed with as much gusto as the skillful pummeling of Jack Dempsey. His prejudices were many, told in the discourteous style which was, to a large degree, the intellectual mode of the 1920s. Races, nations, professions, religions, all were lampooned: some of his harshest words were directed at "the only pure Anglo-Saxons left in the United States."

Not all the articles are of equal quality. One can detect those days when he did not feel like writing and no doubt mounted the stairs to his study with a heavy step. But even in the weakest there is always a turn of phrase or theme that is characteristically Mencken. "The two main ideas," he explained, "that run through all my writing, whether it be literary criticism or political polemic, are these: I am strongly in favor of liberty and I hate fraud."[44]

* *

The Constitution and the Bill of Rights, Mencken believed, were sacred documents setting up clear lines of demarcation across which no government could trespass. "I know of no other man," Mencken once said, "who believes in liberty more than I do."[45] His belief fueled his fight against Prohibition, which he viewed as a violation of civil liberties. Over forty-two "Monday Articles" were written on the subject between 1920 and 1933, when the law was repealed; countless references were made in other articles as well. The Los Angeles *Negro Paper* praised him for his "sterling honest and genuine sincerity that he has always maintained in his splendid crusades . . . for the downtrodden ones."[46] As early as 1917 he addressed the concerns of the black man when he wrote "Negro Spokesman Arises to Voice His Race's Wrongs." When the Senate Judiciary Committee held hearings on the Costigan-Wagner Anti-Lynching Bill in 1934, Mencken testified with force and effect in behalf of the bill and was the only journalist to do so in person (others sent in the usual telegrams), calling lynching a murder, not simply a crime. According to senators on the panel, it was through Mencken's testimony as well as his articles in the *Evening Sun*, which supported the Costigan-Wagner Anti-Lynching Bill and those that repeatedly denounced lynching which were influential in their considering the passing of the bill.[47] His article on Donald Gaines Murray, who was denied entrance to the University of Maryland solely because of his color, prompted G. B. Murphy of the *Afro-American* to thank Mencken for "the splendid and eminently fair article . . . on the Murray case."[48] His continuing fight for equality, as evidenced in the very last article he wrote ("Mencken Calls Tennis Order Silly, Nefarious"), prompted Clarence C. Mitchell, Bureau Director of the NAACP in Washington, D.C., to tell his sons that Mencken was on the side of the black man.[49] Jewish groups, however, reacted angrily after he wrote "Help for the Jews," which proposed that only certain Jewish refugees from Nazi persecution should be admitted to the United States, but that Eastern Jewish refugees should be sent to Russia. He was surprised when it "brought me a greal deal of denunciation and I have been treated as an enemy in the local Jewish paper."[50] Throughout his career, Mencken seemed genuinely perplexed by his reception by the Jewish community.

It was, however, his impassioned defense of the First Amendment, in favor of freedom of speech, which throughout his career can be said to be his *raison d'être*. So thorough was his knowledge of the Constitution and the Bill of Rights that there were journalists who assumed him to be a graduate of Harvard Law School. His defense of this basic right is evident in his series of reports from Tennessee on the Scopes Monkey Trial. He convinced the *Evening Sun* to provide the bond for John Scopes, and persuaded Clarence Darrow to head the young schoolteacher's legal team. Initially, Mencken observed the evangelical passions of a region he had derided. As the case wore on, Mencken used the proceedings to champion the larger issue of freedom of speech. Thousands of words were written on the trial, but it was Mencken's dispatches that attracted national attention. Managing editors from across the country besieged the *Sunpapers* with requests to buy his reports.

In addition to freedom of speech, another First Amendment right Mencken repeatedly sought to defend was freedom of the press. Even in a democracy a press could still be free and fail to do its job. Mencken knew firsthand how opinion could be manipulated and how newspapers could distort the news. His article, "A Neglected Anniversary," was a case in point. In it he facetiously chronicled the seventy-fifth anniversary of the introduction of the bathtub to America. Despite his later published statements that he had written in jest, what became known as the "Bathtub Hoax" made its way into books, its false information repeatedly touted in countless articles that continue to be published long after Mencken's death.[51]

Very few Americans, Mencken thought, say what they believe, freely and frankly; they always try to find out first what will be well received. "The consequence of this cowardice is that, when they find themselves on the side of the majority, they tend to become dogmatical and tyrannical."[52] From this conviction came his determination not to syndicate his Monday columns. He strongly believed that newspapers lost their definite character from such syndications: "in the face of bitter controversy, they try not to offend any considerable faction. This may be prudent, but it is bad journalism."[53]

This decision led to occasional attacks on Mencken from different quarters. After covering a parade of the Ku Klux Klan in Washington, D.C., he was the butt of denunciations by the Knights and Women of the Ku Klux Klan of Little Rock, Arkansas. Articles against the state twice prompted the members of the Arkansas Senate to pass resolutions calling for Mencken's deportation from the country. Reaction to two articles Mencken wrote condemning a lynching in Salisbury, Maryland, in December 1931 caused even more of an uproar, resulting in a boycott of Baltimore's commercial enterprises and the seizing and burning of copies of the *Sunpapers* by the Eastern Shore communities of the Chesapeake Bay. The editor and publisher of the Crisfield *Times* called Mencken "a curse on humanity," and the Easton *Journal* warned Mencken not to venture on the Eastern Shore since "the populace would surely lynch him. Cut off his toes, and perhaps his ears, for souvenirs."[54] One angry reader from Delaware wrote: "Thank God none of his ideas have ever been accepted by responsible people, only by his most loyal followers, negros, outcasts, and Communists."[55] Despite all this, in January 1932, Mencken received an award from the *Nation* for distinguished journalism in the face of personal danger. At the end of all the controversies, even his enemies came to realize that Mencken's great strength was what he once praised in Al Smith: "He will not lie, and he cannot be bought."[56]

Restraint came during the two World Wars, when his highly unpopular views could no longer be printed. He voluntarily withdrew both times, but not without bitterness. He observed that the manufacture of false news, the incessant spy hunts (he himself had come under scrutiny by the FBI), and the savage persecution of all opponents and critics of the war had resulted in the abandonment of decency and self-respect. It is little wonder he would chafe under the wartime censorship of World War II.

* *

In the last analysis, it was politics, and the "frauds" who engaged in it, that fascinated Mencken. Descriptions of the political scene can be found in his early work for the *Herald*. A large percentage of subjects in his "Free Lance" columns of 1911–15 dealt with local politicians; after World War I, his interest in "the politically obscene" overtook his concern with literary criticism, and perhaps two thirds of his "Monday Articles" are devoted to the discussion of this topic.

He was convinced that the politician was actually an enemy of the people. A politician's aim in life, he said, was to get a job, make promises he knew he could not keep, and pretend to admire men he despised. Then, once having made his way into public office, his goal was to hold on to it for as long as he possibly could, increasing the power it gave him. And yet, Mencken declared, "I like politicians even better than I like professors. They sweat more freely and are much more amusing."[57]

Part of the inspiration for his articles on politicians evolved from government documents, dozens of newspapers, and the fifty magazines he received per month. The more revealing glimpses were gleaned from the pages of the *Congressional Record*; he delighted in pointing out all the inconsistencies and chicanery that appeared in its pages. To various editors on the *Sun* he suggested putting a "slave" to work digging out of the *Record* pertinent speeches of various senators which would "serve as ammunition later on,"[58] for, he declared, "such stuff is in the *Record* almost daily. It is full of facts and figures that appear nowhere else. My belief is that the newspaper which first starts to print it will make a sensation."[59]

In 1904 he covered his first pair of national conventions, Chicago's Republican convention and the Democratic convention held in St. Louis. During this period, his style was still in its infancy; nevertheless, his uncanny powers of observation are evident in the articles and would continue until his last coverage of a convention in 1948.

"His most effective personal technique," wrote Alistair Cooke, "is one that combines an affected naiveté with the pose of a conscientious reporter of absurd events."[60] This procedure was employed brilliantly in his coverage of the national conventions, where the men and women who took themselves seriously

Mencken turned into comic characters. He would begin to type his observations almost as soon as he entered the convention hall. There was Andrew Mellon: "If there is anything in his head, which is very doubtful, it has surely left no trace upon his face"; and the delegates, who will "spend the week crossing and recrossing their legs, lunching on stale ham sandwiches and asking the newspaper correspondents what is going on."[61] And there, too, were the members of "The Women's National Committee for Law Enforcement," most of whom Mencken described as being sixty-eight years old and weighing one hundred and sixty pounds, holding a huge sign: "God Keep Us Pure and Strong." ("No one, as far as I could make out, challenged this pious wish.")[62]

No other entertainment gave him greater pleasure than reporting from the conventions; nor did anyone appreciate his efforts more than Mencken himself. One reporter, peering through Mencken's window late at night after one rally, recalled watching him at work alone in his hotel room, pounding out copy on a typewriter propped on a desk. He would type a few sentences, read them, slap his thigh, toss his head back, and roar with laughter. Then he would type some more lines, guffaw, and so on until the end of the article.[63] In 1928 he thus described his method, as he gave advice about the emerging force of radio:

> It is such preposterous bladders who run the Republican party, choose presidents and determine the national policies of the United States in peace and war. . . . The fact that they are venerated by the booboisie is due chiefly to the newspapers, which treat them with utmost gravity. Nine-tenths of the dispatches sent out from here today will discuss them soberly and respectfully as if they were so many Goethes. And now comes the radio to pump them up still more.
>
> In theory, perhaps, the radio ought to expose them, for it reveals clearly the complete vacuity of their utterances and shows how incompetent they are to manage the simple and half-childish business that engages them. But the radio announcers taking their cue from the newspapers insist upon fawning upon them. The absurd little Fess is introduced as a statesman compared to Bismarck or Cavour. Smoot, the Mormon, who believes that the world is soon coming to an end, is depicted as a great patriot and genius. I propose a reform in this department: the newspapers are hopeless.[64]

It took, however, more than humor for Mencken to affect his readers the way he did; wit was a weapon to hammer home a serious point.

For all his insights into the motivations of politicians, Mencken was often wrong in his predictions. At the 1924 Democratic National Convention he was certain John W. Davis would "never be nominated" (he was); in 1928 he predicted Hoover's defeat (he won); in 1932 he was sure of Hoover's reelection (he lost); and like so many others, he picked Dewey, not Truman, as the winner of the 1948 presidential election. "I was never a good reporter," he confessed. ". . . I never got a scoop in my life."[65]

Once the conventions were all over, said Mencken, defeated candidates were a menace to the country, and so he advised the nation that the losers of a race should be flung from the top of the Washington Monument. Fearing controversy, "Lame Ducks" was not printed by the Chicago *Sunday Tribune,* for which it was written; the Baltimore *Evening Sun* carried it instead.

Throughout his dispatches from the conventions the encroaching effects of technological innovations became apparent. No longer did the candidates bawl speeches through hand-held megaphones; by 1928 voices were being carried aloft through loudspeakers, a device which reduced all voices "to one metallic level of cacophonous roaring."[66] Radio, Mencken thought, removed "the natural heat" of an orator; movie cameras made a man "no more than a piece of stage property for the photographers and movie men," the immense lights and banging flashes "blinding and rattling him"; television merely produced "video verbiage."[67] Such were the effects of the mechanized age. If some politicians seemed baffled by the new technology, after the election of 1932 Mencken would encounter a President who, unlike any of his predecessors, knew how to play the media to his advantage: Franklin Delano Roosevelt.

* *

Franklin Delano Roosevelt was Mencken's primary target, and it was precisely Mencken's attacks on the President, as well as his failure to recognize the Depression and the true intent of Adolf Hitler, that alienated many of his readers and contributed to Mencken's decline in popularity. It had not begun that way: in his "Monday Article" for July 5, 1932, Mencken wrote that FDR was one of "the most charming of men," and that furthermore he would vote for Roosevelt—"anything to get rid of Hoover." Moreover, Roosevelt was "a gentleman" and "his own man." The tone changed, however, shortly after Roosevelt increased his power.

Part of Mencken's dislike of FDR was rooted in what he saw as

Roosevelt's abolishment of traditional Constitutional guarantees; in particular, the limitation of government and free speech. Especially distasteful was the President's establishment of a new era of social programs and benefits, with which Mencken did not want to be associated. He despised what he viewed as America's slide into the welfare state. The economy would right itself, he asserted, just as it had during his own childhood, in 1893 and 1894. He resented having to pay more taxes: the concept of the New Deal under "Roosevelt II" "had only one new and genuinely novel idea: whatever A earns really belongs to B. A is any honest and industrious man or woman; B is any drone or jackass."

As editor of the Baltimore *Evening Sun* for a brief period in 1938, Mencken used his position to state his view of the situation. The most explosive example is "Object Lesson," printed on February 10, 1938. Of the seven columns on the editorial page, six were occupied by a broad expanse of gray; on closer inspection, a reader could see that it was a series of fine screen dots made by the Benday photoengraving—1,000,725 dots appeared on the page: each dot, Mencken wrote, represented one of the federal government's "immense corps of jobholders."

Mencken's pertinacity in broaching such a subject vastly irritated those who criticized what they saw as his "attacks on U.S. workers." Editorials across the nation discussed "the Page of Dots." "It brought home to the beholder the meaning of the millions so easily bandied about in discussions of the nation's business," praised one. As one editorial dryly put it, "Many of these federal jobholders, we fear, do as little work as Mr. Mencken's corps of editorial writers did on that particular day."[68]

As Roosevelt continued his economic and social policies, Congress conceded unprecedented powers to the President, raising fears that constitutional checks and balances were being eroded. Some Democrats abandoned Roosevelt, agreeing with Walter Lippmann's assertion that the President was "drunk with power."[69] For Dorothy Thompson, Roosevelt's benign and charismatic "dictatorship" was "the very soul of Fascism."[70] His critics circulated jokes, such as the one about the eminent psychiatrist summoned prematurely to heaven to treat God "because He has delusions of grandeur—He thinks He is Franklin D. Roosevelt."

Mencken's coverage of the Democratic National Convention of 1940 is strident in its descriptions of Roosevelt's maneuverings for his election and the fiction of the spontaneous draft. After a dutiful show of deference, Roosevelt was nominated on the first ballot; he then chose a Vice President who was accepted, albeit reluctantly in some quarters, by the delegates. Mencken wrote to his brother, August, "The whole show is full of unreality. It seems like an idiotic stage play."[71] In such a situation, Mencken asked, what was the difference between dictatorship and democracy? "It was, in form and substance, precisely like the Reichstag sessions that Hitler calls at long intervals," he wrote in one dispatch. "There was only one choice before the so-called delegates: they could vote *Ja* or be damned."[72] One cannot escape the conclusion that such unpopular views must have been somewhat annoying to the *Sun*.

Mencken's bitterness toward Roosevelt was exacerbated by his intensely personal feeling that contemporary newsmen were not doing their duty: "to keep a wary eye on the gentlemen who operate this great nation, and only too often slip into the assumption that they own it."[73] Being naturally cynical of the motivations of politicians, Mencken revolted as Roosevelt's influence over the press grew unchecked. By the time he entered the White House Roosevelt had perfected the craft of dealing with journalists. Contrary to the reticent Hoover, who had done away with press conferences altogether, FDR scheduled a meeting twice a week in the pressroom of the White House (which he fondly called his "schoolroom"), disarming reporters by greeting them by their first name, giving them a warm handshake and the famous Roosevelt smile. The meetings became, in essence, a public relations device which he could manipulate to his own advantage. If reporters were 60 percent in favor of the New Deal, they were 90 percent for Roosevelt personally. Reporters simply became extras in a drama dominated by the actor at center stage.[74]

FDR, moreover, became a successful pioneer of political broadcasting, using the radio as a means of projecting his ideas and policies directly into American homes. "Most Americans in the previous 160 years had never seen a President; now almost all of them were hearing him, *in their own homes*," the historian David Halberstam points out. "It was literally and figuratively electrifying."[75] By 1940 surveys suggested most voters considered radio, and not newspapers, to be their first choice of political news. The challenge to newspapers had become all the greater.

At a meeting of the Society of Newspaper Editors, Mencken warned his colleagues that if the United States entered the war the press would suffer a form of censorship similar to that experienced during World War I. Once again, he cautioned, news which did not serve government policy would be suppressed; newspapers would succumb to "a squeeze play that politicians have been working on them since the cradle days of the Republic."[76] White House press releases would orchestrate the news, and, in effect, control what the press could cover; all other considerations in the press would be subordinated to the main objective of winning the war. To Paul Patterson, Mencken wrote that the independence of a newspaper was especially necessary, "for we confront a high development of government propaganda in both domestic and foreign affairs." He went on:

I do not propose that we denounce the Administration incessantly and unreasonably; I only propose that we view it skeptically, and refuse to assent to its devices and pretensions until we are sure that they are intelligent and sincere. Every public official with large powers in his hands should be held in suspicion until he proves his case, and we should keep him at all times in a glare of light . . .[77]

He concluded by warning against "radicalism" from "the Right or the Left."

After the United States entered World War II Roosevelt's impact on his office became more imperial, prompting Senator Fulbright to accuse the President of usurping the treaty power of the Senate and circumventing the war powers of Congress. But as Congress fell into line, so did the press. Roosevelt warned the networks against the broadcast of false news. The broadcasting companies understood the message: they were to avoid controversy and opinion. The United States Government Office of Censorship handed out a pamphlet for newspaper editors entitled *Code of Wartime Practices for the American Press*, advising what newspapermen could and could not cover. When Roosevelt refused to allow the press to cover his travels throughout the United States, newsmen met in private to complain. Arthur H. Sulzberger of the New York *Times* claimed that his managing editor had been summoned to the White House and upbraided by Roosevelt for the way the *Times* was handling the war news. "Sooner or late," Sulzberger told Mencken, "we may have to throw off the chains with which we have shackled ourselves and begin to tell the truth."[78] Paul Bellamy of the Cleveland *Plain Dealer* declared that the censorship was an outrage. "Your trouble, Paul," Mencken responded, "is that you discovered that Roosevelt is a dictator too late. You should have got to him in 1932."[79]

On January 16, 1941, Mencken met with Paul Patterson and refused to write anymore. Although Patterson protested, it must have been with a mixture of relief. "I quit," Mencken wrote a friend, "because it seemed like an affectation for me to contribute to the editorial page. My belief is that a newspaper should tell the truth, however unpleasant."[80] His strong conviction that a newspaper should serve as a sort of permanent opposition to the existing government was a position, he realized, that could hardly be supported by many papers: "the majority of them, even when they claim to be in opposition, are only feebly so. Even the most vigorous give rather too large a hearing to . . . government press agencies."[81]

It is perhaps for this reason, along with several others, that World War II was "Roosevelt's war" to Mencken: the unrestricted power of the President and his conscious use of the media overshadowed all else. To some extent, Mencken's disagreements with FDR sprung from his own opposition to the war. Pro-German, but anti-Nazi, he never fully comprehended the horrors of the National Socialists. In 1938, in spite of spending a few weeks in Hitler's Germany, Mencken failed to publicly report the fear and tension among the Jewish people which he had privately described in letters to intimates. He equated America's hatred of Hitler (and all Germans) as simply another instance of the mass hysteria he had experienced during World War I. Stubborn by nature, Mencken's long-held views did not change.

Mencken frequently argued against the Roosevelt Administration's power over the press, which to him, was probably more sinister than the act of war itself. What would be the legacy of such inordinate power in the White House? What would be the role of the press, once Roosevelt was long gone and another president in his place? "If anything is plain," Mencken wrote, it is that "there will be radical changes in journalism during the next fifty years. The plan of newspapers will be revised, and they may lose some of their present functions."[82] Once a free press ceased to exist, he thought, the American system would collapse; it was the only remaining impediment to totalitarianism. "My guess is that by 1975 and maybe 1950 the papers will be heavily policed."[83] Increasingly disappointed with his colleagues and with his newspaper, frustrated after meetings with the *Sun* board of directors, he poured his rage into the pages of his diary.

During the period in which he was not writing for the *Sunpapers*, Mencken wrote an entirely new version of *The American Language*, adding supplements and revisions. His nostalgic essays of his youth were expanded into the three volumes of his autobiography: *Happy Days, Newspaper Days*, and *Heathen Days* (which, ironically, the Director of the Office of Censorship in Washington, D.C., asked him to autograph).[84] He assembled a collection of his writings for *A Mencken Chrestomathy* and a smaller volume of notes for *Minority Report*. He noted, "If it is a fact that I am doomed to go unheeded, then I don't care a damn. I write because I like it, not because I want to convert anyone."[85] Nonetheless, he meticulously catalogued a vast array of his newspaper clippings to make sure they would not go unheeded before their disintegration into "impalpable atoms." His collected papers were for students "engaged in critical or historical investigation," and the articles themselves served "in the hope that they may be of some interest to youngsters entering journalism and perhaps also to other persons."[86] He went daily to the *Sun* office, throwing his energy into labor negotiations and in trying to preserve the integrity of the paper. By 1945 he felt weary, privately stating, "I'll be glad to retire . . . It is not as amusing as it used to be."[87] Clumping past a host of new *Sun* employees he did not know, he heard himself referred to as "the old man," but what his own paper was printing he did not know or care: he had lost all interest in reading the newspapers.[88]

Throughout his self-imposed exile colleagues wrote to him, assuring him that his presence had been sorely missed at the national conventions. By 1948, the mounting excitement of the three conventions (the third to be held by Henry Wallace and his Progressive party) weakened Mencken's resolve to stay out of the newspaper. "God knows I itch to see all three . . ."[89] he wrote to Maclean Patterson, and subsequently covered the conventions, writing angry diatribes that were printed with a special slug that contained more white space between each line; the effect was that his words seemed to leap off the page to the eye of the reader. To the novelist Joseph Hergesheimer Mencken wrote: "Either they'll restore me, or they will kill me."[90] He was right; a debilitating stroke on November 23, 1948 ended his career. Incapacitated for further writing and reading, he died eight years later, on January 29, 1956.

* *

What continues to live on in addition to Mencken's style are the ideas set forth by one of the most irritating and irresistible journalists of the twentieth century. Even if the newsprint of his articles fade into yellow dust, if the gift of his style is mutilated by followers thrice removed, if he himself is damned or praised, the liberating force he provided for American culture has become part of our daily existence, and should be so recognized. If a new sincerity and forthright honesty came into American letters and life, some of the credit must be due to Mencken. He lives on in the turns of phrase and ideas in the language of thousands who never even suspect their source. If the body of literature he left behind manages to "stir up the animals," as it inevitably does, then it is testimony to the fact that we are still grappling with those same issues about which he wrote, and with the manner in which they are expressed.

The general tendency of Mencken's journalism was from the start "toward the annihilation of frauds of all sorts,"[91] and the consternation this caused is exactly the sort of reaction he desired. In an age where columnists are pegged as either conservative or liberal, as right or left, Mencken defies categorization. Writing in his study, he felt "quite distinct and separate from the masses of men. It is very comforting on blue days. I belong to no party. I am my own party."[92] One can only admire such refreshing independence.

M.E.R.

Editorial Note

Of the approximately three thousand articles which Mencken wrote during his lifetime, nearly two hundred were culled for this collection. I have concentrated on the major signed contributions to the Baltimore *Herald*, the Baltimore *Sunpapers* (both the *Sun* and *Evening Sun*), the New York *Evening Mail*, the Chicago *Sunday Tribune*, and the New York *American*. Unsigned news items, editorials, and theater reviews written for the Baltimore *Herald* and the Baltimore *Sunpapers* from 1899 to 1910 have been mostly excluded. Miscellaneous articles written for foreign papers, since they are few in number, have been omitted altogether. Not all the articles Mencken wrote were preserved in his scrapbooks: during the process it was necessary to retrieve them from microfilm located at the Enoch Pratt Free Library and the Library of Congress.

In general, Mencken used two different styles in his expository writing: the report, which gave information, and the column, which gave opinion. Most collections of Mencken's essays concentrate on those that offer strict opinion. Yet the reports, with their mixture of prejudice, wit, and acute sense of observation, also make for excellent reading and are a lasting contribution. Thus, included here are Mencken's dispatches from the Republican and National Democratic conventions as well as those from the Scopes Trial, the Disarmament Conference, Pan American Conference, and London Naval Conference. Save for a few random articles, these have never before been assembled.

Most of the classics have been repeated, as no collection of Mencken would be complete without them: "Valentino,"

"Bryan," and the infamous "The Sahara of the Bozart." Others were included since they provided the germ for later work. ("Spoken American," for example, was one of a series of articles that would blossom into *The American Language*.) Still other essays were chosen for their historical and literary value, as the series on the Scopes Trial in 1925. Those essays that dealt primarily with Baltimore politics and issues have been excluded in the attempt to reach a wider audience. Obviously, any columnist writing during a forty-nine-year span will repeat topics and themes; I have tried to choose the best that show the breadth and scope of Mencken's interests, but do not pretend to have included every single one; some readers will inevitably find some favorites missing. Titles separating each section are taken from other articles written by Mencken that seemed applicable here.

Names and places mentioned in the articles are, in general, self-explanatory. However, bridging material is provided for those reports dealing with conventions, the Scopes Trial, and the conferences, otherwise those essays would exist in a vacuum for modern readers. The notes give the background to those names mentioned as well as to the social history of the time: it is provided for readers of a younger generation.

Texts have been reproduced as they were first printed, complete with asterisks and Roman numerals, as well as Mencken's original spelling. The only exception to this has been to italicize titles of those books mentioned in the articles. Misprints, made by what Mencken called "the imbecility of copyeditors," have been corrected. When Mencken himself penned in a correction in his clipping books, I have incorporated it into the text.

Dates have been verified against the original paper in which they appeared. Scholars should note in some instances Mencken's scrapbooks and Betty Adler's *H.L.M.: The Mencken Bibliography* (Baltimore: The Johns Hopkins Press, 1961) are incorrect.

This collection attempts to provide one of the most comprehensive editions of Mencken's articles, showing the full range of his talents and interests, which made him so famous during five decades of American history. At least two thirds of the essays have not been seen since their first appearance in the newspapers where they were praised or damned over sixty years ago. They are assembled in the hope a new set of readers will be intoxicated by the fresh immediacy of HLM's prose, and by the humor and prescience of one of America's foremost journalists.

Reflections on Journalism

Reminiscence

I

Looking back over a dull life, mainly devoted to futilities, I can discern three gaudy and gorgeous years. They were my first three years as a newspaper reporter in Baltimore, and when they closed I was still short of twenty-two. I recall them more and more brightly as I grow older, and take greater delight in the recalling. Perhaps the imagination of a decaying man has begun to gild them. But gilded or not, they remain superb, and it is inconceivable that I'll ever see their like again. It is the fate of man, I believe, to be wholly happy only once in his life. Well, I had my turn while I was still fully alive, and could enjoy every moment.

It seems to me that the newspaper reporters of today know very little of the high adventure that bathed the reporters of my time, now nearly thirty years ago. The journalism of that era was still somewhat wild-cattish: all sorts of mushroom papers sprang up; any man with a second-hand press and a few thousand dollars could start one. Thus there was a steady shifting of men from paper to paper, and even the most sober journals got infected with the general antinomianism of the craft. Salaries were low, but nobody seemed to care. A reporter who showed any sign of opulence was a sort of marvel, and got under suspicion. The theory was that journalism was an art, and that to artists money was somehow offensive.

Now all that is past. A good reporter used to make as much as a bartender or a police sergeant; he now makes as much as the average doctor or lawyer, and probably a great deal more. His view of the world he lives in has thus changed. He is no longer a free-lance in human society, thumbing his nose at its dignitaries; he has got a secure lodgment in a definite stratum, and his wife, if he has one, maybe has social ambitions. The highest sordid aspiration that any reporter had, in my time, was to own two complete suits of clothes. Today they have dinner coats, and some of them even own plug hats.

II

This general poverty, I suspect, bore down harshly upon some of my contemporaries, especially to older ones, but as for me, I never felt it as oppressive, for no one was dependent on me, and I could always make extra money by writing bad fiction and worse verse. I had enough in Summer to take a holiday. In Winter, concerts and the theaters were free to me. Did I dine in a restaurant? Then I know very well that opinion in the craft frowned upon any bill beyond 50 cents. I remember clearly, and with a shudder still, how Frank Kent once proposed to me that we debauch ourselves at a place where the dinner was $1. I succumbed, but with an evil conscience. And Frank, too, looked over his shoulder when we sneaked in.

The charm of the life, in those remote days, lay in the reporter's freedom. Today he is at the end of a telephone wire, and his city editor can reach him and annoy him in ten minutes. There were very few telephones in 1899, and it was seldom that even the few were used. When a reporter was sent out on a story, the whole operation was in his hands. He was expected to get it without waiting for further orders. If he did so, he was rewarded with what, in newspaper offices, passed for applause. If he failed, he stood convicted of incompetence or worse. There was no passing of the buck. Every man faced a clear and undivided responsibility.

That responsibility was not oppressive to an active young man: it was flattering to him. He felt himself a part of important events, with no string tied to him. Through his eyes thousands of people would see what was happening in this most surprising and fascinating of worlds. If he made a good job of it, the fact would be noticed by the elders he respected. If he fell down, then those same elders would not hesitate to mark the fact profanely. In either case, he was almost completely his own man. There was no rewrite-man at the other end of a telephone wire to corrupt his facts and spoil his fine ideas. Until he got back with his story there was no city editor's roar in his ear, and even after he had got back that roar tended to be discreetly faint until he had got his noble observations on paper. There was, of course, such a thing then as rattling a reporter, but it was viewed as evil. Today the problem is to derattle him.

III

I believe that a young journalist, turned loose in a large city, had more fun a quarter of a century ago than any other man. The Mauve Decade was just ending, and the new era of standardization and efficiency had not come in. Here in Baltimore life was unutterably charming. The town was still a series of detached neighborhoods, many of them ancient and with lives all their own. Marsh Market was as distinct an entity as Cairo or Samarkand. The water-front was immensely romantic. The whole downtown region was full of sinister alleys, and in every alley there were mysterious saloons. One went out with the cops to fires, murders and burglaries, riding in their clumsy wagon. Any reporter under twenty-five, if not too far gone in liquor, could overtake the fire-horses.

I do not recall that crime was common in Baltimore in those days, but certainly the town was not as mercilessly policed as it is today. Now the cops are instantly alert to every departure, however slight, from the Y.M.C.A.'s principles of decorum, but in that era they were very tolerant to eccentricity. The dance-halls that then flourished in the regions along the harbor would shock them to death today, and they'd be horrified by some of the old-time saloons. In such places rough-houses were common, and where a rough-house began the cops flocked, and where the cops flocked young reporters followed. It was, to any youngster with humor in him, a constant picnic. Odd fish were washed up by the hundred. Strange marvels unrolled continuously. And out of marvels copy was made, for the newspapers were not yet crowded with comic strips and sporting pages. What was on the police blotter was only the half of it. The energetic young reporter was supposed to go out and see for himself. In particular, he was supposed to see what the older and duller men failed to see. If it was news, well and good. But if it was not news, then it was better than news.

IV

The charm of journalism, to many of its practitioners, lies in the contacts it gives them with the powerful and eminent. They enjoy communion with men of wealth, high officers of state, and other such magnificoes. The delights of that privilege are surely not to be cried down, but it seems to me that I got a great deal more fun, in my days on the street, out of the lesser personages who made up the gaudy life of the city. A mayor was thrilling once or twice, but after that he tended to become a stuffed shirt, speaking platitudes out of a tin throat. But a bartender was different every day, and so was a police sergeant, and so were the young doctors at the hospital, and so were the catchpolls in the courts, and so were the poor wretches who passed before the brass rail in the police station.

There was no affectation about these lesser players in the endless melodrama. They were not out to make impressions even upon newspaper reporters; their aim, in the phrase of Greenwich Village, was to lead their own lives. I recall some astounding manifestations of that yearning. There was the lady who celebrated her one hundredth arrest for drunkenness by stripping off all her clothes and throwing them at the police lieutenant booking her. There was the policeman who, on a bet, ate fifty fried hard crabs. There was the morgue-keeper who locked himself in his morgue, drunk and howling, and had to be clawed out by firemen. There was the detective who spent his Sundays exhorting in Methodist churches. There was the Irish lad who lived by smuggling bottles of beer to prisoners in the old Central Police Station. There was the saloon-keeper who so greatly venerated journalists that he set them a favored rate of three drinks for the price of two. Above all, there was the pervasive rowdiness and bawdiness of the town— the general air of devil-may-care freedom—the infinite oddity and extravagance of its daily, and especially nightly life.

It passed with the fire of 1904. I was a city editor by that time and the show had begun to lose its savor. But I was still sufficiently interested in it to mourn the change. The old Baltimore had a saucy and picturesque personality; it was unlike any other

American city. The new Baltimore that emerged from the ashes was simply a virtuoso piece of Babbitts. It put in all the modern improvements, especially the bad ones. Its cops climbed out of the alleys behind the old gin-mills and began harassing decent people on the main streets. I began to lose interest in active journalism in 1905. Since 1906, save as an occasional sentimental luxury, I have never written a news story or a headline.

(The Baltimore Evening Sun, January 10, 1927)

Twenty-five Years

I

It would be natural, I suppose, to say that the day when the *Evening Sun* was hatched seems only yesterday, but if I were on oath it would certainly be perjury, or something else of like wickedness and the same name. The truth is that, as I look back upon the birthday of this great moral organ, it appears infinitely remote in time, and very vague in outline. I simply can't remember what happened; it was a day like any other. We got out the first issue without any of the pangs and dubieties that seem to be proper on such occasions. We knew in advance that it was going to be bad, and it *was* bad, so we put it out of our minds as quickly as possible. Later on, I am glad to add, the paper improved.

I became a member of the staff by a sort of accident, and never had any recognized office or title. I had come to the *Sunpaper* in 1906 when the *Evening Herald*, of which I was editor, succumbed, and for three years I enjoyed the placid and lordly life of a *Sun* man under the Abell regime. There was never on this earth a more pleasant newspaper office. It was full of charming fellows, and the Abells carried it on as if it were a good club rather than a great industrial plant. I began as Sunday editor, but by 1910 I was writing editorials.

Then came Charles H. Grasty, an apparition from a strange planet. I knew him, but had reason for believing that he didn't like me, so I prepared to shuffle on. But he sent me word that he had no intention of canning me, whereupon I consented coyly to stay, and in a little while we were very friendly. It wasn't long before he began to make plans for an evening edition. Inasmuch as I was one of the few men in the editorial rooms who had had any experience on an evening paper, I was naturally taken into his councils, and when the paper came out at last, on April 18, 1910, I found myself a sort of first mate to J. H. Adams, the editor.

II

My duties, at the start, were rather complicated. I was supposed to be at my desk at 8 o'clock every morning, and to write two editorials before 11 o'clock. In addition, I had to read all the letters received from correspondents, and to translate into English those that seemed suitable for the *Evening Sun* Forum. If any nuts came in with proposals for new laws or unearthly schemes to beat Taft in 1912, I usually had to listen to them for Adams was busy in his cage, damning the telephone and trying to write his own leaders. If he was still busy at 11:30 I made up the editorial page for him. Then to the Rennert for lunch.

Of an afternoon I devoted myself to a long signed article for the next day. It was printed in the column next to the editorials, and was set in such crowded type that it consumed a great many words. When I undertook this job it seemed easy enough, for I was busting with ideas in those days, and eager to work them off. But in a little while I found that writing 2,000 or 3,000 words a day was really a killing chore, and one day I remember especially, when sitting at the typewriter became suddenly unendurable, and I turned to pen and ink for relief.

When Adams found me using such paleozoic implements he was horrified, and, with his usual decency, let me off some of the editorial writing. But soon after that his health began to be indifferent, and he was sometimes disabled, and at such times I had to do a double stint. I don't remember ever having a disagreement with him, though the only thing we had in common, politically speaking, was our belief in the Bill of Rights. But rows are very rare in newspaper offices. Men of all sorts of ideas somehow manage to get along together.

One rather curious incident of our association I recall. At the end of a busy afternoon Adams called me into his office and asked me to find out what I could about airships. "It looks to me," he said, "as if they were actually coming in, and we ought to have somebody in the place who knows something about them. You are a graduate of the Polytechnic, and should be able to find out how they work." I agreed to do it, but had to report my failure a few weeks later. To this day my knowledge of airships is precisely nil. I never see one in the air without expecting it to fall.

III

How long my job lasted I don't remember exactly, but it wasn't very long. By the end of 1910 I was transferred to the last column of the editorial page, and turned loose upon the town under the style and appellation of The Free Lance, and there I performed daily for five years, with only two intervals out for brief trips abroad. This work was a lot of fun, but it brought me so many visitors and so much mail that editorial writing on the side became impossible, and I have never done any since.

I apologize for talking so much more about myself than about the *Evening Sun*. My share in it, in fact, has always been small, and since its first days I have given a good part of my time to other enterprises. But a newspaper man always thinks of his paper in terms of his own job, and that must be my excuse. Some of these days, I hope, the history of this one will be told in more or less detail. It will be a story of a hard and long fight against depressing odds, carried on with magnificent devotion by a gang of strictly non-messianic and very amusing fellows, and ending in an extraordinary success.

The changes that have come over American journalism during the twenty-five years of the *Evening Sun* have been marked and many, and nearly all of them, it seems to me, have been for the good. There are old-timers who pine for the days when every considerable American city had eight or ten newspapers, but I am not one of them. The truth is that the majority of those newspapers were shabby rags that printed very little news, and fell far below the chastity proper to Caesar's wife. They overworked and underpaid their men, and were constantly blowing up. That their treadmills produced some extremely competent journalists is a fact, but it is also a fact that they polluted the craft with a great many shady quacks.

IV

In my early days, I confess, some of these quacks enchanted me, for the romance of journalism—and to a youngster, in that era, it surely *was* romantic—had me by the ear, and the quacks themselves, in many cases, were picturesque characters, and not without a certain cadaverous glow. But chance threw me, when I was still in my early twenties, into the post of city editor, and as such I had to get out a paper with their aid. The experience convinced me that the newspaper business was in need of a wholesale disinfection, and I am glad to be able to say that it came anon, and has left apparently permanent good effects.

The improvement in newspapers has been general, and very great. Their machinery for gathering news is enormously better than it was when I was a young recruit. More news now comes into the *Sunpaper* office every night than came into it in two weeks back in 1900, and that news is better written and more accurate. It is almost impossible today for an event of any significance to be missed, but in my nonage it happened every day. The New York *Sun* was, in many ways, the best of the American papers a generation ago, but it had only the most meager news service, and at the time of the San Francisco earthquake, in 1906, it came out with nothing save a few brief bulletins and a fine obituary of the town of Will Irwin, written in the office.

Newspapers are a great deal more honest than they used to be, and a great deal more intelligent. Some of the Stone Age editorial writers survive in legend as masters of prose and publicists of the first chop, but the truth is that most of them were only third-rate rhetoricians itching for public office. Nothing that any of them wrote, on public questions, whether in their papers or elsewhere, is worth reading today, or is remembered by anyone. Even the prose of William Cullen Bryant, perhaps the most respectable of them, is . . . deadly and . . . dead. . . .

The improvement in newspapers I ascribe mainly to the increased cost of operating them. When a new one could be set up by any adventurer with a hand press and a few cases of type, the trade naturally attracted a great many dubious persons, and their competition kept even the best papers on a low level. But the invention of the linotype made large capital investments necessary, and in a little while the weaker and more vulnerable sheets began to disappear. Those papers that survive today, whatever their faults otherwise, are at least safely solvent, and they show the virtues that always go with solvency, that is to say, they are not purchasable, they spend money freely in discharging their public responsibilities, they stand aloof from the corruptions of party politics, and they are able to attract to their service a well-educated and self-respecting corps of men. Here, as in so many other fields, capitalism shames the mountebanks who deride it.

(The Baltimore Evening Sun, April 15, 1935)

Notes on Journalism

The general success of the tabloid papers, the oldest of which is only seven years old, still seems to puzzle the majority of newspaper men. When they admit it at all they commonly credit it to the looseness and imbecility of the newcomers, which are described as given over wholly to crime and scandal. But this is plainly a prejudiced and highly inaccurate view of them. In the whole country there are not more than three that actually specialize in such matters. The rest at worst are no worse than the usual run of yellows. And at best they are very good newspapers, intelligently edited and carefully printed.

What makes them popular, I believe, is far less their contents than their form. They are made for reading in crowds, and it is in crowds that they are mainly read. A great advertising boom now rages in the United States, and all the old-line papers run to an immense bulkiness. Some of the more prosperous of them, on the days that advertisers favor, come out in two or three sections and weigh a pound or more. To go through such a paper in a jammed street car is quite impossible. The man who attempts it gets only a beating for his pains. But he can manage a tabloid without making his neighbors yell, and so he reads it.

The lightness of the little papers gives them another advantage; they can be distributed much more quickly than the larger papers. A boy on a motorcycle can carry a hundred copies of even the bulkiest of them to a remote junction in ten or twenty minutes, but the old-style papers have to go by truck, which is slower. Not so many can be printed in an hour. Not so many can be carried by a single newsboy. These advantages count up. The majority of readers, when there is news afloat that interests them seriously, look for it in the larger papers, which can give it in full. But these same readers also buy the tabloids for the first bulletins. Thus there is much duplication of circulation. The tabloids take a certain amount of circulation away from the larger papers, but not enough to be disastrous.

* *

They would be even more successful than they are, I believe, if their editors could resist the temptation to improve them. That temptation, of course, is easy to understand. Every newspaper man worthy of the name dreams of making his paper better than it is, and those who run the tabloids are stimulated further by the general professional opinion that their papers are somehow low. So every tabloid, as soon as it gets into safe waters, begins to grow intellectual. The bald, gaudy devices that launched it are abandoned and it takes on decorum. Already there are tabloids with opinions on the French debt, the Philippine question and the music of Stravinsky. I know at least two that are actually liberal.

This, I fear, is a false form of progress. The tabloid, so lifted by its bootstraps, becomes simply a little newspaper, and it must inevitably be inferior to the big ones. If I were a tabloid magnate I'd head in the other direction. That is to say, I'd try to produce a paper interesting and instructive to the uncounted thousands who now read no newspaper at all. That such persons exist may seem incredible, but it is nevertheless a fact. They swarm in every large American city. They include the vast class of illiterates, which is everywhere larger than the statistics show. And they include the even larger class of near-illiterates—that is, those who are able to spell out enough words to get them through the ordinary business of life, but find reading so laborious and painful that they avoid it as much as possible.

Many of them, as the psychologist, Dr. Eleanor Wembridge, has demonstrated, are congenitally incapable of mastering it. They understand only such words as are comprehensible to a child of, say, 10. The rest is simply a fog to them. An ordinary newspaper article, even in a tabloid, is thus mainly unintelligible to them. Half the words in it are beyond them. Even when, by dint of hard sweating, they spell their way through it, the impression it leaves upon them is very vague and unsatisfactory. They may grasp its main propositions, but all its details are lost upon them.

* *

It is my belief that a newspaper aimed at such readers would make a great success in any large American city, and especially in Chicago or New York. It should be printed throughout, as First Readers are printed, in words of one syllable. It should avoid every idea that is beyond the understanding of a boy of 10. It should print no news about anything that morons are not interested in. And its illustrations, instead of being mere decorations, should really illustrate as the pictures in a First Reader illustrate.

I don't think it would be difficult to get together a staff for such a paper. If journalism itself failed to produce the necessary talent, recourse might be had to pedagogy. There are schoolma'ams, male and female, all over this great land who are professionally adept at explaining things to children. They have perfected technical devices that do the trick quickly and effectively, and those devices could be adapted to journalism without the slightest difficulty. Journalists themselves, after a little training, would greatly improve them, for journalists as a class are much more intelligent than pedagogues. In the end there would be a new English (or American) for the submerged, and reading would spread to a vast class that now gets all its news by listening.

To that class, as to children, much of what now passes for news, and is dished up in endless columns every morning, is wholly uninteresting. Its members, despite the alarms of bank directors and other such naive fellows, are not Socialists; they are, indeed, quite incapable of comprehending politics save as a combat between two men, A and B. In the strict sense, all ideas are beyond them. They can grasp only events. Are they interested only in crime? I don't think so. What they are interested in is drama. The thing presented to them must take the form of a combat, and it must be a very simple combat, with one side clearly right and the other clearly wrong. They can no more imagine neutrality than they can imagine the fourth dimension. And when they see drama they want to see it moving.

* *

Soon or late some sagacious journalist will set up a paper made to the tastes and limitations of this immense horde of God's children, and his rewards will descend upon him like a deluge. The earliest movie magnates tapped that colossal till with great skill, and so lifted the movies to the third (or is it second?) place among the country's industries. They did not start out with Balzac, Joseph Conrad and Dostoievski; they started out with "The Perils of Pauline" and filmizations of serials out of the *Fireside Companion.*

But once they got rich, they began to develop, in the immemorial human way, a yearning to be respectable, and even intellectual. That is, they began to turn their backs upon the original clients, who had poured all their wealth into their coffers, and to reach out for customers of a higher sophistication. Thus, the 10-cent movie house passed into the shadows and in its place appeared the blazing hell showing pictures at $2—pictures full of artistic and even literary pretension. Fortunately for the movie magnates, this pretention was mainly buncombe. They lacked the skill and culture necessary to make the movies genuinely intelligent, and so they escaped bankruptcy. But, even so, they converted a business whose profits were as certain as those of a bootlegger into a business full of hazards and calamities.

They will come to a safe harbor again when they return to the *Fireside Companion* level. No one in this world, so far as I know—and I have searched the records for years, and employed agents to help me—has ever lost money by underestimating the intelligence of the great masses of the plain people. Nor has anyone ever lost public office thereby. The mistake that is made always runs the other way. Because the plain people are able to speak and understand and even, in many cases, to read and write, it is assumed that they have ideas in their heads, and an appetite for more. This assumption is a folly. They dislike ideas, for ideas make them uncomfortable. The tabloids, seeking to force such things upon them, will inevitably alarm them and lose their trade. The journalism of the future—that is, the mob journalism—will move in the direction that I have indicated.

(The Chicago Sunday Tribune, September 19, 1926)

Journalism in the Republic

What journalism in America chiefly suffers from today is the lack of alert and competent professional criticism. The doctors, in the trade journals, are always criticizing one another sharply, and so are the lawyers in theirs. As for the clergy, they devote a very large part of their energy to refuting and damning their brethren, and not a few of them do it on public stumps with the laity invited. So, also, in the fine arts. It is impossible for an architect to get away with a botch without hearing from other architects, and it is impossible for a poet to print anything at all without tasting the clubs of other poets. Even dramatists, movie actors, chiropractors, statesmen and barbers criticize one another, and so keep themselves on tiptoe.

But not journalists. The organs of their craft—and there are journals for journalists, just as there are doctors for doctors—are all filled with mushy and feeble stuff, most of it indistinguishable from the bilge emitted by Rotary and Kiwanis. Reading them, one gathers the impression that every newspaper proprietor in the United States is a great public figure and every circulation manager a wizard. The editorial boys, it appears, never fall down on their jobs; they are not only geniuses but also heroes. Some time ago, having read all such journals assiduously for years, I stopped my subscriptions to them. I found that I preferred the clip sheet of the Methodist Board of Temperance, Prohibition and Public Morals.

Now and then, true enough, a Heywood Broun is exasperated into telling the truth about the manhandling of a Snyder trial, or a Walter Lippmann exposes the imbecility of the Russian "news" in a New York *Times,* or an Oswald Garrison Villard turns his horrible searchlight on a Boston *Herald* or a Washington *Star,* but it is surely not often. For the most part, the journalistic quacks and incompetents suffer no challenge whatever. Nine times out of ten, indeed, all they hear is praise—and most of it comes from the very trade journals that ought to deal with them realistically, if journalism among us is ever to take on any serious dignity.

* *

At the moment it is in a low state, mainly due to the decay of the old time reporter, the heart and soul of the American newspapers of the last generation. The current rush to get upon the streets with hot news, even at the cost of printing only half of it, has pretty well destroyed all his old qualities. He no longer writes what he has seen and heard; he telephones it to a remote and impersonal rewrite man. This rewrite man, not infrequently, is a fellow of considerable talent. He knows how to write quickly and clearly; he tries to be as accurate as possible. But it must be manifest that, hanging on his telephone, maybe miles away from the event he is describing, he is completely unable to get into his description any of the vividness of a thing actually seen. He does the best he can, but that best is to the reporting of a fairer era as a mummy is to a man.

To be sure, a certain amount of the news is still written by reporters who have personally covered it, but that amount tends to diminish year by year. On some of the more "enterprising" afternoon papers it is probably already under a third of all the news printed, and even on the morning papers it is less and less all the time. Obviously, this dull business of talking into a telephone is not attractive to the sort of men who are likely to make good reporters. Such men want to do the whole job; they want to see their own words in print. Doomed to handle only the raw materials of news, they quickly tire of journalism and depart for fairer fields.

Some time ago the Hon. Will H. Hays was saying that he knew of "125 former newspaper men occupying key positions in the movies." No doubt he meant as scenario writers, press agents and so on; not as actors. A good many, perhaps, had never been actual newspaper men, at least of any dignity, but among the rest there were probably some very good ones. The desertion of such good ones is steadily weakening the newspapers of the nation. They are not as well written as they were twenty-five years ago, and, considering the vastly augmented facilities at their disposal, they do not cover the news as diligently and accurately.

* *

It is, indeed, professional incompetence that chiefly ails them today, and not the corruption that liberals and other such chasers of ghosts view with alarm. I am quite familiar with the inner organization of journalism in America today, and I know of few offices in which that corruption is a reality. The papers of the land, when they are bad, are not bad because their proprietors, taking the word from Wall street, order them to be so, but because their staffs are incompetent to make them any better. What did Wall street have to do with the grotesque manhandling of the Miami hurricane—one of the worst pieces of reporting ever heard of? Or with the puerile slush cabled from Paris after the Lindbergh flight? And what has it to do with the bad English, the naïve credulity and the militant Philistinism visible in nine American newspapers out of ten every day?

The fake news that pours in from such centers of controversy as Russia and China is not ordered by Wall street, nor even by the dull Babbitts who now own the majority of papers. It is ordered by managing editors who are professionally incompetent to get better—which is to say, by men who are unequal to the demands of their jobs. They know very well that news fakers swarm in such places, and it is their business to detect them and put them down. Some of them actually do it. But the rest swallow whatever comes in, and so the public is informed every Tuesday that the bolsheviki are preparing to throw up the sponge on the ensuing Saturday, and from Shanghai comes news of the complete defeat of the Nationalist army, and twenty-four hours before it marched triumphantly into the city.

Of late every reflective American reader must have noticed the inaccuracy and imbecility of most of the special correspondence issuing from Washington. In it all the frauds, high and low, who flourish in that town are treated with the utmost gravity, and their cheapest and most venal maneuvers are depicted as masterpieces of statecraft. Is this bilge ordered by Wall street? I doubt it. Is it demanded by the customers of the papers that print it? Again I have a doubt. Far easier and more plausible is the explanation that the Washington correspondents write it willingly and in good faith—that they are too stupid to penetrate the fraudulencies by which they are surrounded.

* *

The correspondents of an earlier day were harder to fool. They treated the Washington scene intelligently and realistically, and they produced a great deal of correspondence of a high order—

stuff that was taken seriously in Washington, and greatly feared by the mountebanks and rogues of the town. There are a few Washington correspondents who still maintain that old standard. But there are not many, and they tend to diminish. The rest are simply bad reporters. They are not corrupt, and they are not the victims of corruption; they are simply incompetent professionally, as a lawyer who knows no law is incompetent professionally.

What is to be done about it I don't know. As I have said, the working conditions that a reporter confronts today are likely to be disagreeable to him in direct proportion to his fitness for his trade. The pull is against the enlightened self-interest of genuinely competent men, and so they are gradually elbowed out—into press agentry, into business, into other professions. The reporter of more than local reputation is disappearing. There was a time when every considerable town housed two or three who were known in the craft all over the country, and often to the public as well. But there are not many left today. They disappear into safe and anonymous desk jobs and join Rotary, or they leave the trade altogether.

It is a pity. For the old time reporter of the better sort was not only a useful man in the best sense, he was also a very happy man. His work brought him an immense stimulation. It took him to good shows, and it offered him endless chances for the most agreeable varieties of self-expression. But today he tends to be a dispirited drudge toting the mimeographed pronunciamentos of press agents. Once he lived the news, and sometimes gloriously made it; now he wheels it in cans.

(The Chicago Sunday Tribune, June 26, 1927)

A Gang of Pecksniffs

I

On the first page of the eminent *Sunpaper* of last Friday appeared a dispatch from New York reporting that the American Newspaper Publishers' Association, there assembled for its annual convention and booze-guzzle, had passed a solemn resolution protesting that "the liberty of the press has been seriously threatened during the past year," pledging its members to "resist all interference with the right . . . of the press to free expression under the constitutional guarantees," and instructing its Committee on Federal Laws "to exercise its utmost efforts to maintain the liberty of freedom [*sic*] of the press wherever it may be threatened." On the same page of the *Sunpaper,* two columns away, appeared a dispatch from Philadelphia reporting that two women had been arrested and jailed for "distributing circulars which petition President Harding to grant amnesty to political prisoners."

Humor? Then the obscene is humorous—as, indeed, most normal Americans seem to hold. As for me, I see nothing to cackle over in the resolution of the publishers. Instead, it should be denounced briefly for what it is: a mass of degraded and disgusting cant. In the history of American journalism during the past half dozen years there is certainly nothing jocose. In all their dealings with the question of free speech the newspapers of the country, and especially the larger and more powerful ones, have been infinitely pusillanimous, groveling, dishonest and indecent. If, as they now pretend so boldly, their editors and proprietors are actually in favor of Article I of the Bill of Rights, then their long acquiescence in its violation proves that they are a herd of poltroons. And if, when it was so grossly violated, they were actually in favor of those who violated it, then their belated resolution proves that they are liars. I see no way to avoid these alternatives. I can imagine no process of reasoning, however subtle and ingenious, whereby persons whose words and acts are so heroically at odds could be converted into honest and honorable men.

II

It is my private impression, born of long familiarity with such fauna, that what brought most of the publishers to the side of the Bill of Rights at last, after all their craven consenting to its invasion, was not any belated enthusiasm for free speech, or, indeed, any intelligent respect for it or understanding of it, but simply and solely a fear that the next violation of Article I would probably cut off some of their revenues. The uplifters are up and doing on all sides, and of late they have uncovered some Great Causes that threaten newspaper profits. For example, there is the matter of race-track information. Practically all American newspapers, however moral they may seem on their editorial pages, print such information on their sporting pages—and it sells a good many papers. Now the uplifters propose a Federal law declaring any paper containing it unmailable. At once, waking from their long sleep, the publishers begin shedding crocodile tears over "the right of the press to free expression under the constitutional guarantees!"

It would be difficult to imagine any more gross and obvious pecksniffery. Put beside it, the proceedings of the Anti-Saloon League seem almost honest. Where were all these publishers when the janissaries of the late Woodrow were prowling the country, clubbing and jailing all citizens who presumed to question his divinity—when men by the hundred were railroaded to prison for venturing to exercise the constitutional right to free speech, and other men were harassed and hounded in a dozen other ways, and publications almost without number were tyrannically barred from the mails? The answer is simple: they were not only consenting to the business; they were actively promoting it. It was their newspapers—many of them great and puissant papers—that egged on the Department of Justice, the Chambers of Commerce, the Americanization Leagues, the American Legion and all other such lawless bands. It was their newspapers that raised the idiotic alarm about Bolshevism, and brought on the wholesale jailing and deportation of innocent men. It was their newspapers that distorted and tortured the news to official uses, and debauched the courts, and connived at crime, and made justice in America a joke. And it was their newspapers that fawningly approved every time some smaller and more honorable sheet got into trouble for trying to tell the truth.

III

I am well aware, of course, that there were exceptional journals that shrunk delicately from much of this swinery—that a few of them came forward with protests long before the race-track information bill alarmed the rank and file. I say a few, but at the moment I am sure of but two: the estimable *Sunpaper* aforesaid and the New York *World*. The *World* was the first gag, and then came the *Sunpaper*. By the time the Palmer buffoonery about radicals got its height, both were in full revolt, and trying to tell the truth. But it is not to be forgotten that even these very exceptional and almost miraculous gazettes ran a long way behind some of the week-lies and monthlies—that they were magnificently silent at the times the *Masses* was suppressed and the *Nation* was attacked. In brief, they deserve very little praise for their revolt, for by the time they came to make it it was quite safe. When they were needed most desperately—when the aid of two such rich and pow-erful papers would have been most effective and valuable—they were silent. To have horned in at that time would have been to run grave risks, for Wilson was strutting about in his halo and Palmer and company believed themselves invincible—but it would have been to render a public service of inestimable worth. I believed at that time and I believe now that in a stand-up fight with Wilson they would have won—that public opinion, after the first clash, would have supported them, as it later came to support even the *Masses.* But instead of making the venture they went to the defense of Wilson, and it was not until he was on his knees that they began to gag at his excesses, and, in particular, at his deliberate, cynical and intolerable violations of the Bill of Rights.

Even then they tried ineptly to separate the man from his evil deeds, *e.g.*, to argue that the cad who kept the poor old ass, Debs, in prison was a statesman and a gentleman. Worse, they continued to pussy-foot, even after they had got over that folly. For example, they denounced the crimes against the Constitution perpetrated by the Ku Klux Klan, and were silent about the far more serious crimes perpetrated by the American Legion. But even so, they were a million times more honest and courageous than any other American newspapers. It was at least obvious that something re-sembling a conscience has begun to gnaw them. The rest of the great American journals continued to display, as usual, the morals and public spirit of so many Prohibition enforcement officers, Congressmen, or street-walkers.

IV

These preposterous fakes now begin to snuffle and blubber over the invasion of the Bill of Rights! Hit in the money-bag, they suddenly become fanatical devotees of the Constitution! It is my sincere hope that even Congressmen will have sense enough to penetrate the fraud. To more intelligent and seemly men I offer a ready test of it. Get a copy of any great American journal of Fri-day, April 28, 1922. See how its news department treated the story from Philadelphia—of the two women dragged to the calaboose by the police for exercising their constitutional right to petition the President for the release of men jailed in violation of *their* constitutional rights. Then see what the staff Delane has to say about the business on the editorial page—if anything. Don't bother to read his learned discourse on the Genoa mountebank-ery, the sins of the coal miners, the candidacy of M. Cox. Go straight to his denunciation of this double assault upon the Consti-tution—if it is there. If you find it, let me know.

(The Baltimore Evening Sun, May 2, 1922)

On Being an American

The American

The notion that Americans are a sordid money-grubbing people, with no thought above the dollar, is a favorite delusion of continentals, and even the English, on occasion, dally with it. It has, in fact, little solid basis. The truth is that Americans, as a race, set relatively little store by money; surely all of their bitterest critics are at least as eager for it. This is probably the only country in the world, save Russia under the Bolsheviki, in which a rich man is *ipso facto* a scoundrel and *ferae naturae*, with no rights that any slanderer is bound to respect. It would be a literal impossibility for an Englishman worth $100,000,000 to avoid public office and public honor; it would be equally impossible for an American worth $100,000,000 to obtain either. The moment he showed his head the whole pack would be upon him.

Americans, true enough, are richer than most. Their country yields more than other countries; they get more cash for their labor; they jingle more money in their pockets. But they also spend more, and with less thought of values. Whatever is gaudy and showy gets their dollars; they are, so to speak, constantly on holiday, their eyes alert to get rid of their change. The only genuinely thrifty people among us, in the sense that a Frenchman is thrifty, are foreigners. This is why they are ousting the natives in New England and in large areas of the middle West. But as soon as they become Americanized they begin to draw their money out of the savings banks and to buy phonographs, Fords, boiled shirts, yellow shoes, cuckoo clocks and the works of Bulwer-Lytton.

* *

The character that actually marks off the American is not money-hunger at all; it is what might be called, at the risk of misunderstanding, social aspiration. That is to say, he is forever trying to improve his position, to break down some barrier of caste, to secure the acceptance of his betters. Money, of course, usually helps him in this endeavor, and so he values it—but not for its own sake, not as a thing in itself. On the contrary, he is always willing to pay it out lavishly for what he wants. Nothing is too expensive if it helps him to make a better showing in the world, to raise himself above what he has been.

It is the opportunity that founds the aspiration. The cause of all this unanimous pushing is plainly the fact that every American's position is always more or less insecure—that he is free to climb upward almost infinitely, and that, by the same token, he is in steady danger of slipping back. This keeps him in a state of social timorousness; he is never absolutely safe and never absolutely contented. Such a thing as a secure position is practically unknown among us. There is no American who cannot hope to lift himself another notch—if he is good. And there is no American who doesn't have to keep on fighting for whatever position he has got. All our cities are full of aristocrats whose grandfathers were day laborers, and clerks whose grandfathers were aristocrats.

* *

The oldest societies of Europe protect caste lines more resolutely. A grandee of Spain, for example, is quite as secure in his class as a dog is in his. Nothing he can do in this world can raise him above it, and nothing he can do can bounce him out of it. Once, a long while ago, I met a Spanish count who wore celluloid cuffs, was drunk every afternoon and borrowed money for a living. Yet he remained a count in perfectly good standing, and all lesser Spaniards deferred to him and envied him. He knew that he was quite safe, and so he gave no thought to appearances. In the same way he knew that he had reached his limit. He was a grandee, but he had no hope whatever of making the next step; he knew that he could never be royal.

No American is ever so securely lodged. There is always something just ahead of him, beckoning him and tantalizing him, and there is always something just behind him, menacing him and causing him to sweat. The preposterous doings of what we call our fashionable society are all based on this uncertainty. The elect are surrounded by hordes of pushers, all full of envy, but the elect themselves are by no means safe. The result is a constant maneuvering, an incessant effort to get a firmer hold. It is this effort which inspires so many rich girls to shanghai foreigners of title. A title, however paltry, is still of genuine value. It represents a social status that cannot be changed by the rise of rivals, or by personal dereliction, or by mere accident. It is a policy of insurance against dangers that it is very difficult to meet otherwise.

* *

The mention of social aspiration always suggests the struggle to be accepted as fashionable, but it is really quite as earnest and quite as widespread on all lower planes. Every men's club, even the worst, has a waiting list of men who are eager to get in, but have not yet demonstrated that they are up to it. The huge fraternal orders are surrounded by the same swarms of aspirants: there are thousands of men who look forward eagerly to election to the Masons, the Odd Fellows or the Knights of Pythias. And among women—but let us keep away from women. The dominating emotion of almost every normal woman is envy of some other woman. Put beside this grand passion her deep, delirious affection for her husband, and even for her children, fades to a mere phosphorescence.

As I have said, the fruit of all this appetite to get on, this desire to cut a better figure, is not the truculence that might be imagined, but rather timorousness. The desire itself is bold and insatiable, but its satisfaction demands discretion, prudence, a politic and ingratiating habit. The walls are not to be stormed; they must be wooed to a sort of Jerichoan fall. Success takes the form of a series of waves of protective coloration; failure is a succession of unmaskings. The aspirant must first imitate exactly the aspects and behavior of the class he yearns to penetrate. There follows notice. There follows confusion. There follows recognition and acceptance.

Thus the hog murderer's or soap boiler's wife horns into the fashionable society of Chicago or New York, and thus the whiskey drummer insinuates himself into the Elks, and the rising retailer wins the toleration of wholesalers, and the rich peasant becomes a planter, and the servant girl penetrates the movies, and the shyster lawyer becomes a statesman, and Schmidt turns into Smith, and all of us Yankees creep up, up, up. The business is not to be accomplished by headlong assault; it must be done quietly, insidiously, pianissimo. Above all, it must be done without exciting alarm and opposition lest the portcullis fall. Above all, the manner of a Jenkins must be got into it.

* *

It seems to me that this necessity is responsible for one of the characters that observers often note in the average American, to wit, the character of orthodoxy, of eager conformity—in brief, the fear to give offense. "More than any other people," said Wendell Phillips one blue day, "we Americans are afraid of one another." The saying seems harsh. It goes counter to the national delusion of uncompromising independence and limitless personal freedom. It wars upon the national vanity. But all the same there is a good deal of truth in it.

What is often mistaken for an independent spirit, in dealing with the national traits, is not more than a habit of crying with the pack. The American is not a joiner for nothing. He joins something, whether it be a political party, a church or a tin-pot fraternal order, because joining gives him the feeling of security—because it makes him a part of something larger and safer than he is —because it gives him chance to work off his steam within prudent limits. Beyond lie the national taboos. Beyond lies true independence—and the heavy penalties that go therewith. Once over the border, and the whole pack is on the heretic.

* *

The taboos that I have mentioned are extraordinarily harsh and numerous. They stand around nearly every subject that is genuinely important to man; they hedge in free opinion and experimentation on all sides. Consider, for example, the matter of religion. It is debated freely and furiously in almost every country in the world save the United States. Here the debate, save it keep to the superficial, is frowned upon. Let an individual uncover the fundamentals of the thing, and he is denounced as a disturber of the public peace. Let a journal cut loose and at once an effort is made to bar it from the mails. The result is that all religions are equally safeguarded against criticism, and that all of them lose vitality. We protect the status quo, and so make steady war upon revision and improvement.

Nor is our political discussion much more free and thorough. It concerns itself, in the overwhelming main, with non-essentials; time and again the two chief parties of the country, warring over details, have come so close together that it has been almost impossible to distinguish them. Whenever a stray heretic essays to grapple with essentials he finds himself denounced for his contumacy. Thus the discussion of the capital problem of industrial organization, in so far as it has gone on at all, has gone on under the surface, and almost furtively. Now, suddenly bursting out in wartime, it takes on an aspect of the sinister, and causes justifiable alarm. That alarm might have been avoided by threshing out the thing in the days of peace.

Behind all this timorousness, of course, there is a sound discretion. With a population made up of widely various and often highly antagonistic elements, many of them without political experience, the dangers of a too free gabbling needn't be pointed out. But at the same time it would be useless to deny the disadvantages of the current system of taboos. It tends to substitute mere complacency for alertness and information. It gives a false importance to the occasional rebel. It sets up a peace that is full of dynamite.

(The New York Evening Mail, May 3, 1918)

On Being an American

I

Apparently there are those who begin to find it disagreeable. One of them unburdened his woes in this place last Tuesday, under the heading of "Is America Fit to Live In?" Let me confess at once that his elegy filled me with great astonishment. I had labored under the impression that this Republic was wholly satisfactory to all 100% Americans—that any proposal to fumigate and improve it was as personally offensive to them as a proposal to improve the looks of their wives. Yet here was a 100% American ranting against it like a Bolshevik on a soap box. And here was I, less than 1/2 of 1% American by volume, standing aghast. A curious experience, indeed. Can it be that all the 100% Americans are preparing to throw up their hands and move out, leaving the land that the Fathers sweated and bled for to us Huns?

God forbid! I'd as lief have some poor working girl (mistaking the street number) leave twins on my doorstep. No one would weep saltier tears than I when the huge fleet of Mayflowers sailed away, bound for some land of liberty. For what makes America charming is precisely the Americans—that is, those above 50%, those above proof. They are, by long odds, the most charming people that I have ever encountered in this world. They have the same charm that one so often notes in a young girl, say of seventeen or eighteen, and perhaps it is grounded upon the same qualities; artlessness, great seriousness, extreme self-consciousness, a fresh and innocent point of view, a disarming and ingratiating ignorance. They are culturally speaking the youngest of white races, and they have all the virtues that go with youngness. It is easy to excite them. It is easy to fool them. But it is very hard to dislike them.

Perhaps there is something deeper than the qualities I have rehearsed. I grope for it vaguely, and decide that it is probably a naïve fidelity to good intentions. The Americans do everything with the best of motives, and with all the solemnity that goes therewith. And they get the reward that the jocose gods invariably bestow. I recall a scene in a low burlesque show, witnessed for hire in my days as a dramatic critic. A chorus girl executes a fall on the stage, and Krausemeyer, the Swiss comedian, rushes to her aid. As he stoops painfully to pick her up, Irving Rabinovitz, the Zionist comedian, fetches him a fearful clout across the cofferdam with a slapstick. Here, in brief, is the history of the United States, particularly in recent years. Say what you will against it, I maintain to the last that it is diverting—that it affords stimulating entertainment to a civilized man.

II

Where, indeed, is there a better show in the world? Where has there been a better show since the Reformation? It goes on daily, not in three rings, but in three hundred rings, and in each one of them whole battalions of acrobats tie themselves into fabulous knots, and the handsomest gals in Christendom pirouette upon the loveliest and most skittish horses, and clowns of unbelievable limberness and humor perform inordinate monkey-shines. Consider, for example, the current campaign for the Presidency. Would it be possible to imagine anything more stupendously grotesque—a deafening, nerve-wracking battle to the death between Tweedledum and Tweedledee—the impossible, with fearful snorts, gradually swallowing the inconceivable? I defy anyone to match it elsewhere on this earth. In other lands, at worst, there are at least issues, ideas, personalities. Somebody says something intelligible, and somebody replies. It is important to somebody that the thing go this way or that way. But here, having perfected democracy, we lift the whole combat to a gaudy symbolism, to a disembodied transcendentalism, to metaphysics, that sweet nirvana. Here we load a pair of palpably tin cannons with blank cartridges charged with talcum-powder, and so let fly. Here one may howl over the show without an uneasy reminder that some one is being hurt.

I hold that this exhibition is peculiarly American—that nowhere else on this disreputable ball has the art of the sham-battle been developed to such fineness. Two late experiences in point. A few weeks back a Berlin paper reprinted an article of mine from the *Evening Sunpaper,* with an explanatory preface. In this preface the editor was at pains to explain that no intelligent man in the United States regarded the result of an election as important, and to warn the Germans against getting into feverish sweats over such combats. Last week I had dinner with an Englishman. From cocktails to bromo seltzer he bewailed the political lassitude of the English populace—its growing indifference to the whole political buffoonery. Here we have two typical foreign attitudes; the Germans make politics too harsh and implacable, and the English take politics too lightly. Both attitudes make for bad shows. Observing a German election, one is uncomfortably harassed and stirred up; observing an English election, one falls asleep. In the United States the thing is better done. Here it is purged of all menace, all sinister quality, all genuine significance—and stuffed with such gorgeous humors, such extravagant imbecilities, such uproarious farce that one comes to the end of it with one's midriff in tatters.

III

But feeling better for the laugh. As the 100% *pleurour* said last Tuesday, the human soul craves joy. It is necessary to happiness, to health. Well, here is the land of joy. Here the show never stops. What could be more steadily mirth-provoking than the endless battle of the Puritans to make this joy unlawful and impossible? The effort is itself a greater joy to one standing on the sidelines than any or all of the joys that it combats. If I had to choose between hanging Dr. Kelly and closing all of the theatres in Baltimore, I'd surely shut up the theatres, for nine times out of ten their laborious struggles to amuse me merely bore me, whereas Dr. Kelly fetches me every time. He is, it seems to me, the eternal American, ever moved by good intentions, ever lifting me to yells with the highest of motives, ever stooping à la Krausemeyer to pick up a foundered chorus girl and ever getting a thumping clout from the Devil.

I am sinful, and such spectacles delight me. If the slapstick were a sash-weight the show would be cruel, and I'd probably go to the rescue of Dr. Kelly. As it is I know that he is not hurt. On the contrary, it does him good: it helps to get him into Heaven. As for me, it helps to divert me from my sorrows, of which there are many. More, it makes me a better American. One man likes the republic because it pays better wages than Bulgaria. Another because it has laws to keep him sober, pious and faithful to his wife. Another because the Woolworth Building is higher than the cathedral at Chartres. Another because Roosevelt could not leave the job to his son. Another because, living here, he can read the New York *Journal*. Another because there is a warrant out for him somewhere else. Me, I like it because it amuses me. I never get tired of the show. It is worth every cent it costs.

IV

I have never heard of such a show in any other country. Perhaps one goes on in Russia, but, as the European *Advocatus Diaboli* said last Tuesday, it is difficult to be happy when one is hungry. Here one always gets plenty to eat, even in the midst of war, and, despite Prohibition, quite enough to drink. I remember many postprandial felicities, inconceivable in Europe, Asia, Africa or

Oceania. Four nights, for example, at the Billy Sunday circus; one night in particular. I had got down a capital dinner, with three or four coffin-varnish cocktails and half a bottle of Beni Carlo. (Ah, those days!) Proceeding to the holy place, I witnessed the incomparable spectacle of a governor of Maryland, the president of a bank and the president of the Western Maryland Railroad moaning and puffing in a bull-ring together. Match it in Europe if you can! I defy you to name the country. The governor, prefect, lord lieutenant, *Oberpräsident* of an ancient and imperial province sobbing out his sins in the presence of 20,000 neckstretchers, the while a florid man with an elkhorn mustache played "Throw Out the Lifeline" on a trombone!

Another memory. The other day, in New York, I gave ear to a publisher soured and made hopeless by the incessant forays of the Comstocks—*The "Genius"* and *Jurgen* suppressed out of hand, half a dozen other good books killed abornin', the national letters hamstrung and knee-haltered by a violent arbitrary and unintelligible despotism. That night I went to the Winter Garden to see the new show. During the first part, 40 or 50 head of girls with their legs bare marched down a runway into the audience, passing within four or five centimetres of my popping eyes. During the second part two comedians came out and began to make jokes about what Havelock Ellis calls inversion. Revolve the thing in your mind. Here was I, an innocent young yokel, forbidden by law to read *Jurgen*, and yet it was quite lawful to beguile me with a herd of half-naked vampires and to divert me with jests proper only to banquets of internes at the Phipps Clinic! After the show I met Ernest A. Boyd. He told me that he had a fearful beer thirst and would gladly give $5 for a *Humpen* of 2 3/4%. I raised him $1, but we found that malt was forbidden. But down in Greenwich Village we found plenty of 100-proof Scotch at 65 cents a drink.

V

Let the 100% viewer-with-alarm stay his tears. If this is not joy, then what is?

(The Baltimore Evening Sun, October 11, 1920)

More Notes for a Work
upon the Origin and Nature
of Puritanism

I

The Puritan background.—Dr. Leon Kellner, in his small but extremely acute work upon the history of American literature, accurately sets forth the causes behind the almost total lack of aesthetic aspiration among the original Puritans. The causes behind the same deficiency in the citizens of the new republic are quite as manifest. These citizens, in the overwhelming majority—and despite much hollow romance about fugitive aristocrats—were men of the simplest peasant stocks, and with traditions of unbroken aesthetic bleakness behind them. Moreover, they were face to face with the exigent problems of existence in a country that had yet to reach any coherence of social organization, and was but imperfectly explored, delimited and defended, and they were without the inspirational influence of a court and an aristocracy, for the only aristocrats they knew were, on the one hand, the characteristically ignorant *junkers* of the great estates, and, on the other hand, the even more boorish magnates of the city *bourgeoisie.* Above all, they were incessantly hag-ridden by political difficulties, both internal and external, of an inordinate complexity, and these occupied all the leisure they could steal from the laborious work of every day. It is difficult for an American of the present time, for all the tumult of our campaigns, to understand the capital part that politics played in American thought and life in the days before the Civil War. Setting aside religion, it was literally the only concern of the people. All men of ability and ambition turned to it for self-expression; it engaged the press to the exclusion of everything else; drawing the best literary talent into its service—Franklin, Jefferson and Lincoln may well stand as examples—it left the cultivation of belles lettres to women and second-rate men. And when, breaking through these bonds of indifference, some chance first-rate man gave himself over to a purely aesthetic expression, his reward was not only neglect, but even a sort of ignominy, as if such enterprises were not for men of self-respect. I need not point to Poe and Whitman, the one almost allowed to starve and the other proceeded against with the utmost rigors of outraged Philistinism.

II

Literature, in brief, was clearly disassociated from the actual struggle for existence. Save one counts in such crude political tracts as *Uncle Tom's Cabin,* one finds it difficult, sweeping the whole literary history of that period, to find a single work offering an artistic presentation of the life that Americans were then living. Later on the time found historians and interpreters, and in one work, at least, to wit, *Huckleberry Finn,* there appeared the elements of the grand literature that is perhaps to come; but no such impulse to representation showed itself contemporaneously; there was not even the crude sentimentalization of here and now that one finds in the popular novels of today.

Fenimore Cooper filled his romances not with the people about him, but with the Indians beyond the sky-line, and made them half fabulous to boot. Irving told fairy tales about the forgotten Knickerbockers; Hawthorne turned backward to the Puritans of Plymouth Rock; Longfellow to the Acadians and the prehistoric Indians; Emerson took flight from earth altogether; even Poe sought refuge in a land of fantasy. It was only the frank second raters—*e.g.,* Whittier—who ventured to turn the life around them to literary uses, and the banality of the result is a sufficient indication of the crudeness of contemporary taste, and the mean position assigned to the art of letters. This was preeminently the era of the moral tale, the Sunday-school book. Literature was conceived, not as a thing in itself, but merely as a handmaiden to politics or religion. The great celebrity of Emerson in New England was not the celebrity of a literary artist, but that of a theologian and metaphysician; he was esteemed in much the same way that Jonathan Edwards had been esteemed. Even down to our own time, indeed, his vague and empty philosophizing has been put above his undeniable capacity for graceful utterance, and it remained for Dr.

Kellner to consider him purely as a literary artist, and to give him due praise for his undeniable skill.

III

The Civil War brought that era of utter sterility to an end. The shock of it completely reorganized the American scheme of things, and even made certain important changes in the national Puritanism, or, at all events, in its machinery. Whitman, whose career straddled, so to speak, the four years of the war, was the leader—and, for a long while, the only trooper—of a double revolt. On the one hand he offered a courageous challenge to the intolerable prudishness and dirty-mindedness of Puritanism, and on the other hand he boldly sought the themes and even the modes of expression of his poetry in the arduous, contentious and highly melodramatic life that lay all about him. Whitman, however, was clearly before his time. His countrymen could see him only as immoralist; save for a pitiful few of them, they were dead to any understanding of his stature as artist, and even unaware that such a category of men existed. He was put down as an invader of the public decencies, a disturber of the public peace; even his eloquent war poems, surely the best of all his work, were insufficient to get him a hearing; the sentimental rubbish of "The Blue and the Gray" and the supernaturalism of "The Battle Hymn of the Republic" were far more to the public taste.

Where Whitman failed, indeed, all subsequent explorers of the same field have failed with him, and the great war has left no more mark upon American letters than if it had never been fought. Nothing remotely approaching the bulk and beam of Tolstoi's *War and Peace*, or, to descend to a smaller scale, Zola's *The Attack on the Mill*, has come out of it. Its appeal to the national imagination was undoubtedly of the most profound character; it colored politics for 50 years, and is today a dominating influence in the thought of whole sections of the American people. But in all that stirring up there was no upheaval of artistic consciousness, for the plain reason that there was no artistic consciousness there to heave up, and so all we have in the way of Civil War literature is a few conventional melodramas, a few forgotten short stories by Ambrose Bierce and Stephen Crane and a half dozen idiotic popular songs in the manner of Randall's "Maryland, My Maryland."

IV

In the '70s and '80s, with the appearance of such men as Henry James, William Dean Howells, Mark Twain and Bret Harte, a better day seemed to be dawning. Here, after a full century of infantile romanticizing, were four men who at least deserved respectful consideration as literary artists, and, what is more, three of them turned from the conventionalized themes of the past to the teeming and colorful life that lay under their noses. But this promise of better things was soon found to be no more than a promise. Mark Twain, after *The Gilded Age,* slipped back into romanticism, and was presently in there before the Civil War, and finally in the Middle Ages. Harte, a brilliant technician, like O. Henry after him, had displayed his whole stock when he had shown his technique; histories were not even superficially true to the life they presumed to depict; one searched them in vain for an interpretation of it; they were simply idle tales.

As for Howells and James, both quickly showed that timorousness and reticence which are the distinguishing marks of the Puritan, even in his most intellectual incarnations. The American scene that they depicted with such meticulous care was chiefly peopled with marionettes; they shrank, characteristically, from those larger clashes of will and emotion which one finds in all truly first rate literature; in particular, they shrank from any interpretation of life which grounded itself upon any sense of its endless and inexplicable tragedy. In the vast combat of instincts and aspirations about them they saw only a feeble jousting of comedians. Their reaction to it was not visible in pity, but merely in giggles. Here again one saw the Philistine distrust of a square facing of the facts of existence; the Philistine exaltation of empty social customs, moralities and formulae; the imbecile assumption that, since God was in His Heaven, all was essentially well with the world; in brief, one saw what Nietzsche called "the greengrazing contentment of the herd," and of its prophets and artists no less than of its constituent nonentities.

V

But in addition to this Puritan impulse from within, there is laid upon American literature the heavy hand of a Puritan authority from without, and no examination of the history and condition of that literature can be of much value which does not take it constantly into account, and establish the means of its influence and operation. The one, of course, has depended upon the other. A people unconvinced of the pervasiveness of sin, the supreme importance of moral problems, the need of harsh and inquisitorial laws—in brief, of the whole Puritan theological and political apparatus—would never have permitted the growth of such curious flowers as Comstockery, so obnoxious and so incomprehensible to all foreigners.

There has never been any question before the American public, whether political or economic, religious or military, which did not resolve itself, soon or late, into a moral question. Even so dull a row as that over the currency produced its vast crop of saints and succubi, of martyrs and Pontius Pilates, of crimes, heathenries and crowns of thorns. Nor has there ever been any surcease of that spiritual eagerness which lay at the bottom of the original Puritan's moral obsession; the American has remained, from the very beginning, a man genuinely interested in the eternal mysteries, and fearful of missing their correct solution. The frank theocracy of the New England colonies had scarcely succumbed to the libertarianism of a godless Crown before there came the Great Awakening of 1734, with its orgies of homiletics and its restoration of talmudism to the first place among polite sciences. The Revolution, of course, brought a setback: the colonists faced so urgent a need of unity in politics that they declared a sort of *Treuga Dei* in religion, and that truce, armed though it was, left its imprint upon the First Amendment to the Constitution. But immediately the young Republic emerged from the stresses of adolescence, a missionary army took to the field again, and before long the Asbury revival was paling that of Whitefield, Wesley and Jonathan Edwards, not only in its hortatory violence but also in the length of its lists of slain.

VI

Thereafter, down to the outbreak of the Civil War, the country was rocked, again and again, by furious attacks upon the devil. On the one hand, this great campaign took a purely theological form, with a hundred new and fantastic creeds as its fruits; on the other hand, it crystallized into the hysterical temperance movement of the '30s and '40s, which penetrated to the very floor of Congress and put "dry" laws upon the statute books of 10 States; and on the third hand, as it were, it established a prudery in speech and thought from which we are still but half delivered. Such ancient and innocent words as "bitch" and "bastard" disappeared from the American language; Bartlett tells us, indeed, in his *Dictionary of Americanisms,* that even "bull" was softened to "male cow." This was the Golden Age of euphemism, as it was of euphuism; the worst inventions of the English mid-Victorians were adopted and improved. The word "woman" became a term of opprobrium, verging close upon downright libel; legs became the inimitable "limbs"; the "stomach" began to run from the "bosom" to the pelvic arch; pantaloons faded into "unmentionables"; the newspapers spun their parts of speech into such gossamer webs as "a statutory offense," "a house of questionable repute" and "an interesting condition."

And meanwhile the Good Templars and Sons of Temperance swarmed in the land like a plague of locusts. There was not a hamlet without its uniformed phalanx, its affecting exhibit of reformed drunkards. The Kentucky Legislature succumbed to a traveling recruiting officer, and two-thirds of the members signed the pledge. The National House of Representatives took recess after recess to hear eminent excoriators of the Rum Demon, and more than a dozen of its members forsook their duties to carry the new gospel to the bucolic heathen—the vanguard, one may note in passing, of innumerable Chautauquans of later years.

(The Baltimore Evening Sun, July 19, 1916)

The Psychic Follies

"Patriotism," said the late Dr. Johnson, glowering at Boswell, "is the last refuge of scoundrels." But there is something even worse: it is the first, last, and middle refuge of fools. Especially is this true under democracy, which is to say, in our incomparable republic, the masterpiece of God. Does one ever hear discourses upon patriotism from prudent and dignified men among us, themselves monuments to their own doctrine? One does not. One hears such pronunciamentos only from a dubious rabble of chautauqua orators, circus preachers, skyrocket politicians, bogus war heroes, half witted pedagogues, and professional uplifters, most of them with something to sell. The thing itself becomes a sort of forlorn joke, like Service and Law Enforcement. Whenever it is mentioned the judicious snicker—and reach uneasily for their watches.

Has any one ever figured out calmly what effect the flag drills, patriotic pageants, and other such maudlin buffooneries, now raging everywhere in the federal union, will probably have upon the rising generation? Will they fill the boys and gals with a boiling, patriotic passion, or will they convince them that the whole business is bunk? Go look at one of these exhibitions if you are in doubt. Observe the poor schoolma'm at her dreadful work, reading highfalutin nonsense out of a book, with one eye over her shoulder in fear that some prowling snooper will catch her leaving something out. And observe the children in front of the ma'm going through their tedious exercises like dogs being trained or soldiers being drilled. If this is a good way to inculcate love of country, then a good way to inculcate a love of aquatic sports would be to play upon the kids with a fire hose. It is, in fact, precisely the best way imaginable to make patriotism loathsome. The young emerge from their banal gestures and recitations with a firm conviction, probably never to be broken in after life, that venerating the flag is an operation not distinguishable from learning the multiplication table, taking castor oil, or getting washed behind the ears.

* *

It is a wonder to me that the brethren of the patriotic faculty do not learn a lesson from their colleagues of the Sunday schools. There were Sunday schools in America at least among the barbarous Puritans, so early as 1669, but it was not until 1872, with the adoption of the International Sunday School Lessons, that they became an organized pest. Since that time they have spread to the remotest parts of the country, and that is a rare child, indeed, who does not come under their fire at some time between the ages of 3 and 15. They have a very elaborate machinery for rounding up recruits, and they are greatly favored by parents, even those of an atheistic and wicked nature, because they pen up their scholars for two hours on a day when it is pleasant for elders to take naps.

Well, has any one ever noticed that this rise of Sunday schools in the United States has been exactly coincident with a general decay of piety? In 1850 fully 75 percent of all adult Americans had some sort of formal connection with a church; in 1926 the largest percentage that even the most romantic ecclesiastical statistician claims is less than 50. How are we to account for that backsliding? Is it due to the influence of Darwin and his accursed hypothesis of evolution? Is the blame to be put upon Nietzsche, the kaiser, or the bolsheviki? Is it a product of jazz, or golf, or the automobile, or the radio, or the immoral movies that come out of Hollywood the damned, or smoking by women, or prohibition, or Sunday baseball, or yellow journalism? Is Clarence Darrow at fault? Or Henry Ford? Or the late Luther Burbank?

All of these agents and agencies of the devil have been blamed, and sometimes by eminent experts in the moral sciences. But I choose to believe that the true villain is the Sunday school. Millions of Americans sent into it in youth unwillingly, have come out of their teens full of rebellion. Its banal ceremonials have somehow offended them, its theology has revolted them, its consecrated men have aroused their suspicions. So they head for the Bad Lands the moment they are free, and their souls, by premature and injudicious efforts to save them, are only put into peril. I believe that the Old Testament, taught to children, has sent more Americans to hell than even necking or the cigarette.

* *

Here I speak by the book, and out of my own hard experience and that of other highly respectable and virtuous men. My father was surely not pious, but I was noisy in infancy as in old age, and he liked to snooze on Sunday, and so he apprenticed me to an acquaintance who kept a Sunday school. This Sunday school belonged to one of the evangelical denominations and was typical of its kind. I sat in it for five or six years and acquired many things of value—for example, a wide and affectionate familiarity with old time Gospel hymns. I know all of them yet, and am glad of it, for they are hearty and amusing, and I believe that if any genuinely American music ever rises among us it will come out of them.

But I was also instructed in morals and theology, and here I soon ran aground. The teachers told off to belabor me were all manifestly idiots, even to the eyes of a boy of 10. Their ethical precepts, if I had accepted them, would have made me a Y.M.C.A.

secretary, which I was certainly not eager to be. Their theology was so childish and so full of plain holes that not a boy in my class ever took it seriously. Like the rest, I listened politely, but, like the rest, I let it go in one ear and out the other. The net result of this instruction was that, at the age of 12, I was a violent atheist, and so were most of the other boys. Hell was not a horror to us, but a joke.

It took me years of experience and suffering in this world to recover my natural human fear of it. Even today I often find myself harboring doubts about it. And even worse doubts about the rest of Protestant theology. It is hard for me, in fact, to contemplate a theologian with a candid and impartial eye. He is somehow disgusting to me, and when the chance offers to plant a hoof in his pantaloons I find myself tempted damnably. This is prejudice, and hence offensive to me, a man who loves justice. But I refuse to take the blame. I was poisoned in Sunday school.

* *

As I say, millions of other Americans have been poisoned in precisely the same way. The fact shows itself brilliantly whenever a Sunday school superintendent goes on trial in the criminal courts, which is oftener, alas, than it ought to be. Every lawyer will tell you that it is almost impossible to get a jury that will hear him fairly. On the panel there are invariably men who were sent to Sunday school in their nonage, and remember the adventure unpleasantly, and these men are hot for railroading the poor accused to jail at once without even hearing his defense. The percentage of convictions in America among professional criminals is not above 20 percent, but among Sunday school superintendents it is at least 95 percent. Every one rejoices when one of them is laid by the heels.

In the face of these plain facts I now hear that fanatics are going through the republic in summer setting up vacation Bible schools for the further harassment of the young and to the further damage and scandal of the Christian religion. Could any imaginable enterprise be more unwise? Thousands of mothers who long to go window shopping or to the movies will herd their children into these dens in order to get rid of them, and there they will be bored and battered for seven days a week, as they now are for one. What will be the effect upon them? The effect upon them, if the science of psychology deserves any respect, will simply be to convert them into frantic antinomians. They will go in like convicts climbing the gallows and they will come out ready to burn down the nearest church, even with a prayer meeting in progress. In twenty years Christians will be as rare in the general population of the country as they are now in the bench of bishops.

Such are the inevitable results of bombarding the young with notions beyond their comprehension and outside their natural tastes. The Sunday schools for half a century have been gradually emptying the churches. The vacation Bible schools, if they are not put down promptly by ecclesiastical authority, will complete the process. And the flag drills and patriotic pageants, kept up for a generation, will fill the land with growls and blushes every time the national ensign goes past.

(The Chicago Sunday Tribune, November 7, 1926)

The Gospel of Service

One day toward the middle of August of last year I sent 25 cents to the *Kiwanis* Magazine of Chicago for a copy of its current issue. My desire was to refresh myself with idealism, to bathe my soul in the spirit of service. The *Kiwanis* Magazine, as I knew, was the organ of Kiwanis International. It was read every day by thousands of resilient and eminent men of business—"leaders in their respective lines." One of its principal contributors was the Hon. Roe Fulkerson, a man whose writings had been an inspiration to multitudes. I looked forward to a spiritual debauch, and expected to come out of it full of pep and hot for service in my chosen craft.

But no *Kiwanis* Magazine arrived. It seemed strange. Two weeks passed, and then three weeks, and then a month. What had happened to service? I sent in a complaint. No answer. The year faded into autumn and then into winter. Christmas came, and after it New Year. I began to give up hope. Finally one day—I think it was late in January—there arrived a letter. It was from a firm of public accountants in Chicago. They said they were examining the books of the *Kiwanis* Magazine and wanted to know if the item of 25 cents, there credited to my account, was correct.

I replied instantly that it was. I added that I regretted the fact immensely. What I wanted, I explained at length, was not a credit of 25 cents but a copy of the *Kiwanis* Magazine. My soul ached and thirsted for its inspiration; I yearned to be uplifted; I wanted to learn how to serve. All this I conveyed to the firm of public accountants, closing with a respectful demand that the magazine be sent at once. No answer. I followed with a postcard, perhaps somewhat tart. No answer. Another. No answer.

* *

This January passed, and after it February. March dawned with the usual meteorological phenomena. My rheumatism by now was bothering me, and I was in a low state mentally. I was doomed, it seemed, to draw no inspiration from the fountain head. The boons and usufructs of Kiwanis were not for me. So I turned, on the 4th of the month, to the next best source. That is to say, I went to Washington to witness the inauguration of the Hon. Mr. Coolidge as President of the United States.

The show was disappointing, and I got home with a chill. My mental depression by now was extreme. I was beginning to have hallucinations. The sound of a phonograph set me to trembling. But suddenly and at one benign stroke I was cured. On my reading table, as I rolled into bed, I found a pile of magazines, all arrived while I was in attendance upon Dr. Coolidge. The first was the *Christian Herald*. I threw it into the fire unopened. The second was the *American Standard*. I put it aside for Sunday. The third was *Hot Dog*. I dropped it into my waste basket. But the fourth, O, hallelujah, was the *Kiwanis*.

I was still reading it at 3 A.M.—page after page describing the altruistic work of the Kiwanis of Red Lion, Pa., and Nashville, Tenn.; portraits of eminent Kiwanis orators, lecturers on service, prophets of New and Better Business Ethics, heralds of the millennial dawn; long, juicy exhilarating articles by Dr. Fulkerson and other wizards of the inspirational word; solemn treatises by Kiwanis philosophers on the esoteric meaning of Kiwanis, the secret work of its votaries; sermons in tabloid form by Kiwanis ecclesiastics. I read until 3 A.M., until 3.05, until 3.10. I fell asleep at last to dreams of introducing the principles of Kiwanis into journalism, of launching myself into constructive work, of consecrating myself to the ideal of service.

In the morning, alas, I am always somewhat sour. As I rolled out of bed my mood of exaltation was brutally dashed. I had sent

25 cents for the magazine. The price marked on the cover was 15 cents. Where was my change?

* *

For months thereafter this question worried me. Could it be that the very chiefs and captains general of Kiwanis, the syndics of the *Kiwanis* Magazine itself, would stoop to bilk a poor literary man out of 10 cents? The thought seemed somehow obscene, and so I put it out of my mind. But it kept on recurring. Specifically, it recurred on March 5, on March 11, on March 23, and on March 29. In April it recurred five times; in May eight times; in June three times; in July six times.

Over and over again I was tempted to write to the publisher, to the editor, to the public accountants, to the chief of police of Chicago, to Dr. Fulkerson, to the Kiwanis club in my town, to the secretariat of the League of Nations. The thought of that lost 10 cents began to ride me. It popped up a dozen times a day. But I always put it away as hideous. If Kiwanis itself was engaged in highjacking, then what would become of idealism in the world? If in the citadel of service a Christian and a patriot could be mulcted of 10 cents, then our boys died in vain at Château-Thierry and Dr. Frank Crane was a lobster.

My trust and hope, I need not say, were rewarded. On August 25 I received from the Kiwanis International an elegantly engrossed statement of account. It showed that on some unnamed date in the past I had deposited 25 cents in the Kiwanis treasury. It showed that on March 4, 1925, I had received goods and services to the value or amount of 15 cents. And it showed, by simple mathematical devices, that the sum of 10 cents remained to my credit. This balance was enclosed with the statement. There were five postage stamps of the United States, each bearing the portrait of the immortal Washington and each of the value of 2 cents. Five times two is ten. Kiwanis had made good and to the last cent.

* *

But let us go back. My order, as I have said, was sent in August, 1924. I got my magazine on March 4, 1925, say six and a half months later. I got my change on August 25, 1925, almost exactly a year later. Should I rejoice that my confidence in Kiwanis, in the long run, was justified—that its lofty principles triumphed over every weakness and temptation in the end? My reply is that I have already rejoiced, to the perhaps excessive profit of the ink and paper trusts. What haunts me is the uneasy feeling that I had to be confident far too long.

Is that feeling hypercritical? Do I yield once more to my lamentable tendency to cavil, my lust to destroy? I think not. Kiwanis is not of ordinary flesh. Kiwanis is Kiwanis. Its sworn purpose is to Improve Business Methods, to Give More Than Mere Goods, to preach the Gospel of Service. Once a week in every town of the republic its great minds meet to further that exalted aim. They sing a few songs, they blow a few spitballs, they get down their chicken croquettes and peach pie, and then they belch gently and give ear to their prophets.

The words of such prophets I enjoy immensely. That is why I sent for that copy of the *Kiwanis* Magazine. It delights me to follow their syllogisms. I approbate their eloquent demands for Something More. When I have my shoes shined I like the professor to inquire about my kidney trouble. Buying a box of collars, I am exhilarated when the haberdasher throws in a bottle opener. I chose my tailor because he sings beautifully and is a prominent Elk. My barber's charm is not in his mere shears but in his flow of economic and sociological ideas. No manicure girl can touch me who is not comely, a swell dresser, and a lover of the films. My bootlegger gets my trade because he is supporting ten orphans in a mission on the Yangtze Kiang.

In brief, I am a natural Kiwanian. I believe that business is also a form of idealism. I love and venerate service. But is it service to take six and a half months to fill a 15 cent order? And is it service to rob a poor man of the interest on 10 cents for a solid year? The answer I leave to the president of Kiwanis International, to the vice-presidents and ex-presidents thereof, to the regional directors, to the club secretaries, to the Hon. Mr. Fulkerson, and to the heirs and assigns of the author of "Sweet Adeline."

(The Chicago Sunday Tribune, October 4, 1925)

A Boon to Bores

I

The other day a strange thing happened. I sat down to dinner in my own house without any impertinent and imbecile jackass summoning me from the table to the telephone. The thing, indeed, seemed almost miraculous; you will never convince me that it could have been possible without divine intervention. There, for the first time in years, I wallowed in the luxury of a meal eaten in peace, with no abominable shrilling of a bell to interrupt my engulfing of my victuals, and no choleric conversation with a moron to paralyze my digestion.

Even so, my unaccustomed happiness was not entirely unpolluted. Though the bell never actually rang, I expected it at every moment, and the expectation, at certain of those moments, was almost as bad as the realization. I was uneasy, worried, at strain. It seemed altogether too pleasant to be true. It had never happened before. It has never happened since.

I speak of jackasses and morons, perhaps seeming to lay it on a bit thickly. The truth is that I push politeness to the verge of euphemism. There is in the whole world no more obnoxious and pestiferous idiot, no more villainous enemy of civilized decency and quiet, than the modern telephonomaniac.

Put beside him, all other known varieties of bores and nuisances shrink to what almost seems like amiability. The ox who favors one with unwanted letters, usually asking nonsensical questions, is easily disposed of; the waste-basket was invented by Galileo to entomb his garbage. The ass who drops in at one's office or pulls one's doorbell may be handled almost as readily; janitors know how to deal with him, and he may be circumvented by stout locks and signs reading "Will Return at 6 P.M."

But the numbskull who uses the telephone is almost unbeatable. There is no closed season for him; he rages unimpeded from 8 A.M. until after midnight. Only a private branch exchange can deal with him effectively—and a private branch exchange is a first-rate nuisance on its own account.

II

There are plenty of men, of course, to whom answering the telephone is a necessary part of the day's work, and most of them, I suppose, get used to it. I myself, in the days before I was educated, was the City Editor of an afternoon newspaper, and as such had to answer 60 telephone calls every day as a matter of routine, not to mention from 20 to 30 calls not foreseen. It was, generally speaking, unpleasant, but it was not actively annoying, for I had little else to do, and when the last edition went to press my telephone grew silent.

No one bothered me after I got home and stretched out with a book—that is, not unless some extraordinary news broke loose, which was not often. Those were the arcadian days before the development of the modern telephone bore, *i.e.*, before the enormous increase in telephone calls which telephone company treasurers, Rotary Club orators and other such criminals view with such pride. No one with whom I was unacquainted called me up. It had not yet been discovered by stoneheads that the telephone offered them a cheap and convenient means of torturing their betters.

Today the fact is universally known, and the number of such stoneheads seems to increase annually. Now the nuisance begins to take on the proportions of a national pestilence. There are even performers on the long-distance lines—degraded half-wits who call one up from Washington, or Philadelphia, or some other distant place, and force one to wait idiotically while half a dozen operators chatter along the line.

If I live to be a century I'll never get used to long-distance calls, or cease to swear horribly when they are announced. I have received enough of them in my time to make it absolutely sure that I'll go to hell when I die, but in all these years I have not received a single one that was worth waiting for 10 seconds. A mathematical certainty of imbecility seems to hang about them, like that which hangs about special delivery letters.

I receive special delivery letters almost every day; yet in my whole life I have never received one that contained any news that might not have come by ox-cart at one knot an hour. They are the playthings of a special breed of nuisance—the larvae, perhaps, of telephonomaniacs. I never answer a special delivery letter, and after February 1 next I shall never open one.

III

To get rid of the telephone curse is more difficult. More than once I have thought of ordering my telephone out, but that would simply make it difficult for my friends to communicate with me, or for persons to reach me conveniently who have legitimate business with me. Worse, it would deprive me of a simple and cheap means of ordering things from the stores. It is seldom that I use the telephone more than twice a week, but when I need it I need it badly. Again, I have toyed with the notion of having my name taken out of the telephone book, thus making my telephone what is called "silent." But that would simply cause trouble to my friends —and offer little impediment to the bores. The latter seem to have the numbers of all "silent" telephones. Persons who have such telephones tell me that they are annoyed almost as much as I am.

There remains the scheme of taking the receiver off the hook—a scheme, I confess, that I have often practiced when I had work to do, and was in no mood to listen to donkeys. Unluckily, it is open to all of the objections that lie against the other two plans, and has, in addition, one of its own; it makes the exchange girls swear like sailors (of course inaudibly) and causes them to send a repairman to find out what is wrong. The repairman comes in, jangles the bell for ten minutes, holds long conversations with colleagues somewhere else, and pockmarks the parquetry with his spikes. I dislike putting an honest man to so much trouble in such a dishonest manner; it is like hauling a member of the Medical and Chirurgical Faculty out of bed at 3 A.M. to prescribe a pint of rye for a poker party. To the last one who came to my house I offered my apologies and a bottle of Erbacher 1913. It is almost better to stand the ringing of the telephone bell.

IV

Better, perhaps—but sometimes almost a sheer impossibility. Maybe mine is a special case, but I can only tell my own story. I don't think I am unusually sensitive to noises, or even to more gross interruptions. An old newspaper reporter should certainly be hard-boiled in that department. But it must be obvious that, to do any sort of writing that is based upon reflections as opposed to mere observation, however trivial and erroneous that reflection may be, requires something approaching quiet and peace.

If I start at 9 A.M. to compose a treatise upon the Disarmament buffoonery, and am interrupted at 9.10 by a woman who wants me to subscribe to some brummagem charity, and at 9.17 by another woman who wants to know if I will read her poetry, and at 9.27 by a life insurance solicitor, and at 9.33 by a strange simian who wants to know who publishes this or that book and at 9.41 by a misdirected call for some neighbor, and at 9.50 by another, and at 9.56 by a third, then it is a bet of at least a hundred to one that I'll have very little on paper by 10 o'clock, and that what is there will be blowsy and puerile stuff. It is simply out of the question to do any decent writing under such circumstances—and yet those are the circumstances under which most writing has to be done in America today.

I work in a remote part of my house, removed by a flight of stairs from the nearest telephone station. This means that every time I am called to the telephone I must go downstairs and then come upstairs again. Why don't I have another extension made to my desk? What a question! Would I be any more comfortable if the infernal machine were directly under my nose—if I had to answer all calls, instead of escaping the many that are now flagged downstairs? If I make any change at all, it will be to order out the second floor extension and put the main telephone in the cellar. If it rings down there, however shrilly, I'll scarcely hear it—and the three flights up and down will rid me of all temptation to answer it.

V

So far I indulge in destructive criticism. Now for a brief paragraph of constructive suggestion.

First, I propose that it be made an invariable rule by all telephone users to state their names clearly the moment they are answered. Most of the bores fail to do this now. As a result, I am brought to the telephone at least three times a day to talk to unknowns who turn out to be unmitigated nuisances. The prompt mention of the name would make a man polite to his friends; too often today, I fear, I am brusque to persons whom it pains me to offend.

Second suggestion: let every man (and woman) who is not admittedly a pestiferous idiot take a pledge to refrain absolutely from calling up strangers, unless by the nature of their profession or in some other way, they specifically invite it, and especially to refrain from calling them up at their homes.

Third: let everybody promise to avoid unnecessary calls under all circumstances.

Fourth: let the clergy of the city offer public prayers that famine and pestilence descend upon all who violate the pledge.

(The Baltimore Evening Sun, January 9, 1922)

Radio Programs

I

The radio, I take it, is quite satisfactory to the wowsers who now propose to make the movies safe for morons. That is to say, it is as devoid of ideas as a Kiwanis orator, and as bare of beauty as a city dump. For hour after hour its customers sit listening to bad music, worse speeches, and other entertainment so dreadful that it cannot be described. The height of comedy on the air is reached by the dialogues of Amos and Andy—a kind of humor that drove people out of smalltime vaudeville shops twenty years ago. Music, if it be instrumental, is supplied mainly by gangs of union men sawing away dismally in the dining rooms of second-rate hotels; if it be vocal, it is performed by decayed fugitives from third-rate church choirs and fourth-rate opera companies. As for the speeches, they seem to issue, with few exceptions, from gentlemen trained as ballyhoo men at county fairs.

Nearly a year ago a kind friend, seeking to improve my Americanism, gave me a very good radio outfit, and sent a mechanic to my house to hook it up with the skies. Since then I have made probably 250 attempts to get something out of it that was worth hearing. But though I have tackled it at all hours from daylight to 3 A.M., and swept the pointer from end to end of the dial, I can't recall more than thirty occasions when I have got anything even remotely describable as civilized entertainment. Everything else that has come over the air has been rubbish. I'd have done as well to hire the Salvation Army for both words and music.

During the winter, to be sure, there were a few good concerts—

some by the New York Philharmonic and some by a scratch orchestra at the Roxy Theater. But the latter were given at an inconvenient hour, and the former were regularly cut off in Baltimore by a braying of consecrated Babbitts at the Y.M.C.A. Moreover, both orchestras played only on Sunday. On week days I have never heard any decent music at all, save only from a small ensemble playing at the Savoy-Plaza Hotel in New York. It may be that other good music has been played, but if so I have never found it. All that I have been able to raise has kept to the general level of a dance orchestra or a circus band.

II

Why this should be so I don't know. It simply can't be that all the radio fans are idiots; certainly there must be a respectable minority of intelligent folk among them. The phonograph people have wind of such a minority, and are at great pains to cater to it. They produce records of the best music ever written, and at reasonable prices. One may hear any of the standard symphonies, well played by a good orchestra, and there are also albums of the operas, of concertos and chamber music, and even of such things as Brahms' *Deutsches Requiem* and the Bach B Minor Mass. But on the air there is little save a murrain of dull jazz, broken ever and anon by the gargling of a soprano told off to finish Tosti's "Goodbye," or the horrible heavings and bellowings of a basso dying in *"Gunga Din."*

The speeches, if anything, are even worse. At long intervals some one who knows what he is talking about takes to the air, but that is surely not often. In the main, the radio is monopolized by obscure ignoramuses with nothing what ever to say. Once a year or so the Pope or some other such dignitary is heard (usually speaking in a foreign tongue), or a George Bernard Shaw gives a brief show. But it is almost unheard of for any novelty of that sort to be of American origin. The radio, in the department of oratory, is tolerable only when it is European. Ninety-nine out of a hundred of the native rhetoricians are persons who have absolutely nothing to say, and say it as badly as possible.

Nor do they commonly discuss interesting things. For six days running, seeking to inflame and instruct my mind at lunchtime, I threw the switch—and got harangues on Farm Relief! Another time I horned into an address on the service offered by a garage somewhere down Sparrows Point way. Yet another time I heard a man with a vaseline voice reading from what turned out to be *Science and Health*. Can it be that there are people who listen to such stuff, willingly and with pleasure? Then there are also people who spend their holidays picking Jimsonweeds and spitting at a mark.

III

The contrast between the American air program, at least as we get it here in Baltimore, and the English program is really heart-breaking. The English, though everyone knows that they are a backward and bankrupt people, who would have been laboring as slaves in Germany today if it had not been for General Pershing and the American Legion, yet manage to make the radio an agent of highly civilized entertainment, and even of education. In proof whereof I turn to the announcement of *B.B.C. Talks* (*i.e.,* British Broadcasting Corporation, the national radio monopoly) for April-July of this year. It appears in a neat pamphlet, and copies are free to all.

What strikes one at once is the high competence of the speakers. The man who discusses music every Friday is not a banal newspaper concert-trotter, but Ernest Newman, the best music critic now living in England, and perhaps the best in the world. The theater is not handled by a press-agent, but by James Agate, a recognized authority, and, what is more, an honest man. And the reviewers of the new books are not advertising agents employed by publishers, but Desmond MacCarthy, an excellent critic, and the Hon. Mrs. Sackville-West, a competent novelist. Even the movies have an intelligent commentator—Francis Birrell, a son of old Augustine, and himself a man of letters of respectable position.

So much for the arts. When it comes to the sciences there is the same showing of good names. A series of five talks on life in the sea is by Dr. A. C. Hardy, professor of zoölogy at Hull, and a series of six on chemistry is by six high authorities, including Sir William Pope, professor of that science at Cambridge. The talks on agriculture are not by political propagandists, as in America, but by practical authorities, many of them actual farmers. And the time devoted to religion is not wasted upon Y.M.C.A. bores and other such puerile evangelists; it is given over to what seems to be a capital series on the history of the Bible by Dr. C. H. Dodd, one of the foremost exegetes in England.

IV

Many of the best books that have come out in England of late have been made up of just such radio talks. I offer as examples Sir James Jeans' *The Stars in Their Courses*, and Dr. C. Leonard Woolley's *Digging Up the Past*. Both books are now being read very widely in the United States, and deservedly so, but nothing even remotely comparable to their contents is ever heard on the air on this side. Instead, we have an almost unbroken series of propagandist harangues by quacks with something to sell, and of idiotic comments upon public events by persons devoid of both information and ideas.

The B.B.C. does not stop with its good programs—which include first-rate music and other entertainment, of course, as well as instruction. It also publishes an elaborate series of pamphlets to accompany the talks, and arranges with the public libraries to provide whatever books suggest themselves for auxiliary reading. Among the current pamphlets are one on "India," to accompany a series of talks by eminent Indians and Englishmen; one on the religions of the East, to accompany a series by Dr. Sydney Cave, president of Cheshunt College, Cambridge, and one on psychology, to accompany a series by Dr. William McDougall. These pamphlets are sold at trifling prices, and all of those issued during any year may be obtained postpaid for 75 cents.

Two of the most valuable and interesting of the series of talks are devoted to foreign languages. Every Monday at 8 P.M. there begins a half hour's lesson in French, and every Wednesday at the same time there is one in German. Suitable textbooks are recommended. The French course has now gone so far that "listeners who are completely ignorant of French would be well advised not to join at this stage," but the German half hour is still divided into three parts, for beginners, second-year listeners, and advanced students. Hundreds of thousands of persons listen in on these courses, and they have been widely imitated on the Continent. In Austria one teacher of English by radio is said to have 150,000 listeners.

The B.B.C. is a Government agency, and is supported by a small annual tax on radio outfits. It sends nothing shabby, cheap or vulgar onto the air. There is no bad music by bad performers; there is no pestilence of oratory by ignoramuses; there is no sordid touting of tooth-pastes, automobile oils, soaps, breakfast foods, soft drinks and patent medicines. In America, of course, the radio program costs nothing. But it is worth precisely the same.

(The Baltimore Evening Sun, June 29, 1931)

The Movies

At short intervals one hears news that the movies are about to be uplifted. Does it ever actually happen? It does not. The movies today, if the accounts of those who frequent them are to be believed, are as bad as they have ever been, and in more than one way they grow worse. Has the threat of censorship purged them of their old frank carnality? Perhaps. But in place of it there is only imbecility. Of late, unable to endure the actual films, I have been reading some movie scenarios—that is, the scenarios of movies currently on view, and most of them successes. What I found in those scenarios, at the best, was precisely what the servant girls of my youth used to find in the *Fireside Companion.* In other words, what I found there was simply mawkish and maudlin bilge.

There are, to be sure, films of a better sort, but how many? Certainly not enough to give any color to the general run. In that general run one finds only fodder for half-wits. The transactions depicted all lie upon the level of kitchen wench romance. That play of rational and amusing ideas which one encounters occasionally in the drama, and very frequently in the novel, is simply not there. The best movie ever heard of, put beside the worst play by Bernard Shaw or the worst novel by a Cabell, become sheer idiocy. The worst sinks so low that no other art, not even that of the architect of suburban filling stations, can show a parallel to it.

Where do the authors come from who concoct such depressing drivel? Some of them seem to be recruited from the ranks of the dramatists, and others are novelists of more or less dignity in their own craft. But when they write for the movies something seems to happen to them—or, at all events, something happens to what they write. It may start out, for all I know, as plausible stuff, even as charming stuff. But by the time it gets to the movie parlor it is only garbage. No author of any decent position has ever written a movie that added an inch to his stature as an artist. But many an author, going to the movies, has been ruined.

* *

Why should this be so? I can discern no sound reason in the nature of things. It is perfectly easy to imagine an intelligent and amusing movie, with an idea in it at least as sound as that in the average stage play, and enough ingenuity in its details to hold the attention of a civilized spectator. The technic of the movie, true enough, is still a bit stiff and unnatural, but so is the technic of the opera. Yet there are plenty of operas that do not insult the intelligence. They have true beauty in them; they conceal the clumsiness of their own form; they have intellectual dignity. One may endure them without throwing one's self into the mood of a hotel chambermaid on a holiday. Slightly intoxicated, one may even enjoy them.

But the movies never rise to that level. In order to enjoy them without treason to the higher cerebral centers one must take on so vast a dose of stimulants that one cannot see them at all. Why? If the experts who profess the subject are to be credited, it is because every movie, before it gets to the screen, must be filtered through a dozen intelligences—and many of them are not intelligences at all, but simply vacuums. It is because the confection of movies is not entrusted to artists, nor even to competent artisans, but to gangs of blacksmiths and pants pressers. These blacksmiths and pants pressers decide what is to be played, and then they decide, in detail, precisely how it is to be played. The result is the aforesaid garbage.

No art, however sturdy, could conceivably survive such murderous sabotage. If an opera librettist had to submit his work to a committee of trolley conductors, and the composer had to write every note under the eye of a church choir tenor and an auctioneer, and if the resultant composition had to be produced by a designer of hot dog stands, and the singers rehearsed by an oyster shucker, then opera would be what the movies are today. In brief, they are idiotic because their production is mainly in the hands of idiots—with a few cynics interspersed to watch for the times when even idiots show some sense.

The bondage of the movies to men wholly incapable of grasping the nature of a fine art, and of no more native taste or intellectual dignity than so many curve greasers or Anti-Saloon league congressmen—this bondage is not due to the movies themselves, but simply to a chain of perfectly obvious natural causes.

The movie business, starting out a generation ago on a shoestring, quickly plunged, like most new enterprises, into an era of wildcatting. Any man with money enough to hire a loft above a livery stable could set up a movie parlor, and any man who could borrow a second-hand camera and induce a few jobless actors to trust him was ready to make films. The result was a saturnalia of speculation and roguery. Patents were worth nothing to the wildcatters; copyrights were worth nothing; contracts were worth nothing. To take the word of a movie man, in those gay days, was like believing the oath of a prohibition agent.

But among them were some men of greater rectitude, and, what is more, of greater talent for business—mainly men who had been petty tradesmen, but still fellows with some grasp of business principles. They tried to reorganize and stabilize the movie industry, and after long and desperate struggles they succeeded. It was no mean task, and they well deserved the profits that flowed in upon them. The trade today, so its leaders boast, is as sound as the steel business, and even has its code of honor. There are movie men in Rotary; there will be a movie window in the Cathedral of St. John the Divine.

* *

But the bookkeeper of an opera house, alas, is seldom competent to select its repertory or to rehearse its caterwaulers. The movies, today, suffer from that profound and inconvenient fact. The men who organized them as an industry now attempt to operate them as an art—and the result is exactly the same as that which follows when a rich hog fattener, having decided to retire to the county seat, designs his own house, including the wall paper and the steeple, and loads a fowling piece to make sure that the workmen carry out his plans.

In other words, the movies languish as a fine art because the men who determine what is to get into them haven't the slightest visible notion that such a thing as a fine art exists. Having learned by experience that certain classes of imbecilities fetch the mob and make a great deal of money, they conclude that such imbecilities are somehow worthy and laudable and so admire them themselves. Hence their honest wonder when the movies are denounced: they can no more imagine than you could that what pleases them should be disgusting to other persons. And hence their vigorous, paralyzing policing of the authors, scenario writers, directors, and actors who are their slaves. The ideas of these gentry alarm them, as they would alarm a Baptist evangelist or a policeman. They prefer their own.

But soon or late the authors, scenario writers, directors, and actors—that is, those among them who have any intelligence, which is not many—will have to revolt against this bondage. Soon or late the movie as an art will have to emancipate itself from the movie as a vast, machinelike, unimaginative, imbecile industry. Soon or late the artist must get his chance. He is halted today by a delusion borrowed from his enemy—that movies are possible only on a great scale, that they must inflame the morons or have no being at all. This is nonsense. The theater, once beset by the same folly, has been liberated by the so-called Little Theater—that is, by the amateur. The movie, I suspect, will be liberated in much the same way. Someday someone with an authentic movie mind will make a cheap and simple picture that will arrest the notice of the civilized minority as it was arrested by the early plays of Eugene O'Neill. When that day comes the movies will split into two halves, just as the theater has split. There will be huge, banal, maudlin, idiotic movies for the mob, and no doubt the present movie magnates will continue to produce them. And there will be movies made by artists, and for people who can read and write.

(The Chicago Sunday Tribune, July 3, 1927)

Traffic

I

The increasing pressure of traffic particularly in the downtown sections of our great Babylons and Gomorrahs, has at least one laudable effect: it makes the *Polizei* happy. Naturally pedantic, and trained, like pedagogues, in the doctrine that all human beings are precisely alike and may be handled like stalks of wheat, BB shot or hogs at the stockyards, they delight in the opportunity to make and enforce ever more complex and nonsensical regulations.

The invention of the traffic tower was a godsend to them. Pretty soon every principal street corner will have such a tower, an impediment to traffic by day and source of confusion and bewilderment at night. Where three or more streets come together there will be whole clusters of them. Such clusters, indeed, already exist —for example, at the entrance to Guilford. I defy any sane man to navigate between the Guilford towers at night without feeling that he is being shot at with spit-blowers. Their flashing, chromatic lights would confuse a driver with five eyes, two in the back of his head.

But they are only a beginning. The possibilities lying in such mechanical scare-crows have only just penetrated the constabulary imagination. When the cerebrums of the cops really begin to sweat and stream there will be a dozen such towers at every corner, some mere warts upon the roadway and some rising to ten, twenty and even fifty feet. Now they flash but two colors: white and red. Five years hence they will range the whole spectrum, like the new Christmas tree taxicabs. And to the lights the cops will add pin-wheels, Roman candles and bombs. They have already started to paint the curbstones all over town—now red; later on, green, blue, purple, pink, yellow, orange and violet. Half the crossings are covered with geometrical diagrams, unintelligible to any motorist who does not get out of his car and go down on his hands and knees to study them. The step will be a short one to the more occult figures of a spherical geometry.

II

The other day I read in the *Sunpaper* that so many motorists were herded for trial in the Traffic Court that it took three judges to dispose of them. Two of these learned men sat upon the bench, hearing the complaining cops and levying fines. The third worked in the crowd, sorting out the criminals for his colleagues. Just how many were in that crowd I forget: the number ran into the hundreds.

Obviously, the police, like Judge Elbert H. Gary, have no need to wait for heaven: they enjoy it here and now. What could be more charmingly to their taste than a body of laws which fills two courtrooms to suffocation every day, and keeps three judges leap-

ing and tugging like fire-engine horses? The situation is made the
more intoxicating by the fact that nine-tenths of the criminals are
persons who would not otherwise fall into the toils—that the traffic regulations tap whole new categories of victims. Time was
when the cops seldom got a chance to nab a white woman, and
never a respectable white woman. Now they take them by the
hundred. It is almost Utopia.

But, of course, not quite. The ideal of the *Polizei*, at all times and
everywhere, is to get their hands upon every citizen at least once a
day. Merit is apparently measured among them by the population
of the jails, prisons and hoosegows. If the warden of the City Jail
complains that he is forced to pack one hundred prisoners in a
cell, if over-worked judges swoon, yell for stimulants and fall from
the bench, then there is rejoicing where the constabulary rest
from labor. The traffic laws have been a boon to these worthy
men. It is now quite safe for them to halt and summon at least
twenty motorists out of every hundred. But that is not enough.
The ideal will not be reached until the laws are wholly transcendental and unobeyable—until a hundred out of every hundred
motorists are ripe for the dungeons, twenty-four hours a day—
until a man may commit just as many crimes when he is at home
in bed, with his car in dead storage, as he now commits every time
he passes the corner of Baltimore and Charles streets. Such is the
dream of *gendarmerie*. Such is human idealism.

III

There was a time when the American citizen was an idealist
himself. Now he is only idealism's raw material, as a cow is the
raw material of butter, ice-cream and custard pie—a stuff milked,
tickled, clubbed and pulverized into beauty by ordained virtuosi. I
am still so young that my toupee looks natural, yet I can remember when, if ordered to toe a mark or climb astraddle upon a rail,
the Americano would resist with harsh words, and even with his
fists. Now he leaps to position like a well-trained circus horse.

The other evening, coming downtown from West Baltimore, I
boarded one of the new two-car trains of the United Railways.
Observing that the front door of the forward car had been opened
by the motorman, and that other persons were entering it, I followed. The conductor was at the rear of this first car, or, rather, in
the rear car. He yelled "All fares!" and I went back and dropped

my fare into his box. The rear car was crowded, but there was plenty of room in the front car, so I started back. The conductor then told me politely enough, that this was *verboten*.

"Once you pass me," he said, "you can't go back."

I asked why. He said he didn't know: it was the order. At the next corner, six or eight persons got on and came back to pay their fares. He told them all that they could not go back; they did not ask why. A few blocks farther on the train stopped and the conductor opened the door behind him to let some passengers off. A flapper in waiting thereupon sprang up the steps and was in the car before the conductor observed her. Her appearance seemed to agitate him greatly.

"Get off!" he bawled. "You can't get on here. You hafta go up front."

The sweet one had apparently never heard of entering a street car by the front door; perhaps she had been warned more than once not to attempt it. She stood bewildered and irresolute.

"Off! Off!" bellowed the conductor. "Don't you yer me? You gotta go up front."

So the gal got off and went up front. A minute later she came down the forward car to pay her fare. At once the conductor ordered her to go back into the rear car and stay there.

IV

The United Railways has ably seconded the *Polizei* in this gradual disciplining and regimentation of the people of Baltimore. When I was a boy riding on the street-cars was a free-and-easy and charming business. The cars stopped almost anywhere on hail, and when they were crowded the people helped one another with great good humor. Those who desired to smoke were free to do so on the rear platform. The conductor came around to collect fares. All this continued through the era of the cable cars. It was with the trolley that the New Efficiency came in.

Today riding on the cars of the United Railways, or even on some of its busses, is indistinguishable from running a gantlet. The passenger is no longer a customer, nor even an individual; he is simply an anonymous unit in an endless chain—a sort of sausage fed into an insatiable, and impersonal maw. His desires are no more regarded than if he were a corpse. The instant he steps aboard a car the cogs and levers of a machine grip him, and thereafter, until he escapes, he is its slave. He must deposit his fare at a certain time and place; he must move as ordered; if he happens to be smoking he is in for a sharp reprimand. All his old rights now reduce themselves to one: he may get off if he doesn't like it, and be damned.

I seldom have occasion to use the trolley: I prefer to walk, and so keep up the illusion that I am a free citizen of a free state. But now and then I use the Charles street busses. Those with conductors recall the glorious days of old horse-cars. The conductors are polite and actually collect the fare. One may smoke. One is free to leave by the very door one entered. But the conductorless busses are almost as bad as the new sausage-machine trolley cars. What imbecile invented the rule that fares must be paid on entering coming downtown and on leaving going up? All day long it confuses passengers and irritates them. Strangers stop to jaw with the driver. The whole scheme is inconceivably clumsy, useless and offensive.

Meanwhile, the company hires an expert in psychology, at $50,000 a year and expenses, to improve its public relations—that is, to diminish the clamor that goes on against it all the time. No wonder there is clamor. Don't the hogs in the slaughterhouse squeal?

(The Baltimore Evening Sun, March 23, 1925)

Parade Unlike Anything Since Days of Roosevelt

Washington, Aug. 8.—The klan put it all over its enemies this afternoon. The parade was grander and gaudier, and by far, than anything the wizards had prophesied. It was longer, it was thicker, it was higher in tone. I stood in front of the Treasury for two hours watching the legions pass. They marched in lines of eighteen or twenty, solidly shoulder to shoulder. I retired for refreshment and was gone an hour.

When I got back Pennsylvania avenue was still a mass of white from the Treasury down to the foot of Capitol Hill—a full mile of klansmen and their ladies, shedding patriotism and sweat. There has been no such procession in this imperial capital since the antic days of Roosevelt.

No one seems to know what brought them in. The whole thing is swathed in dense and romantic mystery. When the gentlemen of the press went to klan headquarters this afternoon, asking how and what, they were incontinently kicked out. It is not even established who commanded the parade. The Imperial Wizard, the Hon. Mr. Evans, was in it, but he professed to be only a guest. One tale has it that the klansmen of the North organized the show to annoy and dismay their brethren of the South. Another had it that it was planned by local mayors of the palace to shame and get rid of the august Evans. But if any such evil purpose lurked under the surface there was certainly no sign of it on top. The parade was not only splendiferous; it was also immensely amicable. It rolled on from end to end without a bubble in the tarpot and without a yell.

But not without such a sweating as this earth has not seen since Cheops built his pyramid. As the klansmen swung up past the Willard Hotel, with a yellow, watery sun in their eyes, their faces ranged in hue from a fire-truck scarlet to the most dreadful shades of violet and purple. It was indeed a fiery afternoon, and out in the middle of Pennsylvania avenue it was at its fiercest. The heat rose up from the soft asphalt like a miasma from hell itself. Even on the sidewalk, under the shade of the Washington trees, it was infernal. But the klansmen plodded bravely on, their eyes upon the starry future of the republic, purged of atheism and hyphenism at last. Anon, one would roll his eyes and stagger to the gutters, to be seized by the *polizei* and carted off to their infirmaries. But the rest plodded on, hour after hour, mile after mile, all the long, blistering afternoon and into the damp, muggy evening.

Pennsylvania led the van, and, in fact, dominated the whole parade. After two hours its hosts were still passing. They marched proudly, and showed a lurid fancy in their investiture. The men of Sam D. Rich Klan, of Pittsburgh, were clothed in robes faced with scarlet, and wore mitres of the sort affected by patriarchs of the Greek rite. They had their wives with them—fat, amiable gals mainly, with their make-ups dripping from the ends of their noses. The men of Johnstown wore trench hats; those of Hollidaysburg bore muskets. Altoona was led by a klan intellectual in horn-rimmed spectacles. The Harrisburg band played "Adeste Fidelis." The Lehighton klansmen had a base drum inscribed "Gnaden Huetten."

So they marched past, rank after rank—the beauty and chivalry of Kutztown, Kunkletown, Kratzerville, Kleinfeltersville, Schwenkville, Houtzdale and Hamburg. The klan gown was only the beginning of their attire. Over it some wore the cloaks of Spanish grandees of the sixteenth century and some the robes of Shinto high priests. One platoon was in green baldrics emblazoned with vermilion crosses; another wore huge special shakers bespattered with gilt stars. The example of the Moose has not gone for naught in the mining towns. There is a rising taste for elegance up there, and it showed itself brilliantly in today's parade.

In the kleagles and other dignitaries, of course, this new voluptuousness went to great lengths. Some were clad in billowy gowns of sea-green satin, with turbans on their heads set with synthetic rubies. Others were swathed in yellow, red and blue. They were, in the main, men of girth and so there was plenty of room for showing off their finery. One imperial profligate rode upon a coal black charger, and had a slave to lead his mount by the bridle. His uniform was a mass of glittering gems, the love-offering, no doubt, of his lieges sweating on foot behind him. He acknowledged the huzzahs of the rabble with graceful sweeps of the left hand. A regal fellow, and much happier in patriotic work, you may be sure, than he ever was in the lime and cement business.

So much for the vestment that flapped past, damp, but full of chromatic thrills. Of the fauna within them it is impossible to speak with such unremoved enthusiasm. It is the tragedy of this great Republic, perhaps, that whenever its patriots get together they look like a gang of meat-cutters and curve greasers on a holiday. So, today, if the truth must get out. Until I gave up, I saw perhaps 10,000 march by. There was not, so far as I could observe, an intelligent face or a comely one on a woman. They were common folk, and their commonness radiated from them like heat from a stove. They come from the places where the hard work of the Nation is done, and the marks of their toil were all over them. The wheelbarrow handle, it was plain, was more familiar to the men in that long line than the golf-stick, and the washtub had engaged the women far oftener than the lipstick.

But what of it? The klan is not a club for snobs, it is a device for organizing inferiorities into a mystical superiority; its primary aim is to turn jackrabbits, by amalgamation, into lions. This business, of course, makes for absurdity. It is impossible to look at an imperial duodenum in his green robes without snickering. It is impossible to watch that endless procession of blank faces go by without shivering. Here are the makings of every imbecility, from fundamentalism up. If these poor blockheads are gullible enough to pay $10 apiece for nightgowns worth perhaps 50 cents, then they are gullible enough to swallow any conceivable nonsense. They have, in fact, already made a good start. They believe that the Pope is preparing to land at the Navy Yard and seize the White House, that the scientists in the country are all parties to a conspiracy to destroy Christianity and debauch the young, and that the Jesuits murdered the lamented Harding and the sainted Bryan.

But such foolishness, in all probability, is inseparable from patriotic emotion. What is believed on the lowest levels is, after all, not much more ridiculous than what is believed on the highest. Patriotism is not scientific; it is romantic. The essential question is not whether it is sound in logic, but whether it is genuine in feeling. The ku kluxers, this afternoon, sweated their way into respect. It was no easy thing, you may be sure, for those fat women to waddle two miles under a blazing sun, nor was it much easier for their lords and masters. They faced the music valiantly, and so gave a public proof of their devotion. To sweat for God and country is not beautiful, but neither is it to be laughed at.

That these poor folk are exploited by rogues is an unpleasant detail, but certainly nothing new in the world. It is the penalty of their ignorance, at all times and everywhere. When, in the course of nature, the kleagles begin to devour one another and so let them go they will fall into the hands of political mountebanks, or, worse still, into the clutches of the fundamentalist pastors. They have been marching in idiotic parades, whooping gloriously for charlatans since the dawn of history and they will go on doing it forevermore. Today's procession was probably one of the most creditable that they can boast of. It was earnest and it had a certain modest dignity. If they go back to their forlorn villages and their drab homes behind the gas works believing that they have achieved something they will not be far wrong.

The chief figure of the show was not present in the flesh. As the marchers got to the Treasury and cast their gaze toward his house they found him represented by an armed marine. I allude, of course, to an exalted personage, now temporarily resident at Swampscott, Mass. When he dismissed the klan with a lofty sniff he probably fell into a blunder that will haunt him for many a long day. For hours and hours, until the rain came down, the constituent metazoa of his last colossal majority tramped down Pennsylvania avenue, marking balefully his pointed absence. Perhaps the fact will still be remembered on the Tuesday following the first Monday of November, 1928.

(The Baltimore Evening Sun, August 9, 1925)

Outside, Looking In

When, a few weeks ago, the clans gathered at Berlin to celebrate the sixth anniversary of the German republic, the orator of the day reached the climax of his address in the following sentence:

"We must emancipate ourselves from the mad tendency to permit our national life to become Americanized!"

This remarkable declaration got relatively little attention in the American press; when it was mentioned at all, it was commonly with the declaration that the Germans are still suffering from their war wounds, and envy our vast prosperity. But that, I think, was a shallow reading of it. The Germans, as a matter of fact, give very little attention to their war wounds, which, after all, were not fatal; they devote themselves mainly to looking ahead. And our prosperity does not greatly disturb them, for in it they see a guarantee of their own; what we are accomplishing today, with the odds all in our favor, they plan to do tomorrow, with the odds more nearly even.

They are, in truth, quite as eager for the dollar as we are, and quite as determined to get it, by fair means or foul. That quest, so nearly universal in the modern world, is not what they have in mind when they speak of the dangers of Americanization. What they think of is something different. It may be described, in general, as the decay of spiritual values that has gone on among us during the past two generations. It may be described, in particular, as our growing impatience with the free play of ideas, our increasing tendency to reduce all virtues to the single one of conformity, our relentless and all-pervading standardization. This is what all Europe fears when it contemplates the growing importance and influence of the United States. It hasn't J. P. Morgan in mind, nor even General Pershing; it has Henry Ford. By Americanization it means Fordization—and not only in industry but also in politics, art and even religion.

* *

If you want to see how the United States of today looks to a reflective European you can do no better than get a little book called *Americanization: A World Menace*, written by W. T. Colyer, a member of the British Labor party, and published by the Labor Publishing Company in London. There is also an American edition, but I forget the name of the publisher; it seems to have got little notice and made no impression. Nevertheless, the book is a remarkable one, for two reasons: First, it is written with great grace and charm—certainly something not to be matched on this side of the water, where labor leaders are almost illiterate. Second, it is the work of a man who knows the United States intimately, and supports every statement he makes with names and dates.

Thus it cannot be dismissed as the usual traveler's tale, of casual glances and wrong inferences all compact. Mr. Colyer lived here for a number of years, and moved about from end to end of the country. Everywhere he went he kept his eyes open and his pencil sharp. The result is an immense accumulation of facts about the life that Americans are living in this third half-century of the republic, and a series of extraordinarily sharp and devastating observations upon them. Mr. Colyer is not blind to what we have accomplished. He sees a wilderness broken to the plow and the flivver. But he sees also a people broken to the yoke.

It is this merciless ironing out of the individual, indeed, that chiefly arrests his attention, and he offers it as a solemn warning to his own countrymen. Americans have got on in the world, he says, by the simple process of sacrificing everything else to getting on. They began as a nation by setting up a table of inalienable human rights, but one by one those rights have gone by the board. No other nation of today is so rigorously policed. The lust to standardize and regulate extends to the most trivial minute of private life.

It goes even further, passing beyond acts to thoughts. Such and such an idea is virtuous and "American"; its contrary is full of sin.

Mr. Colyer believes that that principle is intolerably dangerous—
that it is bound, in the long run, to throttle all intelligence and
make for a groveling and ignominious stupidity. More, he believes
the people of the United States have already made some progress
along that depressing way.

* *

His book, if it represented only one man's opinion, might be
interesting and even instructive, but it would not be important. It
represents, however, a great deal more than one man's opinion. If
you have the gift of tongues, get an armful of French, German and
Italian newspapers: you will find echoes of it in almost every issue.
And if you are, like a good American, monolingual, get an armful
of English papers: you will find the same doctrine in at least two-
thirds of them.

Europe sees Americanism, in brief, as a sort of Philistine uprising against the free spirit of man—as a conspiracy of dull and
unimaginative men, fortuitously made powerful, against all the
ideas and ideals that seem sound to their betters. Henry Ford,
with his discovery that history is bunk and science a fraud, seems
to it to be the archetypical American. He is, within his own field, a
man of great energy and very respectable talents. He has done
useful work, and perhaps earned at least a part of his immense
reward. But he insists upon leaving his own field for fields that are
strange and impenetrable to him, and upon laying down laws
therein for the government of their natural inhabitants. This is
what Europe understands by Americanism, by Americanization.
And this is what it fears.

The trial of the infidel Scopes, I believe, greatly added to those
fears. It got more space in the European papers than the election
of Coolidge, even more than the death of Harding. They gave it
the place of honor for days running. And what was the lesson that
they deduced from it? First, that all ordinary intellectual decency
had departed from the American people—that they were willing
and even eager to flaunt their contempt for all sound knowledge
and sound sense before the world. Second, that a nation cherishing such notions and feelings, and with the money and men to
enforce them, deserved to be watched very carefully.

* *

Europe hears relatively little about what is being done, often against cruel difficulties, by American artists and scientists, philosophers and publicists. It has its own supply of such men, and it naturally heeds them first. They have a high position over there, unmatched on this side of the ocean. An Anatole France, in France, is an eminent man, respected by everyone, including even politicians. A Richard Strauss, in Germany, is more than a mere music maker; he is a public institution, and has a solid importance. We put such men much lower, and so we have fewer of them, and Europe, having more and better ones at home, hears little about the few we have.

But Europe has no Henry Fords, or William Jennings Bryans, or Gimlet-Eye Butlers, or Mayor Hylans, or Wilbur Volivas, and so it is interested by them, instantly and hugely, when they appear in America. It observes that the American people or, at all events, the great majority of the American people, take them quite seriously, and it concludes, not without reason, that they accurately represent America. It hears that Bryan was thrice within reach of the White House—and then it hears of him denouncing the theory that man is a mammal. It hears that Butler is an officer wearing the American uniform—and then it hears he is engaged in monkey shines to entertain the Anti-Saloon League. It hears that Ford is the richest man of a country in which riches exceed any other worth—and then it hears him reviling learning like a yokel in a crossroads grocery store.

Such phenomena surprise it—and shock it. They violate all its notions of propriety, of decency. It cannot imagine a civilized people suffering them without immediate and angry rebellion. So it concludes that the Americans, despite their vast success in collaring dollars, have yet to go some distance before they are fully civilized. And when it hears talk of Americanization it shivers.

(*The Chicago Sunday Tribune, August 30, 1925*)

Triumph of Democracy

The Constitution

I

All government, in its essence, is organized exploitation, and in virtually all of its existing forms it is the implacable enemy of every industrious and well-disposed man. In theory, it invades his liberty and collars his money only in order to protect him, but in actuality it always makes a stiff profit on the exchange. That profit represents the income of the professional politicians, nine-tenths of whom are simply professional rogues. They employ a great many technicians to carry on the ostensible functions of government, and some of those technicians are honorable and competent men, but the politicians themselves are seldom either. Their only object in life is to do as little honest work as they can for the most profit, whether in money, in power or in mere glory. The typical politician is not only a rascal but also a jackass, so he greatly values the puerile notoriety and adulation that sensible men try to avoid.

The prevailing view seems to be that the lower orders of the governmental camorra are the most parasitical and anti-social, but this is not really the case. The minor jobholders that everyone disdains are actually much better fellows than the political bigwigs that most people find it so hard not to venerate. Consider, for example, the Postoffice. Its rank and file is made up of poor men who work hard for every nickel they get, and are so closely watched that the slightest aberration means disaster to them. In return for the relative security of their jobs they have to show a constant competence, and to submit, more often than not, to brutal overloading. But as one goes up the line one finds less and less diligence and less and less capacity for the work in hand, until at the top one commonly encounters a professional politician of the most crass and shameless sort, bent only upon serving his party machine.

It is the same in the City Hall. People who go there on business for the first time are usually greatly surprised to find so many polite, industrious and expert men behind the desks. They expect a gang of lazy, impudent ward heelers, but what they discover is a body of functionaries at least as well qualified as those they are used to meeting in stores and banks. But the higher offices are seldom so decently manned, and in the highest of all, that of the Mayor, it is so rare to find reasonable real and genuine competence that when they happen to be encountered, as in the case say, of the Hon. Mr. Jackson, it seems almost a miracle. When the Governor of an American State turns out to be a man of ability and honesty it is a miracle indeed, and of a very rare sort, for most American Governors are shabby and scurvy politicians, and some of them are obvious knaves.

II

The one aim of all such persons is to butter their own parsnips. They have no concept of the public good that can be differentiated from their concept of their own good. They get into office by making all sorts of fantastic promises, few of which they ever try to keep, and they maintain themselves there by fooling the people further. They are supported in their business by the factitious importance which goes with high public position. The great majority of folk are far too stupid to see through a politician's tinsel. Because he is talked of in the newspapers all the time, and applauded when he appears in public, they mistake him for a really eminent man. But he is seldom anything of the sort, and when he loses his office his eminence usually vanishes instantly.

But while it lasts it is very useful to him, and he is well aware of it. One of the favorite devices of politicians whose stupidity or roguery gets them into trouble is to call upon all good citizens to sustain them as a patriotic matter. This is done not only by Presidents of the United States, but also by all sorts of lesser functionaries, down to the members of school boards and county road boards. It commonly works pretty well, for most people are flattered when anyone who seems to be distinguished asks for their aid. So they go on whooping up their own creature until in the end his unfitness for his job can be concealed no longer, and then they turn him out in anger, and put in some one still worse.

Here the public gullibility is reinforced by the common notion that government is a kind of separate and autonomous entity, standing apart from all other institutions. People constantly speak of "the government" doing this or that, as they might speak of God doing it. But the government is really nothing but a group of men, and usually they are very inferior men. They may have some better man working for them, but they themselves are seldom worthy of any respect. Not many of them have ever been able to make their marks at any reputable trade, and not many of them know anything worth knowing, or ever have a thought that is worth having.

III

At intervals in the history of the world, the people of some country or other, or, more accurately, a relatively enlightened and resolute faction of them, become unhappily aware of the nature of the government they live under, and undertake measures to improve it. Sometimes those measures take the form of assassinating its principal dignitaries, or of driving them into exile, but more often the thing is done more gently. There was a good example, known to every schoolboy, in England in the year 1215, when the barons of the realm, tiring of the tyrannous exactions of King John, corralled him at Runnymede, and forced him to grant them a long series of liberties, some of which remain the common liberties of every Englishman to this day. John kept his throne, but only at the cost of surrendering most of his old prerogatives.

At such times, not unnaturally, the concessions wrung from the tyrant brought to bay are commonly reduced to writing, if only that the parties of both parts may remember them clearly. A writing of that sort is variously known as a charter, a constitution, or a bill of rights. In a few countries, notably England, some of the principal articles in the existing Constitution are not written down at all, but only generally understood. But whether they are written down or not, they have a kind of force that is greatly superior to that of all ordinary law, and changing their terms is looked on as a very grave matter, to be undertaken only on long consideration, and after getting the consent of all the persons, or at least of a majority of them, whose rights it is proposed to modify.

In brief, a constitution is a standing limitation upon the power of the government. So far you may go, but no farther. No matter what the excuse or provocation, you may not invade certain rights, or pass certain kinds of laws. The lives and property of the people are at your disposition, but only up to a plainly indicated point. If you go beyond it, you become a public criminal, and may be proceeded against, at least in theory, like any other criminal. The government thus ceases to be sovereign, and becomes a creature of sharply defined and delimited powers. There are things it may not do.

IV

This device is probably the greatest invention that man has made since the dawn of civilization. It lies at the bottom of most of his progress. It was responsible for the rise of free government in the Greek city states, and it has been responsible for the growth of nearly all the great nations of modern times. Wherever it has passed out of use there has been decay and retrogression. Every right that anyone has today is based on the doctrine that government is a creature of limited powers, and that the men constituting it become criminals if they venture to exceed those powers.

Naturally enough, this makes life uncomfortable for politicians, and especially for the more impudent and unconscionable variety of them. Once they get into office they like to exercise their power, for power and its ketchup, glory, are the victuals they feed and fatten upon. Thus it always annoys them when they collide with a constitutional prohibition. It not only interferes with their practice of their nefarious trade—*to wit* the trade of hoodwinking and exploiting the people: it is also a gross affront to their high mightiness. Am I not Diego Valdez, Lord Admiral of Spain? Why, then, should I be bound by rules and regulations? Why should I be said nay when I am bursting with altruism, and have in mind only the safety and felicity of all you poor fish, my vassals and retainers?

But when politicians talk thus, or act thus without talking, it is precisely the time to watch them most carefully. Their usual plan is to invade the constitution stealthily, and then wait to see what happens. If nothing happens they go on more boldly; if there is a protest they reply hotly that the constitution is wornout and absurd, and that progress is impossible under the dead hand. This is the time to watch them especially. They are up to no good to anyone save themselves. They are trying to whittle away the common rights of the rest of us. Their one and only object, now and always, is to get more power into their hands that it may be used freely for their advantage, and to the damage of everyone else. Beware of all politicians at all times, but beware of them most sharply when they talk of reforming and improving the constitution.

(The Baltimore Evening Sun, August 19, 1935)

The Bill of Rights

Now and then one encounters an excellent book which fails of its purpose because it is based upon an erroneous assumption. Such a book is *Congress, the Constitution, and the Supreme Court,* by Charles Warren, an eminent jurisconsult of Boston, whose previous work, *The Supreme Court in United States History,* won the Pulitzer prize in 1922. The excellence of the volume flows out of the author's profound and philosophical knowledge of American legal history. He understands completely the important part that the courts, and especially the appellate courts, have played in our national development, and he is eloquent and convincing in his argument against those reformers who would hobble them. But he quite misapprehends, I believe, the primary causes of that rising discontent with them which is so plainly visible today.

His error, of course, has plausible foundations. If he assumes that the courts are unpopular because they limit the output of so-called progressive legislation, then he assumes only what has been accepted as a fact by his chief opponents: Senator Borah, the late Dr. La Follette, and the late Col. Roosevelt. Roosevelt's whole attack upon the Supreme court was based upon that notion. The learned justices, wrapped in their funereal shrouds, stood firmly against his plan to stretch the Constitution to fit his policies, and he accordingly denounced them as senile, anti-social, and under the hoof of the plutocracy. La Follette echoed the charge, and elaborated it. It bobs up anew in the somewhat muddled specula-tions of Dr. Borah.

But does it cause any genuine excitement among the generality of Americans? Are they actually fevered by the fact that the child labor act of 1919 was upset by the Supreme court in 1922? Is there any widespread indignation because the same puissant tribunal knocked out the District of Columbia minimum wage act a year later? I think not. Certain specialists in utopian legislation may be wrought up and full of bile, but surely not the average man. What annoys that average man is something quite different—something diametrically opposite. He doesn't bellow because the Supreme court guards the Constitution too jealously; he bellows because it doesn't guard the Constitution jealously enough.

* *

In other words, the current discontent with the courts, and es-pecially with the federal courts, rests at bottom upon a fear of Congress, not upon a fondness or respect for Congress. No one believes in its *bona fides* any more; no one believes that its typical member has any thought save for his own hide. When that hide is menaced he will do anything that is wanted of him, and if the Constitution stands in the way then so much the worse for the Constitution. The legislative process becomes a mere leaping of cowards and mountebanks. Given a lobby pertinacious enough, and almost anything imaginable may be put through.

Of late this putting through has been going on at a dizzy rate, and so the statute books are cluttered with oppressive legislation, most of it supported by penalties that clearly violate the guaran-tees of the Bill of Rights. Every one knows how the right to free speech, for example, has been invaded and made a mock of. And the right to free assemblage. And the inviolability of domicile. And the guarantee against unreasonable seizures. And the ancient right to a jury trial. Under the pressure of ruthless fanatics, will-ing to go any length to satisfy their lust to bludgeon and terrorize their fellow men, Congress has violated every one of these rights, and some of them it has violated repeatedly.

The constitutional remedy lies in the courts. They were set up in the fond belief that they would curb the excesses of the legislature. They were given a written constitution—written in the plainest of plain English—to guide and sustain them. In it the inalienable rights of the free citizen were set forth clearly, and the judges were bidden to maintain them. How have they done their job? It must be obvious that, in late years, they have done it very badly. They have not only let Congress run amok; they have not infrequently run amok themselves. In most federal jurisdictions today the Bill of Rights is worth no more than the statutes of Hammurabi. The fact, I believe, is not lost upon the people. It explains their increasing dissatisfaction with the courts—their growing willingness to listen to reformers who propose to reduce the whole judicial system to impotence and absurdity.

* *

Congress began this invasion of the Bill of Rights very early. The first ten amendments were submitted in 1789 and ratified by the end of 1791, but by 1798 they were already flouted by the alien and sedition acts. The Supreme court, at that time, was not yet in full function, and so the people, passing it over, turned to political action for a remedy. But in 1803 came the great case of Marbury vs. Madison, and thereafter the court's right to police congress was recognized, and it exercised that right steadily and effectively—so effectively that there was no other considerable effort to get around the Bill of Rights until the stormy period of the civil war.

But even during that stormy period the court upheld the guarantees of the citizen with great jealousy, as the celebrated Milligan case sufficiently proved, and during the years following it kept Congress rigorously in order. In 1870, for example, a law was passed setting up a sort of double jeopardy in civil cases—that is, allowing the federal courts to retry actions already decided in state courts. The Supreme court promptly declared it unconstitutional—and it was never heard of again until our own time. In 1890 Congress tried to get around the fifth amendment, with its prohibition of prosecutions or infamous crimes save after indictment of the accused by a grand jury—and again the Supreme court came to the rescue.

So in other cases. In 1886 Congress passed an act which provided for searches and seizures in violation of the fourth amendment, and the Supreme court knocked it out. In 1899 Congress passed an act destroying the right of a man accused to be confronted with the witnesses against him, and the Supreme court knocked it out. In 1867 Congress tried to put an *ex post facto* law on the books, and the Supreme court knocked it out. In 1909 Congress tried to set up appeals by the government in criminal cases, and the Supreme court said nay.

* *

This went on down to the end of the first decade of the present century. Then came a sudden change—how caused I don't know. Holes began to be punched in the Bill of Rights, and new laws of a strange and often fantastic shape began to slip through them. The hysteria of the late war completed the process. The espionage act enlarged the holes to great fissures. Citizens began to be pursued into their houses, arrested without warrants, and jailed without any form of trial. The ancient writ of *habeas corpus* was suspended; the Bill of Rights was boldly thrown overboard.

Here was the most noble opportunity that the Supreme court, in all its history, ever faced. It had a chance to do something, perhaps transiently unpopular, that would be of more value to human liberty in this world than a dozen bogus ways to save democracy. How did it meet the challenge? If you want to find out, and crave an authoritative view, go read the dissenting opinions of the war years and immediately thereafter—that is, go read the opinions of those justices who stood out for the Bill of Rights in the face of all pressure and uproar and were defeated only by the votes of their illustrious colleagues.

In those minority opinions, chiefly by Justices Brandeis and Holmes, there is much melancholy history. And in that history lie the roots of the evil esteem in which the courts are held today. Few Americans, I believe, want to upset them altogether, in the manner proposed by Roosevelt and La Follette. Their theoretical value in the state is too vast, however lamentable their practical failure. But few Americans, regarding that practical failure calmly, can escape the conclusion that some way to improve them is needed and that it must be found.

(The Chicago Sunday Tribune, January 17, 1926)

On Liberty

It is the theory of all modern civilized governments that they protect and foster the liberty of the citizen; it is the practice of all of them to limit its exercise, and sometimes very narrowly. This practice is denounced, by the more extreme sort of libertarians, as grossly hypocritical, and not infrequently they try to prove that it is also plainly illegal. What they overlook is the basic fact that liberty itself, like happiness, virtue and salvation, is very nebulous, and that no one has ever managed to draw up a satisfactory definition of it. Governments are thus forced to deal with it in a sketchy and pragmatic manner. They keep it on tap, but they try their best to prevent crowding at the bunghole.

The reason is not far to seek. Liberty, if it means anything at all, means that body of rights which the citizen reserves to himself, even as against the government. It included the right to do certain things without any regard to their effect upon the government, and the right to withhold the doing of certain other things. Thus a conflict is set up between the rights of the citizen and the power and security of the government. In so far as the citizen prevails the government is weak, and in so far as the government prevails the citizen is not a citizen at all, but a subject.

Obviously no government, of its own motion, will increase its own weakness, for that would mean to acquiesce in its own destruction. The instinct of all living organisms is against such acquiescence, and a government, being made up of men, is as much a living organism as an individual man is. So governments, whatever their pretension otherwise, try to preserve themselves by holding the individual down. He is at once the source of all their strength and the author of their most dangerous weakness. Government itself, indeed, may be very reasonably defined as a conspiracy against him. Its one permanent aim, whatever its form, is to hobble him sufficiently to maintain itself.

* *

At the moment, in the United States, this perennial conflict takes the form of a difference and dispute about overt acts. The national government is trying to enforce a law which, in the opinion of millions of otherwise docile citizens, invades their inalienable rights, and they accordingly refuse to obey it. There ensues a bitter trial of strength and endurance. If the protesting citizens prevail, then the government will be materially 'weakened'; and it will have to step softly in future. If, on the contrary, the citizens in rebellion are overcome, then they will cease to be free citizens to that extent and become subjects.

Such conflicts over actual acts are relatively rare in civilized states. They smell of revolution, and are thus avoided as much as possible by all parties. But conflicts over ideas, as opposed to acts, are going on all the time, and it is in this field that the exact nature of liberty is most difficult to define. The American Constitution seeks to dispose of the question with sweeping generalizations. It provides simply that the rights to free speech, to free assemblage, to petition, and to religious freedom shall never be invaded, and it assumes that everyone knows precisely what these things are.

But who does? Certainly not the learned philosophers who have written upon liberty. For their books are full of unsolved problems and baffling dilemmas, and some of these problems and dilemmas have taken on what may be called a classical dignity. Does the right to religious freedom include the right to practice a religion which involves gross offenses against the common morals of the land? Or against its security in time of war? And does the right to free speech include the right to go into a crowded theater and yell "Fire!"?

*　*

Such questions, of late, have arisen frequently, and the American courts, and especially the Federal courts, have had to deal with them. How far may a citizen go in advocating changes in the government? Or resistance to the government? Suppose he argues that the present government ought to be thrown out and a Soviet of Communists substituted: is that within his rights or outside them? Suppose he argues, as a necessary implication, that, if the sitting officials resist, they ought to be heaved into the Potomac: where does that doctrine land him? And what, incidentally, is advocacy? If it is unlawful to urge that an idea be carried out, is it also unlawful to state it academically and point out its possible merits?

Very few American judges have any interest in such fundamental questions of law, or any capacity for dealing with them intelligently. Thus the courts almost always dodge them, sometimes gracefully and sometimes not. Each case that comes up is decided on superficial points, and there is seldom any courageous grappling with the underlying principles. So the whole matter, legally speaking, remains swathed in doubts and dubieties, and it is impossible for a lawyer, called upon to advise a client, to tell him exactly what his rights are. When and where does free speech cease to be a right and become a matter for the police?

In the absence of a clear judicial answer, various unofficial jurists have tackled the problem. One of the most sagacious of them is Prof. Zechariah Chafee, Jr., of Harvard. His proposal, in brief, is that the lawfulness of an idea—say, in a speech—ought to be determined by its immediate effect. If it causes men to proceed to criminal action on the spot, then it is reasonable to call it unlawful and to punish the man who disseminates it. But if it produces no such action, then it ought to be privileged, no matter how violently it collides with common ideas, or how dangerous its remote effects. In other words, it ought to be lawful to advocate any idea, however outrageous, so long as it remains an idea, but the state should retain a right to prohibit any idea, however mild, that provokes instantly a criminal act.

* *

Other legal philosophers, following Professor Chafee, have developed this doctrine, and it is widely accepted as, at worst, an excellent guess. Even some of the judges, more enterprising than the rest, have apparently heard of it. Its defects are obvious. One of them is that it leaves open the question of what is a criminal act. In California, where the police make the laws, they might very readily make one calling it a felony to applaud an anti-capitalist speaker. Thus the speaker himself would be liable to arrest for causing the applause. But a more serious objection lies in the fact that estimating ideas by their effects is a begging of the whole question—that the true test of them ought to be, not their effects, but their truth.

In this emergency I rise to make a modest suggestion, and so pass on. It is that the real danger in free speech lies in the fact that, not infrequently, it is not actually free—that is, that the attempt to exercise it is, in reality, an attempt to prevent its exercise by the other fellow. Go back to the example of the fool yelling "Fire!" in a crowded theater. What is the objection to him? The objection is that he may lie—that the audience may rush for the exits, to the hazard of its life and limb, without any real cause. In other words, the objection is that there is no opportunity for persons who know that there is no fire to state the fact calmly, and prove it.

The implications should be plain enough. The real danger in subversive doctrines is that they are nearly always presented *ex parte*, and to audiences too ignorant to imagine refutations of them. Let it remain a principle of the law, as Professor Chafee suggests, that when they are so presented they be judged by their immediate effects. But let it be another principle that when they are presented in such a way that they may be challenged and refuted (if possible) on the spot, before the same audience—let it be held that, under such circumstances, there shall be no limitation upon them whatsoever, save only the limitation of common decency. That would be free speech, and it would be fair. Moreover, it would not be anything new. But our cops and judges are still to learn the lesson of Hyde Park.

(The Chicago Sunday Tribune, March 21, 1926)

The Land of the Free

I

Carlo Tresca is the proprietor of a small Italian paper in New York, by name *Il Martello*. He runs to Liberal ideas, and when the Fascisti came into power in his native country, and began Ku Kluxing their opponents, he denounced them in his paper, and called upon the Italians in America to repudiate them. His articles were vigorously written, and quickly attracted attention. A great many Italians began to incline toward his views.

That was early in 1923. In July of the same year certain persons in New York gave a public dinner to Judge Elbert H. Gary, chairman of the board of directors of the United States Steel Corporation. Judge Gary, for his services to the Cause of Humanity in America, had been made an honorary member of the Fascisti organization, and one of the guests who came to the dinner to do him honor was Prince Gelesto Caetani, then and now the Italian Ambassador at Washington. Prince Caetani was naturally called upon to make a speech. He made one bitterly denouncing the opponents of Fascismo among the American Italians, and arguing that "a certain Italian paper in New York" ought to be suppressed.

The assembled apostles of Human Liberty knew that he meant *Il Martello*, and applauded him heartily. That there was no law in the United States forbidding a newspaper to criticize a foreign government did not trouble them; they had been through the late war, and knew what could be done. So did the Department of Justice, then still in command of the eminent Daugherty, and the Postoffice Department. Word was conveyed to Washington, and then back to New York. On July 21 the whole issue of *Il Martello* was held up in the mails. Tresca demanded to know why. The Postoffice Department gave him no answer. He kept on denouncing the Fascisti.

Three weeks later, on August 10, he was suddenly arrested. The charge was that he had printed an article three months before, attacking the Italian monarchy. No such crime, of course, is known to American law, but Tresca was nevertheless arrested. He got out on bail, and kept on denouncing the Fascisti. The charge was allowed to drop. On August 18 the whole issue of *Il Martello* was held up because it contained an account of a raffle; two other Italian papers, containing precisely the same account, went through the mails unmolested. On September 8 it was held up because it contained a two-line advertisement of a book on birth control. On October 27 it was held up because it printed an account of how the Fascisti had forced an Italian woman to swallow an immense dose of castor oil; all the American newspapers printed the same story, but were not molested. On November 10 it was held up because it printed a letter from a reader predicting that Mussolini would come to the same end as Rienzi; other papers had made the same prediction without challenge. On November 24 it was held up for charging Mussolini with misappropriating funds.

II

Meanwhile, Tresca kept on denouncing the Fascisti, and the Italian Ambassador, it may be safely presumed, kept on nursing the conviction that *Il Martello* ought to be suppressed. The war, unfortunately, was over, and so it was not easy to accomplish the business. Holding up the paper day after day, and subjecting it to heavy and arbitrary losses—this was apparently easy, but it was impossible, under the law, to suppress it altogether, and very difficult to get Tresca into jail and keep him there.

Finally, however, juridic science solved the problem. The little two-line advertisement of September 8, announcing a book in Italian on birth control, showed the way. Experienced witch-hunters from the Department of Justice were rushed to New York, Tresca was indicted for advertising a means of preventing conception, and his trial was called in hot haste. He appeared before Goddard, J., in the United States District Court, on November 27. The evidence showed some strange things. Tresca, it appeared, had actually never sent a single copy of the offending issue through the mails. The instant he heard that the Postoffice had held it up he withdrew it, and reprinted a new issue without the two-line advertisement. It appeared, indeed, that other charges were mixed up with the complaint. One was that he had printed an article entitled "Down With the Monarchy." This was plainly not illegal, but the prosecution made much of it. Finally, the assistant district attorney offered to drop the whole case if Tresca would leave the country, *i.e.*, go back to Italy, where the Fascisti could deal with him. He refused, and was convicted. Judge Goddard sentenced him to a year and a day at Atlanta.

This was an appallingly heavy sentence—the heaviest ever heard of. In nearly all previous Federal cases the culprit had been simply fined. In none of the State cases had a sentence of more than six months been inflicted, and the average for all of them was less than a month. There was no evidence that Tresca had ever seen the advertisement before it got into his paper. On the contrary, it was shown that the man who brought it in and inserted it was one Vella, the paper's advertising agent. The actual advertiser was one Nieri, an Italian bookseller. He, too, was arrested and convicted. He got four months in jail. But Tresca, who was only constructively guilty, got a year and a day in Atlanta Prison.

And there he sits now, for the Circuit Court of Appeals has upheld his conviction.

III

Such episodes—and they are by no means rare, despite the common superstition that Palmerism has been squeezed out of the Department of Justice and Burlesonism out of the Postoffice—give the student of American history powerfully to think. What becomes of the old notion that the United States is a free country, that it is a refuge for the oppressed of other lands, that here they may voice their grievances and call for help? There was a time when such rebels against tyranny came here as a matter of course, and were received with open arms. The name of Kossuth is even in the school books. But what would happen to a Kossuth today— if the Hungarian Ambassador could convince Judge Gary and company that he ought to be in jail?

Also, what becomes of the old notion that a peaceable man, in this great Republic, should be unmolested—that the *Polizei* should not pursue and harass him day and night, and try by dodge after dodge to get him into their clutches? The Postoffice tackled Tresca at least five times before it finally fetched him. Every one of those times, it must be obvious, he was innocent of any wrongdoing, else he would have been railroaded to jail forthwith. It took six shots to bring him down—and then he was caught on a childish technicality. Every American editor who prints any reference to a book on birth control, even if it be a review denouncing it, is quite as guilty as he was, and perhaps even more guilty. And consider his punishment! The man who offered the book for sale got four months; Tresca, for merely printing two lines about it, got a year and a day!

I attempt no long sermon on the text; it is eloquent enough of itself. The facts, so far as I know, are not disputed by anyone. There was a time when their publication would have caused an uproar; today they go almost unnoticed. The great agencies of Americanism will let Tresca rot in prison before they lift their hands to help him, just as they are letting his fellow Italians, Sacco and Vanzetti, rot in prison. The American Legion, though it still sweats and moans for human liberty, will not protest; on the contrary, it is more likely to pass a resolution urging that the wop be kept behind the bars, guilty or not guilty. The Sons of the Revolution will maintain a magnificent silence. Kiwanis and Rotary will not be heard from.

IV

So far, indeed, but eight persons in all the United States have gone to Tresca's aid. Four are Italian-American politicians. One is a Liberal pastor. Two are old and battle-scarred libertarians, already marked with the scars of a hundred defeats. The eighth is La Sanger, the birth-control agitator, herself an experienced goat of the New Jurisprudence. No one else will take any interest in the case.

(The Baltimore Evening Sun, January 12, 1925)

Communism

I

Why is it that so few Americans succumb to the blather of Communism? There are, of course, several ready answers. One is that the people of this great Republic are too intelligent to believe in any such nonsense. Another is that they are too prosperous and hopeful: a plain variant of the late Marshal Foch's dictum that Bolshevism is a disease of defeated nations. Both of these answers, I fear, are somewhat too facile to be sound. And especially the first.

That Americans, in the mass, have anything properly describable as keen wits is surely far from self-evident. On the contrary, it seems likely that, if anything, they lie below the civilized norm. Nothing is easier than to delude and swindle them. They are forever yielding up their faith and money to bogus messiahs, political, economic, moral and theological. The regular assumption of all persons who operate upon them with noticeable success—for example, politicians, bishops, newspaper editors, cigarette manufacturers, lawyers, pedagogues, professional war veterans and movie magnates—is that they are almost unanimously imbeciles and for that assumption there seems to be very strong pragmatic support.

A Roosevelt, to be sure, would have been a success anywhere:

his gifts as a mountebank amounted to downright genius. And if a Wilson fooled Americans for a time, then it must be remembered that he fooled the rest of humanity almost as long. But it is hard to think of a really civilized people admiring and following such preposterous fellows as Harding and Coolidge, or even Hoover. No match for Coolidge is to be found in any European country today, nor in Latin-America. Here King George of England naturally comes to mind: he is, in many ways, a sort of Coolidge. But if the English profess to respect George it is only because they can't help themselves. They did not choose him; he was wished on them by God, who has treated them badly in many other ways. In America, Coolidge was freely chosen, and if he had consented to stand again he would have been chosen again.

II

The point, of course, needs no laboring, for every time a test of American intelligence is made it turns out to be low. This country is the home of freak economic schemes, as it is the happy hunting ground of the most blatant and absurd sort of charlatans in politics. So, indeed, in the sciences and even in the arts: one searches the world in vain to find anything to match chiropractic, as one searches it in vain for anything comparable to the New Humanism (by Harvard out of Kiwanis), the American gas and filling station, or the aesthetic of Hollywood.

One would naturally suppose that a people so hospitable to the bizarre and the irrational would embrace communism with joy, just as multitudes of them, in a previous age, embraced free silver. But, as everyone knows, they will have none of it. If it survives among us at all, it is only among persons of foreign birth and tradition and in a small band of obvious half-wits. Two-thirds of the native-born Communists that I have encountered are so plainly *mashuggah* that it would be flattery to call them stupid. They are the sort of persons who, if there were no communism, would believe in astrology or witchcraft.

Why do the rest hold off? Is it because, as some authorities say, the American people are all rich, and hence have capitalistic minds? I doubt it. Millions of them, in point of fact, are very poor: they live always at the brink of disaster. They are not as numerous, to be sure, as in England, but they are certainly as numerous, relatively speaking, as in France, Germany, or the Scandinavian countries. Yet all of these countries are infested by Communists, whereas in the United States they are so rare that the cops commonly arrest them at sight, as they might arrest cannibals. And when the prisoners are landed in the hoosegow and subjected to the third degree it usually turns out that their English is far more suitable to vaudeville comedians than to philosophers.

III

I have no ready answer to the problem, but venture to make two suggestions. One is that communism has failed in the United States because, by the time it was first heard of, the plain people had been vaccinated against it. For years they had been following such quacksalvers as Bryan and Roosevelt, and so they had acquired a certain amount of immunity to social and economic perunas. That immunity, of course, was not complete, but it was at least sufficient to protect them against so gross an infection as communism. They had, so to speak, sprouted screens around their psyches. Those screens were not fine enough to keep out the ultramicroscopic organisms of Farm Relief, but they were far too fine to let in the huge, ungainly microbes of Bolshevism.

That is one possibility. The other is somewhat analogous. It is that Americans were rather more sensitive than most other peoples to the lessons of the concrete debacle in Russia. They probably felt themselves, in a subtle and unconscious way, to be nearer to the Russians than any Europeans. Russia was not like Europe, but it was strangely like America. In the same way the Russians were like Americans. They, too, were naturally religious and confiding; they, too, were below the civilized average in intelligence; and they, too, believed in democracy, and were trying to give it a trial.

Perhaps I am a bit obscure here. What I mean to suggest is that a man is always far more sensitive to the deficiencies of his relatives than he is to those of other persons—not primarily because they bear upon him more directly, but because they exaggerate and make the more palpable and unpleasant his own defects. So with races. Every Englishman is more acutely aware of Scotch weaknesses than he is, say, of Spanish or Greek weaknesses. Every Frenchman is more critical of the Belgians than he is of the Swedes or Dutch. And every German, when he discourses upon the crimes of the French, tends to describe acts and ways of thought that are far more Germanic than Latin.

Perhaps Americans, in the same way, were extra responsive to the mass suicide of the Russians. They saw democracy turning upon and devouring itself—and they were the world's chief democrats. Russia, on a colossal scale, was reducing the cardinal articles of their faith to absurdity. What went on at Moscow was simply a burlesque of what had been going on in the United States for a century and a half. So the Americano shivered, as every dry Senator shivers when he gets home from a booze party and finds his son lying drunk in the hallway.

IV

I throw out these suggestions and pass on. They may be worth nothing. On the other hand, they may verge upon Constructive Criticism: I begin to reach the age for it. The central fact remains: that the Moscow clown-show differs very little from the Washington clown-show, save perhaps in the circumstance that some of the chief Bolshevists actually believe in Bolshevism. And the curious phenomenon that I started out with also remains; that Americans who take naturally and automatically to whatever is idiotic, have nevertheless refused to swallow communism.

That they will swallow it later on seems a very remote possibility. It appears, indeed, to be losing believers in the United States much faster than it makes converts. Its appeal, such as it is, is mainly to the very young and the doubtfully sane—to sassy gals who yearn to belabor (i.e., to hug) cops, and are otherwise plain Freudian cases, and to male exhibitionists with complexes even worse. There is no rational ideology in the movement; even its martyrs are apparently in some doubt as to what it is all about. Its literature is as childish as the literature of Christian Science.

It will probably disappear altogether when the Russian experiment comes to a climax, and Bolshevism either converts itself into a sickly imitation of capitalism or blows up with a bang. The former issue seems the more likely. Some of the chief Bolsheviks, as I have said, are almost unique among politicians, for they really believe in the scheme they preach. But they remain politicians all the same, and when the time of genuine stress comes they will think first of all of their jobs. To keep their jobs they will be quite willing to make terms with capitalism, just as Dr. Hoover, to get his, was quite willing to make terms with Methodism.

(The Baltimore Evening Sun, July 14, 1930)

Morals and the Moron

I

Permit me to rehearse briefly the plot of a recent work of fiction:

One day an American of the lower middle class, married and with a son of twelve years, received from a bachelor friend a note reading substantially as follows: "I am down the street with a couple of chickens. Hurry over." The invitation did not affront the gentleman; on the contrary, it delighted him, and he winked lasciviously in expectation. Unluckily, on searching his pockets, he found that he had no money, and so his face fell, for his experience had taught him that it was impossible for a penniless man to make any impression on chickens. Suddenly he bethought himself of his young son's toy bank. There it stood on the mantelpiece, and he knew that it contained 95 cents. Without hesitation he emptied it, pocketed its contents, and prepared to proceed to the rendezvous. But his young son, observing the burglary, challenged him as he was leaving the house, and when he refused to restore the stolen money, struck him behind the ear with a rolling pin. The blow was sufficient to knock him down, but not enough to halt him. Picking himself up, he ran out of the house and down the street, murmuring, "I got 95 cents and a crack on the head. It could have been worse!"

Unluckily, all these crimes and hazards now went for naught. The friend who had sent the note was a practical joker, and when the eager husband and father got to the place of assignation he found that the chickens were not young women amiably free with their persons, as he had imagined, but two dressed hens hanging in a poulterer's shop. Enraged by his disappointment, he gave his friend a violent kick in the gluteus maximus, and sent him sprawling on the sidewalk. Proceeding home disconsolately, he presently encountered colored youths engaged in a game of craps, and the thought struck him that it might be profitable to enter the game. So he staked the 95 cents stolen from his son's bank, took the dice, and there on the public street began shooting with the two Moors. In a few minutes he had won all their money—$18 in all, including his own stake. With this in his pocket he resumed his journey homeward.

But on the way he happened to pass a millinery shop, and the women's hats on display in the window suggested an idea to him. His wife, he reflected, would know of his robbery of their child's bank; the boy himself, indeed, would tell her of it, for didn't he resent it to the extent of assaulting his father with a rolling pin? So the householder decided that it would be necessary to bribe his wife to silence. If he gave her something valuable, she would not upbraid him for robbing their boy. The hats in the milliner's window were conveniently at hand. He went in, bought one for $18, and, on reaching home, presented it to his wife. She was greatly delighted, but still made an embarrassing reference to the robbery of the toy bank. So he decided to lie to her in order to placate her. That is, he told her that, after seeing the hat in the window, he had found that he had but $17.05 in cash, and that he had "borrowed" the 95 cents from the toy bank to make up the needed $18. This explanation completely satisfied her, and she apologized to him for suspecting him of felonious intent.

II

Where do I find this story? Is it in one of the obscene and subversive books of Theodore Dreiser, Sherwood Anderson or James Branch Cabell, suppressed by the Comstocks and only obtainable from bookselling bootleggers? Do I take it from one of the cheap and furtively sexual all-fiction magazines that are always being barred from the mails? Not at all. I take it from the eminent *Sunpaper* of Sunday, March 23, in which issue of which great moral journal it occupied a whole page, and that an outside one, to wit, the first page of the so-called comic section. There, set forth brilliantly in colored pictures, so that even the illiterate might grasp and enjoy it, it appeared under the title "Mutt and Jeff: Mutt Has a Piece of Luck." And, as if confident of its success, the editor added at the bottom of the page, in large type, "Watch Mutt and Jeff Every Day in THE SUN."

I in no way exaggerate or misrepresent the story. It deliberately represented the father of a family as engaged willingly in adultery, robbery, gambling, assault and lying, and it treated all of these acts as humorous. It represented the son of the house as assaulting his father in a manner indistinguishable from an attempt at murder. It represented the mother as a vain, credulous and idiotic creature. And it was set forth baldly, gaudily, without the slightest show of euphemism—in fact, even boastfully, as if sure of approbation and success. It was assumed as a matter of course that the readers of the *Sunpaper* would enjoy it, and that enjoying it would cause them to buy more *Sunpapers*, to get more stories like it. More, it was printed in a part of the paper devoted especially to the entertainment of the young—it was offered as suitable entertainment for readers scarcely able to read at all. Yet more, it was offered on Sunday morning, "the Sabbath of the Lord thy God, who hath brought thee out of the land of Egypt."

III

My regular customers, of course, need not be assured that I rehearse all these facts without indignation—that I by no means set up the contention that printing such imbecile rubbish is immoral, or that it ought to be put down by the *Polizei*. I believe that it should be perfectly lawful to print anything that people in general will read without protest—and in this case, obviously, no protest was anticipated or received, for exactly similar garbage is printed by the *Sunpaper* seven days a week. I go further: I believe that it should be perfectly lawful to print even things that outrage the pruderies and prejudices of the general, so long as any honest minority, however small, wants to read them. The remedy of the majority is not prohibition, but avoidance. It is under no compulsion to read anything it doesn't want to read. It can avoid such things quite as easily as it avoids hearing, say, the music of Beethoven. To prohibit them on the ground that it regards them as immoral, subversive or atheistic—all judgments open to challenge and argument—is just as absurd as it would be to prohibit the music of Beethoven on the ground that the majority regards it as cacophonous.

But this belief of mine in free speech and a free press is obviously not shared by most Americans. It is embodied, true enough, in the first article of the Bill of Rights, but the actual laws of the United States frown upon it, and it has no place in the *mores* of the people. The prevailing American doctrine, in fact, permits the state to condition free speech, and even to suspend it altogether, whenever it is deemed desirable. Our statute books are heavy with laws proscribing ideas. I could make a long list of them. Many of them are ideas that thousands of intelligent persons cherish as true, and even voice freely in private; nevertheless, it is forbidden to print them, and whoever attempts it is commonly punished very severely. I need allude to but one category: that of ideas in the field of sex. Here there are not only a multitude of statutes specifically limiting the right of free speech, but also a multitude of special agencies, some of them public and some private, devoted wholly to seeing that these laws are obeyed. The archetype of these agencies is the so-called Comstock Society.

IV

Now I come to my point. The Comstock Society and its allies have been functioning in the United States since the early seventies—a full half century. During all of that time they have been ceaselessly alert for what they regard as obscene literature, and year after year they have pursued and prosecuted the publishers and vendors of it. Scarcely a month goes by that they do not make a spectacular raid upon some new book, and very often, as in the cases of Cabell's *Jurgen* and Dreiser's *The Genius*, it is a book that is regarded by many persons, including some of ripe judgment, to be honest, competent and worthy of respect—in brief, a genuine work of art, bringing credit to the national letters. Nevertheless, they have at it relentlessly, regardless of such opinions—always on the ground that artistic merit cannot excuse moral obliquity—that the public virtue must be protected at all costs, even at the cost of sound literature.

Now observe the net worth of all this fine frenzy. After fifty years of violent and even savage efforts to put down literary immorality—after scores and hundreds of prosecutions of perfectly well-meaning authors and publishers, many of them frankly amazed by the charges heaped upon them—after a full half century of this fanatical shouting and oppression, this frantic endeavor to protect the young of the nation from the slightest hint or suggestion of impropriety, the leading newspaper in one of the oldest and most conventional of American towns gives over a whole page of its Sunday issue to a silly and stupid story, entirely without any color of artistic value, in which the father of a family is depicted as planning to engage in a low debauch with a loose woman, as stealing the hard-saved pennies of his own child, as using the money to gamble with loafers on the public street, and as employing his winnings to bribe his wife, a woman so degraded that she will take a money compensation for all the other crimes! And this fable is presented, not as a chronicle of acts to be reprehended, but as a chronicle of acts to be laughed at! And it is set forth with gaudy allurements, not for the entertainment of the inmates of brothels, penitentiaries and the two Houses of Congress, but for the entertainment of little children!

So much for the end product of half a century of comstockery! So much for the actual state of public morals in the most moral of republics!

(The Baltimore Evening Sun, March 31, 1924)

Object Lesson

In the six adjoining columns *The Evening Sun* presents today a graphic representation of the Federal Government's immense corps of jobholders.

Each dot stands for one jobholder, and there are 1,000,000 odd of them. The actual enrollment, at 10 o'clock this morning was reported to be 999,264 head, but additions were being made at the rate of more than one hundred an hour, so the million mark will no doubt be passed before the last edition of *The Evening Sun* is on the streets.

This is the first time in human history, so far as can be ascertained, that a million dots have ever been printed on one page of a daily newspaper. Indeed, it is probably the first time in history that a million objects of any sort have been assembled in so convenient and succinct a way that the whole number could be taken in at a glance.

All of us talk about millions, and hear about them, and read about them, and maybe dream of them, but who has ever seen one? Well, here is a chance to enjoy that instructive experience. There are 825 dots in each row counting from side to side, and 1,213 in each row counting from top to bottom. That makes 1,000,725 in all. The extra 725 are thrown in as makeweight for any dots that may be worn off in the course of printing the paper.

The dots, unfortunately, had to be made very small. There are, in fact more than 3,500 to the square inch. Even so, the chart is too large for the taxpayer to paste in his hat. Let him hang it, instead, on his parlor wall, between "The American's Creed" and the portrait of Mr. Roosevelt.

It may not be beautiful, but it will be the most costly picture, at least symbolically, in his house. If there were no Federal jobholders every American taxpayer could afford to buy a hand painted oil painting by a more or less old master, real or bogus. If there were no jobholders at all every taxpayer's income would be increased twenty-seven percent.

Such is the bill for being saved from revolution and ruin by Wonder Men. If it were not for the corps of Federal jobholders, so we are told, millions of Americans would be starving, and next-door neighbors would be shooting off machine guns at one another over the backyard fence. As it is, every American has a fat and easy job, wages are increasing everywhere, and market and store bills are going down steadily.

The chart, as we have intimated, shows the cost of these great boons in jobholders. It may serve also to show the cost in money. If each of its dots is taken to represent a dollar, then the Federal jobholders wipe the chart clean every twenty-two minutes. In the course of every day of eight hours, Sundays and holidays included, they knock off twenty-two charts. In the course of every week they knock off more than 150. In the course of a year they knock off more than 8,000.

Counting a dot to a dollar, the Federal jobholders have consumed nearly 85,000 charts since the New Deal began. The taxpayer, during that time, has supplied the dots for nearly 19,000. The rest have been filed away for future reference.

(*The Baltimore Evening Sun, February 10, 1938*)

The State of the Nation

I

Three years ago, at the height of the late Golden Age, all Americans of any patriotic decency of mind believed firmly in Santa Claus; today they believe as firmly in witches. Both beliefs, I fear, must be set down as unsound. The prosperity of the Coolidge era was really far less vast and far-reaching than was commonly assumed at the time, and the same thing may be said of the Hoover depression. There is a fashion, at the moment, for extreme pessimism. Any man who ventures to hint that he, personally, is getting on fairly well is not only suspected of lying but also of a kind of treason. It becomes immoral to be serene, just as it was immoral before November, 1929, to be dubious.

As a matter of fact, the prospect ahead is by no means as dark as most of the current necromancers profess to believe. The country has lost a great deal of money, largely at gambling, and it will be on relatively short commons for some time to come, but there is no evidence whatever that it is in any danger of actual bankruptcy. It could lose five times as much as it has lost, and still remain a going concern. Suppose all the debts that foreign governments owe to the United States were wiped out tomorrow, and suppose that the so-called private debts to American investors followed the day after: what would be the effect? The effect would be that the national wealth of the country would be diminished by but little more than 5%.

But there is no reason to believe that any such complete loss is ahead of us—that is, in actual money. The war debts to the confident Uncle Sam are no doubt done for—but most of them were done for the day they were contracted, and no rational bookkeeper has ever counted them among the national assets. If, by some miracle, they were ever really paid, it would be in such small driblets that the money would be wasted as fast as it came in, and the American taxpayer would scarcely hear of it. As for the private debts, they are certainly not hopeless, taking one with another.

Some are backed by what, in the long run, will probably turn out to be ample security, and others have behind them the good faith of governments and business men who may be trusted to pay part, even if they can't pay all. The net loss, to be sure, will be large even so, but there is no sign that it will be large enough to incommode the United States seriously.

II

At home the damage, at least on paper, is much heavier, but the honest investor will have to bear much less of it than the speculator. The latter, in many cases, is wiped out, but that is only saying that he never had any right to be wiped in. The investor, at the moment, is suffering a painful decline in his income, and if he tried to unload he would be burned as badly as the speculator, but the essence of his position is that he doesn't want to unload. Let him hang on, and he will find, after the smoke clears away, that he still owns his property, and that most of his income has been restored. If he bought a 100,000th share in a sound concern he still owns that 100,000th share, and when normalcy returns it will again sweat money for him.

Not many American industries are sunk beyond recovery. Is the steel business? Is the power business? Is the telephone business? Is the automobile business? Most businesses, to be sure, show decreased earnings, and their securities decline accordingly, but nearly all of them are still going concerns, and in the long run they will earn fair dividends upon every reasonable investment. The imprudent fellows, who bought heavily during the inflation are bound to be stung, but they would have been stung even if the inflation had kept on, for many of them paid prices which, on the basis of probable earnings, could never have yielded them more than 2%.

In a few areas the current declines promise to be permanent, but only in a few. The street railways, I daresay, are down and out; their one hope of surviving at all lies in being sold down the river to the power companies. And the steam railroads begin to look almost as sick. But the general depression has had relatively little to do with this double debacle; it is mainly the product of automotive competition. And its net effect upon the national wealth will be virtually nil, for what the owners of railroad and street railway securities lose will simply be added to the takings of

those who own automobile and gasoline securities. As the Vander-
bilts go down the Rockefellers and Raskobs go up.

III

This see-sawing is in progress all the time. We live in a country
of constant experiment and a time of rapid change, and even the
most prudent investor must expect occasional serious losses. Very
few American fortunes are a century old, and those few are
mainly based on land. But a man who invests in land must often
wait many years for his income, and all the while he is heavily
mulcted for taxes. In other words, he needs a lot of free capital to
protect his investment, and must somehow earn it outside. Thus
most small investors in land are wiped out soon or late. It would
be easy to fill the Stadium with them here in Baltimore.

But such losses do not impair the national wealth. What A loses
is gathered in by B, and B is just as much an Americano as A. At
the present moment everyone is talking about friends and acquaintances who have been ruined by the decline in stocks, but no
one seems to remember that all of the sick stocks are being bought
by other persons, and that these other persons, as the depression
passes, will make very handsome profits. Many perfectly good
stocks are now selling on a 7% basis, and not a few sound bonds
are correspondingly low. When they go back to their natural
levels there will be whole herds of newly-rich Americans, and the
losers of today will be forgotten. As for the country as a whole, it
will be precisely where it was before.

If I had any gift for making money my depression over the
current depression would be greatly diluted by a hopeful cupidity.
The woods are full of grand opportunities for the man with ready
cash. Unfortunately, my tendency in money matters is to play
safe, and that usually means boarding confidently the proudest
ship in harbor and then going down with it gloriously when it
puts to sea. If I had had any capital thirty years ago I'd have put it
all into street railways, which were then at the top of the gilt-edge
list—and are now at the bottom of the duds. If I had had any in
1929 I'd have followed the advice of the most eminent investment
bankers in America—and gone to the poorhouse months ago. In
such matters, alas, folly is often better than prudence, and luck
than skill. A rich man always credits his wealth to his own genius,

but nine times out of ten all it really proves is that the angels have favored him.

IV

Will the depression pass? Of course it will pass. What ails the pessimists today is that they think too little of normal times and too much of the boom days of 1928. That we'll ever see another such orgy of idiot money-making and wild spending is gravely to be doubted, but soon or late the country is bound to settle down again to a decent prosperity and contentment. It will take some time to convince those who were rich a few years ago that they are now poor, but it can and will be done. They will learn to scale their expenditures to their income; they will begin to live sensibly again. Maybe the national government will learn the same simple trick, and with it the State governments and the cities.

We have all been on a bust. Every American, high and low, has been blowing money like a drunken sailor. We have fallen into the folly of mistaking luxuries for necessities. I could live very comfortably on half of what it has cost me to live since 1926, and so could you. Both of us, in fact, used to do it, and were happy. But now we find it very hard to go back. Baltimore city, though it is growing poorer every day, continues to erect gaudy palaces for the education of its future factory hands, and to hire wizards to teach them soccer, the mixing of salad dressings, and parliamentary law. And thousands of Baltimoreans who can't afford it continue to keep automobiles.

But all this will pass. Another hard squeeze or two, and people will begin to regain their senses. Once they do so they will discover that a truly civilized and contented life is possible without so much fuss and display. They will still be as rich as any other people, and much richer than most. They will still have all their actual property, and it will be plenty. They will eat and (I hope) drink and be merry. Children will be growing up who have never heard of two cars in every garage and a chicken in every pot. We'll go back to hog meat and Shank's mare.

Meanwhile, most of the current agonies are grossly exaggerated, and some of them are downright imaginary. I am old enough to remember the panic of 1893. There was a depression with real teeth in it. I saw scores of poor people plodding through the snow —barefoot. There was no public fund to relieve them. Nobody in

Baltimore had any money. The whole town was flat on its back. Those who could not find shelter from the cold simply froze. And the hungry actually starved.

(The Baltimore Evening Sun, January 4, 1932)

Crime as a Trade

I

A few weeks ago, writing in this place, I offered the somewhat obvious suggestion that putting down the gangs of criminals who now ravage and terrorize the country will never be achieved until there is a radical change in American criminal law—that as it stands it gives them so many advantages that the poor cops are almost helpless before them. And to this I added the modest proposal that statutes be passed making it a capital offense to practice robbery, kidnaping and armed assault as a trade, and that all of its known practitioners (the cops, of course, know who they are) be rounded up, put on trial before the juries of their peers, and, if convicted, handed over to the hangman forthwith.

Some objections to this programme have been offered by friends who have favored me with letters on the subject, including several learned in juristic science, but after prayer and soul-searching I find myself inclined to stick to it. The chief of these objections is typical of the rest: it is to the effect that it would be impossible, under the existing rules of evidence, to prove that any given man was a professional criminal. But to that I can only reply that one of the principal purposes of any scheme of legal reform, whether mine or another's, must be to change the rules of evidence, so that they will begin to have some sort of resemblance, however remote, to the canons of common honesty and common sense.

Does anyone maintain seriously that there was any doubt in any rational man's mind about the profession of, say, the late Whittemore or the late Legs Diamond? Both were open, avowed and notorious criminals, with no other profession. Both went armed habitually, and were known to be quite willing to murder anyone who stood in their way. Both associated constantly with other criminals, both had been jailed frequently without being dissuaded from their courses, and both carried on their operations in bold and cynical defiance of the police. And yet, under our existing system of maudlin penology and worse law, Whittemore could not be hanged until he had committed a brutal murder in the very penitentiary where he was undergoing his eighth or tenth "reform," and Diamond had to be allowed at large, practicing his trade as publicly as an auctioneer, until his own associates got tired of him and put an end to him.

II

Today hundreds of other Diamonds and Whittemores continue in operation, placarded as "public enemies", but otherwise almost unmolested. They have developed the technique of their trade to such a point that taking them *in flagrante* is almost impossible, and yet everyone knows who they are and what they are doing, and the newspapers discuss their acts daily, and accuse them of long lists of heinous crimes without the slightest risk of libel. Their portraits are printed so often that their faces become as familiar as those of the Hollywood actors, and every schoolboy has heard about their heroic deeds. Yet it is rare indeed for one of them to be brought into court on charges commensurate with his crimes, and almost unheard of for one of them to go to the gallows.

What protects them is an elaborate series of legal rules and assumptions, all illogical and long outworn. One is the rule that a man can be tried for but one crime at a time. Another is the rule that, unless he brings it into evidence himself, his known record may not be offered against him. A third is the doctrine that it is a much less serious crime to shoot at a man and miss him than it is to shoot at him and kill him. A fourth is the doctrine that a crime is a sort of thing in itself, and that the character of the criminal and the social damage done should not be taken into account in estimating and punishing it. And a fifth is the theory that capital punishment ought to be reserved for criminal set-pieces of certain sharply limited categories, and that it is somehow brutal and against God to use it for the general purpose of stamping out crime.

My list is short: I might extend it considerably. It is made up, in the main, of notions so palpably absurd that the courts, in practice, spend a great deal of their time and energies trying to get round them. Is it a fact that a prisoner's record cannot be taken into account in determining his guilt? Then it is equally a fact that it is always taken into account in determining his punishment. Is it a fact that crime is a thing in itself, and quite unrelated to the personality of the criminal? Then all our parole and probation laws are nonsense. And would it be brutal to hang a man for declaring war against society and adopting crime as a profession? Then it is a thousand times as brutal to hang a poor wretch, otherwise quite harmless, who kills under the influence of a sudden and irresistible passion.

III

The truth is that all the benign devices invented in recent years to mitigate the punishment of the chance criminal, and so encourage him to resume decent living, have been seized upon by the professional (aided boldly by the kind of shyster lawyer he commonly employs), and turned to his benefit. I doubt if there is a gunman in practice in the United States today who hasn't at least one parole behind him, and at least one term of probation. Whittemore was a graduate, I believe, in both departments, just as Duker was a graduate of more than one reformatory: if I am wrong, then he was unusual indeed. Practically every eminent Chicago murderer has been paroled in his time, and some of the most active are under probation at this moment.

I am not arguing, of course, against probation and parole. They are devices of plain merit, and when employed to relieve chance criminals of the full rigor of the law they undoubtedly do a lot of good. But as they are only too often carried out in this country they are simply schemes for turning loose professionals and restoring them to their trade. As the researches of Dr. Sheldon Glueck and his associates prove clearly, a substantial majority of the prisoners who are paroled come back, and usually they come back for worse crimes than those they committed originally. Certainly it is a manifest absurdity to parole the same criminal twice, or to put him on probation twice, and yet precisely that is being done all over the United States, and every day.

The poor cops, facing this witless system, naturally lose heart. At the risk of their lives they track down a given professional and bring him to justice—and a little while later they find him turned loose upon this pretext or that, and at his business again, and ready again to kill them if they molest him. The hangman might rid them of him in ten minutes, but day by day the hangman has less work to do, and day by day the number of professional criminals, openly practicing their trade, becomes greater and more appalling.

IV

This breakdown of the whole system of justice is largely due, as everyone knows, to the rise of the organized sentimentality known as the New Penology. Advocated principally by persons to whom it offers easy jobs, it has gone so far that the statute-books of every State are full of its inventions, and even some of the judges have begun to swallow them. Its aims are bold, and its proponents state them frankly. The immediate one is to convert every court-room into a sort of clinic and take the handling of criminals out of the hands of judges and juries, and give it over to so-called experts. And the ultimate one is to abolish the concept of crime altogether, and to substitute for it the concept of illness, so that the gunman will not be hanged or jailed at all, but sent to a comfortable hospital instead, where more experts, aided by a staff of handsome nurses, will proceed to cure him.

That these experts are bogus goes without saying. Some of them, to be sure, are earnest and honest, but they remain bogus none the less, just as a chiropractor is bogus, though he may believe in his own magic. There is, in point of fact, no evidence whatever that any known course of medical treatment can cure a criminal of his evil ways, or even abate his symptoms. Nor is there any evidence that what is the matter with him can be described medically, in terms comprehensible to a rational pathologist. The literature of the subject is simply hollow word-chopping, and the great discoveries of its authors have no more logical validity than *Science and Health*.

The one sure cure for the professional criminal is the rope. Once it has been applied to his neck, his days of preying upon his betters are over, and the cops have accomplished something that is lasting and real. Is it a fact that hanging him does not dissuade his brother? Perhaps. But it unquestionably dissuades the man hanged. He will rob and slay no more, and the taxpayer will be at no further cost for his keep. The choice before us is plain. Either the law must be so rationalized that it can detect, snare and dispose of him, or we must reconcile ourselves to a general outbreak of lynching. For the American people are growing very weary of the Capones, and if the law fails to rid the land of them it will be done by the *posse comitatus*.

(*The Baltimore Evening Sun, August 14, 1933*)

On Controversy

Any man engaged habitually in controversy, as I have been for twenty years past, must enter upon his declining days with a melancholy sense of its hollowness and futility. Especially in this great republic, where all ideas are suspect, it tends almost inevitably to degenerate into a mere exchange of nonsense. Have you ever examined carefully the speeches made by the candidates in a presidential campaign? If so, you know that they are of bilge and blather all compact. Now and then, true enough, one of the august aspirants to the Washingtonian breeches is goaded or misled into saying something pungent and apposite, but not often. His daily stint is simply balderdash.

It is rare, indeed, to encounter a controversialist who states his own case clearly, or who shows any sign of understanding his opponent's. Turn, for example, to the current combat between the fundamentalists and the modernists—an academic and puerile duel in our great Sodoms and Ninevehs, but raging like an oil fire in the Bible and hookworm belt, where men are he and hell yawns. Both sides wallow in pishposh. The fundamentalists, claiming a monopoly of faith, allege that they believe the whole Bible *verbatim et literatim*, which is not true, for at least 99 percent of them reject Exodus xxii, 18,* to say nothing of I Timothy v, 23.** And the modernists argue that there is no conflict between science and Holy Writ, which is even less true.

This controversy, in fact, is almost classical in character. Neither side is able to stick to the question at issue. Each tries to dispose of the other by delivering mighty wallops below the belt—

* Thou shalt not suffer a witch to live.

** Drink no longer water, but use a little wine for thy stomach's sake and thine often infirmities.

fundamentalists by passing laws converting the modernists into criminals (that is, as criminality is now defined by American jurisprudence), and the modernists by depicting the fundamentalists as a horde of gibbering baboons, sworn to uproot civilization and not above suspicion of cannibalism.

* *

I have had a hand in this great battle of scattered wits myself, striving in an austere and lofty manner to introduce the sublime principles of Aristotle's *Organon* into it. I have got the traditional reward of one stopping to preach in front of a house afire. The more extreme modernists—which is to say, the professional atheists—discontented because I haven't advocated hanging the fundamentalists, denounce me as a Crypto-Calvinist, and hold me up to obloquy in their papers. The fundamentalists, suspecting me of a secret partiality for Darwin, accuse me of trying to upset the ten commandments, and one of the most eminent of them was lately hinting that I have personally had a bout with No. 7, and come to grief in the manner described by the late Dr. Sylvanus Stall in his well known work on pathology, *What Every Boy of Fourteen Should Know*.

This last accusation was novel, but, as they run in such affairs, very mild. The usual charge against an opponent, in the America of today, is that he is a bolshevist, and in receipt of Russian gold. It has been leveled at me so often that probably a majority of the persons who have heard of me at all believe it, and there are even dismal days when I half believe it myself, though I have been denouncing socialism publicly for twenty years, and am, in fact, an incurable Tory in politics. A short while ago a Boston critic, becoming aware of the latter fact by some miracle, at once proceeded to denounce me because my radicalism, as he thought he had discovered, was bogus.

During the period 1908–1920 I was chiefly engaged in literary controversies, and so my politics were aside from the issue. But when the great wave of idealism engulfed the United States in 1917 I was at once bawled out as a German spy, and open demands were made that my purely esthetic heresies be put down by the Polizei. My principal opponent, in those days, was an eminent college professor, now unhappily dead. He not only attempted to dispose of my literary judgments by hinting that they were inspired by the Kaiser; he even made the same charge against the works of the writers I was currently whooping up. And so did many of his learned colleagues. I met the attack with an elaborate effort to prove that all college professors were asses.

* *

The issue of this forgotten combat was characteristic: thus all controversies in the realm of ideas end. The moment the great war was over there came a revulsion against its idealism, and so it was no longer damaging to accuse me of taking the money of the Hohenzollerns. Thus the professor that I have mentioned found his principal ammunition gone, and in an effort to unearth more he began reading the books I had been advocating. To his surprise he found that many of them were works of high merit, whereupon he began whooping for them himself, and even going beyond my loudest rah-rahs. In the end he was actually searching them for evidences of Teutonic influence, and hailing it with enthusiasm when found.

His poor fellow professors, meanwhile, were the goats. I ceased to revile them, once the war was over, and devoted myself mainly to political and moral concerns, but various other controversialists took up the jehad, and in a short time it was raging from coast to coast. It got far beyond anything I had myself dreamed of. Indignant publicists, quite unknown to me, began grouping all professors with chiropractors, congressmen, and spiritualists as quacks. In dozens of colleges large and small, north, east, south, and west, the students began holding meetings and flinging insults at their tutors. Scores of college papers, for flouting them in contumacious terms, had to be suppressed. In several great institutions of learning the thing actually reached the form of physical assault.

When the smoke cleared away, the college professor, once so highly respected by every one, found himself a sort of questionable character, and he remains so today. In many cases, I believe, he actually is, but surely not in all. The point is that the virtuous have suffered with the guilty. Many an honest and God fearing professor, laboriously striving to ram his dismal nonsense into the progeny of Babbitts, is bombarded with ribald spitballs as a result of a controversy which began outside his ken and speedily got far beyond the issue between the original combatants.

* *

Such are the ways of war in the psychic field. Why they should be so I don't know, but so they are. No controversy, to my knowledge, has ever ended on the ground where it began. Even the historic one between Huxley and Wilberforce, two of the most eminent men of their time in England, ranged all over the landscape before the contestants had enough. It began with Huxley trying to prove that Darwin's *Origin of Species* was a sound book; it ended with Bishop Wilberforce trying to prove that Huxley's grandfather was a gorilla. All its steps are paralleled in the current combat between the fundamentalists and modernists.

Some time ago, contemplating a trip to the west, I wrote to a friend in a California town, telling him that I would visit him. He mentioned the fact casually to a newspaper acquaintance, and the latter suggested to one of the town Babbitts that I be invited to address the local Rotarians. The Babbitt, thinking to have some harmless fun with me, agreed that it was a good idea, and the next day the local morning paper announced my invitation as a fact. That afternoon the evening paper was full of indignant protests. My friend in the town is a Socialist. I am certainly not, but because he is my friend I was denounced as a dangerous radical, and plans were instantly made to prevent me speaking. The row is still raging as I write, with brother against brother. Meanwhile, no one has actually invited me to harangue the Rotarians, and I'd certainly decline if I were asked.

Once, in an effort to keep controversy on a lofty plane, another Socialist and I wrote a book jointly. He advanced the Marxian arguments, and I tried to meet them. We were excessively polite, and kept strictly to the matter in hand. We both spent hard labor upon the writing, and went to great trouble to verify every fact adduced. The book was praised by reviewers as full of information and extremely high toned. It sold less than 200 copies in eight years. Then the publisher unloaded his stock upon a cut rate bookseller, and copies went for ten cents.

(The Chicago Sunday Tribune, October 24, 1926)

The American Scene

The American Scene

I

Some time ago, in the pursuit of my gloomy duties as an itinerant theologian, I made a journey covering ten states. Most of my traveling was done by day, and so I had a good chance to observe the landscape. Save for a few spots, none of them of any extent, it was unbrokenly lovely. In more than one place, indeed, it was genuinely entrancing. I saw beautiful mountains, I saw beautiful river valleys, and I saw even more beautiful plains. But nowhere in those ten states did I see a beautiful town. One and all, they were hideous.

Why should this be so? I'm sure I don't know. In all the countries of Europe, even Spain, the villages along the way are charming, but in the United States they are almost uniformly appalling. The only exceptions that I know of are in the older sections of the Atlantic seaboard, and especially in New England, Pennsylvania, and Maryland. Here, along the limestone belt, one occasionally encounters a village that is clean, substantial, dignified, and soothing. But not often. Pennsylvania, which has some of the most sightly small towns in the United States, also has some of the worst. Maryland, of late, has succumbed to improvement and be-

·104·

comes indistinguishable from Ohio or New Jersey. The whole of New England is in decay. There is nothing anywhere else.

Certainly poverty is not the cause of this depressing ugliness, for prosperity is widespread in America, and even the farming sections share it, despite the yowling of yokels yearning for *panem et circenses*. There are gaudy filling stations in every village in the country, and plenty of pretentious and expensive buildings. But the more pretentious they are, the uglier they are. They sit upon their lots absurdly. They are painted in the wrong colors. They show no feeling whatever for architectural form. And they commonly swear at their neighbors.

* *

The cities of the United States, in recent years, show a vast improvement in this department. Most of them have still to discover the full virtues of architectural unity and coherence, but they are obviously better than they used to be. Their tall buildings downtown grow more graceful year by year, and they show a new feeling for beauty in their residence sections. But the villages seem to grow worse and worse. When they attempt anything ambitious it is usually a warehouse made of concrete blocks—certainly the most horrible building material ever invented—or a bank building with a false Romanesque front. Their new dwelling houses are mainly bungalows—with pillars in front almost fit for the Parthenon. Everywhere is barbaric painting, and everywhere is cheapness and imitation.

In Europe, from Scandinavia to Sicily, the village churches are always graceful, and often they are very beautiful. I can recall no exception. But in America they are usually even worse than the dwelling houses and stores. On my brief journey I saw village churches in North Carolina, and again in Ohio and Indiana, that were downright staggering. They seemed to have been designed by the devil himself, and as a practical joke upon the Christians frequenting them. Half of them were raised idiotically on stilts, and practically all of them had grotesque and preposterous steeples, mainly of scantlings and clapboards. Not one in fifty showed decent surroundings suitable to a house of worship. The church yards, indeed, were even worse than the churches.

Of late there has been some attempt to improve the country churches, especially in the south and middle west. The southern Baptists have a committee at work upon the problem, and it has had competent architects prepare some very charming designs, well within the means of a small town congregation. The Lutherans of the Missouri synod have undertaken the same reform in their territory, and no doubt other demodifications have been likewise. But so far, I can only report sadly, there is little evidence of practical results. Traveling more than 2,000 miles through the heart of a rich and smiling country I saw only half a dozen churches that did not suggest dog houses.

* *

One reason why they are so bad, of course, is that there are too many of them. Very few European villages, even in the Catholic south, have more than one church. It represents the joint wealth and piety of the whole population, extending over generations, and so it is substantially built, and gets a certain grace and beauty out of its very solidity. But in the average American village there are three, four, and sometimes even six or eight churches put up by the warring sects, and all of them cheap and bad. These sects, trying vainly to outshine and exterminate one another, all remain poor. They rush into church building before they can afford it, and the usual result is simply one more libel upon God, with a debt hanging over it and no money to keep it decently painted.

The Catholics, to be sure, are free from that criticism. They never build a church until they are sure of the money to pay for it, and once it is consecrated it is commonly kept in good order. But in the main they seem to patronize very bad architects, for their churches are usually harsh in design and very ungraceful. Even in the big cities, in truth, the Catholic churches are seldom as beautiful as they ought to be, considering how much money is spent upon them. Large numbers of them are of gray granite—a stone which needs expert handling to avoid making it look like cast iron. That expert handling, I fear, is not often given to it.

But the Protestant churches are the worst, for they are the cheapest, and look it. If they are made of stone, then it is the dullest, least vibrant stone that the vicinity affords; if they are of brick, then it is laid like the brick in a sewer manhole; if they are of wood it is badly sawn and worse painted. And always, or nearly always, there is a complete absence of taste in design. The European peasant seems unable to put up even a hog house without making it somehow graceful; his American descendant is apparently quite unable to build even a church without giving it something of the abominable clumsiness and sickliness of a tar paper house along the railroad track.

* *

I offer no remedy for this unpleasant state of affairs, for I know of none. It might be improved, at least theoretically, by setting up authorities to control architecture, whether public or private, but I am cynical of all such authorities—and they do not seem to be needed in Europe. Will time educate and civilize the yokel and make an aesthete of him? I doubt it. Judging from present evidence, its influence actually runs in the other direction, for the oldest villages in America are the most beautiful—not only because age gives even a bad building a certain dignity, but also and more importantly because the early buildings were better than the modern ones. The whalers of the New England coast towns and the Pennsylvania Dutch farmers of Pennsylvania seem to have been alike gifted with a faculty for design; their surviving churches and homes are all lovely. But their progeny build bungalows.

It is a pity, for the American landscape is almost uniformly beautiful. In very few parts of this immense country is there any natural ugliness. Even the pine woods along the south Atlantic seaboard and the monotonous reaches of the western prairie have their high qualities, and it is not surprising to hear that there are men and women who love them. The more broken country is everywhere of great beauty, from the hills and lakes of Maine to the last flutters of the Georgia highlands, and from the gorgeous Piedmont of Virginia to the cliffs that frown down upon the Pacific. Some time ago I spent a summer morning riding through the blue grass country of Kentucky. Where is there anything in Europe more lovely? In color as in contour it is almost perfect.

But its villages, like those of all other parts of the republic, are mainly hideous. They sprawl absurdly; their trees are badly planted; their houses leap out of the ground like flying fish; they show colors that nature would be ashamed of; they fade into outskirts that are not only frowsy but also filthy. A few seemly and winning towns are there, but not many—not a tenth as many as there ought to be. Such a landscape deserves the reverence of man as a beautiful woman deserves it. He ought to be ashamed of doing anything to mar it. But in the blue grass, as in the green grass, the

American peasant flings himself barbarously upon it and tries his level damndest to make it revolting.

(The Chicago Sunday Tribune, August 28, 1927)

New York

I

My view of the above great city, I find, shifts and varies from time to time. There are days when I long to hear that French spies have blown it up; there are other days when I cherish the theory that it is probably the most civilized town the world has seen since the downfall of Constantinople. Maybe the two notions are really not so far apart as they seem to be. It may be that civilization is a disease, as the Methodist Board of Temperance, Prohibition and Public Morals seems to think, and that the human mind yearns instinctively to throw it off. Who, indeed, can escape the race's ancient nostalgia for trees, green fields, cows, horse-flies, the song of the thrush, the soft earth underfoot? When it comes on in New York it engenders only homicidal moods. The town is made solidly of steel and concrete. The only sweet scents that it knows come out of bottles. It is so artificial that even the grass in its so-called parks looks like embalmed sauerkraut.

I inhabit it off and on, and, as I have said, swing between loathing of it and delight in it. The first emotion comes upon me whenever I have to move about. Where in all the world is mere motion more disagreeable? The subways are so dreadful that no rational man ever enters them if he can help it, and on the surface there is such brutal, paralyzing crowding that even walking across the street is uncomfortable. I have seen traffic jams in Sixth avenue at 1:30 A.M., with a dozen cops bawling and waving their arms, a score of taxi drivers plastered with summonses, a hundred drunks, yelling ribaldries, and an old man lying in the gutter with his head broken. Fifth avenue at 5:30 P.M. becomes a sort of grotesque *reductio ad absurdum* of a thoroughfare. Getting from Fifty-seventh street, where my office is, down to Forty-fourth street, where I live, takes a good twenty minutes by bus or taxi. One could walk it faster if the sidewalks were not solidly packed with human sardines, and the crossings were not like gigantic bowling alleys. Far faster is the trolley under the elevated in Sixth avenue. But how is one to get into it? The business is as hazardous as boarding a freight train under way. The legs and arms of those who try it are piled up like cord-wood.

II

With all this goes the infernal uproar of the town—the most appalling noise ever heard in Christendom. In no city that I have ever been in are there more fires, and in none do the fire-engines make so much racket. One can hear them coming when they are still a mile down the street, even above the thunder of the elevated. Reaching the main crossings they set off sounds that are positively staggering, not with the puerile gongs of the provinces, but with mechanical whistles that seem to be worked by steam. Anon there is a sharp bang and a crash of glass, and a taxicab is upset, or an engine has run into an elevated pole, and firemen are scattered all over the street.

In every block at least two new hotels or office buildings are under way—and once one of them starts its building drags on for months. Most of Manhattan island seems to be solid rock, so digging a cellar of four or five stories is a long and arduous matter. For hours the pneumatic drills chatter and scream; then there is sudden silence, and huge cranes drop heavy steel mats over the holes that have been made. There follows a series of alarming explosions, shaking the whole neighborhood, and following them come yells, crashes, and the sharp, exigent clanging of ambulance bells. A couple of Greeks are hauled out and carted away. The drills resume. When their work is done the steel frame begins to rise, and from it, beginning at 7.30 A.M., there issues the dreadful cacophony of riveting.

It took more than six months to run up the new office building next to my hotel. The cellar alone occupied the workmen for at least three months. Every morning I was thrown out of bed by explosions. At night, coming home, I fell into excavations. That was in a quiet neighborhood, peopled mainly by bachelors, who notoriously love ease. One night lately I sought a yet quieter— Riverside Drive. The evening's exercise ran to piano duets. At least ten times my hearty bass was completely drowned out by the uproar of the New York Central shifting-engines down on the water front.

III

But the charm of the town remains, and it is powerful enough, almost any day, to make me forget most of the noise. That charm, I believe, chiefly issues out of money. New York is simply inconceivably rich—richer than all the capitals of Europe put together, with all the lesser towns of America, save perhaps one or two, thrown in for good measure. Is wealth merely flamboyant and stupid? Not necessarily. It may also be luxurious and beautiful. There are more beautiful things in New York, in all probability, than in Paris and London combined—and I am not forgetting beautiful buildings. Is the new Telephone Building a crib from the Germans? Then where is the match for it in Berlin?

It is, however, in the details of everyday living that wealth counts best, not in public monuments. The New Yorker of easy means lives better, despite his crowded quarters, than any other man ever heard of. He has a more elaborate machinery for making him comfortable, and it is run with almost perfect skill. The older hotels and apartment-houses, perhaps, are still horrors—but the new ones! What ingenuity in their arrangement! What excellent taste in their furnishing and decoration! What perfection in the service they offer to their guests! All hotelishness has gone out of them. One encounters no loiterers in their lobbies, for they have no lobbies. There is no sign of onyx or golden oak. Not a slave is in sight. There is not a sound—save, of course, the uproar from outside, and even that is somehow hushed. The whole vast organism works with the precision and excellence of a watch—nay, of a kidney. And it carries the same confident and decorous air.

Nothing ever goes wrong in such masterpieces of the American genius for comfortable living. Unsummoned, no servant is ever visible; summoned, they appear instantaneously. Clean towels always hang on the rack—not two, or four, or a dozen, but enough for a battle for the heavyweight championship of the world. Ordering cocktail glasses, one never gets goblets. Everything works, including the window-curtains and the shower. Hot water comes out of the hot water tap. Bores are trapped at the telephone switchboard downstairs—invisible like the manager, the valet, the chambermaid, the bringer of orange-juice, ice, shakers, powdered sugar, limes.

IV

It costs a great deal of money, but New York is filled with people who seem to have it. Are they rooked? I am inclined to doubt it. They pay huge prices, and out of those huge prices come huge profits, but they actually get something for their money. They get a kind of luxury that is unobtainable in Europe, save as a sort of miracle: the luxury of being surrounded by perfect and unobtrusive slaves, human and mechanical. Nor is all that luxury for the body alone. There were more orchestra concerts in New York last winter than in Berlin. The town has more theaters, and better ones, than a dozen Londons. It has at least five times as many good restaurants as Paris. It has more night clubs, cabarets and other such gilded dens than hell itself.

But what of Prohibition! I can only say that Manhattan island seems to have forgotten it completely. One reads in the papers that this or that restaurant has been padlocked, but nine times out of ten it is open the same night, and magnificently wet. And if it remains closed, then its staff opens another and better one next door or across the street. Getting in is sometimes a bit complicated: one must be introduced. But once inside, it is assumed amiably that one is of ordinary decency, and not a parishioner of the Rev. Dr. John Roach Straton. Drinks are brought if ordered, and the price declines month by month. Very respectable wines are procurable. The hard liquors are safe and full of virtue.

My taste runs rather to beer-houses, and they are unfortunately not numerous on the island, or very attractive. They tend to be crowded to suffocation, especially after the theater, and to run to indifferent brews. But New Jersey is but half an hour away—and in New Jersey, as in Munich, the quality of the malt liquors is seen to by the *Polizei.* I don't know precisely where the best beer houses are over there; in deference to the Constitution I always make the journey blindfolded, led by one of the official guides. But there *Helles* is superb, believe me!

(The Baltimore Evening Sun, July 26, 1926)

San Francisco: A Memory

I

What fetched me instantly (and thousands of other newcomers with me) was the subtle but unmistakable sense of escape from the United States—the feeling that here, at last, was an American city that somehow managed to hold itself above pollution by the national philistinism and craze for standardization, the appalling progress of 100% Americanism, the sordid and pathetic dreams of unimaginative, timorous and inferior men.

The East, it seems to me, is gone, and perhaps for good. All the towns along the seaboard are now as alike as so many soldiers in a row. They think alike. They hope and fear alike. They smell alike. They begin to look alike. What one says all the others say. What one does all the others do. It is as if some gigantic and relentless force labored to crush all personality, all distinction, all tang and savor out of them. They sink to the spiritual and intellectual level of villages, fat, lethargic and degraded. Their aspirations are the aspirations of curb brokers, green grocers and honorary pallbearers. The living hope of their typical citizen is to die respected by bank cashiers, Young Men's Christian Association secretaries and policemen. They are ironed out, disemboweled, denaturized, dephlogisticated, salted down, boiled, baked, dried in a kiln.

Think of Washington: a hundred thousand miserable botches of ninth-rate clerks, all groveling at the feet of such puerile caricatures as Daniels, Burleson and Palmer. Baltimore: mile after mile of identical houses, all inhabited by persons who regard Douglas Fairbanks as a greater man than Beethoven. (What zoologist, without a blood count and a lumbar puncture, could distinguish one Baltimorean from another?) Philadelphia: an intellectual and cultural slum. Newark: a worse one. New York: a wholesale district with an annex for entertaining the visiting trade. New Haven and Hartford: blanks. Boston: a potter's field, a dissecting room. Mental decay in all its forms, but one symptom there is in common: the uneasy fear of ideas, the hot yearning to be correct at all costs, the thirst to be well esteemed by cads.

II

What is it that lifts San Francisco out of that wallow? I am not at all sure. It may be something intrinsic—specifically, something ethnological. The stock out there differs visibly from any Eastern stock that I know. It is not that half of the people are actual foreigners, for that is also true of New York and nearly true of Baltimore; it is that the native born belong to a distinct strain, mentally and physically—that the independence and enterprise of the pioneers are still in them—that their blood is still running hot and clear. Above all, remember the recentness of this heritage. They are not the children of men who were bold and daring in the seventeenth century, but the children of men who were bold and daring in the mid-nineteenth.

I met a man in the Bohemian Club who began to tell me casually of his grandmother. This lady, an Irishwoman of good birth, came to California from Ireland in 1849, by way of Panama. Imagine the journey: the long sea voyage, the infernal struggle across the Isthmus, the worse trip up the coast, the trek inland. Well, she brought a piano with her!—got it aboard ship in Ireland, guarded it all the way to Panama, dragged it through the jungle, then shipped it again, and finally packed it to her home in the hills! I daresay many of us could find such grandmothers, going back far enough. But in 1849—70 years ago? Our Baltimore grandmothers, in 1849, were sitting snugly by the new Latrobe stoves, reading *Dombey and Son* and knitting socks.

III

Mere geography helps, with a polite bow to meteorology. The climate, to an Easterner, is almost too invigorating. The heat of the Sacramento Valley sucks in such cold breezes through the Golden Gate that they over-stimulate like raw alcohol. An Arctic current comes down the coast, and the Pacific is so chilly that sea bathing is almost impossible, even in midsummer. Coming off this vast desert of ice water, the San Francisco winds tickle and sting. One arises in the morning with a gigantic sense of fitness—a feeling of superb well-being. Looking out at the clear yellow sunlight, one is almost tempted to crow like a rooster. It is a land of magnificent mornings.

But of somewhat less magnificent nights, at least to one from the East. The thrill of it leads to over-estimates. One suffers from the optimism of a man full of champagne. Toward evening, perhaps, a clammy fog rolls in, and one begins to feel a sudden letting down. The San Franciscans have learned how to bear it. They are stupendously alive while they are in motion, but they knock off betimes. The town is rich in loafing places—restaurants, theatres, parks. No one seems to work very hard. The desperate, consuming industry of the East is quite unknown. One could not imagine a sweatshop in the town. Puffs of Oriental air come with the fog. There is nothing European about the way life is lived; the color is all Asiatic.

IV

Now imagine the scene. A peninsula with the Pacific on one side of it and the huge bay on the other—a peninsula bumpy with bold, precipitous hills, some of them nearly a thousand feet high. The San Franciscans work in the valleys and live on the hills. Cable cars haul them up in a few minutes, or they make the voyage in astonishing taxicabs—taxicabs that seem capable of running up the side of a house. Monument street, east of the monument, is nothing; here are hills that are genuinely steep. Coming down on foot one hugs the houses. Going up on foot—but I had better confine myself to what I know.

Once up, the scene almost staggers. It is incomparably more beautiful than any view along the Grand Corniche; from the Twin Peaks San Francisco makes Monaco seem tawdry and trivial. Ahead is the wide sweep of the bay, with the two great shoulders of the Golden Gate running down. Behind is the long curtain of California mountains. And below is the town itself—great splashes of white, pink and yellow houses climbing the lesser hills —houses half concealed in brilliant green—houses often sprawling and ramshackle, but nevertheless grouping themselves into lovely pictures, strange and charming. No other American town looks like that. It is a picture out of the East—dazzling, exotic and curiously romantic.

V

This foreign and half barbaric color gets into everything. One notices it at once without being able precisely to define it. There is the thing that no Atlantic town has ever been able to manage— gayety without grossness. In a sense, the place is wide open, but not in the way that New York and Baltimore and Washington used to be wide open—vulgarly, garishly, hoggishly. The business is achieved with an air, almost a grand manner. It is good-humored, engaging, innocent. There is no heavy attitude of raising the devil. One may guzzle as one will, but one may also drink decently and in order, and shake a leg in the style of Haydn, and lift an eye to a pretty girl without getting knocked in the head or having one's pocket picked. It is a friendly place, a spacious and tolerant place, a place heavy with strangeness and charm. It is no more American, in the sense that American has come to carry, than a wine festival in Spain or the carnival at Nice. It is cut off sharply from all the rest of this dun and dour republic.

But how securely? I have my uneasy doubts. Down a side street I saw a Gospel joint and heard its grisly drum. An Italian, while I was there, was jailed for selling grappa, a native brandy fit for embalming heroes. (The judge, true enough, protested against the raid from the bench, but the poor wop had confessed.) During the war the commercial bounders of the town swindled the Government out of millions, and are now organized in the usual booming clubs, anti-Red vereins, and chambers of illicit commerce. China-town is now as respectable as Guilford, and a good deal less naughty under cover. Sailors touring the Barbary Coast drink sarsaparilla. There is a movement by earnest Christian men to prohibit kissing in the parks. Forward-lookers turn their eyes to the East, and sniff its brummagem evangels. . . .

I advise you to lose no time. In two years San Francisco, too, may be 100% American. Go while the going is good.

(The Baltimore Evening Sun, July 21, 1920)

How to Improve Arkansas

I

With the Hon. Charles H. Brough's partiality for Arkansas, the State of his residence for more than a quarter of a century and the scene of his principal labors as pedagogue, orator, public official, patriot, Freemason, Elk, Maccabee, literary critic, historian, economist, sociologist, philosopher and Christian—with this partiality I have every sympathy, for I confess to the same weakness when it comes to the Maryland Free State, where I had the honor to be born. For all I care the United States may be jolly well damned: I am its subject by historical necessity, not its citizen by choice. But for the Free State I have a kind of affection bordering upon the sentimental, and so, when anyone asperses it or tries to injure it— say by befouling it with Prohibition and other such Wesleyan infamies—I commonly get out such weapons as God hath given me, and have at him violently.

Thus I don't blame Dr. Brough in the slightest for belaboring me in a brisk manner for certain late remarks in this place about the Arkansas *Kultur*. On the contrary, it seems to me that he deserves only praise for his ardor, and perhaps I should add—though it goes without saying when he is mentioned—for his courtly manners. But all the same, I find it impossible to accept his defense of his State at the value he sets upon it himself, for in part it is grounded upon contentions that give a false weight to certain indubitable facts, and in part it is made up of contentions which rest upon facts that are really not facts at all. Both errors appear in the open letter from him that was printed in this place last Tuesday.

Perhaps the most salient of those in the second category is his allegation that I have "agencies of publicity" which he has not, and that the fact that a sovereign State may not sue me for libel gives me an advantage in the present controversy. That I have any unusual "agencies of controversy" is simply not true. What I write in this place is printed in this place only, save when some other newspaper reprints it voluntarily, for the *Sunpapers* do not syndicate their contents, and any other paper that wants to reprint anything I write must ask for special permission. I contribute to no other newspaper, and seldom write for any save one magazine, whose contents are protected in precisely the same way. Nor does the fact that the State of Arkansas cannot sue me for libel give me any advantage, for on the one hand I have never written a word about it that was libelous, and on the other hand the members of its State Legislature, who were but lately denouncing me in rebuttal in a grossly defamatory manner, are protected by their legislative immunity, and so stand beyond the reach of my solicitor, as they are very well aware, and Dr. Brough with them.

II

But this is a small matter, and I mention it only because my learned opponent makes much of it. He gets into deeper water, I think, when he makes his other error—that is, when he states undoubted facts, and then proceeds to give them more weight than is really in them. I point, for example, to his long list of eminent "Arkansas business men"—among them Sam W. Reyburn, "president of Lord & Taylor"; R. Hill Carruth, "executive officer of the Maryland Fidelity and Casualty Company"; Meyer Solmson, "editor of the *Ritz*, New York city"; Van B. Sims, "the highest paid auditor in the world"; Morton Carden, "a prominent figure in the councils of Tammany"; and so on—fourteen in all.

These, I believe are all worthy men, especially Dr. Solmson and the Hon. Mr. Carden, but it is certainly absurd to stand thunderstruck before them, as Dr. Brough seems to do. Maryland could offer a similar list, not of fourteen names, but of 400. Judged by the criterion of "Who's Who in America," which Dr. Brough himself has set up, only six of the fourteen are really men of mark at all, and of the six one denies therein that he was born in Arkansas. Only one of the fourteen still lives in the State. The rest have all had to move out to get elbow room for their talents. Altogether Arkansas has hatched 157 magnificoes for "Who's Who," but only 137 can bear to live there. Maryland, with 12 percent less population, has hatched 532 and is attractive enough to be lived in by 578.

Nor is my eminent friend happy in his roster of Arkansas literati. He puts down in all solemnity such fragile champions as Fay

Hempstead (a man, not a woman), "the poet laureate of the world's Masonry since 1886," Mrs. Josie Frazee Cappleman, "The poetess laureate of the Daughters of the Southern Confederacy," and Mrs. Rena Shore Duncan, "a frequent contributor to the *Saturday Evening Post,*" but forgets altogether the one really important author now living in Arkansas, to wit, Charles J. Finger, of Fayetteville—a native, by the way, of England. In exchange for him Arkansas has sent England John Gould Fletcher, the poet, who escaped from Little Rock with loud hosannahs as soon as he left college.

III

It seems to me that Dr. Brough would do well to let "Who's Who in America" alone; it is full of dynamite. Nor does he get anywhere by alleging, as he did in this place on February 10, that Arkansas is "the twin sister of Michigan in the galaxy of American States." As I demonstrated on February 16, Michigan is usually in tenth or eleventh place in all tables showing the cultural rank of the forty-eight States, whereas Arkansas often disputes with Mississippi for last place. Only on the records of lynchings and open-air baptisms is the State near the top.

It would be far more profitable, I think, for Dr. Brough to devote his skill as an economist to finding out why Arkansas is now so hungry and forlorn, and to devising means for keeping the State out of the national bread line hereafter. It is easy enough to blame the drought, but the drought simply does not explain the famine now prevailing there. Arkansas was by no means the dryest State last year. It had 46.6 inches of rainfall during the year, whereas Maryland had but 23.4 inches, or little more than half as much. Only three States, in fact, had more than Arkansas. In North Dakota there were but 14.9 inches and in Nebraska but 9.8 inches. But in these States the farmers are not storming the village grocery stores; they have food of their own, honestly and laboriously grown. And in Maryland they are not appealing to the Red Cross and the national Treasury to aid them; on the contrary, they are contributing to the relief of Arkansas. In Kent county, one of the dryest of the Maryland counties last year, they completed their Red Cross quota so long ago as February 17.

If Dr. Brough really does not know what ails Arkansas, then I direct his attention to a letter appearing in the *Arkansas Gazette,* the leading paper of Little Rock, on February 4. It tells the story so succinctly and so convincingly that I reprint nearly all of it:

The plight of a great many farmers who are without food and are depending upon the Red Cross for something to eat was largely preventable. Any farmer in Arkansas who owns his farm could have raised wheat and oats. These crops would have matured before the drought burned up the corn crop. Whole-wheat flour, made from wheat ground in an ordinary grist mill, makes wholesome, nutritious bread. Wheat is also good chicken feed, and hens fed on it will lay lots of eggs. Oats make mighty fine feed for horses, mules and cows. Last spring was an excellent season for Irish potatoes, and less than one-fifth of an acre would have provided an abundance for the farmer's family for a whole year. It would seem that with whole wheat bread, eggs, potatoes and plenty of milk and butter the farmer would be pretty well fixed.

I have made thirty-six crops in Arkansas and know what I am talking about. The summer of 1881 was as dry where I lived as last summer was. I made no corn that summer—not a nubbin. But I raised wheat, oats, whippoorwill peas and peanuts. I had a few hogs and kept them in good condition on clover pasture, wheat, peanuts and rape. I made a crop the next year without corn for feed and kept my team in fine shape on oats and pea hay.

It would be interesting to know how many farmers sowed wheat last fall to provide against another possible drought. How many will sow oats during this month to provide feed that will be available before crops are laid by?

Let Dr. Brough give over his vain talk of Masonic poet laureates, high-salaried auditors and other such wonders of the Arkansas sideshow and apply his great learning to the relief of his suffering State. Let him, as a sociologist, find out why so many of its farmers are miserable, exploited, chronically half-starved sharecroppers, without reserves and without hope. Let him, as an economist, find out why it accumulates such small stores of food that its people have to ask alms when a calamity hits them. Let him, as a statesman, find out how it acquired its present crushing debt of $165,000,000, and why it can't borrow enough money to feed its own hungry today. And let him prepare himself for this triple labor by pasting in his hat the following from the *Arkansas Farmer* of March 1:

Some of you fellows have fallen down on your job. You've tried to pay your bills, school your children, make your living and keep the wolf from the door with twenty acres of cotton and nothing else. You know better. Why don't you do better?

And this from the Little Rock *Democrat* of February 8:

So long as the Arkansas of today remains the Arkansas of forty years ago the Menckens are going to make it the butt of ridicule, and millions are going to agree with them.

(The Baltimore Evening Sun, March 9, 1931)

The Home of the Crab

The Age of Horses

I

When I was a boy the most romantic neighborhood in Baltimore, at least to me known, was the vicinity of Paca and German streets. It was so to me, I suppose, partly because my father's place of business was nearby: the perfect loafing place for my brother and me on lazy afternoons. But it was so, also, to other boys, and for a different and better reason. That reason was to be found in Louis Coblens' horse-barn and livery-stable, a dark, mysterious, exciting realm which began on Paca street, ran completely around Miller's Hotel on the corner and broke out on Greene street. My father kept his driving horse there in winter, and so I had the run of it. I got to know all the black hostlers, all the washers of wagons and carriages, forever clad in rubber boots and great, shiny aprons. But best of all, I got to know Mr. Felix Coblens, cousin and chief mate to the proprietor.

I believe I admired Mr. Felix more than I admired any other man then extant, save, perhaps, it were my father himself. In one way at least, and it was an important way, he stood far above my father: he knew harness horses and could drive them with great skill. My father had a taste for them, and always kept one; but I'd be carrying filial duty to fanaticism if I said that he knew how to drive. His method, in fact, consisted simply in slapping the reins along the horse's back, and it seldom got him a mile on the road in less than four minutes. But Mr. Felix was a scientist, and full of subtleties. The moment he climbed into a buggy any horse of the slightest self-respect began to show interest, and when he got out into the Pimlico road (now Park Heights Avenue, and a dreadful canyon of architectural horrors), he was wont to give exhibitions that, I daresay, have never been matched in Baltimore to this day.

What was his secret? I don't know, though, in a fashion, he taught it to me. That is, he taught me how to drive a specific horse, my father's sorrel John. John had a mysterious past and was reputed to have speed in him. But in my father's hands he could beat the milk wagons, and that was about all. One day, when my father was away, Mr. Felix took me out on the old road, and put the lines in my hands. "Here," he said, "this is the way to hold them." I held them so. "Now let him go!" I let him go, and I remember the thrill yet! John simply walked away with them all! We got to Belvedere Avenue in what only seemed a few seconds. And the rest were far behind!

II

There were always plenty of horses on the Pimlico road in those days, especially on summer afternoons, and their drivers were eager for a brush. It was harness driving at its simplest and best: nine-tenths of the nags were put to ordinary buggies. But a good road buggy, in those days, was a work of art—high, light, and with wheels so fragile that it seemed they must certainly smash every time they hit a stone. For use on the road the buggies were stripped to skeletons. Even the little squares of carpet were taken out of them, and if a whip was carried it was short and thin.

The plan was to go out through the park, amble along to the first turn, and then look for challenges. They were seldom long a-coming. Out of the dust behind would emerge an ambitious fellow with a fast-stepper, and in an instant the race was on. It was uphill for the first mile, but who cared? Certainly not the horses. They leaped up the long incline to Gray's with vast enthusiasm, and when they got to Halstead's, and a level road at last, they laid back with their ears and strained every nerve. Here it was that old John usually got in his heavy licks. He had what they called class, and hence could stand the gaff longer than the scrubs. At the very time they began to give out he gave his long legs another stretch, and was off to victory.

But he knew when a race was over. Arriving at Belvedere avenue and the end of the course he would drop his brilliant trot for a lazy lope and turn calmly eastward. All the way down to Jones Falls Valley he loafed along. At the bottom of the hill he would stop at a roadside spring, and wait for his check-rein to be loosed. Then, having drunk, he would amble home, ready for his evening oats and hay, and his no doubt agreeable dreams. Now and then he had a dreadful colic in the night, and had to be rolled. He was sold in his old age, and died peacefully a week later.

III

But I have got all the way to Mount Washington, and must return to Paca and German streets. The Coblens stable, I believe, was then the largest in the city. Its influence made the whole neighborhood horsey. Miller's Hotel, once a resort of horsemen, was already given over to offices, but the horsemen still infested the vicinity. They came to the stable to look over yearlings from Western Maryland; they came to transact business with John Rogers, the carriage maker, whose place was next door; and they came to discuss the intricacies of shoeing with Sam Morrison, the blacksmith, at Greene and German streets.

Morrison's shop did a heavy trade in shoeing dray horses, but that was not the business that interested its proprietor. His great moments came when horses of pretension were brought in, and he was consulted about weights and toes. I used to hang about his shop for hours, marveling at the skill of the smiths and feasting upon the display of strange horseshoes on the walls—some as thin as the case of a watch, others full of occult protuberances and incomprehensible curves. Mr. Morrison I remember well—a hearty and amiable Irishman, always immensely interested in his shop. He wore, commonly, a boiled shirt, and was rather elegant. When he stripped off this shirt, it was a sign that some problem of unusual intricacy confronted his staff. On great occasions he would shoe a horse himself. He was a Kreisler of the anvil and bellows: his virtuosity always brought a crowd.

Mr. Rogers, the carriage maker, I also remember chiefly in shirt-sleeves. He apparently transacted most of his business on the sidewalk in front of his establishment, at all events in warm weather.

There he could be found when he wasn't in Coblens' stable. In or out, he devoted himself to talking horse. Having lost an arm, he could not drive himself, but he knew horses from bit to crupper, and had a hand for managing them. He did a big business in the road buggies in use in those days. My father, having bought one from him, mourned its cost for months. But it was a masterpiece.

IV

Every large stable, in that remote age, had a saloon, so to speak, on its staff. It was impossible to imagine a horse-trade without a libation. The saloon serving the clients of Coblens was kept by a German named Ehoff. It was in Paca street, and had a large bowl of pretzels on the bar. Between my sixth and twelfth years I probably devoured a ton of those pretzels. Mr. Felix never emerged without giving me one. They were very salty and made me very thirsty, but honor forbade me to drink in my father's office. I had to go all the way up Cider alley to Greene street, and there drink from a hydrant behind the dead-house of the University of Maryland.

That alley was naturally made romantic by the dead-house. But it was made even more romantic, at least to me, by the fact that the old firm of Isaac Friedenwald & Company, printers and lithographers, had their hell-box in it. A hell-box is the garbage can of the printing office. Into it go broken type, worn out cuts and empty ink cans. I was, beginning at 7 o'clock on Christmas morning, 1889, a printer, and with an ambition to shine. It was not sufficient to print a paper: my fancy leaped toward a paper printed on colored stock and in colored inks, with a new face of type for every line. The Friedenwald hell-box gave me great help. The cheapest font of type cost 60 cents, but in the hell-box, if I was patient, I could assemble one for nothing. I spent a whole summer hunting for some missing E's—and never found them. May hell roar for that foreman!

Coblens' stable was closed long ago. Half of it is now a garage and the other half is a storage-place for old wagons. Mr. Felix is dead, and the art of road driving with him. So, I believe, is Mr. Rogers. The Morrison shop is for rent. At the opposite corner of Greene and German streets there is a garage. At another corner there is a filling station, horrible in its blatant scarlets and uremic greens.

(The Baltimore Evening Sun, February 1, 1926)

On Living in Baltimore

I

Some time ago, writing in this place about the Baltimore of the eighties, I permitted myself an eloquent passage upon its charm, and let fall the doctrine that that charm had vanished. Mere rhetoric, I fear. The old charm, in fact, still survives, despite the boomers, despite the street-wideners, despite the forward-lookers, despite all the other dull frauds who try to destroy it. I am never more conscious of it than when I return to the city after a week in New York. There is a great city, huge, rich and eminent, and yet it has no more charm than a circus lot or a jazzy hotel. Coming back to Baltimore is like coming out of a football crowd into quiet communion with a fair one who is also amiable, and has the gift of consolation for hard-beset and despairing men!

I have confessed to rhetoric, but here I surely do not indulge in it. For twenty-four years I have resisted almost constant temptation to move to New York, and I resist it more easily today than I did when it began. I am, perhaps, the most arduous commuter ever heard of, even in that town of commuters. My office is on Manhattan island and has been there since 1914; yet I live, vote and have my being in Baltimore, and come back here the instant my job allows. If my desk bangs at 3 P.M., I leap for the 3.25 train. Four long hours follow, but the first is the worst. My back, at all events, is toward New York! Behind lies a place fit only for the gross business of getting money; ahead is a place made for enjoying it.

II

What makes New York so dreadful, I believe, is mainly the fact that the vast majority of its people have been forced to rid themselves of one of the oldest and most powerful of human instincts—

the instinct to make a permanent home. Crowded, shoved about and exploited without mercy, they have lost the feeling that any part of the earth belongs to them, and so they simply camp out like hoboes, waiting for the constables to rush in and chase them away.

I am not speaking here of the poor (God knows how they exist in New York at all!); I am speaking of the well-to-do, even of the rich. The very richest man, in New York, is never quite sure that the house he lives in now will be his next year—that he will be able to resist the constant pressure of business expansion and rising land values. I have known actual millionaires to be chased out of their homes in this way, and forced into apartments. Here in Baltimore, of course, the same pressure exists, but it is not oppressive, for the householder can meet it by yielding to it halfway. It may force him into the suburbs, even into the adjacent county, but he is still in direct contact with the city, sharing in its life, and wherever he lands he may make a stand. But on Manhattan island he is quickly brought up by the rivers, and once he has crossed them he may as well move to Syracuse or Trenton.

Nine times out of ten he tries to avoid crossing them. That is, he moves into meaner quarters on the island itself, and pays more for them. His house gives way to a large flat—one offering the same room for his goods and chattels that his house offered. Next year he is in a smaller flat, and half of his goods and chattels have vanished. A few years more, and he is in three or four rooms. Finally, he lands in a hotel. At this point he ceases to exist as the head of a house. His quarters are precisely like the quarters of 50,000 other men. The front he presents to the world is simply an anonymous door on a gloomy corridor. Inside, he lives like a sardine in a can.

III

Such a habitation, it must be plain, cannot be called a home. A home is not a mere transient shelter: its essence lies in its permanence, in its capacity for accretion and solidification, in its quality of representing, in all its details, the personalities of the people who live in it. In the course of years it becomes a sort of museum of those people; they give it its indefinable air, separating it from all other homes, as one human face is separated from all others. It is at once a refuge from the world, a treasure-house, a castle, and the shrine of a whole hierarchy of peculiarly private and potent gods.

This concept of the home cannot survive the mode of life that prevails in New York. I have seen it go to pieces under my eyes in the houses of my own friends. The intense crowding in the town, and the restlessness and unhappiness that go with it, make it almost impossible for anyone to accumulate the materials of home— the trivial, fortuitous and often grotesque things that gather around a family, as glories and debts gather around a state. The New Yorker lacks the room to house them; he thus learns to live without them. In the end he is a stranger in the house he lives in. More and more, it tends to be no more than Job No. 16,432b from this or that decorator's studio. I know one New Yorker, a man of considerable means, who moves every three years. Every time he moves his wife sells the entire contents of the apartment she is leaving, and employs a decorator to outfit the new one.

To me, at all events, such a mode of living would be unendurable. The charm of getting home, as I see it, is the charm of getting back to what is inextricably my own—to things familiar and long loved, to things that belong to me alone and none other. I have lived in one house for 40 years. It has changed in that time, as I have—but somehow it still remains the same. No conceivable decorator's masterpiece could give me the same ease. It is as much a part of me as my two hands. If I had to leave it, I'd be as certainly crippled as if I lost both legs.

IV

I believe that this feeling for the hearth, for the immemorial lares and penates, is infinitely stronger here than in New York— that it has better survived here, indeed, than in any other large city of America—and that its persistence accounts for the superior charm of the town. There are, of course, thousands of Baltimoreans in flats—but I know of none to whom a flat seems more than a makeshift, a substitute, a necessary and temporary evil. They are all planning to get out, to find house-room in one of the new suburbs, to resume living in a home. What they see about them is too painfully not theirs. The New Yorker has simply lost that discontent. He is a vagabond. His notions of the agreeable become those of a vaudeville actor. He takes on the shallowness and unpleasantness of any other homeless man. He is highly sophisticated, and inordinately trashy.

The fact explains the lack of charm that one finds in his town; the fact that the normal Baltimorean is almost his exact antithesis explains the charm that is here. Human relations, in such a place as this, tend to assume a solid permanence. A man's circle of friends becomes a sort of extension of his family circle. His contacts are with men and women who are rooted as he is. They are not moving all the time, and so they are not changing their friends all the time. Thus abiding relationships tend to be built up, and when fortune brings unexpected changes they survive those changes. The men I know and esteem in Baltimore are, on the whole, men I have known and esteemed a long while; even those who have come into my ken relatively lately seem likely to last. But of the men I knew best when I first began going to New York, twenty-five years ago, not one is a friend today. Of those I knew best ten years ago, not six are friends today. The rest have got lost in the riot, and the friends of today, I sometimes fear, will get lost in the same way.

V

In human relationships that are so casual there is seldom any satisfaction. It is our fellows who make life endurable to us, and give it a purpose and a meaning; if our contacts with them are light and frivolous there is something lacking, and it is something of the very first importance. What I contend is that in Baltimore, under a slow-moving and cautious social organization, such contacts are more enduring than elsewhere, and that life in consequence is more charming. Of the external embellishments of life we have a plenty—as great a supply, indeed, to any rational taste, as New York itself. But we have something much better: we have a tradition of sound and comfortable living. A Baltimorean is not merely John Doe, an isolated individual of *Homo sapiens*, exactly like every other John Doe. He is John Doe of a certain place—of Baltimore, of a definite home in Baltimore. It was not by accident that all the peoples of the Western world, very early in their history, began distinguishing their best men by adding of this or that place to their names.

(The Baltimore Evening Sun, February 16, 1925)

Notes of a Baltimorean

I

Some time ago, having occasion to buy one of the adjustable reading stands used by invalids, I visited in succession five Baltimore stores devoted to the sale of office and library supplies. Not one of them had what I wanted, or, indeed, anything of the sort. A kind saleswoman in the fifth store advised me to try a shop selling hospital supplies, and gave me the address of what she said was the largest of them. I went there, and after some delay attracted the attention of a salesman. He was an oldish fellow and apparently in bad humor. When I stated my wants he replied curtly:

"Out of business."

It seemed incredible: the store was obviously in full blast. So I told him what I wanted again. This time his answer was downright surly:

"Didn't I tell you they went out of business?"

"You mean the manufacturers?"

"Of course I mean the manufacturers."

"And the stands are unobtainable?"

This time he gave me a blistering glare.

"How many times have I got to tell you?" he demanded.

I departed abashed—and next day took the train for New York. There, in a store of precisely the same sort, I found at least a dozen such stands—four or five different kinds, each in a choice of woods. I got exactly what I wanted in two minutes. The dealer told me he had more in his cellar. He said the manufacturer was not out of business, and not thinking of going out of business.

II

It is part of my trade that I am constantly deluged with books. They come in by every mail, and from all parts of the world. During busy weeks I sometimes receive 60 or 70. Never a week goes by that I do not receive 25. All these I look through diligently, picking out those that seem worth reading and reviewing. The rest are piled in a corner. Upon the same pile go books expelled from my library, which is constantly changing. Twice a month all these rejected books go to a second-hand bookseller, and he credits me with them on his ledger. When I want to buy a new book I order it from him, and he charges it to me. Once a year the account is adjusted.

The transaction seems simple, surely. That part of it which falls to the bookseller should be within the capacities of a schoolboy, even of a schoolmaster. Yet there exists in Baltimore a bookseller apparently incapable of it. For two years I suffered from his incompetence. When I ordered a book the chances were always even that I'd not get it. When I asked for an accounting I got no answer. At least a dozen times, on busy days, I had to travel all the way downtown to prod him. Now my business is done with a bookseller in Philadelphia. I send him my rejected books by parcel post. When I order a new book he sends it instantly, or tells me when I may look for it. I have done business with him for a year, and I have yet to meet any annoyance at his hands.

III

A while back I toured the Baltimore stores in search of a raincoat for a little girl. The little girl, having reached the age of ten, knew precisely what she wanted. She specified the material, the color and the size. No store in Baltimore had such a coat in stock, but a saleswoman in the last of the eight or ten I visited offered to get one from New York.

"How long will it take?" I asked.

"About a week."

"Why a week? Can't you get it in four days?"

But she stuck to the week, and even hinted that it might be stretched out to eight or nine days. Ten days went by. No coat. Two weeks. I called up the store. The telephone operator there switched me to the wrong department. I complained and tried again. Wrong again. Another complaint, and a third trial. Wrong again. I now called for a floor-walker—any floor-walker—anyone, indeed, male or female, who knew where raincoats were sold in that store. She sent me around the circle another time. Finally, I demanded audience with the manager, the proprietor, the doorman, the owner of the building, anyone who knew how to find the raincoat department. The operator briskly cut me off altogether.

All this had consumed ten minutes, and I faced a tedious trip downtown. Suddenly, I recalled the name of the saleswoman who had taken my order: I had heard a colleague address her by it while I was negotiating with her. I called up the store again and asked for her. The operator said that no one of that name worked in the place. I bade her politely to inquire. In three or four minutes there was a "Well? Who is it?" on the line, and I was talking with the saleswoman. At first she remembered nothing of my palaver with her. Then she suddenly recalled it.

"Oh, yes!" she said. "You wanted a raincoat, didn't you? Well, we couldn't get it. They don't make them any more. Not that kind."

"Why didn't you notify me?" I asked.

She didn't seem to know.

"Don't you notify customers when their order can't be filled?" She rang off.

Four days later, in New York, I found the raincoat I wanted in the first shop I entered.

IV

I trust the nobility and gentry will not mistake these trivial anecdotes for attempts to defame the fair name of Baltimore, and ruin its trade, and send visiting buyers elsewhere. Regular readers of these monographs know very well that I have a weakness for the town. I have, in fact, composed and printed at least forty articles in praise of it, and in denunciation of New York. Few men indeed go to more trouble to live in it: my office has been in New York since 1914, but I continue to live here, and expect to go on doing so, if luck is with me, for eighty or ninety years more. Baltimore is agreeable to me, despite the effort of the boomers to make it a roaring stink-pot. New York irritates me.

But Baltimore, I believe, would be more agreeable still if there were less slackness among its merchants. It has some capital stores —in some lines, the best I have ever encountered. But in other lines it has very bad ones, and they show no sign of improving. Their stocks are incomplete; they make no effort to help the customer; they are manned by incompetent staffs. The things they sell, I find, I gradually cease to buy in Baltimore; it is quicker and more satisfactory to get them in New York. There a poor stock is exceptional; when a store sells an article, A, it sells every variety of A obtainable on earth. And—whether or not it is due to keener competition I don't know—the New York storekeeper seems fanatically devoted to giving his customer quick and intelligent service. He has enough salespeople, and they know his stock. There is no idiotic hoofing around from one to another. No one has to send for Mr. B. to find out if there is a pair of woolen mittens, or a bottle of Dr. John's Medicine, or a copy of *Scientific Salesmanship* in the house. One goes in, one is waited on, one buys, and one departs—that is all.

V

I have, in general, but small skill at business, though I have engaged in it off and on for years. Compared to such masters of the higher commercial sorcery as the Hon. John L. Alcock, president of the Honorary Pallbearers' Association; the Hon. E. Asbury Davis, and the Hon. Aristides Sophocles Goldsborough, LL.B., I am, I suppose, a dud. Nevertheless, I presume to offer these great men a small piece of advice. It is that they turn aside, for one year, from the exalted craft of stinking up Baltimore with new guano works and gasoline distilleries, and devote themselves to Service on a lower plane. Let them set the competent storekeepers of Baltimore to teaching the incompetent ones how to keep store. If necessary, let them bring in eminent professors of the science from the great universities, and open night schools. Let them pump up their Vision and strive for a new Ideal, that the day may come when a lowly Baltimorean with mazuma in his pocket, on going into any store at random, may be certain of finding that it actually sells what it professes to sell, and that its salespeople know precisely what is on its shelves and where. If Alcock, Aristides and company are too busy enthusing over the Katzenjammer Tower to undertake that crusade, then I hand it over to Rotary. And if Rotary has another engagement, then I summon Kiwanis.

(The Baltimore Evening Sun, October 19, 1925)

Aesthetic Diatribe

I

As the years pass, is Baltimore growing more beautiful or less? The question is not easily answered, though the official town boosters, imagining them able to concentrate their minds upon an aesthetic question, would probably shut off the second half with a roaring affirmative to the first. The charm of Guilford—or, at all events, of certain parts of it—and of the Johns Hopkins group undoubtedly gives them a certain support. But what of the city in general? What of the new neighborhoods that now cover what used to be woods and fields—or ash-dumps? Go out and look at them: they will give you doubts.

The two-story houses that were put up in my boyhood, forty years ago, all had a kind of unity, and many of them were far from unbeautiful. Almost without exception, they were built of red brick, with white trim—the latter either of marble or of painted wood. The builders of the time were not given to useless ornamentation; their houses were plain in design, and restful to the eye. A long row of them, to be sure, was somewhat monotonous, but it at least escaped being trashy and annoying. Before every row, in those days, ranged a file of shade-trees. The green against the red, with flecks of white showing through, was always dignified and sometimes very charming. Many such rows survive, but the trees are gone, and new store-fronts, plate-glass front-doors, concrete steps and other such horrors have pretty well corrupted their old placid beauty.

The two-story houses that go up by the thousand today are far less sightly. Nine-tenths of them, instead of being built of the indigenous red brick, with the indigenous white marble trim, are horribly confected of brick showing all the more uremic colors of the rainbow, and with trimmings that make them downright dreadful. Their general tone is a dirty yellow—the most hideous of hues. In front of them, not infrequently, are one-story porches held up by columns heavy enough to support a railroad bridge.

Their puerile bay-windows are unspeakable, and their preposterous galvanized-iron cornices are ghastly.

II

These grotesque houses, it must be confessed, are superior in some ways to their predecessors of the last generation. They are outfitted with tiled bathrooms, they have floors of so-called hard wood, and even the least of them has some sort of central heating. Living in them, I daresay, is somewhat more comfortable and immensely more soothing to the vanity than living in the red-brick houses of 1885. But that is as far as it goes. They are not half so well built as the old-timers, and they are ugly in detail and in gross, inside and out. Of late, I have peeped into some of them. Everything within seems to be bogus, from the birch doors disguised as oak to the scratched plaster disguised as tiles. They are showy, but I suspect that many of them are not sound. Their one undoubted virtue is that they are at least relatively cheap—that a poor man may hope to buy one without going into debt for more than the term of his natural life.

Why they are made so abominably ugly I don't know. Not a few of them, chiefly of red brick, are very much less ugly than the rest, and yet they seem to attract buyers just as readily. There are builders who put them up by the hundred, row upon row. It would not add two percent to their cost to employ good architects to design them; my belief, indeed, is that it would probably reduce their cost. For as they stand, a large part of the money that goes into them goes into senseless and hideous decorations—the absurd front porches that I have mentioned, the idiotic colored glass in the windows and fanlights, the elaborate and ungraceful mantels, and so on. If the cost of these fripperies were put into architects' fees, they might be made more beautiful—and money might be saved.

Even now, of course, such melancholy houses have architects—of a sort. Someone has to design them. This someone, typically, is to architecture in any rational sense as a chiropractor is to the science and art of medicine. There should be some way to discover him and punish him. I am against more laws—but Harry Thaw is still alive. Let him be invited to Baltimore to resume the practice of his chosen art and mystery. The last architect he promoted to bliss eternal was unfortunately a good one.

III

Many of the larger new buildings that are going up in Baltimore are of the same general sort: they testify to the fact that the town is growing and perhaps they also add something to its comfort, but their contribution to its appearance is very questionable. For example, there is the new skyscraper now in progress at the northeast corner of Monument Square. Its owners had directly in front of them, in the case of the Equitable Building, ample proof that brick in light tones is unsuitable for building in downtown Baltimore, but they nevertheless chose it. In a few years their expensive skyscraper will be as grimy and dingy as the Equitable Building was until very lately, and they will have to imitate the owners of the latter another time by calling in the sandblast men.

Such huge buildings, I suppose, are inevitable: the business of the town needs them. But Baltimore has very few that are of any beauty. Perhaps the best of them all, as a spectacle, is the Gas Company's building, though it fronts on two very narrow streets and is at the bottom of a high and steep hill. The worst, undoubtedly, is the Fidelity Building—an immense structure with the air of an improvisation. Baltimore is very unfortunate in this department. Its office buildings add little to its beauty. In New York some of the new ones—whether because of, or in spite of the new set-back law, I don't know—are strikingly beautiful.

Practically all of the new suburbs save Guilford are ugly, and some of them are truly frightful. They all run to bungalows with idiotic pillars in front of them. The houses are badly placed on their lots and badly grouped. Even Roland Park shows many more bad houses than good ones. Like the rows of two-story houses in the city proper, these Roland Park dwellings have appreciably augmented the comforts of living in our midst, but they have contributed very little to the general beauty of the town. Some of them belong to the jig-saw era, and others are simply preposterous, as a flirtatious fat woman is preposterous.

IV

It will be a long time, I suppose, before laws regulating the design of new buildings will be on the books in Baltimore. And when they come their aim will be, as in New York, not to promote beauty but simply to conserve light. Such laws stand in subtle opposition to American ideas of freedom. It is regarded as perfectly proper, in this country, for the Government to decide what a man shall drink at his table and what books he shall read, but the police power is praised when it comes to regulating what he shall expose upon the public streets to the shame and indignation of his neighbors. Some years ago the city spent a great deal of money laying out the Preston Gardens. But today any householder facing them is free to cover his house with hideous signs, and many enterprising men have made avail of that high privilege.

The case of Mt. Royal plaza is still worse, for the signs there reach almost fabulous heights of ugliness. The city of Baltimore, in order to provide a gaudy arena for their display, increased the tax burden of all of us—and then found itself unable to prevent the complete ruination of the new street. Mt. Royal plaza should be one of the town's chief disgraces. I often wonder what visitors must think of it, coming in from Union and Mt. Royal Stations. Let the syndics of the Honorary Pallbearers' Association give their minds to this question.

But the city itself is apparently as hostile to beauty as the most Philistine of its citizens. Everyone will recall how, for years, it made a horror of the Courthouse plaza. I often wondered in those days why the judges did not jail the Mayor and City Council for obscenity: certainly they must be presumed to have more or less jurisdiction over the approaches to their workshop. Now the City Hall plaza is to have its turn. Building after building will be run up around its edges, each more horrible than the last. The lighting devised by political aesthetes will complete the dreadful business.

Is there any remedy? I know of none. The love of ugliness is apparently inherent in the American people. They cherish and venerate the unspeakable. For these few brief hints that Baltimore is not perfectly beautiful, I shall be damned, I daresay, by many an indignant patriot. At the very moment I write builders are crowding the office of the inspector of buildings, and under the arms of some of them are designs for houses even worse than anything we have seen and suffered so far.

(The Baltimore Evening Sun, February 7, 1927)

Spring in These Parts

I

Traveling up and down the seaboard at this season of the year I am always struck by the earliness and loveliness of the Maryland Spring. It comes on at least two weeks before Spring in the latitude of New York, and it is infinitely softer and more genial. The other day I came down from New England, and the contrast was still more striking. Below Boston the rocky fields were still bare and forlorn, and in Connecticut and New Jersey, north and south of New York, there was only the faintest show of green. But when the Pennsylvania line was crossed they began to color brightly, in Delaware they began to glow, and in Maryland they were riots of brilliant and charming shades, ranging from deep, luminous bottle-greens in the woods to vivid and saucy apple-greens in the open fields.

The New England landscape is surely not without its beauty, even at the end of Winter. It is often harsh, but it is never banal. The jutting rocks give it a somber dignity and there is something sturdy and stimulating about the way stone-fences clamber over and defy the irregular hills. A country, obviously, of resolute and somewhat humorless men, determined to establish their high rights and prerogatives at all costs, even in the face of nature. They labored colossally to convert a stone-pile into a garden. It remains, after three hundred years, a stone-pile—romantic but almost useless.

The contrast with Maryland is tremendous. Here there are no signs of struggle. The curves of the hills are gentle, there are no jutting rocks, and the vegetation looks unforced and exuberant. There are meadows along the banks of the estuaries between Baltimore and the Mason and Dixon line that have the immemorial air of English lawns. It is not hard to believe that they have been there since Tertiary times, thrusting their roots further and further into the amiable soil, and contributing their smooth, radiant greens to the splendor of a hundred thousand Springs.

II

Every man, of course, thinks that the place where he was born is beautiful. I know Middle Westerners who actually admire the prairie landscape, which seems to me to be as depressing as an endless series of C major scales. Long Island has a long list of native celebrants, though most of it, to my eye, looks mangy and absurd: its beaches are bald and its interior is a wilderness of jimson weeds. Here, obviously, sentiment must hold the eye. But we Marylanders may look at our State realistically, and still find it lovely. It has variety, it has color, and it has a certain touch of mystery. Above all, it has softness. The landscape is never harsh, as in New England. It does not provoke motor impulses. One may look at it without getting any desire to fight it.

The best of it, I think, lies away from the water. The Eastern Shore, though it is greatly praised, leaves me rather cold. Back from the rivers it is too flat and monotonous to be interesting, and along the rivers, at least in the day-time, there is too much glare. The nights, I grant you, are superb, especially when there is a moon, but there is little charm by day. The whole Shore, seen from the water, suffers, as Holland does, from the fact that its coast is too low. One sees only a feeble ribbon of misty green, separating the blue immensity of the sky from the gray immensity of the Bay. There are no jutting headlands; there are no breakers along the shore. The effect is that of triviality.

The true delights of the shore lie in its towns. They are seldom beautiful, but they all have pretty airs. They belong wholly to the South, and are quite devoid of Northern sickness. The people in them are extraordinarily engaging, even the Prohibitionists, most of whom at least have the decency to be frauds. I have enjoyed more than one Christian session with Eastern Shore Prohibitionists, and have found them to be excellent judges of hard liquor. I have yet to hear of one who was actually dry. Even the most fanatical of them seems to grasp the basic principle that offering a guest water to drink is as bad as sending him a bill.

III

I have said that the Shore and its towns belong to the South. The fact must be instantaneously apparent to every visitor. The very flora of the region is Southern, especially below Easton. The Mason and Dixon line is a wholly artificial boundary, and so is the Potomac river, save in part. The real division between North and South runs along the Potomac down to Washington, leaving the city in the North, and then plunges into Maryland and takes an irregular course. Charles, Calvert and St. Marys counties are Southern, and so is that part of Anne Arundel below the Severn. Annapolis itself is Southern. But the upper part of Anne Arundel is as Northern as New Jersey.

Just where the line strikes the Eastern Shore I don't know, but it is somewhere North of Easton and South of Tolchester. I suspect that it might run accurately by following the long-leaf pine. Wherever that gaunt and solemn tree grows one is in the South; wherever it is lacking, at least in the Coast States, one is in the North. Frederick County is typically Northern; Queen Anne is typically Southern. Baltimore City, it seems to me, is as thoroughly Northern as, say, Buffalo. It may have been a Southern town in the early days, but I don't think it has been one since the Civil War.

At Washington the line between North and South is very sharply defined. The Capital itself is almost completely devoid of Southern characteristics. Its very Negroes are Yankees, just like their brethren of Harlem. But one has but to cross one of the Potomac bridges to plunge into the heart of the South. Alexandria, indeed, is more Southern than Richmond, and almost as Southern as Fredericksburg. Its wide and leisurely streets are Southern, its ancient houses are Southern, and its loafing, guffawing darkies are Southern to the last degree. Virginia, in large part, has been ruined by so-called progress; even Richmond is now tortured and botched by the boomers and realtors. But Alexandria holds out, Confederate and undisturbed. It is one of the most charming towns in all this part of the country.

IV

But my private taste does not run to Southern towns, nor to the Southern landscape. The former are apt to be a bit frowsy, and the latter is often monotonous in color. Of all the parts of Maryland I think the loveliest is that which is distinctly Northern in tone, to wit, the Piedmont. It begins in the western suburbs of Baltimore and runs clear to the mountains. It has definite variety in detail, and every detail of it is beautiful. In the whole United States, indeed, I know of no countryside that is more enchanting.

The best of it lies in Howard and Carroll counties, and especially in Howard. That country is really quite extraordinary, for, so far as I know, there is not an ugly spot in it. The ancient county town, Ellicott City, is still full of an archaic and romantic strangeness, despite the entrance of the city trolley and the erection of half a dozen bastard-Greek bank buildings. The hills that hem it in are still there, and its houses still cling precariously to their precipices. Below the town, bursting out of one gorge and plunging into another, flows the turbulent Patapsco. On the heights beyond begin the rolling hills of Howard, growing ever higher and higher (but never steep and harsh) until they slide into the range of the Blue Ridge.

I give you this region on a Spring day with the trees in leaf, the wheat up, and flowers in bloom along the hedge-rows. It is a countryside that comes to the very edge of perfection. Fat cattle graze in the meadows, there are sheep upon most of the hills, and noble groves of well-kept trees break the monotony of the fields. There are few villages and the few are all small. The farmers live on their farms, surrounded by riches and loveliness. It would be hard to imagine a more tranquil and enviable life. Brooks run down every hill. The city is out of sight, but near at hand. Good roads run everywhere. There are, I hear, convenient stills.

Do I describe Arcadia, beautiful but unattainable? If you think so, go take a look yourself. Get out your flivver next Sunday morning, and run out the Clarksville pike. You will see the heart of Maryland in the full tide of Spring. And seeing it, you will not soon forget it.

(The Baltimore Evening Sun, April 12, 1926)

A Panorama of Patriots

Valentino

I

By one of the chances that relieve the dullness of life and make it instructive, I had the pleasure of dining with this gentleman in New York, a week or so before his fatal illness. I had never met him before, nor seen him on the screen; the meeting was at his instance, and, when it was proposed, vaguely puzzled me. But soon its purpose became clear enough. Valentino was in trouble, and wanted advice. More, he wanted advice from an elder and disinterested man, wholly removed from the movies and all their works. Something that I had written, falling under his eye, had given him the notion that I was an enlightened and judicious fellow. That part, of course, didn't surprise me.

So, the night being infernally warm, we stripped off our coats, and came to terms. I recall that he wore suspenders of extraordinary width and thickness—suspenders almost strong enough to hold up the pantaloons of Chief Justice Taft. On so slim a young man they seemed somehow absurd, especially on a hot summer night. We perspired horribly for an hour, mopping our faces with our handkerchiefs, the table napkins, the corners of the tablecloth, and a couple of towels left by the waiter. Then there came a thunderstorm, and we began to breathe. There was a hostess at the party, a woman as tactful as she is charming. She disappeared mysteriously and left us to commune.

The trouble that was agitating Valentino turned out to be very simple. The ribald New York papers were full of it, and that was what was gravelling him. Some time before, out in Chicago, a wandering reporter had discovered, in the men's washroom of a gaudy hotel, a slot machine selling talcum powder. That, of course, was not unusual, but the color of the talcum powder was. It was pink. The news made the town giggle for a day, and inspired an editorial writer on the eminent Chicago *Tribune* to compose a hot-weather editorial. In it he protested humorously against the effeminization of the American man, and laid it light-heartedly to the influence of Valentino and his sheik movies.

II

It so happened that Valentino, passing through Chicago that day on his way east from the Coast, ran full tilt into the editorial, and into a gang of reporters who wanted to know what he had to say about it. What he had to say was full of fire. Throwing off his 100% Americanism and reverting to the *mores* of his fatherland, he challenged the editorial writer to a duel, and, when no answer came, to a fist fight. His masculine honor, it appeared, had been outraged. To the hint that he was less than he, even to the extent of one-half of one per cent, there could be no answer save a bath of blood.

Unluckily, all this took place in the United States, where the word honor, save when it is applied to the anatomical chastity of women, has only a comic significance. One hears of the honor of politicians, of bankers, of lawyers, even of the honor of the United States itself. Everyone naturally laughs. So New York laughed at Valentino. More, it ascribed his high dudgeon to mere publicity-seeking; he seemed only an actor grabbing space. The poor fellow, thus doubly beset, rose to dudgeons higher still. His Italian mind was quite unequal to the situation. So he sought counsel and comfort—alas in vain!—from the neutral, aged and damned.

I could only name the disease and confess frankly that there was no remedy—none, that is, known to any therapeutics within my ken. He should have passed over the jibe of the Chicago journalist with a lofty snort—perhaps better still, with a counter-jibe. He should have kept away from the reporters in New York. But now the mischief was done. He was both insulted and ridiculous, and there was nothing to do about it. Let the dreadful farce roll along to exhaustion! He protested that it was infamous. Infamous? Nothing is infamous that is not true. A man still has his inner integrity. Can he look into the shaving-glass of a morning? Then he is still on his two legs in this world, and ready even for the fiends of hell. We sweated a great deal, discussing these austere matters. We seemed to get nowhere.

III

Suddenly it dawned upon me—I was too dull or it was too hot for me to see it sooner—that what we were talking about was really not what we were talking about at all. I began to observe Valentino more closely. A curiously naïve and boyish young fellow, certainly not much beyond thirty, and with a disarming air of inexperience. To my eye, at least, not handsome, but nevertheless immensely attractive. There was an obvious fineness in him; even his clothes were not precisely those of his trade. He began talking of his home, his people, his early youth. His words were simple and yet somehow very eloquent. I could still see the mime before me, but now and then, briefly and darkly, there was a flash of something else. That something else, I concluded, was what is commonly called, for want of a better name, a gentleman.

Valentino's agony, in brief, was the agony of a man of civilized feelings thrown into a situation of intolerable vulgarity, destructive alike to his peace and his dignity—nay, into a whole series of such situations. It was not that trifling Chicago episode that was riding him; it was the whole grotesque futility of his life. Had he achieved, out of nothing, a vast and dizzy success? Then that success was hollow as well as vast—a colossal and preposterous nothing. Was he acclaimed by yelling multitudes? Then every time the multitudes yelled he felt himself blushing inside.

In other words, the old story of Diego Valdez, but with a new poignancy in it. Valdez, at all events, was High Admiral of Spain. But Valentino, with his touch of fineness in him—he had his commonness, too, but there was that touch of fineness—Valentino was only the hero of the rabble. Half-wits surrounded him in a dense herd. He was pursued by women—but what women! (Consider the sordid comedy of his two marriages—the brummagem, star-spangled passion that invaded his very deathbed!) The thing, at the start, must have only bewildered him. But in those last days, unless I am a worse psychologist than even the professors of psychology, it was revolting him. Worse, it was making him afraid.

IV

I incline to think that the inscrutable gods, in taking himself off so soon and at a moment of fiery revolt, were very kind to him. Living, he would have tried inevitably to change his fame—if that is what it is to be called—into something closer to his heart's desire. That is to say, he would have gone the way of many another actor—the way of increasing pretension, of solemn artiness, of hollow hocus-pocus, deceptive only to himself. I believe he would have failed, for there was little sign of the genuine artist in him. He was essentially a highly respectable young man, which is the sort that never metamorphoses into an artist. But suppose he had succeeded?

Then his tragedy, I believe, would have only become the more acrid and intolerable. For he would have discovered, after vast heavings and yearnings, that what he had come to was indistinguishable from what he had left. Was the fame of Beethoven any more caressing and splendid than the fame of Valentino? To you and me, of course, the question seems to answer itself. But what of Beethoven? He was heard upon the subject, *viva voce*, while he lived, and his answer survives, in all the freshness of its profane eloquence, in his music. Beethoven, too, knew what it meant to be applauded. Walking with Goethe, he heard something that was not unlike the murmur that reached Valentino through his hospital window. Beethoven walked away briskly. Valentino turned his face to the wall.

Here, after all, is the chiefest joke of the gods: that man must remain alone and lonely in this world, even with crowds surging about him. Does he crave approbation, with a sort of furious, instinctive lust? Then it is only to discover, when it comes, that it is somehow disconcerting—that its springs and motives offer an affront to his integrity. But do I sentimentalize the perhaps transparent story of a simple mummer? Then substitute Coolidge, or Mussolini, or any other poor devil that you can think of. Substitute Shakespeare, or Lincoln, or Goethe, or Beethoven, as I have. Sentimental or not, I confess that the predicament of poor Valentino touched me. It provided grist for my mill, but I couldn't quite enjoy it. Here was a young man who was living daily the dream of millions of other young men. Here was one who was catnip to women. Here was one who had wealth and fame, both made honorably and by his own effort. And here was one who was very unhappy.

(The Baltimore Evening Sun, August 30, 1926)

Sister Aimée

I

This rev. sister in God, I confess, greatly disappointed me. Arriving in Los Angeles out of the dreadful deserts of Arizona and New Mexico, I naturally made tracks to hear and see the town's most distinguished citizen. Her basilica turned out to be at a great distance from my hotel, far up a high hill and in the midst of a third-rate neighborhood. It was a cool and sunshiny Sunday afternoon, the place was packed, and the whisper had gone around that Aimée was heated up by the effort to jail her, and would give a gaudy show. But all I found myself gaping at, after half an hour, was an orthodox Methodist revival, with a few trimmings borrowed from the Baptists and United Brethren—in brief, precisely the sort of thing that goes on in the shabby suburbs and dark back streets of Baltimore, three hundred nights of every year. I caught myself waiting for Dr. Crabbe to pop up, to shake down the boobs for the Anti-Saloon League—or Dr. Howard A. Kelly, to tell what Bible reading has done for him.

Aimée, of course, is richer than most evangelists, and so she has got herself a plant that far surpasses anything ever seen in shabby suburbs. Her temple to the One God is immensely wide—as wide, almost, as the Hippodrome in New York—and probably seats 2,500 customers. There is a full brass band down in front, with a grand piano to one side of it and an organ to the other. From the vast gallery, built like that of a theater, runways run along the side walls to what may be called the proscenium arch, and from their far ends stairways lead down to the platform. As in many other evangelical churches, there are theater seats instead of pews. Some pious texts are emblazoned on the wall behind the platform; I forget what they say. There are no stained glass windows. The architecture, in and out, is otherwise of the Early Norddeutscher-Lloyd Rauchzimmer school, with modifications suggested by the filling-stations of the Standard Oil Company of New Jersey. The whole building is very cheaply made. It is large and hideous, but I don't think it cost much. Nothing in Los Angeles appears to have cost much. The town, save for a few brilliant spots—for example, the Elks' clubhouse and one or two theaters—is inconceivably shoddy.

II

As I say, Aimée had nothing on tap to make my eyes pop, old revival fan that I am. The proceedings began with a solemn march by the brass band, played about as well as the average Salvation Army band could have done it, but no better. Then a brother from some remote outpost filed down the aisle at the head of a party of fifty or sixty of the faithful. They sang a hymn, the brother made a short speech, and then he handed Aimée a check for $500 for her Defense Fund. A quartet followed, male, a bit scared, and with Camp Meade haircuts. Two little girls then did a duet, to the music of a ukulele played by one of them. Then Aimée prayed. And then she delivered a brief harangue.

I could find nothing in it worthy of remark. It was the time-honored evangelical hokum, made a bit more raucous than usual by the loud-speakers strewn all over the hall. A brother who seemed to be a sort of stage manager shoved the microphone of the radio directly under Aimée's nose. When, warmed by her homilic passion, she turned this way or that, he followed with the microphone. It somehow suggested an attentive deck-steward, plying his useful art and mystery on a rough day. Aimée wore a long white robe, with a very low-cut collar, and over it there was a cape of dark purple. Her thick hair, piled high in a curious coiffure, turned out to be of mahogany brown. I had heard that it was a flaming red.

The rest of the orgy went on in the usual way. Groups of four, six, eight or twenty got up and sang. A large, pudgy, soapy-looking brother prayed. Aimée herself led the choir in a hymn with a lively tune and very saucy words, chiefly aimed at her enemies. Two or three times more she launched into brief addresses. But mostly she simply ran the show. While the quartets bawled and the band played she was busy at a telephone behind the altar or hurling orders in a loud stage-whisper at sergeants and corporals on the floor. Obviously a very managing woman. A fixed smile stuck to her from first to last.

III

What brought this commonplace and transparent mountebank to her present high estate, with thousands crowding her tabernacle daily and money flowing in upon her from whole regiments of eager dupes? The answer, it seems to me, is as plain as mud. For years she had been wandering about the West, first as a side-show barker, then as a faith healer, and finally as a cow-town evangelist. One day, inspired by God, she decided to try her fortune in Los Angeles. Instantly she was a roaring success. And why? For the plain reason that there were more morons collected in Los Angeles than in any other town on earth—because it was a pasture foreordained for evangelists, and she was the first comer to give it anything low enough for its taste and comprehension.

The osteopaths, chiropractors and other such quacks had long marked and occupied it. It swarmed with swamis, spiritualists, Christian Scientists, crystal-gazers and the allied necromancers. It offered brilliant pickings for real estate speculators, oil-stock brokers, wire-tappers and so on. But the town pastors were not up to its opportunities. They ranged from melancholy High Church Episcopalians, laboriously trying to interest retired Iowa alfalfa kings in ritualism, down to struggling Methodists and Baptists, as earnestly seeking to inflame the wives of the same monarchs with the crimes of the Pope. All this was over the heads of the trade. The Iowans longed for something that they could get their teeth into. They wanted magic and noise. They wanted an excuse to whoop.

Then came Aimée, with the oldest, safest tricks out of the pack of Dr. Billy Sunday, Dr. Gipsy Smith and the rest of the consecrated hell-robbers. To them she added some passes from her circus days. In a month she had Los Angeles sitting up. In six months she had it in an uproar. In a year she was building her rococo temple and her flamboyant Bible College, and the half-wits were flocking in to hear her from twenty States. Today, if her temple were closed by the police, she could live on her radio business alone. Every word she utters is carried on the air to every forlorn hamlet in those abominable deserts, and every day the mail brings her a flood of money.

IV

The effort to jail her has disingenuousness in it, and the more civilized Angeleños all sympathize with her, and wish her well. Her great success raised up two sets of enemies, both powerful. One was made up of the other town clergy, who resented her raids upon their customers. The other was composed of the town Babbitts, who began to fear that her growing celebrity was making Los Angeles ridiculous. So it was decided to bump her off, and her ill-timed morganatic honeymoon with the bald-headed and wooden legged Mr. Ormiston offered a good chance.

But it must be manifest to any fair observer that there is very little merit in the case against her. What she is charged with, in essence, is perjury, and the chief specification is that, when asked if she had been guilty of unchastity, she said no. I submit that no self-respecting judge in the Maryland Free State, drunk or sober, would entertain such a charge against a woman, and that no Maryland grand jury would indict her. It is unheard of, indeed, in any civilized community for a woman to be tried for perjury uttered in defense of her honor. But in California, as everyone knows, the process of justice is full of unpleasant novelties, and so poor Aimée, after a long and obscene hearing, has been held for trial, and will go before a petit jury some time in January.

The betting odds in the Los Angeles saloons are 50 to 1 that she will either hang the jury or get a clean acquittal. I myself, tarrying in the town, invested some money on the long end, not in avarice, but as a gesture of sympathy for a lady in distress. The local district attorney has the newspapers on his side, and during the progress of Aimée's hearing he filled one of them in the chivalrous Southern California manner, with denunciations of her. But Aimée herself has the radio, and I believe that the radio will count most in the long run. Twice a day, week in and week out, she caresses the anthropoids of all that dusty, forbidding region with her evangelical coos. And twice a day she meets her lieges of Los Angeles face to face, and has at them with her lovely eyes, her mahogany hair, her eloquent hips, and her lascivious voice. It will be a hard job, indeed, to find twelve men and true to send her to the hoosegow. Unless I err grievously, God is with her.

(The Baltimore Evening Sun, December 13, 1926)

Thomas Henry Huxley
1825–1925

I

On May 4, 1825, at Ealing, a third-rate London suburb, there was born Thomas Henry Huxley, the son of a schoolmaster. I mention Huxley *père* in sheer humane politeness; having discharged his august biological function, he passed into the obscurity whence he had come. Young Thomas Henry, it appears, was almost wholly the son of his mother. He had her piercing eyes, he had her dark comeliness, and he had, above all, her sharp wits. "Her most distinguishing characteristic . . . was rapidity of thought." What her lineage was I don't know, but you may be sure that there was good blood in it.

Huxley was educated in third-rate schools and studied what was then regarded as medicine at Charing Cross Hospital. In 1846, having no taste for medical practice, he joined the British Navy as an assistant surgeon, and was presently assigned to the *Rattlesnake* for a cruise in the South Seas. He was gone four years. He came back laden with scientific material of the first importance, but the Admiralty refused to publish it, and in 1854 he resigned from the navy and took a professorship in the Royal School of Mines.

Thereafter, for forty years, he was incessantly active as teacher, as writer and as lecturer. No single outstanding contribution to human knowledge is credited to him. He was not so much a discoverer as an organizer. He found science a pretty intellectual plaything, with overtones of the scandalous; he left it the chief serious concern of civilized man. The change aroused opposition, some of it immensely formidable. Huxley met that opposition by charging it, breaking it up and routing it. He was one of the most pertinacious fighters ever heard of in this world, and one of the bravest. He attacked and defeated the natural imbecility of the human race. In his old age, the English, having long sneered at him, decided to honor him. They made him a privy councillor, and gave him the right to put "The Right Hon." in front of his name and "P.C." after it. The same distinction was given at the same time to various shyster lawyers, wealthy soap manufacturers and worn-out politicians.

II

Huxley, I believe, was the greatest Englishman of the Nineteenth Century—perhaps the greatest Englishman of all time. When one thinks of him, one thinks of him inevitably in terms of such men as Goethe and Aristotle. For in him there was that rich, incomparable blend of intelligence and character, of colossal knowledge and high adventurousness, of instinctive honesty and indomitable courage which appears in mankind only once in a blue moon. There have been far greater scientists, even in England, but there has never been a scientist who was a greater man. A touch of the poet was in him, and another of the romantic, gallant knight. He was, in almost every way, the perfected flower of *Homo sapiens,* the superlatively admirable all-'round man.

Only too often on meeting scientific men, even those of genuine distinction, one finds that they are dull fellows and very stupid. They know one thing to excess; they know nothing else. Pursuing facts too doggedly and unimaginatively, they miss all the charming things that are not facts. Such scientists are responsible for the poor name which science so frequently carries among plain men. They radiate the impression that its service is dehumanizing—that too much learning, like too little learning, is an unpleasant and dangerous thing.

Huxley was a sort of standing answer to that notion. His actual knowledge was probably wider than that of any other man of his time. By profession a biologist, he covered in fact the whole field of the exact sciences and then bulged through its four fences. Absolutely nothing was uninteresting to him. His curiosity ranged from music to theology and from philosophy to history. He didn't simply know something about everything; he knew a great deal about everything. But he was by no means merely learned; he was also immensely shrewd. I thumb his essays at random. Here is one on the Salvation Army—the most realistic and devastating treatise upon that maudlin imposture ever penned. Here is one on capital and labor—a complete *reductio ad absurdum* of the Marxian balderdash in 3,000 words. And here is one on Berkeley's metaphysics—a perfect model of lucid exposition.

III

All of us owe a vast debt to Huxley, especially all of us of English speech, for it was he, more than any other man, who worked that great change in human thought which marked the Nineteenth Century. All his life long he flung himself upon authority —when it was stupid, ignorant and tyrannical. He attacked it with every weapon in his rich arsenal—wit, scorn, and above all, superior knowledge. To it he opposed a single thing: the truth as it could be discovered and established—the plain truth that sets men free.

It seems simple enough today, but it was not so simple when Huxley began. For years he was the target of assaults of almost unbelievable ferocity and malignancy. Every ecclesiastic in Christendom took a hack at him; he was denounced as the common enemy of God and man. Darwin, a mild fellow, threw *The Origin of Species* into the ring and then retired from the scene. It was Huxley who bore the brunt of the ensuing theological assault, and it was Huxley who finally beat it down, and forced the holy clerks to turn tail. It always amuses me today to read of intellectual clergymen championing what they call Modernism. Their predecessors of but two generations ago were unanimously engaged in trying to damn the first Modernist to hell.

The row was over Darwinism, but before it ended Darwinism was almost forgotten. What Huxley fought for was something far greater: the right of civilized men to think freely and speak freely, without asking leave of authority, clerical or lay. How new that right is! And yet how firmly held! Today it would be hard to imagine living without it. No man of self-respect, when he has a thought to utter, pauses to wonder what the bishops will have to say about it. The views of bishops are simply ignored. Yet only sixty years ago they were still so powerful that they gave Huxley the battle of his life.

IV

He beat them—beat them badly, and all their champions with them. His debate with Gladstone remains the greatest intellectual combat of modern times. Gladstone had at him with all the arts of the mob orator—and to them was added the passionate sincerity of a genuinely religious man. Huxley won hands down. Defeat became a rout. Gladstone retired from the field completely undone, with his cause ruined forever. You will find the debate, in full, in the two volumes, *Science and Hebrew Tradition* and *Science and Christian Tradition*. Huxley's contribution to it constitutes one of the glories of the Nineteenth Century. Far more than forty wars, far more than all the politicians of the century, far more even than the work of Darwin, it liberated the mind of modern man.

For Huxley was not only an intellectual colossus; he was also a great artist; he knew how to be charming. No man has ever written more nearly perfect English prose. There is a magnificent clarity in it; its meaning is never obscure for an instant. And it is adorned with a various and never-failing grace. It never struts like the prose of Macaulay; it never simpers like Pater's. It is simple, precise, unpretentious—and yet there is fine music in every line of it. The effects it achieves are truly overwhelming. One cannot read it without succumbing to it. Again I point to the two volumes of the debate with Gladstone. If they don't thrill you, then go back to the sporting page.

V

Huxley visited Baltimore in 1876, and made a speech at the opening of the Johns Hopkins University. The clergy of the town denounced him roundly as an atheist and a scoundrel, and the late Dr. Gilman with him for inviting him. His visit, indeed, took on the proportions of a scandal, and threatened to do grave damage to the new university. High ecclesiastical dignitaries in other places took a hand in the matter; Dr. Gilman was bombarded from all sides. But he stuck resolutely to his guns. That was forty-nine years ago, and Huxley is thirty years dead. What I wonder is this: if he were still alive and invited again, would he come?

(The Baltimore Evening Sun, May 4, 1925)

The Case of Edward W. Bok

It is one of the tragedies of man that he is usually proud of his follies and ashamed of his virtues and good deeds. The strict monogamist seldom boasts of it; when he does, everyone assumes he is a liar. The pants business, it must be plain, is a great deal more intricate and subtle than golf, and a great deal more useful to humanity. Yet all one hears from its professors, in the smoke rooms of Pullmans, is braggadocio about their golf. Years ago, when I was an active journalist, God gave me the supervision of many lady reporters, some of them beautiful.

One day I put this question to a whole herd of them: "Would you rather have me say that you have done a good piece of work or that you have on a pretty frock?"

They decided unanimously in favor of the frock.

These depressing thoughts are inspired by a contemplation of the career of Edward W. Bok, late editor of the *Ladies' Home Journal.* Bok is surely no shrinking violet. No one could accuse him justly of underestimating himself. He has already printed two large volumes about his own career and if he is spared to us long enough he will probably write a third, fourth and fifth. But what does he boast about in these formidable tomes? What makes him glow most brightly when his thoughts turn inward? I discern two chief things. In the first place, he is proud of his autograph collection. In the second place, he is proud of the Bok peace award.

Think of that, Hedda! His autograph collection is simply a monument to his impertinence. He began it in boyhood by addressing cunningly contrived inquiries to eminent men—in other words, by deliberately making a nuisance of himself. And the Bok peace award is so vast a futility that both the winner of the prize and the donor himself have abandoned the prize winning plan! Yet Bok is immensely proud of both the award and the autographs! It is almost as if John W. Davis should be proud of the event of November 4, 1924—as if Mr. Coolidge should sweat his pride in his beauty and his eloquence.

* *

Meanwhile, there are genuine achievements to Bok's credit, and if he should take to bragging about them in high, astounding terms, I, for one, should be disposed to hear the clatter with no more than a few deprecatory coughs behind the hand. I shall not bore you with a complete list of these achievements; that is something for the pastor to look to say at the last sad rites. I content myself with a single one: Bok is the man who reformed domestic architecture and interior decoration in the United States.

What! Is our domestic architecture, then, really reformed? Even so. In this field, if in no other, we may justifiably slap our own backs. Our painting is second rate, our music is third rate and our literature, in more than one of its aspects, is fourth rate and fifth rate; but our architecture, I believe, leads the world. Does it lag behind the German in boldness and originality? Is it second to the French in erudition? Then it is immensely ahead of either of them in simplicity and dignity, in its competent meeting of practical needs, in its freedom from pedantry and affectation, in its adaptation to place and time.

And in no direction has it made more progress in half a century than in that of building houses for people to live in. If we live better than any other people, it is certainly not due solely to the fact that we have more money. The profiteers and the Civil War had plenty of money, but, when they came to build homes, all they could achieve was a succession of gloomy barns, decorated hideously and idiotically. The land was filled with such monsters, and with countless lesser imitations of them. The American home, when it was not a dark box in a city block, was a circus cage. Its ornamentation was borrowed from the candy box and the wedding cake. There was a tower on top and an iron dog on the lawn. At every corner there was a projecting window. All over trailed the curlicues of the jigsaw.

* *

I need not argue, I hope, that there has been vast improvement. In the worst jerrybuilt bungalow in the cheapest suburb of today there is at least a certain honest simplicity. The thing may not be positively beautiful, but it is at least not actively hideous. Its lines are rational and often harmonious; it is firmly fastened to the ground; it somehow manages to fit itself into the landscape. There is little meaningless ornament upon it. It may be cheap, but it is at least as substantial as the clapboard castles of the seventies and early eighties. Its rooms meet their uses admirably. It is comfortable to live in.

Go up the scale a step, and at once you come, not merely to things that are passable, but to things that show solid and inescapable merit. Every large city in America, and nearly every small city likewise, is surrounded by suburbs full of beautiful houses—houses that are admirably designed in themselves and that fit into their surroundings charmingly. They are not all alike; sometimes, alas, two of them clash. But in the overwhelming majority of them there is at all events an obvious effort to avoid downright ugliness. They show grace, restraint, a feeling for line and color, often an unmistakable dignity. The worst of them is infinitely better than the best dwelling house of the last generation.

And so inside. The marks of the jig saw have vanished. The old heavy overcarved furniture is gone. So are the chromatic wallpapers. So are the brussels carpets. So are the imbecile ornaments. Instead, one finds simple surfaces, plain designs, subdued and harmonious colors. The floors in even the most modest suburban cottages are now of hardwood. The walls no longer blaze with scarlets, violets and coppery greens. There are rugs on the floors. The woodwork is inconspicuous. The furniture, at worst, does not assault the eye and trap the shins. Even golden oak has begun to go out.

*   *

Well, who brought about this change? I believe that credit belongs to Bok more than to any other man—more than to any architect or decorator. When he became editor of the *Ladies' Home Journal,* in 1889, he launched almost at once into a violent campaign against the old abominations. Where he got the impulse I don't know. Maybe he brought it from his native Holland. Maybe he borrowed it from some other man—or woman—now unsung. Maybe he was inspired by thumbing his collection of autographs. Maybe he was illuminated and set off by prayer.

Whatever the origin of his crusade, he unquestionably carried it on with vast energy and a great ingenuity. The *Ladies' Home Journal* was already reaching hundreds of thousands of American women; they were, on the whole, rather well to do; aspirations were beginning to stir within them. Bok launched himself magnificently at their vanity. He began to fill his magazine with pairs of pictures, at first in black and white, but eventually in full color.

One picture of each pair would show something hideous—a house covered with nonsensical scroll work, a room broached with ridiculous furniture, a wall hung with gaudy paper and preposterous pictures. The other picture would show the same thing made sightly—the house reduced to simple lines, the room cleared out and rearranged, the wall painted and the pictures removed to the cellar.

It was a subtle attack. Nine readers out of ten recognized something of their own in the first picture. Bok's captions were not cocksure and offensive; he proceeded by stealthy hints and influences. Thus his victims did not bristle to a defense of their possessions; they found themselves blushing. The next month he was at them again. They began, at first quietly, to make away with a few antimacassars, to retire a few walnut tables with marble tops, to have a wall or two scraped, to hand the crayon portraits of Uncle Brewster and Aunt Eliza to the ash man. They ended with a sort of massacre. Today an American house of the era would make even a Congressman or a policeman snicker. If Bok's pictures were reprinted they would have to go in the comic section.

A public service, it seems to me, of the first magnitude. In 10,000 far-flung towns it turned ugliness into dignity, simplicity, something not far from beauty. One man led all the rest. Today he has apparently forgotten it, and is proud of two puerile follies.

(The Chicago Sunday Tribune, June 28, 1925)

On Bald Heads

From a man evidently suffering vastly comes the following despairing note:

What is the origin of the prejudice against bald-headed men? Why are they so persistently sneered at, as mental vacuums and moral anarchists? In the morality play of "Everywoman," on view in Baltimore this week, the only bald characters, two in number, are scoundrels. It is so throughout the drama. Don Juan is always bald, but Don Caesar wears a bushy wig. The actual truth of the matter is that bald-headed men are commonly of unusual intelligence. Shakespeare was bald. So was Aristotle. So was Galileo. Baldness, in fact, is an almost infallible mark of genius.

Alas, why is it? Why is the world so unfair, so stupid, so cruel? The bald-headed man is the butt of its most evil jokes. He is represented as a giddy old fool, a patron of burlesque shows, a foe to all the decencies. It is commonly believed that infants burst into bawling at his approach, that he eats and drinks too much, that his solemn appearance is a mere mask for deviltries. And yet, as this correspondent says, many of the world's greatest men, ancient and modern, have been bald. Darwin had a dome as destitute of flora as a cannon-ball. Ibsen's forehead ran all the way to his summit. Molière and Lope de Vega wore wigs. Socrates had no more hair on his head than a dumb-bell.

* *

What a roster might be made of bald-headed geniuses—philosophers, poets, statesmen, conquerors, reformers! It would fill 20 columns of the *Evening Sun*. The names of Julius Caesar, Oliver Cromwell, William of Normandy, George Washington, Scipio Africanus, Pompey, Aeschylus, Homer, Aristophanes, Virgil, Chaucer, Newton, Bacon, Ben Jonson, Kant, Coleridge, Racine, Swedenborg, the two Bacons, Giordano Bruno, Vesalius, Euripides, Plautus, Horace, Goethe, Calderón, Cervantes, Gogol, Bismarck, Metternich, Berlioz and Johann Sebastian Bach would adorn it.

* *

The compilation of such a roster would be a labor of years, perhaps of centuries. But the idea fascinates, and so let us attempt a sort of rough, preliminary list. Here, then, are the names of a few undoubtedly great men who have been undoubtedly bald, either partly or wholly. No man whose baldness was less than 60 percent has been admitted. So:

PHILOSOPHERS

Aristotle,	Schleiermacher,
Pythagoras,	Hobbes,
Plato,	Bacon,
Socrates,	Berkeley,
Descartes,	al-Ghazālī,
*Locke,	Ibn Tufayl,
Comte,	Empedocles,
Kant,	Prodicus,
Spinoza,	Democritus,
Leibniz,	*Xenophanes,
Fichte,	Heracleitus.

POETS

Homer,	*Simonides,
Virgil,	Warner,
Abū Nuwās,	Theocritus,
Omar Khayyám,	Vogelweide,
Chaucer,	Klopstock,
Horace,	Spenser,
Cooglar,	Herder,
Varius Rufus,	†Rousseau,
*Catulus,	Vigny,
Dryden,	Musset,
Herrick,	Greene,
Dante,	Cowley,
Beowulf,	Kipling,
Heine,	Bertran de Born,
Ovid,	Villon,
Propertius,	Gray.

DRAMATISTS

Aeschylus,	Scribe,
Euripides,	Shakespeare,
Aristophanes,	Terence,
Beaumont,	Calderón,
Goldsmith,	Lope de Vega,
Jonson,	Echegaray,
Molière,	Corneille,
Racine,	*Marlowe,
Ibsen,	Pinero,
Bjrnson,	Sutro,
*Gogol,	Pollock,
Schiller,	Goldoni,
Kotzebue,	Angier,
Jones,	Rostand.

NOVELISTS

Zola,	Cooper,
Turgenev,	Tolstoy,
France,	Trollope,
Boccaccio,	James,
Fielding,	Howells,
Smollett,	Heyse,
*Dickens,	Cervantes,
De Morgan,	Defoe,
*Sudermann,	*Lesage,
Collins,	Lucian,
Hawkins,	Kioden,
Sorel,	Subandhu.

GENERALS

Julius Caesar,	Prince Eugène,
Scipio Africanus,	Marlborough,
*Hannibal,	Bernadotte,

Frederick the Great,   Blücher,
†Washington,   Wellington.

SAILORS

Columbus,   ‡Hobson,
Nelson,   Cook,
Dewey,   Van Tromp.

SCIENTISTS

Galileo,   Darwin,
‡Newton,   Wallace,
Hunter,   Lodge,
Linnaeus,   Osler,
*Volta,   Vesalius,
Koch,   Mueller,
Mendel,   Franklin,
Boyle,   Lavoisier,
†Glauber,   Davy,
Helmholz,   Haeckel,
Behener,   Berzelius,
Priestly,   *Liebig,
Boerhaave,   Guy-Lassac,
Resumur,   Mendeleyev.

STATESMEN

Cromwell,   Metternich,
Bismarck,   Disraeli,
John Adams,   Bülow,
Pitt,   Witte,
Gladstone,   *Wolsey.

ORATORS

Bryan,   Isocrates,
Cicero,   Cato the Censor,
Demosthenes,   *Clay,
Webster,   Fox,
Peter the Hermit,   Mansfield,
Burke,   Athanasius,
Beecher,   Isaeus,
Ingersoll,   Tom Reed.

MUSICIANS

Clementi,   Palestrina,
§J. B. Bach,   Scarlatti,
§P. E. Bach,   Paganini,
§C. P. E. Bach,   Haydn,
§Hans Bach,   Grieg,
§W. F. E. Bach,   Saint-Saëns,
§Veit Bach,   *Glinka,
§Heinrich Bach,   Purcell,
§J. M. Bach,   E. de Reszke,
§J. C. Bach,   Strauss,
§W. F. Bach,   Raff,

Luil,
Cu,
Bülow,
Brahms,
Offenbach,
Von Suppé,
Novák,

†Pleyel,
Planeus,
*Popper
*Rheinberger,
Jadassohn,
Jules Levy,
Stradivarius.

ARTISTS

Raphael,
Rodin,
Wren,
Blake,
Duren,
Doré,
*Cruikshank,
Gibson,
Vedder,
Verrshtchagin,
Watts,
Cotof,
*Dupré,
Rubens,
Wilson,

Van Dyck,
Mignard,
*Correggio,
Van Aelst,
Jan Steen,
Piloty,
Knaus,
Lenbach,
Ribot,
Bastien-Lepage,
Manet,
†Reynolds,
†Gainsborough,
Kneller,
Tiepolo.

MURDERERS

Cesare Borgia,   *Crippen.

ACTORS

†Garrick,
Burbage,
Roscius,
Tree,

Macready,
Talma,
Richard Carle,
Salvini.

*Partly.
†Under his wig.
‡Became bald after leaving the sea.
§Baltitude ran in the Bach family.

(The Baltimore Evening Sun, February 18, 1911)

Two Wasted Lives

One commonly hears of such persons as Emma Goldman and Alexander Berkman only as remote and horrendous malefactors, half human and half reptilian. Editorial writers, on dull days, exhume ancient bills of complaint against them and give thanks to

God that they are safely beyond these Christian shores, and for good. They are denounced by orators before the American Legion, by suburban pastors and by brave Congressmen. While they were still in our midst one heard only that *Polizei* were hot on their trail, that the gallant catchpolls of the so-called Department of Justice were about to trap them, that the hoosegow at Atlanta was being warmed for them. Since the *Buford* sailed the science of jurisprudence has made immense progress among us. Had it leaped a step Berkman would have had a padlock through his snout, and La Goldman, I suspect, would have been outfitted with *ceinture de patrioname*.

All this indignation, unfortunately, conceals something, and that is the somewhat disconcerting fact that both are extremely intelligent—that once their aberrant political ideals are set aside they are seen to have very sharp wits. They think clearly, unsentimentally and even a bit brilliantly. They write simple, glowing and excellent English. Their feelings, far from being those of yeggmen, cannibals and prohibition enforcement officers, are those of highly civilized persons. How, then, is their political nonsense to be explained—their childish belief in the proletariat, their life-long faith in Utopia? Go ask me something easier! I am no professor of morbid psychology. But I know a very intelligent man, a scientist of national fame, who believes that drinking a glass of beer is a mortal sin. I know another man, eminent in public life, who patronizes chiropractors. I know a third, worth at least $10,000,000, who believes in thought transference. I know a fourth—

* *

But it is unnecessary to go on. The fact that a human brain of high amperage, otherwise highly efficient, may have a hole in it is surely not a secret. All of us, in our several ways, are illogical, irrational, almost insane. It is the misfortune of Berkman and La Goldman that the form their private folly takes is very unpopular; that it greatly alarms all the more simpleminded types of men; that it is the custom in America to combat it, not by laughing at it, but by yelling for the police. The fact, I believe, has given them undue eminence in the national demonology. They are ranked with Benedict Arnold, the James brothers, Brigham Young, Sitting Bull and John Wilkes Booth. What is good in them is completely overlooked.

These reflections are inspired by a reading of Berkman's *The Bolshevik Myth* (Boni & Liveright), preceded shortly by a reading of Miss Goldman's *My Disillusionment in Russia* (Doubleday, Page). Both, it seems to me are very good books, books of quite unusual distinction—perhaps, indeed, the best books that the Russian débâcle has yet produced. There is not the slightest hint of the usual propaganda in them. They were not written either to gild the Bolsheviki as angels or to bedaub them as devils. Both, so to speak, were done against the grain; there is in them a confession of profound error. But they are frank, they are fair and straightforward, and they are written with quite extraordinary skill. I attempt no choice between them. Miss Goldman's volume is perhaps the more moving, for there is something finer in her than in Berkman, but his is surely the more dramatic and devastating.

* *

Berkman starts with his departure from the United States on the *Buford*. He was, he says, glad to get away, and I believe him. He had spent more of his years here in prison than in freedom; ahead, at worst, was liberty. He was, of course, an anarchist, and hence an opponent of the Bolsheviki—despite the belief of Federal district attorneys, newspaper editorial writers, members of Congress and other such morons that the two are identical—but he was far more interested in the revolution than in the notions underlying it. Here, at last, the great experiment of his dreams was on. Here, at last, the Chandala had overthrown their masters and were hard at work upon the New Jerusalem.

Berkman stepped upon Russian soil with his heart leaping like that of a Kansas deacon landing at Bimini. The Bolsheviki were instantly polite to him. More intelligent than the rulers of older countries, they had observed the fact that he was a man of parts, and they determined to make use of those parts—perhaps even to win him over by keeping him busy and showing confidence in him. He was received and made much of by the highest dignitaries of the state. He was given important work. He was given authority. He was turned loose.

Alas, for the plans of mice and men! His sharp eyes, it quickly appeared, were just a bit too sharp. Day by day they began to penetrate further and further into the Bolshevik sham. They discovered abuses innumerable—graft injustice, petty tyranny, downright oppression. They found politicians getting rich at the expense of the starving toilers. They found courts run by brutes, and the jails full of innocent men. They found corruption and incompetence everywhere, cynicism and self-seeking in high places, misery almost inconceivable under the surface show. In brief, they found that life in Utopia was ten times as hard, a hundred times as unhappy, a thousand times as savage, as under the hell-hounds of capital—worse, even, than life in a Pennsylvania mining town; almost as appalling (to a humane man) as life in Los Angeles (to an intelligent one).

* *

Poor Berkman was staggered. His bald head, I daresay, steamed with clammy sweat. So this was the revolution! This was the end of a lifelong dream, cherished for years and years in dungeons! It would be difficult to imagine any more crushing disillusionment. Nor any more realistic dealing with it. Berkman wasted no time trying to see the better side. He didn't counsel himself to be patient, and wait for a miracle. Instead, he asked for his passport, went to Berlin, got a comfortable pew in a respectable beer house, spit on his hands and wrote *The Bolshevik Myth*. I believe it will do more to blow up that myth than all the pious snuffing of the late Charles Evans Hughes—nay, more than the hottest tears of 10,000 Charles Evans Hugheses.

For Berkman is a transparently honest man. There can be no question of his bona fides. Nor of the soundness of his information. Nor of his capacity to weigh it, estimate it, determine its bearings. His book constitutes a criticism that is absolutely shattering. Nothing is left of the Bolshevik balderdash when he has finished with it. He searches out its every weakness; he exposes the dreadful fraudulence of all its principal exponents; he turns it completely inside out. When the Department of State attempted the same job only Babbitts believed it; its own fraudulence was too manifest. But Berkman, I suspect, will convince even the liberals.

Now to my point: It was a great mistake, I am convinced, to let so shrewd, forthright and frank a fellow go, and La Goldman with him. The defect in our system is that it utilizes men badly—that it throttles more talent than it makes any use of. The Bolsheviki seem to be surviving Berkman's devastating onslaught; it may even strengthen them at home, if only by making them more careful. But in the United States, where such criticism is needed quite as sorely as in Russia and where it could be turned to use ten times as well—here the only thing we can think of doing to such a man as Berkman is to lock him up in jail. Because his fulminations alarm a few profiteers, we hunt him as if he were a mad dog—and finally kick him out of the country. And with him goes a shrewder head and a braver spirit than has been seen in public life among us since the Civil War.

(The Chicago Sunday Tribune, April 26, 1925)

The Exile of Enzesfeld

I

That there is more than meets the naked eye in the case of the late King Edward is plainly most likely. The row over his proposed marriage was not the beginning of a chain of fatal events, but its culmination. He had been in bad odor with the rulers of England for a long while. They resented his careless and shabby mode of life, and lived in fear that it would produce at any moment a dreadful scandal. And they resented even more his effort to balk and silence them by a resort to what, in any other man, would have been recognized by everyone as deliberate and yet reckless demagogy.

It is hard to account for his pronunciamentoes during his Welsh tour in any other terms. He must have been well aware that the situation of the former miners in some of the valleys he visited was completely and eternally hopeless. The mines that they and their fathers had worked for years had been worked out, or become so depleted that it was no longer possible to operate them at a profit in competition with better ones. If the miners had been men of any sense they would have departed long ago. But they remained at home, hoping idiotically for a miracle, and when they began to starve the Government put them on the dole.

There was nothing else to do. They refused to move away, and there was no work for them where they were. Various demagogues, chiefly professional labor leaders turned politicians, proposed from time to time that the mines be seized and sold to succor the idle miners, but no one wanted them, and if they had actually been put up at auction they would have brought nothing. The Government did the best it could. It fed the hungry and paid their rent. It listened to all the plans of deliverance proposed, whether sane or insane. But in the end it always had to return to feeding the hungry and paying their rent.

II

Edward's public remarks in the blighted areas were plainly intended to be criticisms of the Government's course, and were universally so accepted. What he said, in substance, was that it had done badly by the miners, and that he knew of a way to do better. This was an undisguised usurpation of a prerogative that the Kings of England lost three centuries ago. They are forbidden, under the Constitution now prevailing, to take any side in politics, or to express any views on political questions. If one of them happens to have an opinion about a matter before Parliament, he is supposed to keep that opinion strictly to himself. I am not arguing that this is either a wise arrangement or an unwise one, a good one or a bad one; I am simply stating the fact.

Why, then, did Edward violate the code? I suspect that the fundamental reason was that he was the sort of man who habitually violates codes, but there was also, in all probability, a special reason, to wit, a crafty design to embarrass and handcuff the Government by raising the mob against it. If he could get a big enough crowd behind him, then Baldwin and company would be estopped from bothering him about his private goings-on, for it would be easy to interpret every move against him as a measure of revenge on him, and the mob would be for him right or wrong. In brief, he apparently planned to take the offensive out of the Cabinet's hands, and thus get a great advantage in the row that threatened.

If this was actually his scheme it was certainly a plausible one, and also an exhilaratingly bold one. Unfortunately for its success, the gabble in the American newspapers got out of hand, and he was forced into combat before he was quite ready. When the time came Baldwin had the drop on him, and in the short space of a week he was dispatched with that calm, pious ferocity which has always been one of the great glories of English statecraft. If he had won, he would have been the undisputed boss of Britain, and the first real King on the throne of his fathers since Henry VIII. But he lost, and now he is only an exile at Enzesfeld, the Hoboken of Vienna.

III

It is not necessary, in reverting to his late Majesty's private peccadilloes, to share the blubbering moral indignation of his Grace of Canterbury. Bishops—at least in England—are hardly notable for their common sense, nor are they distinguished for any excess of Christian charity. One hears of them mainly as making public spectacles of themselves, and only too often they do it by violating some cardinal article of the code laid down by the Leader they are supposed to follow. Without doubt there are members of the order who are familiar with Romans XII, but equally without doubt they seldom apply it in their daily business.

But though his Grace's dogmatic assertion that all of Edward's friends were loose characters was an exaggeration, and has been challenged very properly, the fact remains that his late Majesty kept the kind of company that most men of any sense and dignity try to avoid. One never heard of him consorting with persons who knew anything worth knowing, or had ever done anything worth doing; he seemed to prefer nonentities. He had easy access, by virtue of his exalted office, to the most intelligent men and the most amusing women in Europe, but he stuck to trash. When he sought recreation he went to a night club, and pranced to the obscene cacophony of a jazz band. And when he felt the need of female companionship *in camera* he chose the kind of women who know all the head waiters from Carlsbad to Biarritz.

Every man, of course, has his silly moods, and most men, however lofty their customary mien, feel an occasional yearning for low company. The late Theodore Roosevelt delighted in the society of pugilists, and the late W. E. Gladstone is said to have enjoyed talking to streetwalkers. But it is one thing to stoop thus now and then, and it is quite another thing to wallow on such levels all the time. If Edward had gone off on an occasional toot, taking a gang of earnest crap shooters and incessant brides along, no one would have complained seriously, but when it became generally known that he was immersed in such circles every evening, and even all day long, there was a great deal of unpleasant whispering and the responsible officers of the Government began to be alarmed for the dignity of the monarchy, and, toward the end, for its very security.

IV

Here Edward most assuredly did *not* play the game according to the rules. Pursuing always his private inclinations, which were almost inconceivably stupid and vulgar, he forgot altogether his duty to his associates in the Government of his country, to the multitude of his lieges, and to his family. In particular, he forgot his plain duty to his mother—a somewhat stodgy and old-fashioned lady, perhaps, but still one whose prejudices he was bound in honor to respect, at least in outward show. She has borne herself with fortitude in the ghastly weeks just past, but it needs no great fancy to imagine the black depths of her agony.

His project of marrying La Simpson was only the climax of a long series of lesser jackanaperies, all of them unworthy of a man holding responsible office in a civilized state. In its first form, it appears, it actually involved making her Queen; it was only later, and seemingly under pressure, that he switched to a morganatic union. But morganatic unions are unknown to the law of England, and under the *mores* of England, which are quite as potent as laws, though they are not written down, kings do not marry ladies who have other husbands out at pasture. Thus poor Edward made a colossal bust of it, and came horribly to grief.

In the objections raised to multiple connubial bliss by my ghostly brother of Canterbury I can see only hooey. A private man, it seems to me, should be free to marry any woman he fancies, even though she may have a dozen husbands behind her, some dead and some alive. Such multitudinous widows have been espoused, to my knowledge, by men of considerable sense, and to the felicity of both high contracting parties. But what may thus be done by a private man cannot be done by the King of England. It is an essential part of his implied contract with his people that he conduct himself, in all public situations, according to the *mores* of his country. When he fails to do so he breaks the contract, and loses all his rights under it.

The blood-sweating bishops of England may be gloating today over the exile of Enzesfeld, but I doubt if anyone else is. He is a poor fish who has brought his life to complete disaster, and if, in his lonely despair, he now regrets his monumental folly it is certainly no wonder. It will be, indeed, no wonder if he shoots himself before La Simpson shakes off her shackles. But he has no one to blame for his miseries, present and to come, but himself. He walked straight into the buzz saw, his eyes to the front and whistling gaily.

(The Baltimore Evening Sun, December 21, 1936)

Meditations on the Fair

Meditations on the Fair

I

A man's women folk, whatever their outward show of respect, always regard him secretly as an ass, and with something not akin to pity. His most gaudy sayings and doings seldom deceive them; they see the actual man within, and know him for a shallow and pathetic fellow. This is one of the best of proofs, perhaps, of feminine intelligence, or, as it is more commonly denominated, feminine intuition. The mark of that so-called intuition is simply a sharp and accurate perception of realities, a relentless capacity for distinguishing between the substance and the appearance. The appearance is a hero, a magnifico, a demigod. The substance is a poor mountebank.

The proverb that no man is a hero to his valet is obviously of masculine manufacture. It is both insincere and untrue—insincere because it merely masks the egoistic doctrine that he is usually a hero to every one else, and untrue because a valet, being a fourth-rate man, is likely to be the last person in the world to penetrate his master's charlatanry. Who ever heard of a valet who didn't envy his master, who wouldn't willingly change places with his master, who didn't secretly wish that he was his master? A man's wife has no such illusions. She may envy her husband his complacency and his vices, but she never envies him his soul.

This shrewd perception of masculine bombast and make-believe—the acute sense of man as the eternal tragic comedian—is at the bottom of that compassionate irony which passes for the maternal instinct. A woman wishes to mother a man simply because she sees into his helplessness, his need of an amiable audience, his touching self-delusion. That ironical note is not only daily apparent in real life; it sets the whole tone of feminine fiction. The woman novelist never takes her heroes quite seriously. From the day of Jane Austen to the day of Mrs. Watts she has always got into her picture a touch of waggishness, of superior aloofness, of scarcely concealed mirth. I can't recall a single masculine figure created by a woman, from Daniel Deronda to Ethan Frome, who was not, at bottom, an ass.

II

Women, of course, have their own weakness, perhaps to keep their intellectual superiority to men from becoming too obvious and too painful. It is the product of the reaction of male attitudinizing and buncombe upon them, and it takes the form of an affectation of feebleness, a bogus need of aid and counsel. It is by this route that they can most effectively disarm masculine suspicion, and so get what they want. Man is flattered by an acknowledgment, however insincere, of his strength and capacity. He likes to be consulted, leaned upon, appealed to. The result is the vast pretense that characterizes the relations of the sexes under civilization. Man is always looking for someone to boast to; woman is always looking for someone to complain to.

III

This affectation, of course, gradually takes on the vigor of a habit, and so tends to get some support, by a process of self-delusion in reality. The civilized woman, indeed, usually inherits that habit fully formed; she is half convinced, by the prevailing folk-lore, that she is weak, helpless and ill-used, and that she needs a male protector. This delusion visualizes itself in that thirst for martyrdom which one so often finds in women, particularly the least intelligent. They take a heavy delight in suffering; it caresses them to be hard put upon; they like to picture themselves as slaughtered saints. Thus they always have something to complain of.

If, by any chance, they haven't, they are uneasy and unhappy. Let a woman have a husband whose conduct is not reasonably open to question, and she will invent mythical offenses to make him bearable. And if her invention fails she will be plunged into the utmost misery and humiliation. This fact probably explains many mysterious divorces; the husband was not too bad, but too good. For public opinion among women, remember, does not favor the woman who has no masculine torts to report; if she says that her husband is wholly satisfactory she is looked upon as a numbskull. A man, speaking of his wife to other men, always praises her extravagantly. Boasting about her soothes his vanity; he likes to stir up the envy of his fellows. But when two women talk of their husbands it is mainly atrocities that they describe. The most esteemed woman gossip is the one with the longest and most various repertoire of complaints.

IV

This yearning for martyrdom explains one of the commonly noted characteristics of women: their capacity for bearing physical pain. In pain a man sees only an invasion of his self-respect. It floors him, masters him, and makes him subtly ridiculous. But a woman obviously enjoys the effect that the spectacle of her suffering makes upon the spectators. She would much rather be praised for facing pain with a martyr's fortitude than for devising some means of getting rid of it. No woman could have invented chloroform, nor, for that matter, alcohol. Both drugs offer an escape from situations and experiences that, even in aggravated forms, women relish. The woman who drinks as men drink nearly always shows a deficiency of feminine characters and an undue preponderance of male characters. Almost invariably you will find her vain and boastful and full of other marks of that psychic exhibitionism which is so sterlingly masculine.

V

Some time ago I overheard a discussion by several men of a fact often noted—that women of high intelligence usually marry third-rate men. The conclusion reached was that they did it because they couldn't help themselves—that men of their own class were too clever to be ensnared by them. A more idiotic conclusion could not be imagined. The truth is, of course, that first-rate men are often captured by women so shallow and unintelligent that they are almost masculine. But how, then, is the fact to be explained? Why do women of undoubted intelligence so often marry fellows who are mere muttonheads?

For the reason, it seems to me, that a first-rate woman, even more than an average woman, is eager to retain those advantages which her sex gives her, and particularly the advantage of her sharp intelligence, her efficiency in cerebral combats and emergencies, her so-called intuition. That advantage is safe so long as her antagonist is an average man; it is doubly safe when he is appreciably inferior. But it tends to be imperiled as he rises in intelligence, and finally there comes a place where it is actually in doubt. Wise women steer clear of that place. They play safe.

In this discretion there is a good deal more than mere egoism— that is, a good deal more than a mere desire to rule the roost. It is based, at bottom, upon an accurate and instinctive sense of sexual differences, and particularly of the difference in mental alertness. A woman of intelligence wants to safeguard her superiority, not so much because it enables her to boss her husband, but because it preserves that subtle and half-mysterious disparity which is at the heart of sex attraction. The charm of a woman to a man lies in her complete differentness, and the charm of a man for a woman lies in the same thing. A woman could not love a man who wore skirts and penciled his eyebrows, and by the same token she could not love a man who revealed too close an approximation to her own clear processes of mind. A normal woman likes to laugh at her man—half affectionately and half ironically. She likes to observe that he is a fool, dear, but none the less damned. Her love for him, even at its highest, is always somewhat pitying and patronizing.

This is why women of intelligence so often marry stock brokers, sportsmen, business men and other such dull and unimaginative fellows. It is not that they esteem stupidity per se; it is that they know its value for keeping up that illusion of strangeness which is the chief bond between the sexes. There must be, said Shakespeare, some mystery in love. There can be no mystery between two equal minds.

VI

What men, in their imbecility, constantly mistake for a deficiency of intelligence in women is merely an incapacity for mastering small and trivial tricks. A man thinks that he is more intelligent than his wife because he can add up figures more accurately and because he understands the lingo of the stock market, and follows the doings of political mountebanks, and knows the minutiae of some sordid and degrading business or profession, any soap selling or the law. But these puerile talents are not really signs of intelligence; they are merely accomplishments, and they differ only in degree from the accomplishments of a trained chimpanzee.

The truth is that the capacity for mastering them is the sign of a petty mind, and Havelock Ellis, in his great study of British genius, shows that men of genius almost invariably lack it. One could not think of Shakespeare or Goethe or Beethoven multiplying 3,456,754 by 79,999 without making a mistake, nor could one think of them remembering the price of this or that stock last July, or the number of beans in a pound, or the freight rate on steel beams from Akron, Ohio, to Newport News, or concerning themselves about the cost of producing a stick of chewing gum, or the pay of street car conductors, or the credit of some obscure shopkeeper in Memphis, Tenn. Such idiotic concerns are beneath the dignity of first-rate minds.

That women always try to evade them—that they have little capacity for the childish complexity of tricks upon which men base their so-called business and professional skill and cunning—this is but one more proof of their intellectual aristocracy. They are not stumped by such enterprises because they are difficult, but because they are trivial. For precisely the same reason, as Ellis shows, it is rare to encounter a first-rate man who is good at tying neckties, or who understands the more delicate points of cricket or baseball, or who knows how much he spends for tobacco.

In a man's world, of course, such simian aptitudes are rated high, and so not many women get on. To succeed as a lawyer, for example, a woman would have to throttle two of her chief attributes: her disdain for the petty accumulation of useless knowledge, and her sharp feeling for the truth. But once women are politically free there may be a radical overhauling of the values now put upon such ignoble capacities. We may come to the point, indeed, whereat the idiotic mental baggage of a lawyer or a stockbroker, or a soap vendor, is put on a par with the mental baggage of a solver of jigsaw puzzles, where it actually belongs. When that time comes intelligence will be rated at its true worth in the world, and women's superior possession of it will begin to crack skulls.

(The New York Evening Mail, November 15–16, 1917)

Answers to Correspondents

Mothers' Day—From an esteemed stranger comes a polite objection to my late doctrine that the man who will begaud himself with a carnation in order to inform strangers that he loves his mother is a cad. This stranger hymns the custom (apparently a Baltimore invention; how characteristic!) as touching and beautiful, and argues that every decent man should be willing to set aside one day a year for honoring his mother. A typical piece of sentimental reasoning. What should be obvious and indisputable requires a public ceremonial to prove it! Why not a day for wearing little tin bathtubs to prove that one bathes, in the patriotic American manner, once a week? Why not white hatbands for gentlemen who are true to their wives? It is precisely the mark of the cad that he makes a public boast of what is inseparable from decency. He is the fellow who marches grandly in preparedness parades to show off his valor, his patriotism, his willingness to die for his country. He is the fellow who insults his mother by making a spectacle of the fact that he is on good terms with her.

The cad becomes a widespread American type; one hears his mellifluous wind music on all sides; he is the newly hatched right thinker, full of conceit in his new pieties. What passes of late for the American spirit—how Washington would have marveled at it! —is no more than a cad's spirit: it is chiefly made manifest by a booming pretension to a moral grandeur, a noble beauty of character, a lofty detachment from common weakness, which one actually finds in no country so little as in this one. Idealism? Pish! A man does not serve his country by canting, snuffling and marching in parades; he serves her by striving to make her clean, brave, just, intelligent and worthy of respect. And he does not honor his mother by making up like an honorary pallbearer; he serves her by doing his work in the world, whatever it may be, in a way that does her credit, and remembering his debt to her every day of his life.

(The Baltimore Evening Sun, June 13, 1916)

The Holy Estate

As a bachelor and hence a neutral, I find myself completely convinced after thirty years of laborious observation and incessant meditation, that the happiest marriages are those which are the most conventional. Thus the shocking theorizing of my eminent friend, Judge Ben B. Lindsey, leaves me unmoved. All his companionate marriage scheme would accomplish, accepting it at its best, would be to provide an easy means of dissolving marriages that were already wrecked. But what the world needs is something that will save marriages that are merely wobbling.

It is my belief that this salvation is achieved by convention far more often than it is achieved by anything else. And by convention I mean the rules that are made by a sort of general acclamation, and without any regard to the merits of a particular case. The contented husband is that one who is too wise to resist these rules. He accepts them as unquestioningly as he accepts the gradual hardening of his arteries. He says and does, not what it would be most natural and exhilarating to say and do, but what he is expected to say and do. Having acquiesced in the conventional assumption that marriage is for eternity, he acts upon the assumption that it really is. Having made solemn oath to be a good husband, he tries his level damndest to be one.

How he arrives at this program, it seems to me, is of small importance. He may come to it romantically or he may come to it cynically. The essential thing is that, having come to it, he has disposed at one stroke of the one thing that wrecks more marriages than anything else, and that is simple lack of trust. He has become a trustworthy man, and hence, to all intents and purposes, a good husband. For it is mutual trust, even more than mutual interest, that holds human associations together, the small as well as the great. Our friends seldom profit us, but for all that they make us feel safe. We know, or think we know, exactly what they will do in any given situation. They take the hazard out of life, and put in security. Marriage is a scheme to accomplish precisely the same end.

* *

The trouble with the companionate scheme, by whatever name it may be called, is that it destroys this security and this trust. Neither party can ever be quite sure of the other, and hence neither can give the other full confidence. How can any such arrangement be called a marriage, which, as any lawyer will tell you, is not a contract but a status? It is, in point of fact, not a marriage at all, but simply an agreement to live together, and not even for a definite time. Obviously, such an agreement has no substance; it may be terminated for a whim. And equally obviously, the parties to it, knowing its terms, cannot give each other their full confidence.

The advocates of the companionate scheme, seeing clearly enough that it thus destroys the confidence which is at the bottom of genuine marriage, have sought to get rid of the elements which make confidence especially necessary. That is to say, they have tried to get rid of children and of common property. The companions, it appears, are to avoid parenthood, at least for a considerable time. And the wife is to have no claim upon the husband's estate. Once the agreement is terminated, each party is to be restored to the *status quo ante*. Neither has any further interest in the other.

But all that, it seems to me, simply makes the antecedent marriage, or whatever you choose to call it, a mockery. A normal man does not marry a woman thinking of her as a possible enemy; he marries her thinking of her as a perpetual friend. He is not only willing to give her his full confidence; he is eager to do it. His delight in her is his complete merging of their interests, and, in so far as it is humanly possible, of their personalities. But how now, if he finds that she is not his one irrevocable friend, but the one who can desert him the easiest, and at the least risk of her legal and social censure? Is there any chance of happiness in that arrangement? If there is, then all that has been taught about human psychology is false.

* *

I speak, of course, of normal men and women, with the usual tastes, prejudices, yearnings and sentimentalities. There may be extraordinary folk to whom some one or other of the current substitutes for marriage may be satisfactory, but certainly there can't be many of them. One hears of an occasional husband and wife living in separate houses or even in different towns, and pursuing unrelated and disparate avocations, but usually that news is only an advance notice of a lively divorce suit.

For most persons, I believe, such palpable artificialities would be quite impossible. The normal man does not want to keep his wife as far away as he can with no continuing share in it. It is, indeed, precisely her sharing of it that makes her his wife and not a mere casual acquaintance. The essence of their relation lies in its merging of interests, hopes, fears, sorrows, triumphs, glories. Once there is division in that direction the whole thing falls to pieces. It has ceased to be a marriage and become merely an intermittent week-end.

The advocates of the companionate nonsense, to do them justice, see that much clearly. They assume a community of life—the husband and wife are to live together quite conventionally. But they overlook the fact that a true community of life is impossible without a community of interest—that the tie, to be binding, must lie in something stronger than simple physical proximity. More accurately, they recognize the defect, but seek to dispose of it by arguing that the tie ought to be loose—that it is most comfortable when it may be thrown off at will. But that is simply arguing that the solution of the marriage problem is to be not married.

* *

My private belief, the fruit of the excessive meditation I have mentioned, is that the true solution lies in hanging all the current reformers and going back to Bach. The plain fact about marriage is that it is a magnificent sentimentality, or it is nothing. The moment any effort is made to change its ancient terms, that moment it becomes something else, and something a great deal more unpleasant than it was before. The reformers with their novelties only succeed in making their customers unhappy. The really happy married couples, now as always, are those who accept the conventionalities and responsibilities of their holy estate willingly, and even thinkingly. To attempt to rationalize it is to destroy it.

There are, to be sure, persons to whom marriage of the conventional sort, or, indeed, of any sort, is a sheer psychic impossibility. I know plenty of them. They lack that yearning for intimate and unbroken companionship which is normal to the human race. They are slow to yield their confidence. Adventurous by nature, they set no value upon security. But the thing to do with these odd fish is to let them alone, and not try to lure them into marriage by changing its terms. For when they are fetched they are fetched only transiently, and in the ensuing smash there can only be unhappiness for all concerned.

The average man, luckily for posterity, is not of that sort. Adventure does not enchant him; it merely alarms him. He does not want to be free; he wants to be secure. In the presence of women, the chief hazards of the male, such a man is uneasy and unhappy. He sees in every glittering, provocative eye a menace to his peace and safety, and in every flash of rouge a plain warning. What he yearns for with a great yearning is a safe harbor from such perils. He pines for a sweet one who will capture him, and so cease chasing him—and, what is more, protect him from the chase of others.

To the needs of such a man, it seems to me, the monogamy that prevailed among us until the reformers got loose is admirably adapted. It not only makes him feel safe; it also gives him a high purpose in life, and a feeling that he is somehow honorable, laudable and deserving. Giving him someone to trust, it makes him trustworthy himself. He is at peace, and hence happy. The reformers with their prattle only disquiet and alarm him. I renew my suggestion that they be hanged.

(The Chicago Sunday Tribune, January 8, 1928)

How Much Should a Woman Eat?

The meanest man in the United States, unearthed the other day in Chicago, came into public view protesting piteously that his wife's extravagance was ruining him. Her appetite, he said, was gigantic, and on brisk, fair days she ate as much as 30 cents' worth of food. A few days afterward a Bostonian, arrested on a charge of nonsupport, admitted that he gave his wife but 8 cents a day and said that he regarded the money as sufficient for her provisioning. During the same week a Duluth man sought a divorce from his wife on the ground that she fried and consumed a peck of Bermuda onions daily, and so made his house uninhabitable, his bank account a theoretical abstraction and his dream of happiness a mere hallucination.

The world, perhaps, contemplates these men and their acts with mingled amusement and contempt, but in sober truth they have not a little justice and equity on their side. It is easy enough to laugh at them or to dismiss them with sneers, but who shall say that they are wrong? Have they violated any law or ordinance of any nation, State or municipality, or outraged any known principle of jurisprudence? Common honesty compels the admission that they have not. Our American statutes are silent upon the subject, and our courts, with their customary negligence, have never judicially determined, in any way, shape or form, the amount of food necessary to the nourishment of a wife. Failing such rules of law, every husband must solve the problem for himself, and if, in his endeavor so to solve it, his native prejudices lead him to some conclusion obnoxious to humanitarians, he is entitled, nevertheless, to the respect and tolerance due every man who essays a hazardous and difficult enterprise.

Every competent circus man knows to the fraction of an ounce how much food his various and exotic charges require in the course of 24 hours. He knows that an elephant of such-and-such tonnage needs so-and-so much hay; that a snake of such-and-such a distance from fang to rattle needs so-and-so many rabbits, rats and other snakes. And in the army, by the same token, the dietetic demands of the soldier are worked out to three places of decimals. A private carrying 80 pounds of luggage, with the temperature at 65°, can march 18 1/3 miles in 16 2/3 hours upon three ham sandwiches, half a pint of stuffed olives and a plug of plantation twist. A general weighing 285 pounds can ride a cayuse up four hills, each 345 feet in height on 6 ginger snaps and 12 Scotch highballs. Experiments are made to determine these things, and the results are carefully noted in official handbooks, and so attain the force of military regulations. But at the domestic hearth every young husband must figure it out for himself.

We have no doubt that much of the ill-feeling which results is due to an ignorant and romantic misinterpretation of misleading indications. When a girl is engaged in the enterprise of luring a man toward the Aisle of Sighs she affects an air of impalpable spirituality. Schooled by her elders of her own sex in the theory that a man is attracted by evidences of weakness and fragility, she pretends to an abhorrence of all the more vigorous victuals. Let her gentleman friend take her to some eating house and she orders a charlotte russe or a lettuce sandwich. Her favorite viand, judging by appearances, is celery shoots; the very thought of roast beef seems to disgust her.

The poor man marries her, and on their honeymoon she continues her deception. Her meals are made up of toast, fudge and mayonnaise. She orders half, quarter, eighth and sixteenth portions. But by the time the pair set up housekeeping in their own dear little flat the demands of hunger begin to grow irresistibly, and one morning Clarence is astounded and appalled to see his Mayme wade into five mutton chops, a rasher of bacon and half a dozen hot rolls. That night, at dinner, she eats six ears of corn, a quart of lima beans, a joint of mutton, a bowl of potato salad and two thirds of a shad. The next day, getting her true gait, she makes away with a beef-steak that would suffice for a starving commercial traveler.

Is it any wonder that the unfortunate man loses his reason and runs amuck? Is it any wonder that the sharp anguish of disillusionment carries him to fantastic extremes? Is it any wonder that a man thus deceived into believing, by deliberate chicanery, that the girl he is about to marry eats only meringues and radish tops, and led, by these deceits, to make a correspondingly low estimate of his household expenses after marriage—is it any wonder that this man, when his bride begins to consume $4 worth of food a day, should grow discontented, peevish and cruel?

(The Baltimore Sun, August 30, 1908)

The Woman of Tomorrow

The gradual emancipation of women that has been going on for the past century has still a long way to proceed before they are wholly delivered from their traditional burdens and so stand quite clear of the oppressions of men. But already, it must be plain, that they have made enormous progress, perhaps more than they made in the ten thousand years preceding. The rise of the industrial system, which has borne so harshly upon the race in general, has brought them certain unmistakable benefits. Their economic dependence lessens year by year; they learn ways and means of paddling their own canoes; they are no longer the mute and helpless slaves of inordinate and unintelligent masters.

Most women, of course, still hesitate to seize the complete freedom that is now within their grasp. For one thing, the idea of marriage yet intrigues and tantalizes them; they continue to prefer it to the autonomy that is coming in. But the fact remains that they now have a free choice in the matter, and that dire necessity no longer has them in its clutches. After all, they needn't marry if they don't want to; it is always possible for them to get their bread by their own labor in the workshops of the world.

Their grandmothers were in a far more difficult position. Failing marriage, they not only suffered a cruel ignominy, but in many cases faced the menace of actual starvation. There was simply no place in the economy of those times for the free woman, save as a disdained dependent. She either had to enter upon the religious life and so resign the world altogether, or accept the patronage that was as galling as charity. The old maid, down to a few years ago, was the family doormat. She had no rights that any one was bound to respect.

* *

Nothing could be plainer than the effect that the increasing economic security of women is having upon their whole outlook upon the world. The diminishing marriage rate and the no less diminishing birth rate show that the wind has begun to blow from strange quarters. It is usual for statisticians (who are all males, and hence asses) to ascribe the fall in the marriage rate to a growing disinclination to marriage on the male side. This growing disinclination, in point of fact, is on the female side. Women still seek marriage, true enough; but they no longer seek it as blindly and unintelligently as they used to. On the contrary, they grow harder and harder to please, and so it is not surprising to find that they are pleased less often.

There already appears in the world, indeed, a class of women who, while still not genuinely averse to marriage, are yet free from any theory that it is necessary to their happiness, or even invariably favorable. Among these women are a good many some-what vociferous propagandists, almost male in their violent ear-nestness. They range from the man-eating suffragettes to such preachers of free motherhood as Ellen Key and such professional martyrs and boob-shockers as Margaret Sanger. But among them are also many who wake the world with no such strident snorting, but content themselves with carrying out their ideas in a quiet and respectable manner.

The number of such women is larger than is generally imag-ined, and that number tends to increase steadily. They are women who, with their economic independence assured, walk the world as free agents, asking nobody's permission for their comings and goings. Naturally enough, their superiority to the common frenzy for marriage and to all the feminine hocus-pocus that goes there-with—naturally enough, this superiority makes them extremely attractive to the better sort of men. As a result it is not uncommon for one of them to find herself voluntarily sought in marriage, without any preliminary chicanery by herself—surely an experi-ence that very few ordinary women ever enjoy, save perhaps in dreams and while under the influence of narcotics.

* *

The transvaluation of values that is thus in progress will go on slowly and for a long while. That it will ever be quite complete is rather to be doubted. There are, in fact, inherent differences be-tween the mind of man and the mind of woman, and these differ-ences will probably continue to show themselves until the end of time. Women will grow more and more independent, and more and more competent for the laborious tasks of civilization, but I don't believe that they will ever become as competent as men, for those tasks, in the last analysis, demand talents that are peculiarly masculine—in the main, a talent for puerile and largely mechani-cal expertness, a high capacity for stupid assiduity.

To acquire any such competence women would have to sacrifice a good deal of their present intelligence. This spiritual suicide is probably quite beyond them; they are intrinsically incapable of it. Thus a shade of their present intellectual superiority to men will always remain, and with it a shade of their relative inefficiency, and so marriage will continue to hold out attractions to them, or at all events to most of them, and its overthrow will be prevented. Nature, in fact, is on its side. To abolish it entirely, as certain fevered reformers propose, would be as difficult as to abolish the precession of the equinoxes.

At the present time the majority of women wobble somewhat absurdly between two schemes of life, the old and the new. On the one hand their economic independence is still full of conditions, and on the other hand they are in revolt against most of the ancient conventions. The result is a general unrest, with many signs of extravagant and unintelligent revolt. One of these signs is the appearance of intellectual striving among certain classes of women—not a striving, alas, toward the genuine pearls and emeralds of the mind, but only merely toward the acquirement of the rubber-stamps that men employ in their so-called thinking.

* *

Thus we have women who launch themselves into party politics, and fill their heads with a vast mass of useless knowledge about political tricks, customs, theories and personalities. Thus, too, we have the woman uplifter, trailing along ridiculously behind a tatterdemalion posse of chautauquans, utopians and other such quacks, each with something to sell. And thus we have the woman who goes in for advanced wisdom of the sort on tap in the women's clubs—in brief, the sort of wisdom that consists entirely of a body of beliefs and propositions that are ignorant, unimportant and untrue.

Such banal striving, of course, is not peculiar to the United States; but it is surely more widespread here than elsewhere. Its popularity is due to the relatively greater leisure of our people, who work less than any other people on earth, and, above all, to the relatively greater leisure of our women. Thousands of them have been emancipated from any compulsion to labor without having acquired any compensatory intellectual or artistic interest or social duty. The result is that they swarm in the women's clubs, and waste their time listening to bad poetry, worse music, and still worse lectures on Maeterlinck, Balkan politics and birth control.

This enchantment by balderdash is amusing, but it is also a nuisance. Upon it may be blamed the bad housekeeping so generally on view in the United States. Here women reveal one of their subterranean qualities; their deficiency in conscientiousness. They are, in fact, quite without that doglike fidelity to duty which is one of the shining marks and chiefest boasts of men, high and low. They never summon up a lofty pride in doing what is inherently disagreeable; they always go to the galleys under protest, and with vows of sabotage; the whole sex constitutes a sort of domestic I.W.W. or Bolsheviki.

* *

The sentimentality of men connives at this, and is thus largely responsible for it. If men were harsher and more exigent, women would do less shirking. But harshness now goes out of fashion and is replaced by softness. The average *puella* never learns how to cook decently for the simple reason that it is not worth her while. Before she can master a fourth of the culinary subtleties that are commonplaces even to the negro cooks on pullman dining cars, she has caught a man and need concern herself about them no more, for he has to eat, in the last analysis, whatever she sets before him, and his lack of intelligence makes it easy for her to shut off his purely academic criticisms. By an easy process he finally attaches a positive value to her incompetence. It is a proof, he concludes, of her fineness of soul. In the presence of her sublime inefficiency he stands abashed, like a wart viewing the Matterhorn.

But as women, gaining economic autonomy, meet men in more and more serious competition, there will come a rise in masculine distrust and fear of them, and this change will be reflected even in the enchanted domain of marriage, for all its deceptive moonshine. That is to say, the husband, having yielded up most of his old rights, will begin to reveal a new jealousy of those that remain, and particularly of his right by a fair return upon his investment of docile industry. In other words, as women shake off all their ancient disabilities, they will also shake off some of their ancient immunities, and their doings will come to be regarded with a sobering and more critical scrutiny than now prevails.

* *

The extension of the suffrage, I believe, will encourage this awakening. In wresting it from the sentimental and reluctant male the women of the land are sowing dragons' teeth, the which will presently leap up and gnaw them. Once women have the political power to obtain their just rights, they will begin to lose their old power to obtain special privileges by emotional appeals. Men, facing them squarely at last, will consider them anew, not as romantic political and social invalids, to be coddled and caressed, but as free competitors in a harsh and abominable world.

When that reconsideration gets under way there will be a general overhauling of the relations between the sexes and a good many of the fair ones, I venture, will begin to wonder why they didn't let well enough alone.

(The New York Evening Mail, May 2, 1918)

The Dark American

Negro Spokesman Arises
to Voice His Race's Wrongs

Unless I err gravely (in which case I recant and apologize), the
ablest document the war has yet produced in the United States is
the composition of a colored man, Prof. Kelly Miller, A.M., dean
of the college of arts and sciences in Howard University, the
Ethiop Sorbonne at Washington.

It is in the form of an open letter to the President of the republic and it bears the date of August 4, but so far as I can make out its
text was not made public at that time. Now, however, the learned
senior Senator from Washington, the Hon. Wesley Livsey Jones,
A.B., has spread it in extenso upon the instructive papyrus of the
Congressional Record, and there, on pages 7631–34 of the issue of September 12, you will find it.

The epistle of the dark dean is, in form, a solemn protest against
the late pogrom at East St. Louis and a demand that the Federal
government take measures to prevent such astounding massacres
in future. In this protest and demand, of course, there is nothing
new, and nothing remarkable; all the Moorish synods, pleasure
clubs, sodalities and orders of Elks, Odd Fellows and Galilean
Fishermen have been inundating Congress and the White House
with similar papers.

But in two important respects Dr. Miller's confection transcends the ordinary.

On the one hand it is written in a style so suave, so persuasive and withal so graceful and colorful that, even forgetting its content, it is a quite unusual work of art in words.

On the other hand it passes beyond a mere prayer for abatement and relief, and proceeds to the formulation of a definite political theory for the American negro—a theory that, for the first time in the history of the race, shows both a penetrating sense of what is wrong and an acute understanding of what may be done about it.

Dr. Miller wastes no time gabbling about Jim Crow cars, the laws against miscegenation and the rule forbidding negro hog-and-hominy parties at the Plaza Hotel. He does not argue that white society, such as it is, should throw open its doors to its negro cooks and chauffeurs. He looses no maudlin bawl about the exclusion of negroes from the Piping Rock Club, the University of Virginia, the Ancient Order of Hibernians and the B'nai B'rith.

His whole argument is confined to the field of political rights—rights specifically and unqualifiedly guaranteed by the organic law of the land.

He shows how those rights are invaded and made a mock of today, he demonstrates that the existing machinery is insufficient to restore them, and he gives dignified and respectful notice, but nevertheless plain and uncompromising notice, that, unless some better machinery is devised in a reasonable time, the negro will hold himself free to disregard the duties that go with them and are an integral part of them.

In brief, what he says is this:

We blacks are getting tired of this endless rowelling and persecution. We are getting tired of mobbing, lynchings, burnings at the stake. We are getting tired of having no representative in the government, and no means of obtaining common justice.

When we complain, we are put off. When we protest we are reviled. The states either cannot or will not help us. We therefore call upon the Federal government, and we ask for attention. Heretofore, we have got only words. Asking for justice, we have been "given a theory of government"; asking for protection, we have been "confronted with a scheme of governmental checks and balances."

It is now time to do something. You ask us to be patriots, to die for our country, to protect it against aggression. Well, first show us that it is our country. First protect us. First, prove to us that we will get the same return from patriotism that other patriots get.

This in crude outline. The sagacious professor is far more courtly than I have made him appear, and far more convincing. His letter runs to four or five newspaper columns, and I recommend it to your very careful reading.

It bears out, in a striking way, what I have been predicting in various favorite periodicals for a dozen years past: that sooner or later the American negroes would hatch a leader capable of putting their discontents into clear, simple and vivid words, and that the appearance of such a leader would give a new complexion to the race problem, and make it ten times more pressing than ever before.

The first part of the prognostication, it seems to me, is now fulfilled; the Miller manifesto is something quite new under the Afro-American sun. The second part, I venture, will be brought to term during the internal uproars and readjustments that are bound to follow the war.

Down in the South, where the race question is forever on the mat, the difficulties of dealing with it have been steadily mounting up for two decades past, and despite all the alleged thought that has been lavished upon it by corn-fed publicists the southerners are further from a solution than ever before. They wobble eternally between antagonistic theories.

First, they proceed upon the assumption that all their woes would cease if only they could get rid of the darky—and not infrequently they try to bring in that millennium with the shotgun and the torch. Then, when the alarmed raccoons jump freight-trains for the North, they find their fields unplowed and their windows unwashed, and yell for them to come back.

And so in details. First they decide to educate the negroes, and then they decide that education ruins them. First they are in favor of Booker Washington's schemes, and then they are against them.

First they try kindness then they try force. First they pretend that the thing is easy—that any child, if uncontaminated by Yankee blood, can understand it—, and then they throw up their hands.

The trouble down there, at the bottom, is very simple. That section of the American people which has the most difficult and vexatious of all problems on its hands, and not only on its hands, but directly under its nose, is precisely the section which is least accustomed to clear thought, and hence least capable of it.

The southerner, whatever his graces otherwise, is almost destitute of the faculty of sober reflection. He is a sentimentalist, a romanticist, a weeper and arm-waver, and as full of superstitions as the Zulu at his gates.

There are whole areas in the South—areas quite as large as most European kingdoms—in which not a single intelligent man is to be found.

The politics of the region is vapid and idiotic—a mere whooping of shibboleths. Its literature is that of the finishing school. Its philosophy is the half supernaturalism of the camp-meeting, the wind-music of the chautauqua. It has no more art than Liberia.

Add to this intellectual emptiness, a bellicose and amusing vanity, and you have a picture of incompetence that is almost tragic. The whole machinery of so-called southern chivalry, the invention of the feudal aristocracy of ante-bellum days, now almost wholly extinct, has been taken over by the emancipated poor white trash, and the result is a wholesale preening and posturing that must needs make the judicious grieve.

The southerner who is chiefly heard from is apparently all toes; one can have no commerce with him without stepping on them. Thus he protests hysterically every time northern opinion is intruded into his consideration of his problems, and northern opinion, so often called to book, now prudently keeps out. The result is that he struggles on alone, and that he goes steadily from bad to worse.

He was in difficulties while the negro was yet a mere serf, legally freed but still tied to the soil. He is in ten times worse difficulties now that the negro has begun to find leaders, and is beginning to acquire property and self-respect, and is showing signs of demanding an accounting.

The economic progress of the colored brother, in fact, gives the whites of the black belt their worst disquiet. It was relatively easy to deal with the darky separated from starvation by no more than one week's meagre wages, but what of the darky who owns a farm, and has money in the bank, and is perhaps even one of its stockholders and directors?

Such blacks are no longer rare. In state after state of the South, the negro holdings of property are increasing faster than the white holdings, and the negroes are founding banks, merchandis-

ing companies, cotton gins, insurance companies, and even whole
towns.

With property goes self-respect, and with self-respect goes aspiration. That aspiration irritates and outrages the poor whites.
They view it as the Russian muzhik views the accumulations of
the village Jew. It is, at bottom, one of the chief causes of race
antagonism, and in the end, of race conflicts.

So the volcano keeps on smoking, and the more reflective Southerners, in the intervals of fustian, regard the occasional explosions
with uneasy eyes. Worse, the disturbance throws out far ripples.
As Prof. Miller wisely points out, the state of affairs south of the
Potomac makes for trouble north of the Potomac; the Atlanta massacre was the father of the East St. Louis massacre.

The thing, in brief, takes on larger and larger aspects; it becomes, in the true sense, a national problem, for the southerners
are quite unable to deal with it, and so long as their inability
continues, the northerners will have to bear a part of the burden.
Meanwhile, the negroes themselves begin to show signs of restlessness, and the Miller manifesto gives that restlessness definite
voice.

"Mr. President," it says, "negroes all over this nation are
aroused as they have never been before. It is not the wild hysterics
of the hour, but a determined purpose that this country shall be
made a safe place for American citizens to live and work and enjoy
the pursuits of happiness."

A fair plea—and behind it there is an extremely able argument
—perhaps the best argument that any southerner, white or black,
has contributed to American governmental theory in half a century. What will be the answer of the national government?

The Force bill was one answer—and it failed to answer. The
two houses of Congress now jockey with the East St. Louis matter
—a feeble scratching of the surface. One house, if I remember
rightly, has appointed an investigating committee that will bring
in a report heavy with meaningless words. The other house has
delicately put the dynamite behind the clock.

Perhaps it is a southerner, after all, who has seen farthest, and
none other than the redoubtable negrophobe, the Hon. James
Kimble Vardaman, of Mississippi. In the Senate, some time ago, he
raised a warning voice against drilling the blacks. Teach them
how to bring the Turk to account for butchering the Armenians,

and they may come home to inquire into the butchering of their own relatives.

This, of course, is an extreme view, and perhaps an alarmist view. But the Miller manifesto shows that we have already come to the stage where we must give thought to it—that the negro has at last acquired a spokesman who can think clearly, disengaging non-essentials from essentials, and who can put his conclusions into clear and forceful English.

Altogether, that manifesto is a document of the utmost significance. Lost amid issues which seem to be greater, it is getting much less attention than it deserves.

(The New York Evening Mail, September 19, 1917)

The Murray Case

I

Donald Gaines Murray, A.B., is a young colored man of Baltimore. He has been living here since childhood, and his family has been paying State and city taxes for thirty years. In the spring of 1934, after the usual four years of study, he was given his bachelor's degree by Amherst, one of the oldest and best of the smaller American colleges. On January 24 last, having a mind to consecrate his life to the fearsome mysteries of the law, he applied for admission to the Law School of the University of Maryland, a tax-supported institution. He was well qualified for entrance, academically speaking, and indeed much more than qualified, for he had four years in college behind him, whereas the school statutes require but two. But on the ground that he was of African descent, and on that ground alone, his application was peremptorily refused, and the $2 fee that he had sent in with it was returned.

On April 8, dissatisfied with this summary rejection, he filed a suit in the Baltimore City Court, praying most humbly for a mandamus requiring the regents of the University of Maryland to admit him. On April 18 a temporary order to that effect was signed by Stein, J., and the regents were commanded to come into court on May 6 to give an account of themselves. On that day, through their official legal adviser, Attorney-General Herbert R. O'Conor, LL.B., they filed their answer, and on May 21 the plaintiff's attorneys replied to it. On June 25, in the same court, O'Dunne, J., reaffirmed the Stein mandamus, and added an order requiring the regents to examine Mr. Murray's qualifications before September 25, the first day of the Law School year, and to admit him forthwith if he turned out to be eligible.

On August 2, the regents filed an appeal, and at the same time petitioned the Court of Appeals to hear it at a special session before the end of August, on the stated ground that if the hearing were postponed until the regular session in October, the plaintiff would be already enrolled in the Law School. This application the learned judges refused, and so there will be an Ethiop among the Aryans when the larval Blackstones assemble next Wednesday. Moreover, he is likely to remain there for a long while, for it will take some time for the Court of Appeals to hear and dispose of his case, and no matter what its decision may be there will be an appeal to the Supreme Court of the United States, either by him or by the regents.

II

So long as the matter remains *sub judice* it would be an indecorum, and an impertinence, of course, to venture upon any opinion about the constitutional issues that it involves. On all such issues, whatever they may be, the judgment of the Court of Appeals may be awaited with full confidence, for the present judges thereof are not only notable for their wisdom and learning, but also for their courage and impartiality. But there are also some social issues in the case, and inasmuch as they are already being discussed somewhat heatedly, at least in Afro-American circles, it may be proper to advert to them in a chaste and cautious manner.

The first has to do with the question whether the professors and students of the Law School really object to the presence of a colored student in their midst. If they do, then I can find no indication of it in the papers filed in the case. The regents of the university apparently object violently, and so does the registrar of their Baltimore schools, but the gentlemen actually in charge of the Law School are not so much as mentioned in the papers, and neither are the young men who sit under them. The only complainant produced by the regents, outside their own household, is a gentleman who has three daughters at College Park, thirty miles away, and he is a Washingtonian and apparently pays no taxes in Maryland.

Why, indeed, should the professors and students of the Law School object to the presence among them of a self-respecting and ambitious young Afro-American, well prepared for his studies by four years of hard work in a Class A college? Scholastically, he will stand above rather than below the average of his class, and as a matter of common sense and common justice it would not only be brutal but also absurd to turn him out. All the judges among the professors have been listening for years to the pleadings of colored attorneys, and all the practicing lawyers have met them in court and in conference. There has never been any hint that this contact has been revolting to either judges or lawyers, or that it has worked any ponderable damage to either the administration of justice or the dignity of the bar. Indeed, the salient despoilers of both, in late years, have not been black lawyers but white ones, and the Law School itself has been engaged in an heroic effort to raise the intellectual and moral level of its students, hitherto all white. Mr. Murray will need no such lifting up. He already stands on a level clearly higher than that which the Law School has set.

III

The regents of the university, in their official statement of their case, make much of the fact that it has always been the policy in Maryland to educate whites and blacks in separate schools. This is true so far as the public schools are concerned and even so far as the ordinary college courses are concerned. The separation has been resented by a small faction of colored people, but the majority of them do not object to it, and inasmuch as virtually all the whites of the State are in favor of it, it is not likely to be abandoned in the near future.

But the reasoning which supports it fails when one comes to the level of the professional schools, and especially when one comes to the Law School. The students in the Law School are not children, and hence are not likely to divide themselves into hostile camps over anything so superficial as the color of their skins. Nor are they hollow adolescents going through the ordinary college mill, and eager only to dance, neck, and hoodwink the poor gogues told off to struggle with them. They are, instead, grown men and women, and they are in school for the serious purpose of preparing for a learned and honorable profession. To think of them as crackers hugging idiotically their more fortuitous whiteness is to say at once that they are unfit to be admitted to the bar of any civilized State.

I am not arguing here for mixing the races in the public schools. As I have hinted, in the present state of public opinion in Maryland it would probably be most unwise, no matter what may be said for it in the abstract. The public schools are for immature children, and it would be foolish to expect them to rise above the prevailing *mores*. And behind those children are parents who, taking one with another, are of scarcely sounder judgment. But in the professional schools we are dealing not only with adults, but also with adults who are presumed, by definition, to be of more than ordinary intelligence, prudence, and decency. If that presumption is false, then there is no superior class at all in Maryland, and the State must be content to be ranked, intellectually, with Arkansas and Mississippi.

IV

The regents of the university deny that barring Mr. Murray from the Law School would do him any appreciable damage. They advise him, complacently, to go to Washington and enter Howard University, and even hint that, if he is lucky, he may get a grant in aid from the Commission on the Higher Education of Negroes, which was set up by the last Legislature with resources running to the lavish amount of $10,000. But it must be obvious that this answer is really no answer at all. The regents might just as well advise him to go to Addis Ababa or Timbuktu. He wants to get his training, not in Washington, but here in Baltimore, where the laws and procedure of Maryland are at the bottom of the teaching and where he plans to practice after he has completed his course, and the only question at issue is whether he can be denied that choice on the sole ground that he is black.

On all other grounds he is admittedly qualified to enter the Law School. He is of a proper age, he has been prepared in a first-rate college, there is no shadow of objection to him on moral grounds, and his people have been taxpayers since before his birth. The one and only allegation brought against him is that he is not white. And the obvious motive in raising that caveat is not to protect the

Law School, which does not complain, but to protect the huge tax-eater at College Park. What the regents really fear is that if the courts order Mr. Murray admitted to the Law School, other Negroes will apply for admission to the so-called College of Arts.

As for me, I believe that the courts may be trusted to differentiate between the two. The Law School is a first-rate professional school supported by the taxpayer, and there is no institution of its kind in the State for colored students. Either it must let them in, or they must leave the State. But the College of Arts is a fifth-rate pedagogical dump patronized largely by the children of Washingtonians, and it would be easy to bring the Princess Anne Academy, which is for colored students, up to equality with it. Thus the issue is clear. The only question before the house, disregarding purely legal considerations, is whether the Law School is to be abandoned to Ku-Kluxry in order to protect a so-called college that costs the taxpayers immense sums every year, benefits them little if at all, and is in general vastly less an institution of learning than an impudent political racket.

(The Baltimore Evening Sun, September 23, 1935)

Sound and Fury

I

What with their grandiose effort to stampede and paralyze Baltimore with threats of boycott, ruin and desolation, their even more grandiose effort to terrify the sinful *Sunpapers* into leaping to the mourners' bench and accepting lynching as a Christian sacrament, and their announced determination, come what may, to save the Republic and the True Faith from the hellish conspiracies of the Russian Bolsheviki, the Salisbury fee-faw-fums are giving a very gaudy show—so gaudy, indeed, that I marvel to see Baltimoreans so indifferent to it. It is quite as good as any of the similar shows that are set up from time to time in the deeper reaches of the Bible Belt, and it has the prime virtue of being all our own. But very few Baltimoreans seem to be aware that it is going on, and those few take no apparent interest in it.

The local papers of the lower Shore, for a week past, have been bursting with incandescent and highly instructive stuff. They have not only mirrored faithfully the emotions of a pious and patriotic people at an heroic moment; they have also printed a number of new facts about the sublime event of December 4. One item, which I take from the *Berlin-Ocean City News,* is that the ceremony was not performed in churchly silence, as the *Sunpaper's* correspondents reported, but to the tune of "kicking and screaming." Nor was this kicking and screaming, it appears, done by the lynchee, for he was in a strait-jacket and had his head tightly bound, but by the six Salisbury boosters who led the lynchers.

Another interesting item is that the rope was not flung over the fatal tree by "several men," as the lying *Sunpaper* reported, but by a gallant Salisbury "schoolboy"—no doubt a graduate of some seminary in ropecraft, chosen for his talent. A third item I lift from the celebrated *Marylander and Herald* of Princess Anne, a leader in the current movement to bust Baltimore by boycott:

> One member of the mob took his knife and cut off several toes from the Negro's feet and carried them away with him for souvenirs.

What has become of these souvenirs the *Marylander and Herald* does not say. No doubt they now adorn the parlor mantelpiece of some humble but public-spirited Salisbury home, between the engrossed seashell from Ocean City and the family Peruna bottle. I can only hope that they are not deposited eventually with the Maryland Historical Society, or sent to Archbishop James Cannon, Jr., the most eminent of all the living natives of Salisbury.

II

My remarks in this place on December 7, under the heading of "The Eastern Shore Kultur" seem to have upset the *Marylander and Herald,* for it devotes the better part of two columns of black type on its first page to a calm and well-reasoned refutation of them. The essence of this refutation is that, along with the Hon. Bernard Ades, LL.B., I am affiliated with "anarchist and Communist groups, composed for the most part of men and women from the lowest strata of the mongrel breeds of European gutters." To this the Cambridge *Daily Banner* adds the charge that I am a lyncher myself, for didn't I once propose to take William Jennings

Bryan "to the top of the Washington Monument in Washington, disembowel him, and hurl his remains into the Potomac"?

This proposal, unfortunately, I can't recall, but no doubt the editor of the *Daily Banner* has a better memory than I have. In any case, I am constrained to acknowledge it on the general ground that a theologian is capable of anything. The *Worcester Democrat*, of Pocomoke City, though it does not mention my ghastly designs on Dr. Bryan, joins the *Daily Banner* in denouncing me as a lyncher, and offers to bet that both Dr. Edmund Duffy, the *Sunpaper*'s wicked cartoonist, and I "are cussing the luck which prevented [us] from getting [our] hands on the rope that swung 'Mister' Williams to a tree." Going further, it ventures the view that both of us

could have danced with glee around the bonfire of human flesh; and could easily have imagined a barbecue was on hand; could have eaten the flesh of the carcass, and smacked [our] lips over the fine flavor of the gasoline.

This fancy, which I leave to the Freudians, warms up the Pocomoke brother, and he proceeds as follows:

Mencken's soul, if he has one, must have come from a hyena, a rattlesnake, or a skunk. There must have been present at his birth a flock of leathern-winged bats, a nest of rattlesnakes, a swarm of hornets, and a colony of toad frogs—all contributing to his special form of life. There must have been some such scene attending his later existence as portrayed by the immortal William where the witches concoct a charm made up of poisoned entrails, fillet of a fenny snake, eye of newt, toe of frog, wool of bat, tongue of dog, adder's fork, blind worm's sting, lizard's leg, scale of dragon. . . . and all cooled with baboon's blood. With all this, his body was smeared good and plenty, and behold! the creature in its present form!

III

I reprint these brief extracts from a diatribe that runs on to a column because they serve very well to show what effect the lynching spirit, if it is allowed to go unchecked, has upon the minds of simple people—even upon the more literate minority thereof. If a man who is apparently familiar with respectable literature can write so, what is one to look for in the common run of low-down politicians, prehensile town boomers, ignorant hedge preachers, and other such vermin? That a community so debauched is in a mood to restore the orderly processes of civilized government is certainly hard to believe. Inflamed to frenzy by the very men who ought to calm it, it is bound to proceed to other outrages, and unless the decenter people of the region regain the upper hand such outrages will undoubtedly follow.

These decenter people, I should add in fairness, have not been wholly silent. Even some of the newspapers of the Shore, though they are under cruel pressure from the reigning witch burners, have spoken out courageously against the Williams lynching. One such is the Salisbury *Advertiser*. Though it seeks to put the blame for the atrocity upon the Communists, it yet denounces plainly "an ugly blot upon the name and reputation of our peace-loving Christian community which it will take generations to live down, and [which] cannot ever be erased," and goes on to argue that, by now, even "those having part in the consummation of the deed" are probably ashamed of themselves.

The *Star* and the *News* of Elkton, in the upper part of the Shore, speak even more plainly, and especially the former, which does not mention the Communists, but condemns the lynching roundly as the "diabolical act" of a "depraved mob," and calls upon Governor Ritchie and the Wicomico county authorities "to bring the perpetrators of this unspeakable crime to justice, and by doing so give notice that such vicious outrages will not be tolerated in Maryland."

IV

The question before the house is thus quite simple. It is whether the Salisbury lynchers will be permitted to escape punishment for their crime, and so inspire a long series of like atrocities among similar town boomers, or whether the decent people of the lower Shore will band themselves together effectively and see that the guilty are brought to heel. Every schoolboy in Salisbury knows who was in the mob. The names of those who dragged the victim from the hospital, blind and helpless, are known, and so is the name of the hero who made off with the souvenir toes. The leaders are on public display at this moment, bathed in moron admiration.

The Salisbury *Advertiser* is probably right: some of the very men who ran with the pack on December 4 have by now found their "sympathy with such illegal procedure" oozing out of them. There were plenty of other Salisburians who were on the other side from the start. From some of them, in fact, I have received letters during the past week. What remains to be done is to organize this decent opinion against the scoundrels who disgraced the town, and to bring them to justice as quickly as possible lest civilized government be abandoned altogether on the lower Shore. This may take some time, but it can be done if a few resolute leaders step forward, giving notice to Ku Kluxry that they are not afraid. The chief lynchers are already very uneasy, and they have reason to be.

Meanwhile, their attempt to becloud the issue by ranting against Communists and depicting the *Sunpapers* as Red need deceive no one. There were open threats of lynching against Yuel Lee in Snow Hill before any Communist appeared on the Shore, and they were heard again at Cambridge when it was proposed so unwisely to try him there. The judges and district attorneys at Cambridge actually asked Governor Ritchie for troops so early as November 13. In brief, a lynching was brewing among the Shore Ku Kluxers, and everyone knew it. That Williams happened to be the victim instead of Lee was only an accident. The will to lynch was already there.

That the murder of Mr. Elliott was a brutal and revolting one no one denies. Nor does anyone blame his son for attempting, on discovering it, to dispose of his murderer. Any other son would have done the same thing. But it is one thing to yield thus to a sudden and natural passion, and quite another to plan and execute a deliberate and inexcusable crime. The sole question to be determined is whether the civilized people of Maryland will permit such crimes to be perpetrated with impunity. The Salisbury lynchers must make up their minds to the fact that that question is not going to be got rid of by puerile gabble about Communist plots and childish efforts to alarm their betters.

(The Baltimore Evening Sun, December 14, 1931)

The Lynching Psychosis

I

No one, I take it, was surprised when the Wicomico county grand jury reported to Bailey, J., that it could not find the lynchers of Matthews Williams. That result, in such cases, is always expected, and it is rare for anticipation to be disappointed. It must be said for the Salisbury jurymen that, whatever their private hesitations may have been, they showed a rather unusual public diligence. They invited the Attorney-General of the State to sit with them, they accepted the aid of detectives from Baltimore, and they summoned more than a hundred witnesses. Moreover, they let it be known that anyone else who could throw any light upon the business would be heard freely. But no one seems to have come forward, and none of the persons actually examined knew anything. The lynching, it appears, was a sort of transcendental event, taking place in secular space but only dimly visible to mortal eyes. A large crowd turned out to enjoy it, but no one could make out who was running it.

What all this proves is plain enough. It is that lynchings, despite their apparent violation of all the laws of physics, are not really miracles in a vacuum, but incidents in a long and overt series of phenomena, stretching both backward and forward in time. The impulse to perform them, in all probability, is present everywhere and at all times. It shows itself in Baltimore every time a hold-up man is taken in the act or prohibition agents raid a respectable and popular saloon. But in order that it may lead to actual murder there must be a preliminary collapse of the police power, an antecedent breakdown of the orderly process of justice. Once that breakdown occurs a lynching is imminent, and once it has taken place the recovery is usually long enough delayed to let the lynchers escape.

That is what happens from time to time all over the Bible Belt, and that is what happened at Salisbury. The makings of the lynching there were visible on the lower Shore for six weeks before Williams murdered Mr. Elliott; they were later described in detail by the Court of Appeals in its declaratory judgment in the Yuel Lee case. First, gangs of ruffians began to menace various prisoners, and the local police, too weak to protect them, had to flee with them to safety. Then the same or other ruffians threatened a lawyer in attendance upon the court, and the local judge failed to punish them for contempt. What followed was probably inevitable. The mob, sensing its power, awaited its chance. That chance came at Salisbury on December 4.

II

The time to stop all this, plainly enough, was at the start. If the first show of mob spirit had been met by vigorous resistance there would have been no lynching, and the Court of Appeals would have been spared the embarrassing need of describing a complete collapse of fair process in the Maryland Free State. But the local police on the lower Shore were either too feeble or too timorous to cope with the mob, and no one stepped forward to give them adequate reinforcement. All the natural leaders of the region—politicians, bankers, lawyers, clergymen, and so on—failed to function. Half a dozen of them might have organized a *posse comitatus* and put the ruffians to flight. But no one spoke up, and so the situation went on from bad to worse.

The tragedy of Salisbury does not lie in the fact that it houses a sufficiency of brutes to make a lynching. Just as many, no doubt, are to be found in any other Maryland country town, and in Baltimore there are countless more. The tragedy lies in the fact that, on its day of trial, Salisbury turned out to be quite without resolute and intelligent leaders. Not a single bigwig came forward in the emergency, though the whole town knew what was afoot. Any one of a score of such bigwigs might have halted the crime, if only by threatening to denounce its perpetrators, but none spoke. So Williams was duly hanged, burned and mutilated, and Salisbury made the first pages of the whole country.

That any considerable number of educated Salisburians regard the lynching with satisfaction is too much to believe. In the feverish week of charge and counter-charge that followed it some of them were misled into defending it, or at least into condoning it, but no doubt they now blush on remembering the fact. They must be well aware, on reflection, that the crime disgraced and defamed the town, and they must also be well aware that their own lack of public spirit, courage and initiative was a salient factor in making it possible. They cannot complain if the worst element in the whole lower Shore is now triumphant and defiant. They had their chance to strike for law and order, and they muffed it.

III

How to prevent such things in future? The problem is not easy. In all the rural sections of the United States it is hard to organize a sound and effective public opinion. The cities tend to draw off most of the more intelligent young men, and the relatively few who stick it out at home are submerged in the general stupidity. It is to the interest of all the local professional politicians, revivalist clergymen, town boosters and other such racketeers to keep that stupidity at a maximum of density, and they devote themselves to the business with great energy. No one speaks out boldly for sense and decorum. The civilized minority, contemplating the odds against it, commonly withdraws into cynicism.

There was a time in the history of America when a landed aristocracy set the tone of rural opinion, and supplied impeccable if not always intelligent men for the principal local offices, but that time is no more. Politics in the country is now mainly in the hands of professionals out of the lower orders, and they are worse, if anything, than the politicians of the cities. They maintain friendly relations, on the one hand, with the local Babbitts—mortgage sharks, labor sweaters, dubious promoters, and so on, including the kept clergy—and on the other hand they have their lieutenants in the rustic underworld of bootleggers. The combination is hard to beat. It controls practically all the local agencies of public information. It knows how to hold and use its power. It is financed out of the public till.

Can it ever be overthrown? Perhaps, but surely not easily. It is, in the typical American county, so firmly intrenched that only a revolution could dispose of it. But not everywhere. In many a rural region, especially in the older States and certainly in Maryland, there is still a minority of unquestionably civilized men and women. It is small, and at the moment it is usually resigned to impotence and despair, but there are still powerful potentialities in it. If it were organized it could make itself felt, and once it began to show some strength it would attract many unexpected supporters. After all, no rational man wants to live in a place where shabby politicians go unchallenged, and there is no outlet for an enlightened public opinion, and public order is at the mercy of the worst element. The trouble is that, as things stand, too many Americans have no other choice.

IV

The specific campaign against lynching drags on ineptly. The various laws that have been suggested to put it down do not promise much. I myself once suggested fining the offending county some large sum—say $50,000 or $100,000—and making the fine a first lien upon all the local property. But that, I conclude on reflection, would simply penalize innocent people. The county Babbitts, who are mainly responsible for the bad government which makes lynchings possible, would know how to escape their fair share, and the burden would fall upon the poor farmers.

In some of the Southern States an effort has been made to insure the conviction of lynchers by compulsory changes of *venue*, sometimes to adjoining counties and sometimes to distant ones. But there seems to be little in that plan either, for if the witnesses refuse to identify the lynchers at home there is not much chance that they will do so anywhere else. Nor is there much apparent utility in cashiering a sheriff who permits a lynching, for it is seldom possible to prove that he actually consented to it, and if he is removed the local politicians are sure to make just as dubious a fellow his successor.

The one really promising remedy lies in organizing decent local opinion. That decent local opinion, in most of the rural parts of the United States, is now silent and hence without influence. It is seldom voiced in the county newspapers, and encounters only an implacable opposition from the clergy. The local politicians are naturally hostile to it, and in their ranks are at least two-thirds of the county lawyers. What it needs is new leaders—leaders who want nothing, and have nothing to sell. I believe that wherever and whenever such a leader bobs up in rural America, whether North or South, East or West, he will meet with a very hearty response, and have a lot of fun. And if he is lucky he may also achieve some good.

(The Baltimore Evening Sun, March 28, 1932)

Mencken Calls Tennis Order
Silly, Nefarious

When, on July 11 last, a gang of so-called progressives, white and black, went to Druid Hill Park to stage an inter-racial tennis combat, and were collared and jugged by the cops, it became instantly impossible for anyone to discuss the matter in a newspaper, save, of course, to report impartially the proceedings in court.

The impediment lay in the rules of the Supreme Bench, and the aim of the rules is to prevent the trial of criminal cases by public outcry and fulmination. I am, and have always been, in favor of the aim. I was in favor of it, in fact, long before any of the judges now extant arose to the bench from the underworld of the bar, and I argued for it at great length in the columns of the *Sunpapers*. But four months is a long while for journalists to keep silent on an important public matter, and if I bust out now it is simply and solely because I believe that the purpose of the rule has been sufficiently achieved. The accused have had their day in court, and no public clamor, whether pro or con, has corrupted the judicial process. Seven, it appears, have been adjudged guilty of conspiring to assemble unlawfully and fifteen others have been turned loose.

To be sure, the condemned have petitioned the Supreme Bench, sitting *en banc*, for new trials, but it is not my understanding that the rule was designed to protect the reviewing lucubrations of the Supreme Bench. I simply can't imagine its members being swayed by newspaper chit-chat; as well think of them being swayed by the whispers of politicians. Moreover, I have no desire to sway them, but am prepared to accept their decision, whatever it is, with loud hosannahs, convinced in conscience that it is sound in both law and logic. As for the verdict of Judge Moser below, I accept it on the same terms precisely.

But there remains an underlying question, and it deserves to be considered seriously and without any reference whatever to the cases lately at bar. It is this: Has the Park Board any right in law to forbid white and black citizens, if they are so inclined, to join in harmless games together on public playgrounds? Again: Is such a prohibition, even supposing that it is lawful, supported by anything to be found in common sense and common decency?

I do not undertake to answer the first question, for I am too ignorant of law, but my answer to the second is a loud and unequivocal No. A free citizen in a free state, it seems to me, has an inalienable right to play with whomsoever he will, so long as he does not disturb the general peace. If any other citizen, offended by the spectacle, makes a pother, then that other citizen, and not the man exercising his inalienable right, should be put down by the police.

Certainly it is astounding to find so much of the spirit of the Georgia Cracker surviving in the Maryland Free State, and under official auspices. The public parks are supported by the taxpayer, including the colored taxpayer, for the health and pleasure of the whole people. Why should cops be sent into them to separate those people against their will into separate herds? Why should the law set up distinctions and discriminations which the persons directly affected themselves reject?

If the park tennis courts were free to all comers no white person would be compelled to take on a colored opponent if he didn't care to. There would be no such vexations and disingenuous pressure as is embodied, for example, in the Hon. Mr. Truman's Fair Employment Practices Act. No one would be invaded in his privacy. Any white player could say yes or no to a colored challenger, and any colored player could say yes or no to a white. But when both say yes, why on earth should anyone else object?

It is high time that all such relics of Ku Kluxry be wiped out in Maryland. The position of the colored people, since the political revolution of 1895, has been gradually improving in the State, and it has already reached a point surpassed by few other states. But there is still plenty of room for further advances, and it is irritating indeed to see one of them blocked by silly Dogberrys. The Park Board rule is irrational and nefarious. It should be got rid of forthwith.

Of equal, and maybe even worse, irrationality is the rule regarding golf-playing on the public links, whereby colored players can play on certain links only on certain days, and white players only on certain other days. It would be hard to imagine anything more ridiculous. Why should a man of one race, playing *in forma pauperis* at the taxpayers' expense, be permitted to exclude men of another race? Why should beggars be turned into such peculiarly obnoxious choosers?

I speak of playing *in forma pauperis* and that is precisely what I mean. Golf is an expensive game, and should be played only by persons who can afford it. It is as absurd for a poor man to deck himself in its togs and engage in its witless gyrations as it would be for him to array himself as a general in the army. If he can't afford it he should avoid it, as self-respecting people always avoid what they can't afford. The doctrine that the taxpayer should foot the bills which make a bogus prince of pelf of him is New Dealism at its worst.

I am really astonished that the public golf links attract any appreciable colored patronage. The colored people, despite the continued efforts of white frauds to make fools of them, generally keep their heads and retain their sense of humor. If there are any appreciable number of them who can actually afford golf, then they should buy some convenient cow-pasture and set up grounds of their own. And the whites who posture at the taxpayers' expense should do the same.

In answer to all the foregoing I expect confidently to hear the argument that the late mixed tennis matches were not on the level, but were arranged by Communists to make trouble. So far as I am aware this may be true but it seems to me to be irrelevant. What gave the Communists their chance was the existence of the Park Board's rule. If it had carried on its business with more sense they would have been baffled. The way to dispose of their chicaneries is not to fight them when they are right.

(The Baltimore Evening Sun, November 9, 1948)

On Babbitts

On Banks

I

In the House of Representatives last Monday the Hon. Brent Spence, LL.D., of Kentucky, a Democrat in faith, arose to smear the Hon. Alf M. Landon, LL.D., of Kansas, the Presidential nominee of the Republicans. The smearing took the familiar form of reading a speech made by Dr. Landon some years ago. It was loosed upon the State Bank Division of the American Bankers' Association at Chicago on September 6, 1933, during the first delirious days of the New Deal honeymoon. Dr. Spence was plainly of the opinion that unearthing it would make Dr. Landon look foolish. My own view, after a diligent perusal of it, is that it makes Dr. Spence himself look foolish. For seldom have these eyes encountered a document by an American politician in which there was a larger assay of common sense. If this is the sort of thing that the Democrats are going to denounce during the campaign, then most persons of any intelligence will be driven into Dr. Landon's arms.

The subject of the speech was the insurance of bank deposits, then before Congress as part of a banking bill introduced in the Senate by the Hon. Carter Glass, LL.D., of Virginia, Secretary of the Treasury under Woodrow Wilson. Dr. Glass had just refused to enter the Roosevelt Cabinet in the same capacity and in a little while he was to come to the fore as a severe critic of the New Deal, but in those miasmatic days he couldn't escape the prevailing vapors altogether, and one of his chance whiffs of them seems to have had possession of him when he wrote his bill. At all events, he put into it a provision that the honest operators of Federal Reserve banks should be taxed to protect depositors against the crooked ones, and that provision remains in the law to this day.

Dr. Landon's objections to it were very clearly stated. The insurance of bank deposits, he said, was nothing new: it had been tried in eight mid-Western States. Everywhere it had failed miserably. Its sole effect was to prosper wildcat banking. The depositor, assuming that all banks were safe, succumbed to the high-pressure salesmanship of the sharpers operating bad ones, and when the inevitable crash came the good banks not only had to make good his loss but also to face dangerous and perhaps even disastrous runs. In Kansas the guaranty fund went broke to the tune of $7,000,000, and in Iowa it blew up with a shortage of $17,000,000.

"When five sound banks," said the Hon. Mr. Landon, "must pay the loss of one rotten one, the drain on the five necessarily impairs their strength. One of them breaks under the strain and the remaining four are weakened by the added strain, and so on."

II

Such sensible talk, coming from a candidate for the Presidency, naturally amazes and upsets a Congressman, who expects all candidates for public office, whether high or low, to confine themselves to puerile rubbish of the sort that Dr. Roosevelt emitted in his Baltimore speech. Has the success of Federal deposit insurance refuted Dr. Landon? It has not. The Federal insurance scheme has worked up to now simply and solely because there have been very few bank failures. The next time we have a pestilence of them it will come to grief quickly enough, and if the good banks escape ruin along with the bad ones it will be only because the taxpayer foots the bill.

This Federal insurance scheme, as I recall it, insures only deposits of $5,000 or less. The idea behind it is one of the immemorial postulates of demagogy, to wit, that all persons who have any considerable amount of money got it by thievery, and deserve to be relieved of it by other thieves. The same notion was at the bottom of the Brain Trust's recent proposal to seize and dissipate the reserves of all American corporations of any size—a proposal so insane that even Dr. Raymond Moley, the original cortex of the Trust, was moved to denounce it violently in his weekly paper, *Today*.

The insurance of small deposits, even if the insurance is actually paid when it is needed, will certainly not suffice to prevent wildcat banking. Indeed, it will give very little real protection against such banking to even the small depositor. He may get his own deposit in cash, but if his boss goes broke he will be out of a job, and the money he has rescued will soon be gone. The objection to destroying corporation surpluses is pretty much the same. As a More Abundant Life mountebank describes them, they are nefarious accumulations of ill-gotten wealth, but actually they are insurance funds against lean years, and the principal beneficiaries are not the holders of a corporation's securities but its employes. If it had not been for such surpluses, some of the largest corporations in the United States would have had to suspend operations altogether five years ago, and not a few would have stopped forever.

III

What is to be done about crooked banks, nitwit banks, bad banks in general? The problem seems to be beyond the capacities of American legislators, for every solution that they have arrived at in the past has turned out, in the light of experience to be no solution at all. So far as I can make out, there is nothing in the present laws to prevent another Baltimore Trust Company being launched tomorrow. Indeed, if the current business recovery develops into a boom we'll have one almost inevitably, and all the innocents who were hornswoggled the last time, including especially the great public journals of this town, will be taken for another dizzy ride.

Even another Chesapeake Bank or Park Bank is quite possible. In theory, of course, the State Banking Department would head it off, but that same theory was generally entertained six years ago. The truth is that bank examinations, like physical examinations, are very far from infallible. The most careful insurance doctor sometimes misses something that kills the applicant in six weeks, and in the same way the most diligent bank examiner may be fooled. Moreover, his authority is limited, and he is seldom able to order that radical cleaning out which is the one effective cure for banks run by rogues or fools. Only too often he sees what is coming, and yet can't stop it.

In his voluminous final report on the Baltimore Trust Company's death and autopsy the Hon. Simon E. Sobeloff was lately indulging in some interesting speculations in this direction, but his conclusions were too cautious to be of much practical use. It may be that, like so many other problems of legislation, this one is essentially insoluble, at least by legislative means. The real remedy is not to put all bankers in the position of dangerous criminals on parole, but to prevent men who need such watching from entering the banking business. How is that to be done? I am surely not able to give you a ready answer.

IV

But it would probably help if the operation of banks were confined to men of a reasonable training in banking and their ownership to men of substantial financial responsibility. Under our present laws, any ambitious ass is free to set up a bank, and anyone else, however limited in resources, is free to buy stock in it. What this last comes to has been shown in the case of the Baltimore Trust, many of whose stockholders have got rid of their double liability by the simple process of showing Judge O'Dunne that they haven't the money to pay up. Why should such poor fish be engaged in banking? They lack the first requisite, which is sufficient means.

A bank's directors, under our present laws, are hardly more than false-faces. They have neither the time nor the skill to scrutinize the doings of their officers. Most of them, if the Baltimore Trust case may be taken as typical, are business men with no special knowledge of banking, and little apparent desire to acquire any. They seek the office, in some cases, because they want an inside track to the bank's strongbox, but in most cases what moves them is only vanity. It is an eminent and enviable thing, in the world they inhabit, to be a bank director (or, at all events, it was until recently), and so they succumb. When the sheriff appears at the door they are as honestly surprised and outraged as Dr. Kelly was when it turned out that some of the ladies he had saved from lives of shame were operating a fancy house at his expense.

I am no constructive critic, but a few suggestions occur to me.

One is that bank boards be made much smaller, and that only men who know something about banking and are of large means be admitted to them. Another is that no director, officer or stockholder be permitted to borrow money, whether directly or indirectly, from his own bank. A third is that, when a bank suspends payment, it would simplify matters to hang (or, in any case, to jail) all its officers and directors at once, whether its suspension be due to their roguery, to their stupidity, or only to their bad luck. That is their trade risk, and they should take it. The depositors demand a victim. They want what the Greeks called *katharsis*. The fact that they didn't get it in the Baltimore Trust case has filled this town with bitterness, and paved the way for the enactment of banking laws that will put heavy burdens on the good banks without curbing bad ones in the least.

(The Baltimore Evening Sun, June 22, 1936)

Hard Times

One of the things that will have to be learned in the United States, soon or late, is that men of business, and especially bankers, are usually very poor economists and even worse psychologists. When I was a boy they were bellowing against the eight-hour day just as loudly as they are now bellowing against communism. The general improvement in the condition of the American working-man, so plainly visible since the Civil War, was not effected by their initiative or even with their consent, but against their will. They take alarm far too easily, and they are too easily deceived by their own sophistries.

Certainly there is something radically wrong with a system which enables a Henry Ford to posture magnificently as one who pays lavish wages, and then, when a pinch comes, to lay off men by tens of thousands, and throw them on public charity. I do not allege that Ford is a conscious fraud; I simply argue that the scheme he stands for is a bad one, and could be improved. Perhaps improving it will not be easy, but surely it should be possible to the master-minds that Dr. Hoover and most newspapers admire; if not, then better men should be given a chance. For it is an absurdity to call a country civilized in which a decent and industrious man, laboriously mastering a trade which is valuable and necessary to the common weal, has no assurance that it will sustain him while he stands ready to practice it, or keep him out of the poorhouse when illness or age makes him idle.

At the moment, of course, there is no time to discuss these things at length. The pressing business is to relieve actual suffering, and there is every reason to believe that it will be attended to competently. There is enough money in the country to feed the whole population on terrapin and canvas-back duck: the immediate problem is simply that of getting enough away from those who have more than they need to succor those who have nothing. But once the emergency is over there should be a frank consideration of the fundamental question. The poverty of the unfit and slothful, I suppose, can never be cured. But certainly there should be some way to keep want from the doors of the fit and willing.

(The Baltimore Evening Sun, March 23, 1931)

On Babbitts

I

In Chicago, during the Leopold Loeb trial, the highly respectable word *moron* began to take on an evil and even revolting significance. Applied to the two murderers by careless newspaper reporters and passed by copyreaders professionally ignorant of English, it came to mean what used to be called (with equal imbecility) a *degenerate, i.e.,* one given to the practice of exotic and abominable vices. Today, no Chicagoan dares to use it in its proper sense. If he speaks, however affectionately, of his stenographer, his pastor or his brother-in-law as a moron, he gets only a beating for his pains, with a suit for damages following. Even the professors at the University of Chicago have had to abandon the word. Once they were full of learned gabble about the morons in their care. Now they have to use various clumsy euphemisms, *e.g.,* pre-Kluxers, Cro-Americans, osseocaputs, pithecanthropi and delayed adolescents.

In much the same way the word *Babbit* has been mauled and ruined by ignorant journalists. One sees and hears it applied indiscriminately to all varieties of business men, from bank presidents in their lascivious marble and onyx boudoirs to humble gas adulterators in their lonely filling-stations. It seems to be generally assumed that any man who engages in traffic for gain is a Babbitt —that the mark of the species is simply commercial assiduity. Nothing could be more absurd—as anyone may readily discover by reading Sinclair Lewis' novel. Is the George F. Babbitt of that book Any Business Man? Certainly not. He is a business man of a special and narrow type. His marks are as plain as day, and two in number. The first is that he is not very successful—that his business, as such things go, is petty and piddling—that he is anything but a leader in his line. The second is that he is full of highfalutin fraud and bombast—that he talks like a millionaire and a chautauqua orator rolled into one—that he tries to make the world believe, and even to convince himself, that his trivial and sordid money-grubbing is all altruistic—in brief, that he is not a business man at all, but a philanthropist yearning and sweating for Service.

II

Obviously, the average business man, and especially the average successful business man, is no such person. I have known many of the tribe in my time, some of them very intimately, but I can't recall a single one who wasted any breath cackling about Service, or who made any pretense, in any other way, that he was in business for any purpose save to make profits. I see nothing discreditable in that motive. It is honest, it is honorable and it is sound. There is no nonsense about it. But has it, of late, gone under a cloud? Then blame the Babbitts who shrink from confessing it frankly, and try to pretend that they are in business for purely philanthropic and even messianic purposes. Blame the windjammers who go about the country arguing that Christ was the first Rotarian, and Washington and Lincoln charter members, *post mortem*, of Kiwanis.

It seems to me that these mountebanks have done a great deal of damage to business as a profession—first by convincing the generality of outsiders that it has come to be run in America like a revival or a land boom, and secondly by filling many business men with a feeling that there is something disgraceful about carrying it on in a straight-forward and unsentimental manner, with the idea of making profits out of it. The natural inference from the current blather is that the only decent business men are those who spend all their time slobbering over one another and playing Santa Claus to everyone else. The man who devotes himself wholly to his job becomes a sort of slacker, and is afraid to admit it.

All this, I think, is nonsense, and, what is more, very evil nonsense. The best business man is not the one who roves the world searching for opportunities for Service. He is not the one who wastes his time listening to idiotic speeches. He is not the one who bellows for Idealism. He is, instead, the one who devotes himself strictly and wholeheartedly to his business, who likes it and gets fun out of it, and who masters every least detail of it. He is the one who believes that the only sort of Service worth a hoot is to sell honest goods at a fair price. This man gets and holds customers, and makes money. You never hear of him making speeches on Idealism. But neither do you ever hear of him failing at 8 cents on the dollar.

III

Such business men, I believe, are far more numerous than the yawping, uplifting, bugaboo-chasing, Chamber of Commerce variety. They constitute the majority in every line, including even real estate. They are the men actually responsible for the great progress that business has made in this country, not only in profits, but also in dignity and integrity. They are the concealed leaders, but nevertheless the real leaders, not the Dr. Frank Cranes and Billy Sundays who are in the newspapers everyday.

Certainly it must have occurred to everyone who gives heed to such things that the rhetoricians who profess to speak for business men, and fill the air with wind music about Service and Idealism, are not themselves business men of any genuine eminence. Take a look around Baltimore. Put down the names of the presidents or cashiers of the six largest banks, or the names of the men who run the six largest manufacturing plants. How many of them ever take to the stump to blubber for Service? How many of them are ever heard of on the subject of American Ideals? How many respond to the Hon. Aristides Sophocles Goldsborough's order to rise upon their hind legs and enthuse?

Not many, you may be sure. Probably none. Such men are too

busy doing their work to become evangelists; they leave the exhorting and the psalm-singing to the lesser fry. The danger is that these lesser fry will be mistaken for actual leaders—that fair men, standing on the sidelines, will conclude that *all* business men are jackasses. The reality of that danger is shown by the extension of the meaning of the word Babbitt, already mentioned. The Babbitts make so much noise that the impression has gone about that they are genuinely representative—that what they say is what all other business men think. This is a grave error. The worst Babbitts, in fact, are not business men at all, but simply professional elocutionists. They no more speak for business than Lydia Pinkham, in her day, spoke for medicine.

IV

I have spoken of the desire for profit as the fundamental motive of the actual business man. I believe that it is, and I believe that the fact is fortunate for all of us. In the long run the only way to get a profit is to offer sound goods at fair prices. If the goods are bad customers will not come back; if the prices are too high they will not come back. When a man has a good business, making money year in and year out, it simply means that his customers have learned to trust him—that he is offering something that people want, and at prices they can comfortably pay. This is service with a small *s*, but it is real; whereas the kind with the capital *S* is a fake.

But there is something more. A man in business is not a mere machine for making money. The same vanities that are in all of us are in him; he likes to do his job a bit better than the next fellow; he likes to be admired, and maybe envied. In other words, he has pride of workmanship. It pleases him to hear people say that what he sells is good, and to see them part with their money willingly and come back for more. The profits, true enough, caress him, but so do the friendly feelings and the general respect. Good will is not only an asset on his books; it is also something that tickles his midriff.

This pride of workmanship is in all men above the rank of earthworms. It is, beyond even the desire for gain, the thing that makes men labor in the heat of the day. No other incentive to industry offers so powerful a stimulus, or brings such satisfying rewards. The man who has done a good job, and knows it, is a man who comes as near to happiness as anyone ever gets on this lugubrious ball. A cataract of molasses runs down his back; his nostrils are enchanted by the sniff of genuine pre-Prohibition stuff; a sweet singing, as of angels well grounded in solfeggio, is in his ears.

Such a man doesn't want to listen to maudlin harangues by itinerant chautauquans, designed by God to be chiropractors. He doesn't want to be belabored by hired back-scratchers and eye-rollers. It is not necessary to teach him how to enthuse. He leaves all such things to men who are incompetent, and know it in their secret hearts, and try to get rid of the knowledge by making noises. That is, he leaves it to Babbitts.

(The Baltimore Evening Sun, December 21, 1925)

Empty Pessimism

The business man of today is a stranger to his wife. He hardly knows his own children. Our fathers had time for church, religion and books. The man of today falls into bed at night worn out by the day's struggle.

This from a sermon preached in Baltimore lately. Such sophomoric pessimism, if it were rare, might be dismissed lightly, as a folly too trivial to be combatted seriously, but, unluckily enough, it is howled from the housetops by thousands of eager sophists, and a great many unreflective folk have begun to accept it as sound philosophy. No fallacy, indeed, is in better credit at the moment than the fallacy that human life is growing more fatiguing every year. Upon it depends all of the latter-day nonsense about neurasthenia, hysteria, nervous prostration and other such terrible diseases. It is assumed, as a matter of course, that civilization is reducing the human race to a frazzle, and there are even persons who advocate a frank return to barbarism as the only means of preventing the extinction of the genus homo.

But what are the facts? Is it a fact that the average man of today works harder than the average man of, say, three or four centuries ago? Is it a fact that his mode of living makes him more vulnerable to disease? Is it a fact that his mind is tortured by cares and anxieties unknown to his forbears? Is it a fact that he is "a stranger to his wife," that he "hardly knows his own children," that he "falls into bed at night worn out by the day's struggle"? Is it a fact, in brief, that he is more harassed, gets less out of life and dies earlier and more horribly, than the man of the fifteenth century or of the eighteenth century, or of 1875? I think not. It seems to me, on the contrary, that if there is anything certain in history it is the fact that the average man of today finds life a far more agreeable adventure than the average man of any other age. He works less and he has more pleasure. He lives longer, and he is happier and cleaner and more of a man while he lives.

The picture of the modern business man drawn by the shallow pessimists of the moment is a picture no more accurate than Cicero's portrait of himself. It shows that business man as a stoop-shouldered, putty-faced slave, bending from 7 o'clock in the morning until midnight over a book of unpayable debts, his eyes fishy, his hands trembling, his bald head spattered with drops of freezing sweat. He is constantly on the verge of bankruptcy; the heel of some trust is always on his neck; he can never wrest enough money from the world to meet the exactions of his extravagant wife, his heartless daughter, his dissolute son. He suffers incessantly from a host of loathsome diseases—neurasthenia, eczema, dandruff, chilblains, paranoia, malnutrition, adenoids, sciatica, smoker's throat, alcoholism and dyspepsia. He dies miserably at the age of 16 or 17, having crowded the labor and waste of a decade into every year.

So much for the ideal business man of the jeremiads and patent medicine circulars. What about the real one? A very different fellow! Go seek him out in the wholesale district. You will find him paunchy, clear-skinned and well-barbered. He arrives at his office at 8.30 or 9 o'clock. At 1 o'clock he saunters out and engulfs a square meal. At 4.30 o'clock he falls asleep in his chair. At 5 o'clock the head bookkeeper awakens him and he goes home. His profits for the day have been $42.65. He has worked four hours. His "extravagant" wife, in the evening, spends two hours getting $6 out of him to buy a hat for their daughter. He is sound asleep at 10.30 o'clock.

Seriously, does any one really believe that the modern business man is overharassed and overworked? He has worries, true enough, but who hasn't? Did his predecessor of 50 or 100 or 500 years ago escape them? I think not. The merchant of the Middle

Ages had to face not only the ordinary hazards of trade but also the hazards of piracy, of robbery on land, of confiscation, of ecclesiastical anathema. Even down to a century ago piracy and confiscation were very real dangers. A man put his all into a single venture by sea, and for two, three or four years heard nothing of his ships. Did that sort of trading conduce to untroubled repose?

Today the merchant is beset by no such troubles. The whole power of civilization is concentrated upon the task of protecting him, of safeguarding his property, of relieving his agonies of doubt and dread. Communications are quick, banks are sound, pirates have vanished, kings no longer raise money with the rack and wheel, elaborate and efficient laws protect a trader, not only in his legitimate enterprise but also in his chicaneries. A man engaged in commercial ventures may go to sleep at night with sure knowledge that, short of what insurance policies call acts of God, nothing can harm him save his own inefficiency.

But the working man—hasn't civilization ground him to a pulp? If the reduction of his working hours by 50 per cent, and the increase of his reward in beef and beer by 1,000 per cent—if this is grinding, then he has been ground. But his wife? Well, what of her? Co-operative industry has relieved her of two-thirds of the tasks which made her great-grandmother old at 40. But neurasthenia increases? Nonsense! Neurasthenia is one of the rarest of diseases—save in the Emmanuel movement books. All nervous disorders, great and little, are far less prevalent today than they ever were before. Hysteria, once an almost universal plague, is now rare. All save a few maladies are decreasing rapidly. The death rate is falling every year. The average man of today lives fully five years longer than the average man of but two generations ago.

But men have ceased to read, to meditate, to live the larger life. Balderdash! The common man of the eighteenth century didn't read Homer and Milton. Instead, he read the newsletters on weekdays and Baxter's *Saint's Rest* on Sunday. Today the common man reads the newspapers and magazines—a distinct step forward. The sporting page of the worst yellow journal in the land offers far more healthful reading than the immortal *Saint's Rest*. Prizefighters, whatever their faults, at least inculcate an honorable self-reliance, a faith in man, a cleanly optimism. But the thing that Baxter taught was a pessimism so abject, so preposterous and so degrading that it is impossible for a man of today to read him without disgust. His philosophy, in brief, is abhorrent to the instincts of every man who respects himself and the race to which he belongs, just as other shallow booming, vapid and maudlin pessimism, whatever its authority, must be.

(The Baltimore Evening Sun, October 27, 1910)

The Choice of a Career

An estimable customer writes to me from a town of the middle west, saying that he is a medical man in modest but comfortable practice, with four sons, and asking me, as an elderly and notoriously judicious fellow, what I think he ought to do with them. My answer, already in his hands, is that I think he ought to train them all for business. And my reasons are the same that would have prompted me to advise a Prussian Junker, in the old days, to put his sons into the army, or a Münchener, in this our own day, to make brewers of them. For business is the national art of the American people, and not only the national art but also the national delight and passion. No man among us gets more of the benefits which flow out of being an American than the successful business man. No man is more lavishly admired and willingly honored. No man is more safe, satisfied, and comfortable.

There are bilious souls who protest against all this and argue that it is somehow discreditable to the nation. For my present purpose I am not interested in that contention, which may be either sound or false. What I point to is simply a plain fact. In every American community, whether it be large and complex or small and primitive, at least eight of the ten principal citizens are business men, and in many communities, and indeed in whole states, the ratio runs ten to ten. There is no eminence in any of the professions comparable to the eminence of such vastly successful business men as Henry Ford, John D. Rockefeller, and the late Judge Elbert H. Gary. Judge Gary did not honor business, in the American view, by entering it from the bench; he honored the bench by making it an avenue into business.

I do not forget here, of course, such transient heroes as Lindbergh, Babe Ruth, Jack Dempsey and the movie stars. But their fame, it must be manifest, is almost as evanescent as that of poor Judd Gray. One day they are applauded furiously, and the next day they are completely forgotten. But once an American becomes an Andy Mellon or a Charlie Schwab he is secure in his celebrity as long as he lasts, and even after he is dead he is remembered. For a successful business man, in such a country as this one, gets beyond being a mere man; he becomes a public institution, and even a public monument. For a century after his death old John D. will be venerated. But who will remember the leader of the American bar of his time, or the greatest American doctor?

* *

This respect for wealth and the power that goes with it is common, of course, throughout the world, but I know of no other country in which it runs to such lengths as in the United States. In other lands there is also a great deal of public respect for other kinds of achievement, and it often exceeds that which goes to the mere amassing of money. But here we have no heroes, not even of the military or political varieties, who stand above the Fords and Rockefellers. There was a time when we had them, but it is no more. In other fields the most august man, compared to a Judge Gary or a J. Pierpont Morgan, is as a wart to Ossa.

There are proofs of it almost every day. Not long ago a very great biologist died among us—perhaps the greatest who had ever breathed American air. His achievements were revolutionary in character, and he was the recipient of many honors. But practically all of these honors came from abroad. At home he was scarcely a name. When he was discussed at all, it was only idiotically and in the chromatic Sunday supplements of yellow journals. The United States, as a nation, took no notice of him. When he died the fact went unnoted officially. The President of the United States had no regrets. I allude to Jacques Loeb—and perhaps I had better explain that he was attached to the Rockefeller institute, and was not the Loeb of Leopold and Loeb.

The passing of Judge Gary was no such *pianissimo* affair. News of it was flashed around the country with the thrilling speed of tips from Tijuana. All the newspapers of the nation broke out into long memoirs of him, and flattering eulogies. The editorial writers performed upon his clay in high, astounding terms. Arthur Brisbane, the chief of their clan, compared him to Aristotle. A thousand clergymen preached upon his career. Legislatures passed encomiastic resolutions. And the President of the United States was moved to assure the relict of the late lamented, by telegraph and at great length, of his complete and inconsolable grief.

But what had Judge Gary done? He had simply amassed money for himself and for others. There was no sign throughout his long life that he had any other talent. He never said anything new or startling, even about the steel business. All the larger problems that beset it in his time were solved by other men, and mainly in the face of his protests. He was, judging him by any fair standard, as hollow as a jug. But he was an immensely successful business man, and so his death became an official calamity, and the President, speaking for the nation, mourned copiously.

* *

As I say, I do not attempt to determine whether all this is to be lamented or viewed with joy. All that concerns me is the plain fact. It is a fact with many facets. The attitude of the nation toward Gary is the attitude of every American community toward its rich traders and manipulators. They are its recognized leading men, and they get whatever they want. Desiring a high tariff, they get a high tariff. Convinced [erroneously, it now appears] that prohibition would profit them, they got prohibition. Eager for the United States to enter the late war, they readily put it in.

Obviously, such powers are worth having. They give a man a sense of security. They make him think well of himself, and with sound reason. And the satisfactions that they give rise to are durable, for money commonly lasts longer than men. A great poet or bacteriologist or composer or general seldom leaves his son anything save an inconvenient if honorable name, but an eminent man of business can transmit much of his power and even a good deal of his honor. John D. Rockefeller, Jr., without his father, would probably be an obscure bookkeeper or garage keeper, but with his father he is a magnifico, and when he dies the then President will lament it officially, and there will be a lot of writing about him by men who sincerely admire him and envy him today.

I thus advise not only my middle western customer, but also all other American fathers of laudable ambition to breed their sons to business. It is, I daresay, as amusing a trade as any other, and its rewards make those of all others look silly. Here I do not set up any valuation of my own; I accept the current American valuation. After all, we are living in the United States, and cannot escape its fundamental ideas. One of those fundamental ideas is to the effect that a Judge Gary is a better man than a Jacques Loeb. It may be true or it may be false; the only important thing is that nine Americans out of ten believe it, and that their belief is turned into very valuable realities by the Judge Garys. I assume that every normal father wants to see his son safe, honored and happy. Well, the best way to make sure of it is to put him into business. He may long sentimentally, in the after years, for the life of an artist, but he will never long for it as steadily and as painfully as the average American artist longs for money.

For the national prejudices affect even those who profess to reject them. I know many artists of various sorts, and not a few of them affect a vast scorn of money, and of those who have it. They allege that they have renounced it willingly and gladly. But the more willingly and gladly they allege that they have renounced it, the more violently, I note, they appear to yearn for it. They, too, are Americans. They can no more escape it than a dog can escape having fleas.

(The Chicago Sunday Tribune, January 29, 1928)

National Conventions

1904

After becoming President upon McKinley's assassination in 1901, Theodore Roosevelt was frequently frustrated by condescending references to his "Accidency." Nevertheless, he became widely loved and acclaimed as no other President before him. His battles against "the malefactors of great wealth" and his stand on foreign matters (he took as his motto the old African proverb, "Speak softly and carry a big stick") all had popular appeal. An intellectual who had written over fourteen books, he was, admitted Mencken, one of the most literary Presidents the United States ever had in office. Moreover, his enthusiasm was contagious. "Life fascinated him," Mencken observed, "and he knew how to make his doings fascinating to others." However popular, Roosevelt bemoaned the fact that he had not been elected to office, saying, "I'd rather be elected to that office than have anything tangible of which I know."

The Republicans convened in Chicago on June 23; presiding over the convention was "Uncle Joe" Cannon, the permanent chairman. All 994 delegates voted unanimously for Roosevelt on the first ballot, and added Charles W. Fairbanks, a wealthy conservative from Indiana, to the ticket for vice presidency.

The Democrats were confounded, as they had no one who could match

Roosevelt. William Jennings Bryan, the former Nebraska congressman who had roused enthusiasm with his "Cross of Gold" speech at the convention of 1896, was in slow decline after his defeats in the elections of 1896 and 1900. The eastern wing of the party (the "Safe-and-Saners") was now in control, and the delegates turned to Alton B. Parker, chief justice of the New York Court of Appeals, in the hope that his stand on issues would be more appealing to conservative businessmen. When informed of his selection, Parker wired that he was a firm adherent of the gold standard, and if any delegates were to disagree, he would decline the nomination. Opposing Parker, William Jennings Bryan asked for a renewal of the party's former free-silver declaration and demanded that an income tax resolution be included in the platform. He was voted down. William Randolph Hearst, the publisher, also opposed Parker, but could not gain enough support to offer any serious threat. Thus Parker, nicknamed "the Enigma from New York," became the Democratic candidate. Eighty-one-year-old Henry G. Davis from West Virginia was chosen as his Vice President. The millionaire Davis had a singular asset—deep pockets—and he was expected to reach into them to finance the campaign; he did not.

Roosevelt relished having the virtually unknown Parker as his opponent. On November 8, he won in a landslide that astonished even him, taking every northern state plus Davis's own West Virginia. It was the most decisive victory since Jackson beat Clay in 1832. "I am no longer a political accident!" Roosevelt crowed happily. In his exuberance he made the rash announcement: "On the fourth of March next I shall have served three and a half years and this . . . constitutes my first term. The wise custom which limits the President to two terms regards the substance and not the form, and under no circumstances will I be a candidate for or accept another nomination." He would regret this statement when he broke away from his party and ran as a Progressive candidate in 1912—and lost to the Democratic Party leader, Woodrow Wilson.

The two selections which follow are Mencken's weakest reports from a convention; however, they are his first, written when he was twenty-four years old, when his style had not yet developed its confidence and vibrancy. (Its ease and mastery would not be reflected until 1920.) But the exuberance and attention to human detail are still there, albeit in larval form. Mencken caught the poignancy of Bryan's demise, and so it is little wonder that it is the stronger of the two. They have been included to show the range and development of Mencken's convention reporting, which began with the nomination of Theodore Roosevelt in 1904, and, save with a few breaks, spanned forty-four years, finishing with the election of Truman in 1948.

Theodore Roosevelt Named for President; Charles W. Fairbanks for Vice-President

Chicago, Ill., June 23.—With perspiration standing out in beads upon its forehead and its collar wilted and its spirits depressed, the republican party, by its representatives in convention assembled, today nominated Theodore Roosevelt, of New York, to succeed himself as President of these United States and of the territories thereof, and sovereign lord of the dominions beyond the seas. At the same place and a few minutes later it named Charles W. Fairbanks, of Indiana, for the second place on the ticket that will go before the American people in November. Then it mopped its brow, heaved a sigh of genuine relief, and as the band played "Auld Lang Syne" started for home. . . .

It was twenty degrees warmer than yesterday when the delegates assembled this morning, and before the convention was called to order everyone was fuming and puffing painfully. High up, along the roof of the gigantic Coliseum, but one ventilator in three was open, and along the walls nearly every window was closed. Why this was the case did not appear, and neither did it appear why more air was not admitted two hours later, when the air in the vast barn grew stifling, and hundreds of spectators fought their way out to avoid being overcome by the heat.

A call had been issued for 10 o'clock, but it was half an hour later before Chairman Cannon called for order. Just as he stepped forward a woman appeared upon the platform and handed him a bunch of lilies.

Then a chaplain read an interminable and unintelligible prayer from manuscript and there was pottering about on the platform and delay while senators whimpered to the chairman and deputy assistant sergeants-at-arms climbed over the rail with messages and escorted late comers of prominence to the forefront of the impending fray.

Finally the perspiring delegates demanded more expedition, and after that in response to their noisy calls, things were rushed along at better speed. At one o'clock exactly, the chairman announced that nominations for President of the United States were in order and the clerk began calling the roll of states.

Alabama, the first on the roll, responded by waving her claims, as her spokesman said, to "the Empire State of New York," then former Governor Black arose from his seat behind Senator Chauncey M. Depew, and unlimbering his long legs crawled through the crowd to the platform.

He is a man of almost freakish height and of well nigh unbelievable ungainliness, and as he lumbered out to the end of the jutting speakers' stand, and threw back his long-tailed black cutaway he looked exactly like the affable undertaker immortalized in *Huckleberry Finn.*

"Mr. Chairman and Gentlemen of the Convention," he shouted —and the big show was on.

Yesterday "Uncle Joe" Cannon battered the democrats with ridicule of a sort not too finely pointed. Some of his jokes might have fitly graced a musical comedy and some of his terrific gestures might have made the reputation of a team of refined acrobatic comedians. Today Governor Black followed him in ridiculing the democrats' faith and men sharpened his barbs more carefully.

"Uncle Joe's" weapon was the meat cleaver of burlesque. Governor Black's was the keen-edged, razor-tipped arrow of satire and sarcasm. He gripped a handkerchief in his right hand and held it behind him all the while he was on the platform, and his gestures with his other hand were few and awkward. So, too, he indulged in no vocal eccentricities or pyrotechnics, and his speech might just as well have been read. But his telling points went home and aroused tremendous enthusiasm, and the hearty laughs that began amid the mutton-chops of Senator Depew echoed and reechoed throughout the hall.

"The democratic party," said Mr. Black, "is like a regiment so much at odds with itself that its soldiers have to sneak out and butcher their comrades in the next tent before they may safely sally forth to tackle the enemy."

"Good!" yelled a hundred delegates and uproar like this followed uproar.

"The main business of the democracy," continued Mr. Black, "is to forget its past sins. It has no hope for the present and none for the future. When a great public question arises it spends weeks wondering what Thomas Jefferson or Andrew Jackson would have done about it if they were alive. Not so with Theodore Roosevelt. (Tremendous applause.) Everybody knows where and how he stands. (Cheers and yells of "Roosevelt!") Everybody knows what he thinks. (Laughter and cheers.) Thomas Jefferson is dead. (Roars of laughter.) Theodore Roosevelt is alive."

Directly before Mr. Black, in the section allotted to the New York delegation, sat a group of the Empire State's republican leaders—Senator Depew; Senator Platt, who once sought to slay Mr. Roosevelt by making him Vice-President; Governor Odell, Mr. Elihu Root and former Governor Timothy L. Woodruff, the immaculate.

Each time Mr. Black delivered one of his broadsides Senator Depew would slap the knee of Mr. Root and lean back that he might roar his mirth more comfortably.

The rest of the delegates and spectators took their cues from these New Yorkers, and when Mr. Black's speech ended with the name of the candidate there began, with a terrific whoop, the nineteen minutes of ear splitting din.

In a flash the Indiana delegates opened gaudily striped umbrellas bearing portraits of Mr. Roosevelt and Senator Fairbanks, and from every row of seats popped up flags and banners.

In the gallery, opposite the platform, sat Gen. Fred D. Grant, and beside him was a grizzled veteran waving a huge flag.

Someone rushed to the platform with another star-spangled banner that had been first flung to the breeze at the convention of 1860, which nominated Lincoln, and Chairman Cannon grabbed it and rushed down to the front of the speakers' stand with it.

Ten ushers came struggling out of a cellar door with a gigantic and evil looking crayon portrait of Mr. Roosevelt. It toppled over upon the Iowa delegation and one of the delegates, to save himself, reached up a dusty hand to ward it off. Thereafter the President wore a black smudge on his right cheek.

Far back in the hall the Californians arose with a huge banner and near them a woman alternate from one of the Western states took off her hat and hoisted it high above her on a marker pole.

A youth with a megaphone appeared on the platform and urged the crowd to do something, but no one could understand him and he was elbowed out of sight.

Half a dozen children—boys and girls—were lifted to the platform and set to work waving flags. One little chap, with long Fauntleroy curls, appeared seated on the head of one of the reading clerks. A little girl robbed him of the center of the stage by looming into view standing upright on the shoulders of a national committeeman.

The tumult rolled in waves. Now and then the din of the band, which had begun playing "The Star-Spangled Banner" as soon as Mr. Black finished, could be heard above the other uproar and once the delegates near the gallery tried to sing the anthem. But then there came a succession of yells that reminded one of the merry-making of college boys on the night following a big football game, and by and by the band ceased playing "Oh, say, can you?" and swung into the more appropriate measures of "There'll Be a Hot Time in the Old Town Tonight."

Then the Alaskans, with their stuffed eagles, began parading the aisles, and the Californians, with their bands, the Indianians, with their umbrellas, and hundreds of other delegates with flags, canes, markers and streamers dropped into line.

At this minute "Uncle Joe" stepped forward and motioned for silence. But his appearance merely started the uproar anew and for almost as long again it continued unabated. Then the picturesque old chairman forced his way to the front a second time and, being beyond the row of tables, painfully stooped and banged on the floor.

"We have here," he began half a dozen times, and after a while there was quiet long enough for him to point out the Lincoln convention flag or to have the reading clerk read a brief account of its history.

"Uncle Joe" raised the flagstaff, and assuming a statuesque pose, upheld the tattered old banner after the fashion of a color bearer hero in a war lithograph while the audience heard the story. As he turned to resume his seat a gust of wind blew the flag about his head and he was almost capsized.

. . . Harry S. Cummings, the colored lawyer of Baltimore, was the last of the half dozen spellbinders chosen to second the nomination of the President. He faced an audience made savage by the torture of a succession of disappointing speeches, but he had not been on the platform ten seconds before the air cleared and when he stepped down, a short while later, there was an outburst of applause that fairly shook the rafters. Certainly no other speaker made a more favorable impression or scored a greater personal success.

"I realize," he began, "that the best way I can make a hero of myself today is by making my speech short." And, following his own hint, he spoke briefly and to the point.

There was some fear among the Southern delegates that he might dive too deeply into the race question, but though he discussed it, after a fashion, his remarks were studious and careful, and every word he said was heard with respectful attention.

When he ended Postmaster General Henry C. Payne, "Uncle Joe" Cannon and a score of the other republican leaders on the platform congratulated him in a manner that left no doubt of their sincerity.

At 6.10 o'clock, after the crowd had perspired through rather more than two hours, less nineteen minutes, of oratory, the roll call of states began.

Alabama, at the head of the list, was the first to cast her vote. "We name that gallant soldier and brilliant statesman, Theodore Roosevelt, of New York," said her spokesman, "and give him all our votes."

Down the line then went the reading clerk, to Arkansas, to California, to Florida, to Georgia. The name of Arkansas she pronounced so that it rhymed with apple sass, and the spokesman of the state, in responding, gently corrected by calling the state Arkansas, with a mighty emphasis on the "saw."

Senator Beveridge cast Indiana's votes in a fashion that would have made the fortune of the tinsel hero of a ten, twenty and thirty cent melodrama, and "Gas" Addicks bobbed up to the say of little Delaware. Senator Cullom cast Illinois' solid block, and "Tom" Platt, who four years ago tried to give Mr. Roosevelt his final quietus, bared his neck to the yoke of the inevitable by announcing that New York stood by the Rough Rider to a man.

This last was really a dramatic incident, but Platt seemed so pitifully weak as he couched there in his chair that the regiment of original Roosevelt men present pitied him instead of gloating over him.

New Jersey moved that the call of the roll be suspended and that the nomination be made by acclamation, but this proposal was frowned down by delegations that wanted to embroider their voting with little speeches of exultation.

"We cast our eight votes for Theodore Roosevelt," said Rhode Island's spokesman, "and we wish we had a hundred." This pleased the crowd, as did the statement of the spokesman of Texas, that his state gave her solid vote "to her adopted son, the Rough Rider, who rode from the Alamo to San Juan hill."

When Virginia was called Congressman Campbell Slemp and another delegate bobbed up together and there was a good-natured laugh at their expense. Oklahoma—"the next star in the nation's bright galaxy," said her spokesman—Arizona, New Mexico and Alaska came in order and then at the end came Hawaii and Porto Rico.

"Porto Rico casts her first vote for Theodore Roosevelt, of New York," said the palm-clad island spokesman, and the balloting was over.

There followed a moment of purely formal reckoning, and then "Uncle Joe" slowly stalked forward.

"It is the sense of the republican party," he said, "that Theodore Roosevelt, of New York, be its candidate for President of the United States of America in the month of November in the year 1904."

The main business of the convention was over. The Rough Rider had been nominated without a dissenting voice.

"In the democratic party," one of the speakers had said earlier in the day, "the leaders select candidates for the people. In our party the people have selected a candidate for the leaders," and it seemed to be true. There was far more genuine enthusiasm among the rank and file in the back rows than among the reverend seigniors on the stage.

With the air becoming more and more suffocating every moment, the chief duty of the day's work done, the delegates, though some of them tried hard and managed to force themselves into a pseudo-enthusiastic state, manifested but little interest in the balloting for the vice presidential candidate.

The withdrawal of Congressman Hitt, of Cyrus Walbridge and of the other rivals of Senator Fairbanks had been discounted, and so when Senator Cullom arose to formally announce that Mr. Hitt was not a candidate and a Missouri delegate did the same gentle work for Mr. Walbridge, there was little cheering.

Senator Dolliver, of Iowa, who was once a vice-presidential possibility himself and came within an ace of taking Mr. Roosevelt's road to the White House, nominated Senator Fairbanks, and the seconding speeches, all of which were inexpressibly dull, were made by Senator Depew, who told one ancient story and no new ones; Senator Foraker, of Ohio, who mercifully made his oration brief, Governor Pennypacker, of Pennsylvania, who spoke in place of Senator Boies Penrose, and a former senator, Tom Carter, the favorite of Montana.

Senator DePew moved that the roll call be dispensed with, and the nomination was made by acclamation, with a tremendous whoop-ee-dee. Then half of the crowd rushed for the exits and the other half yelled "Fairbanks!" Those with flags and banners rushed toward the Indiana section, and not finding the candidate there assaulted the stage.

Meanwhile the uproar increased, and for a while it seemed likely that the nineteen minutes of loud noise that followed the nomination of Mr. Roosevelt would be repeated.

"Uncle Joe" saved the day. "Order!" he shouted, advancing toward the edge of the speakers' stand, and then, when the silence was restored, he told of the sly and bashful Indianian's escape.

"Senator Fairbanks," he said, "is not in the hall. He slipped out —and now let's have a motion to adjourn."

It was made and seconded and by 3 o'clock the Coliseum was empty.

(The Baltimore Morning and Sunday Herald, June 24, 1904)

Hon. Henry G. Davis for Vice-President. Judge Alton B. Parker's Stand for Gold Indorsed by the Democratic Convention; Crowds Held on Throughout the Night to Witness William Jennings Bryan's Gallant Fight Against the Power He Downed Eight Years Ago

St. Louis, Mo., July 9.—With the soft red glow of the dawn paling the harsh glare of arc and incandescent light, and 20,000 heavy-eyed men and women rousing themselves to hear what he had to say, William Jennings Bryan, of Nebraska, fought his last fight in the big convention hall here this morning, and went down to defeat with the yells of his enemies ringing in his ears.

For fifty hours he had been tireless and sleepless, struggling in committee room and on the floor, by word and deed, for the things that seemed to him sacred. Now, with his voice a mere whisper, his collar a rag, his hair disheveled, his eyes sunken and his face pallid and deep-lined, the old leader arose before his old retainers and his victorious foes, an imperial and a mighty figure, and said good-by.

It was the tragic climax of what many an observer says has been the most melodramatic national convention in years. When he stumbled out, half an hour later, Bryan was half carried to his hotel by his brother, and sank upon his bed limp and unconscious.

"It's a bit of a bore," said the dilettante millionaire Belmont upon the platform, rubbing his eyes.

For eight years Bryan had battled against men of Belmont's breed, and now Belmont was smiling upon him patronizingly and saying that his eloquence was a bore.

None who sweltered in that foul-smelling, steaming hall during those exciting ten hours will ever forget the sight. Thirty thousand men and women were there—delegates, alternates, native Bryanites of Missouri, and a Hearst clique that earned its wages to the last cent.

On the platform Chairman Champ Clark wore out his voice in three hours, and in the galleries the shouters had to work in relays. Coats and collars were shed, and an ocean of ice water was gulped down, but the physical discomforts of the place increased hour by hour and before long everyone was perspiration-soaked and impatient and out of humor.

Scarcely a corporal's guard deserted, and at midnight there were still 25,000 in the hall. Men grew weak and red-eyed in that sickening heat as the hours dragged on and women grew ghastly pale. Still men and women remained, and when the dawn came and Bryan arose to fight his last fight, 20,000 were there to cheer him.

It was broad daylight when the crowd left—broad daylight of a hot summer morning—and the thousands filed out slowly. They had seen a drama more stirring than all the tragedies that Shakespeare ever wrote and it was not make-believe, either. So they dragged along to their homes and hotels in silence and went to sleep.

This afternoon when the convention reassembled not 8,000 persons were in the hall. The Vice-President had still to be named, but who would arise heavy-eyed to see a sham battle when he had watched the clash of arms at Appomattox or Waterloo? One who judged the strength of men merely by the cheers they brought forth would have said, before the roll call of states, that Bryan had won his fight and that Hearst was the democracy's choice for the presidency. But all of this was the work of the galleries.

When the great Hearst outburst came it was the galleries more than the few loud-yelling delegates from Hearst states that made the tumult. Hearst men were everywhere, with handkerchief signals to other and lesser Hearst men. They had planned this riot of ear-splitting noise months ahead and they carried it through their program without a hitch.

On the floor they waved standards. From their leaders on the platform they took their cues. In the galleries they yelled, calmly and steadily and with the business-like air of men receiving fixed wages for performing certain well-defined work.

The majority of the delegates—the men whose votes were to count for more than the loudest of cheers—sat in silence throughout this turmoil. It was a show worth seeing and hearing, and they enjoyed it, but it did not make their blood course through their veins a bit faster than usual, and it did not lift them to their feet as did Bryan's speech at Chicago in 1896.

So, too, it was again when the great Nebraskan himself arose before them, after the night had been spent and the dawn had come. The galleries had been calling for him since midnight, and once, when he had arisen in his place to make a commonplace announcement, there had been a mighty cheer. But when he struggled to the platform at last, in his familiar alpaca coat and his old white string tie, scarcely a delegate gave him greeting.

Bryan looked weak and haggard as he faced the huge crowd and his voice was hoarse and scarcely audible. But as soon as he began to speak a hush fell that was eloquent in itself, and nearly every word he said was heard and understood.

"Eight years ago," he began, "the democratic party gave me its standard to bear. Four years ago that commission was renewed. Tonight I come to you to give it back. You say that I have run my course, and some of you may say that I have not fought a good fight, but none of you"—and the Nebraskan's shattered voice rose to a height that reminded his hearers of the old days—"none of you can deny that I have kept the faith!"

There was more eloquence in this than can ever be set down in black and white. It was a surrender and a defiance, and as Bryan paused and stepped back, with head erect and eyes flashing fire, there arose a whoop that made the formal cheering for Parker and the machine-made "enthusiasm" for Hearst seem puny.

Again and again his hearers yelled. The delegates, perhaps, did not applaud, and on the platform Mr. Belmont thought that it was all a bore, but, as one of the other speakers said, the democrats in the galleries were democrats just as much as the democrats in the delegates' seats, and their votes were as good as any other man's vote.

Three-fourths of the people in the hall thought that Bryan had arisen to second the nomination of Hearst, for whom he had battled valiantly the day before, but instead he named Cockrell, of Missouri—a democrat ungilded by the yellow metal of the East.

Before this the Cockrell shouters had distributed flags throughout the hall, and when Bryan concluded these flags were waved. It was a pretty demonstration, but it was scarcely in keeping with the rest of the drama. Flag-waving is for Fourth of July clambakes and Sunday school picnics and not for the funeral of a mighty chieftain.

There were other speeches—dozens of them—and some, such as Rose's philippic against Parker and Darrow's disguised defense of anarchy and Champ Clark's stirring appeal for the South, brought forth tremendous cheers.

Rose made a speech that the republicans will probably use in full as a campaign document. It arraigned Parker before the bar of his party and of his countrymen for high crimes and misdemeanors, and after a while it grew so warm that a cautious delegate arose to protest that a democratic convention was not a fit place to attack the democratic party.

Clark had spoken a short while before Rose and had aroused the Southerners to the point of frenzy with an eloquent tribute to the solid democratic phalanx of Dixieland.

"You Southerners," cried Rose in reply, "don't know what it means to be a democrat. In your country a democratic victory is as certain as the sunrise and your fights are among yourselves. But think of us democrats on the firing line."

It was five minutes before Rose could proceed. When he finally resumed his speech again he placed in nomination Wall, of Wisconsin. Scarcely had he come to this part when the crowd howled him down. It didn't care to hear about Wall, of Wisconsin.

Fighting all night, with the temperature at a hundred degrees, is a strenuous business, but the faithful 20,000 managed to have a good time, nevertheless. Low comedy relieved the tragedy, as it does in *Othello*, and diversions of all sorts distracted attention from the work in hand.

Once a Westerner arose to make a long speech in favor of his chosen candidate. He launched into a verbose and rhetorical eulogy that might have fitted any one of the half dozen men brought forward, and after a while the crowd grew impatient with him.

"Name your man!" yelled the galleries, but still the spellbinder rambled on.

"Who is it?" cried a man on the floor. "Dr. Mary Walker?"

"No!" bawled another voice; "it's James J. Corbett."

"It's Dr. Munyon!" yelled a third.

Then someone said that the speaker has called his candidate a "gallant soldier."

"It's General Booth of the Salvation Army!" said a long-whiskered Missourian.

Finally it was discovered that the orator was nominating Gen. Nelson A. Miles, and the crowd laughed derisively, as if the idea of General Miles' candidacy were a huge joke.

Strangely enough, the women seemed to bear the discomforts and tortures of the long night better than the men. When they left the hall in the morning their hair was stringy and their complexions pale, but they didn't have that sunken-eyed, ghastly look of many of the delegates. Perhaps that was because they hadn't been sitting up all the night before waiting for the report of the committee on resolutions and playing poker and drinking sour mashes.

Senator Daniel, of Virginia, chairman of the resolutions committee, seemed on the verge of collapse as the dawn broke. He was so weak when he brought in the platform, early in the night, that his voice couldn't be heard, and the terrific turmoil afterward left him exhausted.

Richmond Pearson Hobson, who had addressed the convention in the afternoon, sat faithfully till the end—an interesting spectator. Near him was the Hon. J. Hamilton Lewis, of the red beard;

"Ham" rose once to get a better view of things, and the reporters, whose view he obstructed, yelled at him to step down.

"Outside, Ham!" they shouted, and Lewis turned and with a smile sat down. Late in the night he sent an usher out for a bottle of beer and calmly drank it from the bottle in full view of the sweltering 20,000. It was envy more than disapproval that brought forth satirical cheers for him.

David B. Hill, the god in the machine, sat through it all stolidly and in silence. When the Parker outburst came—it was the first cheer for the New Yorker, by the way, in the convention—he smiled with a satisfied air and mopped his brow.

When the Hearst shouters began their thirty-six-minute demonstration and kept it up until all convention records, old and new, were broken, he leaned back in his chair and yawned. And finally, when the tumult and the shouting died and the roll call came, he smiled again—this time with the happy air of a man who looks upon his handiwork and sees that it is good.

There had been yells for Hearst and cheers for Bryan, but before the clock struck 6 the convention had decided that Alton B. Parker, of New York, was its unanimous choice for President of the United States.

Maybe Hill felt sorry for the pathetic figure that had stumbled out of the hall a short while before. More likely he remembered the lean years that had been his and forgot to be merciful to his foe. Thus the old order had changed and given place to the new.

The king was dead and the crowd was merging out into the sunlight of another day, crying "God save the king!"

(The Baltimore Morning and Sunday Herald, July 10, 1904)

1920

With World War I now over, the country discovered new threats at home: "Red Scares" and "Un-American" strikes, a revival of the Ku Klux Klan, a destruction of the unions by big business. Anyone was considered subversive who was not "100 percent American."

The Republicans felt confident they could win the election and end the Wilson era. The favorite candidate was General Leonard Wood, a Rough Rider and confidant of Theodore Roosevelt, who stated that the idea that Wilson's League of Nations could prevent war was "idle twaddle and a dream of mollycoddles." Two other front-runners were Governor Frank O. Lowden of Illinois, who favored agricultural interests; and the liberal contender, Senator Hiram Johnson, who championed free speech and condemned the Red Hunts by Wilson's Attorney General Palmer. Other candidates in the race included Herbert Hoover, the successful Wartime Food Administrator; Senator William Edgar Borah of Idaho; Calvin Coolidge, the governor of Massachusetts; and Warren Gamaliel Harding, newspaper publisher and senator from Marion, Ohio, whose "America First" speeches contributed to the slogan "Back to Normalcy."

The Republican Convention, held at the Coliseum in Chicago during June 8–12, was the first convention held during Prohibition. The influence of big business pervaded the atmosphere more heavily during this convention than during any other for the past quarter century. In the primaries the main battle was fought between Johnson, Wood, Lowden and Harding. Senator Borah, a friend of Johnson's, charged that Wood's managers had tried to buy control of the convention; subsequent investigations uncovered that Lowden had even bribed delegates. The hot, exhausted delegates remained in a deadlock between Wood and Lowden. Harry Daugherty, Harding's promoter, later would receive credit for predicting his candidate would end the deadlock by being chosen by the Republican bosses during the small hours of the morning in a smoke-filled room. In the end the handsome, genial Warren Harding was considered at 2 A.M. on June 12 along with "Silent Cal" for second place. The delegates, eager to go home, nominated both and adjourned.

Ten days before the Democratic Convention opened, Wilson told the New York World he would not endorse any candidate; inwardly, he was hoping to be renominated for President, otherwise the League of Nations would *die. The convention was held June 28–30 and July 1–3, 5–6, at the Civic Auditorium in San Francisco. Democratic aspirants for the presidency were James M. Cox, a former congressman and governor of Ohio, who endorsed the ailing President's League of Nations, as did the patrician Franklin Delano Roosevelt, Wilson's assistant secretary of the Navy. Among the twenty-two other contenders were President Wilson's son-in-law and former Secretary of the Treasury, William Gibbs McAdoo; Attorney General Alexander Mitchell Palmer; Governor Alfred E. Smith of New York; James Watson Gerard of New York; Homer Stille Cummings of Connecticut; William Randolph Hearst of New York; and the perennial cnadidate, William Jennings Bryan. James Cox emerged as the leading contender, with Franklin D. Roosevelt as his running mate. His nomination, Mencken believed, was done to "perfume the ticket. . . . Roosevelt, perhaps, will fetch a few right thinkers. He is a civilized man and safely wet." Although Cox and Roosevelt lost in the general election, the stage was set for FDR's future triumphs—which would both delight and exacerbate Mencken for years to come.*

The 1920 Democratic Convention at San Francisco would always remain Mencken's personal favorite: "Take wine, women and song, add plenty of A-No. 1 victuals, the belch and bellow of oratory, a balmy but stimulating climate and a whiff of patriotism, and it must be obvious that you have a dose with a very powerful kick in it. This, precisely, was the dose that made the Democratic national convention of 1920, holden in San Francisco, the most charming in American annals. No one who was present at its sessions will ever forget it. . . . Whenever I meet an old-timer who took part in it we fall into maudlin reminiscences of it, and tears drop off the ends of our noses. It came within an inch of being perfect."

A Carnival of Buncombe

All of the great patriots now engaged in edging and squirming their way toward the Presidency of the Republic run true to form. This is to say, they are all extremely wary, and all more or less palpable frauds. What they want, primarily, is the job; the necessary equipment of unescapable issues, immutable principles and soaring ideals can wait until it becomes more certain which way the mob will be whooping. Of the whole crowd at present in the ring, it is probable that only Hoover would make a respectable President. General Wood is a simple-minded old dodo with a delusion of persecution; Palmer is a political mountebank of the first water; Harding is a second-rate provincial; Johnson is allowing himself to be lost in the shuffle; Borah is steadily diminishing in size as he gets closer to the fight; Gerard and the rest are simply bad jokes. Only Hoover stands out as a man of any genuine sense or dignity. He lacks an intelligible platform and is even without a definite party, but he at least shows a strong personality and a great deal of elemental competence. But can he be elected? I doubt it.

What will fetch him in the end, it seems to me, is Knownothingism in all its new and lovely forms. He is altogether too much the foreigner to be swallowed by the great masses of the plain people. They will listen, for a while, to his sweet words; they will hear his protestations of undying loyalty to the flag and to the inspired maxims of Andrew Jackson; but in the long run they will remember that he fled from the republic as a youngster and became, to all intents and purposes, an Englishman, and they will remember, too, that his boom, in its early stages, showed a suspiciously English cast of countenance. Was it actually launched by Viscount Grey? Well, what are the odds? The accusation will be quite as potent as the proof. In such matters one does not need convincing evidence; one merely needs an effective charge.

William Randolph Hearst, a politician of large and delicate gifts, has already raised the issue, and in his journals of public education, with their 5,000,000 circulation, he devotes himself daily to pumping it up. Hoover, it appears by these Hearstian blasts, is actually no more than a pussyfoot sent out by Lloyd George, Sir George Paish and company to insinuate himself into the confidence of innocent Americans, seduce them into voting for him, so hoist himself into the White House—and then hand over the country to the unholy English. His ultimate aim, like that of young Pulitzer, young Reid, the Pierpont Morgan partners, *Ladies' Home Journal* Curtis and other such Anglomaniacs, is to restore the United States to its old place as a loyal British colony, and unload upon it the goat's share of Great Britain's war debt.

Thus Hearst. The Irish-American weeklies go even further. The very mention of Hoover's name lifts them to frenzies. Imagine him President—and taking orders from the Colonial Office! It is a dream more terrible than that of the League of Nations. In all these fears, of course, one discerns a certain exaggeration. It is probably untrue that Dr. Hoover is being financed by English money, or that he'd rather be the Premier of a British colony than president of a free nation, or that he has visions of being promoted from the White House to the House of Lords. In such notions there is a pervasive unlikelihood. But under even the most grotesque of them there remains a sediment of sense, and this sediment of sense takes the form of the doctrine that the interests of England and of the United States, since the close of the war, have begun to diverge sharply, and that it would thus be somewhat unsafe to entrust the interests of the United States to a man so long schooled in promoting the interests of England.

This feeling, it seems to me, is growing very rapidly, and it will be strong enough in the end to eliminate Hoover. It shows itself in many current phenomena—for example, in the acrimonious newspaper duel now going on between the two countries and in the revival of the old sport of pulling the lion's tail on the floor of Congress. The English, usually so skillful at leading the Yankee by the nose, now show a distressing lack of form. Their papers begin to go on at a furious rate, denouncing everything American as dishonest and disgusting. The doctrine that Americans won the war—a very tender point—is laughed at. American rapacity is blamed for the present demoralization of exchange. There is more or less open talk of repudiating England's American debt. Even Lord Grey's very discreet letter has not much improved the situation, for what he has gained by his mollifying words he has lost by his blow to the extreme wing of League of Nations advocates, most of whom are more English than the English, and now feel themselves repudiated and deserted.

In brief, one begins to hear hymns of hate in the offing, and Dr. Hoover will be lucky indeed if they do not drown out his self-sacrificing offer to serve the state. If he speaks against them, then Hearst and the Irish will have all the proof that is needed, speaking politically, to convict him of being a British spy. And if he essays to join in, then even the persons who are now friendly to him will begin to suspect him of a dark and treacherous hypocrisy. The times, in other words, are unfavorable to a candidate bearing his marks. England and the United States are fast drifting apart and the inner causes of that separation will produce important effects upon American domestic politics. The thing that holds up the peace treaty is not any notion that it is dishonest and unjust, or any desire to kick the corpse of Woodrow. It is suspicion of England, pure and simple, as anyone may quickly discover by reading the debates in the Senate, and the harangues of the anti-treaty missionaries on the stump.

Palmer is even weaker than Hoover, if only because he is a man of much inferior ability and of infinitely less intrinsic honesty. His medieval attempts to get into the White House by pumping up the Bolshevik issue have had the actual effect of greatly diminishing his chances. The American people, as a general thing, enjoy the public pursuit of criminals. They esteem and respect a prosecuting officer who entertains them with gaudy raids and is on the first pages of the newspapers every morning. To provide such sport for them is the surest way to get on in politics: every intelligent district attorney prays every night for a Thaw, a Becker or an O'Leary, that he may follow in the illustrious footsteps of Folk, Haney, Whitman and Hughes. But Palmer went a bit too far. He carried the farce to such lengths that the plain people began to sympathize with his victims, nine-tenths of whom were palpably innocent of any worse crime than folly. Today he faces a public conviction that he is a silly fellow, despotic and without sense. That conviction does little violence to the truth.

Aside from his efforts to scare the boobery with Bolshevist bugaboos, Palmer seems to put most reliance in his fidelity to Dr. Wilson's so-called ideals. Here he simply straps himself to a cadaver. These ideals, for two years the marvel of Christendom, are now seen to have been mere buncombe. Dr. Wilson himself never made any actual effort to give them force and effect. On the contrary, it is now evident, by the testimony of all who were privy to the facts, that he heaved them overboard as so much rubbish at the first opportunity. Palmer does not actually believe in them. He has probably done more than any other one man, save only Mr. Wilson himself, to break down democratic self-government in America and substitute a Cossack despotism, unintelligent and dishonest. His final appeal for votes is with the affecting slogan: "Equal rights for all; special privileges to none." And this from the creator of the Chemical Foundation!

In brief, the fellow is a hollow charlatan. Wood is more honest. He is the simple-minded dragon, viewing all human phenomena from the standpoint of the barrack-room. His remedy for all ills and evils is force. Turn out the guard, and let them have a whiff of grape! One somehow warms to the old boy. He is archaic, but transparent. He indulges himself in no pishposh about ideals. He has no opinions upon any public question save the primary one of protecting property. His is a policeman's philosophy, and hence a good deal more respectable than that of Palmer, which is a detective's. But what chance has he got? I can't see much. There is no emotional push in his candidacy. The Red issue is dying fast; it will be forgotten before election. And the issue of Americanism is being murdered by idiots. Day by day its exponents pile up proofs that to be an American, as they conceive it, is to be a poltroon and an ass.

Two issues show some likelihood of surviving. One is the issue of national independence—what is now visible as the anti-English issue. The other is the issue of personal freedom. Between Wilson and his brigades of informers, spies, volunteer detectives, perjurers and complaisant judges, and the Prohibitionists and their messianic delusion, the liberty of the citizen has pretty well vanished in America. In two or three years, if the thing goes on, every third American will be a spy upon his fellow-citizens. But is it going on? I begin to doubt that it is. I begin to see signs that, deep down in their hearts, the American people are growing tired of government by fiat and denunciation. Once they reach the limit of endurance, there will be a chance again for the sort of Americanism that civilized men can be proud of, and that sort of Americanism will make an issue of a thousand times as vital as the imitations put forward by the Prohibitionists, the Palmer White Guard, the Wilson mail openers and the press agents of the American Legion.

Well, imagine Hoover or Palmer nominated by the Democrats, and Wood or some other glorified gendarme nominated by the Republicans. What then? In the offing lurks William Jennings Bryan. I have a suspicion that Bryan is a better politician than any of them. He must see, as every impartial man must see, that both the great parties are sick unto death—that both are thinking in terms of 1914. And he must see, too, the vast body of miscellaneous malcontents in the middle ground, all sore, all eager to strike, all waiting to be led. There are, to begin with, probably a million Socialists; Palmerism in State and nation has been manufacturing them by whole brigades and army corps. There are I.W.W.'s and their like—extravagant fanatics, fools ready to believe anything, but hard used, evilly done out of their common rights. There are racial groups, each with its bitter grievances. There are the revolutionary yokels out in the Northwest, marching like the Bolsheviki.

There are the Irish, ready to repudiate Tammany, and the blacks, eager to punish the Republican party. There are, finally, the growing thousands of plain men, who tire of government by Burlesons, Palmers, Lusk committees, profiteers and newspapers, and begin to long for a restoration of peace, freedom and common decency.

Jennings is an oily fellow, an adept opportunist. His specialty is capitalizing grievances. Prohibition, at the moment, rather handicaps him, but he will know how to get rid of it if necessary. He is at home where men groan under atrocities and are beset by devils. He has the soft words that soothe the fevered brow. He can weep. Already one of his legs is over the side of the Democratic ark. Suppose he takes a bold header into the wild waters of miscellaneous radicalism? Suppose he sets out to round up all who have scalded necks, and despair in their hearts, and a great yearning to raise blue hell? The chance is there—and there, perhaps, stands the statesman foreordained—there stands the super-Debs, the white Touissant L'Overture. Spartacus come back to earth. He, too, has suffered. He lost his job because he wasn't English enough. He is a laborer, a farmer, an Irish patriot, an oppressed war veteran, a poor coon.

Given his health, there is fun ahead for Jennings.

(The Baltimore Evening Sun, February 9, 1920)

It's All in Wilson's Hands,
Mencken Concludes
After Looking Around
at Frisco

San Francisco, June 29.—In Chicago the one permanently active force in the convention, constantly felt and borne in mind, was a sick man at the end of 1,000 miles of telephone wire. In San Francisco there is a different sick man and a much longer wire, but the effect is almost precisely the same.

The personality of President Wilson so heavily dominates the whole scene that all lesser egos shrink to nothing. He can get whatever he wants, provided only he names it plainly. He can veto anything that offends him, whether it be the actual nomination of a candidate or a trivial slip upon some point of etiquette, honor or literary style. No delegate not liquored beyond all that is seemly would dare to flout him. For he is "the cook and the captain bold, and the mate of the *Nancy* brig, and the midshipmate and the bosun tight, and the crew of the captain's gig."

Yesterday's opening session resolved itself almost instantly into a gaudy Wilson feast, with no one save a few Irish volunteers to disturb the loud harmony. The Palmer delegates tried to capitalize the enthusiasm on tap by setting up yells and songs for their darling, but immediately the first Wilson rocket was set off the Pennsylvanian was forgotten, and the net result is that he begins the second day a good deal further down the pole than he was the first day. The high point came when a huge American flag that hung over the platform was lifted up, and there appeared behind it a large oil painting of the President, showing him wearing a blue mail-order suit, a purple necktie and a Camp Meade haircut. The thing itself was hideous, but the spirit behind it was inspiring, and so the crowd began whooping like mad, and all the demonstrations planned for the nomination day were given a preliminary airing.

Homer S. Cummings' keynote speech, as delivered, was devoted almost entirely to praise and defense of the president. The text given to the press associations, I suppose, showed an elaborate discussion of other issues. Homer himself, in fact, assured one of the Irish volunteers who interrupted him that he had something soft and suave to say about the woes of Erin. But he never got to it. Practically the whole of his hour and a half was devoted to an extremely effective defense of the League of Nations and of the President's doings at the peace table—in truth, to the most persuasive defense that I have ever heard. Homer is no orator. His voice lacks resonance. He is tall, bald and unimpressive. But for all that he delivered his arguments with fine force, and they exploded torpedoes all over the hall.

Altogether it was an extremely lively opening session. The weather was almost perfect—cool and yet not chilly; bright overhead and yet without glare. Through the opening doors at the back of the hall one glimpsed the fronds of swaying palms, a spectacle so unheard of at national conventions that it enchanted the delegates instantly. The hall itself is small, but very well arranged and even beautiful. Behind the speaker's platform is a large pipe organ and to either side of it there is a gallery, one for the band and the other for a choir. Overhead hangs a gigantic canopy, so huge that it conceals the whole roof. The seats are roomy. The attendants are polite. Outside, in the convention building, there is a clean lunchroom. The acoustics are perfect.

The contrast with Chicago constantly obtrudes itself. There the hall was hot and unlovely, the sets were small and cramped, the aisles were constantly blocked by the inefficient police, and when a delegate sneaked out to refresh himself with a sandwich or a bottle of pop he had to descend to a dirty cellar and stand up to his meager and disgusting meal. The dirtiest man that I have ever seen in my life was in charge of the sandwich counter at Chicago.

In San Francisco the business is in charge of women in clean white uniforms and the sandwiches are large and appetizing, and there are chairs to sit down on while devouring them. The difference is enormous and important. It is easy for a delegate to be happy when he is decently housed and fed.

The simple fact is that San Francisco is doing the thing in the grand manner and making a colossal impression on the visitors. One goes to a national convention expecting to live for a week or 10 days, like a hog in a sty. Here things are not only comfortable; they are almost luxurious. The oldest frequenters of conventions remember no such hall, no such smooth and admirable arrangements, no such attentive and unobtrusive hospitality. The town is scarcely more than a fifth the size of Chicago, and yet its hotels have swallowed the convention crowd without straining, and there is not the slightest breakdown or confusion. If one rings for a bellboy he comes. If one falls over and smashes a chair or a dressing table a new one is put in at once. If one complains that a delegate next door is drunk and noisy an anaesthetist or a mental healer is sent for to silence him.

As I have said, the Palmer delegates, chiefly those from Pennsylvania, tried to capture the opening session, but when the hymn to Woodrow was turned on by Cummings, they quickly subsided and were heard of no more. My private notion is that they discharged their whoops too soon, and so diminished the effectiveness that they will have when they are more sorely needed—to wit, when the ground begins to heave and rock beneath the fighting Quaker and the time has come for heroic measures. Their pièce de résistance was and is a song running, "Palmer, Palmer, Pennsylvania," to the tune of "Glory, Glory, Hallelujah." They have some good voices in their crowd and their singing is very caressing to the ear. Now and then a fat woman in blue leaps up from the interior of the delegation and lets off a falsetto cheer. In the intervals of song a cheer leader directs a raucous rah, rah, rah.

So much for the Palmer music. By the time it was shut off by roars for the Cummings doctrine—said to have been okayed with blue exclamation points by the White House itself—that the learned doctor is immortal, it had pumped most of the air out of the Palmeristas, and they were all, save the buxom gal in blue, somewhat limp. The official music of the convention then swung grandly into the woodrowiad. It was led by a brass band, supported by the pipe organ, and graced and embellished by a quartet and a choir. The choir sang through megaphones and quickly got out of time, but the thing was thrilling for all that. "The Star-Spangled Banner" went off with a bang, and, what is more, with unaccustomed dignity. And the marches and battle ballads that followed every time a speaker stopped for breath were given heartily and stirringly.

The genial dampness continues. No honest delegate need go unkissed by stimulants, provided he has a good nose and is not full of fears that every side street is peopled by highwaymen. Simultaneously, the wets give up all hope of getting a ringing declaration for beer and light wines into the platform. They declare that they will be able to knock out Bryan's dry plank on the floor, but that is as far as they go. In this hope there is probably some substance. The convention is pre-eminently a Wilson gathering and not a Bryan one. Bryan, I believe, gives away his uneasiness about his dry plank by leaping into the ring with a League of Nations plank, coupled to a characteristic demand for an amendment to the Constitution. What he obviously plans to do is to conceal a decisive defeat under a vague and inconclusive battle.

The convention, as I have said, is overwhelmingly for Wilson, not for Bryan. Wilson will have whatever platform he wants, down to and including the punctuation thereof. He can name the candidate if he wants to. Not one of the current aspirants would have a ghost of a show against his active opposition. But that he desires to exercise this last power is anything but clear. He may exercise it to break a hopeless deadlock or to prevent the leaderless convention running amuck. But it is difficult to imagine so shrewd a politician taking the open responsibility of naming his own successor and then running the risk of finding himself with a Taft on his hands.

(The Baltimore Evening Sun, June 29, 1920)

Mencken Says All's Set
to Put "Young William" Over
If Wilson Gives the Word

San Francisco, July 1.—Barring acts of God and the public enemy, it would seem to be Son-in-Law McAdoo. He is the favorite this morning by odds of at least 2 to 1.

Both the Palmer boom and the Cox boom came to grisly ends in the convention hall yesterday afternoon, the first coming down with paralysis at 2 P.M. and the other drowning in a mixture of light wines, beer and well-water an hour later. Thus, while the two corpses were being hauled out by the catchpods, the Rev. Burris Jenkins, of Kansas City, got upon his legs, made a modest little speech for the Crown Prince, and instantly set off a volcano.

The McAdoo demonstration that followed was not only longer and louder than either that for Palmer or that for Cox, it was also incomparably more hearty and spontaneous. All that is needed to put young William over with a bang is a single wink from the White House. Everything is apparently set to nominate him. All he wants is the imprimatur.

It was a session full of thrills, surprises and buffooneries, and also a session strangely full of charm. The crowd stuck almost solidly from 11 A.M. until after 6, hugely enjoying every minute of the show. The first whoop was generated by the Governor of Arkansas when he rose to second the nomination of Senator Owen. He is a sad-looking man, with a Chauncey M. Depew nose and brilliant bald head, and no one expected him to make any use of the seltzer siphon. But in his first sentence he loosed a pun worthy of Weber and Fields.

"Arkansas," he said, "is the only State mentioned in the Bible.

Turn to the book of Genesis. There you will find the immortal and prophetic words, "And Noah looked out the ark and saw."

Higher flights of wit, of course, are imaginable, but it somehow tickled the crowd, and the rest of the Governor's speech brought forth storms of yells.

On his heels came a fair suffragist of Massachusetts, Mrs. Susan W. Fitzgerald. Mrs. Fitzgerald has dignified gray hair and carries herself like a professor at Vassar, but when she stepped to the front of the platform and the leader of the band searched hurriedly for some tune to greet her, he hit upon "Oh, You Beautiful Doll."

The crowd roared, Chairman Robinson nervously concealed a snicker in the water pitcher, and Mrs. Fitzgerald herself smiled good-humoredly. Her speech was a bad one, but her bearing in this somewhat trying situation pleased everybody, and so she was applauded mightily, and when she sat down there was a tumult.

After that whoop followed whoop. All the girls who rose to second nominations were given receptions fit for Lillian Russell, in the last century, and when Mrs. Lillian R. Sire spoke for Governor Smith, of New York, one delegate grew so giddy with joy that he rushed out of the hall, lifted a wreath from a passing hearse, and then fought his way to the platform to present it to her.

Both the Palmer demonstration and the uproar for Cox were helped by this general disposition to be happy, but all the same they showed a feebleness that revealed the collapse of hopes behind them. The delegates were polite, but not enthusiastic.

Of the two, the Palmer demonstration was the better staged. It rested principally upon music. Instantly the name of the eminent foe of anarchy was mentioned, the band burst into the Palmer song, "Palmer, Palmer, Pennsylvania," to the tune of "Glory, Glory, Hallelujah!"

This was precisely at 11.43. Thereafter, save for two breaks of one minute each, the chorus was played continuously until 2.07. It took four seconds to get through it. I thus figure that it was done 95 times—enough to last me until the next war.

The "Palmeristas" bawled the song through megaphones and tramped around the hall as they bawled, but when the music stopped at last they were done for. The singing seemed to exhaust their ingenuity. The best they could provide in the way of comedy was a red-haired youth, who leaped upon the chair and swung his arms about him in the manner of a Russian dancer doing the ballet, "The Czar is down with smallpox! Hurrah, hurrah!" They had no banners, and their marching quickly got them tied into knots. Finally they grabbed a pretty girl, hoisted her high in the air and so attempted to revive enthusiasm; but the demonstration plainly lacked grip and substance. It went on for 34 minutes, but after the tenth minute it was purely artificial.

The Cox hullabaloo was even less spontaneous. The efforts of the Cox leaders to seduce the drys have shaken the faith of the wets, and the result is that the Ohioan is regarded with suspicion on all sides, and his nomination seems, at this writing, to be impossible without a miracle. His whoopers had a band of their own in one of the galleries and it tore the air for 20 minutes running with the Cox song, which uses the tune of "Oh, Didn't He Ramble." Once this song was worn out, the demonstration was done, though Chairman Robinson let it struggle and gasp along until it had outlived the Palmer demonstration by one minute. The Cox-ites sent a college cheer leader to the platform to inflame the crowd, but he failed miserably. It was obvious, as the pumped-up tumult died, that Cox was fading with it.

What followed was unexpected and a vast success and next to the McAdoo demonstration, the most hearty uproar of the whole day. It came when Bourke Cocoran, the silver-tongued, appeared on the platform to pay New York's formal tribute to Gov. Alfred E. Smith.

Bourke was in poor form, his speech was childish, and Smith was not regarded seriously as a candidate, but on the heels of the light applause the band swung into "Tammany" and then into "The Sidewalks of New York," and then into "Sweet Rosie O'Grady," and then into a whole series of the sentimental songs of a yesteryear, and bit by bit, without the slightest intent or pre-arrangement there grew up a demonstration that made the other two seem silly. It had no leaders and it had no plan, but it came from the heart and when it subsided at last a few electric cantos of rhetoric might have set off such a Smith boom that all the king's horses and all the king's men would have been needed to scotch it.

That rhetoric, unluckily for Smith, was not poured out. The man sent up to second Cocoran's speech was young Franklin D. Roosevelt, and young Franklin D. Roosevelt botched and butch-ered the thing for two minutes. What was demanded by that golden opportunity was a flash of genuine eloquence, a ringing appeal to the delegates to turn from the cadavers of Palmer and

Cox and cast their votes for Alfred. But all that Roosevelt had on tap was a line of puerile and ineffective bosh about the great achievements of the navy. As the delegates listened all their enthusiasms oozed out of them. Thus the Smith boom died in the hour of its birth and it will take strong medicine to revive it.

But while the thing lasted it made the most charming episode of this most delightful of all conventions. Ten thousand men and women, carried away by the homely music of those bedraggled old songs, sang with the band, danced around the hall and yielded themselves unashamed to a debauch of sentiment.

In the Maryland delegation J. Walter Lord was the first to succumb. He resisted "After the Ball" and he resisted "The Bowery," but when the band got to "Two Little Girls in Blue" he gave a low moan, clutched the Maryland standard to his heart and leaped into the dance. Governor Ritchie was the next to fall. He was knocked out by "A Bicycle Built for Two." Then Mrs. Lord, who was sitting with the delegation, followed her husband. Then Robert Crain fell for "Sweet Rosie O'Grady." Then John J. Mahon, too proud to sing or even to stand up, began to blow his nose romantically.

All over the hall were singing delegates, alternates, guests, newspaper reporters, policemen and firemen. A row of elderly suffragettes, stored for safety in the organ loft, converted themselves into a choir. The Cox band joined the regular convention band, a Palmer cornetist helped with fearful blasts. The very magnificoes on the platform began to buzz and sway. In the midst of the sweet saturnalia a lady delegate from the West was so softly overcome that she tried to kiss the Hon. Daniel J. Loden. "Dan" was willing, but an usher hauled her off. Telling about it later on, "Dan" courteously reduced her age from 47 to 32. This morning he is telling everyone that he will start a boom for her for the Vice-Presidency.

A fine piece of musical psychology was hidden in this pretty score. The "Tammany" song, which came immediately after Cocoran's speech, left the crowd cold, but the moment the band dropped into "The Sidewalks of New York" singing began all over the hall. The explanation is simple. "The Sidewalks of New York" is in three-four time, which is to say, the waltz time, and waltz spells sentiment all over the world. "After the Ball" is in the same time, so is "Sweet Rosie O'Grady." So is "Two Little Girls in Blue." So is every other song that the 10,000 whooped and hummed. Instantly the band went back to "Tammany" in common time and the show was over. The march beat thrills, but it cannot mellow.

The crowd will go home delighted with San Francisco. There will be another convention here four years hence, if the delegates and alternates have to hock their false teeth to pay the fare. San Francisco has simply knocked them out. There is an air here that is simply unmatchable in the East and it is social as well as atmospheric. One notices at once a touch of spaciousness and freedom. The town is genuinely gay. There is a touch of the exotic in its life, almost a touch of the Asiatic. One gets a sense of deliverance from the oppressive Puritanism of the East.

Do not misunderstand me here. There is no sign of debauchery. Nothing gross and hoggish. But when I rode along the shores of the Pacific last night, with the moon shining over the waters and a good dinner filling me with optimistic reflections, when I bounced along in a comfortable night hack and saw a thousand young fellows in other night hacks happily sailing by, each innocently hugging his girl and the cops looking on as if there were no laws against honest joy, it somehow made me glad that I had traveled the desert and renewed acquaintance with civilization.

The hospitality of San Francisco, in some of its manifestations, almost verges upon low cunning. Imagine a town in which every hotel keeper starts off every morning by sending every one of his guests a basket of fruit or a box of flowers. The women visitors are tickled half to death. In all other convention cities the delegates are herded into their pens by ward heelers schooled in the art at iron molders' picnics and on cheap excursion boats. Here the ushering in is done by pretty girls in white. Instead of clubs, they employ smiles. Imagine what good order there is. Imagine how the delegates are delighted.

(The Baltimore Evening Sun, July 1, 1920)

Battle at San Francisco
Absolutely Free and Open,
Henry Mencken Affirms

San Francisco, July 7.—Don't let anyone tell you that this was a bossed convention—that the whisky trust, or Charles F. Murphy, or Tom Taggart, or Wall street, or any other such power put over something on the great, trusting herd of pure and patriotic delegates. As a matter of plain fact, the thing was no more bossed than a rough-house at an Irish wake.

The battle was absolutely free and open. No leader or faction had any advantage that was denied to any other leader or faction. The victory went to the combination of big-city organizations, simply because they chose a candidate intelligently and then stuck to him resolutely.

First they broke down the morale of the Palmer men, few of whom honestly believed that Palmer could defeat Harding if nominated. Then they disposed of the McAdoo men, all of whom were haunted by doubts as to what the crown prince really wanted and what he would ultimately do. Thus, facing war on two fronts, the big-city wets gained their victory by the ancient device of digging themselves in, husbanding their blood and iron, letting their antagonists go magnificently to smash upon their barbed-wire entanglements.

What chiefly facilitated the business, of course, was the division in the ranks of the enemy. If the White House had taken a hand there would have been a far different story to tell, but after flooding the town with whispering agents and attorneys the White House finally decided to keep hands off. It was a decision marked by no little political sagacity. A few rounds of inspired drum-fire might have sufficed to beat Cox, but the party would have been left torn and distracted, with victory in November out of the question. Tammany, saddled with another load of idealism, would have gone back to New York with shooting pains in both legs. The Cook county democracy would have cheered bravely and then died. What the boys wanted was a practical man, one to woo and seduce the boobery and yet fundamentally safe and sane. They got him and they are happy.

My private notion is that the White House never had the slightest thought of dictating the nomination. All the dark hints that were thrown out by Burleson, Glass, Colby and the rest of the emissaries from Government headquarters were simply buncombe. The mysterious frauds did not represent the White House at all; they simply represented themselves and the fact became obvious when each began to root desperately on his own account, without the slightest regard to the teamwork or major strategy.

Colby offers an excellent example. For three or four days he operated behind the palms in the hotel lobbies, letting it be known that revelations were in his knapsack. Then he suddenly threw off all disguise and became a candidate himself—a candidate with no more actual support from the Llassa on the Potomac than McAdoo had, or even Carter Glass.

Thus left free and untutored, the delegates chose the nominee without let or hindrance, and he represents, as he stands, the honest desires of the great majority of them. Whether he represents the desire of a full two-thirds I do not quite know, and in fact rather doubt. Swallowing him was a bitter business for the right-thinkers from the South and Middle West, and some of them kept on gagging until the last bugle call. William Jennings Bryan, the natural prophet of all the right-thinkers, is bawling pathetically today. But even Bryan finds it difficult to argue that Cox was not chosen freely, and so it seems likely that he will have to support the ticket. The most he can pump up is indignation against a mythical beer trust. Bryan himself probably believes in this hobgoblin; at all events, now and then. The old peerless leader is now a mere weeper and martyr, grotesque and a bit tragic. But I doubt that many delegates actually share his hallucinations.

Bryan's allegation that Carter Glass hit him under the belt in the platform committee is unfair and ridiculous. As a matter of fact, he was given so much rope that he almost monopolized the sessions of the committee, and so delayed the convention itself for a day and a half, and caused the adjournment over Sunday. Then he got his second chance on the floor, and for one whole day he whooped and gibbered all over the platform, half drowning the delegations in his pious balderdash. A more pathetic spectacle I have not witnessed since the Rev. Billy Sunday was in Baltimore and the damned fought their way into his theological rat trap.

Bryan also hints that Colby done him dirt. But what was Colby's actual offense? Simply that he stood up in the midst of all the Bryan caterwauling and blew the nonsense of the Commoner to pieces with a few blasts of plain common sense. Colby made one of the best speeches of the convention. It was brief, it was good-humored, it was pungent and it was devastating.

It seems to me that the general run of delegates at the convention was a good deal above the average—that is, above the Democratic average. Even the Southern States sent well-dressed, well-behaved and apparently decently educated men and women. The wool-hat boys of the past were all missing. What has become of them, God knows; perhaps prohibition and the Young Men's Christian Association have denatured them.

In the old days it was common for half of the delegates from some Southern States to be stewed from beginning to end of a convention; but this time, though plenty of hard liquor was on tap, nine-tenths of them kept sober, at least during the sessions. When it was discovered, one day, that a Texan had brought in a jug of corn juice concealed in a megaphone, the fact caused a great lifting of eyebrows. Another day an eminent journalist went down on the floor to borrow a chew of tobacco. On his return he told me with a great astonishment that only two men in the North Carolina delegation had plugs on them. To such fantastic lengths has the uplift gone.

But if the South thus showed a high level of culture and rectitude, it failed miserably to produce effective leaders. The best speeches were made by Northerners—Colby, Cocoran, and so on —and the Northern organization men showed a stupendous superiority on the floor. Glass, the most conspicuous of the sub-Potomac magnificoes, made a very poor impression, and his personal boom was dead and buried two minutes after he had started to read the platform. An under-sized and cocky-looking fellow, with the oratorical manner of an East Side ward leader, he simply let all the gas out of his boom. Virginia, instructed for him, stuck to him even after he had thrown up the sponge, but he was never seriously considered elsewhere. Neither was any of the other Southern candidates.

The nomination of Franklin D. Roosevelt for the Vice-Presidency was done to perfume the ticket. Roosevelt is the leader of the anti-Tammany Democrats in New York and it was desired to rid the ticket of the Tammany bouquet that began to cling to it when Murphy was gradually forced into the leadership of the Cox forces. But Roosevelt's politics, like those of his lamented cousin on the other side, stop short of converting idealism into down-right mania. He was willing enough the other day to make a speech for Gov. Alfred Smith of New York, the favorite son of Tammany, and though it was a wretchedly bad speech it was nev-ertheless free from sneers. Roosevelt, perhaps, will fetch a few right-thinkers. He is a civilized man and safely wet.

Wetness, in fact, drips from the ticket. Now that he is nomi-nated, Cox supporters begin to forget their late effort to hoodwink the drys. After Woodrow had been canonized, the League of Na-tions issue sank to second place; all thoughts turned upon the battle between the drink and the chaser. Bryan saw it so. Tam-many saw it so. The victory, when it came, was far more alcoholic than political.

(The Baltimore Evening Sun, July 7, 1920)

Bayard vs. Lionheart

I

One discerns in all the current discussion of MM. Harding and Cox a certain sour dismay. It seems to be quite impossible for any wholly literate man to pump up any genuine enthusiasm for ei-ther of them. Each, of course, is praised lavishly by the profes-sional politicians of his own party, and compared to Lincoln, Jef-ferson and Cleveland by the surviving hacks of the party press, but in the middle ground, among men who care less for party success than for the national dignity, there is a gone feeling in the stomach, with shooting pains down the legs. The Liberals, in par-ticular, seem to be suffering badly. They discover that Harding is simply a third-rate political wheel-horse, with the face of a mov-ing-picture actor, the intelligence of a respectable agricultural im-plement dealer, and the imagination of a lodge joiner, and that

Cox is no more than a provincial David Harum with a gift for bamboozling the boobs.

These verdicts, it seems to me, are substantially just. No one but an idiot would argue seriously that either candidate is a first-rate man, or even a creditable specimen of second-rate man. Any State in the Union, at least above the Potomac, could produce a thousand men quite as good, and many States could produce a thousand a great deal better. Harding, intellectually, seems to be merely a benign blank—a decent, harmless, laborious, hollow-headed mediocrity perhaps comparable to the late Harrington, of Maryland. Cox is quicker of wit, but a good deal less honest. He belongs to the cunning type; there is a touch of the shyster in him. His chicaneries in the matter of prohibition, both during the convention and since, show the kink in his mind. He is willing to do anything to cadge votes, and he includes in that anything the ready sacrifices of his good faith, of the national welfare, and of the hopes and confidence of those who honestly support him. Neither candidate reveals the slightest dignity of conviction. Neither cares a hoot for any discernible principle. Neither, in any intelligible sense, is a man of honor.

II

But it is one thing to yield to virtuous indignation against such individuals and quite another thing to devise any practicable scheme for booting them out of the synagogue. The weakness of those of us who take a gaudy satisfaction in our ideas, and battle for them violently, and face punishment for them willingly and even proudly, is that we forget the primary business of the man in politics, which is the snatching and safeguarding of his job. That business, it must be plain, concerns itself only occasionally with the defense and propagation of ideas, and even then it must confine itself to those that, to a reflective man, must usually appear to be insane. The first and last aim of the politician is to get votes, and the safest of all ways to get votes is to appear to the plain man to be a plain man like himself, which is to say, to appear to him to be happily free from any heretical treason to the body of accepted platitudes—to be filled to the brim with the flabby, banal, childish notions that challenge no prejudice and lay no burden of examination upon the mind.

It is not often, in these later days of the democratic enlightenment, that positive merit lands a man in elective office in the United States; much more often it is a negative merit that gets him there. That negative merit is simply disvulnerability. Of the two candidates, that one wins who least arouses the suspicions and distrusts of the great masses of simple men. Well, what are more likely to arouse those suspicions and distrusts than ideas, convictions, principles? The plain people are not hostile to shysterism, save it be gross and unsuccessful. They admire a Roosevelt for his bold stratagems and duplicities, his sacrifice of faith and principle to the main chance, his magnificent disdain of fairness and honor. But they shy instantly and inevitably from the man who comes before them with notions that they cannot immediately translate into terms of their everyday delusions; they fear the novel idea, and particularly the revolutionary idea, as they fear the devil. When Roosevelt, losing hold upon his cunning at last, embraced the vast hodgepodge of innovations, some idiotic but some sound enough, that went by the name of Progressivism, they jumped from under him in trembling, and he came down with a thump that left him on his back until death delivered him from all hope and caring.

III

It seems to me that this fear of ideas is a peculiarly democratic phenomenon, and that it is nowhere so horribly apparent as in the United States, perhaps the nearest approach to an actual democracy yet seen in the world. It was Americans who invented the curious doctrine that there is a body of doctrine in every department of thought that every good citizen is in duty bound to accept and cherish; it was Americans who invented the right-thinker. The fundamental concept, of course, was not original. The theologians embraced it centuries ago, and continue to embrace it to this day. It appeared on the political side in the Middle Ages, and survived in Russia into our time. But it is only in the United States that it has been extended to all departments of thought. It is only here that *any* novel idea, in any field of human relations, carries with it a burden of obnoxiousness, and is instantly challenged as mysteriously immoral by the great masses of right-thinking men. It is only here, so far as I have been able to make out, that there is a right way and a wrong way to think about the beverages one drinks with one's meals, and the way children ought to be taught in the schools, and the manner in which foreign alliances should be negotiated, and what ought to be done about the Bolsheviki.

In the face of this singular passion for conformity, this dread of novelty and originality, it is obvious that the man of vigorous mind and stout convictions is gradually shouldered out of public life. He may slide into office once or twice, but soon or late he is bound to be held up, examined and incontinently kicked out. This leaves the field to the intellectual jelly-fish and inner tubes. There is room for two sorts of them—first, the blank cartridge who has no convictions at all and is willing to accept anything to make votes, and, secondly, the mountebank who is willing to conceal and disguise what he actually believes, according as the wind blows hot or cold. Of the first sort, Harding is an excellent specimen; of the second sort, Cox.

IV

Such tests arise inevitably out of democracy—the domination of unreflective and timorous men, moved in vast herds by mob emotions. In private life no man of sense would think of applying them. We do not estimate the integrity and ability of an acquaintance by his flabby willingness to accept our ideas; we estimate him by the honesty and effectiveness with which he maintains his own. All of us, if we are of reflective habit, like and admire men whose fundamental beliefs differ radically from our own. But when a candidate for public office faces the voters he does not face men of sense; he faces a mob of men whose chief distinguishing mark is the fact that they are quite incapable of weighing ideas, or even of comprehending any save the most elemental—men whose whole thinking is done in terms of emotion, and whose dominant emotion is dread of what they cannot understand. So confronted, the candidate must either bark with the pack, or count himself lost. His one aim is to disarm suspicion, to arouse confidence in his orthodoxy, to avoid challenge. If he is a man of convictions, of enthusiasm, of self-respect, it is cruelly hard. But if he is, like Harding, a numskull like the idiots he faces, or, like Cox, a pliant intellectual Jenkins, it is easy.

The larger the mob, the harder the test. In small areas, before small electorates, a first-rate man occasionally fights his way through, carrying even the mob with him by the force of his personality. But when the field is nationwide, and the fight must be waged chiefly at second and third hand, and the force of personality cannot so readily make itself felt, then all the odds are on the man who is, intrinsically, the most devious and mediocre—the man who can most adeptly disperse the notion that his mind is a virtual vacuum.

The Presidency tends, year by year, to go to such men. As democracy is perfected, the office represents, more and more closely, the inner soul of the people. We move toward a lofty ideal. On some great and glorious day the plain folks of the land will reach their heart's desire at last, and the White House will be adorned by a downright moron.

(The Baltimore Evening Sun, July 26, 1920)

1924

Behind the successful veneer of President Harding's administration, the corruption of key cabinet figures would eventually supersede all else. One such figure whose influence was often for sale was the President's principal and trusted adviser, Attorney General Harry Daugherty; another was Charles R. Forbes, head of the Veterans Bureau, who accepted bribes for awarding contracts for hospital buildings and supplies; and perhaps the most flagrant was the notorious "Teapot Dome" scandal, traced to Secretary of the Interior Albert B. Fall, which involved the secret leasing of the nation's oil reserves to private parties in return for bribes. When Harding suddenly died of a heart attack in August 1923, the taciturn "Silent Cal" took office. The shocking revelations of Harding's administration surfaced shortly thereafter, yet Coolidge himself was not implicated, and his reputation remained intact. A man of simple manners and few words (it was said he could be silent in five different languages), his reserved and aloof personality contrasted sharply to Harding's. In 1924, voters decided to "Keep Cool with Coolidge," and he was quickly nominated on the first ballot at the Republican National Convention, held at the Municipal Auditorium in Cleveland, Ohio, during June 10–12.

The Cleveland convention is said to have been the most boring in Republican history. Sessions were, at times, poorly attended. "It is traditional at national conventions for hotel lobbies to swarm with fanatics whooping up their favorites. . . ." observed Mencken. "They ooze and radiate enthusiasm. But the man who could be a Coolidge fanatic could also be a fanatic for double-entry bookkeeping. Even the sworn friends of the President—the men who brought him up to his present Arctic eminence . . . —even these professional Coolidgestas carry on their business with the air of grocery clerks wrapping up packages of ginger snaps. As for the common run of delegates, they are simply standing in line waiting. A whoop for Coolidge would be almost as startling as a whoop for parallel longitude." He added, "The contemplation of his character can freeze a sober man to silence, but could it freeze a man kissed by the grape? I doubt it." Indeed, thanks to the efforts of George C. Southwell, boss of the Dry Maintenance League, the most popular drink was a "Keep-Cool-with-Coolidge" highball made of raw eggs and fruit juice. The first dry national convention in human history was, to Mencken, "as appalling and as fascinating as a two-headed boy."

The Clowns March In

I

At first blush, the Republican National Convention at Cleveland next week promises to be a very dull show, for the Hon. Mr. Coolidge will be nominated without serious opposition and there are no issues of enough vitality to make a fight over the platform. The whole proceedings, in fact, will be largely formal. Some dreadful mountebank in a long-tailed coat will open them with a windy speech; then another mountebank will repeat the same rubbish in other words; then a half dozen windjammers will hymn good Cal as a combination of Pericles, Frederick the Great, Washington, Lincoln, Roosevelt and John the Baptist; then there will be an hour or two of idiotic whooping, and then the boys will go home. The LaFollette heretics, if they are heard of at all, will not be heard of for long; they will be shoved aside even more swiftly than they were shoved aside when Harding was nominated. And the battle for the Vice-Presidency will not be fought out in the hall, but somewhere in one of the hotels, behind locked doors and over a jug or two of bootleg Scotch.

A stupid business, indeed. Nevertheless, not without its charms to connoisseurs of the obscene. What, in truth, could more beautifully display the essential dishonesty and imbecility of the entire democratic process. Here will be assembled all the great heroes and master-minds of the majority party in the greatest free nation ever seen on earth, and the job before them will be the austere and solemn one of choosing the head of the state, the heir of Lincoln and Washington, the peer of Caesar and Charlemagne. And here, after three or four days of bombarding the welkin and calling upon God for help, they will choose unanimously a man whom they regard unanimously as a cheap and puerile fellow!

I don't think I exaggerate. Before the end of the campaign, of course, many of them will probably convince themselves that Cal is actually a man of powerful intellect and lofty character, and even, perhaps, a gentleman. But I doubt seriously that a single Republican leader of any intelligence believes it today. Do you think that Henry Cabot Lodge does? Or Smoot? Or any of the Pennsylvania bosses? Or Borah? Or Hiram Johnson? Or Moses? Or our own Weller? These men are not idiots. They have eyes in their heads. They have seen Cal at close range. . . . But they will all whoop for him in Cleveland.

II

In such whooping lies the very soul and essence of humor. Nothing imaginable could be more solidly mirthful. Nor will there be any lack of jocosity in the details of the farce: the imbecile paralogy of the speeches; the almost inconceivable nonsense of the platform; the low buffooneries of the Southern delegates, white and black; the swindling of the visitors by the local apostles of Service; the bootlegging and boozing; the gaudy scenes in the hall. National conventions are almost always held in uncomfortable and filthy places; the one at San Francisco, four years ago, is the only decent one I have ever heard of. The decorations are carried out by the sort of morons who arrange street fairs. The hotels are crowded to suffocation. The food is bad and expensive. Everyone present is robbed, and everyone goes home exhausted and sore.

My agents in Cleveland report that elaborate preparations are under way there to slack the thirst of the visitors, which is always powerful at national conventions. The town is very well supplied with bootleggers, and regular lines of rum ships run into it from Canadian ports. Ohio has a State Volstead act and a large force of spies and snoopers, many of them former jail-birds. These agents of the Only True Christianity, no doubt, will all concentrate in Cleveland, and dispute with national Prohibition blacklegs for the graft. I venture the guess that bad Scotch will sell for $15 a bottle in the hotels and at the convention hall, and that more than one delegate will go home in the baggage car, a victim to methyl alcohol.

Ohio is run by the Anti-Saloon League, and so the city of Cleveland will be unable to imitate the charming hospitality of the city of San Francisco, four years ago. The municipality there ordered 60 barrels of excellent Bourbon for the entertainment of the delegates and alternates, and charged them to the local smallpox hospital. After the convention the Methodist mullahs of the town exposed the transaction, and proved that there had not been a patient in the hospital for four years. But the city officials who were responsible, when they came up for reelection soon afterward, were re-elected by immense majorities. Despite Prohibition, the people of San Francisco are still civilized, and know the difference between entertaining human beings and entertaining horned cattle.

III

The managers of the Hon. Mr. Coolidge's campaign are apparently well aware that the nomination of the Hon. Al Smith by the Democrats would plunge them into a very bitter and serious fight, and so they are trying to weaken Al by weakening Tammany Hall. One of the principal arguments used to bring the Democratic convention to New York was that Tammany would see that the delegates and alternates got enough sound drinks at reasonable prices to keep pleasantly jingled—an unbroken tradition at Democratic national conventions since the days of Andrew Jackson. Now the Coolidge managers have hurled hundreds of Prohibition agents into Manhattan, and a desperate effort is under way to make the town bone-dry. The Dogberries of the Federal bench, as usual, lend themselves willingly to the buffoonery: dozens of injunctions issue from their mills every day, and some of the principal saloons of the Broadway region are now padlocked.

But all the New Yorkers that I know are still optimistic. There are, indeed, so many saloons in the town that all the Federal judges east of the Mississippi, working in eight-hour shifts like coal miners, could not close them completely in the month remaining before the convention opens. Every time one saloon is closed two open. Meanwhile, the 12-mile treaty with England seems to have failed absolutely to discourage bootlegging from the Bahamas. On the contrary, the price of Scotch has declined steadily since it was signed, and the stuff now coming in is of very excellent quality. It is my belief that the theory that it is heavily adulterated is spread by Prohibitionists, who are certainly not noted for veracity. I have not only encountered no bad Scotch in New York for a year past; I have never heard of any. All the standard brands are obtainable in unlimited quantities, and at prices, roughly speaking, about half those of a year ago.

IV

Moreover, very good beer is everywhere on sale, and nine-tenths of the Italian restaurants, of which there must be at least two thousand in the town, are selling cocktails and wine. Along Broadway the difficulty of concealing so bulky a drink as beer and the high tolls demanded by the Prohibition enforcement officers make the price somewhat high, but in the side-streets it is now only 60 per cent above what it was in the days before the Volstead act. The last time I went into a beer-house in New York, two or three weeks ago, the *Wirt* greeted me with the news that he had just reduced the price 10 cents a *Seidel*. His place was packed to the doors.

I am thus inclined to believe that the efforts of M. Coolidge's partisans to employ the Eighteenth Amendment against M. Smith will fail. When the white, Protestant, Nordic delegates from the Christian Endeavor regions of the South and Middle West arrive in the big town, their tongues hanging out, they will get what they have dreamed of all these months. It will cost them somewhat more than the dreadful corn liquor of their native steppes, but they will quickly get too much aboard to bother about money. In brief, I formally prophesy that the Democratic National Convention will be as wet as Democratic national conventions have always been, and that the Prohibitionist delegates, as always, will do more than their fair share of the guzzling. The soberest men in the hall, no doubt, will be the Tammany delegates and their brethren from the other big cities of the East. To these cockneys drinking has vastly less fascination than it has for the hind of the hinterland; decent drinks are always under their noses, and so they are not tortured by the pathological thirst of the rural Ku Kluxers. Moreover, they will have a serious job in hand, and so they will avoid the jug. That job will be to get the bucolic Baptists drunk, and shove Al down their gullets before they recognize the flavor.

(The Baltimore Evening Sun, June 2, 1924)

Mencken Forced to Flee
Before Burton's Oratory;
"Babbitry" Appalls Him

Cleveland, Ohio, June 11.—More than any other convention that I have ever known or heard of this one is marked by vulgarity and imbecility. There is absolutely no relief from the steady stream of depressing slush. It is really quite appalling. The delegates, herded about like cattle at the stockyards, show the faces and manners of children on holiday from a home for the feeble-minded. And the so-called leaders, at the highest points of their leading, seldom get beyond the average sense and dignity of the speakers at a luncheon of the Kiwanis Club.

Here democracy is making its lowest recorded dip. If it ever gets any lower it will cease to be human.

This almost pathological stupidity is something new at a national convention and particularly at a Republican National Convention. The Republican party in the past has been led by men who, whatever their faults otherwise, were at least decently educated and urbane and civilized of habit. Even its clowns showed something of the grand manner. For example, Chauncey M. Depew. When he was put up to make the crowd roar, he made it roar with genuine wit. One somehow felt that he was superior to his buffoonery—that he was deliberately unbending in a healthy spirit of play. And of his more solemn brethren one felt that, even if they were scoundrels, they were also gentlemen.

The present show is not run by gentlemen, but by the worst sort of political and commercial bounders. It is cheap, common, dull and irritating. The character of the official hero has colored the whole ceremonial of his elevation to Valhalla. There are no Chauncey M. Depews on the program, but only a long series of dreadful dullards, each new one worse than all who have gone before. All the sleek elegance of yesteryear has vanished; what remains is mainly a parade of small town Rotarians in mailorder clothes. When Andrew W. Mellon was put up yesterday to read a resolution he stood out as brilliantly as a lovely cutie at a caucus of lady democrats. He was a ghost out of happier days, before the lath-factory and the cow-stable were set up in the Forum Romanorum. No other such ghosts, I venture, will be permitted to walk. The Lodges, the Roots, the Cumminses and the rest of the old-timers are all secure in the hold, with the hatches battened down over them. Babbitt is on deck.

Yesterday's opening session was so vilely blowsy and nonsensical that even the local sightseers could not stand it, and long before it was over the galleries were half empty. The keynote speech of the Hon. Theodore E. Burton was undiluted drivel—nine thousand words of bad English without an idea in it. Burton is an ancient political hack, with long legs and a small bald head, and looks a great deal like a barber out of work. He plainly fancies himself as an orator, and has a way of stopping expectantly every time he makes what he regards as a telling point. The crowd yesterday seldom took up these cues and never with anything approaching joy. There would be a mild rattle of applause, and then he would plunge and stagger on. For an hour and thirty-five minutes this pathetic clowning kept up.

I stood it for 20 minutes and then withdrew. But there was no escaping that deadly rattle of hollow words. Directly in front of the speaker's pulpit there was the receiver of a voice amplifier and wires from it were strung, not only to all parts of the huge hall, but also to the esplanade in front of it. Thus I was pursued by Burton's rubbish when I got outside. Hundreds of other persons, including many of the delegates, were similarly in flight. We retreated foot by foot until we were brought up the shore of Lake Erie. Even there the noise was still audible, and so we gave it up and came back. Just after we got to the hall again someone discovered that there was a place in the basement that was beyond reach of the amplifier. It was crowded to suffocation in five minutes.

This idiotic harangue, remember, was not an impromptu by a spellbinder far gone in liquor. It was very carefully delivered by an elderly, highly respectable and quite sober man, and it had been composed long in advance of its delivery and elaborately revised by all the master-minds who now run the so-called Republican party, including the President of the United States. In other words, it represented the deliberate and highest thought of all those master-minds; it embodied a statement of the lofty principles upon which they now propose to ask for the votes of the

American people. I can only report quite simply that, as I heard it delivered, its content would have insulted the intelligence of an audience of 9-year-old schoolboys; that the manner of its delivery would have done discredit to a barker in front of a circus side-show.

Once Burton had got it out there was an attempt at a dramatic interlude. Somewhere down on the floor an ancient was discovered who had been a member of the convention which nominated Lincoln in 1860, and he was dragged to the platform to exhibit his wounds to the mob. Some one rashly suggested that he make a speech, and he instantly launched into a violent philippic against slavery, with very caustic animadversions upon the character of the late Jefferson Davis. His voice, of course, was very feeble, but the amplifier magnified it into an uncanny roar. The effect was that of a baby in arms breaking out into a bass solo. At the end of 10 minutes he was settling down to tell the whole history of the foul conspiracy to disrupt the Union, with graphic sketches of the principal villains. Then Burton, who seemed a mere youth beside him, rushed up to him, grabbed him by the hand, congratulated him vociferously, and so elbowed him off the platform. The crowd applauded and guffawed.

This was the first day's show. That of the second day, now in progress, differs from it only as one bad egg differs from another. There is not even anything to laugh at—that is, heartily, decently, with innocent good humor. What one gapes at, hour after weary hour, is simply a performance of marionettes—worse, a performance of marionettes without heads—mere inanimate sticks. I hear that on tomorrow, the great day, a vast demonstration for the Honorable Mr. Coolidge will be staged. A glee club from Massachusetts is rehearsing somewhere, a band has been hired, and Y.M.C.A. cheer leaders are on the premises. It may be that these professors will be able to make the welkin ring, but I doubt it. If they succeed with the harsh job before them—if they actually make this mob of morons cheer with any lustiness for the vacuum in the White House, then I shall hire them on Thursday to make William Jennings Bryan cheer for Darwin.

Bryan himself is here—a bit older than the last time, a bit more seedy and a bit more pathetic. He is now quite bald and looks thin and forlorn. He is writing for a syndicate of Christian newspapers, mainly in the South. Compared to the counter-jumpers who are running this great patriotic orgy he seems almost an intellectual. Bryan is the only man I have encountered here who appears to be glad that the town is dry. The delegates and alternates view the fact with extreme dis-ease. All day long and all the evening they shuffle about, exchanging whispered tips about concealed jugs. Many of them are professional prohibitionists in their home towns and all of them will vote for a dry plank in their party platform today, but so far I have not encountered one who was not only willing but also eager to get a drink. The only thing talked of in the hotel lobbies is the rum situation. The business of the convention needs no discussion. It has been decided to the last place of decimals, and by process of predestination.

The town is still dry, but not quite as dry as it was on Sunday. Several rum-ships, it is reported, have broken through the blockade and landed cargoes. The Michigan Red Cross is said to have sent in a caravan of motor trucks. But prices remain very high, and most of the stuff on tap is of dubious quality. This morning a local newspaper reporter called me up and asked me if I knew where he could get a drink. I gave him the addresses of 250 saloons in Baltimore and 2,000 in New York. Try to imagine a newspaper reporter unable to get a drink in his own town!

(The Baltimore Evening Sun, June 11, 1924)

Vice-Presidential Battle
Thrills Mencken
After Dull Business
of Naming "Cal"

Cleveland, June 13.—It was not until the depressing business of canonizing good Cal had been got out of the way that this convention began to show any genuine life of dignity. The usual roles of the candidates were then reversed. The Vice-President, for long concealed mysteriously in a black cloak, became both hero and villain, and the President, though the halo rode upon his ears and the scepter was in his hand, sank to the ignominious estate of a walking gent.

The spell-binder who put up to offer the name of Dr. Coolidge to the delegates was a very good one, and he made an excellent speech, but the theme he struggled with was too much for him. What he essayed to prove was, as he said himself, that the eminent candidate was and is a human being. The thesis apparently amused not a few of the delegates: they laughed somewhat indelicately at some of the learned speaker's illustrative anecdotes. What is more, he was constrained to laugh, at times, himself, and so the whole transaction took on a jocosity that was appropriate but disconcerting.

This orator was Dr. Marion Burton, president of the University of Michigan, and a distinguished exponent of the latest modes in the higher learning. The University of Michigan does not confine itself to the training of astrophysicists and philogians; it also teaches the art of paper-hanging and the science of fire insurance; not even the Johns Hopkins is more broadly devoted to service.

Thus Dr. Burton lacks the pedantic manner and academic pallor of the old-time savant. Instead he is a tall, lean, brisk, ingratiating and go-getting fellow, and the instant he got upon his legs it became apparent he was by no means abashed. Nor was his confidence unfounded. He turned out to be a capital mob orator, with a clear, agreeable voice and a halting staccato style, and in two minutes he had his crowd with him and was making the praise of Dr. Coolidge a pleasant and even merry business.

But for all his eloquence he could not make it thrilling, and the fact became horribly apparent the moment he discharged the name of the candidate and fell into the arms of Chairman Mondell. It is the custom at national conventions to hold back the name until the last instant, and then to snap it out dramatically, for the sound of it is the signal for the formal demonstration to begin. But this time, for the first time in political history, no demonstration followed. There was a feeble round of applause, a few delegates began parading the aisles with their State standards and then the whole thing died. Three minutes after it began there was absolutely no sound in the hall save the shuffling of feet.

Perhaps the man in charge of the lights and music was partly to blame for this unprecedented fiasco. He should have started the band playing "The Star-Spangled Banner," "Yes, We Have No Bananas," or some other such stimulating tune; instead he kept it silent for at least five minutes. He should have turned on all the spotlights and bathed the delegates with great beams of blinding light; instead he turned on dim reds and blues, appropriate only to a funeral parlor.

When, after what seemed to be a geological epoch, the band began to play at last, it played, "Onward, Christian Soldiers." It was too late. The crowd in the galleries essayed to sing, but at once got out of tune with the band. Then the pipe organ horned in —out of time with both the band and the galleries. A Y.M.C.A. song leader, hurriedly rushed to the platform, tried to lead all three, but made a mess of it. The singing died down as quickly as the applause, and again there was an appalling silence.

In 10 minutes it was all over and the seconding speeches began. They quickly converted tragi-comedy into burlesque. A fat woman from Kansas, swathed in apricot-colored silk of dazzling brilliance, mounted the platform, squared off like a heavyweight ready for the gong, and bawled "Mr. Chairman" into the amplifier in a voice so raucous that the crowd yelled. Then a colored intellectual from New Jersey, with the beard of a Harvard professor, climbed into the pulpit and was riotously booed down. Then came the Hon. Isaac M. Meekins, of North Carolina, a chunky, baldheaded fellow in horn-rim spectacles and an alpaca coat. The Hon. Mr. Meekins planted himself firmly in front of the amplifier, cleared his throat and launched head-first into the following lofty and mellow stuff:

"Under the wide and tender light of the full orbed moon, I stood by the inlet of the sea, and saw the mighty tide ebb and flow. I saw the ebb tide, lay and flow. I saw the ebb tide, lay and ashamed, taking out the filth and debris from the rivers, bays and sounds to be swallowed up in the ocean's vastness, and I said: 'How like the body politic is that scum upon the face of the waters moving seaward!' "

There was a great deal more to the same elevated and ennobling effect. The Hon. Mr. Meekins, in fact, had taken care to distribute printed copies of his prose-poem before he began to recite it. But the delegates and alternates, alas, failed to rise to it, and the burghers of Cleveland in the galleries even professed to regard it as humor.

This greatly offended Dr. Meekins, and he showed it. He glared about him truculently, he tried to bawl down the uproar; he defiantly draped himself over the pulpit rail to wait for it to end. Four or five times he started again and as many times he was brought up by the bawling Philistines in front of him. Finally he came to this purple passage:

"As the shepherd loves the flock he leads afield, so he, in whose heart his countrymen are enshrined, serves and leads them best. Never to tire, never to grow cold; to look for the budding flower and the opening heart; to hope always; to love always—this is service; this is duty; and Calvin Coolidge is all service—all duty."

To the best of my knowledge and belief, this gem of Kiwanis poetry was never shot into the amplifier. I sat not more than 50 feet from the talented speaker, and I strained my ears to hear him, but all I got was a hurricane of guffaws and cat calls, and a voice from the gallery yelling, "When do we eat?".

It was a dreadful quarter of an hour for the Hon. Isaac M. Meekins of Elizabeth City, N.C. As he disappeared through the trapdoor in the platform and then emerged below to struggle back to his place on the floor, his bald head glistened as if it were red-hot, and the prudent cops and sergeants-at-arms fell back to give him way. It was the high point of the whole nomination ceremony. North Carolina supplied the martyr to make the Roman holiday. . . .

(The Baltimore Evening Sun, June 13, 1924)

In contrast to the lethargy and harmony of the Republican convention, the Democratic National Convention met in Madison Square Garden in New York on sixteen days between June 24 and July 9, amid a heat wave and a spirit of dissension. Senator Pat Harrison of Mississippi, the keynote speaker, spoke mostly of the Harding scandals, but the main issue was the Democratic Party's violent division over the Ku Klux Klan. The forces were divided between the anti-Klan delegates, mostly from the East and other large cities; and those who supported the Klan or felt it should not be openly disavowed. The champion of the anti-Klan forces was the popular governor of New York, Alfred E. Smith, who received a seventy-three-minute ovation after Franklin D. Roosevelt, now crippled with polio, nominated him as "the 'Happy Warrior' of the political battlefield." To the Klan, Smith's liberalism and Catholicism were anathema; their own candi-

date (though he disavowed much of their positions) was William Gibbs McAdoo.

Sixty candidates were nominated for the presidency; as ballot after ballot was taken, the favorite sons dropped out, but neither Smith nor McAdoo could command the two-thirds majority. It took thirteen stifling days and 103 ballots before the delegates, deadlocked over Smith and McAdoo, abandoned their choices and nominated the former ambassador to London and Solicitor General to President Wilson, John W. Davis of West Virginia; for the vice presidency they chose Charles W. Bryan, governor of Nebraska and brother to William Jennings Bryan.

For the most part, Mencken enjoyed being among "the witch-burners"—his desk was directly in front of the delegates from Georgia ("What faces!"). But as the convention dragged on, he and others felt as if they were doomed to remain at Madison Square Garden all summer. Will Rogers complained New York City had invited the delegates to visit the place, not to live there; to a friend, Mencken wrote: "I pray that our Redeemer may inspire them to call it off tomorrow. I have on my last shirt and must go naked if they continue."

Mencken Decides Klan's Enemies Have Hurt Their Cause by Drawing Issue

New York, June 26.—The klan, having grabbed the center of the stage yesterday, hangs on to it somewhat dubiously today, wondering what to do with it. There is such a thing, it appears, as being burnt by the spotlights. When the wizards, goblins, mastodons and imperial duodenums came to town, and began bawling for a plank pledging allegiance to the Invisible Empire and a candidate sworn to its lofty principles, I doubt that even the most optimistic of them had any hope of getting anything more than a lot of free and gaudy advertising. It was obvious even to idiots that the Democratic party in convention assembled could not afford to indorse the klan, and that Dr. McAdoo, its candidate, could not conceivably win if he did so.

McAdoo, in fact, devoted most of his energies, once he got upon the battleground, to trying to make it appear that he was not the klan candidate at all. He kept away from the wizards, goblins and other sorcerers; he let it be known delicately that he was hot for religious liberty; he tried to start flirtations with the less intransigeant of the Smith delegates; he deliberately chose a Catholic to put him in nomination. But the whooping of the wizards, unfortunately for him, had gone too far to be disposed of by any such devices. It had gone so far, in fact, that it had stirred up a great deal of very bitter anti-klan sentiment.

This anti-klan sentiment is now raging furiously—so furiously that it threatens to get away from the leaders and bring on a genuine battle to the death. It was responsible for all the hard swearing done by the resolutions committee in the heat of yesterday and it was responsible for the ludicrous and yet ugly episodes that put melodrama into the session of yesterday afternoon. Today the convention is full of electricity. Before the session is over there may be some really thrilling thunder claps.

It was the anti-klan men, of course, and not the klansmen, who brought the issue on to the convention floor, and they did it with every sign of malice aforethought. The session had been droning along for more than two hours with no more life in it than a dead fish on the beach. The speech of Senator Thomas Walsh, the permanent chairman, had been so dull that twice while he was at it the delegates and alternate arose, like a bleachers crowd in the seventh inning, and stretched their arms and legs. Great waves of heat pulsated through the hall. Sweat in its gaseous form rode the thick and lazy air.

It would have been hard enough, in that miasma, to look at a hanging. Listening to poor Walsh was almost unendurable. When he finished there was a cheer of thanksgiving, as of ship wrecked mariners sighting a 30-knot Cunarder, her bands playing and her smokestacks belching the inspiring smell of ham and cabbage.

Then came the roll of States, and from the delegation of the first one called, Alabama, there uprose a brisk and dapper little fellow named Fordney Johnston to put the eminent name of Oscar W. Underwood in nomination. Underwood was plainly a dead one and Johnston turned out to be a poor speaker, and so the crowd settled down wearily to another spell of boredom. Most of the male delegates and alternates took off their collars. There was a great shuffling of feet, and much lugubrious grunting and wheezing.

Two or three times Walsh hammered for order, but it never lasted more than a moment. Meanwhile, Johnston worked his way desperately through his speech—a long and incredibly tedious account of good Oscar's lifelong services to the Democratic party, the republic and the human race in general. Finally, he got so tired of it himself that he lounged against the speakers' stand, and began to rattle it off as if he were reading the annual report of the Pennsylvania Railroad.

But something was in reserve, and suddenly Johnston came to it. The huge audience saw him stand back and square himself, and the noise in the hall fell to a whisper. He had come to the klan section of his discourse, and everyone wanted to hear it, for everyone knew that Underwood had been slaughtered by the klan in the South and was sore and eager for blood—that he was dead as a candidate, in fact, precisely because the klan had fallen on him.

Johnston began gently with the usual platitudinous rubbish about religious freedom. It was feeble stuff, but it seemed to be leading to something, and so the attentive silence continued. Presently that something came. It was a brief, harsh, staccato denunciation of the klan—by name!

The fat was then in the fire. It was too late to call the firemen. With a roar a thousand foes of the klan sprang to their feet and began to pour into the aisles, and in half a minute a great demonstration against the Invisible Empire was in progress. It was unpremeditated and so it was without order, but it was formidable enough for all that as is mounted in volume some of the klan delegations began to look alarmed. But, so far as I could make out, no direct affront was actually offered to them. In the Colorado delegation the anti-klan men tried to carry the State standard into the parade and the klansmen of the delegation held on to it and refused to let them take it, but the battle was stopped by the cops before it got very far. The standard itself was damaged, but no one was hurt.

The alert reporters have already furnished the public and posterity with painstaking and, I hope, accurate lists of the State standards that were carried in the anti-klan parade and of those that were guarded throughout by klansmen. Suffice it to say here that the non-marching States, with very few exceptions, were the McAdoo States. Georgia stood like a stone wall and so did Kansas. It was, in its way, a demonstration of relative strengths, and it seemed to me that the klansmen, despite their silence, got the better of it.

The whole fight upon the klan, in fact, is probably helping Mc-Adoo. The anti-klan whoopers, by incautiously showing their teeth, have put every 100 percent American on his guard, and I believe that it will be far more difficult now to mollify and bamboozle them than it would have been if the whole issue had been permitted to subside, like prohibition, into a platitude in the platform.

There may not be enough kluxers in the convention to nominate McAdoo, but there are probably enough to beat any anti-klan candidate so far heard of, and they are all on their tiptoes today, their hands clutching their artillery nervously and their eyes apop for dynamite bombs and Jesuit spies. . . .

(The Baltimore Evening Sun, June 26, 1924)

"I can recall no national convention at which there were more and longer speeches, nor at which the general average of eloquence was so low," Mencken reported on June 27. Bryan's oratory, which had once captivated so many, had become *"a decay of platitudes."* The best speech, he admitted, *"was that delivered by the Hon. Franklin D. Roosevelt yesterday, putting Dr. Smith in nomination, and Dr. Roosevelt, compared to such champions of the past as Bryan and Bourke Cocoran, is certainly no orator. His advantage . . . lies in the simple fact that he is a charming man. He won the crowd yesterday the instant he stood up, and he held it for half an hour without the slightest resort of artifice."* But Mencken did not credit this triumph to what many saw as Roosevelt's charisma or ringing rich tenor: *"Roosevelt, of course, was on absolutely sure ground. He was nominating Al Smith, and any speech nominating Al Smith would have gone with a roar, even if it would have been made in Lithuanian."*

New York, Mencken discovered, had made Al Smith its demigod. *"Win or lose, Al is and will remain one of the folk-heroes of the New York populace. I know of none other quite like him in American history. He is not merely popular; he is worshipped. For human beings here, as elsewhere, make their gods in their own image, and in Al every poor boy in New York sees himself—sees all his secret aspirations realized and made visible, and on a plane of dignity almost beyond his loftiest hopes."* This pride in Al Smith was universal, Mencken found, and was *"genuinely touching. I never come into my hotel without being stopped by the doorman and the elevator boy and asked for news. Is all going well with Al? Will he be put over? Are those scoundrelly Ku Kluxers licked? Who could say no when so much happiness is hidden in a little yes? I lie 40 times a day, and every time I do it, I am proud of the gift which makes my lies so realistic."*

Conventions Have Become Ill Managed and Inefficient Carnivals, Thinks Mencken

New York, June 28.—Democracy, after all, must be a sound scheme at bottom, else it would not survive such cruel strains. Here at this so-called national convention it is being subjected to the hardest strain of all, to institutions or to men; it is being made ridiculous. The proceedings of the assembled Democrats, in theory, are the most solemn that the delegates of a free people can engage in; in actuality, they are so vulgar, so tawdry, so downright preposterous that a synod of chimpanzees should and would be ashamed of them.

The convention system, at bottom, is certainly not a bad one. It gives the people of all parts of the country their chance to be heard; it provides for free debate; it insures voting in the open; it is fundamentally fair and honest. But in practice it has become so horribly enmeshed in formulae that two-thirds of the ends that it was designed to achieve are defeated. The delegates spend nearly all their time and energies not in considering the business before them, but at the hollow maneuvers of trained animals. Half the time they can scarcely hear what is going on before them and the rest of the time it is almost impossible for them to take an active and intelligent part in it.

For three days now the delegates to the present convention, sitting for hour after hour in a hot and hideous hall, have been listening to speeches—perhaps 40 or 50 in all. Of the whole lot only one has shown the remotest approach to sense or dignity, and even that one was twice too long. I allude to the speech of the Hon. Franklin D. Roosevelt nominating Al Smith. It was surely no great shakes as oratory, but it was at least clear in substance and agreeable in manner. All the rest of the harangues so far launched upon the sweating delegates have been undiluted bilge.

Why, then, are such speeches made? Why do the delegates and alternates listen to them with such heroic patience? Simply, I believe, because the custom of listening to them has gradually grown up—because there is in human beings in the mass an almost irresistible tendency to do docilely whatever has been done before—because politicians, in particular, are such humorless followers of rules and precedents that a realistic dealing with the business before them is well-nigh beyond their imagination.

Perhaps the fact that lawyers run our politics enters here. A lawyer practicing his craft under Anglo-Saxon jurisprudence becomes a pedant almost inevitably. The system he follows is expressly designed to shut out common sense. He is forbidden to exercise his fancy and his reason, such as they are; he must follow the law and the precedent. When he carries this habit of mind into politics its result is just such dreary clown shows as the present convention.

Consider, for example, the matter of the so-called keynote speech. Years ago it occurred to some one that it would be a good idea to open every party convention with a statement of the party's claims to public support. The idea was plainly not a bad one, but see what it has come to in the course of time. The keynote speech has grown longer and longer, and sillier and sillier. It is now almost completely devoid of intelligible content. Some hollow party hack is put up to rant and snort for an hour and a half, and when he has finished it is discovered that he has said precisely nothing. I can recall no keynote speech in my time that would have done any credit to a boy of 12. The best have been masses of puerile platitudes; the worst have been idiotic and disgraceful.

Not even politicians are fools enough to believe that such nonsensical harangues have any immediate utility. The delegates and alternates pay little heed to them, and are certainly not influenced appreciably by what they hear. The theory is, however, that they are read by the country. But is it sound? I doubt it. Not one newspaper in a hundred attempts to print the whole text of a keynote speech, and not one reader in a thousand gives any serious study to the extracts and summaries that are actually printed. Why, indeed, should he? Why should he waste his time plowing through a nobody's gaudy vaporings about nothing?

But it has become the custom to open every national convention with just such a discharge of rubbish, and so it is done with all solemnity every time. No one thinks to object to it; a challenge of it would shock the heavy-witted mountebanks who run the show as much as any other intrusion of common sense.

Worse, there is now a growing tendency to have two keynote speeches, one by the temporary chairman and then one by the permanent chairman. Yet worse, there appears a threat to add still another—by some female rabble-rouser honored with the hollow office of vice-chairman. The three, four years hence, will probably consume five hours. The time would be better spent playing marbles or getting drunk.

The nominating speeches, in the main, are just as bad. In theory, their purpose is to make the delegates acquainted with the past achievements of the various candidates and to argue for their votes. In actuality, all these speeches reduce themselves to idle and tedious fustian. The delegates loll through them hopelessly: now and then, when a speaker turns out to be extraordinarily imbecile, even for a politician, they make cruel sport of him, and even chase him from the platform. All such harangues follow a silly formula. The name of the candidate advocated is never mentioned until the last sentence. In consequence, it often happens that the delegates have to listen to a speech for half an hour without knowing clearly whom it praises.

The uproar which follows the mention of the candidate's name is now wholly artificial, and thus devoid of all significance. Now and then true enough, a minor candidate gets some genuine applause. There was an example in the case of Governor Ritchie Thursday, but the larger demonstrations are all deliberately stage-managed, and most of them are extremely vulgar and unimpressive.

No sane person enjoys such ear-splitting noises, and such preposterous parades of bewildered hirelings. The more intelligent delegates, in fact, usually go out of the hall while they are in progress. They become mere buffooneries for the entertainment of the galleries. Yet they are kept up absurdly because at some remote time in the past there was one that was real.

Such exhausting interruptions, added to the huge size of the usual convention hall, make it impossible for the delegates to take any active and useful part in the proceedings. The gallery is now more important than the convention; the tail has begun to wag the dog. Only formal speeches are practicable, and formal speeches, as everyone knows, are seldom illuminating. Free debate is completely shut off. A delegate cannot ask a question from the floor without great difficulty, and if he attempts to interrupt and cross-examine a speaker he is quickly submerged in an uproar.

The fact comes to the front every time there is an effort to deal with a routine parliamentary matter, say the question of a recess. If there is a division of opinion it is quickly reduced to a formal debate between two champions and they are chosen, not by the delegates, but by those bosses on the platform. The delegate on the floor, though he may have something apposite and important to say, simply cannot say it. And when the time comes to put the question to a vote, the galleries vote as well as the delegates and nine times out of ten a decision is reached, not by the majority voice, but by the private prejudice of the chairman.

The delegates, true enough, are still able to vote when the time comes to choose the candidates, but the business is so clumsily managed that it wastes hour after hour of time. One of the reasons, therefore, lies in the fact that many of the delegations are too large, and it is thus very difficult to poll them. Some in this convention are made up of delegates who have but a half, a quarter or even a sixth of a vote apiece. Absentees are common, especially at long sessions, and there are frequent disputes about the rights of alternates, the unit rule and the duties of delegates under their instructions.

These disputes, at their best, cause interminable delays; at their worst they end in profanity, fist fights and threats to walk out. Whenever a convention lasts more than the first week large numbers of the delegates and alternates begin to go home. A candidate for the Presidency is often chosen by the votes of persons who are a thousand miles away.

The present convention has been so tedious and uncomfortable so far, and it promises to be so long, that many of the delegates have begun to talk of overhauling the whole convention procedure. Even some of the leaders have come to see that the limit of endurance is nearly in sight.

One of the proposals that I have heard many times is that the number of delegates be reduced by half, and that future conventions be held in smaller halls, with room only for the delegates, the alternates and the newspaper reporters. The gallery has got to be an almost unbearable nuisance. It is not much interested in the business of the convention; what it wants is simply a vulgar show, and giving that show has brought the national conventions of both great parties down to the level of street carnivals.

Another proposal that I have heard is that conventions avoid such big towns as New York and Chicago hereafter and go to smaller places where the local politicians have smaller gangs behind them. Tammany, I believe, has tried to be decent during the present show, but the legions of Tammany are not used to parliamentary forms and in this contest they have a passionate interest. Many of the country delegates are genuinely alarmed. They believe seriously that the whoopers in the galleries will try to rough the convention when the tide begins to run against good Al, and that the New York police will help them. It is probably not true, but it is surely not pleasant to sit through a long convention with such fears in mind.

(*The Baltimore Evening Sun, June 28, 1924*)

The mercury rose and the air dripped with moisture, but still the delegates, now in shirtsleeves and fanning themselves futilely with palm-leaf fans, remained deadlocked as "the greatest bore in history" continued. "The whole machine is going to pieces," Mencken wrote. "The collapse is mental, spiritual and even physical. Not only are the delegates and alternates in a state of Katzenjammer, with overtones of malaria; the very hall itself has begun to disintegrate. As I sit in the Evening Sun *office in the dungeon beneath the platform, laboriously composing these lines, carpenters are at work tearing down walls and pulling out electric wires all around me. A colleague comes in and accuses me of stealing his typewriter; I do not trouble to even kick him out. A delegate falls down the steps; the carcass is shoved into a corner and forgotten. All over the place waste paper is a foot deep and hidden in it are the fragments of countless ham sandwiches, hot dogs, bottle openers, hatbands, walking sticks and wilted collars. It is a scene of filth and sadness. Hidden under the debris are blasted hopes and broken hearts. Two weeks ago the pulse of life was throbbing here and men rushed hither and thither, their blood leaping and their eyes apop. But now there is nothing but weariness and the yells that come from the hall are feeble and brief."*

Post-Mortem

I

On the morning after the final adjournment of the late Democratic National Convention, as I snored in the Biltmore Hotel, dreaming of this and that, a colleague of the *Sunpaper* came in and shook me. My eyes, as I opened them, were half blinded by the flash of sunlight from his bald head. Under his union suit rolled the lovely curves of his matronly but still heroic form. His aspect was stern. Obviously, he was agog.

"What I want you to do," he said, "is to take down my words. Wake up Hyde. I want two witnesses."

I woke up Hyde, and besought him to proceed. He plunged at once into the oath laid down in the Maryland statutes: "In the

presence of Almighty God, I do solemnly promise and declare"—
But what? Simply that he was done with national conventions
forever—that he would never attend another one in this life—that
if, by any chance, I ever caught him at one or within a hundred
miles of one, I should be free to knock him in the head, boil him
down, and sell his bones to a dice factory.

I have never seen a more earnest man. His eyes flashed blue and
awful flames. His whole hide glowed scarlet through his union
suit. Had there been any hair on his head it would have bristled
like the *vibrissae* of a Tom cat. In one long and indignant sentence
he recited a great catalogue of hardships—meals bolted suicidally
or missed altogether, nights spent in pursuing elusive and infamous politicians, hours wasted upon the writing of dispatches that
were overtaken by fresh news before they could get into the *Sunpaper*, dreadful alarm and surprises at 3 o'clock in the morning, all
the horrors of war without any of its glory. Twice he swore his
oath, and then, for good measure, he damned the whole universe.

II

But Hyde and I were not impressed. We had heard such high
talk before. We knew that the deponent was an honest man, but
we also knew that he was mistaken. We knew that he would be on
hand for the next great show, as he had been on hand for this one
and for all others in his time—that, for all his protestations and
high resolves, he could no more break himself of the convention
habit than he could break himself of the habit of breakfasting on
five fried eggs and two Manhattan cocktails. The fellow was
doomed, as we were ourselves, and if he didn't know it, it was
simply because he was not himself.

For there is something about a national convention that makes it
as fascinating as a revival or a hanging. It is vulgar, it is ugly, it is
stupid, it is tedious, it is hard upon both the higher cerebral centers and the gluteus maximus, and yet it is somehow charming.
One sits through long sessions wishing heartily that all the delegates and alternates were dead and in hell—and then suddenly
there comes a show so gaudy and hilarious, so melodramatic and
obscene, so unimaginably exhilarating and preposterous that one
lives a gorgeous year in an hour.

There were three such supreme shows in the late Democratic
convention—one given by the Hon. Homer Cummings when he

begged for more time for the resolutions committee, one supplied by the Ku Kluxers and their enemies when they had their great combat on the floor, and the last furnished by the whole company when it went crazy in ten seconds and nominated the Hon. Mr. Davis. I missed all of these shows. I was asleep during the first and second, and during the third I was hard at work in *The Evening Sun* office under the stand, writing an article proving that Dr. Davis could never be nominated.

Nevertheless, I had my fair share of the fun—enough, at all events, to take me back in 1928—if God spares me, and I can still walk with two sticks. Hyde will be there too, slaving away in the press-stand for hot hour after hot hour, wearing out lead pencils by the box, with one eye up and one eye down. And somewhere not far away, tracking down the masterminds, will be John Owens, with his noble dome and his bloody oaths.

III

But what does the general public get out of it? The general public gets precisely the same show—a bit diluted, perhaps, by distance, but still incomparably humorous and thrilling. Herein, indeed, lies the chief merit of democracy, when all is said and done; it may be clumsy, it may be swinish, it may be unutterably incompetent and dishonest, but it is never dismal—its processes, even when they irritate, never actually bore.

The Coolidge convention at Cleveland came nearer doing it than any other convention that I can recall, but even the Coolidge convention, as dull as it was, was redeemed by the revolt of the La Follette husbandmen. The thing, as planned, was to be infinitely decorous—a musicale in the afternoon. Into the drawing-room stomped the prairie peasants in their muddy boots, and at once the musicale was converted into a dog-fight. A mere farce, tawdry and degrading? Not at all. There was also some genuine drama in it. The dogs were all caught and dispatched in the end, but not until they had done thrilling execution among the dog-catchers.

The New York convention was riotous from end to end. Even during the long days of balloting there was always melodrama under the surface. The volcano slept, but ever and anon it sent up a warning wisp of smoke. When it belched actual fire the show was superb. The battle that went on between the Ku Kluxers and their enemies was certainly no sham battle. There were deep and implacable hatreds in it. Each side was resolutely determined to butcher the other. In the end, both were butchered—and a discreet bystander made off with the prize.

It seems to me that the essence of comedy was here. And a moral lesson no less, to wit, the lesson that it is dangerous, in politics, to be too honest. The Hon. Mr. Davis won the nomination by dodging every issue that really stirred the convention. The two factions lost everything that they had fought for. It was as if Germany and France, after warring over Alsace-Lorraine for centuries, should hand it over to England.

IV

The judicious will not fail to extract other lessons from the two conventions. For example, the lesson that politicians, in the main, are poor hands at practical politics—that their professional competence is very slight. Very few of them, indeed, show any sign of ordinary good sense. Their tricks are transparent and deceive no one, not even other politicians. When they accomplish anything, it is usually by accident.

Consider some of the master-minds on exhibition in New York. Tom Taggart, McAdoo and William Jennings Bryan are typical. It would be hard to think of three men who, while the sessions lasted, were talked of more, or with greater fear. Every rumor dealt with them. Every scheme took account of them. Taggart, it was whispered, was playing both ends against the middle; when the crash came he would grab everything for himself. McAdoo was too astute and too desperate to be beaten: if he could not actually win, he would at least break up the convention and ruin the Democratic party. As for Bryan, he had sworn a mighty oath to prevent the nomination of Davis, and every time he rose on the floor the Davis men trembled.

Well, what happened to all these great professors? In brief, all of them came to ridiculous ends. Taggart managed his machinations so badly that he got exactly nothing; his candidate, Ralston, had blown up long before the final struggle began. And McAdoo? McAdoo, on the day of fate, saw even his Ku Kluxers deserting him: he stood on the burning deck alone, and when he leaped into the water and swam ashore there was no one left to give him a cheer. Bryan fared even worse. They not only shoved his arch-enemy, Davis, down his throat; they shoved his brother, the Nebraska

John the Baptist, after Davis, and so made it impossible for him to yell.

This joke upon Bryan was worth all the long sessions, all the lost sleep, all the hard usage of the *gluteus maximus*. I shall be snickering over it for many long years. I shall recall it upon the scaffold, and so shock the sheriff with a macabre smirk.

(The Baltimore Evening Sun, July 14, 1924)

Breathing Space

I

This would seem to be a good time for the prudent voter to keep his ears open and his mind in the same state. Of only one of the four eminent men on the two major tickets is much known, and even that one, the Hon. Mr. Coolidge, there is less known than there ought to be. It is established that he is a stubborn little fellow with a tight, unimaginative mind, but it is certainly not established that he is a man of any genuine ability. He made a dreadful mess of the Daugherty business and of the Denby business, trying to hang on and to let go at the same time, and he even made a worse mess of the business of handling Congress. He seems to have very little capacity for dealing with men, and indeed, despite his bucolic stubbornness, very little resolution of any kind. The chances are that if he is elected in November his administration will be one of turmoil and difficulty, and that it will end in scandal and disaster.

Big Business, it appears, is in favor of him, and with it Little Business. The fact should be sufficient to make the judicious regard him somewhat suspiciously. For Big Business, in America, is almost wholly devoid of anything even poetically describable as public spirit. It is frankly on the make, day in and day out, and hence for the sort of politician who gives it the best chance. In order to get that chance it is willing to make any conceivable sacrifice of common sense and the common decencies. Big Business was in favor of Prohibition, believing that a sober workman would make a better slave than one with a few drinks in him. It was in favor of all the gross robberies and extortions that went on during the war, and profited by all of them. It was in favor of the crude throttling of free speech that was then undertaken in the name of patriotism, and is still in favor of it. It was hot against the proceedings which unveiled the swineries of Fall, Doheny, Daugherty, Burns and company, as Dr. Coolidge himself was. Now it is in favor of Dr. Coolidge. He may be, as they say, a virtuous and diligent man, but he is surely in very bad company.

II

What is to be said of Dr. Davis? His press-agents, it appears, lay stress on two things: that he is highly intellectual, a man who reads books, and that he is a very successful lawyer. The two merits, alas, do not often go together, nor is there any evidence that either is of much public value in a President. The last reader of books who sat in the White House got the United States into a ruinous war, increased the public debt by $25,000,000,000, destroyed the Bill of Rights, and filled in the Government service with such strange fowl as Bryan, Lansing, Palmer, Burleson and Colonel House. This bookworm was also a lawyer, though a bad one.

Dr. Davis is said to be a good one. But is there any reason to believe that, among lawyers, the best are much better than the worst? I can find none. All the extravagance and incompetence of our present Government is due, in the main, to lawyers, and, in part at least, to good ones. They are responsible for nine-tenths of the useless and vicious laws that now clutter the statute-books, and for all the evils that go with the vain attempt to enforce them. Every Federal judge is a lawyer. So are most Congressmen. Every invasion of the plain rights of the citizen has a lawyer behind it. If all lawyers were hanged tomorrow, and their bones sold to a mah jong factory, we'd all be freer and safer, and our taxes would be reduced by almost a half.

Dr. Davis is a lawyer whose life has been devoted to protecting the great enterprises of Big Business. He used to work for J. Pierpont Morgan, and he has himself said that he is proud of the fact. Mr. Morgan is an international banker, engaged in squeezing nations that are hard up and in trouble. His operations are safeguarded for him by the man-power of the United States. He was one of the principal beneficiaries of the late war, and made millions out of it. The Government hospitals are now full of one-legged soldiers who gallantly protected his investments then, and the public schools are full of boys who will protect his investments tomorrow. Mr. Davis, it would seem, approves this benign business, and, as I say, is proud of his connection with it. I knew a man once who was proud of his skill at biting off little dogs' tails.

III

This brings us to the candidates for the Vice-Presidency. Of the Hon. Mr. Dawes it is sufficient to say that he is a shining light in both Big Business and the law. He is what they call well heeled and is frankly sympathetic with other men who are well heeled! When, after the war was over, certain Congressmen began asking what had become of some of the money appropriated for its conduct, Mr. Dawes appeared before them, gave them a good round cursing, and so scared them into silence. What became of the money was never found out. Then the learned gentleman turned his attention to schemes for policing labor. His masterpiece, it appears, involved the copious cracking of heads. All the Rotary Clubs and Chambers of Commerce are in favor of Mr. Dawes. He is the pet candidate of the country bankers. Most of them, in fact, are sorry he doesn't head the ticket.

Of the Hon. Mr. Bryan I can tell you little, save that he wears a skullcap and is a brother to the eminent Jennings. Jennings was hot against Dr. Davis and threatened to bolt the ticket if he was nominated. So they put Brother Charley on it, and thus spiked him. Brother Charley has gone on in politics out in the cow States by promising, if elected, to reduce the price of coal and gasoline. His opponents, in the main, have promised to raise the price of corn and wheat. Confronted by such a choice, the husbandmen have commonly voted for Charley, as for the least of two swindlers. In brief a politician rather above the average. Unlike Brother Jennings, he is said to be doubtful about the scientific accuracy of Genesis, but the eloquence of Jennings will suffice to hold the rustic Fundamentalists in line. In his early days Charley was sporty, and had something to do with horses. But now, with his skullcap, he looks like a country undertaker. The job he aspires to has been held in the past by John Adams, Thomas Jefferson, John C. Calhoun and Hannibal Hamlin. More recently it has been held by Garrett A. Hobart, Charles W. Fairbanks and the Hon. Mr. Coolidge.

IV

The Hon. Mr. La Follette remains. He has no hope, it would seem, of actually seizing the throne; all he dreams of accomplishing is to throw the election into the House of Representatives, where, holding the balance of power, he will be able to dictate the election. But what good will that do him? His right of dictation, practically considered, will be simply a right to choose between the Hon. Mr. Coolidge and the Hon. Mr. Davis. Dr. La Follette himself will probably be the third man, but no one believes that either side will consent to his election—and the House will be restricted to three high men; it cannot go outside for a candidate.

In brief, his power, assuming he keeps both Dr. Coolidge and Dr. Davis from getting a majority in the Electoral College, will have only what the lawyers call a nuisance value. He will be able to scare everyone half to death, and yet he will be unable to get anything for himself. But won't it be possible for him, with both gangs at his mercy, to strike a bargain with either one or the other? Won't both be willing, in return for his support, to adopt his program, and so give him a great moral victory? Of course, of course! Both sides will be willing to promise anything, on a stack of Bibles a mile high. And whichever side promises most, and so fetches Dr. La Follette, will ditch him two hours after its candidate is inaugurated.

But another possibility remains. La Follette is surely no flapper in politics. It may be that he will refuse to believe either party. In that case there will be no election at all, and March 4 will come without a new President in waiting. What will happen then? Dr. Coolidge, I presume, will try to hold on—and ten thousand eager patriots will apply for injunctions and mandamuses against him. In other words, the whole comedy will be transferred to the Supreme court of the United States. In yet other words, it will become infinitely low and buffoonish, infinitely amusing. Nine lawyers, including one good one, will elect the President. I give warning that I shall need the Stadium to laugh in.

V

But this is not yet. The time has not come for overt mirth. The perspicacious subject of the Republic, for a month or two, will listen much and say little. We'll know more about the candidates by September 1. And what we find out about them may make the show even more charming than it is today.

(The Baltimore Evening Sun, August 4, 1924)

1928

Coolidge and the country prospered on the principle of laissez-faire government. He made no attempt to work closely with Congress, take issues to the people, nor use his executive powers in a forceful manner. Nevertheless, he was a popular President. The country liked his dry wit, frugal habits, and what they saw as his "good conscience," which enabled him to sleep an average of eleven hours a day. As his term drew to a close, Mencken observed, "He will pass from the Presidency as he came into it—a dull and docile drudge, loving the more tedious forms of ease, without imagination, and not too honest." In 1927 Coolidge told reporters he did not choose to run again for the presidency.

The strongest contender for office was Herbert Hoover, the Secretary of Commerce and Wartime Food Administrator. When the Republican delegates met in Kansas City on June 12–15, Hoover was chosen on the first ballot; Charles Curtis, the Senate majority leader, was chosen as his running mate. The greatest asset in their campaign was economic prosperity, and Hoover emphasized it, calling for more of the same: tax reduction, the "American system" of free enterprise, high tariffs, and full enforcement of the Eighteenth Amendment, which he called "a great social and economic experience, noble in motive and far-reaching in purpose."

The year 1928 appeared more bleak for the Democratic Party than 1924. The Democratic National Convention was held at Houston, Texas (to please the southern Democrats), on June 26–29, and delegates immediately chose the popular Al Smith, four-term governor of New York. Franklin Roosevelt, once again, placed "the Happy Warrior" on the nomination. Joseph T. Robinson of Arkansas was chosen as Smith's running mate. Disturbed by the crime spawned by the Eighteenth Amendment, Smith favored "fundamental changes in the provisions of Prohibition," thus arousing the wrath of the Anti-Saloon League, the Women's Christian Temperance Union, and other militant dry groups. To make matters worse, Smith had chosen millionaire John J. Raskob as his campaign manager (like Smith, he was a "wet" and a Catholic); Smith's associations with Tammany Hall also hurt him in many cities of the South and West.

Religion was another major issue throughout the campaign; even though Smith made it clear he believed in "the absolute separation" of church and state, rumors persisted that the Catholic candidate would annul Protestant marriages, that Protestant children would be declared illegitimate, and that the Pope had his bags packed, ready to move to Washington once Smith was elected. "A Vote for Al Smith Is a Vote for the Pope," shouted Klansmen; a Smith victory would be "Rum, Romanism, and Ruin." Fiery KKK crosses threatened his route to an auditorium in Oklahoma City; preachers told their congregations, "If you vote for Al Smith, you're voting against Christ and you'll be damned."

On July 10 Mencken subscribed to all of the Baptist and Methodist papers to discover, firsthand, what was being printed of the Catholic candidate: ". . . there are journals which pile indignation upon indignation, and devote practically all their space to philipics against Al, Raskob, Tammany, the Beer Trust, and the Pope," wrote Mencken in his Monday column, "Onward, Christian Soldiers!" In the Baptist and Commoner Pastor J. A. Scarboro told readers the texts of Daniel and Revelation supported his case against Al Smith, concluding: " 'The Devil's crowd—Catholics, political demagogues, brewers, bootleggers, prostitutes—the whole motley bellygang are for Smith!' "

To Mencken, the fury of their diatribes was amusing, but there was a deeper issue involved. "I daresay the extent of the bigotry prevailing in America, as it has been revealed by the campaign, has astounded a great many Americans," he wrote. Hoover had said little to check the anti-Catholic crusades of some of his supporters. "He muttered three sentences against religious intolerance," Mencken wrote before election day, "but the bigots kept on supporting him, and they will support him tomorrow, and he knows it and is counting on it."

The campaign promised to be a bitter one. "Smith will make a gaudy show," Mencken predicted, "but I don't think he will gather any votes by it. The American people prefer safer men. That is to say, they prefer vacuums." An admirer of Smith, Mencken followed his long campaign throughout the country, writing some of his best articles for the Evening Sun. In the East, enthusiastic crowds turned out to hear Smith speak; although many turned out in the South to see the controversial candidates's brown derby and cigar, the receptions were cool: Smith, a Catholic, a wet, a New Yorker, and a Tammany man, was simply a foreigner among them. Prosperity was on Hoover's side, and he reassured his audiences that the poorhouses were vanishing, that there was "a chicken in every pot and two cars in every garage." Smith retorted, "Let's look at the record!" but the voters ignored his dire warnings. The Hoover landslide carried forty states, including Smith's own state of New York. As it turned out, the euphoria was short-lived.

Strife Rends Democrats,
Says Mencken,
Making Smith Men Less Secure

Houston, Texas, June 25 (Special).—Harmony is the watchword, but there is blood in every eye. True enough, the combat which impends will be largely a sham battle, but all the same it promises to have its moments. When two Republicans meet at a national convention they retire behind the nearest potted palm and embrace. When two Democrats meet they clear a space in some crowded hotel lobby, leap in air with fearful whoops and proceed to tear each other limb from limb. This year, for the first time in a long while, the party has a candidate with the vast majority of convention votes behind him and excellent chance of victory in November ahead of him. The cue would seem to be for brotherly love. But all one hears is rumors of black plots and conspiracies. Every ambitious statesman in town is trying to make the first pages, not by reconciling the warring factions and forming a solid front, but by stirring up every smoldering hatred and lighting new ones where none glower now.

The plain fact is that the Democratic party is scarcely a party at all, but simply a loose federation of discordant minorities, chiefly devoted to civil war. The distance separating some of the hostile factions is far greater than that separating either of them from the Republicans, or even from the Socialists. Worse, they are all more or less at odds with the official doctrine of the party as a whole, so that Thomas Jefferson, if he came back to earth and inveigled some boozey delegates into putting him in nomination, would not poll two dozen honest votes.

The thing goes to fantastic lengths. If there was any idea that Jefferson cherished, it was the idea of limiting the scope and power of government, even at the cost of armed rebellion, yet here the party is about to give its highest honor to a man who first came into notice as an advocate of a long string of paternalistic panaceas. He is, to be sure, against prohibition, and there Jefferson would be with him, but he cannot be either nominated or elected without the aid of prohibitionist votes.

For years the party has advocated a tariff for revenue only, and I suppose that this year's platform will advocate it again. But at least two-thirds of the Southern delegates are actually protectionists, and so are many of the delegates from the North and West. The chief argument I have heard against the availability of Cordell Hull, of Tennessee, is that he is honestly in favor of a low tariff and had delivered powerful licks for it in the past. Next to that comes the argument that he is really a prohibitionist and would accept literally the sop that the platform will throw to the drys.

Not many of the other dry aspirants labor under that suspicion. Some of them are hearty boozers and make little effort to conceal the fact. Others are honestly in doubt about prohibition, but keep it to themselves. I was told today that one of the principal Southern prohibitionists, a man who is personally dry, is convinced that prohibition is a complete failure and that it should be abandoned in favor of the Ontario plan of regulation. But in the convention he will advocate law enforcement to the last gasp and gurgle.

Almost the only genuine Jeffersonians on the battle ground are Governor Ritchie and Senator Reed, and the first has already thrown up the sponge. In theory, his advocacy of States' rights ought to be balm to the Southern delegates, for their fathers fought a long war on that issue, but if he set forth his ideas in this convention they would probably mob him, for the prohibition blather has converted them into irreconcilable federalists and they regard every mention of States' rights as an attack upon the Eighteenth Amendment and hence upon female virtue, the sanctity of the home, white domination and God.

The chief animosity to Senator Reed lies in the circumstance that he opposed American entry in the League of Nations, and thereby came into conflict with the late Dr. Wilson. The fact that at least nine Democrats out of ten are now against having anything to do with the League of Nations makes no difference. The row with Wilson is remembered and its cause is forgotten. It is also forgotten that Senator Reed and Wilson agreed about prohibition and that the Senator voted to sustain Wilson's veto of the Volstead act. This veto itself is forgotten. Moreover, it is officially denied by the prohibitionists. They are taught by their pastors that the libel was invented by the Jesuits.

The Smith men profess to believe that they could nominate Al on the first ballot if they would, but most of them seem to think that it will be more politic to let the favorite sons have a turn or two. The allies against Smith are even more discordant than the allies against Hoover at Kansas City. They range from the extreme wets of the Missouri delegation to the extreme drys from the Bible belt. It would be as difficult to make these drys agree upon Reed as it would be to make them agree upon Smith, and there is not the slightest chance that any of the Reed men will ever fall behind a dry. Their second choice is Smith.

Al will be nominated, when, as and if the deed is done, by the votes of many delegates who are by no means hot for him. They will vote for him simply because they believe he is the only candidate who can win and thus provide them with jobs. It is easy, going among them, to uncover traces of the Ku Klux spirit. Especially among the Southern delegates there is much uneasiness. Many of them believe more or less in prohibition and more of them fear the Pope. What has been ground into them by their pastors is not to be got out by a few speeches. They are for Al, but they wish heartily that he was a sound Baptist.

This morning a Texas newspaperman told me a story.

"In my town," he said, "there lives the worst scoundrel in the world. He killed his uncle, ran away with his young sister-in-law, deserted her in Norfolk, Va., and then came home and robbed his brother's orphans. He has plenty of money and a great deal of political influence, and so he escapes his just deserts. More than one effort has been made to jail him, but his high-powered lawyers always get him off."

The journalist paused and then asked me:

"Do you believe the story?"

"Why not?" I replied. "It sounds dreadful, but you are a newspaperman and he lives in your town. You ought to know."

"Exactly," he responded. "But I'll tell you at once that the man is a pure myth. I invented him this very minute. I did it to show you how the yokels in these wilds get their information about the Pope. They have never seen him, and so they rely upon their pastors, who pretend to be experts. Many of them have never even seen a priest. I myself was 12 years old before I saw one. Then I peeped at him through a knothole, and I remember to this day that I plainly saw his horns and tail."

Just such a boy of 12, grown up to 33, is Dan Moody, Governor of

Texas, who is being groomed to lead the fight for a bone-dry plat-form on Wednesday. Moody was born in a prairie village, forty miles from Austin, and was probably well into his teens before he ever saw any human being not a Baptist. He is against the klan, but its essential ideas and points of view got into him in infancy, and he has not grown out of them since. He is a practicing teeto-taler, which makes him rare among dry politicians. But his funda-mental fear, in all probability, is not of the jug, but of the Pope.

How far he will get in the convention remains to be seen. As the Governor of the host State he will have to be treated politely, but every effort will be made to prevent him attempting a stampede. Probably he wouldn't bring it off, even with a clear field. But it is the immemorial custom of Democrats in convention assembled to fight whenever the chance offers publicity and to the last ditch, and so the managers of the Smith campaign are probably a good deal more nervous than they profess to be.

(The Baltimore Evening Sun, June 25, 1928)

Episode

I

LOUISVILLE.

Three days of barnstorming, with bands braying day and night, had tired Al out, so his chamberlains and robbers decided to allow eleven hours for the five-hour run from Nashville to Louisville, and to put in the slack on a quiet country siding. It was a humane and charming idea. When Hyde hauled me out in the morning I stepped into a world almost too placid and lovely to be real. Birds trilled and gurgled from every rail along the trackside, and a bril-liant yellow sun beat down upon all the colors of a Kentucky autumn.

Immediately in front of me, as I climbed down from the silent train, there was a field, and beyond it and to each side stretched bits of woodland. The scene was downright theatrical: it seemed like a backdrop for some colossal performance of *As You Like It*. At first I discerned no actors, but presently two girls came out of the grove to the right, and I saw that it concealed a white farmhouse. The girls crossed the field and bade me good-morning. Would Al show himself? I didn't know. Would he stop at Lebanon Junction, half a mile down the track? Again I didn't know. Could it be arranged? Perhaps I might try.

Two more girls now came up, along with a couple of half-grown boys and an older woman. The older woman turned out to be the mother of the rest. She was perturbed, it appeared at once, by the pull of conflicting duties. There was the obligation to respect the snores of a tired visitor, and there was the obligation to offer him cheer. Did I think he would care for an old-time Kentucky chicken breakfast? I had my doubts. Would he like a stoup of country wine, made by her own hands? He was, I feared, on the wagon. But cider? I doubted that he had ever heard of it.

II

Now Hyde emerged from the train, dripping courtliness and talcum powder, and with him another man of the Smith entourage. Hyde polled the family at once. The four daughters were all for Al, but mamma inclined toward Lord Hoover. What! She would vote against a man who had come to sleep in her very dooryard? She began to wobble and presently was as good as lost. She eyed us with that wise, shrewd humorous fashion that aging women have. Were we Tammany thugs? Catholics? Friends of the saloon? Then perhaps the present talk about such fowl was exaggerated. She invited us politely to step over to her house.

All this palaver had been carried on across the fence which separated her field from the railroad right of way. To get to her house we had to walk down the track to her gate, maybe a city block away. As we started she and the four girls and two boys scurried across the field for the house, and by the time we reached it they were on the back porch, ready to receive us. It was a peaceful and romantic old farmhouse, hugging the ground and freshly painted white. Surrounding it was a lordly grove of oaks, now gaudy in saffron and crimson. Chairs were brought and the old lady dived into the house.

In a moment she came out with a carafe of dark red wine and a tray of glasses. The wine, it appeared, was of her own making. The grapes whence issued were in her own yard—had fattened and purpled there in the autumns of many years—had yielded up their royal juices, indeed, back in the days of her husband, now long dead. What we saw were last year's vintage—only a year old, but old enough. It would cure whatever we had. She began to fill the glasses.

An old guzzler, scarred and blistered from uvula to pylorus, I nevertheless felt a qualm. Wine at 7.30 A.M.? It somehow seemed fantastic, unearthly, even a bit dangerous. I hinted idiotically that I was a Prohibitionist. The old lady gave me a swift and derisive glass.

"Here," she ordered, "take your glass."

III

It was sound country wine, as thick and rich as minestrone, and the three of us got it down with a hearty smacking of the lips. The first half we drank to our hostess and her four charming daughters; the second half to Al. There followed beakers of cider, again her own making—rich, aromatic, beady, and almost as dark as Münchner. As my eye caught the blue sky through the bottom of my glass the old lady announced her conversion. She would put away the sophistries and treasons of Sir Herbert, and cast her vote for Al. Her four daughters applauded and cheered.

At once, in the fashion of converts to holy causes, she applied for a job. Not to be sure, for herself, but one for her daughters, or rather for two of them. What she wanted was an honorable post of postmistress at the Lebanon Junction, half a mile down the track. The two girls, it appears, were schoolma'ams, but had no vocation for the birch. Both longed for public life. If one was appointed, then the service would be slavery, for the people of Lebanon came for mail at all hours, seemly and unseemly. But if both were appointed, jointly and severally, then one could be enjoying life while the other stood in attendance.

It seemed ingenious to us, warmed as we were by her excellent wine, and what is more, reasonable. So we forthwith entered into a contract to get the job for both girls, as of 12 midnight of March 4, 1929. We agreed, in case Al bucked, to harry him until he yielded. We agreed to defy and set at naught, if necessary, the whole Democratic machine of Bullitt county, Kentucky. We agreed to chase away and dispose of all other candidates, male or female. And to all these promises we affixed our respective sign manuals and pledged our lives, our property and our sacred honor.

IV

Back on the train, Hyde began to be uneasy. His chivalry is not of this world: he is a man of the Thirteenth Century. Had we thanked our hostess sufficiently? Had we throttled the puerile haughtiness of slick city jakes? Had we shaken hands impartially with all four of the charming daughters, and with the other schoolma'am that appeared at the last minute, dropping in on her way to school? We checked up, compared notes, searched our hearts, found that we had. But then we discovered that, upset by bibbling so early in the morning, we had committed the foulest *faux pas* of them all. We had forgotten to ask the lovely old lady her name!

Hyde almost fainted. His courtliness froze within him. The talcum-powder rained from his face like thistle-down. He turned vermillion, then white, then crimson, then white again, then a pale blue, like the bottom of a mackerel. Something must be done about it, and at once. The Smith man had no suggestion to offer, and neither had I, but Hyde was equal to the business. He disappeared down the train, going at a gallop. He came back in a minute with a white satin badge—the same badge that all of us were wearing. In the center of it was a small lithograph of Al. Above, painted in blue, were the words, "Governor Smith." Below were the words, "Personal Party."

So we went back to the house for the presentation ceremony. Hyde affixed the badge to our late hostess with a great flourish. "You are now," he said, "one of Al's personal friends. Wear this badge and you can see him whenever you please. It is good on his train this morning. It will be good at the big meeting in Louisville tonight. It will be good at the White House after March 4. Simply show it and they will pass you in."

The old lady refused to believe it, but she kept the badge, and as she waved us good-by she was still wearing it. Back on the train, we discovered that we had again forgotten to ask her her name! Hyde locked himself in the car where they keep the movie photographers.

V

As the train pulled out we saw the old lady and her four daughters clambering into their Ford. It seemed impossible that they should beat us to the Lebanon Junction, but they managed somehow to do it. As we passed the station and the assembled crowd set up a huzzah, there they were—the four daughters waving their handkerchiefs and the old lady with her badge. Al was in the last car, and they were all set to give him a whoop. But he was hidden, *non est*, invisible—engaged, no doubt, in witless statecraft with idiot politicians, bringers of false news, back-scratchers, *pediculoe*. And thus, I fear, he lost a vote that Hyde had collared for him by chivalry and I by thirst.

(The Baltimore Evening Sun, October 15, 1928)

Analysis Fails Mencken, Pondering Smith's Sway of Crowds; Just Has "IT"

Sedalia, Mo., Oct. 17.—What is it that fetches the boobs is something that still eludes me, after many years of following and observing politicians, evangelists, chautauquans, movie magnates and other such professional fly-traps. I doubt that they know themselves. They succeed, when they succeed at all, by a sort of instinctive process and the weaknesses they play upon are too irrational to be described in words. If Al could put the thing into intelligible principia he would be the most profound of political philosophers—a veritable Aristotle of his craft. As it is, he is simply an immensely competent politician.

It is instructive to watch him do his stuff, but the essential mystery remains. Why should the flourish of a brown derby inflame and upset the aurignacian men of Tennessee, North Carolina, Kentucky and Missouri, where brown derbies have been unknown and meaningless for years? Why should people troop in for miles to see him flash by roosting on the folded top of an automobile, wearing a grin as fixed and unconvincing as any grin must be which goes on in the morning with its owner's pantaloons and stays there all day long? And why, having seen him flash by, should multitudes flop to him, as his spies and moppers-up now report them to be flopping, against the rabid exhortations of their pastors and the solemn warnings of Holy Writ?

In his actual utterances there has certainly been very little for the plain people to get their teeth into. He has high skill as a rabble-rouser, but on this tour he has very little rabble-rousing. Instead he had spent most of his time discussing subjects which, even to metaphysicians, remain dark, baffling and irritating. Myself trained as a newspaper copyreader, I can read a certain plausibility into any imaginable combination of words, however idiotic, but what he thinks, precisely, about the tariff, farm relief, Government ownership and so on is still over my head, though I have heard all his speeches from the front seats and, in addition, have listened to him in camera. What have the Bible-searchers got out of it, craning to hear from the edges of the crowd? Probably no more than they would have got out of so many speeches in Choctaw. Yet the news is that many of them went away convinced— that the tide is running Al's way in large areas of the hookworm country.

Obviously, there must be something else, perhaps impalpable to ordinary instruments of precision, like the arenas that entertain the dog. There is a something about Al's aspect that the plain people like, not knowing why, and they seem to like it almost as well where cops are curiosities as where cows are curiosities. I have watched them at a dozen country railway stations, crowding up to the observation platform. Maybe the stop is for but two or three minutes; sometimes there is no more than a slowing down. They crane their necks expectantly, waiting for they know not what. Suddenly Al is on view, waving the brown derby, reaching out to shake hands, hauling in the bouquets brought for Mrs. Smith and joshing the local worthies. They regard him quizzically for a moment, and even with a certain hostility, but then, of a sudden, he has landed them, and as the train rolls out they are howling.

To account for this phenomenon various theories are bandied among the publicists in attendance upon him. There is a school which holds that his singularly brilliant complexion should have the credit—that the American people love and admire a man with a red face. Al's is surely red enough, but the theory somehow seems inadequate. There is another school which holds that he wins them by his free and unashamed sweating. When he is fully in action the perspiration literally pours from him. It runs down his long nose and leaps into space. It gushes from the back of his neck. He uses handkerchiefs of extraordinary size and has one in every pocket. In the course of an hour's speech he hauls out four or five of them, and swabs himself elaborately at every pause. But I have seen him knock off half a county when he wasn't sweating at all, and even when his usual crimson complexion was abated to a faint sea-shell pink. Thus the theorists must guess again.

Nor is there anything magical about his gestures or about his voice. He waves the brown derby almost mechanically, first with one hand and then with the other. With the disengaged hand he holds to the folded automobile top. In speaking he gesticulates relatively little, and mainly in a commonplace manner. There is resonant, but somewhat clouded; there is nothing of the tenor clarity of Wilson's in it, and still less of the cello like quality of Bryan's. In any case, not many of his auditors hear it. What they hear is simply the loud speaker, and the loud speaker, like the radio, reduces all voices to one raucous stridency, as inhuman and undistinguished as the sound of an automobile horn.

Nor is Al any more striking in appearance than he is in manner. He is somewhat short in stature, and looks even shorter than he is. His shoulders slope like a woman's, and his body looks too long for his legs. His skull is well made, with a wide leap between the temples and a bulging occiput, but his head as a whole lacks the massiveness and is not set gracefully upon his neck. His nose is too long; his face is too long; his neck is too long. There is no brilliant flash of teeth when he smiles. His ears are thick and badly draped. He is certainly no beauty, even by bucolic standards. Compared to him Dr. Coolidge seems almost a pretty fellow, and the late Dr. Harding was an Apollo. The newspaper gals say that he has it all over Lord Hoover, but that is too easy to be worth mentioning.

The plain fact is that Al's points are mainly infra-red and ultra-violet. It is impossible to chart or label them. He simply has the thing that the movie folk call IT—and the movie folks discovered long ago that it could not be described with any precision. There are grand and gaudy beauties who lack it altogether, and there are shabby little girls who radiate it at a pressure of a million volts. Al has it as no American politician has had it since Roosevelt. He has more of it, indeed, than Roosevelt, for the popularity of Roosevelt was largely logical: the plain people admired him because he had waded in blood and saved American womanhood from the Spanish Hun. But they know very little about Al, and what little they know, at least in these back reaches of the land, is mainly unfavorable. I don't think it would be exact to say that they admire him, even after they have seen him. But it is as plain as day that they delight in him. He somehow thrills them and makes them happy. When he casts his magic over them it penetrates to their gizzards.

But even the most powerful magic cannot prevail against such dullness as resides in official statistics, and the fact was never more dismally demonstrated than in Sedalia last night. Al had before him an audience that was simply raring to yell, and when he came before it he plainly delighted it. The applause, indeed, was really almost terrifying. I have never heard such ear-splitting sounds come out of human throats, not even at a national convention. His first banal pleasantries renewed the uproar, and he seemed to be facing the greatest success of his whole trip—perhaps even the greatest success of his career. But then he plunged into the trackless morass of government finance, and in ten minutes the meeting was dead. For a while the crowd grabbed pathetically at every excuse to applaud, however feeble, and once or twice it even made excuses when there were none in the text, but presently it gave the thing up as hopeless, and the end was boredom and silence, with hundreds already escaped from the hall.

Al, of course, is no Reed Smoot, the human adding machine. His natural humor plays over and illuminates even so depressing a subject as the expenditures of Government. He had, despite the common report, very little actual wit, but his humor seldom fails him. It searches out and exposes absurdities; it runs to grotesque comparisons and homely incongruities. But it would have to be ten times as pungent and as effective as it is to disarm a country audience that has come out to see a skinning match, with blood spattering the ceiling, and is confronted by a statistical attach upon the operations of the post office.

Last night's yokels had rolled in, many of them from hundreds of miles away, and over roads not too smooth. Many had come from Kansas, and even from Oklahoma. They struggled into town all day, wet and muddy, but hot for the show. The town eating houses were quickly swamped and helpless; most of the visitors got only hot dogs to eat and only coca-cola and its allies to drink. They packed the hall at 2 P.M. and waited for Al until 8, with relays by local orators to flog and flay them and two banks to boil their blood. For all that battering they were fresh and eager when he appeared at last. They arose as one man and gave him such a cheer as must have been disclosed on every radio machine in Missouri.

But what they thought when he got to the end of his speech I can't tell you, and what they will report to their neighbors when they get home must remain a mystery until the votes are counted on November 6.

(The Baltimore Evening Sun, October 17, 1928)

Al in the Free State

I

It is difficult to make out how any native Marylander, brought up in the tradition of this ancient Commonwealth, can fail to have a friendly feeling for Al Smith in the present campaign. He represents as a man almost everything that Maryland represents as a State. There is something singularly and refreshingly free, spacious, amiable, hearty and decent about him. Brought up in poverty, and educated, insofar as he got any education at all, in the harsh school of the city streets, he has yet managed somehow to acquire what is essentially an aristocratic point of view, the habit and color of a gentleman. He is enlightened, he is high-minded, he is upright and trustworthy. What Frederick the Great said of his officers might well be said of him: he will not lie, and he cannot be bought. Not much more could be said of any man.

The contrast he makes with his opponent is really appalling. Hoover stands at the opposite pole. He is a man of sharp intelligence, well schooled and familiar with the ways of the world, and more than once, in difficult situations, he has shown a shrewd competence, but where his character ought to be there is almost a blank. He is the perfect self-seeker, pushing and unconscionable; it is hard to imagine him balking at anything to get on. His principles are so vague that even his intimates seem unable to put them into words. He is an American who came within an inch of being an Englishman, a Republican who came within an inch of being a Democrat, a dry who came within an inch of being a wet. He is what he is today because it has paid him well so far, and promises to pay still better hereafter.

It is a commonplace of the campaign that no one is passionately for him: all his most ardent support comes from those who are passionately against Al. In that support there is a grimly eloquent summing-up of the two men. Al naturally arouses the distrust and dislike of all the anti-social elements, of all the mountebanks who prey upon vulgar ignorance and credulity, and all the racketeers, high and low. The goblins of the Klan are against him, and so are the water-power exploiters. He is dreaded by the spies and boob-squeezers of the Anti-Saloon League, and hated by the witch-chasing Methodist bishops. The friends of Fall and Daugherty detest him, and the dupes of Heflin and Straton tremble at his name. All these sweet babies are for Hoover.

II

The issues of the campaign, as usual, have become tangled and obscured. There have been pointless, murky debates about the tariff, farm relief, government ownership, and other such inanimate and meaningless things. The true realities lie in the characters of the two candidates. Which is the more enlightened and courageous, the more likely to formulate rational and effective policies, the least likely to yield to privilege and power, the more trustworthy? The question almost answers itself. Al is for the free man because he is a free man himself. If his head failed him, his heart would carry him irresistibly that way. But Hoover will hedge. He will find excuses to hesitate. He knows who his masters are, and he will serve them.

On the one hand, he denounces every effort to hobble the water-power hogs as socialist and tyrannical; on the other hand, he swallows calmly the intolerable contempt for private right that is Prohibition. On which side does he actually stand? What would he say if he were man enough to say what he really thinks? I believe that he is honest when he defends private right in the name of the water-power hogs, and dissembling when he denounces it in the name of the Anti-Saloon League. But he needs the votes of the dry fanatics, and so he is dry. He admits the failure of the Volstead act, but he is for it. He is against too much government, but he calls for more.

Certainly it would be hard to imagine a more devious fellow. He has all the limber knavishness of the low-down American politician without any of the compensatory picturesqueness. He is like a lady of joy who lacks the saving grace of being beautiful. He is a Ziblman, but not so transparent; a Goldsborough, but not so dumb. Hoover is not dumb. He has a good head on him, and knows what he wants. Almost by instinct, he turns to scoundrels. They swarm around him like flies around a molasses barrel. They, too, know what they want.

III

Compared to this sorry zany, with his fluid principles and tricky evasions, Al stands forth as every inch a man. It has been urged against him that his knowledge of some of the things he discusses is defective—that his equipment in certain fields of statecraft is less than it might be and ought to be. But that is mainly empty talk. He knows enough, and he can learn more. The basic sort of knowledge is his beyond a doubt: he can tell a rogue from an honest man through eight feet of oak and the basic sort of integrity no one denies him: he is for the honest man at once, and until the last galoot's ashore.

In all his speeches there has been that simple note. It has been the *leitmotiv* of his whole career. Does he discuss the tariff? Then it is to discover why its benefits are so unequal, and to make them more equitable. Does he plunge into the Bad Lands of farm relief? Then it is because only charlatans have been there before him, and he wants to find out what fairness and candor can do. Does he play with the buzz-saw of government ownership? Then it is because bitter experience has taught him, as it has taught the rest of us, that the water-power hogs are incurably dishonest and disreputable—that a truce with them would be as hopeless as a truce with Adam-Zad the Bear.

His politics are thus simple, and to those debauched by the customary obscurantism they must inevitably seem somewhat naive. But they have sufficed him in New York, and they would suffice him at Washington. There is, after all, no mystery in government, no arcanum closed to all save Vermont lawyers, minestock promoters, Pittsburgh note-shavers, and other such adepts. The main and perhaps the only thing is to make being governed bearable, to hold down the rascals who live by the toll of the rest of us, to keep the brutal hoofing and looting of the plain man within bounds, to get a reasonable honesty and decency into the business. To this aim Al has addressed himself since his first days of power. He found New York one of the worst-governed States in the Union; he will leave it one of the best-governed.

IV

So much for his virtues; there remains his charm. It seems to me that it is not enough that a President of the United States should be full of learning and rectitude; it is also important that he have good humor in him, and be likable as a man. His business is not merely discharging words of wisdom; he must also manage men. If he is too vain and haughty to do it, as Wilson was, then the result is bound to be turmoil and disaster. If he is too idiotic, as Harding was, then it is a riot and scandal. If he is too boorish, as Coolidge is, then it is sour and witless burlesque.

We have surely had enough such inept and preposterous fellows in the White House. Do all the major problems confronting the country, from farm relief and foreign policy, remain unsolved? Then it is mainly because the ship of state has lacked a competent pilot, able to win and command the crew. I don't think Hoover could do it. No one likes him in Washington, save the porch climbers who hope to work him. He is too cautious, suspicious, secretive, sensitive, evasive, disingenuous. He is another Coolidge, only worse. There is nothing in him, no human juices. He is like a balloon tire inside, as he is without. His administration, if he is elected, will be one of whispers, as his campaign has been.

Al is at the other end of the human race. Frank, amiable, tolerant, modest and expansive, he has the faculty of taking men into camp. They trust him at sight, and the better they know him the more they trust him. No man in American politics has ever had firmer friends among his enemies. His career, indeed, has been made by their aid, and it is Republicans who are his most devoted partisans today. He would bring to the White House the equipment of a genuine leader. He would face Congress with assurance and break it to his will. And he would give us the liveliest, gaudiest, most stimulating show ever seen in Washington since the days of Roosevelt.

I can imagine aging men and women voting for Hoover as the safer of the two. They fear Al because he is so much alive. But what of the young? What of the first voters? Show me one who is not instinctively for Al, and I will show you one whose soul yearns for the robes of a Y.M.C.A. secretary or the white satin badge that goes with consecrated B.Y.P.U. work.

(The Baltimore Evening Sun, October 29, 1928)

The Eve of Armageddon

I

It has been, by God's will, a very bitter campaign, which is to say, an unusually honest one. Every effort to conceal the real issues— and both sides moved in that direction at the start—has gone to pot. If Al wins tomorrow, it will be because the American people have decided at last to vote as they drink, and because a majority of them believe that the Methodist bishops are worse than the Pope. If he loses, it will be because those who fear the Pope outnumber those who are tired of the Anti-Saloon League.

No other issue has got anywhere, nor will any other swing any appreciable number of votes. Al and Lord Hoover seem to be at one on the tariff, both say they are for economy, and both promise relief to the farmer though neither says how he is going to achieve it. When Hoover denounced Al as a Socialist it fell flat, for everyone knows that he is not, and when Al tried to hook up Hoover with Fall and Doheny it fell flat, for Americans are not opposed to corruption. Both sides have appealed alike to Negroes and Negro-baiters, and neither knows which way either group is going to jump. Labor, foreign policy, water power—all these questions are off the board.

There remain only Prohibition and religion, or more accurately, only religion, for Prohibition, in the dry areas, has long ceased to be a question of government or even of ethics, and has become purely theological. The more extreme drys, real and fake, simply refuse to discuss it. Throughout the Bible country belief in it has become a cardinal article of faith, like belief in the literal accuracy of Genesis. Men are denounced as traitors for so much as arguing that it ought to be discussed. Practically every one in those wilds guzzles more or less, as explorers quickly discover, but to suggest that Prohibition has failed and that something better is imaginable is as grave an indecorum as it would be to suggest to a Catholic theologian that the question whether the wine is really turned into blood at mass be submitted to a committee of chemists. In such fields *Homo sapiens* scorns and abominates human evidences. Challenged, he merely howls.

II

I daresay the extent of the bigotry prevailing in America, as it has been revealed by the campaign, has astounded a great many Americans, and perhaps even made them doubt the testimony of their own eyes and ears. This surprise is not in itself surprising, for Americans of one class seldom know anything about Americans of other classes. What the average native yokel believes about the average city man is probably nine-tenths untrue, and what the average city man believes about the average yokel is almost as inaccurate.

A good part of this ignorance is probably due to the powerful effect of shibboleths. Every American is taught in school that all Americans are free, and so he goes on believing it his whole life—overlooking the plain fact that no Negro is really free in the South, and no miner in Pennsylvania, and no radical in any of a dozen great States. He hears of equality before the law, and he accepts it as a reality, though it exists nowhere, and there are Federal laws which formally repudiate it. In the same way he is taught that religious toleration prevails among us, and uncritically swallows the lie. No such thing really exists. No such thing has ever existed.

This campaign has amply demonstrated the fact. It has brought bigotry out into the open, and revealed its true proportions. It has shown that millions of Americans, far from being free and tolerant men, are the slaves of an ignorant, impudent and unconscionable clergy. It has dredged up theological ideas so preposterous that they would make an intelligent Zulu laugh, and has brought the proof that they are cherished by nearly half the whole population, and by at least four-fifths outside the cities. It has made it plain that this theology is not merely a harmless aberration of the misinformed, like spiritualism, chiropractic or Christian Science, but the foundation of a peculiar way of life, bellicose, domineering, brutal and malignant—in brief, the complete antithesis of any recognizable form of Christianity. And it has shown, finally, that this compound of superstition and hatred has enough steam behind it to make one of the candidates for the Presidency knuckle to it and turn it upon his opponent—basely to be sure, but probably wisely.

III

Certainly something is accomplished when such facts are exposed to every eye, and with overwhelming reiteration. It may be uncomfortable to confront them, but it is surely better to confront them than to be ignorant of them. They explain many phenomena that have been obscure and puzzling—the rise to power of the Anti-Saloon League, the influence of such clowns as Bishop Cannon, the Rev. John Roach Straton and Billy Sunday, and, above all, the curious and otherwise inexplicable apparition of the Klan, with its appalling trail of crime and corruption.

All these things go back to one source, and that source is now known. The problem before the civilized minority of Americans is that of shutting off its flow of bilge-water. Can that be done? I am not so sure. The majority of rural Americans, with the best blood all drained to the cities, are probably hopelessly uneducable. Sound ideas make no more appeal to them than decent drinks. They prefer nonsense to sense as they prefer white mule to Burgundy. Abandoned for years to the tutelage of their pastors, they have now gone so far into the darkness that every light terrifies them and runs them amuck.

But though the job of enlightening them may be difficult, it should be worth trying. And if, in the end, there is only failure, then the way will be open for other and more radical remedies. For in the long run the cities of the United States will have to throw off the hegemony of these morons. They have run the country long enough, and made it sufficiently ridiculous. Once we get rid of camp-meeting rule we'll get rid simultaneously of the Klan, the Anti-Saloon League and the Methodist Board of Temperance, Prohibition and Public Morals. We'll get rid of the Cannons and

Heflins, the Willebrandts and Wayne Wheelers. And we'll get rid, too, of those sorry betrayers of intelligence who, like Hoover and Borah, flatter and fawn over the hookworm carriers in order to further their own fortunes.

IV

It seems to me that Dr. Hoover has been exposed in this campaign as no candidate for the Presidency ever was before, not even the ignoramus Harding or the trimmer Davis. He went into it as a master-mind, a fellow of immense and singular sagacities; he comes out of it a shrewd politician, but nothing more. His speeches have been, on the one hand, so disingenuous, and, on the other hand, so hollow, that even his most ardent followers now take refuge behind the doctrine that he will, at all events, be safe— that he will not invite the Pope to Washington, or monkey with such divine revelations as the tariff and Prohibition, or do anything to alarm stock speculators, or make any unseemly pother about stealing.

Hoover, since the day he abandoned mine-stock promoting for Service, has always had the help of a good press. He knows how to work the newspapers. The Washington correspondents, in large majority, dislike him, but still they fall for him, for he is adept at the art of taking the center of the stage and posturing there profoundly. In the past his futilities were only too often overlooked, in the blinding light of his publicity. He went to the Mississippi in all the gaudy state of a movie queen, but came back with no plan to stop the floods there. He issued tons of reports of dull subjects, but said nothing. But always he got lavish press notices.

In the campaign, however, his old devices failed. His original plan, obviously, was to look wise and say nothing. His speech of acceptance was a mass of windy platitudes, almost worthy of Coolidge. But gradually Al forced him into a corner and he had to talk. What has he said? I defy anyone to put it into reasonable propositions. No one, to this moment, knows what he really proposes to do about the tariff, or about Prohibition, or about foreign affairs, or about water power, and in the matter of farm relief he has simply passed the buck. Theoretically an abyss of wisdom, he has chattered like a high-school boy. Once he muttered three sentences against religious intolerance. But the bigots kept on supporting him, and they will support him tomorrow, and he knows it and is counting on it.

(*The Baltimore Evening Sun, November 5, 1928*)

1932

"General prosperity had been a great ally in the election of 1928," but "General Depression," wrote Hoover in his Memoirs, *"was a major enemy in 1932." Stock market speculations, overexpansion, inadequate purchasing power among the masses, and the uncertainty of foreign markets led to the collapse of the stock market in 1929, and the mounting despair of 1930 and 1931 destroyed Hoover's reputation as a great engineer and humanitarian.*

The Republican Convention met in Chicago Stadium on June 14–16. Urged not to seek the renomination, Hoover felt obliged to run again. The convention was dispirited and colorless: on June 17 Mencken reported: "The Republicans are going home today in a frame of mind that is anything but exultant. They are aware that Mr. Hoover has failed to win back the public esteem that he never really had, and that he remains one of the most unpopular Presidents on record." He went on: "The one real hope of the Republican leaders lies in the strong possibility that the Democrats, when they meet on June twenty-seventh, will be divided even more seriously, and that whatever compromise they reach will be worse."

The Democrats, however, were confident of victory when they met June 27–July 2 at Chicago. Eleven contenders vied for the candidacy, many from former elections: James Cox of 1920, John W. Davis of 1924, Joseph T. Robinson and Alfred E. Smith from 1928. Although Smith had the support of many of the party regulars, to many of his partisans, "the Happy Warrior" was no longer the same—he had gone "high-hat, highbrow, and high-life." Other candidates in the race included Governor Albert Ritchie from Maryland and Senator James A. Reed, as well as the popular John Nance Garner, the Texan Speaker of the House. But it was Franklin D. Roosevelt, two-term governor of New York, who was the front-runner; his vigor and resourcefulness in meeting the economic catastrophe in his state had earned him a huge following.

The battle to win the presidential nomination was between Roosevelt and Al Smith, and it promised to be "an old-time Democratic battle royal," Mencken predicted. "The air will be full of hair and ears within twenty-four hours." Reviewing his description of the event once it was over, Mencken admitted "a tired air is in it, but when I recall the circumstances under which it was concocted I marvel that it is not worse." The delegates met at eight P.M.*—they would not adjourn until the next morning. During the early part of the night the heat of the hall was intense. "All the brethren in the press stand, like the delegates on the floor, were dripping with perspiration," wrote Mencken. "As for me, my seersucker suit came to resemble a bathing-suit, and my necktie took on the appearance of having been fried." At three o'clock in the morning a violent thunderstorm broke, and a cool breeze swept through the hall as the last of the nominating speeches finally ended at four in the morning. The remaining delegates were anxious to go home, but Roosevelt's managers, anxious to begin the balloting, began the process at 4:28 A.M. At seven o'clock Mencken went out for breakfast, and as he chewed a roast beef sandwich and drank a glass of beer, the delegates continued their voting until finally adjourning at 9:15 in the morning. During the next few hours FDR's managers worked frantically to line up additional votes so their candidate could go over the top. The two dispatches which Mencken sent to the Baltimore* Evening Sun *show his talent for accuracy. How FDR's nomination was contrived did not become generally known until much later.*

The 1932 convention not only ushered in the long reign of Roosevelt and the collapse of Al Smith, but with it came the death of Prohibition. ". . . I believe it is quite safe to say that Prohibition died on June 29, 1932, aged twelve years, five months, and thirteen days," Mencken wrote in an editorial in the Evening Sun. *"The sponge, in fact, was up in the air before the Democratic assassins got to Chicago, and even before the Republicans got there. . . . The legend of its invincibility has blown up."*

Of the forty million men and women who went to the polls, one in every three was without work or regular income. Roosevelt's overwhelming victory was a reversal of the Democratic defeat of 1928: he won by a landslide. Part of Hoover's defeat, Mencken observed, was not only "his long and preposterous efforts to deny that there was any Depression," but "his almost incredibly incompetent dealing with Prohibition. He was too stupid to see that the vast majority of people were sick of it, and too cowardly to risk the crumbling fangs of the Anti-Saloon League, and in consequence he hung on to the Eighteenth Amendment at least two years too long. . . ."

On April 17, 1933, the Anheuser-Busch clock in Times Square at Manhattan chimed "Happy Days Are Here Again" as Prohibition ended. Throughout the United States thirsty citizens drank an estimated 1,500,000 barrels of beer within twenty-four hours. In Baltimore, H. L. Mencken drank his own glass of the brew at the bar of the Rennert Hotel. "Not bad at all," he said. "Fill it again."

Drys Are Done for,
Mencken Says,
and Is Sad at the Thought

Chicago, June 15.—This convention of county postmasters, Federal marshals and receivers in bankruptcy, masquerading as the heirs of Lincoln, is the stupidest and most boresome ever heard of; nevertheless, it will probably get its paragraph in the history books, for it is witnessing the death struggles of prohibition.

If the delegates were really free agents they would vote the imposture out by a majority of at least five to one. They quibble and compromise only because such is the word that comes from Washington. But even that compromise is a dreadful defeat for the drys, and they know it. Four years ago they would have cracked their whip and sent Lord Hoover sailing through their hoop like an arrow. But now he heaves and blunders through the air like a doormat, and half of him lands inside and half outside.

The whole sad drama was played out in miniature at the hearing before the resolutions committee yesterday afternoon. Approaching the parlor in the Congress Hotel where it was held, I found a sweating, fuming crowd milling around the closed doors, and was amazed to discover Bishop James Cannon, Jr., in the midst of it.

He greeted me pleasantly, but it was plain to see that he was very unhappy. And no wonder! Try to imagine Bishop Cannon waiting outside the door of Republican politicians four years ago! Or even a year ago! But there he lingered for a bad half hour, elbowed horribly by wet cuties with huge repeal banners flapping across their facades, and when he was admitted at last the committee did not even hear him.

The contrast with the scene at Houston four years ago was really most pathetic. There the bishop and his allies faced a frankly hostile candidate in Al Smith, and he was notoriously in favor of a dripping wet platform. But they beat him down in the resolutions committee, and put through a platform precisely to their taste, and Al was reduced to the perilous device of repealing and reenacting it with his own amendments. But this year the tide is roaring the other way, and the best they can get, even in the house of their friends, is a disingenuous and preposterous straddle.

They made a good fight before the resolutions committee, and put forward some of their most effective argufiers—Ernest H. Cherrington, Daniel A. Poling, F. Scott McBride, Col. Raymond Robbins and the saintly Mrs. Ella A. Boole, grand goblin of the W.C.T.U. They even produced a pretty and well-dressed young woman—a Mrs. Rushman Patterson, of Washington—the most sightly creature, and by long odds, ever witnessed by these eyes on the dry side of the fence.

But the wets had orators just as adept and lady supporters even more pulchritudinous, and, however, destiny was plainly with them. They had all of the assurance. They were full of a contagious confidence. The battle was going their way. The drys fought gamely, but it was without any visible hope.

Even the bishop was scarcely himself. He told me that he would go on fighting to the last ditch, and I believed him, but I observed that he said nothing whatever about winning. The other dry spokesmen took the same cautious line. They admitted freely that the opposition to prohibition was formidable, and that it was growing. They talked frankly of a time when it might be necessary, and even advisable, to put the whole thing to another test at the polls. All they ventured to plead for was the kind of test provided for by Article V of the Constitution, and at least one of them, Colonel Robbins, admitted categorically that it would give the dry side a great advantage, and that without the advantage they would probably lose.

All of this, I confess, was music to my ears. I could not help recalling the many other occasions when I had heard the same apostles do their stuff, or refrain from contrasting their old cockiness with their present despairs. It was pleasant to see them palpably licked, but it was also somewhat sad. Here were the most accomplished political manipulators ever on display in the America of my time, and now they were brought down at last and their old enemies were gloating over them.

They still have some good fights in them, and the formal clearing off of the prohibition rubbish will probably be a long and difficult business, but there can be no doubt hereafter that it will be cleared off.

The scene of the dry Waterloo was a garish parlor in the convention headquarters hotel—the sort of apartment in which Rotarians blow their spitballs and brass-band weddings are staged. At one end was a long table for the officers of the resolutions committee, with the excessively polite Dr. James B. Garfield, its chairman, in the center. Dr. Garfield gave each side half an hour and banged his gavel the instant time was up. For the wets Pierre S. du Pont was floor manager, and for the drys Dr. Cherrington. Each operated by pulling coattails. There was very little applause for either side.

In front of the chairman's place were a couple of rows of chairs for members of the committee and behind them a few more rows for the more eminent and infirm among the wets and drys. They were thrown together indiscriminately. The celebrated Cannon Chase, of Brooklyn, was flanked by two wet sweeties and on the other side Dr. Nicholas Murray Butler found himself cheek by jowl with Dr. McBride. The chairs filled less than half of the room. The rest of the space was for standees. They sweated painfully, for the day was hot. Tobacco smoke filled the room.

A dozen or more newspaper photographers, including a Jap, set off flashlights at intervals of ten or fifteen seconds. When a speaker came forward to address the committee they closed in on him and shot him from all four sides. Sometimes they made so much noise that the proceedings had to be halted to clear them off. They always came back. Thus the drys fought their last great fight, with smoke strangling them and flashlights blinding them.

As I have said, the scene was full of melancholy. These were tough babies, and in their day they had drawn buckets of blood. I have seen some of the most eminent statesmen in America blanch at their frown. They put Hoover into the White House and kept Al out. They once owned all the State Legislatures, hoof and hide. They still own a working majority in Congress. But it is fading. Every day another serf throws off his shackles. The poor dogs are licked.

Their last repeal bite, I suspect, is reserved for Lord Hoover. He has saved them from complete disaster, but only to make it certain on some near tomorrow. What they will do about it I don't know, but it is obvious that the old love affair is at an end.

Mrs. Boole, in her speech, hinted that many of them, next November, will stay away from the polls. But a good many others will probably vote for the Democrat—provided he is wet enough. For in their present low mood they have far more inclination toward an open enemy than toward a false friend.

(The Baltimore Evening Sun, June 15, 1932)

Allies Block Stampede
in "Horrible" All-Night Session,
Mencken Says

Chicago Stadium, July 1.—The plan of the Roosevelt managers to rush the convention and put over their candidate with a bang failed this morning, and after a turbulent all-night session and two roll-calls the anti-Roosevelt men fought off a motion to adjourn until this afternoon and the delegates proceeded to a third test of strength.

A few minutes before the first roll-call began, at 4 o'clock this morning, Arthur F. Mullen, of Nebraska, Farley's chief of staff, told me that Roosevelt would receive 675 votes on the first ballot and 763 on the second, and that the third would bring him the two-thirds needed for his nomination.

But the first ballot actually brought him only 666 1/4 and the second only 677 3/4, and the third had not gone halfway down the roll of States before it was plainly evident that a hard fight was ahead of him, with his chances much slimmer than they seemed to be the time the voting began.

In brief, the Roosevelt runaway was stopped.

The first two ballots were taken amid the utmost confusion and to the tune of loud and raucous challenges from unhappy minorities of various delegations. On the first ballot Minnesota demanded to be polled, with the result that its 24 votes under the unit rule went to Roosevelt. New York, which was also polled, split unequally, with 28 1/2 votes going to Roosevelt and 65 1/2 to Al Smith.

This was a somewhat unpleasant surprise for the Roosevelt men and they got little consolation out of the second ballot, for on it Roosevelt made a gain of but a single vote. Their total gain of 11 1/2 came mainly from Missouri, where the 12 Roosevelt votes of the first ballot increased to 18, with a corresponding loss to former Senator James A. Reed.

By this time it was clear that the Roosevelt assault had been hurled back, and the allies, who had been apparently trying all night to manufacture as many delays as possible, suddenly demanded action on their own account. This demand was sufficient to block an effort that the Roosevelt men made at 8.05 to adjourn until 4 P.M. It was opposed violently by New York, speaking through the clarion voice of Dudley Field Malone, and a standing vote showed such a formidable party against the adjournment that the proposal was withdrawn.

The second ballot probably took more time than any ever heard of before, even in a Democratic National Convention. The roll-call was begun at 5.17 A.M. and it was not until 8.05 that the result was announced. Thus the running time was nearly three hours. Two large States, Ohio and Pennsylvania, demanded to be polled, and there was a battle in the District of Columbia delegation that consumed a full hour.

Two of the District delegates were Ritchie men, and they fought hard to throw off the unit rule and have their choice recorded, but Chairman Walsh decided that the rule bound them, and their votes were thus credited to Roosevelt. The same fate befell six Ritchie votes in the Michigan delegation on the third ballot.

Governor Ritchie polled 21 votes on the first ballot—Maryland's 16, 4 from Indiana and 1 from Pennsylvania. On the second ballot he gained 2 1/2 in Pennsylvania, making his total 23 1/2. Meanwhile Al Smith, who started off with 201 3/4, dropped to 194 1/4, and slight losses were also shown by Traylor, White, Byrd and Baker, and six of former Senator Reed's Missourians departed for the Roosevelt camp. Altogether the allies polled 487 3/4.

On the first ballot, a few minutes before the roll-call began, Howard Bruce of Maryland estimated that they would poll 484 and that their irreducible minimum of shock troops, good for fifty ballots if necessary, was 425—40 more than would be needed to prevent Roosevelt from ever polling a two-third majority.

The all-night session was a horrible affair and by the time the light of dawn began to dim the spotlights, a great many delegates had gone back to their hotels or escaped to the neighboring speak-easies.

When the balloting began shortly after 5 A.M. scores of them were missing and the fact explained the worst delays in the voting and especially some of the quarrels over the rights and dignities of alternates. When New York was called Jimmy Walker could not be found, but by the time the dreadful business of polling the immense State delegation, with its ninety regular members and eight members-at-large, neared an end, he somehow turned up and was presently saying something for the microphone and getting a round of applause for it.

The third ballot showed plainly that Roosevelt was not going to run the convention amuck, but the same evidence proved that the allies had likewise failed to knock him out.

He was holding all his principal delegations, and in addition he was making some small gains in the territory of the enemy. His total vote was 682 $79/100$, which showed an increase of five and a fraction over the second ballot and of sixteen over the first. This was surely not disaster. Nevertheless, it was still sufficient to fill the allies with hope and courage, for they had been in fear that the first Roosevelt rush would shake and break their lines, and that had certainly not happened.

The way the tide of battle was going was revealed dramatically by the attitude of the leaders on the two sides. All during the infernal night session the Roosevelt men had been trying to wear out and beat down the opposition, and to push on to a showdown.

They opposed every motion to adjourn, and refused every other sort of truce. They wanted to get through with the speeches as soon as possible, but they were confident enough to be still willing to match speech with speech, and they did so until daylight. But after the first ballot they began to play for time, and after the second all of their early bellicosity had gone out of them.

The allies, meanwhile, were gaining in assurance. They knew that Al Smith was ready to talk of delivering his vote to one or another of them after the third ballot, and they were eager to reach it. But the Roosevelt men, by that stage, saw clearly that a hard fight was ahead, and so took their turn at playing for time.

The combat of rhetoricians and rooters during the long, hot and weary hours of the night was depressingly typical of a Democratic national convention. The show was almost completely idiotic, with now and then a more or less rational speech to relieve it.

Senator Tydings made one such speech, putting Governor Ritchie in nomination, and another was made by Richard F. Cleveland, son of Grover Cleveland, seconding him. A third came from William G. McAdoo in the interest of Garner. But the average was as low as one might look for at a ward club in a mean street and few of the delegates and fewer of the visitors seemed to pay any attention to what was said.

All sorts of grotesque female politicians, most of them with brassy voices and hard faces, popped up to talk to the radio audience back home. The evening session, in fact, had been postponed to nine o'clock to get a radio hookup and every fourth-rate local leader in the hall, male or female, tried for a crack at the microphone.

More than once weary delegates objected that the Niagara of bilge was killing them and along toward four in the morning Josephus Daniels went to the platform and protested against it formally. But all of the nine candidates had to be put in nomination, and when they had been put in nomination all of them had to be seconded, not once, but two, four, six or a dozen times. Worse, their customers had to parade obscenely every time one of them was launched and some of the parades ran to nearly an hour.

Here one gang helped another. The Texans, who had a band, lent it to every other outfit that had a candidate, and it brayed and boomed for Ritchie, Byrd, Reed and Al Smith quite as cruelly as it performed for Garner. This politeness, of course, had to be repaid by its beneficiaries, and with interest.

The Byrd band, clad in uniforms fit for Arctic exploration, did not let up for hours on end. And while it played one tune, the band of the Texans played another, and the official band in the gallery a third, and the elephantine pipe-organ a fourth. At one stage in the uproar a male chorus also appeared, but what it sang I can't tell you, nor which candidate it whooped and gargled for.

It was hard on the spectators in the galleries, but it was even harder on the delegates, for they had to march in a good many of the parades and they were hoofed and hustled when they kept their seats.

Most of them, as is usual at a national convention, are beyond middle life, and a good many of them show obvious marks of oxidation. Two have died since the convention began, a matter of only five days. Scores had to clear out of the hall during the night and seek relief in the corridors.

Toward three o'clock, a thunderstorm came up, and the extreme heat of the early evening began to lessen. By that time, a full half of the spectators had gone home, so the cops were able to open the great doors of the hall without running any risk of being rushed off their feet, and by dawn the place had become relatively comfortable.

But then the sun began to shine down through the gallery windows, and presently the floor was a furnace again, and the delegates got out their foul handkerchiefs and resumed their weary mopping and panting.

Under such circumstances, there is always plenty of ill-humor. There is more of it than usual when Democrats meet, for they are divided into implacable factions, and each hates all the others. Many of the more wearisome maneuvers of the three roll-calls were apparently suggested by mere malignancy.

The Pennsylvanians, I was told, demanded to be polled simply to bring back to the hall some of their own delegates who had deserted the battlefield and gone home to bed. The row in the District of Columbia delegation was apparently two-thirds personal and only one-third political. And the Smith men carried on their relentless campaign of motions, protests and parliamentary inquiries mainly to annoy the Roosevelt men.

Toward the end the thing became a mere endurance match. It was plain after the second ballot that neither side was going to break, but the allies by now were hungry to punish the Roosevelt outfit, and they did so by opposing adjournment and by raising all sorts of nonsensical difficulties, some of which could be resolved only after long conferences on the platform and a copious consultation of precedent books and parliamentary lawyers.

Old Tom Walsh, the chairman, held out pretty well until eight o'clock, but then he began to cave in, and during the last hour the temporary chairman of the convention, the wet bridegroom, Senator Alben W. Barkley, of Kentucky, operated the bungstarter and struggled with the riddles that were thrown at him from the floor.

All the more sensible delegates wanted to take a recess until 9 o'clock tonight, for they knew that long and wearying conferences were ahead, and they yearned for a few hours of honest sleep.

(The Baltimore Evening Sun, July 1, 1932)

Mencken Finds Both Sides Sour, Thinking Only of Their Losses

Chicago Stadium, July 2.—The great combat is ending this afternoon in the classical Democratic manner. That is to say, the victors are full of uneasiness and the vanquished are full of bile. It would be hard to find a delegate who believes seriously that Roosevelt can carry New York in November, or Massachusetts, or New Jersey, or even Illinois. All of the crucial wet States of the Northeast held out against him to the last ditch, and their representatives are damning him up hill and down dale today.

Meanwhile the Southern and Middle Western delegates are going home with a tattered Bible on one shoulder and a new and shiny beer seidel on the other, and what they will have to listen to from their pastors and the ladies of the W.C.T.U. is making their hearts miss every other beat.

The row ended quietly enough last night, but without the slightest sign of genuine enthusiasm. The galleries kept on howling for Al Smith to the finish, but Al himself sulked in his hotel, and placards in the lobbies this morning announced that most of his true friends would leave for Manhattan at noon. When, at 10.32 last night, Chairman Walsh announced the final vote, there was only the ghost of a cheer, and in less than a minute even the Roosevelt stalwarts were back in their seats and eager only for adjournment and a decent night's rest.

The convention was worn out, but that was only part of the story. It was also torn by rancors that could not be put down. The Smith men all knew very well that the result was a good deal less a triumph for Roosevelt, who actually seemed to have few genuine friends in the house, than a defeat and rebuke for Smith. As for the Roosevelt men, they found themselves on their repeal honeymoon wondering dismally if the bride were really as lovely as she had seemed last Wednesday. Both sides had won and both had lost, but what each thought of was only the loss.

In all probability the Marylanders, though they lost their fight for Governor Ritchie, came out of the struggle with fewer wounds than any other delegation that played a part of any actual importance in the ceremonies. They had been beaten, but they had not made any enemies. They were on the bandwagon, but the Smith *bloc* had no cause to complain of them. They owed this comfortable result to the fine skill of Governor Ritchie himself. He was his own manager here, just as he had been his own manager in the preliminary campaign, and his coolness resisted a dozen temptations to run amuck and get into trouble. He took the whole thing calmly and good-naturedly, and showed not the slightest sign, at any stage, of the appalling buck fever which so often demoralizes candidates. He kept on good terms with the Smith outfit without getting any of its sulphurous smell upon him, and he submitted to the inevitable in the end in a dignified manner, and without any obscene embracing of Roosevelt. If Roosevelt is elected in November there is a swell place in the Cabinet waiting for him—that is, assuming that he wants it. And if Roosevelt is butchered by the implacable Smith men, then he will have another chance in 1936, and a far better one than he had this week, with the corpse of Al incommoding him.

As you all know by now, the final break to Roosevelt was brought on by the Garner men from California. Garner's friends from Texas were prepared to stick to him until Hell froze over, but in California he was only a false face for McAdoo and Hearst, and McAdoo was far more bent upon punishing Smith for the events of 1924 than he was for nominating Texas Jack, just as Hearst was more eager to block his pet abomination, Newton D. Baker, than to name any other candidate. Hearst was quite willing on Thursday to turn to Ritchie, who was satisfactory to him on all the major issues, including especially the League of nations. In fact, negotiations with him were in full blast Thursday afternoon, with Arthur Brisbane as the intermediary. But McAdoo had other ideas, chiefly relating to his own fortunes, and he pulled Hearst along. For one thing, McAdoo had a palpable itch for the Vice-Presidency. But above all he yearned to give Smith a beating, and he saw after the third ballot that Roosevelt would be the handiest stick for the job.

The actual nomination of Roosevelt after the turmoils of the all-night session went off very quietly. The delegates appeared in the hall all washed up, with clean collars, pressed suits and palpable auras of witch hazel and bay rum. The scavengers of the stadium had swept up the place, the weather had turned cool and there was the general letting down that always follows a hard battle. No one had had quite enough sleep, but everyone had had at least some. Chairman Walsh, who had been wilting visibly in the horrible early hours of the morning, was himself again by night, and carried on his operations with the bungstarter in his usual fair, firm and competent manner. He is a good presiding officer and he had got through the perils of the night session without disaster. Now he was prepared for the final scene and every spectator in the packed galleries knew where it would lead the plot and who would be its hero.

California comes early on the roll, so there was no long suspense. McAdoo went up to the platform to deliver the State delegation in person. He must be close to seventy by now, if not beyond it, but he is still slim, erect and graceful, and as he made his little speech and let his eye rove toward the New York delegation he looked every inch the barnstorming Iago of the old school. Eight years ago at New York he led the hosts of the Invisible Empire against the Pope, the rum demon and all the other Beelzebubs of the Hookworm Belt, and came so close to getting the nomination that the memory of its loss must still shiver him. The man who blocked him was Al Smith, and now he was paying Al back.

If revenge is really sweet he was sucking a colossal sugar teat, but all the same there was a beery flavor about it that must have somewhat disquieted him. For he is Georgia cracker by birth and has always followed his native pastors docilely, and it must have taken a lot of temptation to make him accept the ribald and saloonish platform. Here, indeed, revenge was working both ways, and if Al were a man of more humor he would have been smiling, too.

The other rebellious States fell into line without much ceremony, always excepting, of course, those which held out for Al to the end. Illinois was delivered by Mayor Cermak of Chicago, a Czech brought up on roast goose and Pilsner, and showing the virtues of that diet in his tremendous shoulders and sturdy legs. He spoke also for Indiana, which had been split badly on the first three ballots. When Maryland's turn came Governor Ritchie spoke for it from the floor, releasing its delegates and casting their votes for the winner, and a bit later on former Governor Byrd did the business for Virginia. In the same way Missouri was delivered by former Senator James A. Reed, who somewhat later came up to the platform and made a little speech, denouncing Samuel Insull and Lord Hoover in blistering terms and calling upon the Smith men to "fall in line like good soldiers and face the common enemy." Senator Reed spoke of the time as "this afternoon," though it was actually nearly ten o'clock at night. But no one noticed, for the all-night session had blown up all reckoning of time and space.

The whole proceedings, in fact, showed a curiously fantastic quality. Here was a great party convention, after almost a week of cruel labor, nominating the weakest candidate before it. How many of the delegates were honestly for him I don't know, but certainly it could not have been more than a third. There was absolutely nothing in his record to make them eager for him. He was not only a man of relatively small experience and achievement in national affairs; he was also one whose competence was plainly in doubt, and whose good faith was far from clear. His only really valuable asset was his name, and even that was associated with the triumphs and glories of the common enemy. To add to the unpleasantness there was grave uneasiness about his physical capacity for the job they were trusting to him.

Yet here they were giving it to him, and among the parties to the business were a dozen who were patently his superior and of very much larger experience. For example, Tom Walsh, the chairman, one of the most diligent and useful Senators ever seen in Washington and a man whose integrity is unquestioned by anyone. For example, Carter Glass of Virginia, an irascible and almost fanatical fellow, but still a very able man and an immensely valuable public servant. For example, Reed of Missouri, the very picture and model of a Roman senator, whose departure from the Senate cost it most of its dramatic effectiveness and a good half of its power. Even McAdoo is certainly worth a dozen Franklin D. Roosevelts. As for Al Smith, though he is now going down hill fast, he was once worth a hundred. But the man who got the great prize was Roosevelt, and most of the others are now too old to hope for it hereafter.

The failure of the opposition was the failure of Al Smith. From the moment he arrived on the ground it was apparent that he had no plan, and was animated only by his fierce hatred of Roosevelt, the cuckoo who had seized his nest. That hatred may have had logic in it, but it was impotent to organize the allies and they were knocked off in detail by the extraordinarily astute Messrs. Farley and Mullen. The first two ballots gave them some hope, but it was lost on the third, for the tide by then was plainly going Roosevelt's way. Perhaps the Al of eight or ten years ago, or even of four years ago, might have achieved the miracle that the crisis called for, but it was far beyond the technique of the golf-playing Al of today. He has ceased to be the wonder and glory of the East Side and becomes simply a minor figure of Park Avenue.

But in the midst of the débâcle he could at least steal some consolation from the fact that his foes were facing a very difficult and perhaps almost impossible campaign before the people. His sardonic legacy to his party is the platform, and especially the Prohibition plank. It will harass Roosevelt abominably until the vote is counted, and after that it may take first place among his permanent regrets. If his managers had had their way, there would have been a straddle comparable to the one made by the Republicans. But the allies rushed them so savagely that they were taken off their feet. That rush required little leadership. It was spontaneous and irresistible. The big cities poured out their shock troops for it.

The delegates went back to their hotels last night to the tune of "Onward, Christian Soldiers." It was the first time that the tune had been heard in the convention, and probably the first time it had been heard in the hall. But playing it was only a kind of whistling in the dark. For five days the bands had been laboring far different hymns, and their echoes still sounded along the rafters.

(The Baltimore Evening Sun, July 2, 1932)

Mencken Tells How
Magic Word "Beer"
Brought the Cheers

Governor Roosevelt begins to look a little tired. The whispering about his legs, of course, has come to nothing; he gets about on them very nimbly, and it will be many a day before they give out. But even a centipede would be somewhat frazzled by what he has been through during the past two months. For weeks on end he has put in noisy, exigent, nerve-wracking days and broken nights. Lights running to millions of candle power have beaten down upon him and fried him. He has been bombarded by bands and rowelled by handshakers. All the worst bores in America have had free access to him. He has breathed and eaten tons of train dust.

So it is no wonder that his eyes look a bit fishy, that his forehead has some new wrinkles, and that there is a shade more grey in his hair than there was last July. His scalp, in fact, begins to show through plainly, like a photograph coming up in the developer. By 1936 he will be bald.

His speech at the Fifth Regiment Armory last night was surely no great shakes, either in substance or in delivery. His voice shows heavy strain, and he begins to force his tones like a wornout opera tenor. The loud-speaker helps out, but not enough. Since July he has uttered more than half a million words, most of them before large audiences, in drafty, smoky halls.

The bull of Bashan himself, put to such a test, would show some wear. Dr. Roosevelt, being no bull, shows more. He was built for lyrical work, not for whooping and howling. He is at his best in a close-up, talking across a table. But fate condemns him to huge barns, full of folk yearning to be deafened and set afire.

The crowd last night listened to him politely, but it would be idle to say that he inflamed it. Al Smith, speaking from the same pulpit four years ago, gave it a far better show. For thirty of his forty-five minutes Dr. Roosevelt performed variations upon a metaphor that left nine-tenths of his hearers cold. How many of them had ever heard of the Four Horsemen of the Apocalypse? Probably just as many as had heard of Duns Scotus.

They applauded feebly and at the wrong places. When the hon. gentleman said that 258 American factories had been moved abroad since the enactment of the Smoot-Grundy tariff there was the loudest clapping of the evening. That is, up to 8.39 o'clock.

At that moment precisely the magical word beer burst out of the loud speaker and the whole house arose to its legs and cheered. That is what the crowd had come for—that and nothing else. Beer in our time. Beer tomorrow. Beer this afternoon. Beer right now. Get the home brewers out of the cellar by Christmas, before Christmas, at once. Let us have Münchner, Pilsner, Würzburger, Kulmbacher, even Bauernschmidt's, Brehms's, Wiemer's, Steil's Goldbran. What this country needs is a good 5 cent glass of beer.

Dr. Roosevelt named no day, but he let it be known that the wait would be cut as short as possible. There can be no question that he was believed. He looked very thirsty himself. The crowd, taking him at his word, performed the loudest and longest applause of the evening. It ran probably half a minute.

But there is nothing of the rabble-rouser about Roosevelt. He can make, on occasion, a pretty good speech, but he seldom reaches the midriff. Al, in his day, would cause them to leap in the air and holler like converts at a revival. But with Roosevelt they stay in their seats.

The loud speaker, in truth, has pretty well killed oratory. You will never see another Col. Bill Kilgour or another John P. Poe. I remember when Mr. Poe used to come down to the front of the stage at the Lyric (then the Music Hall) and begin business by howling "Had I a voice of brass"—It would shake the windows and lift the roof; nay, it would knock locomotives off the track in the Bolton Yards two blocks away. Mr. Poe was small in stature— it would have taken two of him to make a Ritchie or a Tydings. But one and a half of him would have been enough to make a bombardment of Fort McHenry.

All that is now gone and done for. The loud speaker makes all voices sound alike, and their volume is regulated not by their owners, but by a union man in overalls, sitting at the controls under the platform. He can, at will, make a lady politician scream like a Comanche. At the Republican National Convention last July he made the Hon. Ogden L. Mills bellow so terribly that the echoes, coming back from the walls and roof, deafened and paralyzed Mills himself, and he staggered from the platform at the end like a man kicked by a mule. Whether the union man did it deliberately or accidentally I don't know, but certainly it used up poor Mills.

Dr. Roosevelt is tired, but he is sustained by a kind of hooch that beats anything that ever came out of a distillery. It is the hooch of success. His eyes will be bloodshot by November 7, but they will still permit him to see the White House, even over long leagues of space and through forty feet of concrete. His voice will be worn down to a faint *pizzicato*, but he will still be able to say "Yes" with the astounding clarity of a June bride. He is a happy man, and he has a right to be.

For when he flew to Chicago last July to accept the nomination there were not many who thought he could beat Lord Hoover. Certainly not many Democrats in the actual hall thought so. They saw Al Smith sulking and scowling, and they believed that Roosevelt was too mild and wishy-washy a fellow to fetch him in, and soothe all the other soreheads, and unite the party, and win the people. They prepared to go home in the traditional mood of Democrats—that is to say, holding their heads, damning their luck, and wishing that the Confederates had won.

Their pessimism was grounded upon two errors. On the one hand, they greatly underestimated the unpopularity of Hoover—and especially the unpopularity that he had accumulated for himself by his devious and unconvincing dealings with the beer question. On the other hand, they underestimated almost as much the skill and energy of Dr. Roosevelt. They thought that what they had on their hands was old Teddy boiled down to an almost homeopathic attenuation—one part Roosevelt to 10,000,000 parts *aqua destillata*. But when the campaign opened they found that they really had solution of Rooseveltian alcohol that was fully 50 proof.

In brief, the amiable Franklin has made a very adroit and effective fight. He has Hoover on the ropes, and is still punching hard. Seen and heard in a smoky hall, with Klieg lights blistering him and the bad air corroding his larynx, he pleases mildly without exciting at all, but he goes very well over the radio, and he reads well in the newspapers the next morning.

Here he has it all over Hoover. Hoover sounds flat through the ether, and his literati, though they have done far better than he could do himself, have never got any real punch into his speeches. Moreover, it hurts him to smile, and every patron of the newsreels is well aware of it.

But most of all, these same people distrust him, even when he seems to be right, and for that distrust they have sound reasons. They don't care much what he has to say about the budget, or the gold standard, or farm relief, or any other such tiresome matter, but they remember with relentless tenacity how shabbily he tried to fool them on prohibition. That is the one question that really interests them. It is the only honest issue in the campaign. Roosevelt meets it squarely, but Hoover still dodges. On March 5 he will be headed back for the gold mines of Australia.

No wonder Dr. Roosevelt smiles almost continuously, even when discussing bankruptcy and starvation. That smile of his will come off by this time next year, for he has some tough sledding ahead of him. But until he actually gets into the White House and tries to make good on beer, the budget and the rest, it will continue to irradiate and gladden the universe. Even for a Roosevelt, he is a very lucky man.

(The Baltimore Evening Sun, October 26, 1932)

1936

Breaking with the philosophy of past governments, from 1932–1935 Roosevelt decided to step in with far-reaching programs of social and economic legislation. A host of federal agencies came into being to relieve the distress of the vast numbers of unemployed: the Federal Emergency Relief Administration (FERA), the Works Progress Administration (WPA), the Civil Works Administration (CWA), the Public Works Administration (PWA), the National Recovery Administration (NRA), the Civilian Conservation Corps (CCC), and the Tennessee Valley Authority (TVA). All of these measures did not produce prosperity, but they did pull the country out of its angst and provided jobs for millions of people. But to Mencken, the concept of government which Roosevelt was promoting was that of "a milch cow with 125,000,000 teats," and there were many who agreed with him. Across the country, the President became the center of both passionate adoration and hatred.

To unseat Roosevelt, the Republicans met in Cleveland June 9–12 and chose Alfred M. Landon, governor of Kansas, on the first ballot. An oilman from a farm state, he pleased businessmen and held a good chance of winning the support of Western farmers; moreover, his folksy manner caused him to be dubbed "the Kansas Lincoln." Republicans sang their praises to Landon to the tune of "O Susanna":

> *Landon, oh, Landon*
> *Will lead to Victory—*
> *With the dear old Constitution,*
> *And it's good enough for me.*

Colonel Frank Knox, publisher of the Chicago Daily News, *was chosen as his running mate. Alfred E. Smith crossed party lines to support the ticket, as did Mencken, who accompanied Landon on his campaign trip, ultimately voting for him: "To a lifelong Democrat," he confessed in one of his columns, "it will be something of a wrench, but it seems to me that the choice is one that genuine Democrats are bound to make."*

Mencken felt his candidate would advocate "a return to the Jeffersonian doctrine that the only tolerable government is a relatively weak one. That doctrine, it seems to me, is still quite as sound as it was in Jefferson's day, and if it were put into practice it would make an end to the many abuses and nuisances which now afflict the country." But it was hoping against hope: "Unfortunately, only a small number of living Americans appear to believe in it, and the Hon. Mr. Landon not infrequently offers excuses for the suspicion that he is not one of them. On the metaphysical plane, to be sure, he may be a convinced Jeffersonian, but as a practical matter he is a Kansan, and in Kansas the notion that the Treasury was set up to pay the debts of clod-hoppers is as axiomatic as the notion that a horse-hair put into a bottle of water will turn into a snake."

Nineteen thirty-six raised the curtain on many small parties. The Socialist party, Communist party, Socialist Labor party, and the Prohibitionist party all put up candidates. The new Union Party nominated William Lemke, Republican congressman from North Dakota. Its followers were those who supported Francis Townsend and Father Charles E. Coughlin, Michigan's "radio priest," and the backers of Gerald Smith, from Louisiana. The party believed FDR's policies were communistic (a "Brain Trust cake baked in Moscow," howled Smith). In a fit of rhetorical passion during the campaign, Father Coughlin ripped off his clerical collar and called the President "Franklin Double-Crossing Roosevelt," a "liar" and "a betrayer." In the press stand, Mencken watched his antics, chortling to himself. His own opinion of the priest was "very low"—"a fraud of the first calibre."

Roosevelt dominated the proceedings of the Democratic Convention, held in Philadelphia on June 23–27. John "Cactus Jack" Garner was renominated as Vice President. Roosevelt arrived at Franklin Field in Philadelphia to give his acceptance speech. As he made his halting way toward the microphones, he stopped to shake the hand of the poet Edwin Markham, and in doing so the knee-lock of his left brace snapped and he lost his balance. In the confusion that followed, the pages of his speech fell and splattered across the stage. Roosevelt continued to smile and wave to his audience, but, as he confided off-the-record to a group of reporters, inwardly he was furious. He was mad at Jack Garner for mangling his name in the introduction, calling him "Delaney"; at Ed Halsey, the Senate secretary, for stepping in front of him, thus blocking FDR as he waved to the crowd; at the mayor of Philadelphia, who kept leaning over to confide to him how many police were stationed in the park, and in doing so, blowing a fresh gust of halitosis into FDR's face. He was mad at the blinding lights; at the speech, which had fallen to the floor; and especially, at "the damned brace which had picked that moment of all moments to break down." Still mad, with the brace now adjusted into place, he began his speech. His voice, carried by loudspeakers to every corner of the field, rang out strongly. One hundred thousand spectators listened to it in silence; many more millions listened to the speech on their radios at home:

There is a mysterious cycle in human events. To some generations much is given. Of other generations much is expected. This generation of Americans has a rendezvous with destiny. . . . here in America we are waging a great and successful war. It is not alone a war against want and destitution and economic demoralization. It is more than that; it is a war for the survival of democracy. We are fighting to save a great, a precious form of government for ourselves and for the world.

He spoke on, saying the country had shaken off the power of royalists in politics, declaring that the power to give or refuse jobs, to charge high or low prices, and to permit or block new competing firms, were the powers of "economic royalists."

When he reached this part of his speech, a roar broke out in the crowd, and FDR's anger dissipated: "I knew I had them . . ." It was one of the most memorable addresses of his life, but Mencken remained unimpressed as his article illustrates.

"Three Long Years" Usurps Honor Given "Oh, Susanna" as GOP Campaign Song

Convention Hall, Cleveland, June 10.—The campaign song of the Republicans, it appears, is not to be "Oh, Susanna" after all, but a parody of "Three Blind Mice."

It was born last night of the fortunate conjunction of a phrase in the speech of the Hon. Frederick Steiwer and a happy thought in the head of Louis Rich, bandmaster of the convention. By noon today it was all over town, and when the Hon. Bertrand H. Snell, the permanent chairman of the convention, let go with his inaugural address this afternoon it actually broke into his remarks.

The Hon. Mr. Steiwer's phrase, as readers of these dispatches will recall, was "three long years." It was his answer to a series of rhetorical questions, and after he had intoned it *andante lamentoso* two or three times the crowd began to join in.

This gave Mr. Rich his idea. Turning to his artists he shouted

"F sharp, E and D, all in unison," and the last time "three long years" was chanted the band supported the crowd with the notes. They constituted the opening measure of "Three Blind Mice."

All this went out by radio, and in a little while Mr. Rich began to receive telegrams from fans. One of them was a Mrs. Wilder Tileston, of New Haven, Conn. It was as follows:

> Three long years (repeated)
> Full of grief and tears (repeated)
> They've all added on to the farmers' debt,
> They've put all the taxpayers into a sweat,
> They're the worst the country has ever seen yet.
> These three long years.

This seemed swell stuff to Mr. Rich, and he was soon in communication with the convention press agent, the Hon. Theodore G. Huntley. Mr. Huntley saw the point at once, and in half an hour he had a staff of six poets at work, writing parodies. Six of these parodies were mimeographed by noon, and when the convention reassembled for today's first session Mr. Rich had the melody scored for his band.

Twice, as I have said, it broke into the Hon. Mr. Snell's speech, and this evening, as the crowd assembled for the Hoover session, the band played it over and over, and the crowd made efforts to sing it. Tonight Mr. Rich is still bombarded by telegrams, many of them containing suggestions for additional stanzas. He is the musical director of Station WHK, Cleveland, and a very up-and-coming professor.

The Hon. Mr. Snell had less to say than the Hon. Mr. Steiwer, but he said it rather more effectively. Instead of banging away at machine-gun speed, as Steiwer did, he permitted himself a more leisurely tempo, with plenty of room for gestures.

He was done out in a swell new Palm Beach suit and a neat haircut, and altogether made a pretty good job of his harangue, though what he had to say was hardly more than a repetition of what Steiwer had said last night. The first burst of really hearty clapper-clawing came when he shoved his fists into the air, threw back his head, rolled his eyes, and had at the delegates and alternates with this one:

"Thank God no Republican President has ever violated his constitutional oath by calling upon the members of his party in Congress to violate theirs!"

It was dreadfully hot down on the floor, but the hearts of the delegates and alternates were still full of veneration for the Constitution, and when Dr. Snell staggered back from the microphone to give them a chance they leaped to their feet and gave a loud holler—in fact, the loudest to be heard in this somewhat gummy convention until Hoover tackled them tonight.

The rest of Dr. Snell's speech was largely made up of echoes from Revolutionary times.

"Can this be America," he roared, "where citizens live and breathe only by the gracious consent of an ambitious ruler?"

The nays plainly had it, and the hon. gentleman went on:

"Against this demoralizing reign of irresponsible incompetence I hear today America's earnest prayer for deliverance."

A fine stage pause followed, and one could almost hear the minute men marching down the road, praying against deliverance from both New Deal professors and hit-and-run automobilists.

"The voice of the people," continued Dr. Snell, "calls us not merely to oppose another political party as in the past, but rather to resist the encroachments of an alien system of capricious personal government. Shall we measure up to this patriotic duty?"

This time the ayes prevailed, and the learned speaker proceeded to quote George Washington and Abraham Lincoln, both of whom he spoke of in the highest terms. He ended with a polite reference to God, who, by orthodox Republican theory, has been an *ex officio* member of the Republican National Committee since Civil War days.

The speech, intellectually speaking, seldom got above the level of a high school commencement address, but it served its purpose very well, and its success with the delegates and alternates was considerably above that of Dr. Steiwer's hour of high-speed gargling last night. But it was Steiwer who launched the campaign song, and for that great service to his country he will probably get some notice in the school books. The reward of Snell will be only the happy memory of a hot and useless duty gallantly done.

(The Baltimore Sun, June 11, 1936)

Roosevelt and Garner
Told of Nomination
in Open-Air Ceremony
at Philadelphia

Franklin Field, Philadelphia, June 27.—The solemn business of notifying President Roosevelt and Vice-President Garner that they had been chosen by the Democratic National Convention as the party candidates to succeed themselves was got through in the open air in Franklin Field this evening.

It had been raining off and on all day, and until 7.30 it seemed likely that the notification ceremony would have to be transferred to the Convention Hall. But the clouds began to break after sunset, and save for a few brief sprinkles there was no more rain. The President went on the air promptly at 10 o'clock, daylight time. The whole show was over in less than an hour, though its preliminaries had consumed all the time since 6 o'clock.

The Franklin Field Stadium, which belongs to the University of Pennsylvania, seats 85,000 persons, more or less, and in addition 17,000 chairs had been placed on the field itself. The official stand was so low that few, if any, of the spectators on the field could see it.

It had to be made so because of the President's lameness. He is unable, without great difficulty, to ascend stairs, so a ramp was built in the alley behind the stand. Up this ramp his automobile would ascend. Inasmuch as it could not be made very high, the height of the stand was limited. The stand was decorated in gray, with long pennants showing the national colors. Along the fence behind it were large portraits of all the Democratic Presidents since Jefferson.

In front of the official stand was the stand for the band. The musicians, led by their talented Kappelmeister, Lieut. Joseph Frankel, began playing at 6 o'clock, and kept it up *fortissimo* until driven to shelter by the rain at 6.40. They remained under cover for ten minutes or so and then emerged to play some more. Thousands of umbrellas went up on the field and on the unsheltered parts of the stadium, but not many spectators cleared out.

Across the alley behind the official stand rose Weightman Hall, one of the university buildings. It is a three-story structure with towers at both ends, and the windows of the two towers and of the third story of the building itself looked down upon the stands. In every window were squads of Philadelphia police armed with revolvers, riot guns and machines for discharging gas bombs. They were taking no chances with Communists, pacifists and other such dangerous characters. If they had ever opened with their artillery for the protection of the President, they would have decimated the band and raked the delegates and alternates.

The first spectator, a policeman's wife, took her place at 8.30 this morning, but it was half an hour before the second arrived, and when the band began to play there were still thousands of vacant seats, especially at the far end of the stadium, a good city block from the stand. As the afternoon wore into evening the reserved seats filled first, for it had been announced that none save those for distinguished guests would be held after 8 o'clock.

The long wait was pretty tedious. It was damp and muggy in the stadium even when no rain was falling, and many of the spectators had on hot raincoats. In the intervals of the music the loud-speaker brayed all sorts of inquiries and announcements. "Will Mrs. Bartel please come to the Arizona delegation?" "Mrs. Jones desires to tell her husband that their party is in Section B, near the front row." "Eddie Peabody, the world's greatest banjoist, will now play for us, 'Is It True What They Say About Dixie?'"

Once a wag induced the announcer to bellow "Will Charles Ross please come to the moving-picture stand?" Charlie Ross was a Philadelphia boy whose kidnapping back in the 70's shook the whole country. He has never been found, but every now and then an impostor claiming his name turns up in Philadelphia, and gives the local papers a two-day sensation. The last one, on investigation, turned out to have been born six years after poor Charlie was snatched.

At 7.30 Colonel Halsey, sergeant-at-arms at the convention, announced through the loud-speaker that the ceremonies would be duly held on the field, rain or no rain. The news got a somewhat feeble round of applause. The time of the President's appearance was still two hours and a half ahead, and the gray skies seemed likely to leak again at any moment. The Indian princess who yo-deled in the convention hall the other night was put up to try her magic upon them. She loosed a lugubrious chant to the accompaniment of Professor Peabody's banjo, but the firmament remained very forbidding. Nearly all the vocal music of the evening was equally depressing. A torch singer performing "If I Should Lose You" was almost heart-breaking.

At 7.45 there was another sprinkle of rain, but it lasted only half a minute, and as it ceased there was a glow of bright light from the setting sun. In this heavenly radiance an airplane began to circle the empyrean above the field trailing a streamer reading, "Wine Dine Benny The Bums 1508 Pine." Simultaneously the loud-speaker made another call for Charlie Ross. The first call, it appeared, had not fetched him.

There was a third call for him at 8 o'clock, accompanied by a third sprinkle of rain. A few minutes later the exercises of the evening began with the entrance of a drum corps of lovely she-gals from Cheyenne, Wyo. They played with great ferocity and marched down to the far end of the field. Its size may be gauged from the fact that when they were at one end of it only the boom of their bass drum could be heard at the other. As they came back toward the stand Mayor S. Davis Wilson of Philadelphia arrived with his suite of aides and was received with loud ejaculations by his admirers.

The loud-speaker kept on calling for Charlie Ross, but he never turned up, either dead or alive. At 8.15 the crowd was warned that, on the entrance of the President, it would be expected to "avoid any demonstration in the form of marching."

It was stated that if marching were attempted "the lives of many persons would be endangered," but the nature of the danger was not explained. Perhaps it had something to do with the cops posted on the battlements of Weightman Hall. Every time there was any sign of turmoil down on the field, they leaned forward hopefully and fingered the lanyards of their artillery.

The band and its horrible torch singers and other prop sets of doom retired at 8.30 and was succeeded by what was described as the Philadelphia Symphony Orchestra. It brought along eight bull-fiddles and some big drums, but after Lieutenant Frankel's band, it sounded rather thin. In all probability, not 5 percent of the people in the Stadium could hear it at all. While it struggled with Dvorak's *Carnival* overture, the President's venerable mother appeared on the stand, and the applause that greeted her drowned out its music altogether.

It did better with Strauss' beautiful *Blue Danube* waltz, but in the midst of the finale from Tchaikovsky's Fourth Symphony it was choked off again by the entrance of other notables. The boys sawed away manfully, but most of the time the only sound that could be heard fifty feet away was an occasional bing of the cymbals.

Whose idea it was to put an orchestra into a six-acre field, surrounded by 1,000,000 people I don't know. The stage management of this convention has been extraordinarily stupid. Even when the orchestra played "Dixie" only a few thousand heard it, and the usual frantic shrieks and bellowings did not follow.

When Lily Pons, formerly of the Metropolitan Opera Company was put up to warble with the orchestra efforts were made to get her a better hearing and more attention. There was a vociferous announcement of her impending wrestle with "Lo, Hear the Gentle Lark" through the loud speaker, and a microphone was set up in front of her to magnify her coloratura to stupendous proportions.

She turned out to be too short in stature to reach the mike, and when search was made for the convention Bible to put under her feet it could not be found, so the stem of the mike was bent to accommodate her. She trilled and gurgled beautifully, and got a loud hand. But she refused to sing again, and the orchestra burst into "The Stars and Stripes Forever." It sounded like the performance of a Swiss music-box in the Catacombs of Rome.

In brief, the show was a very poor one, and after 9 o'clock the crowd began sweating and fuming for the main bout. There were long stage waits, broken only by raucous yells from the loud speakers for the missing Charlie Ross. The cops, bestirred at last, searched for him under the stands, and arrested forty or fifty suspects, but they all proved they were not Charlie, and were released after warnings.

At 9.25 the loud speaker announced that the President had arrived at the Baltimore and Ohio station and was being greeted there by Vice-President Garner and the Hon. Jim Farley and snapped by "myriads of photographers." The machine was then hooked to the radio, and continued reports on his progress followed.

When he finally got into an automobile and drove off, the radio began telling what was going on in Franklin Field under the noses of its hearers. It appeared at once that nothing was going on, so the report was quickly shut off. There were still some vacant seats in the stands, but not many. The official announcer warned the crowd again that if it attempted to parade either before or after Dr. Roosevelt's speech, "serious consequences" might follow.

A spooky silence followed, broken by occasional outbursts of nervous applause. The people on the field rose to their feet, but none save those in the first few rows could see anything. At 9.40 the President suddenly came down to the stand on the arm of Jim Farley with Cactus Jack beside them, and two Ambassadors, Daniels and Bullitt, leading the way. There was a great wave of applause, but it broke up into ripples, and in a few minutes Jim waved for silence and La Pons undertook to sing "The Star-Spangled Banner."

While she was at it the President's two elder sons, James and John, stood at attention in front of the stand. Her efforts were but meagerly rewarded. The crowd didn't want to hear any more music. The stars of the evening were before it, and it was eager for them to begin their performance. A Philadelphia Divine, put up to solicit heavenly approval of the proceedings, was hardly heard.

At 9.45 Jim introduced Senator Pat Harrison, of Mississippi, who read the speech of Senator Alben Barkley, the temporary chairman of the convention, notifying Cactus Jack of his nomination. Barkley had already left Philadelphia. The Hon. Mr. Garner put on horn-rimmed spectacles and read his speech in a clear, level voice. He made very few gestures, and was beautifully brief.

Lights of at least a million candle-power glared down upon him, some of them from the top rows of the stadium and the rest from the news-reel stand which rose in the middle of the delegates' section. Dr. Garner allowed that he was a good soldier, and would obey any lawful order received from his chief.

When he shut down Farley introduced Old Joe Robinson, whose job it was to notify Dr. Roosevelt. Joe made a slip at the start by speaking of the convention as having been held at Chicago. His mind, no doubt, was flitting back to the Golden Age of four years ago before the New Deal arose to afflict Democratic statesmen. He had prepared a speech running to eight or ten minutes, but because it was necessary to get Dr. Roosevelt on the air promptly at 10 o'clock, daylight time, he delivered only a small part of it.

The President began exactly on time. He drew his first applause when he spoke of the "grave responsibility" lying upon him, and more followed when he praised "the millions of Americans who have borne disaster bravely and have dared to smile through the storm." His resonant tenor voice rang out clearly, and he was heard for the most part in a silence that was broken only by the rattle of typewriters and telegraph keys in the press stand.

The press stand was surrounded by a solid wall of Philadelphia cops and on the battlements of Weightman Hall the cop machine gunners continued their expectant vigil. No other public ceremonial within my experience has ever been policed more tremendously.

The speech was over in a little less than half an hour. It was received in a friendly way by the huge crowd, but it would certainly be an exaggeration to call it a big success. There were very few really loud outbursts of applause. The loudest followed His Excellency's excoriations of the money-mad werewolves who flourished under Harding, Coolidge and Hoover and his boasts that the New Deal had liberated the great mass of the plain people from their fangs. The clapper-clawing, such as it was, seemed to come mainly from the upper reaches of the stadium. There was very little from the surviving delegates and alternates on the field.

Once the speaker got off the text of his manuscript, but he recovered himself quickly and without confusion. While he spoke, his wife, his mother and his two sons sat directly behind him. The young men's caps were just on a level with his waist. In front of him was a phalanx of police captains, each of them a specialist in the tricks of radicals. Others stood in the corners of the small stand, searching the nearby areas with eagle eyes. A kind of uneasiness seemed to hang over the scene. The repeated warnings against rowdy demonstrations had had their effect. The people appeared to be almost afraid to yell.

Dr. Roosevelt finished a few minutes before ten thirty. As he gulped a glass of water and stepped back from the microphone, the band, which had returned to displace the orchestra, broke into "The Stars and Stripes Forever," and then into "Anchors Aweigh." There was applause, but not much, and in a minute it was over.

The President acknowledged it with waves of his arm. With the members of his family and Dr. Garner, he posed for the newsreels. There was no attempt at the forbidden demonstration. The upper galleries of the stadium began to empty the moment the speech was ended, and in ten minutes whole rows of seats were empty.

It was, all things considered, a very feeble affair. The crowd was huge, but it showed nothing properly describable as enthusiasm. I have heard crowds a tenth as large make ten times as much noise.

(The Baltimore Sun, June 28, 1936)

Coroner's Inquest

I

The Hon. Mr. Roosevelt's colossal victory in last Tuesday's plebiscite gave him plenty of excuse to leap and exult, but if he is really the smart politician that he seems to be he must be entertaining certain stealthy, *pizzicato* qualms today. He now carries all the burdens of omnipotence. There is no one to say nay—that is no one he is bound to heed. He has in his hands a blank check from and upon the American people, authorizing him to dispose of all their goods and liberties precisely as he listeth. The Congress that was elected with him will no more dare to challenge him than a pussy cat would dare to challenge a royal Bengal tiger, and even the nine old metaphysicians on Capitol Hill may be trusted to recall, if only subconsciously, that it is imprudent to spit too often into Caesar's eye.

In brief, he has become a sort of chartered libertine, and it will be interesting to note how he reacts to his franchise. The great majority of his lieges believe firmly in the Utopia that he has been preaching since 1933, and they will now expect him to bring it in at last. He can no longer make the excuse that wicked men are hindering him, nor can he plead that he is navigating unmapped waters and must proceed cautiously. He has been engaged, for nearly four years, in exploring and mapping the way, and in that work he has had the aid of a vast band of transcendental engineers of his own choice. What everyone will look for now is full steam ahead. Either we must soon see the glorious shores of Utopia or the whole argosy will be wrecked.

For a year or two past, as everyone knows, it has been making heavy weather. Not one of its greater objectives has been attained. The rich continue rich, and many millions of the poor remain on the dole. Business has improved, but it has improved a great deal more for stockmarket speculators than for honest men. The one-crop farmers continue to bellow piteously for help. Labor is still torn between sweat-shop employers on the one hand and racke-teering labor leaders on the other. For all these woes and malaises the right hon. gentlemen must now find something colorably re-sembling remedies, and with reasonable dispatch. Either he is ac-tually a wizard and knows how to cure them, or he is the worst quack ever heard of on earth.

II

Against his success in this great moral enterprise stand two in-convenient facts. The first is the fact that many, and perhaps in-deed most of the woes and malaises aforesaid appear to be inher-ently incurable. The second is the fact that people in the mass are very mercurial, and especially the sort of people who believe in miracles. They are all with him today, but that is no assurance that they will be with him tomorrow. On the contrary, there is every reason to believe that they will turn on him, soon or late, as they have turned on all popular messiahs since the dawn of his-tory.

The melancholy careers of Wilson, Roosevelt I and Hoover offer cases in point, to keep to recent times and the boundaries of this great Republic. Dr. Roosevelt himself, in truth, has already had a couple of warnings, and thus has good excuse for the qualms that I have surmised. After his great victory at the mid-term elections of 1934 there was a rapid descent in his popularity, and by the middle of 1935 he seemed headed for repudiation and disaster. In Septem-ber, 1935, the very accurate poll of the Institute of Public Opinion showed that only a bare majority of the people canvassed were for him.

He recovered a bit toward the end of the year, and kept on gaining favor until the national conventions met last June. He then showed a headlong drop, and by the middle of July he was very near the low point he had touched in September, 1935. But when, on July 23, the speech of acceptance of the Hon. Mr. Lan-don was broadcast, there was a rise in the stock of the Hon. Mr.

Roosevelt, and as the campaign developed it went on rising. Toward the very end, in all probability, there was another recession, but if so it was not sufficient to affect the result on election day. The hon. gentleman was reelected by an unprecedented majority.

But it is not to be forgotten that 16,000,000 Americans voted against him. These may be trusted to stay put, and millions of those who voted for him may be trusted to begin suffering the pangs of *Katzenjammer* very shortly.

III

The immense improbability of the Hon. Mr. Landon's election was manifest from the day he made his first speech. It was, as such things go, a pretty good speech, and it was followed by many even better ones, but there was nothing in any of them to lift and frenzy multitudes, and there was nothing in the hon. gentleman's delivery of them to compensate for their ineffectiveness. He turned out, indeed, to be one of the worst public speakers recorded in the archives of faunal zoölogy. Over and over again, facing an eagerly friendly audience, he scotched its nascent whoops and reduced it to scratching itself.

I traveled with him on three of his four campaign trips, and witnessed his performance at close range. In all my life I have never encountered anything more depressing than his elocution. Most of his speeches were not delivered at all; they were simply recited. And what a recitation it was! If it was possible, by any device, however tortured, to stress the wrong word in a sentence, he invariably stressed it. If the text called for a howl of moral indignation he always dropped his voice, and if a sepulchral whisper was in order he raised it. The audience was never given a fair chance to applaud, and when it barged in notwithstanding it was cut off.

At Philadelphia and again at Pittsburgh the hon. gentleman started off with unaccustomed fire, and it seemed likely that he would make good speeches at last. But both times he subsided into his usual forbidding manner after a few minutes. Off the platform he is certainly not cold. On the contrary, he is a very amiable and charming fellow, and, what is more, a shrewd one. Sitting in his private car, he talked amusingly and persuasively, and often had something penetrating to say. But once he got before the microphone he became a schoolboy reciting a piece, and it was in that character that he appeared before the country. I can recall no audience that showed any sign of being genuinely aroused by him. And encountered no radio fan, however willing, who got any kick out of his soughings.

IV

Worse, the content of his speeches was often as ineffective as their manner of delivery. There was only one way to beat Roosevelt, and that was to attack him with horse, foot and dragoons, denouncing his mountebankeries in a voice of brass and allowing him no virtue whatever. Above the level of the dole-birds, at the start of the campaign, there was a great deal of doubt about the New Deal, and if the opposition candidate had belabored its Father Divine in the grand manner, keeping him constantly on the defensive, there might have been a different tale to tell last Tuesday.

But the Hon. Mr. Landon, it quickly appeared, was quite incapable of that sort of war. He was too mild a fellow for it, and, perhaps I should add, too candid, too conscientious. He conceived it to be his high duty, not to flog and flay Roosevelt, but to submit his own ideas to the country, and the more he submitted them the more it became evident that some of them, and not the least important, were indistinguishable from the fundamental hallucinations of the New Deal. When he came out for more and bigger bonuses for mendicant farmers he simply surrendered to the enemy, and from that time on his campaign was dead.

In a word, the Republicans nominated the wrong candidate. They got an honest man, and one who, if he had gone to the White House, would have made a diligent, reliable and courageous President, but the majority of them took him unwillingly, and never agreed with the notions he expounded so laboriously and so futilely. The old-time professionals of the party, when they reached Cleveland last June, found themselves hamstrung. The stench of Hoover was so strong upon them that they were clapped into quarantine instantly; indeed, many of them went there voluntarily. The Western Progressives, save for the old moo-cow, Borah, were *non est;* they had gone over to the New Deal in a body, bellowing "Glory, glory, hallelujah!" This left the show to the Kansas Gang, an unearthly combination of former stooges of the Anti-Saloon League, county chairmen from the Dust Bowl and irresponsible amateurs out for a lark. It was only this Kansas Gang that had a presentable candidate ready, and he was nominated by default.

Could some other hero have won? I am inclined to believe that it was possible. Roosevelt, skillfully and relentlessly bombarded, would have got into difficulties quickly, for he was vulnerable in front, in the rear and on both flanks. But Landon's earnest homilies upon the issues of the hour left him unscathed. Until the last week of the campaign he did not even bother to answer them. All his radio time was devoted to the intoning of mellifluous dithyrambs, with music by dulcimers and accordions.

(The Baltimore Evening Sun, November 9, 1936)

1940

During Roosevelt's second term he continued to fight for social progress. The Republican minority was powerless to oppose his proposals; their hopes rested upon "the Nine Old Men" in the Supreme Court, who resisted Roosevelt's sweeping changes. The Court invalidated some of the key New Deal legislation, and FDR began to fear that if it should decide against the National Labor Relations Act or the Social Security Act, it would be the end of the New Deal. So he spoke to the people, telling them he had decided to infuse the Supreme Court with young blood, appointing up to six new justices so there would be a total of fifteen justices in the Court.

The outcry that followed lasted from February until June, eclipsing all other issues. FDR was seen by many as a dictator who wanted to kill constitutional government by destroying the independence of the judiciary. FDR ultimately shelved his plan, but during the controversy the Court gradually committed itself to New Deal policies—which had been Roosevelt's aim all along.

Meanwhile, unemployment rose and wages fell in August 1937 as the country entered "the Roosevelt depression" and five thousand strikes erupted throughout the country. A new Farm Security Administration was created, along with the Fair Labor Standards Act. During the congressional election of 1938, Roosevelt traveled across the country, criticizing those senators who were opposed to the New Deal. His interference in the Southern primaries was met with strong criticism.

In 1938, domestic problems took second stage to foreign issues: Americans wondered if they would have to enter a war to help Britain fight Nazi Germany. The country became divided as isolationists postured to keep the United States out of European affairs and not participate in any upcoming war and the interventionists argued if dictators such as Hitler and Mussolini were not checked, America would become the next victim..

The Republicans had enjoyed some success during the midterm election of 1938, thereby encouraging a flurry of Republican presidential contenders. The popular candidates were New York's District Attorney, Thomas E. Dewey; Robert Alphonso Taft, senator from Ohio and son of former President Taft; Michigan's Senator Arthur H. Vandenberg; and Wall Street lawyer and utilities executive Wendell L. Willkie, who had voted for the Democrats in 1938 but who had now become a Republican. Willkie was without any political experience, but he had a lively homespun quality that appealed to many. Other potential nominees were New York publisher Frank Gannett, and ex-President Hoover.

The Republican Convention met in Philadelphia on June 24, only two days after France was forced to sign the armistice with Germany. Formerly, Dewey and Taft had been the front runners, but during the months preceding the convention Willkie had gained the lead: "Willkie for President" and "Win with Willkie" clubs had emerged all over the country. Drumming up support in a well-organized campaign for Willkie were Oren Root, Jr., and Russel Davenport, aided by the publicity director for the Committee of Utility Executives, as well as other prominent advertising men. Henry Luce of Time *magazine and other newspaper publishers, plus wealthy New York bankers and businessmen, were also backing him. When the delegates began to ballot, Dewey took first place, but by the fourth ballot, Willkie was in the lead, with 306 votes compared to Dewey's 250 and Taft's 245. The galleries chanted, "We want Willkie! We want Willkie!" The hall was tense with excitement. On the sixth ballot, when Michigan released its pledge to Vandenberg and threw its votes to Willkie, the roar of the galleries was deafening. It was the triumphant victory of an amateur.*

Hon. Herbert Hoover
Brings Down House at Convention

Convention Hall, Philadelphia, June 25.—It was reserved for the Hon. Herbert Hoover, who led the Republican party down to disaster in 1932, to set going the first genuine uproar that its 1940 National Convention has staged.

When he got to the hall at 9.37 P.M., daylight time, arrayed in his traditional double-breasted blue suit, dark necktie and high white collar, there was a wild yell from the delegates and alternates, supported instantly by antiphons from the galleries, but it was not until he approached the mike to begin his speech, four minutes later, that the steel rafters really trembled.

The demonstration lasted six minutes by the clock, and was manifestly spontaneous and honest. During the brief interval be-

tween the entrance of the right hon. gentleman and his first attempt to turn on his eloquence there was prayer by a colored
bishop wearing a doggy morning coat, gray-striped trousers and a
lavender rabat, and a song by a lady soprano arrayed in all the
colors of the rainbow.

The former President, aided by various literary ghosts of high
skill, had prepared a fluent and well-reasoned harangue, and the
parts of it dealing with foreign relations were marked by really
extraordinary good sense. But it quickly appeared that his seven
years of retirement had not improved his elocution, and he had
not been going ten minutes before his audience was somewhat
subdued.

He stood before the mike like a schoolboy reciting a piece, and
seldom varied his intonation or made a gesture. For three or four
minutes running he would lean on the speakers' table, and then
for as many minutes he would prop his hands on his hips or let
them hang loosely at his side.

He had a print of his speech propped up before him, but he had
apparently memorized large sections of it, for he often proceeded
with only an occasional glance at the text. Once or twice the
rotund terminology of his ghosts seemed to baffle him, and when
he came to the word eleemosynary he hesitated for a second or
two and then pronounced it elemeetsinory.

Whenever he loosed a jocosity, which was not infrequently, and
the audience seized the chance to laugh, he smiled himself in a sly
and satisfied way. But most of the time his somewhat pale face,
now much thinner than it used to be, was virtually expressionless,
and at no time did he employ the arts of the orator to warm and
point up his remarks.

He seldom misplaced emphasis in the maddening manner of the
Hon. Alf M. Landon; he simply omitted emphasis altogether. The
effective phrases in his speech—and there were plenty of them—
had to be discovered by the audience for itself. He never gave it
any help—not even by such elementary devices as shaking a fist,
winking an eye or pretending to pause for a word.

The section of his discourse dealing with the war showed evidences of unusually careful preparation, and, in fact, the text of it
was not perfected until late this afternoon, hours after printed
copies of the remainder of the speech had been distributed to the
reporters.

The audience heard it with close attention and it was interrupted by applause much more often than the other parts, for the conflict between the implacable isolationists and the more extreme interventionists has worried the assembled politicoes since they got to Philadelphia, and Hoover's somewhat ingenious effort to reconcile the two factions thus got a very eager and friendly hearing.

The loudest approval of the whole evening followed his declaration that "if we are to keep cool and not stimulate war there must be an end to provocative speech by our officials."

For a moment, at this point, it looked as if a real demonstration were in the making. Hundreds of delegates leaped to their feet and what had begun as mere handclapping quickly rose to yells. But Hoover, as if alarmed by the noise, hastily resumed his anesthetic sing-song, and in a few seconds the crowd had been restored to reason and reduced to silence.

Once the war section was passed and the right hon. gentleman launched into his solemn peroration, people began to move out of the galleries. It was hot in the hall, especially upstairs, and a whole hour of monotone was rather too much to bear. There was no actual walkout, but it seemed to be threatening as the speech ended.

The last sentence, a rhetorical question, "Republicans, are you prepared to go into the fight?" brought the delegates to their feet again, and Hoover bowed politely and backed away from the mike.

Chairman Martin rushed forward to foment the applause, held up the speaker's right arm in the manner of a referee indicating the winner of a prize fight, and signalled to the photographers to do their duty. Some of the delegates began parading the aisles with their State standards, but this was apparently not to Hoover's taste, for he presently broke away from Martin and made off, followed by the photographers.

At 11 o'clock Martin rapped for order, and after a few routine announcements the Convention adjourned until 2 o'clock tomorrow afternoon. At that time the Resolution Committee is expected to come in with the platform, and before the end of the day the long and tedious job of putting a dozen or more candidates in nomination may be started.

Today's morning session of the convention was given over mainly to the second-chop keynote speech of the Hon. Joseph W. Martin, Jr., of Massachusetts, the permanent chairman. In view of the lesser importance of his pronunciamento he was given but half the time allotted to the Hon. Harold E. Stassen last night. He hollered precisely thirty minutes to the second.

The radio brethren are now the dictators of all great public gatherings, and the Hon. Mr. Martin had to sit in his place until they were ready for him, like a pugilist waiting for the opening gong. A committee composed of State Governors, Senators and other such dignitaries, along with several more or less beautiful lady delegates, had been appointed to escort him to the platform. It fumed and fussed down on the floor until the radio signal came.

The Hon. Mr. Martin's speech was standard convention stuff, and caused no visible pother among the delegates and alternates. The purple passages that they applauded were the following:

1. We are here to rally all patriots in a crusade for Americanism. (Brisk handclapping.)

2. The early patriots came here to form a nation. We came here today to protect and preserve that nation. (A little louder handclapping, with a few exultant yells.)

3. My countrymen, we can, if we will, achieve concerted effective effort just as efficiently as any subject peoples can. We can do it without surrendering the Bill of Rights. (Hearty whoops.)

4. We must preserve our country from the schemes and treachery of those unsympathetic to our constitutional republic, who would destroy it. (Defiant yells.)

5. All Fifth Columnists must be rooted out and thrown out. (More yells.)

6. We must not permit political liberty to be used as a mask for plotters against the American system. (Ditto.)

7. The Constitution must not be misused to destroy the Constitution. (Ditto, but not so loud.)

8. We want an America at peace with the world (a really gusty roar); an America untainted by hatreds and fears (another).

9. The record of the New Deal will never be approved by the American people. (Mild applause.)

10. America wants to get back to sanity, progress and peace. (Howls.)

11. We must preserve free America for the generations to come, cost us what it may. (Noises of an order inferior to howls.)

These specimens give a fair idea of the style and content of the speech. The rest of it was much worse and got no applause at all.

Martin looked small beside the gigantic Stassen, and showed no sign of oratorical virtuosity. He has made an excellent record as minority leader of the House of Representatives, but is supposed to be barred from the Presidency by the circumstance he is a Catholic. As a matter of fact, he is an Irish Protestant, born in Massachusetts.

When he took command of the convention, vice Stassen, wafted back to oblivion, a delegation from Illinois rushed to the platform to present him a gavel. It apparently had some connection with the late Abraham Lincoln, but in the noise and confusion no one could make out whether it was made of the actual bones of Old Abe or only the surviving timbers of his natal log cabin.

(The Baltimore Sun, June 26, 1940)

Wonder Man

I

Though it was unquestionably surprising, there was really nothing mysterious about the nomination of the Hon. Wendell L. Willkie in Philadelphia last Thursday. He was embraced by the assembled heirs of Lincoln for two reasons, both of them plain enough. The first was that he was obviously the only candidate in the running who stood the slightest chance of beating Roosevelt in November, and the second was that there was no one on the fire-ground with sufficient skill and authority to arrange and command the nomination of any of the more orthodox aspirants.

The second reason, politically speaking, was more important than the first. If there had been any bosses on the bridge, the odds are that the convention would have nominated Taft, despite his palpable weaknesses, for his nomination would have tended to preserve the party organization, and preserving the party organization is more important to a professional than winning an election. But seven lean and hungry years had virtually denuded the G.O.P. of bosses. Every State delegation was on its own, and most of them were hopelessly divided.

The leading professional candidates, Taft, Dewey, Vandenberg and Gannett, were not only not able to effect the nomination of one or another of their own number by delivering delegates; they were even unable to hold their delegates for themselves. Defections began on the second ballot, and by the time the third got under way whole delegations were raring to go to Willkie. The professional plan, in so far as there was any plan at all, appeared to be to concentrate on Taft, but there was no one on hand with enough power to put it into effect, and so it blew up.

Thus the first reason for favoring Willkie came into effect, with nothing to impede it. The howling of the galleries was not needed to convince the delegates that he was the popular choice; and they knew by the events of his whirlwind canvass that he was a bold and effective campaigner. So they leaped to his standard, convinced that if he could not beat Roosevelt, then certainly it could never be done by such palpably feebler and less-enterprising fellows as Taft, Dewey, Vandenberg or Gannett.

II

Whether or not he is actually capable of the trick remains to be seen. The issue, in fact, depends upon the progress of the war. If England walks out on Roosevelt, as it has already walked out on Poland, Norway (twice), Belgium and France, he will become a comic character, and it will be easy for so resourceful a campaigner as Willkie to knock him off. But if the war goes on, and he succeeds in his plain purpose to get the United States into it, he will be able to wrap himself in the flag, and the flag will save him. Once he is wrapped, indeed, Willkie will be almost helpless, for he is himself a warlock, and will have to stand silent with his hat off.

Roosevelt, at the moment, appears to be doing some heavy sweating. As a lifelong Anglomaniac, he probably finds it hard to take in the notion that England may be licked; but other Anglomaniacs, during the past few weeks, have managed somehow to entertain it, and it may be that it has got him, too. If so, he is very likely to announce at the last minute that he is not a candidate for a third term. He may, in fact, say that he has *never* been a candidate, though everyone knows that he has. Hints to that effect already emanate from the White House, and the Hon. Frank Knox is said to have been given to understand, on accepting his appointment to the Cabinet, that Roosevelt would not run again unless forced into it by his inescapable duty to morality and religion.

If he pulls out, Willkie will have a walkover, for no other imaginable Democrat could stand up to his ferocious assault upon the New Deal, with its horrible record of billions wasted on the buying of moron votes, and the defenses of the country neglected. Old Hull, who has never been anything more than a rice New Dealer, would wither and perish under his *Blitzkrieg*, and any such selling-plater as the Hon. Robert H. Jackson would hardly be in the running. Just as the Republican party has suffered by the decay of its bosses, so the Democratic party has suffered by the dominance of a super-boss, semi-celestial in character and obliterating all others. Take away Roosevelt, and there will be little left of it save a mob of crackpots and frauds, mendicants and dupes.

III

Willkie is no more a wizard than Roosevelt, but he has something of the same capacity to convince idiots that he is, and so he is likely to be a very popular candidate, and to make a picturesque campaign. Once he gets under way his slightest utterances will take on an oracular character, and mothers will begin carrying their babies to him to be cured of cramps, windgalls and distemper. For the plain people of the world are always looking for messiahs, and whenever one wears out they resort to another. They are never content with hard diligence and common sense; what they always pant for is magic.

Whether or not Willkie, if elected, will make a competent President is on the knees of the gods, but I, for one, have some doubts of it, for I believe that successful businessmen usually make poor public administrators. They always share the popular delusion that running a government is precisely the same thing as running an electric company, a wholesale house, or a chain of grocery stores. It is, of course, nothing of the kind. The public official drafted from business invariably discovers to his dismay that dealing with politicians is an art quite new to him, beyond his talents and experience, and nine times out of ten they quickly wreck him.

Of Willkie's intrinsic ability there can be no question. He is a highly successful man, and he has been successful in a business that is widely unpopular and is afflicted by a dreadful array of hostile legislation. To operate a public utilities company at a profit in a democracy dominated by demagogues calls for cleverness of the first caliber. It takes courage, ingenuity, patience, boldness, and a tough hide, not to mention a sense of humor. Willkie has all of these things.

His sale of a large group of Commonwealth and Southern properties to the Government at a reasonable price was a feat equal to squaring the circle or talking one's self out of the deathhouse. Everything was against him. The New Deal goons had him down, and were bent upon making a moral example of him. Yet he managed, strapped to the board, to blarney them into paying at least sixty per cent of the actual value of the properties. No wonder the economic royalists of the country let go an almost incredulous huzzah and began to groom him for a higher destiny.

IV

He is, in private, a charming fellow, with a good line of talk, a sense of the ludicrous (even in himself), and a plentiful stock of hard common sense. There is a kind of sloppiness about him that is somehow attractive, and will be a valuable asset on the stump. His hair is tousled, he perspires freely, his pants hang loosely, and he enters upon no conspiracy with his tailor to conceal his paunch. No one, on meeting him, appears to dislike him, and most persons fall for him at once. During the week of the convention virtually all the gossip about him was favorable. Talk against the other candidates went on day and night, and they all acquired opprobrious nicknames, but not Willkie.

That he will make a gaudy campaign, whether against Roosevelt or against one of Roosevelt's false-faces, goes without saying. He is not only a frank man, saying what he thinks in plain English; he also appears to love combat for its own sake, and will get a considerable spiritual satisfaction out of slambanging the New Deal imposture. On the war issue, as I have noted, he will be stymied, at least until England blows up; moreover, he will be handicapped by running on a platform out of harmony with his own known views. But on all other issues he will be able to bellow in a large and free manner, and there is every evidence that he will do so joyously, and to the considerable damage of the quacks he belabors.

(The Baltimore Sun, June 30, 1940)

The Democratic party convention met at Chicago Stadium in Chicago, Illinois, on July 15–18. Arriving early, Mencken surveyed the stadium where he was to work for the next few days. The "prissy, tearoomy style" of decoration prevailing at recent conventions, he noticed, had been abandoned in favor of the traditional flags and ribbons. More than 250 American flags hung from the stadium ceiling, and along the gallery rails were huge streamers and festoons of bunting. "The effect is that of a high-toned country fair in the hog-and-hominy belt." Spotlights lit the hall for the accommodation of newsreel photographers, lighting up the bright red chairs. "In the glare of the movie lights they look downright incandescent," Mencken observed. "Some of the delegates sat down in them as gingerly as a condemned fellow takes position in an electric chair." Directly behind the platform palatial glass-enclosed quarters had been erected for the radio reporters, but, as Mencken dryly noted, there was no position for television broadcasters. "The television rights are open to anyone who wants them, but no one has applied. Whether this is or not a fact will cause delegates from the Bible Country to recall the ominous words of Proverbs xxix, 18 . . . ('Where there is no vision, the people perish; but he that keepeth the law, happy is he.')"

Franklin Roosevelt had shrunk from openly seeking the nomination: he wanted to be drafted by the party, but this had to be cleverly managed. When the Democratic Convention opened, three fourths of the delegates were pledged to the President. On Roosevelt's behalf, Harry Hopkins was in control of the situation. From the privacy of his bathroom in the Blackstone Hotel, Hopkins installed a private telephone line to the White House, and kept in close touch with the President throughout the convention. When Senator Barkley in a feisty speech first uttered Roosevelt's name, Mayor Ed Kelly signaled to his superintendent of sewers, Thomas F. Garry, and Garry's voice, piped from a room beneath the auditorium, boomed from all the loudspeakers: "We Want Roosevelt! The World Wants Roosevelt!" The "voice from the sewers," as it later came to be called, continued to repeat the slogans for twenty-two minutes before the demonstration died down. Barkley concluded his speech:

I and other close friends of the President have long known that he had not wished to be a candidate again. We knew, too, that in no way whatsoever has he exerted any influence in the selection of delegates, or upon the opinions of the delegates to this convention. The President has never had and has not today any desire or purpose to continue in the office of the President, to be a candidate for that office or to be nominated by the convention for that office. He wishes in all earnestness and sincerity to make it clear that all delegates to this convention are free to vote for any candidate. This is the message I bear to you from the President of the United States.

Another demonstration followed, and the "voice from the sewers" took up the chant again. The next day, Mencken reported after "the demon voice" kept roaring, "The party wants Roosevelt . . . The world needs Roosevelt . . . Everybody wants Roosevelt!" the delegates voted for FDR on the first ballot. Those opposed to a third term proposed James Farley of New York as an alternative to the President, along with John Garner of Texas and Millard Tydings of Maryland. But Roosevelt carried the first ballot with 946 votes against Farley's 72, Garner's 61 and Tydings's 9. "The two-term tradition, held almost sacred in American politics for nearly a century and a half, went out of the window" Mencken wrote, as the great name of Roosevelt was "cheered—just as scheduled."

Roosevelt Statement
Flabbergasts Delegates

Chicago, July 16.—For a full minute after Senator Alben W. Barkley, of Kentucky, the permanent chairman of the convention, made the Roosevelt announcement tonight the delegates sat as if flabbergasted.

There were a few cries of "No," and others of "We want Roosevelt," but they were not numerous, and it was plain to see that the news left everyone still uncertain—indeed, twice as uncertain as before.

As if to cover up their confusion some of the delegates began parading the aisles with their State standards, but they moved slowly and almost in silence. This went on for perhaps five minutes. Then someone got to the mike and shouted, "We want Roosevelt," and the show promised to brisken a bit, but almost instantly it collapsed again.

At no time did more than a fifth of the delegates take any hand in it. They simply stood on their chairs staring expectantly, each apparently hoping that someone else would start something. It was a curious scene indeed, and perhaps without parallel in the whole history of national conventions.

An hour before, set going by Barkley's first mention of Roosevelt, they had staged a demonstration that at least showed a certain heartiness, though it was certainly not uproarious and did not last long, as such things go. But now they simply gaped about them while small groups paraded the aisles.

After this funeral festivity had gone on for perhaps ten minutes, the band tried to give some help, but even the loudest music failed to set anything going. Then someone began to yell "New York wants Roosevelt" from a mike on the floor, and presently the same bellow came from various other States. But for a while the voice was always the same, and it was not until nearly all the States had been spoken for that any actual spokesmen for most of them appeared.

After that the thing became a free-for-all and various variations appeared in the call, some of them satirical. A stentorian voice from the Hague stronghold began with "New Jersey wants Roosevelt" and then proceeded to "The party wants Roosevelt" and "The country wants Roosevelt." On the heels of this, in a different voice, came "Jim Farley wants Roosevelt," and then "Willkie wants Roosevelt," and then "Tammany Hall wants Roosevelt."

In the course of ten minutes all other voices were drowned out by a dreadful one that kept on shouting "Roosevelt, Roosevelt, Roosevelt" in the manner of a colossal lunatic. It issued, according to reports reaching the press stand, from Congressman Eddie Hart, of New Jersey, one of the followers of Mayor Hague.

The spectacle, by this time, had become almost unearthly. There stood the delegates on their chairs, most of them blinking in a puzzled sort of way and looking far more glum than cheerful. And out of the crowd, amplified in a horrible manner by a loudspeaker system, roared that ghastly voice, sounding hardly human.

It was the first mechanized demonstration ever seen and its complete artificiality was always obvious. The relatively few delegates who had left their seats were grouped in front of the platform with their standards held aloft.

The rest remained in their places, plainly wondering what the Roosevelt statement meant. Did it mean that he had really withdrawn? Or simply that he wanted his renomination made unanimous? They would have to wait until morning to find out.

Gradually the demonical voice began to show signs of wearing out, and other whoopers began to be heard. Some of the new voices were feminine, but not many. One of the male ones shouted "Virginia wants Byrd." The uproar began to sound like the noise of children at some rowdy game—exaggerated, of course, 100,000 times. But it never showed any sign of spontaneity. From first to last it was plainly manufactured—and not too adroitly.

Barkley made various efforts to slap it down. Once he adopted the device of bringing his wife to the platform mike, and introducing her. It did not work, for the demon voice kept on roaring. Finally everyone in the hall began to grow sick of the bedlam, and it died down of itself. Order was finally restored a few minutes after midnight.

Barkley began his own speech a little before 10 o'clock. It had been reported that he would occupy but twenty minutes, and in view of the sufferings that the convention had endured at the hands of the Hon. William B. Bankhead last night, this report was very well received.

But the chance to holler at length presented temptations that no politician could resist, so Barkley went on fattening his speech, and in the end it presented formidable proportions.

He is a hack politician of long experience on the stump, and at one time served the Anti-Saloon League as a full-time rabble-rouser. His voice is clear and powerful, and he made the most of all his points, some of which were far from ineffective.

He got his first round of applause when he denounced the Hon. Wendell L. Willkie as "a political chameleon" and his second when he referred to the Willkie battle for the Republican nomination as "the heroic battle of the kilowatt."

When he mentioned the name of the Hon. Herbert Hoover the delegates booed and laughed, and when he first loosed the name of Roosevelt there was a considerable demonstration—the first seen so far in this convention.

The Hon. Sumner Welles, Under Secretary of State in the Roosevelt Administration, seized one of the Maryland standards and toted it up to the open space in front of the platform. He was attended by Richard O'Connell, W. Preston Lane, Brooke Lee and other esquires. But Senator Tydings hung on to the other standard and was still guarding it valiantly when the uproar ended.

There were no bands on the floor, and so the show began to bog down after ten minutes. Aside from the State standards the only banners seen on the floor were the State flag of Pennsylvania and a placard reading "North Carolina's twenty-six votes for Roosevelt." The Maryland standard interned by Senator Tydings was not the only one that did not join the parade. Those of Missouri, New York, Virginia, Louisiana and Oklahoma also stood fast.

At the end of fifteen minutes of somewhat dull stomping and yowling Barkley began banging for order, and a little while later he got it by announcing that a woman had been hurt in the parade and needed medical assistance. Six doctors rushed for the stand, and the fourth of them to reach it was Dr. Page C. Jett, of Prince Frederick, one of the Maryland delegates. Despite his celebrity he arrived too late, for the lady had been rushed to an ambulance by doctors 1, 2 and 3. Her injuries were reported to be not serious.

Barkley resumed his bellowing at 10.30, having got about a fourth of the way into his speech when he was stopped. In what remained of it there was little that the delegates could get their teeth into, so they heard most of it listlessly, quietly sweating in the glare of the movie lights. There was only a scattering of hand-clapping when he denounced the "grasping, greedy totalitarian states" of Europe, and only a little more when he bawled against fifth columnists at home.

But there was an appreciably better response, when he declared that "at least one continent on this earth shall be kept free for the exercise of the individual and collective rights and privileges of free men." Most of this response appeared to come from the delegates and alternates. Despite reports that the galleries had been packed by goons of the Kelly-Nash-Nudelman machine, they were relatively quiet all evening, even during the Roosevelt demonstration.

Whether or not there will be a minority report remains to be seen. It is reported this evening that certain malcontents, including Senator Byrd, of Virginia, and Senator Tydings, of Maryland, have two in hand, and will take them to the floor. One condemns conscription and the other declares against a third term. Neither will be adopted by the convention.

The Vice-Presidential lightning ran wild today and began to flash all over the lot. At least twenty different candidates were trotted out, ranging from New Dealers who actually believe in the New Deal to Bourbons who put it somewhere between spiritualism and cannibalism. Even Mrs. Roosevelt was mentioned, and one bright fellow suggested that Roosevelt himself be given both the Presidential and Vice-Presidential nominations.

There was also an under-current of sentiment for the Hon. Wendell L. Willkie, of Wall Street, Ind., some holding that it would be a smart idea to give him the second place on the ticket and others inclining toward going the whole hog.

The statesmen in command of the negotiations that went on in every hotel room and behind every potted palm were the Hon. Eddie Flynn, of New York, representing Tammany Hall; the Hon. Frank Hague, Mayor of Jersey City and captain general of New Jersey; the Hon. Joe Guffey, of Pennsylvania, and the Hon. Edward J. Kelly, Mayor of Chicago and head of the highly scented Kelly-Nash-Nudelman machine.

On the part of the New Deal G.H.Q. the chief whisperers were the Hon. Harry L. Hopkins, the Hon. Harold L. Ickes and the Hon. Henry A. Wallace, all of them members of the Cabinet. Wallace and Ickes are Republicans and Hopkins is a former Socialist.

Poor Jim Farley had a dreadful day of it. On the one hand the New Dealers mauled and scorched him in an effort to make him withdraw his own candidacy and continue as chairman of the Democratic National Committee, in charge of the campaign, and on the other hand the anti-New Dealers begged him as a patriot and a Christian to stick to his loathing of a third term and save the faces of his friends. . . .

(The Baltimore Sun, July 17, 1940)

———————

It was the vice-presidential nomination which produced the real battle of the Democratic Convention. When FDR let it be known that he had chosen his Secretary of Agriculture, Henry A. Wallace, as his candidate, the delegates demurred at his "dictation." There was such an arousal of ill feeling that Barkley adjourned the afternoon session without allowing any nominating speeches. The recess gave Harry Hopkins and others time to round up the necessary votes for Wallace's nomination. An angry President barked to Hopkins on the long-distance phone: "Well, damn it to hell, they will go for Wallace or I won't run, and you can jolly well tell them so." He then prepared a speech, refusing the nomination.

The recess over, the delegates gave vent to their feelings about the hand-picked Vice President. To quell the mood, Eleanor Roosevelt flew to Chicago to make a gracious speech for Wallace, and after Hopkins and others had finished working on the delegates, Henry Wallace was chosen on one ballot.

In the early hours of the morning Roosevelt addressed the convention:

> *Only the people themselves can draft a President.*
> *If such a draft should be made upon me, I will,*
> *with God's help, continue to serve with the*
> *best of my ability and with the fullness of my*
> *strength.*

Disgusted with the entire process, Mencken duly reported the events, and then followed the Willkie campaign.

Triumph of Democracy

It needed only an ordinary pair of ears at Chicago to discover that loyalty to the Throne was far from a universal pestilence among the delegates and alternates in convention assembled. There was bitter resentment of the Hon. Mr. Roosevelt's hypocritical maneuvering for a third term, and there was resentment even more bitter of his imperious insistence that the Hon. Henry A. Wallace be made his running mate. At the moment Wallace was shoved through on Thursday night, with the steam roller laboring and sputtering like Behemoth in travail, it is probable that a secret poll would have shown fewer actual votes for him than for any other statesman in all this great Republic, not excluding the Hon. Wendell L. Willkie.

It was, indeed, a common joke of the convention that large numbers of the delegates were for Willkie even as against Roosevelt himself, and would so vote in November. How much truth was in this I do not profess to say, but certainly it was plain that the anti-third-term tradition was dying hard, and to the tune of grave dubieties. The show in progress was not merely a political combat; it was a downright revolution, and even the stupidest delegate must have given some uneasy consideration to its possible consequences.

If a third term, why not a fourth? And if a fourth, then why have any parties at all? As a convinced monarchist of long standing, I am not upset by such speculations, but they unquestionably had the effect of highly wayward thoughts upon men brought up to and living by the party system. They saw all their immemorial rights and prerogatives snatched out of their hands. They were not consulted about anything; they were simply told what they had to do. And what they had to do was to connive at an imposture whose true character was blisteringly plain to all of them, however facilely it may have fooled the radio audience. What they were asked to consent to—or, rather, *ordered* to consent to—was a bold and successful attempt, unparalleled in American history, to hand over the reins of power to one man, and make him the impeccable and unchallengeable sovereign, not only of his party but also, if his luck continued, of his country.

* *

Politicians are usually not reflective men, but there must have been plenty of them who pondered sardonically, as the Great Croon of Croons proceeded early Friday morning, on the dramatic contrast between its pious denunciation of dictators and the hard reality that stared them in the face. They had spent the whole week flat on the ground, with the aforesaid steam roller bumping over them. Every sign of opposition, however rational, was instantly slapped down—or anticipated and circumvented. All orders came from the White House, and from nowhere else.

Even the rebellion of the surviving isolationists was thus disposed of, quickly and effectively. They came to Chicago determined to make a fight in the open against the Hon. Mr. Roosevelt's palpable and long-continued efforts to get the United States into the war, and some of them were full of boasts that they would battle on to the last ditch. But there was never any contest, for the mendacious plank that came from the White House flooded their carburetors, and left them to console themselves, if they could, with its transparent false pretenses.

At that, they were more fortunate than any of the other groups of dissentients. They at least got something to cherish, even though it was bogus; the others were simply run over by the steam roller. It had its operating crew on the scene—half of it supplied by the odoriferous Kelly-Nash-Nudelman machine of Chicago and the even worse Hague machine of New Jersey, and the other half made up of New Deal idealists—but all orders came direct from Washington, and when they came it was at the convenience of the commanding authority, not at that of the delegates.

How the thing worked was shown amusingly on Thursday afternoon when the convention actually stopped on a dead center because no one knew what it was expected to do. This ignorance was not inferred; it was openly announced from the platform by the Hon. Jimmy Byrnes, of South Carolina, one of the New Deal loud-speakers. He explained frankly that he had been promised a telegram from the White House, but that it had not come, and while he waited for it the convention had to divert itself with small-town vaudeville.

* *

The Croon of Croons made many things plain. It not only elucidated at length the theory of the Indispensable Man; it also indicated clearly the program of the campaign. That program will have the one end of keeping the boobs alarmed. They will be terrified and lathered by an endless series of nightmares. One day Hitler will be coming by air from the eastward, and the next day the Japs will be coming by water from the west. And on all days Fifth Columns at home will be carrying on a sinister war upon religion, morality, and all the rest of it, and only the ceaseless vigil of One whose soul is all sacrifices will be potent to save.

This, of course, is the buncombe that demagogues have ladled out at all times and everywhere since the earliest dawn of human society. First set up a bugaboo—and then give chase to it with loud yells. First scare the boobs out of their pants, and then rush up to save them. Whether or not it will work again this time will depend very largely upon the progress of events abroad. If the war is still going on in November, it will be worth millions of votes; but if the war has blown up, it will be worth very much less.

On this point I undertake no prophecy, but simply indicate the emerging facts. The Croon of Croons was, on all counts, a masterly document. It established firmly—at all events, for vote-getting purposes—the dogma that the long and devious campaign for the third-term nomination was never made at all, and that the candidate had to be drafted in the end. And it launched the theory that the conflict now joined is not one between the usual gangs of politicians, eager only to grab places at the public trough, but one between the hosts of Heaven, sweating innocence and righteousness, on the one hand, and the scabrous rabble of Satan on the other.

* *

It is interesting to speculate upon the possible effects, in the long run, of this stupendous fraud. There were men who left the convention at Chicago—and not all of them foolish men, by any means—convinced that it might go down into history as the last Democratic National Convention ever held—and maybe, indeed, as the last convention of any great party, in the sense that parties have been understood in the United States in the past. If the fraud succeeds, there will be no more Democratic party, but only a Roosevelt party, and even the Republican party, though it may survive on paper, will be reduced to impotence.

In case this happens, it will hardly be fair to lay all the blame on Roosevelt, though unquestionably he will be the chief instrument of the revolution. It has been in the making, in fact for many years —at least since the Jackson era. Even in those remote days judicious men saw what was coming. They realized the essential weakness of democracy, and predicted some of its worst excesses —now unhappy and inescapable realities. They warned that giving the vote to incompetent, despairing and envious people would breed demagogues to rouse and rally them, and that the whole democratic process would thus be converted into organized pillage and rapine.

It has come to pass under Roosevelt, and no one seems to be able to fetch up a plausible remedy. Beating him with Willkie may help a little, but it will probably not help much, for the best that Willkie may be expected to attempt is a lame compromise. There is, indeed, no evidence before the house—at all events, up to the present—that he is not a potential demagogue himself. Thus the process seems destined to go on to full turn. What will happen after that, I do not profess to know, and perhaps I should add in candor that I do not greatly care.

(*The Baltimore Sun, July 21, 1940*)

There He Is!

The Willkie funeral train which now drags its glittering length through the great open spaces of the West is a purely American phenomenon, and unmatched on earth since Apostolic times. In no other country do candidates for the purple go out for votes in any such gaudy and vociferous manner. Even in this incomparable republic it was not always done. So recently as 1892 it was hardly heard of, and even in 1896 the immortal McKinley made his campaign from the anchorage of his front porch in Canton, Ohio. But his opponent, the yet more immortal William Jennings Bryan, had an itch for the plain people like a cat's itch for catnip, so he packed his carpet-bag and went out to see them, mooing like a cow every time he encountered a few gathered together. All other aspirants to the hot pants of Washington and Lincoln have been doing the same ever since.

Just after he was nominated the Hon. Mr. Willkie announced that he would tour the country by air, not by train, but his professional advisers soon talked him out of that. It was, in fact, a silly idea, and proof enough, if proof were needed, of his amateur status. Every politician of any seasoning knows that the set speeches a candidate makes are only a small part of his campaign. The main thing is to let the plain people see him—and many more can see him as his train rolls along than could even hope to do so at a few airports. It is not in halls that he operates on the boobs, but from his back platform. Whenever the train passes a settlement of more than five houses he comes out to wave, and whenever it hits a town big enough to support a drugstore or Kiwanis club it slows down and he bows and smiles.

Moreover, the local politicos all prefer a train to an airship, for it enables them to get aboard at junctions and be photographed with the candidate. To that end they always bring their own photographers along, and usually they travel for forty or fifty miles. The ensuing photographs, appearing in the local papers the next morning, prove to all (a) that the candidate whose arm appears round the neck of Bill Jones and Fred Smith is a friendly and engaging fellow, well worthy of poor men's votes, and (b) that Bill and Fred are big shots, and will be able to get their share of jobs for the faithful in case the election goes the right way.

* *

Seeing these local politicos is one of the heaviest chores of a touring candidate. Most of them are as vacant of ideas as so many clothing-store dummies, but they are all rated as wizards locally, so they deem it their duty to offer him advice. When they come in large squads they are received in a club-car, and the candidate goes from one to another, slapping their backs (if male), tickling their chins and ears (if female), and listening solemnly to their revelations. The really important dignitaries among them are asked into the private car and given not only a hearing but also a couple of stiff drinks, along with autographed photographs of the candidate.

These photographs are always inscribed, "To my dear old friend, Julius So-and-so," or "To that lovely lady and smart politician, Mrs. Rudolph J. This-and-that," though in most cases the candidate has just met the recipients for the first time and knows nothing about them save that they are nuisances. His worst headaches naturally come from his female visitors. They are commonly of excessive bulk and low oomph, and when a gang of them begins fluttering and sweating in a narrow space the effect is very unhappy. If any cuties show up, which happens rarely but still *does* happen, the candidate's wife, if aboard, diverts them to her own quarters, and there immobilizes them until they reach their jumping-off place, and the danger is over.

They often bring presents—sometimes a chocolate cake, sometimes a sweater or a pair of pulse-warmers. During Prohibition they often brought hooch, and the candidate was supposed to go through the motions of taking a drink from every jug. He begged off whenever he could, always on the ground that he had a long speech to write and wanted to keep more or less sober, but usually couldn't. In 1920, when female politicos first began to impend in numbers, I hazarded the insane prophecy that drink would be supplanted as the vice of American politicians by a mass attack upon the Seventh Commandment, but that was before I had seen the ladies.

* *

A candidate thus touring gets very little sleep, and after a couple of weeks he is so worn out that he can hardly stand up. No matter how early in the morning his train pulls into a junction there is always a crowd of half-wits waiting to see him, and if he doesn't appear promptly they set up a cater-wauling and beat on his car windows. In case there is a heavy rain and the crowd has been dispersed, the railroad men working in the yard perform this friendly office. Sometimes the candidate refuses to come out, but more often he does. Even when he doesn't his rest has been interrupted, and he seldom gets back to sleep.

Once it is clear daylight there is a gathering at every station, however small, and not infrequently lines of yokels roost on the fences along the track. The country boys always put pennies on the rails for the train to run over. If the candidate is elected these squashed pennies take on magical properties, and are useful for curing heaves in horses and warts in human beings. In case he is defeated they are inert, and must be charged off to profit and loss. It has been estimated by statisticians that a candidate's train runs over an average of sixty-seven pennies to the mile of distance run.

All day long the candidate divides his time between listening to the local politicians, male and female, and dashing back to the rear platform to greet his prospective lieges. If word comes that a really big crowd is collected anywhere ahead, the train is stopped, and he makes a little speech. On any given day he makes precisely the same speech everywhere. He always praises the town by name, and nearly always has to be told what its name is by one of his secretaries. Not infrequently he doesn't even know what State he is in.

Toward the end of the afternoon he is supposed to rest in preparation for his speech of the evening, which usually involves a halt in a biggish town, sometimes for overnight. But this is the only time of the day when the newspaper reporters aboard the train can get at him, and in consequence he enjoys very little repose. Reporters are romantic fellows, so most of them like and even admire the candidate, but they are also pessimists; and not many ever believe that he will be elected. In his presence, however, they are politely cheering.

* *

Next to the candidate himself, the hardest working persons on the train are the secretaries who produce the enormous number of mimeographed hand-outs that are issued every day. They are expected to find out the names of all the local politicos who come aboard, and if a name is misspelled and a heart broken they catch hell for it. They also provide the reporters with transcripts of all the speeches the candidate makes, however trivial. Whenever he opens his mouth stenographers take down what he says.

When he makes a set speech of an evening the text is usually distributed to the reporters early in the day, and the press associations send it out at once, so that it is in type all over the country long before the candidate starts to croon. When he speaks extemporaneously, as Willkie says he will often do, the business is more complicated and onerous. A mimeograph is brought to the hall and installed under the platform, and it grinds out pieces of the speech as fast as the stenographers take it down and transcribe it. These pieces, numbered serially, are then distributed in the press stand. In a long speech they may run to a dozen, or even more. The first ones have gone out over the wires long before the candidate has gurgled his last gurgle.

All this, as you may imagine, costs a lot of money. In truth, a campaign train is immensely expensive. But the party campaign fund is drawn on only for the actual fares of the candidate and his entourage. Even the local politicos who come aboard commonly buy their own tickets. The newspaper reporters, newsreel men, radio announcers, telegraph agents and other such fellows pay their way as if they were on an ordinary train. The reporters take nothing from the National Committee save only the services I have just described. Their only graft, in fact, is copy paper, which is supplied gratis by the telegraph companies. Sometimes the companies also lend them typewriters, but most of them tote their own.

(The Baltimore Sun, September 15, 1940)

Music and Spellbinders
Entertain Willkie Crowd

New York, Nov. 2.—The cops began to let the people into Madison Square Garden at 3.30 this afternoon, and in half an hour floor and galleries were virtually filled. Thereafter nobody could get nearer than half a block to the Garden without passing a police line.

Inasmuch as Willkie was not booked to let go his message until 10.15, this involved a long delay for the customers, and it had to be filled with conciliatory entertainment and food for reflection.

The entertainment was chiefly music. It ran all the way from solos for soprano, contralto, tenor, baritone and bass to mass attack upon fireside favorites by the whole congregation, and from virtuoso pieces for cornet and saxophone to communal whistling. There were two bands and an orchestra, and when one was not going the others were usually hard at it. Sometimes all three played at once.

No less than three song sheets were circulated. Most of the songs appeared in parody, with Willkie whooped up and Roosevelt slapped down, but that was not true of "The Sidewalks of New York" and "My Wild Irish Rose." Both have something approximating a sacred character in New York, and it would be a grave indecorum to parody them, even in the cause of patriotism.

Some of the best singing of the evening was done by a male chorus alleged to be the National Republican Glee Club. Confidential reports reaching the press stand were to the effect that it was made up mainly of members of the glee club of the New York Police, wearing a false face to prevent misunderstanding and recrimination. Whether cops or not, its members warbled beautifully, and in the midst of the prevailing cacophony they actually attempted polyphony.

One of the parodies was sung to the tune of "Oh, Susanna," which was the Alf Landon theme song in the campaign of 1936. It ran as follows:

> He comes from Indiana
> On the shoulders of the crowd,
> He's free from obligations
> And he has no ax to grind;
> A 1940 honest Abe,
> A friend to all mankind.

Another, to the tune of "Sailing, Sailing," ran thus:

> Sailing, sailing, steering us into war.
> That is the way they planned it all,
> With whispers behind a door;
> Sailing, sailing, better get out the oar,
> We've got the vote to steer the boat
> And we are the crew, what's more.

The rest were of even lower literary visibility. It was a relief when the band returned to "East Side, West Side" or to the gemlike purity of "The Beer-Barrel Polka."

The song leader was George Ira Everett and he did a very competent job. On several occasions the beat of his baton synchronized almost exactly with both the tempo of the bands and that of the audience.

The general manager of the entertainment was Walter O'Keefe, a radio star who traveled to the coast with Willkie and is an old hand at such work. He broke in occasionally with brief monologues of his own. In one of them he told of attending the recent Willkie meeting at the Chicago Stadium, and said that the smell of the Democratic National Convention still hung about the place. The crowd thought that this was a new one, and laughed loud and long.

He also got a howl by saying that he had a 5-year-old boy who was afraid of the draft and had written to the White House asking for a captaincy in the Boy Scouts.

O'Keefe allowed that the only election returns he would be interested in on Tuesday night would be the return of the whole Roosevelt family to Hyde Park. (Tumultuous acclaim.)

The decorations of the Garden were credited in the official program to Walter Dorwin Teague. They consisted mainly of bunting. The portraits of but two Presidents were displayed—to wit, Washington and Jefferson. Beside each portrait, in immense letters, was the legend: "No third term."

A large circular portrait of Willkie hung behind the speakers' stand. It was so large that it cut off view of the stand from the people in the upper gallery. In the midst of one of O'Keefe's turns they set up so loud a chant of "Raise that picture" that he had to suspend.

The cops permitted no one without a ticket to approach within a street width of the Garden, but outside those limits it was free for all, and many thousands gathered—just how many no one could determine accurately, though it was annotated from the platform that there were at least fifty. They stretched for blocks, and heard all the going-on within the hall through the loud-speaker system. From time to time, they were invited to join in the songs, but their singing could not be heard inside, for the loud-speakers worked only one way.

In the intervals of melody various spellbinders, mainly of small talent, were put up to enchant and harass the faithful. They ranged from such political professionals as the Hon. Kenneth F. Simpson, who wrecked the President aspirations of the Hon. Tom Dewey, to such amateurs of eminence as Gene Tunney.

The Hon. Newbold Morris, president of the New York City Council, denounced Fiorello La Guardia in harsh terms, and accused him of neglecting his job in order to go about the country whooping up the New Deal. This excoriation produced applause that was really deafening.

While Simpson was hollering, something happened to the loud-speaker system and the people in the far parts of the hall began to chant "we can't hear." At once the folks marooned behind the circular portrait of Willkie responded with "We can't see."

"What are we to do?" demanded Simpson of the loud-speaker engineers. "This is a good speech—what is left of it."

He turned out to be right, for when the loud-speaker resumed business he soon had the crowd yelling. He also wrung from it some colossal boos for Ed Flynn, chairman of the Democratic national committee and boss of the Bronx.

Another time-killer who did well was former Judge Joseph M. Proskauer. He is no great shakes as an orator, but as a living proof of the fact that all the Jews of New York are not for Roosevelt he got a hearty welcome, and made effective use of it.

He is a Democrat, and was one of the confidential advisers of Al Smith in 1928.

"No true Democrat," he said, "can be a New Dealer."

A moment later, he quoted Dorothy Thompson in support of

his argument and the mention of her name brought forth a vast boo in two waves, even louder than those that had greeted the name of Boss Flynn.

The wide platform behind the speakers' stand was almost as densely crowded as the floor of the hall. Fat cats of the utmost juiciness sat in row after row, many of them accompanied by their ladies.

They gaped respectfully when Joan Crawford, the movie star, swept upon the platform, and she was accommodated with a seat in the front row. The Hon. Joe Martin, chairman of the Republican National Committee, had just got to the mike, but all the photographers deserted him in order to snap La Crawford.

Joe's speech consisted mainly of a series of rhetorical questions, the answer to each of which was "No." The crowd whooped it wildly. He was followed by the Hon. Roscoe Conklin Simmons, an old-time colored orator of the flowery school. Brother Simmons devoted himself to painting a picture of the life and character of the late Abraham Lincoln, extremely favorable in character. He gave a good exhibition, but talked rather too long. When he shut down the whole audience arose to cheer, and the band played "The Battle Cry of Freedom."

The zero hour before the appearance of Willkie was given over to the New York local candidates, but it was wrecked for these unhappy gentlemen by the appearance of Clare Boothe, author of *The Women* and wife of the proprietor of *Time, Fortune* and *Life*.

La Boothe presented a really tremendous contrast, both in manner and appearance, to the average female politico, and the crowd was quick to see it. Slim, beautiful and charming, and wearing a simple black dress, with no ornaments save two immense pearl earrings, she outshined even La Crawford, and when she began to unload her speech, it appeared at once that she was also a fluent and effective talker.

In large part, her remarks were aimed at Dorothy Thompson, with whom she has been carrying on an oratorical hair-pulling match for several weeks past.

"New Deal policies," she said, "make some very strange bedbugs. Dorothy will have plenty of time to scratch herself after election day."

This somewhat sassy *bon mot* delighted the crowd, and the rest of the lady's remarks were liberally sandwiched with applause.

When she concluded there was so long and hearty a roar that many persons thought that Willkie was coming into the hall.

He actually arrived at 10.15 precisely. Bruce Barton, candidate for the United States Senate, was then at the mike. A tremendous shout outside the hall cut short his observations, and he retired precipitately. Joan Crawford and her attendant maids of honor were moved back from the front row to make room for Mrs. Willkie and hers, and Willkie himself leaped to a table on the platform and waved to the crowd.

It responded with a roof-shaking chant of "We want Willkie." Radio time was coming on, and Chairman Kenneth Simpson banged violently for order, but it was twelve minutes before he could get enough of it to introduce the candidate. The Willkie son, Philip, stood in the crowd at the head of the main aisle, just under the speakers' stand. He howled with the others, and also joined in the chant of "We want Willkie."

The speech of the evening is reported at length by other hands. Willkie's rest since yesterday afternoon, though it was brief, was plainly beneficial, for his voice was clearer than it had been for a week past. As usual, he prefaced his prepared speech with a few sentences *extempore*, and again, as usual, he made a number of verbal changes in the text.

It was, in the main, serious argument, offering few occasions for loud gloats and ejaculations. The crowd heard the first half of it, almost the first half hour of it, with only the most formal signs of approval. It was not until near the end, when the candidate came to his denunciation of racial intolerance, that there was any really heavy applause.

Sensing the mood of the crowd, he began extemporizing on the theme, and it was these extemporizations that pleased it most. The more he labored that theme, the louder rose the applause, and in his final ten minutes he was interrupted by it at least twenty times. More than once it developed into the chant of "We Want Willkie," and he had to stop until the uproar died down.

When his prepared text ran out at last, which was at 11.12, he launched into the peroration that he had been gradually perfecting by trial and error during the past two weeks. It went over just as well in New York as it had been going over in the hinterland. In its final form, in fact, it turned out to be very nifty stuff. If the campaign were to go on for another three months, Wendell L. Willkie would be an orator.

He came to the end of his remarks at 11.17. The crowd began calling for Mrs. Willkie, and she was lifted to a table on the platform with her husband beside her. While Willkie waved his arms, the two bands and the orchestra played "The Star-Spangled Banner." Willkie then waved some more, and the music played some more. This went on for, perhaps, ten minutes, with thousands pushing toward the platform for a better view.

Presently there appeared in the aisle directly before the speakers' stand a weird-looking tall man in what appeared to be a theatrical makeup. He had on a strange looking hat and a long-tailed coat and wore a mustache that looked somewhat artificial.

As he came in front of the stand, not twenty feet from Willkie, he reached into a pocket and brought out a small revolver. A spectator noticing it, called to Sergeant Edmund Unger who was standing a few feet away, and Unger had the stranger collared in two seconds. He was led out quietly and not a dozen people noticed what had gone on.

Willkie went home without hearing anything about it. The campaign of 1940 was over.

(The Baltimore Sun, November 3, 1940)

Coroner's Inquest

Willkie did well, God knows. In the face of a war scare and a war boom, it was certainly no mean feat to cut down the Roosevelt majority of more than 11,000,000 in 1936 to less than 5,000,000. Nevertheless, he was licked, and the causes of his licking are far from occult. *Imprimis,* it is impossible to beat a sitting President with $17,000,000,000 to spend, and an enlightened willingness to spend it where it will be best appreciated. *Zum zweiten,* it is impossible to beat a demagogue by swallowing four fifths of his buncombe, and then trying to alarm the boobs over the little that is left.

The truth is that Willkie swallowed rather more than four fifths. He went along on each and every one of the New Deal schemes to uplift the downtrodden and bring in Utopia at home, and he went along in a large and hearty way on the New Deal scheme to succor "morality and religion" abroad. In the closing days of his campaign, he was reduced to concentrating all his hol-lering upon the third term, which he described as a foul attempt upon what he called "the American way of life."

There was plenty of weakness in that position, and I have pointed it out more than once in this place. The third term, in itself, is actually as inert as the second term. It may indicate, in fact, a departure from "the American way of life"; but, on the other hand, it may indicate the exact opposite. Anyone with half a fancy can imagine a campaign in which a sitting President, run-ning to succeed himself in a second time, might be pitted against an open and avowed totalitarian, whether Fascist or Communist. That very thing, in truth, may one day happen—and sooner than the fans of democracy believe.

Willkie's real opportunity lay in disregarding all such theo-rizing, and directing his whole hullabaloo to the overt Roosevelt record, both at home and abroad. If he had any chance of election at all, it was founded upon two fears—first, the fear of millions of hard-working, self-sustaining Americans that the New Deal's wholesale buying of votes with public money is heading the coun-try for ruin, and, second, the fear of the same or other millions that the New Deal foreign policy is heading it into a highly expen-sive and probably disastrous war. But he not only failed to de-nounce these colossal follies in a forthright and effective manner; he actually ratified them, the first by plentiful evasions and the second categorically.

* *

I heard him make at least 100 speeches during the campaign, and I read perhaps fifty more. In none of them did he ever utter a word against the *beneficiaries* of the New Deal pillage and bribery. So far as the argument showed, they were all worthy, and even noble, characters. When he was out in the stocks, he assured the gimme farmers that his election would not deprive them of a cent of their loot, and when he was in the cities he assured the urban dole-birds and shovel-leaners that theirs would be just as safe. If he ever criticized this insane waste of the taxpayers' money, it was on the ground that increased production would make it "unneces-sary," and get the beneficiaries even better usufructs—at the cost, alas, of more or less honest work.

But there was nothing new in that, for Roosevelt himself had been saying the same thing. Moreover, Roosevelt, if only belatedly, had been *doing* something to increase production, whereas all Willkie had to offer was the prediction that his election would induce various unnamed private entrepreneurs to do more. Maybe so—but before the very eyes of the boobs stood factories humming with war orders, and every man Jack of them knew that jobs were growing plentiful, and that pay for actual work was being reinforced by all sorts of New Deal schemes for extra compensation, most of it not earned at all.

In the face of this massive and inescapable evidence, it is no wonder that Willkie lost all the industrial States. I was with him in no less than nine of them, and in every one smoke was pouring out of every chimney. Factories so long abandoned that not a single pane of glass was left in them were working day and night. Here was New Deal money pouring out like beer from a cosmic keg. Here was the first great gush of the $17,000,000,000. The crowds listened politely, with no more than an occasional boo or egg, but it was plain to anyone that only a miracle could induce them to abandon the fat bird in hand for a shadowy and perhaps imaginary one in a remote bush.

* *

On the war issue Willkie quickly got into difficulties, for he proposed on the one hand to back the English philanthropists to the limit, and he promised on the other to keep Americans out of the war. Unhappily, Roosevelt was making precisely the same proposal and promise, and there was thus nothing left to argue about. To be sure, no one not insane believed that Roosevelt would keep his promise, but neither did anyone believe that Willkie could keep his. The most that he really offered was the theory that, as a businessman, he would produce war materials faster than the New Deal quacks, and so, by inference, get into the war sooner.

But no one believes in businessmen any more, and I am not convinced that the boobs, taking one with another, are in favor of going to war, or have any confidence in the idealism of England, or even the good faith of England. Willkie always got loud bellows from them when he denounced Roosevelt's open warmongering, but they cooled off when he followed with tall talk against the dictators. My guess is that most of them believe that war is inevitable. They are against it, but, with the heads of both great parties out to save "religion and morality," they see no way to avoid it, and so resign themselves to it gloomily, just as they resign themselves to coryza and monogamy.

There was, in fact, something hollow about Willkie's doctrine that his business friends, if given charge of the war preparations, would carry them on more competently than the Rooseveltian Chaldeans and soothsayers. What of their record in 1917–18? Has he never heard of Hog Island? Or of the airship contracts? We are probably doomed to see the same thing repeated, and on a grander and gaudier scale. The prehensile patriots of the higher brackets are already swarming in Washington, and by the time the show is over they will probably be as fat as they were in 1919.

* *

The fact that Willkie polled 21,000,000 votes and gave Roosevelt a very real scare will enable him to escape the oblivion which engulfed Alf M. Landon four years ago, and there is every reason to believe that he will hold a large part of his following during the third term. He is a tremendously healthy, vigorous and attractive fellow, and as his campaign went on he developed into an adroit and effective rabble-rouser. There is much more honesty in him than in Roosevelt, and now that he is a free agent he can afford to think more clearly and to speak more plainly.

It is highly probable that he will carry himself wisely, and that his influence will increase. In the popularity of Roosevelt there has always been something false and meretricious: it is the popularity of a radio crooner or movie actor. But that of Willkie, such as it is, is rather the popularity of a champion athlete. He got through his campaign without once violating popular notions of the seemly, and he has behind him a wife who has a level head and is a much better asset than the messianic and gullible Lady Eleanor.

Roosevelt, I assume, will presently make some effort to rope him into the defense racket, and thereby sterilize him politically; but I believe he is far too smart to fall for any such clumsy canoodling. If he keeps clearly in opposition, he will be in a superb position to strike hard when the war is over and the inevitable *Katzenjammer* develops. The boobs, by that time, will be full of repining, as they were in 1920. And the country will be bankrupt at home, and maybe badly nicked abroad.

There will be a chance for Willkie here, and a good one. But he will have to extend the range of his ideas, and get rid of some delusions. If he thinks he can talk down the class bitterness that Roosevelt has so diligently fomented, he will find that he is wrong. His only hope, I suspect, lies in recognizing it as a fact, and in organizing the looted and oppressed against the New Deal rabble of panhandlers. If it turns out that the latter are in a permanent majority, then "the American way of life" will be out of the window, Willkie or no Willkie.

(The Baltimore Sun, November 10, 1940)

1948

On April 12, 1945, shortly after the beginning of his fourth term, President Roosevelt died of a cerebral hemorrhage at Warm Springs, Georgia. The end of the war was in sight as Vice President Truman was catapulted into the limelight. The conservative middle class approved of Truman's policies, but he was criticized by liberals over his foreign policy, and assailed by the South because of his stand on civil rights. During the midterm election of 1946, the country voted Republican, giving them a majority in the House and Senate, while taking almost all the governorships outside the South.

Truman was the Democratic party candidate at the Democratic party convention held July 12–14 at Convention Hall in Philadelphia; his running mate was Alben William Barkley, senator from Kentucky, chosen after his "give 'em hell" keynote speech at the convention. General Eisenhower, Truman's only serious potential rival, had removed himself from the race.

Truman sounded a populist theme, denouncing the Republican Congress, which was interested more in "the welfare of the better classes" than in ordinary men. Democrats were resigned to the fact that their President would be defeated, but Truman felt differently. He went on the campaign trail, meeting voters, blaming Congress, and getting more and more popular. His earthy humor and friendly manner evoked a warm response, and "Lay it on, Harry!" became the battle cry of his followers.

The Republican favorites were New York's Governor Thomas E. Dewey, and Senator Robert A. Taft, a conservative. Others in the race were Senator Arthur Vandenberg, of Michigan; California's Governor Earl Warren; Harold Edward Stassen, of Minnesota; and General Douglas MacArthur. Cheering demonstrations greeted every name at the Republican Convention, also held at Philadelphia, on June 21–25. But Dewey was the acknowledged favorite, nominated unanimously on the third ballot. Certain of victory, Dewey behaved as if he were already President, carefully avoiding specific issues and speaking in generalities. The month of the election, he took a week off from campaigning.

Also running as a presidential candidate was Henry A. Wallace, who led the Progressive party. His advocacy of peaceful negotiations with the Russians rather than a "cold war" resulted in his being labeled a Communist. The convention was held in Philadelphia on June 24–25.

Other parties were also in the running, among them the Socialist party, Probibition party, the American Vegeterian party, and the States' Rights Democratic Party Convention ("Dixiecrat party"), who nominated James Strom Thurmond of South Carolina for president by acclamation on the first ballot.

On election night, Republicans in New York City went to hotels to celebrate in their evening dress and drink champagne. So confident were they of Dewey's victory that many of them had not even bothered to vote. In a surprising turn of events, Truman won by a plurality of over 2 million popular votes, and carried twenty-eight states (303 electoral votes) to Dewey's sixteen (189 electoral votes).

* *

The convention and campaigns of 1948 harbingered the end of an era. It would be the last time presidential candidates campaigned across the country by train; it was the first time conventions were televised. The electric bulbs of the television lights exuded heat into the hot, unair-conditioned auditorium; facial makeup melted into one's clothing. A new age had begun.

After a hiatus of eight years, Mencken had returned to cover the national conventions. He started off for Philadelphia on June 18, agreeing to simply accompany publisher Paul Patterson of the Sun *and not write anything. But it was plain to him that once he arrived, it would be "psychologically impossible" to refrain from writing; he was hard at work within an hour. "The show promises to be good," he wrote to a friend. "But I am getting rather feeble and have some fear that the long hours and endless excitement may knock me out." He was, however, in old form, twirling his cigar and gaping with gusto at the young radicals at Wallace's Progressive Convention. ". . . a magnificent obscenity," Mencken confided in his diary. "All the worst idiots in the United States were there, and the Communists played on them with great skill and facility." Dizzy spells foreshadowed the debilitating stroke that would hit him three months later, but the thrill of being seated once more at what he viewed as the greatest show on earth added to his energy and output. "It delighted me to discover that my old facility for rapid writing in the face of a moving news story had not been lost," he happily wrote in his diary; "I worked, indeed, with such facility that my last word was always written within five minutes after the show ended."*

It would be his last convention.

Television Lamps Stir Up
2-Way Use for Beer

Philadelphia, June 20.—Television will take its first real bite at the statesmen of America tomorrow, and this afternoon there was a sort of experimental gumming or rehearsal in Convention Hall.

It passed off well enough, all things considered, and no one was actually fried to death.

But I doubt if any politician, however leathery his hide, survives that unprecedented glare of light without a considerable singeing. I was sitting quietly in the almost empty press-stand when the first 10,000-watt lamp was turned on.

The initial sensation was rather pleasant than otherwise, for it was a good deal like that of lolling on a Florida beach in midsummer. But in a few minutes I began to wilt and go blind, so the rest of my observations had to be made from a distance and through a brown beer bottle.

Of these 10,000-watt lamps there are ten in the galleries, all focused on the speakers' stand. And a little above and directly in the front of the stand there is a cluster of ten more, though each of these rates but 5,000 watts.

Once during the afternoon the whole battery was in action at once. The effect was very little less than that of an atomic bomb. The few hard-boiled fellows who faced it out on the platform began by looking almost transparent, and then showed a phosphorescent glow. The hardiest stood it only a few minutes.

How often this whole battery will be turned on I do not know. Today, fortunately, most of it was usually dark, for the business before the House was a rehearsal for the newsreels, not for television.

I recall the day when the newsreel lights were frightening, but now they seem like small potatoes. Every politician of any experience faces them bravely. But what the television lights will do to these same great patriots tomorrow remains to be determined.

The ladies who will cavort before them are running about town tonight seeking advice about television makeup. The report circulates that it differs enormously from makeup for the movies, for the newsreels, or even for stoking a blast furnace.

One female politico told me that she had learned that all the ordinary pigments were ineffective, and that it would be necessary to lay in purple, green and even black grease paints. Inasmuch as it was Sunday, no theatrical supply house was open, and the poor girls had to postpone their inquiries until tomorrow morning.

The star of the newsreel performance was the Hon. Dwight H. Green, Governor of Illinois, who will be the keynoter.

He appeared in a neat double-breasted blue suit, a checkered white-and-black necktie and shoes with white tops, and wore a gilt badge with six bars. He is of about the stature and bulk of President Truman, but like Truman is a pert and lively fellow, and so he made an excellent impression upon the newsreel boys.

First they posed him shaking hands with the Hon. Walter S. Hallanan, chairman of the committee on arrangements of the Republican National Committee; then they posed him shaking hands with the Hon. Carroll Reece, chairman of the national committee, and then they posed him waving his arm at the empty benches.

So much done, they put him to intoning his speech, after first sending a man to the mike to warn a few persons present that what he said was not to be revealed until his actual speech began tomorrow night.

All of this hocus-pocus was necessary because the newsreel boys know by bitter experience that during the delivery of this actual speech it will be difficult to mug him, what with the crowding in the aisles, the inevitable breaking-down of the lighting system, and other such hazards.

The pictures made today went to New York at once, and there they will be developed and printed tonight, and the prints packed in cans.

These cans will go out by air to hundreds and perhaps even thousands of movie parlors, and tomorrow evening at the precise moment the hon. gentleman bursts into his first sentence, they will begin to unroll, and while he roars on movie audiences from Omaha to Atlanta will follow him yell for yell and blow for blow.

His whole speech, of course, will not be sent out, but only its more palpitating moments.

I violate no confidence when I tell you that there will be plenty of them, and that every enemy of the American way of life on earth, from Stalin to Truman, will get a severe mauling.

The Hon. Mr. Hallanan was also mugged today and likewise the Hon. Mr. Reece.

Reece blew up in the fourth sentence of his speech calling the convention to order, but it made no difference to the newsreel boys, for they simply ordered him to go back to the start and do it again. This time he was letter-perfect, but as an added precaution they made him do it twice more.

The whole business went on with the halts and stumbles of a wedding rehearsal in a church. When all was ready for the start some one discovered that there was no gavel on the platform, so there was a long delay until one was found in the basement.

Even under the mild newsreel lights Reece did some very free sweating. Tomorrow, under the television superglare, he may faint or even catch fire. But no one is worried about that, for the National Committee has a blanket accident policy on all participants in the convention, with a very juicy indemnity for the widow of any who is actually put to death.

The decorations of the hall were completed tonight, and it is ready for the opening orgies tomorrow morning.

The city of Philadelphia some time ago spent a lot of money having it repainted, and it is now rather charming in its color scheme, with thin blue lines relieving flat surfaces of a sightly yellow, and high points of gilt here and there.

But politicians cannot endure such simple effects, which strike them as fit only for churches and tearooms. In order to enjoy a homey feeling they have twined the galleries, the platform and the high shelves which bear the television and movie lights with streamers of red, white and blue bunting, apparently borrowed from a street carnival.

Along the front of the platform they have set a row of seven gilded eagles, and linking the eagles are festoons of gilded oak leaves. Directly in front of the speakers' stand is a spray of gladiola larger than any ever seen at a funeral since that of John L. Sullivan.

A small portrait of Abraham Lincoln hangs from the proscenium arch above the platform.

The seats on which the delegates and alternates will suffer appear to be upholstered, but this is mainly an optical delusion, as the occupants will quickly discover. The upholstery is actually wafer-thin, and the hardwood below will come into action with little amelioration.

The only chairs in the Hall that are really cushioned are those reserved for the members of the national committee. Their seats and backs have thick pads filled with steel wool, and their arms and legs are of gas-pipe plated with chrome. The seats in the press stand and galleries have no upholstery at all.

The markers indicating the places of the different state delegations, traditionally made by nailing crude cardboard signs to broomsticks, are of white on black plastic, with pink borders, and metal standards.

The standards fit into clasps at the floor-level, and may be removed without any unseemly tugging and cussing whenever there is a parade.

Unhappily, getting them back when the parade is over will be something else again. It is thus very probable that they will wander, as usual, to far places, and that Marylanders may end the proceedings as Hawaiians and honest Georgians as fiends in human form from New Hampshire or Vermont.

The television brethren are not only encroaching on the newsreel boys, but also on the radio boys. There was a time when the latter occupied all of a long glass-enclosed perch high up on the wall behind the platform. But now the television brethren have got a lodgement in this perch. Indeed, they are already hogging both ends of it, and the poor crooners are squeezed between them.

(The Baltimore Sun, June 21, 1948)

Anti-Rights Rebs Due, All Armed to the Jaws

Philadelphia, July 10.—Save for some cavalry patrols and a few spies who arrived by air, the Confederate Army, sworn to knock off President Truman, had not yet got to Philadelphia tonight, and as a result there was an air of confidence among the Yankee hordes already assembled.

A good many of the Federal job-holders on the ground, indeed, were sure that the rebels would begin falling to fragments before they crossed the Chickahominy, but it should be added at once that this ease of mind was not shared by those most familiar with the behavior patterns of sub-Potomac politicos.

The species, in fact, is excessively bellicose and even blood-thirsty, and there has not been a Democratic convention in history in which it did not stage a gory bout.

Even at the lovey-dovey convention of 1936, with everyone gassed and enchanted by the smell of jobs, some of the southern-ers, led by the late Cotton Ed Smith, of South Carolina, put on an insurrection against letting colored delegates from the North make speeches.

This time there is more ground for an uproar than at any time for years, for the convention can hardly escape discussing the Hon. Mr. Truman's civil-rights program, and if any attempt is made to indorse it as it stands there will certainly be some loud hollering by the Confederate firebrands, and the more fiery of them may actually take the walk they threaten.

The convention bosses, despite their brave talk, are a little anx-ious about this possibility, and everyone hopes that a way may be found to compromise and reconciliation.

To this end a subcommittee of the resolutions committee has been sweating behind closed doors all day, trying to draw up a plank that will both save civil rights and placate the southerners.

According to the gossip oozing through the locked doors, the lead in this great feat of sophistry is being taken by the Hon. Philip B. Perlman, solicitor general of the United States.

There are many smart lawyers on the ground, but none other is so well fitted for the task as the Marylander, for he not only knows both canon and civil law inside and out; he also had the advantage, before he tackled Blackstone, of serving on the staff of *The Evening Sun*, and is thus hep to every trick of journalistic double-talk.

How far he has got with his dismal job I don't know, for I have been unable to get through his barbed wire today, but it is a fact that he has been getting a great many suggestions through the keyhole, not only from specialists in legal pathology but also from former colleagues in newspaper work.

One of the latter, a cynic on the staff of the St. Louis *Post-Dispatch*, sent in a proposed plank this afternoon reading as fol-lows:

We are for all of President Truman's civil rights recommendations—and for white supremacy.

Chairman Francis J. Myers, of the resolutions committee (he is not a member of the subcommittee of sophists), submitted to a long press conference today without letting even the smallest kitten out of the bag. He declared, no doubt truthfully, that he had no idea how the plank would read when completed, but seemed to incline toward the theory that it would resemble the 1944 plank, which said nothing.

That plank was drawn up, however, before Dr. Truman cut loose with his revolutionary program, and hence before the Confederates took to the war path. What was a spray of rose water in 1944 may turn out to be a squirt of gasoline next week.

The agendum of the convention postpones the report of the resolutions committee until Wednesday, but there will undoubtedly be demands that it be brought in on Tuesday, or maybe even Monday.

Myers reported that extraordinary precautions will be taken to keep it secret until it is presented on the floor, but that plan may very easily upset by the advance of journalistic science.

Three weeks ago the Republicans had the same idea, but a woman reporter sneaked into their Kremlin and had the whole platform in type for her paper before their resolutions committee tumbled to what was happening.

Though Supreme Court Justice William O. Douglas has declared categorically that he doesn't itch to grab the nomination from Truman, he has not said that he wouldn't take it if it were thrust upon him, so his propagandists keep up a noisy clatter.

They are chiefly very young men, and seem to be innocently unaware that nominations are made by the votes of delegates, to be sure, but not enough to make any impression upon the great swarm of Truman jobholders, and it is hard to be imagine the Confederates coming over to their man.

Myers was asked today if he was for Douglas for second place on the ticket, but got rid of the question in a delicate flow of words. He was then asked if the White House inclined that way, but replied that he had not discussed the matter with the White House.

The report about town is that Truman, as a middle westerner, favors a running mate from either the West Coast or the East Coast.

This turns a baby spotlight on Senator Tydings, of Maryland, who is the official choice of the State delegation, but most of the members of the delegation seem to be actually for Governor Lane, who can't be an open candidate.

The Eisenhower boom is dying in dreadful agony. The General himself has taken a Sherman runout powder, but his more rampant followers, led by his old mess sergeant, Marty Snyder, are still going about the Philadelphia streets in a jeep fitted with a loudspeaker, whooping and howling for him.

Comrade Snyder told me today that he would stick until the last galoot was ashore—that is until the convention had made a nomination, whether of his hero or another.

He hands out the words of an Eisenhower song written by Mayhew Lake, a student of the late George M. Cohan, and when the phonograph hitched to the loudspeaker sounds the music a good many idlers join Marty and his aide-de-camp, John Schwarz, in the singing.

The words have only the palest sort of literary merit, but the music is not bad and if the General could be kidnapped and nominated the combination would make a good campaign song—at all events, one better than Truman's poets and composers are likely to fetch up.

With the Eisenhower campaign headquarters reduced to a jeep, the only one that remains open is that of the Douglas boys. No one ever drops in to hear their message, so they go on the street and flag passers-by.

They pin a button on every one who doesn't wave them off, and distribute pamphlets and handbills describing the learned Justice as a forward-looker beyond compare with a heart that busts whenever he thinks of the underprivileged.

I doubt that they will discover any concern for the underprivileged in the approaching legions of Lee, Longstreet, Stonewall Jackson and Jeb Stuart.

The heelers in charge of the arrangement of the hall added the flags of all the states to the bunting left over from the Republican convention.

The flag of the Free State, though it has a bad spot on the gallery rail, shines out among the ill-designed and banal ensigns of the other states like a wart on a bald head. Saving the flags of Texas and Alaska, it is the only one that may be plausibly described as beautiful.

The same heelers have done some reshuffling in the press stand. Such Republican papers as the Chicago *Tribune*, the New York *Herald-Tribune*, and the Boston *Herald* have been demoted to places further from the speakers' platform than they had three weeks ago, and the principal Democratic papers have been moved up.

I record without comment the news that the pew of the *Sun-papers* is now two rows forward of what it was before.

This morning some wag pasted a huge photograph of Eisenhower upon the front of the speakers' stand. It will be torn off, I daresay, before the orgies begin.

(The Baltimore Sun, July 11, 1948)

Mencken Finds Several Raisins
in Paranoic Confection

Philadelphia, July 25.—After another long and dismal day of pathological rhetoric relieved only by the neat and amusing operations of the party-line steamroller, the delegates to the founding convention of the third and maybe last Progressive party, began shuffling off for home tonight.

On the whole, the show has been good, as such things go in the Republic. It has provided no sharp and gory conflict of candidates like that which marked the Republican Convention. It has offered no brutal slaughter of a minority like that which pepped up the Democratic Convention, but it has at least brought together a large gang of picturesque characters, and it has given everyone a clear view of its candidates and its platform.

The former certainly do not emerge from it with anything properly describable as an access of dignity. Wallace started off by making a thumping ass of himself in his preliminary press conference, and did nothing to redeem himself by his bumbling and boresome delivery of his speech of acceptance (otherwise not a bad one) last night.

As for Taylor, he has made it plain to all that there is nothing to him whatever save a third-rate mountebank from the great open spaces a good deal closer to Pappy O'Daniel than to Savonarola. Soak a radio clown for ten days and ten nights in the rectified juices of all the cow-state Messiahs ever heard of, and you have him to the life. Save on the remotest fringes of the intellectually underprivileged it is highly unlikely that he will add anything to the strength of the new party.

Wallace's imbecile handling of the Guru matter revealed a stupidity that is hard to fathom. He might have got rid of it once and for all by simply answering yes or no, for no one really cares what foolishness he fell for ten or twelve years ago.

He is swallowing much worse cases of hokum at this minute, and no complaint is heard. But he tried disingenuously to brush off the natural and proper questions of the journalists assembled, and when they began to pin him down and press him he retreated into plain nonsense.

Worst, he had begun this sorry exhibition by a long and witless tirade against the press. He went into the conference with every assumption in his favor. He came out of it tattered and torn.

The convention naturally attracted swarms of crackpots of all sorts and for three days and three nights they did their stuff before the sweating platform committee, ostensibly headed by the cynical Rexford Tugwell.

But the platform was actually drawn up by the Communists and fellow-travelers on the committee, and when it got to the floor this afternoon they protected it waspishly and effectively against every raid from more rational quarters.

When an honest but humorless Yankee from Vermont tried to get in a plank disclaiming any intention to support the Russian assassins in every eventuality, no matter how outrageous their doings, it was first given a hard parliamentary squeeze by the Moscow fuglemen on the platform, and then bawled to death on the floor.

No one who has followed the proceedings can have any doubt that the Communists have come out on top. Wallace, a little while back, was declaring piously that he didn't want their support, but certainly made no effort to brush it off during the convention.

In any case, his effort to climb from under, like Eleanor Roosevelt's, came far too late, and no persons of any common sense took it seriously.

As for Taylor, he has been cultivating the Kremlin, openly and without apology, all week, and the comrades in attendance seem to have no doubt of his fealty. When he got up in Shibe Park to make his so-called speech of acceptance—an effort worthy of a corn doctor at a county fair—he actually held it up long enough to throw them a bucket of bones.

The delegates, taking them one with another, have seemed to me to be of generally low intelligence, but it is easy to overestimate the idiocy of the participants in such mass paranoias.

People of genuine sense seldom come to them, and when they do come they are not much heard from. I believe that the percentage of downright half-wits has been definitely lower than in, say, the Democratic Convention of 1924, and not much higher than in the Democratic Convention of this year.

This is not saying, of course, that there were not plenty of psychopaths present. They rolled in from North, East, South and West, and among them were all of the types listed by Emerson in his description of the Chandos street convention of reformers, in Boston more than a century ago.

Such types persist, and they do not improve as year chases year. They were born with believing minds, and when they are cut off by death from believing in a F.D.R. they turn inevitably to such Rosicrucians as poor Henry.

The more extreme varieties, I have no doubt, would not have been surprised if a flock of angels had swarmed down from Heaven to help whoop him up, accompanied by the red dragon with seven heads and ten horns described in Revelation XII, 3. Alongside these feeble-minded folk were gangs of dubious labor leaders, slick Communists, obfuscaters, sore veterans, Bible-belt evangelists, mischievous college students, and such-like old residents of the Cave of Adullum.

But it would be unfair to forget the many quite honest, and even reasonably intelligent folk, male and female, who served as raisins in the cake. Some of them I recalled seeing years ago at other gatherings of those born to hope. They were veterans of many and many now-forgotten campaigns to solve the insoluble and remedy the irremediable.

They followed Bryan in their day, and T.R. and the elder La-Follette and all the other roaring magicians of recent history. They are survivors of Populism, the Emmanuel movement, the no-more-scrub-bulls agitation, the ham-and-eggs crusade of Upton

Sinclair, the old-age pension frenzy of Dr. Francis Townsend, the share-the-wealth gospel of Huey Long, and so on without end.

They are grocery-store economists, moony professors in one-building "universities," editors of papers with no visible circulation, preachers of lost evangels, customers of a hundred schemes to cure all the sorrows of the world.

Whether they will muster enough votes on Election Day to make a splash remains to be seen. In the United States new parties usually do pretty well at the start, and then fade away. Judging by the speeches they listen to here in Philadelphia their principal current devil is the embattled gents furnisher, Harry S. Truman. I heard very little excoriation of Dewey, but they screamed against Harry at every chance.

(The Baltimore Sun, July 26, 1948)

Truman's Election:
Mencken Says Country
Jolly Well Deserves It

The super- or ultra-explosion that staved in the firmament of heaven last Tuesday not only blew up all the Gallups of this great free Republic; it also shook the bones of all its other smarties. Indeed, I confess as much myself. Sitting among my colleagues of the *Sunpapers* as the returns began to come in, I felt and shared the tremors and tickles that ran up and down their vertebrae.

How could so many wizards be so thumpingly wrong? How could the enlightenment play so scurvy a trick upon its agents? Certainly there must have been very few Americans in the IQ brackets above 35 who actually expected Truman to win. I met a great many politicos during the campaign, some of whom whooped for the right hon. gentleman and some of whom whooped against him, and yet I can't recall a single one who showed any sign of believing that he could beat the rap.

* *

Even his running mate, the Hon. Alben W. Barkley, who hollered in Baltimore on October 22, was plainly full of doubts. A professional jobholder and rabble-rouser for 43 years, he did his stuff as in duty bound, but if there were any high hopes welling within him he certainly kept them concealed from the customers. His general air was that of a country pastor preaching the funeral services of a parishioner plainly bound for hell, and all the other jobholders present looked and acted a good deal more like pallbearers than wedding-guests.

But, meanwhile, the Missouri Wonder was roving and ravaging the land, pouring out hope and promise in a wholesale manner. To the farmers he promised a continuance of the outrageous prices that are reducing the rest of us to eating only once a day. To the city proletariat he promised ever higher and higher wages, with the boss a beggar at his own gate. To the jobholders he promised more and more jobs, and juicier ones. To the colored brethren he promised the realization of their fondest hopes and hallucinations. And so on to the glorious end of the chapter.

What had Dewey to offer against all this pie in the sky? Virtually nothing. His plan in the campaign, as in that of 1944, was to chase what appeared to be the other fellow's ambulance. He seemed eager to convince everyone that he was for everything that Truman was in favor of, but with much less heat. Never once in his canvass, so far as I can recall, did he tackle Truman's buncombe and blather in a frank and forthright manner. His speeches were beautiful songs, but all of them were sung *pianissimo*.

His literati have been blamed for this tender gurgling, but it seems to me that the fault was all his own. The late Al Smith, in the campaign of 1928, was afflicted by literati even more literary, but he got rid of them by tearing up their speeches and striking out on his own. To be sure, he didn't win, but that was surely not because he did not make a good fight; it was simply because the Bible searchers everywhere had become convinced that if he got to the White House the Pope would move into the cellar.

Dewey had no such handicap and yet he came to grief in the grand manner. His defeat ran against all the probabilities and was complete, colossal and ignominious. Its springs, I believe, are to be sought in defects of his own personality. He is by nature cute but cautious. He is a good trial lawyer, but an incompetent rabble-rouser. He addresses great multitudes as if they were gangs of drowsing judges, all of them austere in the hangmen's gowns, but consumed inwardly by an expectant thirst.

* *

Truman made no such mistake. He assumed as a matter of course that the American people were just folks like himself. He thus wasted no high-falutin rhetoric upon them, but appealed directly to their self-interest. Every one of them, he figured, was itching for something, and he made his campaign by the sempiternal device of engaging to give it to them. A politico trained in a harsh but realistic school, he naturally directed his most gaudy promises to the groups that seemed to be most numerous, and the event proved that he was a smart mathematician.

Neither candidate made a speech on the stump that will survive in the schoolbooks, but those of Truman at least had some human warmth in them. Like Al Smith, he frequently disregarded the efforts of his literati, and proceeded on his own, and it was precisely at such times that he was most effective. While Dewey was intoning essays sounding like the worst bombast of university professors, Truman was down on the ground, clowning with the circumambient morons. He made votes every time he gave a show, but Dewey lost them.

One of the most significant phenomena of the campaign was the collapse of Henry Wallace's effort to convert the plain people to the Russian whim-wham. They simply refused to be fooled, and if the battle had gone on for another month his support would have been reduced to the Communists. At the start Truman was plainly afraid of him, but only at the start. It soon appeared clearly that all the actual Progressives behind Wallace were made uneasy by the Communists' collaring of him, and in the end most of them were fetched by Truman.

* *

He was out to get all the soft-heads, and he got them triumphantly. Unhampered by anything resembling a coherent body of ideas, he was ready to believe up to the extreme limits of human credulity. If he did not come out for spiritualism, chiropractic, psychotherapy and extra sensory perception it was only because no one demanded that he do so. If there had been any formidable body of cannibals in the country he would have promised to provide them with free missionaries fattened at the taxpayers' expense.

So we now have him for four years more—four years that will see the country confronted by the most difficult and dangerous problems presented to it since 1861. We can only hope that he will improve as he goes on. Unhappily, experience teaches that no man improves much after 60, and that after 65 most of them deteriorate in a really alarming manner. I could give an autobiographical example, but refrain on the advice of counsel. Thus we seem to be in for it. I can only say in conclusion that the country jolly well deserves it.

(The Baltimore Sun, November 7, 1948)

Lame Ducks

Lame Ducks

I

One of the unpleasant byproducts of the democratic form of Government is that it fills the land with disappointed and embittered men, savagely gnawing their finger nails. A salient specimen is the Hon. Hiram W. Johnson, Senator in Congress from the great State of California and an eminent member of the knights Templar and the Native Sons of the Golden West. Hiram was baffled of the Presidency in 1924, and has been full of psychic staphylococci ever since. When he arises in the Senate it is only to radiate malicious animal magnetism. Not long ago he even went to the length of denouncing a Federal judge—an act almost verging upon Bolshevism under our jurisprudence.

Countries under the hoof of monarchism escape such lamentable exhibitions. Unsuccessful aspirants for the crown are either executed out of hand or exiled to Paris, where tertiary lues quickly disposes of them. The crown prince, of course, has his secret thoughts, but he is forced by etiquette to keep them to himself, and so the public is not annoyed by them. He cannot go about praying publicly that the King, his father, come down with endo-

---

Original title by H.L.M. The article appeared under the heading, "A Noose or Poison for Beaten Presidential Candidates," in the Baltimore *Evening Sun*.

carditis, nor can he denounce the old gentleman as an idiot and advocate his confinement in a home for the feebleminded. Everyone, of course, knows what his hopes are, but no one has to listen to them. If he voices them at all it is only to friendly and discreet foreign ambassadors and the ladies of the half and quarter worlds.

Under democracy such reticence is unknown. The land swarms with open and undisguised candidates for the highest office, and they urge their claims without disguise. One may laugh at them, but one has to listen to them. Worse, one also has to listen to their repinings when they are defeated. A few of them, more high toned than the rest, may retire *pianissimo* to the sewers, but the rest remain on deck, exhibiting their ghastly wounds and bellowing for justice until the mortician knocks them off.

II

That the presence of such soreheads upon the public stage constitutes a public nuisance must be obvious. That they offer a menace to the common welfare must be also plain, at all events to attentive students of history. The names of Clay and Calhoun bob up at once. Clay, like William Jennings Bryan after him, was three times a candidate for the Presidency. Defeated in 1824, 1832 and 1840, he turned his back upon democracy, and became the first public agent and attorney for what we now call the interests. When he died he was the darling of the Mellons of his time. He believed in centralization and in the blessings of a protective tariff. Those blessings yet remain with us.

Calhoun, deprived of the high plum of an unappreciative country, went even further. He seems to have come to the conclusion that its crime made it deserve capital punishment. At all events, he threw all his strength into the plan to break up the Union. The doctrine of Nullification owed more to him than it owed to any one else, and after 1832, when his hopes of getting into the White House were finally extinguished, he devoted himself wholeheartedly to preparing the way for the Civil War. He was more to blame for the war, in all probability, than any other man. But if he had succeeded Jackson, the chances are very good that he would have sung a far different tune.

There are plenty of other examples. One is so plain that it has actually got into the school history books. It is that of Aaron Burr. If he had beaten Jefferson in 1800 there would have been no duel with Hamilton, no conspiracy with Blennerhassett, no trial for treason, and no long exile and venomous repining. Burr was an able man and his talents were of great value to the young republic. But his failure to succeed Adams made a misanthrope of him, and his misanthropy more than once brought it close to disaster. I add a few lesser names: Greeley, Frémont, Hancock, Blaine. All these men were soured and made useless by defeat. If Blaine had been elected in 1876 he would have ceased to wave the bloody shirt. As it was, he was still waving it in 1884.

III

But there is no need to go back into history. In our own time we have seen what biliousness consumes the defeated and what damage they can do. The case of Roosevelt is typical. His debacle in 1912 converted him into a sort of political killer, and until the end of his life he was constantly on the warpath. The outbreak of the war in 1914 brought him great embarrassment, for he had been the most ardent American spokesman for years past of what was then generally regarded as the German scheme of things. But in order to damage Wilson he swallowed the convictions of a lifetime and took the other side, and thereafter he became the most violent of the war hawks. Some of the fruits of his reckless bellowing are still with us.

Bryan was even worse. His third defeat in 1908 convinced even so vain a fellow that the White House was beyond his reach, and so he consecrated himself to reprisals upon his enemies. He saw very clearly who they were: the superior minority of his countrymen. It was their almost unanimous opposition that had thrown the balance against him. Well, he would now make them infamous. He would raise the mob against everything they regarded as sound sense and intellectual decency. He would post them as sworn foes to all true virtue and all true religion, and try, if possible, to put them down by law. There ensued his frenzied campaign against the teaching of evolution.

Those who regarded Bryan in his last years as a mere religious fanatic were far in error. It was not religious enthusiasm that moved him but hatred. He was a walking boil, as anyone could quickly see who encountered him face to face. His one aim was to get revenge upon the class he held to be responsible for his own disaster. He wanted to hurt it, proscribe it, if possible destroy it.

To that end he was willing to sacrifice everything else. He passed out of life at last at a temperature of 110 degrees, his eyes turned horribly upon 1600 Pennsylvania avenue northwest and its leaky copper roof. In the suffering South his fever lives after him.

IV

Bryan was perhaps the worst. Going beyond Calhoun and even beyond Burr, he was willing to slaughter civilization itself in order to get a poultice for his wounds. Put into the White House he would have mellowed; with every deserving Democrat in a job and grape juice on the table, his dreams of international peace would have sufficed to entertain him. But barred out, he suffered publicly and damnably, and his sufferings resolved themselves into a serious menace to public order and public decency.

Even a McAdoo, absurd as he is, can be dangerous. McAdoo, safe in a good job, is a competent and useful man. But baffled of a job, he resorts instantly to the worst sort of demagogy. At the last Democratic National Convention he was quite willing to march with the klan; in fact, he wooed it openly and unashamed. Now that the klan is in decay, and the chances of his nomination seem more remote than ever, he shows all the classical symptoms of a statesman with a very sore head. What remains of his old strength converts itself into what the lawyers call a nuisance value. He can't win, but he can at least punish those responsible for the fact. You may be sure he will try to do it. They always do it if they can.

The damage, of course, falls upon the country. It has to pay the cost of all these grotesque and indecent wars of revenge. It is damaged when a Hiram Johnson, boiling inwardly, become useless as a Senator. It is damaged far worse when a Bryan hoists the black flag and declares a holy war upon all intelligence and decorum. That damage goes with the Democratic system. But is it inevitable? Is there no way of escape? I offer one at once. Let us have a Constitutional amendment providing that every unsuccessful aspirant for the Presidency, on the day his triumphant rival is inaugurated, shall be hauled to the top of the Washington Monument and there shot, poisoned, stabbed, strangled, and disemboweled and his carcass thrown into the Potomac. What we'd have gained if that amendment had been on the books in 1896! and in 1912!

(The Baltimore Evening Sun, April 11, 1926)

The Men Who Rule Us

Imperial Purple

I

Most of the rewards of the Presidency, in these degenerate days, have come to be very trashy. The President continues, of course, to be an eminent man, but only in the sense that Jack Dempsey, Lindbergh, Babe Ruth and Henry Ford are eminent men. He sees little of the really intelligent and amusing people of the country: most of them, in fact, make it a sort of point of honor to scorn him and avoid him. His time is put in mainly with shabby politicians and other such designing fellows—in brief, with rogues and ignoramuses. When he takes a little holiday his customary companions are vermin that no fastidious man would consort with—dry Senators with panting thirsts, the proprietors of bad newspapers in worse towns, grafters preying on the suffering farmers, power and movie magnates, prehensile labor leaders, the more pliable sort of journalists, and so on. They must be pretty dreadful company. Dr. Harding, forced to entertain them, resorted to poteen as an analgesic; Dr. Coolidge loaded them aboard the *Mayflower,* and then fled to his cabin, took off his vest and shirt, and went to sleep; Dr. Hoover hauls them to the Rapidan at 60 miles per hour, and back at 80 or 90.

The honors that are heaped upon a President in this one hundred and fifty-sixth year of the Republic are seldom of a kind to impress and content a civilized man. People send him turkeys, opossums, pieces of wood from the Constitution, goldfish, carved peach-kernels, models of the State capitols of Wyoming and Arkansas, and pressed flowers from the Holy Land. His predecessors before 1917 got demijohns of 12-year-old rye, baskets of champagne, and cases of Moselle and Burgundy, but them times ain't no more. Once a year some hunter in Montana or Idaho sends him 20 pounds of bear-steak, usually collect. It arrives in a high state, and has to be fed to the White House dog. He receives 20 or 30 chain-prayer letters every day, and fair copies of 40 or 50 sets of verse. Colored clergymen send him illustrated Bibles, madstones and boxes of lucky powders, usually accompanied by applications for appointment as collectors of customs at New Orleans, or Register of the Treasury.

II

His public rewards come in the form of LL.D.'s from colleges eager for the publicity—and on the same day others precisely like it are given to a champion lawn-tennis player, a banker known to be without heirs of his body, and a general in the Army. No one ever thinks to give him any other academic honor; he is never made a Litt.D., a D.D., an S.T.D., a D.D.S., or a J.U.D., but always an LL.D. Dr. Hoover, to date, has 30 or 40 such degrees. After he leaves office they will continue to fall upon him. He apparently knows as little about law as a policeman, but he is already more solidly *legum doctor* than Blackstone or Pufendorf, and the end is not yet.

The health of a President is watched very carefully, not only by the Vice-President but also by medical men detailed for the purpose by the Army or Navy. These medical men have high-sounding titles, and perform the duties of their office in full uniform, with swords on one side and stethoscopes on the other. The diet of their imperial patient is rigidly scrutinized. If he eats a few peanuts they make a pother; if he goes for a dozen steamed hard crabs at night, washed down by what passes in Washington for malt liquor, they complain to the newspapers. Every morning they look at his tongue, take his pulse and temperature, determine his blood pressure, and examine his eye-grounds and his knee-jerks. The instant he shows the slightest sign of being upset they clap him into bed, post Marines to guard him, put him on a regimen fit for a Trappist, and issue bulletins to the newspapers.

When a President goes traveling he never goes alone, but always with a huge staff of secretaries, Secret Service agents, doctors, nurses, and newspaper reporters. Even so stingy a fellow as Dr. Coolidge had to hire two whole Pullman cars to carry his entourage. The cost, to be sure, is borne by the taxpayers, but the President has to put up with the company. As he rolls along thousands of boys rush out to put pennies on the track, and now and then one of them loses a finger or a toe, and the train has to be backed up to comfort his mother, who, it usually turns out, cannot speak English and voted for Al in 1928. When the train arrives anywhere all the town bores and scoundrels gather to greet the Chief Magistrate, and that night he has to eat a bad dinner, with only ginger-ale to wash it down, and to listen to three hours of bad speeches.

III

The President has less privacy than any other American. Thousands of persons have the right of access to him, beginning with the British Ambassador and running down to the secretary of the Republican country committee of Ziebach County, South Dakota. Among them are the 96 members of the United States Senate, perhaps the windiest and most tedious group of men in Christendom. If a Senator were denied admission to the White House, even though he were a Progressive, the whole Senate would rise in indignation, even though it were 80% stand-pat Republican. Such is Senatorial courtesy. And if the minister from Albania were kicked out even the French and German Ambassadors would join in protesting.

Many of these gentlemen drop in, not because they have anything to say, but simply to prove to their employers or customers that they can do it. How long they stay is only partly determined by the President himself. Dr. Coolidge used to get rid of them by falling asleep in their faces, but that device is impossible to Presidents with a more active interest in the visible world. It would not do to have them heaved out by the Secret Service men or by the White House police, or to insult and affront them otherwise, for many of them have wicked tongues. On two occasions within historic times Presidents who were irritable with such bores were reported in Washington to be patronizing the jug, and it took a lot of fine work to put down the scandal.

All day long the right hon. lord of us all sits listening solemnly to quacks who pretend to know what the farmers are thinking about in Nebraska and South Carolina, how the Swedes of Minnesota are taking the German moratorium, and how much it would cost in actual votes to let fall a word for beer and light wines. Anon a secretary rushes in with the news that some eminent movie actor or football coach has died, and the President must seize a pen and write a telegram of condolence to the widow. Once a year he is repaid by receiving a cable on his birthday from King George V. These autographs are cherished by Presidents, and they leave them, *post mortem*, to the Library of Congress.

There comes a day of public ceremonial, and a chance to make a speech. Alas, it must be made at the annual banquet of some organization that is discovered, at the last minute, to be made up mainly of gentlemen under indictment, or at the tomb of some statesman who escaped impeachment by a hair. A million voters with IQ's below 60 have their ears glued to the radio: it takes four days' hard work to concoct a speech without a sensible word in it. Next day a dam must be opened somewhere. Four dry Senators get drunk and make a painful scene. The Presidential automobile runs over a dog. It rains.

IV

The life seems dull and unpleasant. A bootlegger has a better time, in jail or out. Yet it must have its charms, for no man who has experienced it is ever unwilling to endure it again. On the contrary, all ex-Presidents try their level damndest to get back, even at the expense of their dignity, their sense of humor, and their immortal souls. The struggles of the late Major-General Roosevelt will be recalled by connoisseurs. He was a melancholy spectacle from the moment the White House doors closed upon him, and he passed out of this life a disappointed and even embittered man. You and I can scarcely imagine any such blow as that he suffered in 1912. It shook him profoundly, and left him a wreck.

Long ago I proposed that unsuccessful candidates for the Presidency be quietly hanged, as a matter of public sanitation and decorum. The sight of their grief must have a very evil effect upon the young. We have enough hobgoblins in America without putting up with downright ghosts. Perhaps it might be a good idea to hand over ex-Presidents to the hangman in the same way. As they complete their terms their consciences are clear, and their chances of going to Heaven are excellent. But a few years of longing and repining are enough to imperil the souls of even the most philosophical of them. I point to Dr. Coolidge. He pretends to like the insurance business, but who really believes it? Who can be unaware that his secret thoughts have to do, not with 20-year endowment policies, but with 1600 Pennsylvania Avenue? Who can fail to mark the tragedy that marks his countenance, otherwise so beautifully smooth and vacant, so virginally bare of signs? If you say that he does not suffer, then you say also that a man with *cholera morbus* does not suffer.

On second thoughts, I withdraw my suggestion. It is probably illegal, and maybe even immoral. But certainly something ought to be done. Maybe it would be a good idea to make every ex-President a Methodist bishop.

(The Baltimore Evening Sun, August 17, 1931)

Harding Faces Task
with Air of Confidence

Washington, March 4.—The Warren Gamaliel Harding who stood in front of the Capitol this afternoon, his feet planted firmly upon the spot made sacred by Abraham Lincoln, Chester A. Arthur and Rutherford B. Hayes, his voice raised to the intoning of a great state paper that began with a sentence in bad English and ended with a noble phrase from Holy Writ—this Warren Gamaliel differed vastly from the simple rustic who was lifted out of oblivion on that Hades hot day in Chicago last summer.

He was, to begin with, infinitely better dressed. There was a delicate and indescribable touch to the set of his coat, his collar fitted perfectly, distinction radiated from his necktie; he was shod like the leading actor in a Broadway play. But more important than the change in the vestments of the man was the change in the man himself. One found him somehow more solid, more deliberate in movement, more conscious of the glare upon him. And, most of all, one observed two large and sinister bags beneath his eyes—two mute and far from beautiful proofs that the last eight months have surely not left him to snore in a hammock.

* *

Romance interprets these bags as signs that the colossal responsibilities upon him have begun to shake him—that he spends half his nights, perhaps, praying for relief from the agony of greatness. But as an amateur psychologist I presume to doubt that this agony gives the honorable gentleman any genuine concern. His inaugural harangue, in fact, showed confidence rather than fear; he was full of facile hopes and easy promises.

But what does flabbergast him, I suspect, is the sheer annoyance of being President—the great complex of little irritations and petty inhibitions that tortures any man in that exalted office. Dr. Harding is, by nature, an offhand and easygoing fellow, a provincial politician quite true to type. But as President of the United States he is the center of a thousand blazing spotlights, the target of a multitude of unintelligible prohibitions and urgencies, and it is all this, I suspect, that has paled him and stiffened him and put those unbeautiful bags beneath his eyes.

* *

I saw him yesterday for the first time since he was nominated. At Chicago he and Mrs. Harding inhabited a modest suite in a far-from-brilliant hotel and anyone who desired to have speech with him was free to engage him. One simply rang him up from the lobby and told him that one was coming up. Arriving at his door, one knocked politely and then walked in. But yesterday afternoon, when he received the newspaper correspondents for a last palaver before the White House engulfed him, he was surrounded by all the oppressive ceremonial of an Oriental potentate.

His visitors, three-fourths of whom he knew very well, were first herded into a stuffy ante-chamber and carefully scrutinized by detectives. Then, as they filed into the Harding reception room, one by one, two detectives glared at them from each side of the doorway, and directly ahead of them stood James H. Preston, boss of the Senate press gallery, eagerly alert for anarchists, Japanese spies, liberals, Industrial Workers of the World and believers in the government ownership of railroads. Not a man or a woman got past that door who was not recognized by Mr. Preston, who knows everyone. Had a ringer appeared in the line, the gyves would have been upon his wrists before he could have got his bomb out of his hat.

Within there stood, not the amiable and unaffected Harding of Chicago, the obscure Senator come up to the big town to see what would turn up, but a gentleman somewhat tight and furtive in manner—a man in the elegant coat aforesaid, already blistered and made jumpy by eight months in the glare. A Senator says whatever is in his mind, trusting to the decency of the reporters to save him from scandal. But a President has to measure every word, and to look behind him twice before he utters it, and every time he looks two or three Secret Service men get down upon all fours to examine the carpet. It would be unpleasant to even the most formal of men. To a Harding it must be almost maddening.

* *

But though Gamaliel thus suffers from his greatness, and begins to look strangely weary and dissipated, it must give him certain comfort to see how the business is agreeing with Mrs. Harding. I hope I may not be suspected of trying for office via the kitchen door when I say that the improvement in her since those roasting Chicago days is little short of marvelous. She is a far better looking woman than her photographs make her appear, but historical justice demands the admission that her raiment in Chicago was far below the high mark of the Avenue de La Paix. All over it, in fact, there were the telltale thumbprints of the leading costumier of Marion, Ohio, and to the general horror there was added the high white collar affected by presidents of Ladies' Aid Societies in the remote prairie towns of the Middle West. The lady was respectably clothed, but her garb was quite devoid of inspiration. Any handy grandmother might have designed such confections as she wore.

But that was eight months ago. The Mrs. Harding who showed herself at the Capitol today was a woman simply and beautifully dressed—a woman in a frock that showed the highest sort of skill in every line, and with a hat on her head that would have got more than one glance at Longchaps. More, there was a change more subtle—a change in the woman herself. Ease and grace and assurance were in her carriage; she showed all the marks of the grand manner, with a certain delicate dauntiness to set it off. The new

President, in fact, appeared before his subjects with a decidedly handsome wife. . . .

(*The Baltimore Evening Sun, March 4, 1921*)

Gamalielese

I

On the question of the logical content of Dr. Harding's harangue of last Friday I do not presume to have views. The matter has been debated at great length by the editorial writers of the Republic, all of them experts in logic; moreover, I confess to being prejudiced. When a man arises publicly to argue that the United States entered the late war because of a "concern for preserved civilization," I can only snicker in a superior way and wonder why he isn't holding down the chair of history in some American university. When he says that the United States has "never sought territorial aggrandizement through force," the snicker arises to the virulence of a chuckle, and I turn to the first volume of General Grant's memoirs. And when, gaining momentum, he gravely informs the boobery that "ours is a constitutional freedom where the popular will is supreme, and minorities are sacredly protected," then I abandon myself to a mirth that transcends, perhaps, the seemly, and send picture postcards of A. Mitchell Palmer and the Atlanta Penitentiary to all of my enemies who happen to be Socialists.

But when it comes to the style of a great man's discourse, I can speak with a great deal less prejudice, and maybe with somewhat more competence, for I have earned most of my livelihood for twenty years past by translating the bad English of a multitude of authors into measurably better English. Thus qualified professionally, I rise to pay my small tribute to Dr. Harding. Setting aside a college professor or two and half a dozen dipsomaniacal newspaper reporters, he takes the first place in my Valhalla of literati. That is to say, he writes the worst English that I have ever encountered. It reminds me of a string of wet sponges; it reminds me of tattered washing on the line; it reminds me of stale bean-soup, of college yells, of dogs barking idiotically through endless nights. It is so bad that a sort of grandeur creeps into it. It drags itself out of the dark abysm (I was about to write abscess!) of pish, and crawls insanely up the topmost pinnacle of posh. It is rumble and bumble. It is flap and doodle. It is balder and dash.

II

But I grow lyrical. More scientifically, what is the matter with it? Why does it seem so flabby, so banal, so confused and childish, so stupidly at war with sense? If you first read the inaugural address and then heard it intoned, as I did (at least in part), then you will perhaps arrive at an answer. That answer is very simple. When Dr. Harding prepares a speech he does not think it out in terms of an educated reader locked up in jail, but in terms of a great horde of stoneheads gathered around a stand. That is to say, the thing is always a stump speech; it is conceived as a stump speech and written as a stump speech. More, it is a stump speech addressed primarily to the sort of audience that the speaker has been used to all his life, to wit, an audience of small town yokels, of low political serfs, or morons scarcely able to understand a word of more than two syllables, and wholly unable to pursue a logical idea for more than two centimeters.

Such imbeciles do not want ideas—that is, new ideas, ideas that are unfamiliar, ideas that challenge their attention. What they want is simply a gaudy series of platitudes, of sonorous nonsense driven home with gestures. As I say, they can't understand many words of more than two syllables, but that is not saying that they do not esteem such words. On the contrary, they like them and demand them. The roll of incomprehensible polysyllables enchants them. They like phrases which thunder like salvos of artillery. Let that thunder sound, and they take all the rest on trust. If a sentence begins furiously and then peters out into fatuity, they are still satisfied. If a phrase has a punch in it, they do not ask that it also have a meaning. If a word slides off the tongue like a ship going down the ways, they are content and applaud it and wait for the next.

Brought up amid such hinds, trained by long practice to engage and delight them, Dr. Harding carries over his stump manner into everything he writes. He is, perhaps, too old to learn a better way. He is, more likely, too discreet to experiment. The stump speech, put into cold type, maketh the judicious to grieve. But roared from an actual stump, with arms flying and eyes flashing and the old flag overhead, it is certainly and brilliantly effective. Read the inaugural address, and it will gag you. But hear it recited through a sound-magnifier, with grand gestures to ram home its periods, and you will begin to understand it.

III

Let us turn to a specific example. I exhume a sentence from the latter half of the eminent orator's discourse:

I would like government to do all it can to mitigate, then, in understanding, in mutuality of interest, in concern for the common good, our tasks will be solved.

I assume that you have read it. I also assume that you set it down as idiotic—a series of words without sense. You are quite right; it is. But now imagine it intoned as it was designed to be intoned. Imagine the slow tempo of a public speech. Imagine the stately unrolling of the first clause, the delicate pause upon the word "then"—and then the loud discharge of the phrase "in understanding," "in mutuality of interest," "in concern for the common good," each with its attendant glare and roll of the eyes, each with its sublime heave, each with its gesture of a blacksmith bringing down his sledge upon an egg—imagine all this, and then ask yourself where you have got. You have got, in brief, to a point where you don't know what it is all about. You hear and applaud the phrases, but their connection has already escaped you. And so, when in violation of all sequence and logic, the final phrase, "our tasks will be solved," assaults you, you do not notice its disharmony—all you notice is that, if this or that, already forgotten, is done, "our tasks will be solved." Whereupon, glad of the assurance and thrilled by the vast gestures that drive it home, you give a cheer.

That is, if you are the sort of man who goes to political meetings, which is to say, if you are the sort of man that Dr. Harding is used to talking to, which is to say, if you are a jackass.

IV

The whole inaugural address reeked with just such nonsense. The thing started off with an error in English in its very first sentence—the confusion of pronouns in the *one-he* combination, so beloved of bad newspaper reporters. It bristled with words misused: *Civic* for *civil*, *luring* for *alluring*, *womanhood* for *women*, *referendum* for *reference*, even *task* for *problem*. "The *task* is to be *solved*"—what could be worse? Yet I find it twice. "The expressed views of world opinion"—what irritating tautology! "The expressed conscience of progress"—what on earth does it mean? "This is not selfishness, it is sanctity"—what intelligible idea do you get out of that? "I know that Congress and the administration will favor every wise government policy to aid the resumption and encourage continued progress"—the resumption of what? "Service is the supreme *commitment* of life"—*ach, du heiliger!*

But is such bosh out of place in a stump speech? Obviously not. It is precisely and thoroughly in place in a stump speech. A tight fabric of ideas would weary and exasperate the audience; what it wants is simply a loud burble of words, a procession of phrases that roar, a series of whoops. This is what it got in the inaugural address of the Hon. Warren Gamaliel Harding. And this is what it will get for four long years—unless God sends a miracle and the corruptible puts on incorruption. . . . Almost I long for the sweeter song, the rubber-stamps of more familiar design, the gentler and more seemly bosh of the late Woodrow.

(The Baltimore Evening Sun, March 7, 1921)

The Coolidge Buncombe

I

One of the chief arguments made for Dr. Coolidge is that the majority of business men are for him. If this were true, then it would be fair to conclude, not only that business men put their private profits above the public good—which they probably do in fact, precisely like the rest of us—but also that they are singularly lacking in sense and prudence. For if anything is plain today, it must be that another Coolidge administration, if it is inflicted upon us, will end inevitably in scandal and disaster. The day good Cal is elected every thieving scoundrel in the Republican party will burst into hosannas, and the day he is inaugurated there will be song and praise services wherever injunctions are tight and profits run to 50 percent. There will follow, for a year or two, a reign of mirth in Washington, wilder and merrier, even, than that of Harding's time. And then there will come an explosion.

How all this will benefit legitimate business I can't make out. The only business men who will gain anything by it will be the one who manages to steal enough while the going is good to last him all the rest of his life. All the others will get burnt in the explosion, and they always do when political dynamite is set off. Do they quake today before the menace of LaFollette? If so, let them consider how LaFollette came to be so formidable. Three years ago he was apparently as dead as Gog and Magog. The Farmer Labor party snored beside him in the political morgue; Socialism was already in the dissecting room. Then came, in quick succession, the oil scandal, the Veterans' bureau scandal, and the intolerable stench of Daugherty. In six months LaFollettism was on its legs again, and now it is so strong that only a miracle can keep the election out of the House.

II

When so-called radicalism is denounced this sequence of cause and effect is only too often overlooked. It is assumed that men become radicals because they are naturally criminal, or because they have been bribed by Russian gold, or because they have not been properly Americanized. But the thing that actually moves them, nine times out of ten, is simply the conviction that the Government they suffer under is unbearably and incurably corrupt. The Doheny-Denby oil arrangement made thousands of them. The wholesale burglary of the Veterans' Bureau made thousands more. And the exposure of the Department of Justice under Daugherty and Burns lifted the number to millions. The notion that a radical is one who hates his country is naïve and usually idiotic. He is, more likely, one who loves his country more than the rest of us, and is thus more disturbed than the rest of us when he sees it debauched. He is not a bad citizen turning to crime; he is a good citizen driven to despair.

Where the government is honestly and competently administered radicalism is unheard of. Why is it that we have no radical party of any importance in Maryland? Because the State government is in the hands of reasonably decent men—above all, because the State courts are honest and everyone knows it. And why is radicalism so strong in California? Because the State is run by a dreadful combination of crooked politicians and grasping Babbitts —because the fundamental rights of man are worth nothing there, and anyone who protests against the carnival of graft and oppression is railroaded to jail—above all, because the State courts are so servile, stupid and lawless that they almost equal the Federal courts under the Anti-Saloon League. No honest man in California is safe. There are laws especially designed to silence him, and they are enforced by kept judges with merciless severity. The result is that California is on fire with radicalism—that radicals pop up twice as fast as the Babbitts and their judicial valets can pursue and scotch them.

III

What I contend is that the Coolidge Administration, if it is inflicted on us is bound to be quite as bad as the Harding Administration, and that the chances are that it will be a great deal worse. In other words, I contend that it is bound to manufacture radicalism in a wholesale manner, and that this radicalism will be far more dangerous to legitimate business than the mild stuff that Dr. LaFollette now has on tap.

I believe that the Coolidge Administration will be worse than that of Harding for the plain reason that Coolidge himself is worse than Harding. Harding was an ignoramus, but there were unquestionably good impulses in him. He had a great desire to be liked and respected; he was susceptible to good as well as to bad suggestions; his very vanity, in the long run, might have saved him from the rogues who exploited him. Behind Harding the politician there was always Harding the business man—a man of successful and honorable career, jealous of his good name. Coolidge is simply a professional politician, and a very petty, sordid and dull one. He has lived by job-seeking and job-holding all his life; his every thought is that of his miserable trade. When it comes to a conflict between politicians and reputable folk, his instinctive sympathy always goes to the politicians.

He showed this sympathy plainly in the Denby and Daugherty cases. To say that he was not strongly in favor of both men is to utter nonsense. He not only kept them in office as long as he could, despite the massive proofs of their unfitness; he also worked for them behind the door, stealthily and ignominiously. To this day he has not said a single word against either of them; all his objurgations have been leveled at those who exposed them and drove them out. He kept the asinine Teddy Roosevelt, Jr., in office until a week or so ago, and then gave him a parting salute of twenty-one guns. He is even now trying to promote Captain Robison, the man who arranged the Doheny oil grab. Who has forgotten that he wanted to appoint Daugherty to "investigate" that colossal steal? Or that he was in close and constant communication with Ned McLean, Daugherty's and Fall's friend, during the whole of the inquiry?

IV

No amount of campaign blather will suffice to wipe out this discreditable record. Coolidge pulled against the oil investigation from the start; he pulled against the Daugherty investigation from the start; he let Daugherty and Denby go at last only under pressure, and after trying to hit their opponents below the belt. His sympathy has been with such oppressed patriots all his life, and it is with them today. If he is elected for four years every professional politician in the republican party will rejoice, and with sound reason. There will be good times for the boys—and Fall, Daugherty and company will be safe.

But will the country be safe? It is not so certain. Those business men who think only of easy profits tomorrow might do well to give a thought or two to the day after. They have seen a very formidable radical movement roll up under their noses. If they have any sense, they will not be deceived by the argument that it has been set in motion by "agitators." What agitators? Who and where are they? I can find no such persons. LaFollette stumped the country for years and got nowhere. Only his own State heeded him. But last winter he began to get a response, and soon it was immense and vociferous. That response came from men and women who had become convinced at last, and with good logic, that government by professional politicians was intolerably and hopelessly rotten—that the only remedy was to turn them out, and then make laws to prevent them coming back.

Personally I doubt that such laws, if made, will work. In other words, I am not a radical. I believe that all government is evil, and that trying to improve it is largely a waste of time. But that is certainly not the common American view; the majority of Americans are far more hopeful. When they see an evil they try to remedy it—by peaceful means if possible, and if not, then by force. In the present case millions of them tire of the degrading Coolidge farce, with its puerile evasion of issues, its cloaking of Denby and Daugherty, its exaltation of such political jugglers as Slemp and Butler, its snide conspiracy to rob LaFollette of honest votes in California. They tire of it and want to end it. What now, if they are forced to stand four years more of it? What if they must see it grow ever worse and worse?

To timorous business men, in this year 1924, LaFollette may look dangerous. But let them ask themselves what sort of radicalism will probably be afoot in 1928, after four more years of Coolidge.

(The Baltimore Evening Sun, October 6, 1924)

The Coolidge Mystery

I

The brethren who had the job of writing eulogies of the late Dr. Coolidge made very heavy weather of it, and no wonder, for such papers are difficult to do at best, and they become almost maddening when they must be done under pressure. The right hon. gentleman, who had always been more or less baffling to journalists, and hence a source of serious professional concern to them, threw them the hardest of all his hard bones in the end by dying so unexpectedly. I dare say that a poll of the editorial offices of the country would have given him at least thirty years more of life. He seemed, in fact, to be precisely the sort of man who would live to a vast and preposterous age, gradually mummifying in a sort of autogenous vacuum. But he fooled all the amateur actuaries by dying suddenly and melodramatically, and in what for a Vermont highlander was only the beginning of his prime.

I have accumulated a large number of obituaries of him, and examined them with some care. Their general burden seems to be that he was "a typical American." But was he? Alas, the evidence brought forward to support the thesis runs against it instead. For it appears that a typical American, in the view of the journalistic *Todsäufer*, as in that of the author's schoolbooks, is one who wins his way to high place by heroic endeavors and against desperate odds—and that was certainly not the history of Dr. Coolidge. On the contrary, his path in life was greased for him like that of a royal prince, and there is no evidence that he ever met a single serious obstacle from birth to death, or had to pause even once to get his breath and bind up his wounds.

He came into the world under one of the luckiest stars that ever shined down on mortal man. There was nothing distinguished about his family, but it was at least very respectable, and his father was a man of local importance, and rich for his place and time. If young Cal was ever on short commons no record of the fact survives. He was well fed, he was well schooled, and when the time came for him to launch into life he got a quick and easy start. Going direct from college into a prosperous law office—apparently by the influence of his father—he got into politics almost immediately, and by the time he was 27 he was already on the public pay roll. There he remained continuously for precisely thirty years, advancing step by step, always helped by fortune and never encountering anything properly describable as opposition, until he landed finally in the gaudiest job of them all, and retired from it at 57 with hundreds of thousands in gilt-edged securities.

II

The typical American, whether in politics or out, is a far different fellow. Whatever his eventual success, his life is normally one of struggle, and he goes through it flogged by a demon. If it has its perihelions of triumph and glory, it also has its nadirs of defeat and despair. But no defeat ever stopped Coolidge, and no demon gnawed at his liver. His life, for all its blinding lights, was as placid as that of a nun in a convent. The heavenly hierarchy seemed to be in a conspiracy to protect him, and help him along.

Asking for nothing, he got everything. In all history there is no minute of a more implacable destiny, or of an easier one.

I recall well the day that he was nominated for the Vice-Presidency in Chicago—a blistering July Saturday in 1920. There had been, as everyone knows, a bitter battle for the Presidential nomination, and it went to the late Dr. Harding by a despairing sort of compromise, and only because he was too obscure to have any serious enemies. The battle over, half the delegates rushed out of the steaming hall and started for home. The nomination of a Vice-President was almost forgotten, and when some one recalled it the only candidates who turned up were fifth-raters. Hiram Johnson, defeated for the Presidential nomination, refused it scornfully, as beneath his dignity. So Henry Cabot Lodge, who was presiding, suggested Coolidge, who came from his own State and was one of his satellites, and Coolidge it was. The balloting took perhaps ten minutes. Then the remaining delegates also rushed out, for the hall was an inferno.

Immediately afterward I retired to the catacombs under the auditorium to soak my head and get a drink. In one of the passages I encountered a colleague from one of the Boston papers, surrounded by a group of politicians, policemen and reporters. He was making a kind of speech, and I paused idly to listen. To my astonishment I found that he was offering to bet all comers that Harding, if elected, would be assassinated before he had served half his term. Some one in the crowd remonstrated gently, saying that any talk of assassination was unwise and might be misunderstood, for the Armistice was less than two years old and the Mitchell Palmer Red hunt was still in full blast. But the Bostonian refused to shut down.

"I don't give a damn," he bawled, "what you say. I am simply telling you what I know. I know Cal Coolidge inside and out. He is the luckiest ———— in the whole world!"

III

This Bostonian knew a lot, but not all. He was right about the early translation of Harding to bliss eternal, but wrong in assuming that it would have to be effected by human agency. He had not yet learned that Coolidge was under the direct patronage and protection of the Archangels Michael, Raphael and Gabriel, who are to ordinary angels as an archbishop is to an ordinary man, and to archbishops as an archbishop is to a streptococcus. It is quite impossible to account for his career on any other theory. There were massive evidences of celestial intervention at every step of it, and he went through life clothed in immunities that defied and made a mock of all the accepted laws of nature. No man ever came to market with less seductive goods, and no man ever got a better price for what he had to offer.

The achievements of the deceased, in fact, almost always turn out on inspection to have been no achievements at all. Did he actually break up the celebrated Boston police strike? He did not. It was broken up by other men, most of whom were not even in his confidence; all he did was to stand on the side lines until the tumult was over. Did he tackle and settle any of the grave problems that confronted the country during his years in the White House? He tackled few of them and settled none of them. Not a word came out of him on the subject of Prohibition. Not once did he challenge the speculative lunacy that finally brought the nation to bankruptcy. And all he could be induced to do about the foreign debts was to hand the nuisance on to poor Hoover.

His record as President, in fact, is almost a blank. No one remembers anything that he did or anything that he said. His chief feat during five years and seven months in office was to sleep more than any other President—to sleep more and to say less. Wrapped in a magnificent silence, his feet upon his desk, he drowsed away the lazy days. He was no fiddler like Nero; he simply yawned and stretched. And while he yawned and stretched the United States went slam-bang down the hill—and he lived just long enough to see it fetch up with a horrible bump at the bottom.

IV

It was the snoozing, I suspect, that was at the bottom of such moderate popularity as he enjoyed. The American people, though they probably do not know it, really agree with Jefferson: they believe that the least government is the best. Coolidge, whatever his faults otherwise, was at all events the complete antithesis of the bombastic pedagogue, Wilson. The itch to run things did not afflict him; he was content to let them run themselves. Nor did he yearn to teach, for he was plainly convinced that there was nothing worth teaching. So the normalcy that everyone longed for began to come back in his time, and if he deserved no credit for bringing it in, he at least deserved credit for not upsetting it.

That this normalcy was itself full of dangers did not occur to anyone. The people generally believed that simple peace was all that was needed to cure the bruises and blisters of war time, and simple peace was what Dr. Coolidge gave them. He never made inflammatory speeches. He engaged in no public combats with other statesmen. He had no ideas for the overhauling of the government. He read neither the *Nation* nor the *New Republic,* and even in the *New York Times* he apparently read only the weather report. Wall Street got no lecturing from him. No bughouse professors, sweating fourth-dimensional economics, were received at the White House. The President's chosen associates were prosperous storekeepers, professional politicians, and the proprietors of fifth-rate newspapers. When his mind slid downhill toward the fine arts, he sent for a couple of movie actors.

Is anything to be said for this *Weltanschauung?* Perhaps a lot. The worst fodder for a President is not poppy and mandragora, but strychnine and adrenalin. We suffer most when the White House bursts with ideas. With a World Saver preceding him (I count out Harding as a mere hallucination) and a Wonder Boy following him, he begins to seem, in retrospect, an extremely comfortable and even praiseworthy citizen. His failings are forgotten; the country remembers only the grateful fact that he let it alone. Well, there are worse epitaphs for a statesman. If the day ever comes when Jefferson's warnings are heeded at last, and we reduce government to its simplest terms, it may very well happen that Cal's bones now resting inconspicuously in the Vermont granite will come to be revered as those of a man who really did the nation some service.

(The Baltimore Evening Sun, January 30, 1933)

Little Red Ridinghood

I

Once more the alibi boys of the White House gang are trying to depict the Hon. Mr. Hoover, their patron and pattern, as a political innocent, beset by sinful and designing men. Now it is the Hon. Robert H. Lucas who has deceived, betrayed, embarrassed and undone him. A little while back it was the Hon. Simeon D. Fess, A.B., A.M., LL.D. Before that it was the Hon. Claudius H. Huston, B.S. And before that it was Colonel Mann, Bishop Cannon, Ma Willebrandt, the Emperor Simmons and a long line of other such wicked virtuosi, reaching back to the Original Hoover Man. Always it appears that Dr. Hoover is greatly amazed and chagrined when one of them is found out and put to flight. And always it is hinted that he marvels that such gentry should ever get into places of honor and puissance in the party he heads and adorns.

I wonder how many people take such blather seriously? How many really believe that Dr. Hoover is as innocent politically as his whitewashers try to make him look? Probably not many. There was a time, no doubt, when their excuses and protestations were swallowed pretty widely, but that time is no more. The country has now taken the measure of Dr. Hoover, and knows him for what he is: a politician of a highly practical sort, eager for the main chance, and anything but squeamish. When it comes to choosing men he chooses bad ones almost infallibly, whether it is for places at the public trough or posts in the Republican organization. And when they depart in scandal, which is often, he plainly deserves to be held to account.

The notion that Huston was wished upon him is sheer nonsense. It was he who wished Huston on the Republican National Committee. The fellow, indeed, was an almost perfect specimen of the Hoover man, and had been a member of the intimate Hoover circle for years. He was in the Department of Commerce when Dr. Hoover was Secretary, and sat upon his right hand. In 1927 and 1928 he was in charge of the Hoover pre-convention campaign in a large sector of the Bible country, and helped to round up the blackamoors, the Ku Kluxers and the Methodist clergy. He was a towering figure at the Kansas City convention, and afterwards he led the embattled evangelists of Tennessee against the Pope.

II

It would be impossible to imagine a hero nearer to the Hooverian ideal. He not only measured up to it magnificently in a purely political way: he also measured up to it in every other way. He was what they call, in the Hookworm Belt, a sterling Christian business man. That is, he divided his time (forgetting politics) into two halves, and devoted the one-half to money-getting on a big scale, and the other half to saving and uplifting his fellowmen on an even bigger scale. He ran an oil company, a wheel-barrow factory and a furniture company; he was vice-president of a trust company and of a bank; he was president of the Chattanooga Manufacturers' Association and of the Chattanooga Chamber of Commerce, and, as the Senate investigation committee discovered, he often played the stock market. And on the other side he was chairman of almost every Y.M.C.A. drive that came along, an ardent supporter of prohibition and a consecrated Presbyterian.

This is precisely the sort of man that Dr. Hoover seems to admire. Whenever he has a choice between a politician who is also hot for the Y.M.C.A. and one who is not hot for the Y.M.C.A. he always chooses the former. And whenever he has a choice between one who is what is called a Babbitt and one who is not, he picks the former again. Huston met his specifications perfectly. The common run of politicians are suspicious of Christian business men, but Dr. Hoover prefers them. So Huston, as Hoover's man, was forced upon the Republican National Committee—with what result readers of the Washington scareheads will remember.

There followed Dr. Fess, a Methodist pedagogue who had got on in the world and jimmied himself into the United States Senate by eager and doglike services to the Anti-Saloon League. Rather curiously for a fellow of his kidney, Fess was actually religious and had a tender conscience, and one day it led him to blurt out a somewhat disconcerting truth, to wit, that he was a liar. This confession, made on the floor of the Senate, appalled the other Senators, for it is not etiquette among them to admit anything. But Hoover apparently had no aversion to liars, for presently he was slipping Fess into the place vacated so unwillingly by Huston. Now Fess is about to be canned by acclamation, and the next in line is the Hon. Raymond Benjamin, of California.

III

Of Benjamin the chief thing known is that he is the author of the California Anti-Syndicalist Act, perhaps the most drastic, cruel, disingenuous and nonsensical statute ever passed in America. He thus qualifies as a Babbitt of the most malignant sort, and, *per corollary*, as a 100% Hoover man. With thousands of Republican lawyers to choose from, some of them learned, and all of them willing, Dr. Hoover chose without hesitation the one whose chief claim to fame is that he launched the foulest blow ever delivered at the Bill of Rights and so opened the way to railroad scores of foolish and harmless men and women to prison.

Nevertheless, Dr. Benjamin is at least above the Hoover average. He may be, in his public aspect, a Babbitt of the most implacable and blood-sweating type, but in private life he is an Elk, and that is at least a fair indication that he has never taken any money from the Anti-Saloon League. The Elks, in general, are almost as wet as bankers, movie actors, newspaper editors or university presidents. Dr. Benjamin is not only a member of the order, he was once its Grand Exalted Ruler, with the rank and uniform of a field marshal. The fact is somehow reassuring. It may even mean that Dr. Hoover is preparing to turn damp.

But somehow I doubt it. His principles in this area, of course, are conveniently vague. He has never come out flat-footedly for the Noble Experiment. I believe that, if he thought it would re-elect him in 1932, he would turn himself into a thumping wet tomorrow. I go further: I believe that he would turn Moslem or Single Taxer or New Humanist to the same end. Here I do not sneer at him: I simply call attention to the fact that he is President of the United States in this melancholy year 1930. It takes a very resilient and open-minded man, things being what they are, to get and keep that pretty job. But there is no sign that turning wet would help Dr. Hoover in the slightest; on the contrary, it would only split his party and insure his defeat. So there is every reason for believing that, no matter what the Wickersham committee reports, he will keep on good terms with the Methodist bishops and the Anti-Saloon League.

He will, in fact, need the brethren far more in 1932 than he needed them in 1928. The Pope will not be in front of him next time, and so the Ku Klux idealism will not help him. Nor will there be a united party behind him. If he is to keep enough yokels in line to offset the bitter enmity of the cities, he must do it on the issue of prohibition, and there his principles must be in strict accord with those of Bishop Cannon, the very pattern and archetype of the Christian business man. How far the bishop will be forced to compromise remains to be seen, but you may be sure that Dr. Hoover will not compromise any more. Thus I look for many successors to Messrs. Huston and Fess. More judges of the caliber of the Hon. Richard J. Hopkins will go upon the god-forsaken Federal bench, and more visionaries of the type of the Hon. Mr. Lucas will supply copy for the sweating Washington correspondents.

IV

Why Presidents of the United States, in these later days, should prefer such associates I don't know, but there is the fact. There was a time when the White House was frequented by interesting and amusing persons, notably during the reign of Roosevelt, but of late it is only a hangout for trash. The daily list of visitors reads like the roll call of a third-rate oyster roast, and Dr. Hoover fills his camp at the week-ends with the same dull and preposterous folk who used to snore with Dr. Coolidge on the *Mayflower*. In Harding's time it was even worse.

A President of the United States, if he has the taste for it, has access to the best society in the country. Very few men would refuse an invitation to visit him, and not many more would decline his call to the public service. But with 125,000,000 people to choose from Dr. Hoover almost always finds his man, not among the best million, but among the worst. When there is a Federal judge to be appointed he does not commonly canvass the leaders of the bar and choose a sound lawyer and an honorable man; he canvasses the dope-sheets of the Anti-Saloon League and gets a dub. So when God lays upon him the solemn duty of selecting managers for his tattered and demoralized party almost always he fixes upon candidates so dubious that they are in trouble the instant they take office.

Viewed in the most human light imaginable, this habit is surely most unfortunate. One hates to think of a President of the United States seeking his associates and intimates in such circles. But the facts are the facts, and the historian cannot evade them. Perhaps on some doomed and distant tomorrow it will become the custom, when news arrives that this or that man has been invited to the White House, to throw him out of all decent clubs.

(The Baltimore Evening Sun, December 29, 1930)

The Men Who Rule Us

I

For his harangue to the learned brethren assembled for the re-opening of Columbia University, on September 23, Dr. Nicholas Murray Butler chose the title of "Midgets in the Seats of the Mighty," and in the course of his remarks he indulged himself in some very sad reflections. The world, he said, and especially that part of it which prefers democratic government, is now run mainly by obvious third-raters. How many Presidents of the United States, since the first group of four, have fairly represented "the flower of the nation's intellect and character"? Probably five out of the twenty-six, and possibly six: Dr. Butler is not quite sure. And how many of the Prime Ministers of the Third French Republic—forty-nine in all—"will survive the same test of excellence"? "Perhaps," answers Dr. Butler, "Not more than five."

Which Presidents he would nominate as superior if the police got him into a back room at headquarters and proceeded to loosen his tongue with lengths of rubber hose filled with BB shot—this I can only guess. Most Americans, I suppose, would agree upon Abraham Lincoln, and four out of five would add Andrew Jackson. That makes two. The contenders for the third place would be Cleveland, Roosevelt and Wilson, and probably all three would get a majority of votes. We now have five. What of the possible sixth? I search the list in vain. John Quincy Adams? Hardly. Van Buren? Grant? McKinley? Taft? All are plainly impossible. Coolidge? Harding? Hoover? The quest becomes ridiculous.

My suspicion, indeed, is that Dr. Butler is a good deal too generous. Grover Cleveland undoubtedly had the "intellect and character" that he speaks of, and I suppose we must throw in Lincoln whether he had it or not, for he has become one of the national deities, and a realistic examination of him is thus no longer possible. But what of Roosevelt and Wilson? The first was a politician long before he was a statesman, and if he were running for the Presidency today, under the conditions that Lord Hoover faces, there is every reason for believing that he would take the same hopeful view of the Noble Experiment. His Progressive world-savers, in fact, were always ready to flirt with the Prohibitionists. As for Wilson, he was simply a pedagogue thrown up to 1000 diameters by a magic lantern, and he never got over the shabby opportunism of the campus. If his campaign in 1916 was honest and honorable, then honesty and honor are words quite without meaning.

II

Intelligence has been commoner among American Presidents than high character, though Grant ran against the stream by having a sort of character without any visible intelligence whatever. He was almost the perfect military man—dogged, devoted and dumb. In the White House he displayed an almost inconceivable stupidity. Whatever was palpably untrue convinced him instantly, and whatever was crooked seemed to him to be noble. If the American people could have kept him out of the Presidency by prolonging the Civil War until 1877, it would have been an excellent investment. A more honest man never lived, but West Point and bad whiskey had transformed his cortex into a sort of soup.

Very few Presidents have had IQ's as low as Grant's: even Harding was appreciably brighter. Among them, in fact, there have been some extremely sharp fellows—for example, Van Buren, Johnson and Arthur. Arthur was a Broadway character on the order of Jimmie Walker—fond of good living, full of humor, but with no more character than a Prohibition agent. He made, on the whole, a good President—certainly a better one than Garfield would have made. He was too intelligent to attempt any great reforms, and so the country got on very well during his term, and when he died at 56—the youngest ex-President, save one, to become an angel—he was sincerely regretted, especially by bartenders and philosophers. Washington, in his time, was gayer than it has ever been since. The oldtimers there still talk about his parties.

Why some ribald historian doesn't do a book on the Arthur administration I can't make out, and often wonder. Washington swarmed with rogues returning after the scare they got at the end of Grant's second term, and every sort of graft prospered. After four years of Hayes' depressing Methodism, with prayer meetings in the White House, the town was itching for a roughhouse, and

Arthur was the boy to provide it. It was his theory, as it is Jimmie Walker's that public office is a private bust. But he was no village guzzler like Harding: he preferred vintage wines to hard liquor, and permitted only the best to lave his tonsils.

III

There is also room for a study by some competent psychologist —if one exists—upon the character of Roosevelt. He was, by long odds, the most interesting man who ever infested the White House, not excepting Jefferson and Jackson. Life fascinated him, and he knew how to make his own doings fascinating to others. He was full of odd impulses, fantastic ideas, brilliant phrases. He was highly intelligent, and, for a politician, very widely read. Instead of consorting with the dull jackasses who seem to satisfy Lord Hoover he made contact with a great variety of able and entertaining men, ranging from prizefighters to metaphysicians, and managed to dredge a lot of useful knowledge out of them. The White House, in his day, was a sort of *salon*. Today it is more like a garage.

Unfortunately, Roosevelt's extraordinary mentality was not supported by character of equivalent voltage. He was, on occasion, a very slippery fellow, and he knew how to sacrifice principle to expediency. His courage, which he loved to display melodramatically, was largely bluster: he could retreat most dexterously when ballot-boxes began to explode. On many of the capital questions which engaged the country in his time he seems to have had no settled convictions: he was, for example, both for a high tariff and against it. He belabored the trusts publicly, but granted them favors behind the door. He was a Progressive for votes only, and had little respect for most of his followers.

Roosevelt's operations during the World War were shameless. His sympathy, at the start, naturally went to Kaiser Wilhelm, for the two men were very much alike, and he defended the German invasion of Belgium with great plausibility. But later on his yearning to get back into the White House inspired him to begin badgering Wilson, and toward the end he carried that badgering to extravagant and preposterous lengths. Poor Wilson, a pedagogue and hence full of vanity and pomposity, bore the racket very badly, and it drove him into extravagances of his own. In the end, of course, he won the bout. Roosevelt passed from the scene in the melancholy rôle of a politician out of a job—and mourning for it with heavy sobs. When he died in 1919 Wilson was almost an arch-angel.

IV

Coming down to Harding, Coolidge and Hoover, one finds the word character losing all intelligent meaning. Did Harding have it? Then so has any other serf of the Anti-Saloon League. Did Coolidge? Then so has a cast-iron dog on a lawn. As for Hoover, it is perhaps too soon to judge him, but certainly it is fair to say that he has shown few signs of genuine character so far. The thing we look for in men who indubitably have it—the assurance that they will act in a certain way in any new situation, and that it will be an honest, resolute and unselfish way—this excessively rare and valuable something is simply not in him. The word principle seems to have no meaning to him. The only thing he appears to think of is his job.

His intelligence, I suspect, has been vastly overrated. He be-longs to a class of shiny, shallow go-getters who were much es-teemed during the late Golden Age. They swarmed in the coun-try, and were everywhere mistaken for master-minds. But now their essential vacuity is plain to all. Facing genuine difficulties, they have gone to pieces unanimously—with Hoover leading the pack. If medical men were as generally incompetent and fraudu-lent as these busted wizards, then all of us would be down with smallpox, cholera and yellow fever. If lawyers were as bad, then the wizards themselves would all be in jail. Hoover, like the rest of them, is a brisk and successful salesman—but it will be a long time before there is another seller's market.

What is the remedy? Dr. Butler casts a somewhat trembling eye toward a dictatorship. Experience shows, he says, that it brings "into authority and power men of far greater intelligence, far stronger character and far more courage than the system of elec-tions." But I fear we are not yet ready for the change. The com-mon people still have a great fear of their betters. Even Hoover is a shade too fancy for them. Before we get rid of the democratic imposture at last, we must first go through a file of sub-Hoovers and worse-than-Hoovers. Some day, I believe, a marveling world will see a Charlie Curtis, a Puddler Jim Davis, a Jim Watson, maybe even a Cole Blease in the White House. Then for the whirl-wind!

(*The Baltimore Evening Sun, October 5, 1931*)

Roosevelt

I

About some of Dr. Roosevelt's schemes to save us all from ruin, revolution and cannibalism there are rising doubts, but the popularity of the man himself continues, and if he suffers a combat with Congress this winter he is pretty sure to have the public on his side. In part this is due to his sheer skill as a politician, or as one would say if he were not President of the United States, as a demagogue, but probably in larger part it is due to a widespread and not irrational confidence in his intelligence and courage. We have had so many Presidents who were obvious numskulls that it pleases everyone to contemplate one with an active cortex, and so many who hugged their corners that it is stimulating to have one who leaps out into the ring, and can give as well as take.

The contrast with Hoover is very striking. I pass over Hoover's long and preposterous efforts to deny that there was any Depression, and point to his almost incredibly incompetent dealing with Prohibition. He was too stupid to see that the vast majority of the people were sick of it, and too cowardly to risk the crumbling fangs of the Anti-Saloon League, and in consequence he hung onto the Eighteenth Amendment at least two years too long, and when he turned on it at last he seemed a traitor rather than a hero. Centuries ago some wise man said that though many welcome treason, no one loves a traitor. Poor Hoover discovered the truth of this on the Tuesday following the first Monday in November, 1932. With both drys and wets distrusting and disliking him he went down to ignominious defeat.

The course of Dr. Roosevelt was much more shrewd, candid and bold. He saw clearly back in 1929, when he was a candidate for Governor of New York, that Prohibition was on its way out, and he got upon the wet bandwagon forthwith. In the past he had been more or less friendly to the dry delusion, but he had studiously avoided incurring any debt to the Methodist bishops, and his conversion was thus free of the smell of treason. In the Presidential campaign he spoke out unequivocally, promising the immediate return of beer and the immediate resubmission of the amendment in case of his election. Elected by a huge majority, he straightway undertook to make good on both promises. His resurrection of beer, in fact, was so swift that it lifted the wets to heights of joy from which they have not yet descended, and when repeal followed almost at once they were still sailing the stratosphere, and throwing down tons of roses on Dr. Roosevelt.

II

He showed his mettle again in the matter of lynching. At the time of the last public butchery on the lower Eastern Shore he was heading for Chestertown, which is on the upper Shore, to receive an honorary degree, an attention inspired by a pedagogical itch to get some free notice and prestige out of him, but the sort of thing that a President can hardly avoid. Obviously, it would have been an indecorum if he had denounced lynching in his address of thanks, for he was in the position of a guest, and could not question the common decency of the neighbors of his hosts. But when the California obscenity followed he was not incommoded by any such obligation, and what he had to say was said quickly, plainly and forcefully. The Eastern Shore assassins, if they have any sense left, now know what he really thinks of them, and what all civilized men think of them.

Hoover was also heard on the subject of the San José civic pageant, but he spoke only as a very private citizen, and after four years of dense silence in the White House. During those four years there were scores of lynchings in the Bible country, and more than one delegation of Aframericans had at him with demands that he denounce the sport, but he said nary a word. It was not difficult to surmise reasons for his holding his tongue. He had carried a large part of the South in 1928 through the efforts of the evangelical Ku Kluxers, which is to say, through the efforts of convinced and habitual lynchers, and he was in hopes of carrying it again in 1932. It is possible, of course, that he had some nobler reason, but if so it did not appear. The colored brethren believed, and still believe, that he was afraid of offending his homicidal friends, and so believing, they voted for Roosevelt.

It took no courage for Hoover to denounce Governor Rolph a few weeks ago. Having learned a lot since 1932, he knows very well that he can never collar another elective office in this life, and so the enmity of bucolic and barbaric evangelical sects is now nothing to him. But it may mean a very great deal to men who are still in politics, as the recent earnest silence of the Maryland jobholders has demonstrated. Not a word has come out of the Goldsboroughs, or out of any other professionals of their class. The local Roosevelts have been few, and when I have mentioned Governor Ritchie, Attorney-General Lane, and the Secretary of State, Mr. Winebrenner, I can think of only two or three others. The rest, like Warden Martin of the City Jail and President Ames of the Johns Hopkins, have been extremely careful not to offend the lynchers.

III

I suspect that a large part of Dr. Roosevelt's hold on the plain people is that they recognize him to be what is called, for a lack of a better word, a gentleman. Most of them, I suppose, would have difficulty defining the term, but all the same they know what it means. A gentleman is one who is somehow superior to the common run. He will fight longer, and he can be trusted further. There is a point, perhaps, at which he, too, will turn and run, and another at which he will sell out his friends to his own advantage, but both points lie far out in space, and much beyond the spot at which an ordinary politician will be ready and even eager to barter his grandmother's false teeth for a job.

The very superiority of such a man causes him to be viewed with a certain uneasiness, for some of his processes of mind are incomprehensible to his inferiors, and he commonly strikes them as a bit stiff and pedantic. He may be, in the ordinary relations of life, what they call a good fellow, and very often he is, but he nevertheless keeps up a considerable dignity, and is never quite a swine among swine. This dignity is resented increasingly as one goes down the scale, and on the lowest levels it encounters an implacable hostility, shot with envy, no doubt easily explicable on Freudian grounds. When a gentleman, by any chance, gets into politics, and especially if he arises to any sizable office, the vermin at the bottom feel uncomfortable in his presence, and are always ready, when it seems safe, to fall on him.

Here, perhaps, we may find a clue to some of the adventures of Governor Ritchie. It is pretty generally recognized that he is superior, in tradition and character, to the common run of Maryland politicians, and this superiority has probably had quite as much to do as his mere political skill with keeping him at Annapolis. The more reflective sort of people have confidence in his fundamental decency. They may believe that he is unwise on occasion, but they do not believe that he is knavish. There are obviously things that he will not do, even to continue in office. But all his qualms and points of honor are bound, soon or late, to alienate the low-down variety of politicians, who have no more notion of honor than so many street-walkers, and with them go the simian half-wits who are their customers. It is useful, in politics, to be decent, if only because it is so rare, but only up to a point. After that it is hazardous, as Grover Cleveland discovered.

IV

Whether or not Dr. Roosevelt will hang on to his *principia* as long and as tenaciously as Dr. Cleveland, and pay for it in the end by going out of office unthanked and unpopular—this remains to be seen. He is a Roosevelt, and hence, by American standards, a gentleman, and he shows plain signs of being aware of the obligations that go with the character. But as a Roosevelt he is also—a Roosevelt, and that means a born politician. Some of his appointments have certainly involved little apparent sacrifice of political advantage to the public interest. But in this field, perhaps, it is imprudent to ask too much, for a President is elected for four years only, and on the day he takes office he has to begin laying his plans to be reelected. The persons he must rely upon to achieve that end need not be as dreadful as Hoover's evangelists, but at best they are likely to be pretty bad.

So far, though he has made some lamentable concessions to them, Dr. Roosevelt has kept the whip-hand over the whole outfit, including both the professional politicians and the Brain Trust. He knows how to get rid of men when they become too manifestly liabilities, and he does it without any vain gurgle of apologies. More than any other President since Cleveland, he is his own man. The well-heeled yearners who put up the money for his campaign have all been taken care of, but they have been taken care of in such a way that they have done a minimum of damage to the public interest, and some of them are already on their way out. So with the Brain Trust. Its members have rolled and hollered in the catnip of publicity, and will never be fit for flogging sophomores again, but it must be evident by now that they are not running the White House. All orders still come from the front office, and not infrequently they leave the Brain Trust looking silly.

On this fact we must pin what remains of our trust. The science of government is really very simple, else the world would have gone to pot long ago. The country will remain safe enough for all practical purposes so long as it is in the hands of a man of character, honest, gallant, and mellowed and moderated by a sense of humor. Most Americans, I take it, still believe that Roosevelt answers to these specifications. He will have a free hand while he can keep them thinking so.

(The Baltimore Evening Sun, January 2, 1934)

How Legends Are Made

Brief Battle Was Hopeless
for Carpentier from First

New York, July 2.—In the great combat, staged there in that colossal sterilizer beneath the harsh Jersey sun, there was little to entertain the connoisseur of gladiatorial delicacies. It was simply a brief and hopeless struggle between a man full of romantic courage and one overwhelmingly superior in every way.

This superiority was certainly not only in weight nor even in weight and reach. As a matter of fact, the difference in weight was a good deal less than many another championship battle had witnessed and Carpentier's blows seldom failed by falling short. What ailed them was that they were not hard enough to knock out Dempsey, or even to do him any serious damage. Whenever they landed, Dempsey simply shook them off. And, in the intervals between them, he landed dozens and scores of harder ones. It was a clean fight, if not a beautiful one. It was swift, clear-cut, brilliant and honest.

Before half of the first round was over it must have been plain to even the policemen and Follies girls at the ringside that poor Carpentier was done for. Dempsey heaved him into the ropes at the end of the first minute, and thereafter gave him such a beating that he was plainly gone by the time he got to his corner. Blow after blow landed upon his face, neck, ribs, stomach and arms.

Two-thirds of them were uppercuts at very short range, blows which shook him, winded him, confused him, hurt him, staggered him. A gigantic impact was behind them. His face began to look blobby, red marks appearing all over his front.

Where was his celebrated right? Obviously he was working hard for a chance to unlimber it. He walked in boldly, taking terrific punishment with great gallantry. Suddenly the opportunity came and he let it fly.

It caught Dempsey somewhere along the frontiers of his singularly impassive face. The effect upon him was apparently no greater than that of a somewhat angry slap with an ordinary ax. His great bulk hardly trembled. He blinked, snuffled amiably and went on. Five seconds later Carpentier was seeking cover behind the barricade of his own gloves and Dempsey was delivering colossal wallops under it, over it and headlong through it. He fought with both hands and he fought all the time. Carpentier, after that, was in the fight only intermittently. His right swings reached Dempsey often enough, but as one followed another they hurt him less and less. Toward the end he scarcely dodged him. More and more they clearly missed him, shooting under the arms or sliding behind his ears.

In the second round, of course, there was a moment when Carpentier appeared to be returning to the fight. The crowd, eager to reward his heroic struggle, got to its legs and gave him a cheer. He waded into Jack, pushed him about a bit, and now and then gave him a taste of that graceful right. But there was no left to keep it company and behind it there was not enough amperage to make it burn. Dempsey took it, shook it off and went on. Clout, clout, clout. In the space of half a minute Carpentier stopped 25 sickening blows, most of them short and all of them cruelly hard. His nose began to melt, his jaw sagged. He heaved pathetically. Because he stood up to it gamely and even forced the fighting, the crowd was for him and called it his round, but this view was largely that of amateurs familiar only with rough fights between actors at the Lambs Club. Observed more scientifically, the round was Jack's. When it closed he was as good as new and Carpentier was beginning to go pale.

It was not in the second but in the third round that Carpentier did his actual best. Soon after the gong he reached Jack with a couple of uppers that seemed to have genuine steam in them, and Jack began to show a new wariness. But it was only for a moment.

Presently Carpentier was punching holes through the air with wild rights that missed the champion by a foot, and the champion was battering him to pieces with shorts that covered almost every square inch of his upper works. They came in pairs, right and left and then in quartet and then in octets, and then almost continuously. Carpentier decayed beneath them like an autumn leaf in Vallombrosa. Gently and pathetically he fluttered down. His celebrated rights by this time gave Jack no more concern. It would have taken 10 of them to have knocked out even Fatty Arbuckle. They had the effect upon the iron champion of petting with a hotwater bag. Carpentier went to his corner bloody and bowed. It was all over with the high hopes of that gallant Frenchman. He had fought a brave fight and kept the faith, but the stars were set for Ireland and the Mormon.

The last round was simply mopping up. Carpentier was on the floor in half a minute. I doubt that Dempsey hit him hard in this round. A few jabs and all the starch was out of his neck. He got up at nine and tried a rush. Jack shoved him over and gave him two or three light ones for good measure as he went down again. He managed to move one of his legs, but above the waist he was dead. When the referee counted 10, Dempsey lifted him to his feet and helped him to his stool. With his arms outstretched along the ropes he managed to sit up, but all the same he was a very badly beaten pug. His whole face was puffy and blood ran out of his nose and mouth. His facade was one great mass of hoof prints. Between them his skin had the whiteness of a mackerel's belly. Gone were all his hopes. And with them the hard francs and centimes, at ruinous rates of exchange, of all the beauty and chivalry of France.

Many Frenchmen were in the stand. They took it as Carpentier fought, bravely and stoically. It was a hard and square battle and there was no dishonor in it for the loser.

But as a spectacle, of course, it suffered by its shortness and its one-sidedness. There was never the slightest doubt in any cultured heart from the moment that the boys put up their dukes that Dempsey would have a walkover. As I say, it was not only or even mainly a matter of weight, for between the two of them as they shook hands there was no very noticeable disparity in size and bulk. Dempsey was the larger, but he certainly did not tower over Carpentier. He also was a bit the thicker and more solid, but Carpentier was thick and solid, too.

What separated them so widely was simply a difference in fighting technique. Carpentier was the lyrical fighter, prodigal with agile footwork and blows describing graceful curves. He fought nervously, eagerly and beautifully. I have seen far better boxers, but I have never seen a more brilliant fighter—that is, with one hand. Dempsey showed none of that style and passion. He seldom moved his feet and never hopped, skipped or jumped. His strategy consisted in the bare business (a) of standing up to it as quietly and solidly as possible and (b) of jolting, bumping, thumping, bouncing and shocking his antagonist to death with the utmost convenient dispatch.

This method is obviously not one for gladiators born subject to ordinary human weaknesses and feelings. It presents advantages to an antagonist who is both quick and strong. It grounds itself, when all is said, rather more on mere toughness than on actual skill at fighting. But the toughness is certainly a handy thing to have when one hoofs the fatal rosin. It gets one around bad situations. It saves the day when vultures begin to circle overhead. To reinforce it Dempsey has a wallop in his right hand like the collision of a meteorite with the Alps and a wallop on his left hand like the bump of a ferryboat into its slip.

The two work constantly and with lovely synchronization. The fighter who hopes to stand up to them must be even tougher than Jack is, which is like aspiring to be even taller than the late Cy Sulloway. Carpentier simply fell short. He could not hurt Dempsey and he could not live through the Dempsey bombardment. So he perished there in that Homeric stewpan, a brave man but an unwise one.

The show was managed with great deftness, and all the usual rumors of a frame up were laid in a manner that will bring in much kudos and mazuma for Mons. Rickard hereafter. I have never been in a great crowd that was more orderly, or that had less to complain of in the way of avoidable discomforts. Getting out of the arena, true enough, involved some hot work with the elbows; the management, in fact, put on some small fry after the main battle in order to hold some of the crowd back and so diminish the shoving in the exits, which were too few and too narrow. If there had been a panic in the house thousands would have been heeled to death. But getting in was easy enough, the seats, though narrow, were fairly comfortable, and there was a clear view of the ring from every place in the monster bowl. Those who bought bleacher tickets, in fact, saw just as clearly as those who paid $50 apiece for seats at the ringside.

The crowd, in the more expensive sections, was well dressed, good humored and almost distinguished. The common allegation of professional moralists that prize fights are attended by thugs was given a colossal and devastating answer. No such cleanly and decent looking gang was ever gathered at a Billy Sunday meeting, or at any other great moral outpouring that I have ever attended. All the leaders of fashionable, theatrical and sexual society were on hand, most of them in checkerboard suits and smoking excellent cigars, or, if female, in new hats and pretty frocks. Within the ring of my private vision, long trained to aesthetic alertness, there was not a single homely gal. Four rows ahead of them there were no less than half a dozen who would have adorned the Follies. Behind me, clad in pink, was a creature so lovely that she caused me to miss most of the preliminaries. She rooted for Carpentier in the French language and took the count with heroic fortitude.

I saw nothing rough, nothing vulgar, nothing disgusting. The Mayor of Jersey City and the Governor of New Jersey climbed into the ring before the great battle to be presented to the crowd. If they ever faced more decorous and well-washed multitudes in the course of their political tours of Jersey, then no news of such miracles has ever reached me. The spectators took it all calmly. There was no yelling beyond the seemly; the sight of blood reduced no one to the frenzies of a camp meeting; even the wheezes of the volunteer comedians, in so far as I heard them, were always of a polite and amiable character. I sweated there from 10 o'clock in the morning until 4 o'clock in the afternoon and heard only one man loose a damn. And that single damn was addressed, not to any human enemy, not in anger or in blasphemy, but simply in courteous remonstrance to high heaven against the heat that poured down through the thin clouds.

In but one particular did the show fall short. The preliminaries were second-rate, and bored almost everybody. Who wants to see a mob of third-raters clouting one another when the big boys are being greased and powdered down under the stage? It is an anticlimax turned upside down, and hence made doubly obnoxious. What such a day's sport needs is a touch of refined humor. My suggestion is that Dr. Rickard, when he gives his next show, reject the services of all the Soldier Joneses and Battling McGinnisses and that in place of their banal struggles he put on six eight-round bouts between gentlemen chosen by lot from the audience. This would be a show indeed.

(*The Baltimore Sun, July 2, 1921*)

How Legends Are Made

I

The late herculean combat between Prof. Dempsey and Mons. Carpentier, in addition to all its other usufructs, also had some lessons in it for the psychologist—that is, if any psychologist can be found who is not an idiot. One was a lesson in the ways and means whereby legends are made, that man may be kept mis-informed and happy on this earth, and hence not too willing to go to hell. I allude specifically to a legend already in full credit throughout the length and breadth of Christendom, to wit, the legend that Mons. Carpentier gave Prof. Dempsey some fearful wallops in the second round of their joust, and came within a micromillimetre of knocking him out. Loving the truth for its own sake, I now tell it simply and hopelessly. No such wallops were actually delivered. Prof. Dempsey was never in any more danger of being knocked out than I was, sitting there in the stand, between the Hon. Henry Morrow Hyde and some anonymous Frenchman, with a very pretty gal just behind me and five or six just in front.

In brief, the whole story is apocryphal, bogus, hollow and null, imbecile, devoid of substance. The gallant Frog himself, an honest as well as a reckless man, has testified clearly that, by the time he came to the second round, he was already substantially done for, and hence quite incapable of doing any execution upon so solid an aurochs as the Hon. Mr. Dempsey. His true finish came, in fact, in the first round, when Dr. Dempsey, after one of M. Carpentier's flashy rights, feinted to his head, caused him to duck, and then delivered a devastating depth-bomb upon the back of his neck. This blow, says M. Carpentier, produced a general agglutination of his blood corpuscles, telescoped his vertebrae, and left him pal-sied and on the verge of Cheyne-Stokes breathing. To say that any pug unaided by supernatural assistance, after such a colossal shock, could hit von Dempsey hard enough to hurt him is to say that a Sunday-school superintendent could throw a hippopotamus. Nevertheless, there stands the legend, and Christendom believes it as firmly as it believes that Jonah swallowed the whale. It has been printed multitudinously. It has been cabled to all the four quarters of the earth. It enters into the intellectual heritage of the human race. How is it to be accounted for? What was the process of its genesis?

II

Having no belief in simple answers to the great problems of being and becoming, I attempt a somewhat complex one. It may be conveniently boiled down to the following propositions:

(a) The sympathies of perhaps a majority of the intelligentsia present were with M. Carpenter, because (1) he was matched with a man plainly his superior, (2) he had come a long way to fight, (3) he was the challenger, (4) he was an ex-soldier, whereas his opponent had ducked the draft.

(b) He was (1) a Frenchman, and hence a beneficiary of the romantic air which hangs about all things French, particularly to Americans who question the constitutionality of prohibition and the Mann act; he was (2) of a certain modest social pretension, and hence palpably above Professor Dempsey, a low-brow.

(c) He was polite to newspaper reporters, the surest means to favorable public notice in America, whereas the oaf, Dempsey, was too much afraid of them to court them.

(d) He was a handsome fellow, and made love to all the sob-sisters.

(e) His style of fighting was open and graceful, and grounded itself upon active footwork and swinging blows that made a smack when they landed, and so struck the inexperienced as deft and effective.

All these advantages resided within M. de Carpentier himself. Now for a few lying outside him:

(a) The sporting reporters, despite their experience, often succumb to (e) above. That is, they constantly overestimate the force and effect of spectacular blows, and as constantly underestimate the force and effect of short, close and apparently unplanned blows.

(b) They are all in favor of prizefighting as a sport, and seek to make it appear fair, highly technical and romantic: hence their subconscious prejudice is against a capital fight that is one-sided and without dramatic moments.

(c) They are fond, like all the rest of us, of airing their technical knowledge, and so try to gild their reports with accounts of mysterious transactions that the boobery looked at but did not see.

(d) After they have predicted confidentially that a given pug will give a good account of himself, they have to save their faces by describing him as doing it.

(e) They are, like all other human beings, sheep-like, and docilely accept any nonsense that is launched by a man who knows how to impress them.

III

I could fish up other elements out of the hocus-pocus, but here are enough. Boiled down, the thing simply amounts to this: that Professor Carpentier practiced a style of fighting that was more spectacular and attractive than M. Dempsey's, both to the laiety present and to the experts; that he was much more popular than M. Dempsey, at least among the literati and the nobility and gentry; and that, in the face of his depressing defeat, all his partisans grasped eagerly at the apparent recovery he made in the second round—when, by his own confession, he was already quite out of it—and converted that apparent recovery into an onslaught which came within an ace of turning the tide for him.

But why did *all* the reporters and spectators agree upon the same fiction? The answer is easily given: *all* of them did *not* agree upon it. Fully a half of them knew nothing about it when they left the stand; it was not until the next day that they began to help it along. As for those who fell upon it at once, they did so for the simple reason that the second round presented the only practicable opportunity for arguing that M. Carpentier was in the fight at all, save perhaps as an unfortunate spectator. If they didn't say that he had come near knocking out Dr. Dempsey in that round, they couldn't say it at all. So they said it—and now every human being on this favorite planet of Heaven believes it, from remote missionaries on the Upper Amazon to lonely Socialists in the catacombs of Leavenworth, and from the Hon. Warren Gamaliel Harding on his alabaster throne to the meanest Slovak in the bowels of the earth. I sweat and groan on this hot night to tell you the truth, but you will not believe me. The preponderance of evidence is against me. In six more days I'll be with you, rid of my indigestible facts and stuffed with the bosh that soothes and nourishes man. . . . Aye, why wait six days? Tomorrow I'll kiss the book, and purge my conscience.

IV

Meanwhile, I take advantage of my hours of grace to state the ribald and immoral truth in plain terms, that an occasional misanthrope may be rejoiced. Mons. Carpentier never for a single instant showed the slightest chance of knocking out the eminent Dempsey. His fighting was prettier than Dempsey's; his blows swung from the shoulder; he moved about gracefully; when he struck the spot he aimed at (which was very seldom), it was with a jaunty and charming air. But he was half-paralyzed by that clout on the posterior neck in the first round, and thereafter his wallops were no more dangerous to Dempsey than so many cracks with a bag stuffed with liberty cabbage. When, in the second round, he rushed in and delivered the two or three blows to the jaw that are alleged to have shaken up the ex-non-conscript, he got in exchange for them so rapid and so powerful a series of knocks that he came out of the round a solid mass of bruises from the latitude of McBurney's point to the bulge of the frontal escarpment.

Nor did Dempsey, as they say, knock him out finally with a right to the jaw, or with a left to the jaw, or with any single blow to any other place. Dempsey knocked him out by beating him steadily and fearfully, chiefly with short-arm jabs—to the jaw, to the nose, to the eyes, to the neck front and back, to the ears, to the arms, to the ribs, to the *kishgish*. His collapse was gradual. He died by inches. In the end he simply dropped in his tracks, and was unable to get up again—perhaps the most scientifically and thoroughly beaten a man that ever fought in a championship mill. It was, to my taste, almost the ideal fight. There was absolutely no chance to talk of an accidental blow, or of a foul. Carpentier fought bravely, and for the first minute or two, brilliantly. But after that he went steadily down hill, and there was never a moment when the result was in doubt. The spectators applauded the swinging blows and the agile footwork, but it was the relentless pummeling that won the fight.

Such are the facts. I apologize for the Babylonian indecency of printing them.

(The Baltimore Evening Sun, July 5, 1921)

Thoughts on Eating

Notes on Victuals

I

One hears constantly that it is impossible to obtain a bad meal in France. Like everything else that one hears constantly, this is nonsense. A few months ago, having occasion to pass from Cherbourg to Paris, I was confronted on the train by one of the worst meals in my recollection. The victuals themselves were inferior, the cooking was vile, and the service was atrocious. And a week later, in Paris, I encountered something that I did not know existed in the world—a roast goose that was uneatable. Worse, it was in a *kosher* restaurant—Chez Feigenbaum, or some such name. As a lifelong venerator of both the French and the *kosher* cuisines I was doubly dismayed, for the French and the Jews had joined in failing me. It was, indeed, a bad night for a German Presbyterian.

I should add that these reverses were the only ones I encountered in France. Every other meal that I had the honor of eating there was excellent, and half a dozen of them came close to the sublime. The noblest of them all revolved around a fish, of species and name unknown to me. It was, perhaps, two feet long and nine inches wide, and it came to the table in a large earthenware dish, with a thick, pinkish sauce embracing it. As I say, I don't know what this fish was called, either in French or in English, but I shall remember it clearly on the gallows. It had a flavor almost inconceivably lovely. And the sauce, though it looked somewhat like the dreadful lobster sauce that the English put on turbot, was a masterpiece. I recall nothing else of the meal. The fish was enough.

The blow that Feigenbaum delivered to my *kishgish* in Paris was atoned for by another searcher of the Old Testament in Vienna. His name I forget, but his place of business is in the Leopoldstadt, the Jewish quarter, and any hotel *portier* can direct you to it. On a calm night the wild, surf-like sounds made by patrons sparking soup off spoons may be heard a block away. Again I called for roast goose—and this time it was perfection. The waiter there always inquires: *"Vorn oder hinten?"* Order the *hinten*. It includes a magnificent goose ham. Ask for sauerkraut with it, and wash it down with Pilsner.

II

Another thing that one constantly hears is that the laws in England are enforced very strictly, and that no patriotic Englishman ever thinks of violating them. This is more nonsense. The English liquor laws, in so far as they are oppressive, are violated very widely, and I know of at least one place in the country, with drinking going on all night, that has no license at all. More, the constituted authorities know about it, too, but for reasons that no doubt seem sufficient to them they do not molest it.

In London the saloons have to close at 11 P.M. or thereabout, varying slightly with the neighborhood, and the barmaids and bouncers make a great show of hustling their clients out on time. The nearest cop always pokes his nose through the door for a few minutes after the hour, and if he finds any boozers still in action he makes a great pother. But all that is necessary to get another drink is to move to the nearest restaurant with a late license, and there order a plate of soup. Once it is on the table one may keep on ordering drinks until 12.30, and delay the drinking of them until 1 A.M. And after that one may go to the nearest hotel, and keep it up all night, for a hotel may serve drinks to its guests at any hour of the twenty-four, and anyone is a guest who has written his name on the register.

So much for Law Enforcement in the Motherland. The laws there, like the laws everywhere else, are enforced only in so far as public sentiment is behind them. The English are a naturally orderly people, and so they do not admire gunmen: thus a gunman has every hand against him, and is very likely to come to grief. But they sweat under Prohibition after 11 P.M. just a painfully as we sweat under it before 11 P.M., and they prove their discontent by violating it whenever they can. It may be enforced very strictly against the poor, but it is certainly not enforced against those who happen to be rich or otherwise influential. The West End of London swarms with drunks all night.

III

The badness of English cooking is proverbial all over the world, but no one seems to have investigated its causes. I suggest that it may be due, at least in part, to two things, the first being that the English have a Puritan distrust of whatever is bodily pleasant, and the second that it is practically impossible to grow good food in their country. The first point needs no laboring. Every American who has been in England in winter knows how the whole population shivers and freezes. The simple device of putting in adequate stoves has apparently never occurred to anyone—or, if it has, it has been rejected as unmanly. The English prefer to be uncomfortable, and think of their preferences as heroic.

So at the table. Most Englishmen have been abroad, and know very well what good victuals taste like. But when they are at home they take a gloomy, stubborn, idiotic delight in eating badly. To say that they have a diseased taste and actually enjoy their flabby, flavorless, badly cooked dishes—this is to go beyond plain facts. It takes only a glance to see that they suffer almost as much as visitors to their country. But they can't get rid of the feeling that it is virtuous to suffer so—that eating better stuff would be frenchified, wicked, and against God. So they remain faithful to a cuisine which Nietzsche long ago described as next door to cannibalism.

I have hinted that the native victuals of the English are all bad. An exception, of course should be made of their incomparable mutton, and another, perhaps, of their sole, but beyond that the judgement holds. Their beef, for all their touching veneration of it, is distinctly inferior to ours, as anyone may discover by eating it in the form of steaks. Their pork, at best, is only so-so, and their veal is not better. They seldom eat lamb at all. Of the stuff they get out of the sea, not much is really good. Their oysters are vile, and their turbot is flabby and almost tasteless. Their salmon is better, but it is surely not to be mentioned in the same breath with our mackerel, blue-fish and shad. That leaves their excellent sole—usually ruined in the cooking.

But it is in the vegetable department that the English suffer most cruelly. The commonest vegetable on their tables is what they call cabbage or greens—a headless and arsenical bunch of flaccid leaves, something like our sprouts, but not nearly so good. It is boiled in plain Thames water and brought to the table without any apparent seasoning. The effect is ghastly: I'd as lief eat stewed hay. With it, as a rule, comes a plate of potatoes, cooked likewise. Or something worse. The repertory is very small. The same depressing vegetables are dished up day after day.

They are eaten, I suspect, not because the English really like them, but because it is impossible to grow better in England. The climate of the island is very generous to grass, but not to plants of greater complexity and delicacy. In France every vegetable that will grow at all is at its best (consider, for example, the incomparable peas and string beans!), but in England they are all weedy and coarse. So the English have forgotten that vegetables may be succulent and charming, and what they eat in that department is eaten in a resigned, medicinal manner. To try and cook it beautifully would be to flout the plain will of the Lord. If anything is plain, it is that He intended it to fall just short of uneatable.

What saves England from complete culinary darkness is the mutton. At its best, it is probably the most magnificent red meat to be had in the world. It has a lordly flavor, and is almost unbelievably tender. The fat, instead of being tallowy, is bland and delicate. It is so good that even the crude, barbaric English way of roasting it cannot ruin it, so that one may order it safely almost anywhere. I believe that it is one of the great glories of the English people—a greater glory, indeed, than their poetry, their policemen, their hearty complexions, or their gift for moral indignation. It is the product of English grass—unquestionably the best grass on this piebald ball. Ah, that the English nobility and gentry could dine as well as their sheep!

(The Baltimore Evening Sun, April 7, 1930)

Victualry as a Fine Art

Some time ago, functioning as a magazine editor, I essayed to get hold of some articles on the American cuisine. At once I discovered that the number of American authors capable of writing upon the subject, charmingly and at first hand, was so small as to be substantially equal to the number of honest prohibition agents. After six months' search, in fact, I found but three, and one of them had been living abroad for years and another had lived there since childhood. Even the first was scarcely a 100 percent American, for he had traveled extensively, and though he was holding a public office in Washington when I found him he confessed in the first sentence of his article that he wished the Volstead act were repealed and the Hon. Mr. Volstead himself in hell.

I speak here, of course, of authors competent to write of victualing as a fine art. Of cooking-school marms, of course, we have a-plenty, and we also have a vast and cocksure rabble of dietitians, some of them more or less scientific. But it must be obvious that the cooking-school marm knows very little about voluptuous eating, and that the dietitian is its enemy. The marm, indeed, seldom shows any sign that the flavor of victuals interests her. The thing she is primarily interested in, to borrow a term from surgery, is the cosmetic effect. In the women's magazines she prints pretty pictures of her masterpieces, often in full color. They look precisely like the dreadful tidbits one encounters in the more high-toned sort of tearooms, and at wedding breakfasts. One admires them as spectacles, but eating them is something else again.

Moreover, the marm is primarily a cook, not an epicure. She is interested in materials and processes, not in gustatory effects. When she invents a new way to utilize the hard heel of a ham, she believes that she has achieved something, though even the house-cat may gag at it. Her efforts are to the art of the cordon bleu what those of a house painter are to those of a Cézanne. She is a pedagogue, not an artist. The fact that she is heeded in the land, and her depressing concoctions solemnly devoured, is sufficient proof that Americans do not respect their palates.

* *

Why this should be so I don't know, for here in this great republic we have the materials for the most superb victualry the world has ever seen, and our people have the money to pay for it. Even the poorest American, indeed, eats relatively expensive food. His wife knows nothing of the hard pinching that entertains her French sister. He has meat in abundance and in considerable variety, and a great wealth of fruits and vegetables. Yet he eats badly, gets very little enjoyment out of his meals, and is constantly taking pills. The hot dog is the *reductio ad absurdum* of American eating. The Sicilian in the ditch, though he can never be President, knows better: he puts a slice of onion between his slabs of bread, not a cartridge filled with the sweepings of the abattoirs.

The national taste for bad food seems all the more remarkable when one recalls that the United States, more than any other country of the modern world, has been enriched by immigrant cuisines. Every fresh wave of newcomers has brought in new dishes, and many of them have been of the highest merit. But very few of them have been adopted by the natives, and the few have been mainly inferior. From the Italians, for example, we have got only spaghetti; it is now so American that it is to be had in cans. But spaghetti is to the Italian cuisine simply what eggs are to the Spanish: a raw material. We eat it as only those Italians eat it who are on the verge of ceasing to eat at all. Of the multitudinous ways in which it can be cooked and garnished we have learned but one, and that one is undoubtedly the worst.

So with the German sauerkraut—a superb victual when properly prepared for the table. But how often, in America, is it properly prepared? Perhaps once in 100,000 times. Even the Germans, coming here, lose the art of handling it as it deserves. It becomes in their hands, as in the hands of American cooks, simply a sort of stewed hay, with overtones of the dishpan. To encounter a decent dish of it in an American eating house would be as startling as to encounter a decent soup.

* *

What ails our victualry, principally, is the depressing standardization that ails everything else American. There was a time when every American eating house had its specialties, and many of them were excellent. One did not expect to find the same things everywhere. One went to one place for roast goose, and to another for broiled soft crabs, and to another for oysters, and to yet another for mutton chops. Rolls made the old Parker House in Boston famous, and terrapin à la Maryland did the same for Barnum's and Guy's hotels in Baltimore.

This specialization still prevails in Europe. The best restaurants in Paris—that is, the best in the epicurean, not in the fashionable sense—do not profess to offer the whole range of the French cuisine. Each has its specialty, and upon that specialty the art of the chef is lavished, aided by prayer and fasting. His rivals in other places do not try to meet and beat him on his own ground. They let him have his masterpiece and devote themselves to perfecting masterpieces of their own. Thus victualing in France continues to show a great variety and a never-failing charm. One may eat superbly every day and never encounter a dish that is merely eatable. The Parisians look forward to dinner as a Tennessean looks forward to his evening bout with the Scriptures.

But in America the public cooks have all abandoned specialization, and every one of them seems bent upon cooking as nearly as possible like all the rest. The American hotel meal is as rigidly standardized as the parts of a flivver, and so is the American restaurant meal. The local dishes, in all eating houses pretending to any tone, are banned as low. So one hunts in vain in Boston for a decent plate of beans, and in Baltimore for a decent mess of steamed hard crabs, and in St. Louis for a decent rasher of catfish. They are obtainable, perhaps, but only along the wharves. One must take a squad of police along to enjoy them in safety.

* *

What remains? A series of dishes fit only for diners who are hurrying to catch trains—tasteless roasts, banal beefsteaks, cremated chops, fish drenched in unintelligible sauces, greasy potatoes, and a long repertoire of vegetables with no more taste than baled shavings. The bill of fare is the same everywhere, and nowhere is it interesting. Within the last year I have been in the heart of New England and in the heart of the south. In both places the hotels offered the same standardized cuisine. In neither was there any culinary sign that I was not in Chicago or New York. In New England the brown bread was indistinguishable from the stuff served on Pullman dining cars, and in the south there was no corn bread at all.

I dare say that the Pullman diner has done much to bring in this standardization. Distances are so great in the federal union that the man who does much traveling eats most of his meals on trains. So he gets used to dishes that all taste alike, whatever their ostensible contents, and ends by being unable to distinguish one from another. Thus he is indifferent to novelty, and perhaps hostile to it. The hotels give him what he wants. If he protested often enough and loudly enough they would turn out their present crews of street railway curve greasers and locomotive firemen and put in cooks.

I leave the meals served on Pullman diners for a separate treatise. They are botched by the effort to give them the delusive variety of the appalling meals served in American hotels. In a kitchen two feet wide and eleven feet long four or five honest but uninspired Aframericans try to concoct fifteen or twenty different dishes. They naturally spoil all of them. On the continent of Europe all meals served on trains are table d'hôte. Their principal dishes are cooked, not on the train, but at the terminals. They are always appetizing and often excellent. Light wines or beers wash them down. The dining cars are hideous with gaudy advertisements—one sees inside what one sees outside in America—but the chow does not insult the palate. At home I have to eat many meals in Pullman diners. I always order the same thing. It is impossible for even a Pullman cook to spoil ham and eggs.

(The Chicago Sunday Tribune, June 13, 1926)

Callinectes Hastatus

The Frenchman, Jules Hoche, author of a once-celebrated book on Bismarck, listed among the proofs of the eminent Pomeranian's barbarism the fact that he liked fried oysters—"which is treason," said the horrified Jules, "to gastronomy."

The soundness of this notion need not be argued. No civilized man, save perhaps in mere bravado, would voluntarily eat a fried oyster—the dose is too nauseating to be endured. Down in Maryland, where the dish originated among the negro slaves, it is to be had only in cheap lunchrooms and at what are called oyster-suppers, usually held in the cellars of bankrupt churches. The first-class hotels would no more serve it than they would serve pig liver. The stranger who craves for it must go to a car conductors' coffee joint to wallow in it.

In New York, however, there is no such refinement of palate and dignity of feeling. I have seen fried oysters served in one of the most expensive hotels of the town, and the head waiter didn't even put a screen around the table—which would have been done in Baltimore had a United States senator, a foreign ambassador or some other untutored magnifico insisted upon having them. And in the so-called sea food eating houses, so I hear, they are dished up without the slightest question, and all the year 'round. Imagine a Christian eating fried oysters in summer!

*   *

Well, the people of New York do even worse; they eat Chesapeake soft crabs fried in batter! What is cannibalism after that? I'd as lief eat a stewed archdeacon. Think of immersing a delicate and sensitive soft crab, the noblest of decapods, in a foul mess of batter, drenching it and blinding it, defacing it and smothering it—and then of frying it in a pan like some ignoble piece of Pennsylvania scrapple! As well boil a cocktail, or a smelt, or a canvasback duck.

There is, of course, but one civilized way to prepare soft crabs for the human esophagus, and it goes without saying that it is the one way never heard of by the Greek bootblacks who pass as chefs in New York. It is, like all the major processes of the bozart, quite simple in its essence. One rids the crab of its seaweed, removes the devil, and then spears it with a long, steel fork upon the prongs of which a piece of country bacon, perhaps three inches long, has been already made fast. Then one holds the combination over a brazier of glowing charcoal or a fire of hickory *(carya ovata)*, say for three or four minutes.

What happens belongs to the very elements of cookery. The bacon, melted by the heat, runs down over the crab, greasing it and salting it, and the crab, thus heated, greased and salted, takes on an almost indescribable crispness and flavor. Nothing imaginable by the mind of man could be more delicious. It is a flavor with body, delicacy and character. Slap the crab upon a square of hot toast and then have at it. No plate, remember! No knife or fork! Above all, no catsup, Worcestershire sauce, chow-chow, pa-

prika, tabasco, horseradish or any other such condiment. The crab
and the bacon—that is all.

* *

This is the way an enlightened Marylander, respecting his
stomach and his ancestors, prepares the soft crab of the Chesapeake for his pylorus. As I say, the theory of the process is absurdly simple, but in the details, of course, there is room for a
delicate and highly arduous technic. Along the remote coasts of
the eastern shore of Maryland, where slavery still exists under
cover, a negro cook able to prepare soft crabs to perfection sells
for $2,000 or $3,000 at public vendue. And when such a slave wins
his freedom, by swimming the Chesapeake Bay, he can get $100 a
week for his talents in Baltimore.

More, the art is practiced by white persons of high respectability, and a gift for it is much esteemed. The present sheriff of Baltimore was elected to office on account of his remarkable merits as a
crab cook. Though a Democrat by faith, he ran as an independent,
and upon a platform containing but two planks—one a formal
acknowledgment of the genius of Thomas Jefferson, Andrew Jackson, Robert E. Lee and George Washington, and the other a blanket offer to prepare soft crabs for any club or other organization
unable to engage a professional. During his campaign he officiated
at 700 parties, and at the election he won by a 10 to 1 vote.

* *

This gentleman specializes in soft crab and crab soup, of which
last there are two varieties—the so-called shore soup, with vegetables and a shinbone, and the kind with cream. Both are perfect,
both require an able and resourceful cook, and both are unknown
in New York. To cook the shore soup properly is a long and laborious business. The best cooks go to the shore the night before and
have the pot boiling by 4 A.M. At least 100 different vegetables,
including certain wild herbs of the Chesapeake swamps, go into it.

For both kinds of soup, of course, hard crabs are used, and it is
usual, in preparing the shore variety, to throw in the shells with
the meat and fat—not the top shell, but the shells of the legs,
feelers and body. First, of course they are cracked with an axe—a
delicate job in itself. The bungler either mashes them to mush or
doesn't break them up enough to let out the flavors of the meat.
This soup is served in deep plates, and eight plates make a meal.

Nothing is eaten with it save rye bread. Nothing is drunk save light beer. After eating it is ethical to take a siesta.

Crab soup with cream is prepared more quickly. Once the crab meat is picked, indeed, and the cream and butter and seasoning have been properly blended, the soup itself may be cooked in a chafing dish and in five or ten minutes. But that blending requires an artist. A pinch too much of this or that, and the whole potful is fit only for the hogs. This creamed soup, of course, is rather too rich for serious eating; one large plate commonly suffices; I have never heard of anyone eating more than three. But there are men who have eaten fifteen or twenty plates of shore soup in the course of a day, and without the slightest damage.

* *

The most ancient of all crab dishes is boiled hard crab. Superficially, it seems within the talents of any cook, however bad, but actually the process of preparing it is very intricate. The king of all boiled hard crab artists is Hen Wagner; he is, indeed, perhaps the only genuinely first-rate expert left in the world. Just what Hen puts into the pot to give his crabs their incomparable flavor I don't know, though I believe that celery seed, bay leaves, parsley and mushroom juice are among the ingredients. Whatever the formula I can bear witness to the crabs. They are absolutely superb. Nothing even remotely approaching them is produced by any other crab cook that I know—and I think I know all the good ones, at least in Christendom.

Once an epicure of my acquaintance, thinking to penetrate Hen's secret, filched a can of liquor from his pot and took it to a chemist for analysis. The chemist worked at it for a week or so, and then brought in a report showing no less than 217 ingredients, among them, calcium dioxide, levulose, ethyl chloride, tributyrin, stearin, oleic acid, potassium palmitate, elaidic acid, manganese fluoride, haematin, oxyhaemoglobin and chlorophyll. The formula, of course, was useless; no cook could possibly understand it. Moreover, it appeared that Hen, getting wind of what was afoot, had emptied a bottle of Peruna into the pot before the burglary.

* *

In the Neck of Virginia probably 100 different crab dishes are prepared by the native cooks, but in the eating-houses of New York, high and low, I have been able to find but a dozen or so, and very few of these are fit to eat. Most of them are of the chafing dish variety, and consist merely of a heavy cream-of-crab soup, thickened with grated cheese, cracker dust or some other such filler. The devilled crabs of New York—they are always plain "devil" crabs in the South—are apparently made of one part crab-meat (four days old, and probably embalmed) and five parts stale bread. They are almost invariably served in shells that show fork-marks, and have been used before. Eating one of them is almost as revolting a business as dining in Pittsburgh.

One of the noblest of crab dishes, hard to get at in New York and usually very bad, is crab meat a la creole. It may be cooked in five minutes, but the selection and blending of the ingredients takes hours. They include mushrooms, sweet corn, green and red peppers, celery, tomatoes, parsley, garlic, onions and gumbo, and the proportions must be exactly right. The medium of suspension is melted butter. A few Bulgarian bacilli help, but are not necessary. The mixture should be served upon thin toast, and on red-hot plates. The minute the colloids begin to coagulate it is spoiled.

The crab cake is another very delicate victual, usually ruined by being made too gummy. It should be held together, not by glucose or Portland cement—the most favored binders apparently, in the Broadway hotels—but by the whites of newly-laid eggs. Moreover, the cook should wash his hands before forming the cakes—an important point, particularly if he has been spending the morning picking chickens or peeling onions. Fry them in butter, not in axle-grease. Serve them on very hot plates. Garnish them with parsley. No cracker-dust. No sawdust. No plaster of Paris.

* *

But here I wander into reminiscences. The truth is that the Chesapeake crab, like the Chesapeake oyster, is rapidly passing into the shadows. The eastern shoreman, avid for gain, have almost exterminated him; at his best, he is now watery, diabetic and degenerate. I remember the time when crabs were so numerous in the bay that whenever a Sunday school went for an outing on an old-time side-wheeler millions of them followed the boat, fairly leaping out of the water in the hope that a scholar or two would fall overboard. And so large and active that four of them could dispose of even a superintendent before the lifeboats could be lowered.

But no more. I have seen, in the late years, hard crabs so small and skinny that a dozen of them could hardly dispatch a sea-nettle. I have eaten twenty or thirty, and then sent out for a ham sandwich. The world is changed in many ways, and in all ways for the worse.

(The New York Evening Mail, June 3, 1918)

Meditations on a Day in June

The inner springs of Puritanism, once the Freudians uncover them, will be found, I venture, to lie in the Puritan kitchen. The blue-nose is simply a fellow who eats badly, and who suffers from it violently. No man with a sound meal under his belt ever cares a hoot for the peccadilloes of his neighbor around the corner. Moral endeavor and enlightened victualing are as incompatible as baseball and counterpoint.

The explanation of such grisly phenomena as Jonathan Edwards is to be found in the infernal cooking of New England, which is still the worst in the world, despite the importation of Greek bootblacks disguised as chefs. The early Puritans, even when they feasted, feasted upon unappetizing and indigestible food; it is no wonder that they cut short their meals in order to leave more time for sermons. And on ordinary days they wolfed such chow as might have gagged a hyena—parched corn, boiled venison, dried beans, chicory coffee, black-strap molasses, and so on. A decent soup, in those bleak days, would have got its cook into jail. A well-made entree would have brought out the stocks.

It is the Puritan domination that makes American cookery so depressing to this day. The Puritan, brought up on bad food, comes in the end to regard all decent eating as immoral. His favorite victualing place is a quick-lunch room; his favorite dishes are baked beans and tough apple pie. Gorged upon such disgraceful provender, he grows bilious and saturnine, and regards everything better with a sinister eye. Thus he navigates a vicious circle—first poisoned, and then demanding more poison.

His salvation lies in making him eat better food. A hundred thousand competent cooks, turned loose in the United States, would dispose of prohibition in a year, and not only of prohibition, but also of vice crusading, Sabbatarianism, book-censoring and all the other disgusting symptoms of the Puritan murrain. I do not speak theoretically, but by the book. Who has not seen the transformation of an American Puritan in France—the gradual bleaching of the blue nose, the appearance of civilized instincts, the final emergence of an amiable and self-respecting man? The cause is plain. It is simply impossible in France to get food bad enough to keep a Puritan liver going. Such garbage is utterly unknown to French cookery; to concoct it would be inconceivable to a French cook.

I have personally witnessed the process of transformation. I well remember a Boston man in a little hotel near the Opera, just arrived from Cherbourg. He spent his first morning hunting for a plate of some abominable American breakfast food—the leavings of a mule stable. Unable to find it, he was forced to put up with a plate of French rolls. For second breakfast he had a piece of sole—capitally done. At dinner that evening he got down the first civilized meal of his life. In five days he was in a sort of trance—discovering the beauty of the world, unloading his old theology, sniffing the air of Christendom. In two weeks I met him at St. Cloud, lunching with a cutie with blue-black eyebrows. And it was Sunday afternoon!

(The New York Evening Mail, June 5, 1918)

Hot Dogs

I

The hot dog, as the phrase runs, seems to have come to stay. Even the gastrologists have given up damning it, as they have given up damning synthetic gin. Indeed, I am informed by reliable spies that at their convention in Atlantic City last May they consumed huge quantities of both, with no apparent damage to their pylorus. In such matters, popular instinct is often ahead of scientific knowledge, as the history of liver eating shows so beautifully. It may be that, on some near tomorrow, the hot dog will turn out to be a prophylactic against some malady that now slays its thousands. That this will be the case with respect to gin I am willing to prophesy formally. Meanwhile, hot dog stands multiply, and millions of young Americans grow up who will cherish the same veneration for them that we, their elders, were taught to give to the saloon.

My own tastes in eating run in another direction, and so it is very rarely that I consume a hot dog. But I believe that I'd fall in line if the artists who confect and vend it only showed a bit more professional daring. What I mean may be best explained by referring to the parallel case of the sandwich. When I was a boy there were only three kinds of sandwiches in common use—the ham, the chicken, and the Swiss cheese. Others, to be sure, existed, but it was only as oddities. Even the club sandwich was a rarity, and in most eating-houses it was unobtainable. The great majority of people stuck to the ham and the Swiss cheese, with the chicken for feast day and the anniversaries of historic battles.

Then came the invasion of the delicatessen business by Jews, and a complete reform of the sandwich. The Jewish mind was too restless and enterprising to be content with the old repertoire. It reached out for the novel, the dramatic, the unprecedented, as it does in all the arts. First it combined the ham sandwich and the cheese sandwich—and converted America to the combination instanter. Then it added lettuce, and after that, mayonnaise—both borrowed from the club sandwich. Then it boldly struck out into the highest fields of fancy, and presently the lowly sandwich had been completely transformed and exalted. It became, as the announcements said, a "meal in itself." It took on complicated and astonishing forms. It drew on the whole market for materials. And it leaped in price from a nickel to a dime, to a quarter, to fifty cents, even to a dollar. I have seen sandwiches, indeed, marked as much as a dollar and a half.

II

The rise in price, far from hurting the business, helped it vastly. The delicatessen business, once monopolized by gloomy Germans who barely made livings at it, became, in the hands of the Jewish reformers, one of the great American industries, and began to throw off millionaires. Today it is on sound and high-toned basis, with a national association, a high-pressure executive secretary, a trade journal, and a staff of lobbyists in Washington. There are sandwich shops in New York which offer the nobility and gentry a choice of no less than a hundred different sandwiches, all of them alluring and some of them downright masterpieces. And even on the lowly level of the drug-store sandwich counter the sandwich has taken on a new variety and a new dignity. No one eats plain ham anymore. At its worst it at least has a dab of cole-slaw to set it off. At its best it is hidden between turkey, Camembert and sprigs of endive, with anchovies and Russian dressing to dress it.

What I have to suggest is that the hot dog *entrepreneurs* borrow a leaf from the book of the sandwich men. Let them throw off the chains of the frankfurter, for a generation or more their only stay, and go seeking novelty in the vast and brilliant domain of the German sausage. They will be astonished and enchanted, I believe, by what they will find there, and their clients will be astonished and enchanted even more. For there are more different sausages in Germany than there are breakfast foods in America, and if there is a bad one among them then I have never heard of it. They run in size from little fellows so small and pale and fragile that it seems a crime to eat them to vast and formidable pieces that look like shells for heavy artillery. And they run in flavor from the most delicate to the most raucuous, and in texture from that of feathers caught in a cobweb to that of linoleum, and in shape from straight cylinders to lovely kinks and curlicues.

In place of the single hot dog of today there should be a variety as great as that which has come to prevail among sandwiches. There should be hot dogs for all appetites, all tastes, all occasions. They should come in rolls of every imaginable kind, and accompanied by every sort of relish, from Worcestershire sauce to chutney. The common frankfurter, with its tough roll and its smear of mustard, should be abandoned as crude and hopeless, as the old-time sandwich has been abandoned. The hot dog should be elevated to the level of an art form.

III

I call upon the Jews to work this revolution, and promise them confidently even greater success than they have found in the field of the sandwich. It is a safe and glorious business, lying wide open to anyone who chooses to venture into it. It offers immense opportunities to men of genuine imagination—opportunities not only for making money but also for Service in the best Rotarian sense. For he who improves the eating of a great people is quite as worthy of honor as he who improves their roads, their piety, their sex life, or their safety. He does something that benefits everyone, and the fruits of his benefaction live on long after he has passed from this life.

I believe that a chain of hot dog stands offering the novelties I have suggested would pay dividends in Baltimore from the first day, and that it would soon extend from end to end of the United States. The butchers and bakers would quickly arise to the chance it offered, and in six months the American repertoire of sausages would overtake and leap ahead of the German, and more new rolls would be invented than you may now find in France. In such matters American ingenuity may be trusted completely. It is infinitely resourceful, venturesome and audacious. I myself am acquainted with sausage-makers of this town who, if the demand arose, would produce sausages of hexagonal or octagonal section, sausages with springs or music boxes in them, sausages flavored with malt and hops, sausages dyed any color in the spectrum, sausages loaded with insulin, ergosterol, anti-tetanus vaccine or green chartreuse.

Nor is there any reason to believe that the bakers would lag behind. For years their ancient art has been degenerating in America, and today the bread that they ordinarily offer is almost uneatable. But when the reformers of the sandwich went to them for aid they responded instantly with both wheat and rye breads of the highest merit. Such breads, to be sure, are not used in the manufacture of drugstore sandwiches, but they are to be found in every delicatessen store and in all of the more respectable sandwich shops. The same bakeries that produce them could produce an immense variety of first-rate rolls, once a demand for them was heard.

IV

I believe in my scheme so thoroughly that I throw it overboard freely, eager only to make life in the United States more endurable. *Soli Deo gloria!* What we need in this country is a general improvement in eating. We have the best raw materials in the world, both quantitively and qualitively, but most of them are ruined in the process of preparing them for the table. I have wandered about for weeks without encountering a single decent meal. With precious few exceptions, the hotels of America all cook alike —and what they offer is hard to distinguish from what is offered on railway dining cars.

Prohibition, I believe, is largely responsible for this degeneration of the American cuisine. Certainly it is responsible for the degeneration of the cuisine here in Maryland. The classical Maryland dinner of the old days—oysters, clear soup, terrapin and wild duck—is simply unimaginable without the proper wines and liquors. Served with water, it is as preposterous as beer without foam. The booticians struggle heroically to supply what it needs, and day by day they achieve a greater success. Already they bring in wines that are drinkable; soon or late they will bring in wines really distinguished. But meanwhile their prices remain high, and the great majority of people, unable to patronize them, turn to substitutes that their forefathers ate—specifically, to sandwiches and hot dogs. Let us, while waiting for the end of the Methodist hellenium, do the best we can. Let us keep on improving the sandwich, and let us give some attention to the dog.

(The Baltimore Evening Sun, November 4, 1929)

Music

Beethoven

I

The patriotic hunger strike against German artists having collapsed, the Beethoven Association of New York has at last published Alexander Wheelock Thayer's celebrated life of the composer. The combination of "celebrated" and "at last" is not without its humors. The first volume of the work came out in a German translation so long ago as 1866, and since then it has taken a secure place among the classics of musical biography in that tongue, and German diligence has expanded the original three volumes to five. But in English, the language in which Thayer wrote it, it has just got into type—43 years after he finished the first draft of his manuscript, and 25 years after his death. Even so, the printing had to be financed by a private society, nearly all the members of which are foreigners. No American publisher had confidence enough in the civilized curiosity of Americans to risk his money upon one of the noblest works that American scholarship has ever produced.

It is a work of extraordinary merits and of very few defects, and reading it amounts to a disease. I tackled Vol. I two or three weeks ago, and have been gradually gnawing my way toward the end ever since. Theoretically, it is possible to dispatch such a book by making liberal skips; at that art, in fact, I am professionally adept. But when the subject is old Ludwig, skipping becomes not only shameful but also impossible—at all events, if one is as besotted a Beethovenianer as I am. I find myself reading absolutely everything, including even the footnotes disputing whether this or that composition should be marked Opus 56 or Opus 57. More, I find myself warming strangely to the American editor, H. E. Krehbiel. This Krehbiel, in the past, I have frequently denounced as a blowsy pedant and bore, a collector of nonsensical names and dates, a preposterous dodo—in brief, as the worst music critic in America, saving only his half-fabulous friend, Henry Theophilia Finck. All such denunciations, though true, I now formally withdraw. Krehbiel has purged himself. No other American could have done the work that he has here done one-half so competently. It shows intelligence, good judgment and enormous learning. I retire to my cellar and drink to him very respectfully.

II

Well, what sort of man emerges from these almost endless pages of fact and surmise, gossip and tradition? In brief, a man who somehow lives up fully to his music—a man who, in spite of his puns, his lawsuits, his braggadocio, his dirty cuffs, his grotesque amours, his feuds with publishers and his moods of almost operatic despair, was obviously and unquestionably great. Surrounded all his life long by men of his own craft, and some of them the first talents of the time, he differed from them enormously, not only in degree but also in kind. The mind that he brought to the problems of his art was different in every way from their minds. He saw music differently: he sensed possibilities in it that they were entirely unaware of; he began his study of it where even the best of them left off. And the feelings that he put into tone, once he had conquered the old technic and invented his super-technic, were infinitely nobler than the feelings of any of those men, and infinitely more subtle and profound.

It was a bizarre jest of the gods to pit Beethoven, in his first days in Vienna, against Papa Haydn. Haydn was undeniably a genius of the first water, and after Mozart's death, had no apparent reason to fear a rival. If he did not actually create the symphony as we know it today, then he at least enriched the form with its first genuine masterpieces—and not with a scant few, but literally with dozens. Tunes of the utmost loveliness gushed from him like oil from a well. More, he knew how to manage them; he was a master of musical architectonics. If his music is sniffed at today, then it is only by fools; there are at least six of his symphonies that are each worth all the cacophony hatched by a whole herd of Strawinkis and Eric Saties, with a couple of Tchaikovskys thrown in to flavor the pot.

But when Beethoven stepped in, then poor old Papa had to step down. It was like pitting a gazelle against an aurochs. One colossal bellow, and the combat was over. Musicians are apt to look at it as a mere contest of technicians. They point to the vastly greater skill and ingenuity of Beethoven—his firmer grip upon his materials, his greater daring and resourcefulness, his far better understanding of dynamics, rhythms and clang-tints—in brief, his tremendously superior musicianship. But that was not what made him so much greater than Haydn—for Haydn, too, had his superiorities; for example, his far readier inventiveness, his capacity for making better tunes. What lifted Beethoven above the old master, and above all other men of music save perhaps Bach and Brahms, was simply his greater dignity as a man. The feelings that Haydn put into tone were the feelings of a country pastor, a rather civilized stockbroker, a viola player gently mellowed by Kulmbacher. When he wept it was with the tears of a woman who has discovered another wrinkle; when he rejoiced it was with the joy of a child on Christmas morning. But the feelings that Beethoven put into his music were the feelings of a god. There was something Olympian in his snarls and rages, and there was a touch of hellfire in his mirth.

III

The older I grow, the more I am convinced that the most portentous phenomenon in the whole history of music was the first public performance of the Eroica Symphony, on April 7, 1805. The manufacturers of program notes have swathed that gigantic work in so many layers of childish legend and speculation that its intrinsic merits have been almost forgotten. Was it dedicated to Napoleon I? If so, was the dedication sincere or ironical? Who cares —that is, who with ears? It might have been dedicated, just as well, to Louis XIV, Paracelsus or Pontius Pilate. What makes it worth discussing, today and forever, is the fact that on its very first page Beethoven threw his hat into the ring and laid his claim to immortality. Bang!—and he is off! No compromise! No easy bridge from the past! The Second Symphony is already miles behind. A new order of music has been born.

The very manner of it is full of challenge. There is no sneaking into the foul business by way of a mellifluous and disarming introduction; no preparatory hemming and hawing to cajole the audience and enable the conductor to find his place in the score. Nay! Out of silence comes the angry crash of the tonic triad, and then at once, with no pause, the first statement of the first subject—grim, domineering, harsh, raucous, and yet curiously lovely—with its astounding collision with that electrical C Sharp! The carnage has begun early; we are only in the seventh measure! In the thirteenth and fourteenth comes the incomparable foil down the simple scale of E flat—and what follows is all that has ever been said, perhaps all that ever *will* be said, about music making in the grand manner. What has been done since, even by Beethoven, has been done in the light of the perfect example. Every line of modern music that is honestly music bears some sort of relation to that epoch-making first movement.

IV

The rest is Beethovenish, but not quintessence. There is a legend that the funeral march was put in simply because it was a time of wholesale butchery, and funeral marches were in fashion. No doubt the first night audience in Vienna, shocked and addled by the piled-up defiances of the first movement, found the lugubrious strains grateful. But the scherzo? Another felonious assault upon poor Papa Haydn! Two giants boxing clumsily, to a crazy piping by an orchestra of dwarfs. No wonder some honest Viennese in the gallery yelled: "I'd give another kreutzer if the thing would stop!" Well, it stopped finally, and then came something reassuring—a theme with variations. Everyone in Vienna knew and esteemed Beethoven's themes with variation. He was, in fact, the rising themewithvariationist of the town. But a joker remained in the pack. The variations grew more and more complex and surprising. Strange novelties got into them. The polite exercise became tempestuous, moody, cacophonous, tragic. At the end a harsh, hammering, exigent row of chords—the C Minor Symphony casting its sinister shadow before.

It must have been a great night in Vienna. But perhaps not for the actual Viennese. They went to hear "a new grand symphony in D-sharp" *(sic!)*. What they found in the Theater-an-der-Wien was a revolution.

(The Baltimore Evening Sun, April 24, 1922)

Bach at Bethlehem

I

A dusty, bottle-green hillside rising from a river front made harsh and hideous by long lines of blast furnaces; the sunshine blazing down through a haze shot through with wisps of golden orange smoke. Thick woods all the way to the top. In the midst of the solid leafage, rather less than half way up, half a dozen stretches of dingy granite, like outcroppings of the natural rock. Coming closer, one discovers that they are long, bare stone buildings—the laboratories, dormitories and so on of Lehigh University. Low down the hillside one of them stands up more boldly than the rest. It is Parker Memorial Church, a huge tabernacle in austere, apologetic pseudo-Gothic, with a high square tower—the chapel, in brief, of the university, made wide and deep to hold the whole student body at once, and so save the rev. chaplain the labor of preaching twice.

It is here that the Bach Choir, for eleven years past, has been lifting its hosannas to old Johann Sebastian—a curious scene, in more ways than one, for so solemn and ecstatic a ceremonial. Bethlehem, in the main, surely does not suggest the art of the fugue, nor, indeed, any form of art at all. It is a town founded mainly on steel, and it looks appropriately hard and brisk—a town, one guesses instantly, in which Rotarians are not without honor, and Judge Gary is read far more than Anatole France. But, as the judicious have observed in all ages, it is hazardous to judge by surfaces. Long before the first steel mill rose by the river, the country all about was peopled by simple Moravians with a zest for praising God by measure, and far back in 1742 they set up a *Sing-akademie* and began practicing German psalm-tunes on Saturday nights. The great-great-grandchild of that *Singakademie* is the Bethlehem Bach Choir of today.

II

What, indeed is most astonishing about the whole festival is not that it is given in a Pennsylvania steel town, with the snorting of switching-engines breaking in upon Bach's colossal "Gloria," but that it is still, after all these years, so thoroughly peasant-like and Moravian, so full of homeliness and rusticity. In all my life I have never attended a public show of any sort, in any country, of a more complete and charming simplicity. With strangers crowding into the little city from all directions, and two takers for every seat, and long columns of gabble in the newspapers, the temptation to throw some hocus-pocus about it, to give it a certain florid gaudiness, to bedeck it with bombast and highfalutin must be very trying, even to Moravians. But I can only say that they resist that temptation utterly and absolutely. There is no affectation about it whatever, not even the affectation of solemn religious purpose. Bach is sung in that smoky valley because the people like to sing him, and for no other reason at all. The singers are business men and their stenographers, schoolmasters and housewives, men who work in the steel mills and girls waiting to be married. Their leader is one of them; he was born among them, learned most of his music among them and served them as organist for twenty years. If not a soul came in from outside to hear the music, they would keep on making it just the same, and if the Parker Memorial Church began to disturb them with echoes from empty benches they would go back to their bare Moravian church.

I can imagine no great public ceremonial with less fussing and running about to it. No committee swathed in badges buzzes about; there is none of the usual sweating, fuming and chasing of tails. If one has a ticket, one simple goes to one's pew, plainly numbered on a simple plan, and sits down. If one lacks a ticket, one is quite free to lie in the grass outside, and listen to the music through the open doors. No bawling of hawkers is heard; a single small stand suffices for the sale of programs and scores; there is no effort to rook the stranger. The cops have nothing to do; there is no confusion, no parade, no noise save from the railroad yards. Dr. Wolle, the conductor, slips into his place unnoticed; when a session is over he slips out the same way. It is indeed not a public performance at all, in the customary sense; it is simply the last of this year's rehearsals—and as soon as it is over next year's begin. . . .

(The Baltimore Evening Sun, May 30, 1923)

Brahms

I

My excuse for writing of the above gentleman is simply that I can think of nothing else. A week or so ago, on an evening of furious heat, I heard his sextet for strings, opus 18, and ever since then it has been sliding and pirouetting through my head. I have gone to bed with it and I have got up with it. Not, of course, with the whole sextet, nor even with any principal tune of it, but with the modest and fragile little episode at the end of the first section of the first movement—a lowly thing of eight measures, thrown off like a perfume, so to speak, from the second subject.

What is the magic in such sublime trivialities? Here is a tune so slight and unassuming that it runs but eight measures and uses but six of the twelve tones in the octave, and yet it rides an elderly and unromantic man, weighing 180 pounds and with a liver far beyond hope or caring, as if it were the queen of the succubi. Is it because I have a delicately sensitive ear? Bosh! I am almost tone deaf. Or a tender and impressionable heart? Bosh again! Or a beautiful soul? *Dreimal* bosh! No theologian not in his cups would insure me against hell for cent per cent.

No, the answer is to be found in the tune, not in the man. Trivial in seeming, there is yet the power in it of a thousand horses. Modest, it speaks with a clarion voice, and having spoken, it is remembered. Brahms made many another like it. There is one at the beginning of his trio for violin, cello and piano, opus 8—the loveliest tune, perhaps, in the whole range of classical music. There are others in his waltzes. There is one in his double concerto for violin and cello, opus 102—the first subject of the slow movement. There is one in the coda of the Third Symphony. There is an exquisite one in the Fourth Symphony.

·465·

But if you know Brahms, you know them as well as I do. Hearing him is as dangerous as hearing Schubert. One does not go away filled and satisfied, to resume business as usual in the morning. One goes away charged with something that remains in the blood a long while. If I had a heavy job of work to do, with all hands on deck, I'd certainly not risk hearing any of the Schubert string quartets, or the quintet with the extra cello, or the Tragic Symphony. And I'd hesitate a long time before risking Brahms.

II

It seems an astounding thing that there was once a war over Brahms, and that certain competent musicians, otherwise sane, argued that he was dull. As well imagine a war over Schubert's Serenade or the Twenty-third Psalm. The contention of these foolish fellows, if I recall it aright, was that Brahms was clumsy in his development sections—that he flogged his tunes to death. I can think of nothing more idiotic. Turn to the sextet that I have mentioned, written in the early sixties of the last century, when the composer was barely 30. The development section of the first movement is not only sound and workmanlike: it is a masterpiece. There is a magnificent battle of moods in it, from the fieriest to the tenderest, and it ends with a coda that is sheer perfection.

True enough, Brahms had to learn—and it is in the handling of thematic material, not in its invention, that learning counts. When he wrote his first piano trio, at twenty-five or there about, he started off, as I have said, with one of the most lovely tunes ever put on paper, but when he came to develop it his inexperience showed itself and the result was such that years later he rewrote the whole work. But by the time he came to his piano concerto in D he was the complete master of his materials, and ever thereafter he showed a quality of workmanship that no other composer has ever surpassed, not even Beethoven. The first movement of the *Eroica*, I grant you, is *sui generis*. It will be matched the next time two great geniuses collide again. But what is in the rest of the eight symphonies, even including the Fifth, that is clearly better than what is in the four of Brahms?

The first performance of his First, indeed, was as memorable an event in the history of music as the first performance of the Eroica. Both were furiously denounced, and yet both were instantaneous successes. I'd rather have been present at Karlsruhe on November 6, 1876, I think, than at the landing of General Pershing in France. And I'd rather have been present at Vienna on April 7, 1805, than at the baptism of the immortal Coolidge.

III

In music, as in all the other arts, the dignity of the work is simply a reflection of the dignity of the man. The notion that shallow and trivial men can write great masterpieces is one of the follies that flow out of the common human taste for scandalous anecdote. Wagner wore a velvet cap and stole another man's wife: *ergo,* nothing is needed to write great music save a bold spirit and a pretty knack. In other words, a Wagner and a movie actor are on all fours. Nothing could be more preposterous. More than any other art, perhaps, music demands brains. It is full of technical complexities. It calls for a capacity to do a dozen things at once. But most of all it is revelatory of what is called character. When a trashy man writes it, it is trashy music.

Here is where the immense superiority of such a man as Brahms becomes manifest. There is less trashiness in his music than there is in the music of any other man ever heard of, with the sole exception, perhaps, of Johann Sebastian Bach. It was simply impossible for him, at least after he had learned his trade, to be obvious or banal. He could not write even the baldest tune without getting into something of his own high dignity and profound seriousness; he could not play with that tune, however light his mood, without putting an austere and noble stateliness into it. Hearing Brahms, one never gets any sense of being entertained by a clever mountebank. One is facing a superior man, and the fact is evident from the first note.

I give you his Deutsches Requiem as an example. There is no limit of what is commonly regarded as religious feeling in it. Brahms, so far as I know, was not a religious man. Nor is there the slightest sign of the cheap fustian of conventional patriotism. Nevertheless, a fine emotion is there—nay, an overwhelming emotion. The thing is irresistibly moving. It is moving because a man of the highest intellectual dignity, a man of exalted feelings, a man of brains, put into it his love for and pride in his country. That country is lucky which produces such men.

IV

But in music emotion is only half the story. Mendelssohn had it, and yet he belongs to the second table. Nor is it a matter of mere beauty—that is, a matter of mere sensuous loveliness. If it were, then Dvořák would be a greater man than Beethoven, whose tunes are seldom inspired, and who not infrequently does without them altogether. What makes great music is the thing I have mentioned: brains. The great musician is a man whose thoughts and feelings are above the common level, and whose language matches them. What he has to say comes out of a wisdom that is not ordinary. Platitude is impossible to him. He is the precise antithesis of Mr. Babbitt.

Above all, he is a master of his craft, as opposed to his art. He gets his effects in new and ingenious ways—and they convince one instantly that they are inevitable. One can imagine improvements in the human eye, and in the Alps, and in Beauvais Cathedral, but one cannot imagine improvements in the first movement of the Eroica. The thing is completely perfect, even at the places where the composer halts to draw breath. Any change in it would damage it. But what is inevitable is never obvious. John Doe would not and could not write thus. The immovable truths that are there—and there are truths in the arts as well as in theology—became truths when Beethoven formulated them. They did not exist before. They cannot perish hereafter.

So with Brahms. There are plenty of composers of more romantic appeal. I need mention only Schubert. Schubert, had he lived, might have been the greatest of them all, but he died before any patina had formed on him: he was still going to school in his last days. But Brahms seems to have come into the world full bloom. A few experiments, brilliant even when they failed, and he was a master beside Beethoven and Bach. In all his music, done after his beard had sprouted, there is not the slightest sign of bewilderment and confusion of trial and error, of uncertainty and irresolution. He knew precisely what he wanted to say, and he said it magnificently.

(The Baltimore Evening Sun, August 2, 1926)

Night Club

I

I hadn't been in one for three or four years, but save in the wine-list there was no visible change. The same side-show murals on the walls, and the same cacochromatic play of lights. The same sad youths laboring the same jazz. The same middle-aged couples bumping and grunting over the dance floor like dying hogs in a miasmatic pen. The same interludes of dismal professional entertainment, with the same decayed vaudevillians. The same crooners, male and female, bawling maudlin jingles into the same mikes. The same shuffling and forgetful waiters. The same commonplace food. The same poky service.

The wine-list showed some cuts in price. Highballs had come down from the 75 cents of Prohibition days to half a dollar, and some of the simpler kinds of cocktails were but 40 cents. There were champagnes as low as $5 a quart, and still wines at $2.25, $2, and even, in a few cases, $1.75. But the transcripts of the labels (often misspelled) were empty of temptation: they all seemed to be third-rate trade-goods. Every beer listed was, to my unhappy personal knowledge, bad. Of the good beers now on the market there was no mention. It was a task to make up one's mind what to drink. I chose an almost anonymous white wine, and regretted it heartily.

What the mark-up is in such places I don't know, but it can't be much less than 100%. For the overhead is heavy, and the flow of business is not swift. While the clients are performing the lethargic obscenity that they call dancing they are not drinking, and most of them seem to dance every number. I observed one crème de menthe frappe that lasted, by my watch, more than an hour, and one bottle of indeterminate red wine that sufficed for four people all evening. There was nowhere in the place, so far as I could see, any high-pressure boozing, and certainly no one was tight, save maybe my waiter—an habitual heel-drainer, or I am no criminologist. The dancers, with few exceptions, looked very silly, but they were all sober. No carcasses of the stewed, whether male or female, hung along the bar.

II

Why do people go to such places? It is hard to make out. To lose themselves in the color and gayety? I could discern no more gayety than is usual in a Bible class, and the standard color scheme is far more exhilarating to bulls than to human beings. To be soothed and carried away by the music? There is no music, but only an idotic beating of tom-toms, with occasionally a few measures of a banal tune. To seek grace and exercise in the dance? There is no grace in such stupid wriggling, and no exercise in doing it over a few square yards of floor. To dally with amour? But surely the place for amour is not under 5,000 candle-power of red, yellow, green and blue lights, with strangers ricocheting from the cabooses of the high contracting parties, and catapulting them hither and yon.

The music interested me most, for one often hears, even from good musicians, that jazz is not to be sniffed at—that there is really something in it. But what, precisely? I can find nothing in what is currently offered. Its melodies all run to a pattern, and that pattern is crude and childish. Its rhythms are almost as bad; what is amusing in them is as old as Johann Sebastian Bach, and what is new is simply an elephantine hop, skip and jump. Nor is there anything charming in jazz harmony, once it has been heard a couple of times. The discords, three times out of four, seem to be due to ignorance far more than to craft, and the modulations, in the main, are simply those of a church organist far gone in liquor.

As for the instrumentation, it appears to be based frankly on the theory that unpleasant sounds are somehow more pleasant, at least to certain ears, than pleasant ones. That theory is sound, and it has many corollaries; indeed, the love of ugliness is quite as widespread, and hence quite as human, as the love of beauty. But it still remains a scientific fact that a thin and obvious tune, played badly on an imperfect reed instrument, is hideous, and no metaphysics, however artful, can ever reduce that fact to fancy. And it is likewise a fact that a single fiddle, if it be pitted against three or four saxophones, a trumpet, a bull-fiddle and a battery of drums, gives a very bad account of itself, and can make little more actual music than a pig under a fence.

III

My guess is that jazz remains popular, not because of any virtue (even to anthropoid ears) in its melodies, harmonies and instrumentation, nor even to any novelty in its rhythm, but simply to its monotonous beat. No matter what syncopations may be attempted in the upper parts, the drums and bull-fiddle bang along like metronomes, and that is the thing that apparently soothes and delights the customers. It is music reduced to its baldest elementals, and hence music that they can follow. It might be made just as well by a machine, and some day, I suppose, the experiment of so making it will be tried.

That there are artistic possibilities in it may be granted, for on rare occasions some unusually competent composer develops and reveals them. But they are certainly not apparent in the sorry trash that loads the radio every night. It is simply undifferentiated musical protoplasm, dying of its own effluvia. There is no more ingenuity in it than you will find in the design of a series of fence-posts. One tune is so much like another that it is hard to tell them apart, and the cheap harmonies that support the first also support all the rest. Every squeal of the clarinets is an old and familiar squeal, and there is seldom any effort to break the monotony by introducing new instruments, or by working out new ways of using the old ones. The muted trumpet is still offered gravely as something novel and saucy.

The dancing that goes with this noise is, if anything, even worse. It is the complete negation of graceful and charming motion. In its primeval form I used to watch it in the Negro dives of Hawk street thirty-five years ago. There would be a dance-floor packed to the walls, and on it the colored brethren and their ladies, policed by Round Sergeant Charles M. Cole and his storm troopers, would stamp and wriggle, each sticking to a space of a few square feet. In those days the proud Aryan pursued the waltz and two-step, and ballroom dancing had sweeping linear patterns, and went to tripping and amusing tunes. But now the patterns are gone, and dancing everywhere degenerates to what it was in Hawk street—a puerile writhing on a narrow spot.

IV

It is a feeble and silly art at best, and so its decay need not be lamented. It comes naturally to the young, whose excess of energy demands violent motion, but when it is practiced by the mature it can never escape a kind of biological impropriety, verging upon the indecent. The real damage that the new mode has done is to music, the cleanest and noblest of all the arts. There is in the repertory a vast amount of dance music, and in it are some of the loveliest tunes ever written. But now they are forgotten as if they had never been, and people heave and pant to rubbish fit only for tin whistles.

That we owe the change to Prohibition is certainly arguable. By putting all social intercourse in America on an alcoholic basis, it forced people to dance when they were not quite themselves, and in consequence they had to avoid the complications of the waltz and its congeners, and to seek safety in more primitive measures. The simple beat of the tomtom was the safest of all, so it came in. Simultaneously, ears and brains were dulled, and it became painful to follow the complicated and exciting tunes of Johann Strauss, so the crude banalities of jazz were substituted. Thus we have music purged of everything that makes it music, and dancing reduced to a ducklike wabbling, requiring hardly more skill than spitting at a mark.

This is not my hypothesis: I have heard it from authorities worth attending to. They seem to agree that the gradual deboozification of the country, following upon Repeal, will eventually restore decent music to the ballroom and with it a more seemly kind of dancing. As I have noted, the people that I saw in that night club the other evening all seemed to be soberer than was common in Anti-Saloon League days. I should add that most of them looked a bit sad, and that many even looked a bit shamefaced. They had little applause for the music, and were plainly not having anything properly describable as a high old time. In the main, they were old enough to have the pattern of the waltz packed in their knapsacks. What if the professor had choked his horrible saxophones and burst into "Wiener Blue?" My guess is that a wave of genuine joy would have rolled over that dismal hall.

(The Baltimore Evening Sun, September 3, 1934)

The American Language

Spoken American

Why doesn't some painstaking pundit attempt a grammar of the American language—of English, that is, as she is spoken by the great masses of people in this fair land? That grammar will lack many of the rules laid down with so much earnestness in the treatises of Messrs. Harvey and Fewsmith and rammed with such violent exercise of pedagogical muscle into the crania of school-boys. The rule forbidding double negatives, for example, will be missing. There will be no prohibition of "I didn't do nothing." Neither will there be any denunciation of "I have saw," "He would have went," "My father taken me by the ear," "I seen," and "The milkman has came," for all of these forms, while of the dubious authenticity as English, are perfectly regular American, and in daily use by at least 50 percent of the people of the United States.

The argument that they are not worthy of serious investigation because they are mere evidence of ignorance is not a very valid one. Any spoken language, however barbarous, is worthy of investigation. Our philologists spend a lot of time studying the dialects of the Eskimo, the Hausa and the Navajo, not one of which has even a refined grammar, and some of them have begun to turn their attention to Yiddish, that most ghastly of all dialects, but so far not one of them has thought to devote any time to American.

Their German brethren are less fastidious. Every one of the dialects of Germany, bad grammar and all, has been studied and plotted. The same has been done with the dialects of France and Spain.

There is, in fact, no such things as a really scientific grammar—if we count out the grammar of Esperanto, Volapuk, and other such impossible tongues. Languages change from century to century, almost from year to year. In Shakespeare's day "more larger" was perfectly good English, and such phrases as "I have saw" and "I would have went" were at least defensible. No doubt they are defensible today, but whether they are or not the fact remains they are in constant use, and that the conditions for their use should be studied, for the information and amusement of posterity. Our written English will be easily accessible to the philogist of a thousand years hence. But our spoken American, unless his predecessors of today go on their duty, will be as much a mystery to him as the slang of Babylonian or the pronunciation of Periclean Greek.

Some of the principal rules of spoken American are easily discernible. It is particularly original and daring in the matter of conjugating verbs. Instead of "I write" and "I wrote," it uses "I write" and "I written." Instead of the customary form of the past perfect tense it uses "I have wrote." Its second person form in the past tense is "he written." But perhaps the best way to exhibit its rules is to give a sample conjugation. Here, then, is the American manner of conjugating "to see" in the indicative mode:

PRESENT TENSE.

Singular	*Plural.*
I see.	We see.
You see.	Youse see.
He sees.	*They see.

PRESENT PERFECT TENSE.

I have saw.	We have saw.
You have saw.	Youse have saw.
He has saw.	*They have saw.

PAST TENSE.

I seen.	We seen.
You seen.	Youse seen.
He seen.	*They seen.

PAST PERFECT TENSE.

I had saw.	We had saw.
You had saw.	Youse had saw.
He had saw.	*They had saw.

FUTURE TENSE.

I will see.	We will see.
You will see.	Youse will see.
He will see.	*They will see.

FUTURE PERFECT TENSE.

[No such tense is met with in American grammar. In place of it, the future tense is used, as in the phrase "I'll be dead by then."]

Here is a synopsis of "to go":

INDICATIVE MODE.

Present I go.
Present perfect I have went.
Past I went.
Past perfect I had went.
Future I'll go.
Future perfect (?).

SUBJUNCTIVE MODE.

Present If I go.   *Past perfect* If I had went   *Past* (?).

POTENTIAL MODE.

Present I can or must go.
Present perfect I can or must have went.
Past I could or would go.
Past perfect I could, or would, or should, or ought to have went.

Now observe the manner of conjugating "to take," and particularly the manner of forming the past perfect in the potential mode:

INDICATIVE MODE.

Present I take.
Present perfect I have took.
Past I taken.

*These forms, while correct, according to the rules of American grammar, are seldom actually used. Instead of "They have saw" it is more common to hear "Them men have saw." "They," in fact, is a pronoun in little use. "Them" nearly always takes its place.

Past perfect   I had took.
Future   I'll take.
Future perfect   (?).

SUBJUNCTIVE MODE.

Present If I take.   *Past perfect* If I had took.   *Past* If I taken.

POTENTIAL MODE.

Present   I can or must take.
Present perfect   I can or must have took.
Past   I could, or would, or should have took.
Past perfect   I could, or would, or should or ought to, or had ought have took, or had a right to take.

This form of conjugation, however, is limited in its use to certain irregular verbs. Others are conjugated in a manner more clearly approaching that of orthodox English grammar. In the phrase "I hadn't ought to have bought," for example, the verb itself is in good English form, however much the remaining members may alarm. In practice, indeed, even "I written" and "He taken" have a serious rival in a sort of hybrid tense form. This may be called the form of the past-present or present-past tense. It is common to Zulu, Hausa, Plattdeutsch, and other barbarous dialects and is achieved by advancing past actions to the present. Thus, instead of saying "I saw what he was up to," or more correctly in American, "I seen what he was up to," a good many Americans say "I see (or sees) what he is up to, and so I says to him," etc. The American word "sez" thus originated. It is often assumed to be a debased form of "said," but as a matter of fact it is an authentic phonetic form of "says." "Says" is pronounced in American, as if spelled "sez." Therefore, "sez" is perfectly defensible.

But let us return to the subject another day.

(*The Baltimore Evening Sun, October 19, 1910*)

Essay in American

The following attempt to translate the Declaration of Independence into American was begun eight or ten years ago, at the time of my first investigations into the phonology and morphology of the American vulgate. I completed a draft in 1917, but its publication was made impossible by the Espionage act, which forbade any discussion, however academic, of proposed changes in the canon of the American Koran. In 1920 I resumed the work and have since had the benefit of the co-operation of various other philologists, American and European. But the version, as it stands, is mine. That such a translation has long been necessary must be obvious to every student of philology. And this is Better Speech Week.

The great majority of Americans now speak a tongue that differs materially from standard English, and in particular from the standard English of the eighteenth century. Thus the text of the Declaration has become, in large part, unintelligible to multitudes of them. What, for example, would the average soda-fountain clerk, or City Councilman, or private soldier, or even the average Congressman make of such a sentence as this one: "He has called together legislative bodies at places unusual, uncomfortable and distant from the depository of their public records, for the sole purpose of fatiguing them into compliance with his measures" ? Or this one: "He has refused for a long time, after such dissolutions, to cause others to be elected, whereby the legislative powers, incapable of annihilation, have returned to the people at large for their exercise" ? Obviously, such sonorous Johnsonese is as dark to the plain American of 1921 as so much Middle English would be, or Holland Dutch. He may catch a few words, but the general drift is beyond him.

This fact, I believe, is largely responsible for the disaster which overtook those idealists who sought to wrap the Declaration around them during and immediately after the war. The members of the American Legion, the Ku Klux Klan and other patriotic societies, unable to understand the texts upon which the libertarian doctrines of such persons were based, set them down as libelers of the Declaration, and so gave them beatings. I believe that that sort of faux pas might be avoided if the plain people, civil and military, could actually read the Declaration. The version which follows is still far from perfect, but it is at all events in sound American, and even the most advanced admirers of the Hon. Mr. Harding, I am convinced, will find it readily intelligible.

When things get so balled up that the people of a country have to cut loose from some other country and go it on their own hook, without asking no permission from nobody, excepting maybe God Almighty, then they ought to let everybody know why they done it so that everybody can see they are on the level, and not trying to put nothing over on nobody.

All we got to say on this proposition is this: First, you and me is as good as anybody else, and maybe a damn sight better; second, nobody ain't got no right to take away none of our rights; third, every man has got a right to live, to come and go as he pleases, and to have a good time however he likes, so long as he don't interfere with nobody else. That any government that don't give a man these rights ain't worth a damn; also people ought to choose the kind of government they want themselves, and nobody else ought to have no say in the matter. That whenever any government don't do this, then the people have got a right to can it and put in one that will take care of their interests. Of course, that don't mean having a revolution every day like them South American coons and Bolsheviki, or every time some jobholder does something he ain't got no business to do. It is better to stand a little graft, etc., than to have revolutions all the time, like them coons, Bolsheviki, etc., and any man that wasn't a anarchist or one of them I.W.W.s would say the same. But when things gets so bad that a man ain't hardly got no rights at all no more, but you might almost call him a slave, then everybody ought to get together and throw the grafters out, and put in new ones who won't carry on so high and steal so much, and then watch them. This is the proposition the people of these Colonies is up against, and they have got tired of it, and won't stand it no more. The administration of the present King, George III, has been rotten from the jump-off, and when anybody kicked about it he always tried to get away with it by strong-arm work. Here is some of the rough stuff he has pulled:

He vetoed bills in the Legislature that everybody was in favor of, and hardly nobody was against.

He wouldn't allow no law to be passed without it was first put up to him, and then he stuck it in his pocket and let on he forgotten about it, and didn't pay no attention to no kicks.

When people went to work and gone to him and asked him to put through a law about this or that, he give them their choice: either they had to shut down the Legislature and let him pass it all by himself or they couldn't have it at all.

He made the Legislature meet at one-horse tank-towns out in the alfalfa belt, so that hardly nobody could get there and most of the leaders would stay home and let him go to work and do things as he pleased.

He give the Legislature the air and sent the members home every time they stood up to him and give him a call-down.

When a Legislature was busted up he wouldn't allow no new one to be elected, so that there wasn't nobody left to run things, but anybody could walk in and do whatever they pleased.

He tried to scare people outen moving into these States, and made it so hard for a wop or one of them poor kikes to get his papers that he would rather stay home and not try it, and then, when he come in, he wouldn't let him have no land, and so he either went home again or never come.

He monkeyed with the courts and didn't hire enough judges to do the work, and so a person had to wait so long for his case to be decided that he got sick of waiting, and went home, and so never got what was coming to him.

He got the judges under his thumb by turning them out when they done anything he didn't like, or holding up their salaries, so that they had to cough up or not get no money.

He made a lot of new jobs and give them to loafers that nobody knowed nothing about, and the poor people had to pay the bill, whether they wanted to or not.

Without no war going on, he kept an army loafing around the country, no matter how much people kicked about it.

He let the army run things to suit theirself and never paid no attention whatsoever to nobody which didn't wear no uniform.

He let grafters run loose, from God knows where, and give them the say in everything, and let them put over such things as the following:

Making poor people board and lodge a lot of soldiers they ain't got no use for and don't want to see loafing around.

When the soldiers kill a man, framing it up so that they would get off.

Interfering with business.

Making us pay taxes without asking us whether we thought the things we had to pay taxes for was something that was worth paying taxes for or not.

When a man was arrested and asked for a jury trial, not letting him have no jury trial.

Chasing men out of the country, without being guilty of nothing, and trying them somewheres else for what they done here.

In countries that border on us, he put in bum governments, and then tried to spread them out, so that by and by they would take in this country, too, or make our own government as bum as they was. He never paid no attention whatever to the Constitution, but he went to work and repealed laws that everybody was satisfied with and hardly nobody was against, and tried to fix the government so that he could do whatever he pleased.

He busted up the Legislatures and let on he could do all the work better by himself.

Now he washes his hands of us and even declares war on us, so we don't owe him nothing, and whatever authority he ever had he ain't got no more.

He has burned down towns, shot down people like dogs, and raised hell against us out on the ocean.

He hired whole regiments of Dutch, etc., to fight us, and told them they could have anything they wanted if they could take it away from us, and sicked these Dutch, etc., on us without paying no attention whatever to international law.

He grabbed our own people when he found them in ships on the ocean, and shoved guns into their hands, and made them fight against us, no matter how much they didn't want to.

He stirred up the Indians, and give them arms and ammunition, and told them to go to it, and they have killed men, women and children, and don't care which.

Every time he has went to work and pulled any of these things, we have went to work and put in a kick, but every time we have went to work and put in a kick he has went to work and did it again. When a man keeps on handing out such rough stuff all the time, all you can say is that he ain't got no class and ain't fitten to have no authority over people who have got any rights, and he ought to be kicked out.

When we complained to the English we didn't get no more satisfaction. Almost every day we warned them that the politicians over there was doing things to us that they didn't have no right to do. We kept on reminding them who we were, and what we were doing here, and how we come to come here. We asked them to get us a square deal, and told them if this thing kept on we'd have to do something about it and maybe they wouldn't like it. But the more we talked, the more they didn't pay no attention to us. Therefore, if they ain't for us they must be again us, and we are ready to give them the fight of their lives, or to shake hands when it is over.

Therefore be it resolved, That, we, the representatives of the people of the United States of America, in Congress assembled, hereby declare as follows: That the United States, which was the

United Colonies in former times, is now free and independent, and ought to be; that we have throwed out the English King and don't want to have nothing to do with him no more, and are not in England no more; and that, being as we are now free and independent, we can do anything that free and independent parties can do, especially declare war, make peace, sign treaties, go into business, etc. And we swear on the Bible on this proposition, one and all, and agree to stick to it no matter what happens, whether we win or we lose, and whether we get away with it or get the worst of it, no matter whether we lose all our property by it or even get hung for it.

(The Baltimore Evening Sun, November 7, 1921)

Making New Words

The word *scofflaw* passed into history at 5.32 P.M., Eastern Standard Time, on December 5, 1933, at which moment precisely a State convention in Utah cast the vote needed to complete the repeal of the Eighteenth Amendment. The age of *scofflaw*, at the time of its demise, was nine years, ten months, and twenty days. The news of its birth had gone out over the wires of the Morse electric telegraph on the evening of January 14, 1924, and was published in all the morning papers of the next day. Within a week the word was in wide use, and within a month every man, woman and child in the United States knew its meaning.

It had, like all of the higher organisms, two parents, though at the time of its birth they had never met. They were Henry Irving Shaw, of Shawsheen Village, near Andover, Mass., and Miss Kate L. Butler, of Dorchester in the same great State. Late in 1923, Delcevare King, a well-heeled dry of Quincy, Mass., had offered a prize of $250 for a term to designate "the lawless drinker," specifying that it should be sufficiently pungent to "stab awake his conscience." Both Mr. Shaw and Miss Butler sent in *scofflaw*. There were thousands of other entries, but Mr. King preferred *scofflaw* to all the rest, and so his prize was divided between its pa and ma.

* *

In all the history of words there have been few records of deliberate inventions that have been so quickly successful. As a rule, a new word comes in by a process that is mainly accidental. Someone devises it to meet a sudden and maybe transient need—and is amazed a week later to hear other people using it.

It was thus, for example, with the late Mr. Harding's *normalcy*. The truth is that he did not invent it at all, but simply used it ignorantly, or perhaps I should say inadvertently. The word he was fishing for was *normality*, but somehow he got hold of the rare mathematical term, *normalcy*, and so stuck it into his inaugural address. The next day all the intellectual snobs of the country were cackling over it—but by the end of the week it was in common use, and it retains a certain vogue to this day.

Mr. Hoover's phrase, *noble experiment*, was also put forth without any apparent design to contribute to the American vocabulary. He first used it in a letter to Senator William E. Borah, dated February 28, 1928, but at that time it seems to have attracted no notice. But when he repeated it in his speech of acceptance in July of the same year, it caught on at once, and during the four years following it plagued him dreadfully. The wets used it much more than the drys, and in consequence it came to have a bitterly satirical significance. In November, 1932, it probably cost Mr. Hoover at least 5,000,000 votes.

* *

Newspaper writers probably make more new words than any other class of men. They have to work the ordinary vocabulary so hard that they grow tired of it, and are thus impelled to augment and embellish it. *Steamroller*, in the political (and military) sense, was first used in 1912 by Oswald F. Schuette, the Washington correspondent of the Chicago *Inter-Ocean*. It was suggested by the violent tactics used to seat the Taft delegates at the Republican National Convention of that year.

George Ade, I believe, invented *rubberneck*. And Walter Winchell was the father of *whoopee*—an old word put to new use, and almost instantly popular. Jack Conway of *Variety*, who died in 1928, had a long string to his credit, including *palooka*, to *scram*, *belly-laugh*, *sex-appeal* and *bolony*, the last of which was afterward borrowed by Al Smith and is commonly believed to be his own.

I have myself been credited with *Bible Belt*, but whether or not I actually invented it I simply can't tell you. All I can recall is that I began experimenting with various *Belts* in 1924 or thereabout—the *Hookworm Belt*, the *Hog-and-Hominy Belt*, the *Total Immersion Belt*, and so on. Finally, I settled down to *Bible Belt*. Maybe I really fetched it up from the depths of my unconsciousness. But maybe I only borrowed it from some better theologian.

(The New York American, March 7, 1935)

Hopeful Purists

The pedagogues at Princeton, it is announced, have declared a holy war on bad English. Hereafter every freshman entering the university will be put through rigid tests, and if it turns out that his grammar and syntax are shaky he will be condemned to a special correctional class, carried on by a gogue with a lynxian ear for double negatives and split infinitives. If, after an intensive course, he is found to be still deficient he will be given a one-way bus ticket to Yale or Harvard and ordered off the lot.

The scheme deserves the prayers of every lover of elegance in speech, but that it will work is hardly to be hoped. The average American college graduate, no doubt, speaks and writes English measurably better than the average policeman, but not more than one graduate in a thousand ever acquires anything properly describable as a mastery of the language.

I know something of this matter at first hand, for I spent twenty years reading manuscripts for American magazines. It was my observation that only the graduates of West Point could be trusted to write even correctly. Why a military academy should thus beat the great universities in teaching English I don't know, but there is the fact.

* *

The general tendency in this country is against the Princeton purists, and most teachers of English have begun to yield to it. So long ago as 1926 the College Entrance Examination Board admitted "It is me," which had been denounced by finicky grammarians for two centuries, and four years afterward the late Prof. Sterling A. Leonard, of Wisconsin, on consulting the principal American authorities, found that 75 per cent of them were disposed to admit as in good usage not only "It is me" but also "None of them are," "Who are you looking for?" "Try and come," and "We only had one left." A large majority voted for *loan* as a verb, for *slow* as an adverb, and "We haven't but a few left."

An analagous form, "but that," now has behind it the august authority of the Supreme court of the United States. Turn to the decision in *Principality of Monaco* vs. *State of Mississippi,* handed down last May, and you will find Mr. Chief Justice Hughes writing, "There is no question but that." The Supreme Court also uses to *loan* as a verb, forgetting the more ancient and respectable *to lend.*

In Congress almost anything goes. Open the *Congressional Record* at random and you'll find "He don't," "Either of these three," and "It looks like they mean business," and even such monstrosities as "Let us remember those whose it's our duty to serve" and "I will only take but a few minutes of the committee's time."

* *

Outside such relatively austere circles a grammatical free-for-all is in progress. I have myself heard "He ain't only got but one leg," and "He never goes hardly nowhere," and a correspondent sends me, as a souvenir of the Depression, "I ain't scarcely got practically nothing."

Pedagogues are proverbially hopeful men, and those of Princeton run true to form, but what an appalling task faces them! Have they never heard that even Woodrow Wilson, their colleague and grand master, once wrote, "No man or woman can hesitate to give what *they* have"? If not, let them go to the Princeton library and read the speech he made in New York on Sept. 27, 1918.

(The New York American, July 30, 1934)

Why Are We Yankees?

When etymologists feel their professional libido rising within them, and the mood for performing prodigies seizes them, they tackle the word *Yankee*—but never with anything properly de-

scribable as brilliant results. After more than a century of investigation it remains one of the baffling mysteries of their craft. At the
moment the dominant school holds that it is of Dutch origin, but
there remains a minority that believes it came from some Indian
language, or arose out of Indian misadventures with English or
French. The former school, it seems to me, has the better of the
argument, but it can prove its case only half way. That is to say, it
can show that a word roughly similar to *Yankee* was in the vocabulary of the Dutch settlers of Knickerbocker New York, but it can't
show how that word came to be applied to New Englanders.

The first proponent of the Indian origin of the word seems to
have been the Rev. John Gottlieb Ernestus Heckewelder, a
learned Moravian who, despite his German name, was born in
England. His parents brought him to Pennsylvania in 1754, and in
1771 he became a missionary to the Indians who then raged in the
vicinity of what are now Pittsburgh and Cincinnati. In 1818 he
published an account of them, and in it he recorded his belief that
Yankee was simply a product of their unhappy effort to pronounce
the word *English*. He said that they made the word *Yengees*, and
argued plausibly that from this to *Yankees* was but a step.

A bit later on some reader of Heckewelder in Canada sent in
news that the Indians there made *Yankee*, or something closely
resembling it, of the French *Anglais*, and then someone recalled a
report by one of Cornwallis's officers, dated 1789, that the Cher-
okees of the Carolinas had a word eankke, meaning slave or cow-
ard, and were fond of applying it to white men. So *Yankee* came to
be thought of as an Indian loan-word.

*   *

But there were difficulties in the way of accepting the theory,
for further study showed that *Yankee* was apparently first applied,
not to the English, but to the Dutch. So early as 1683, it was found,
Yankey was a common nickname among the pirates who then
raged the Spanish Main, and investigation revealed that the men
who bore it were always, or nearly always, Dutchmen. Someone
then suggested that it was probably derived from either *Janke*, a
diminutive of the Dutch given name *Jan*, or maybe from *Jankees*
(pronounced Yon-case), a blend of *Jan* and *Cornelius*, two Dutch
names which often appeared in combination. Analogues were easily found—for example *Dago* (Diego) for Spaniard (now trans-

ferred to Italians), *Fritz* or *Heine* for a German, *Sandy* for a Scotsman, and *Pat* for an Irishman.

But how did this nickname for Dutchmen come to be applied to Englishmen, and particularly to the people of New England? To this day no really convincing answer has ever been made. All that may be said with any certainty is that it was already in use in 1765 as a term of derision, and that by 1775 the Yankees began to take pride in it. In the latter year, in fact, John Trumbull spoke of it in his poem *McFingal* (now forgotten by everyone save teachers of literature) as connoting "distinction." But he neglected to elucidate its transfer from Dutch pirates to New England Puritans, and no one has been able to do so to this day.

* *

During the Civil War, as every schoolboy knows, *Yankee* became a term of opprobrium again, and was used by Southerners to designate all Northerners. But its evil significance began to wear off after the turn of the century, and when in 1917 the English applied it to the men of the A.E.F., Southerners and Northerners alike, the former seem to have borne the affliction without protest.

At that time a characteristic clipped form, *Yank*, came into popularity at home, launched by its use in George M. Cohan's war song, "Over There." But *Yank* was not invented by Cohan, for you will also find it in Kipling's "The Three Sealers," written long before the war.

Incidentally, the verb *to yank* is also American—and its origin is as mysterious as that of *Yankee.* Whether they have any connection no one knows.

(The New York American, January 7, 1935)

The National Letters

The American Novel

I

The young American literatus of today, with publishers bowing and scraping before him as he waits upon them with his manuscript under his arm and magazine editors competing to pay him the income of a movie actor or a Prohibition enforcement officer, can scarcely imagine the difficulties which beset his predecessor of the last generation. Yet it is but 23 years ago that Theodore Dreiser, coming into New York with *Sister Carrie*, was knocked about from publisher to publisher, only to see his book, when it was printed at last, instantly suppressed. Certainly the last two decades have seen some flowing of water under the bridges. I am one who habitually views with alarm, and yet I must confess that there has been enormous progress in my time, and that the American imaginative writer of this year 1923 is probably quite as free as he deserves to be. He may write, within reason, anything he pleases, and if it has the slightest merit it will get into type. More, it will be read. Yet more, it will be praised.

That such complete freedom now exists is still sometimes disputed—a lamentable proof of the resistance which the human mind always offers to a novel fact. Those who dispute it, I think, make the mistake of overestimating the importance and puissance of comstockery. The Comstocks, true enough, still occasionally raid a new book, but that their monkeyshines actually *suppress* any book of the slightest consequence I doubt very much. The flood is too vast for them. While they chase a minnow a whole school of sharks gets by. In any case, they confine their operations to the scarlet field of sex, and it must be obvious that it is not in the field of sex that the hottest battles against the old American tradition have been fought and won. *Three Soldiers* was far more subversive of that tradition than all the stories of sex ever written in America —and yet *Three Soldiers* came out with the imprint of one of the most conventional of American publishers, and was scarcely challenged. *Babbitt* scored a victory that was still easier. It was so devastating a triumph that even Dr. Stuart P. Sherman joined in the whooping. Yet *Babbitt* was a plain *attentat* against Sherman's dearest principles; if his whole contention was not against just such ribald books, then his contention was without any sense whatever.

II

What the new freedom consists of is simply the right to depict the life of the American people as it appears to the novelist, without any regard for current delusions about it. The old tradition, culminating in Howells, put those delusions first and the facts afterward. Howells himself, though he was fond of calling himself a realist, actually denounced "unpleasant" novels on the ground that the American people were all good and happy—that the disagreeable incidents which he encountered and approved in Russian fiction could have no proper place in American fiction. This naïve nonsense was occasionally challenged by stray novelists of greater intelligence—for example, John Hay and Henry Adams— but in the main it was sustained by the native Dostoevskis and Balzacs and supported by the native Georg Brandeses and Matthew Arnolds. The typical American novel of the period 1895–1905 was either romantic guff of a quasi-historical nature or bucolic comedy that overlooked completely the rustic's mortgages, superstitions, adulteries and chilblains.

It was not Frank Norris who blew up this puerile artificiality, as is widely believed, but Theodore Dreiser. Norris had the professional equipment for the job—there have been few American novelists, indeed, before or since, of greater skill—but he lacked the pugnacity. Had he lived longer, the chances are that he would have been wooed and ruined by the Hamilton Wright Mables, as Hamlin Garland had been wooed and ruined before him. Dreiser, fortunately for American letters, never had to face any such wooing. The critical schoolmarms fell upon him with alarmed, falsetto objurgations the instant he appeared over the rim of the prairie, and soon he was the storm center of a battle royal that kept up for nearly twenty years. The man was solid, massive, immovable. Very little cunning was in him, but he had an appalling tenacity. No conceivable assault could daunt him. The more his harsh, searching, horribly persuasive novels were denounced, the more resolutely he stuck to his formula. That formula is now every American novelist's formula. They all try to write better than Dreiser, but they all imitate him in his fundamental purpose—to make the novel true.

III

True? Do I mean photographic? Am I advocating the "slice of life" nonsense? Certainly not. The novel is not a blueprint; it is a work of art. Life itself, to be sure, may be quite as dramatic as anything even a Joseph Conrad could imagine, as everyone knows who has ever gone to a hanging or peeped through a keyhole, but in the main it is too aimless and dispersed to hold the interest of an observer. Its high days are followed by low days; we are all dead at least twenty hours out of the twenty-four. It is the business of a novelist to boil the thing down, to select what is basic and significant, to relate the apparently fortuitous and meaningless to some intelligible chain of causation—in brief, to interpret and criticize life as well as to depict it.

Here it must be plain that this function cannot be performed if any artificial impediments halt its free play. The novelist, within the bounds of ordinary decorum, must be at liberty to describe his people exactly as he sees them, and to interpret them exactly as he understands them. If he is surrounded by taboos and warnings—if he is forbidden, say, to hint that his hero submitted to the draft reluctantly, or that his heroine is a mammal, or that the scenes in which he sets them are anything but idyllic and serene—then his whole enterprise goes to pieces, and the work he produces, whatever its merits as a piece of writing, is false and vicious as record of human transactions, and worthless as a criticism of human life.

Such taboos greatly damaged the American novel during the time between the Civil War and the appearance of Dreiser. It was an era of uncritical sentimentality. The so-called realism of Howells seldom got beyond the cautious facetiousness of a suburban pastor arising to address his Men's Club. That a ferocious struggle for existence was going on in the Republic, that for every great drygoods jobber or railroad wrecker who came to glory there were a thousand Americans who went down to disaster, that the shine on the surface of the national life was chiefly only shine—all this was scarcely hinted at. It was Dreiser who leaped into that bowl of mush, a wild man from the steppes. When the uproar ceased at last, the bowl was broken.

IV

Today, as I said before, the American novelist is free. There is no longer any convention that he must call a cabbage a rose. He may depict the national scene, or any part of it, precisely as he sees it, yielding to his prejudices and prepossessions as much as he pleases. He is free to accentuate its shadows as much as Howells and company accentuated its pink and lavender lights. If he has any skill at all, publishers stand waiting for him. If he is persuasive, he gets an audience. I can imagine no point of view, however at clash with ordinary points of view, that would bar a beginning novelist from print in America today. So long as he supports his ideas plausibly, so long as his scenes are recognizable and his men and women keep their feet on the ground, he is heard and attended to.

Well, then, what has he done with this new freedom? Does his work show that he has gained anything by it? I believe it does. But does it show that the national literature has gained anything by it? Again I believe it does—but perhaps with a few precautionary coughs. No genuinely great American novel, it may be, is yet upon us; no novelist now in practice among us may be capable of writing it. But at least the ground is cleared for him if he is on his way—at least there is nothing to prevent him doing it if he has the skill. His liberty is yet new, and perhaps he is not yet accustomed to it; the dying moans of the schoolmasters and the occasional buffooneries of the Comstocks may keep him a bit timorous and doubtful. But soon or late, I believe, he will justify all the toil and moil that went into his liberation. Soon or late, leaping from the facile springboard of *Babbitt,* he will plunge down into the strata of motive and impulse that lie beneath the surface, and depict the essential Americano with new truthfulness and new understanding.

(The Baltimore Evening Sun, August 27, 1923)

The Sahara of the Bozart

*Alas! for the South, her books have
grown fewer—
She never was much given to literature.*

In the lamented J. Gordon Coogler, author of these memorable lines, there was the intuition of a true poet. He was the last bard of Dixie. Down there a poet is now rare as a philosopher or an oboe-player. That vast region south of the Potomac is as large as Europe. You could lose France, Germany and Italy in it, with the British Isles for good measure. And yet it is as sterile, artistically, intellectually, culturally, as the Sahara Desert. It would be difficult in all history to match so amazing a drying-up of civilization.

I say a civilization because that is what, in the old days, the South had, and it was a civilization of manifold excellences, and lavish fruits. Down to the middle of the last century and even beyond, the main hatchery of ideas in America, despite the pretensions of the Yankees, was below the Potomac. It was there that all the political theories we still cherish were born; it was there that statesmen were bred; it was there, above all, that the gentler adornments of life were cultivated. A certain noble spaciousness was in the Southern scheme of things. It made for reflection, for tolerance, for the vague thing we ineptly call culture.

But I leave it to any fair observer to find anything approaching culture in the South today. It is as if the civil war stamped out all the bearers of the torch and left only a mob of peasants on the field. In all that gargantuan empire there is not a single picture gallery worth going into, nor a single orchestra capable of playing a Beethoven symphony, nor a single opera house, nor a single monument or building (less than fifty years old) worth looking at, nor a single factory devoted to the making of beautiful things. Once you have counted Robert Loveman (an Ohioan by birth) you will not find a single Southern poet above the rank of a neighborhood rhymester. Once you have counted James Branch Cabell you will not find a single southern novelist whose work shows any originality or vitality. And once you have—but when you come to composers, historians, critics, scientists, painters, sculptors and architects you have to give it up, for there is not one between Alexandria and the gulf.

Even in politics, the old specialty of the South, there is an astounding collapse. In the early days Virginia led the nation; today Virginia is content to tag along after the brummagem uplifters of the middle West, bawling for prohibition, populism, all the claptrap of Bryanism. On the theoretical side the politics of the State is imitative, childish, almost idiotic. On the practical side it is cheap, ignorant, dishonest—a mere matter of rival gangs of job-seekers struggling for the salary teat. Both sides make indecent bargains with Anti-Saloon League rabble rousers. Neither side can show a man capable of leadership.

These characters, of course, are common to the politics of many other states, north and south. No sane man would look for intelligible political ideas, for example, in Delaware, or in Arkansas, or in Georgia. But in Virginia they are especially noticeable and significant because of what has gone before—because of the state's old preeminence, not only as the home of political leaders, but also as the home of political philosophers. The ancient Virginians were not mere boob-bumpers and job-chasers; they were men of thought, of originality and of honor. They lifted politics to the level of a science and an art. But in the Virginia of today it is merely a trade, and a very sordid one at that. It has borrowed the orgiastic numskullery of the middle West without borrowing its honest passion. It is as ignoble a business as running a peanut stand, and it attracts as empty and disgusting a class of men.

But it is not on the political side that the decay of Southern culture is most visible, for here the whole country has gone down hill, and the bray of the Chautauquan sounds throughout the land. What is most salient and depressing to an observer is the almost entire absence of that cultural striving on the gentler side which so plainly marks the West and the North. There is scarcely a second-rate city between the Ohio and the Pacific which isn't struggling to establish an orchestra, or setting up a little theatre, or going in for an art gallery, or giving some other sign that it is lifting its thoughts above the chase of the dollar. These efforts often fail, and sometimes they succeed rather absurdly, but under them there is at least an impulse that deserves respect, and that is the impulse to seek beauty and to experiment with ideas, and so to give the life of everyday a certain dignity and purpose.

You will find no such impulse in the South. There are no committees down there cadging subscriptions for an orchestra; if a string quartet is ever heard there, the news of it has never come out; an opera troupe, when it roves the land, is a nine days' wonder. The little theatre movement has swept the whole country, enormously augmenting the public interest in sound plays, giving new dramatists their chance, forcing reforms upon the commercial theatre. Everywhere else the wave rolls high—but along the line of the Potomac it breaks upon a rock-bound shore. There is no little theatre beyond. There is no gallery of pictures. No artist ever gives exhibitions. No one talks of such things. No one seems to be interested in such things.

Part of my job in the world is the reading of manuscripts, chiefly by new authors. I go through hundreds every week. This business has taught me some curious things, and among them the fact that the literary passion is segregated geographically, and with it the literary talent. Boston produces better writing than the far West; it is suaver, more careful, finer in detail. Los Angeles leads the whole country in quantity; its weekly output of manuscripts even surpasses that of Greenwich village. Kansas and Oklahoma are producing capital poets; they tremble on the verge of literature. Chicago leads them all in ideas, originality, vigor; it is the great hatching place of American letters. But the South? The South is an almost complete blank. I don't see one printable manuscript from down there a week. And in my more than three years of steady reading the two Carolinas, Georgia, Alabama, Mississippi, Florida and Tennessee have not offered six taken together.

As for the causes of this practically unanimous sterility I do not profess to be privy to them, but a theory forms and forces itself, and so I pass it on. It is to the following effect: That the civil war actually finished off nearly all the civilized folk in the South and thus left the country to the poor white trash, whose descendants now run it. The war, of course, was not a complete massacre; it didn't kill them all. But those first-rate Southerners who actually survived were bankrupt, broken in spirit and unable to get along under the new dispensation, and so they came North. A few of them still live and their progeny are numerous. A Southerner of good blood does well in the North. But in the South he tends to throw up his hands and give it up.

This explains the tragic degeneration of politics in Virginia, and the general cultural decay of such states as Georgia and South Carolina. One looks in vain for the old names. They are as extinct as the name of Percy. In place of their bearers one finds a new hierarchy of southern notables—a hierarchy made up of pushful gentlemen from below, sharp in business, loud in pretensions, vulgar in soul and as empty of the old urbanity and politesse, as devoid of any comprehension of civilized culture as so many Sicilian immigrants. They make the public opinion of the South and represent it before the nation. They control its newspapers (it has no other printing), fashion its laws and establish its point of view. That point of view, once so spacious and gentle, is now that of fourth-rate commercial bounders—the point of view, in brief, of Leeds or Manchester, of Providence (R.I.), Youngstown (Ohio) or Omaha (Neb.).

In such an atmosphere, it must be obvious, the arts cannot flourish. The philistinism of the emancipated poor white is not only indifferent to them; it is positively antagonistic to them. That philistinism regards human life, not as an agreeable adventure, but as a mere trial of rectitude. It is distinctively and overwhelmingly moral. Its judgments are all based upon moral certainties; it is unable to rise to that innocence which is the essence of aesthetic understanding and endeavor; to the gross utilitarianism of the earth it adds a sort of celestial utilitarianism, whereby the acts of man are estimated chiefly by their capacity for saving him from hell.

Here, perhaps, we have an explanation of the astounding orgy of puritanism that goes on in the South—an orgy of repressive legislation not often to be matched in the whole history of Christendom. Down there is the true home of prohibition, with its endless spyings and denunciations, its pursuits and house-searchings, its general turmoil and dirtiness. In the middle West the thing has a certain austere dignity; there is a touch of asceticism in it; one feels somehow that those oafs on their lonely prairies really believe in it. But in the South, as in Maine, it is a mere malicious badgering of the other fellow, a struggle to force rectitude upon him, a conspiracy against his effort to let some joy into his life.

Does he recreate himself after work when he might be working more? Then let him go to the rockpile! Does he reach out for an easier, looser habit, disdaining the sordid fears and aspirations of the upstart? Then let him be jailed. Is he, perhaps, a poet? Then let him keep to hymns—or take his turn.

(The New York Evening Mail, November 13, 1917)

A Chance for Novelists

I

Of novels of Washington life there have been a-plenty since Pennsylvania avenue was paved, but I can recall only one, Harvey Fergusson's *Capitol Hill*, of any value either as work of art or as social document. The badness of the others has not been due, in most cases, to the ignorance of their authors—that is, to ignorance of the people and the scene. Certainly Samuel G. Blythe knows Washington quite as well as the devil knows Paris; nevertheless, his tales of human existence there, when cast into the form of fiction, have all been dull. Why? Simply, I believe, because Blythe, like all of the other Washington novelists save Fergusson, has made the mistake of assuming that the essential conflict in Washington is between ideas. This is not true. The essential conflict there, as in Summit, N.J., and Vladivostock, is between desires.

In *Capitol Hill* there is no division of the *dramatis personae* between Democrats and Republicans, progressives and reactionaries, materialists and idealists, patriots and traitors; the only division is between men and women who have something, and men and women who want it. In that simple fact lies most of the book's curious reality. For the truth about Washington is that it is not a town of politics, in the ordinary sense; it is, if anything, a town almost devoid of politics. The people in the industrial cities and out on the farms take political ideas seriously; what they cherish in that department they refuse passionately to surrender. But so far as I know there are not a dozen men in Washington, high or low, who would not throw overboard, instantly and gladly, every political idea they are assured to be devoted to, including especially every political idea that has helped them into public office, if throwing the outfit overboard would help them to higher, grander, and more lucrative office. I say high or low, and I mean it literally. There has not been a President of the United States for half a century who did not, at some time or other in his career, perform a complete *volte face* in order to further his career. There is scarcely a United States senator who does not flop at least three times within the limits of a single session.

II

The novelists who write about Washington are partly recruited from the ranks of the Washington newspaper correspondents, perhaps the most naïve and unreflective body of literate men in Christendom, and for the rest from the ranks of those who read the dispatches of such correspondents, and take them seriously. The result is a gravely distorted and absurd picture of life in the capital city. One carries off the notion that the essential Washington drama is based on a struggle between a powerful and corrupt senator and a sterling young uplifter. The senator is about to sell out the republic to the steel trust, J. P. Morgan, or the Japs. The uplifter detects him, exposes him, drives him from public life, and inherits his job. The love interest is supplied by a fair stenographer who steals the damning papers from the senator's safe, or by an ambassador's wife who goes to the White House at 3 a.m., and, at the peril of her virtue, arouses the President and tells him what is afoot.

All this is poppycock. There are no senators in Washington powerful enough to carry on any such operations single handed, and few of them are corrupt: it is far too easy to bamboozle them to go to the expense of buying them. The most formidable bribe that the average senator receives from year's end to year's end is a bottle or two of very dubious Scotch, and that is just as likely to come from the agent of the South central Watermelon Grower's association as from John D. Rockefeller or the Mikado of Japan. Nor are there any sterling young uplifters in the town. The last was chased out before the Mexican war. There are today only gentlemen looking for something for themselves—publicity, eminence, puissance, jobs—especially jobs. Some take one line and some another. Further than that, the difference between them is no greater than the difference between a prohibition agent and a bootlegger, or tweedledum and tweedledee.

Ideas count for nothing in Washington, whether they be political, economic, or moral. The question isn't what a man thinks, but what he has to give away that is worth having. Ten years ago a professional prohibitionist had no more standing in the town than a professional astrologer, Assyriologist or wart remover; today, having proved that his gang can make or break congressmen, he gets all the deference that belongs to the chief justice. If William Z. Foster were elected President tomorrow, the most fanatical Coolidge men of today would flock to the White House the day after, and try to catch his eye. Coolidge, with Harding living, was an obscure and impotent fellow, viewed with contempt by everyone. The instant he mounted the throne he became a master mind.

III

Fergusson got all of this into *Capitol Hill*, which is not the story of a combat between the true and the false in politics, but the simple tale of a typical Washingtonian's struggle to the front—a tale that should be an inspiration to every Rotarian in the land. He begins as a petty job holder in the capitol itself, mailing congressional speeches to constituents on the steppes; he ends at the head of a glittering banquet table, with a senator to one side of him and a member of the cabinet to the other—a man who has somehow got power in his hands, and can dispense jobs, and is thus an indubitable somebody. Everybody in Washington who has jobs to dispense is somebody. The Hon. James John Davis, supreme emperor of the Moose and secretary of labor, is somebody. So is the Hon. Wayne B. Wheeler. So is the superintendent of the Zoological garden. So, even, is Mr. Coolidge—now.

This eternal struggle for jobs is sordid but, as Fergusson has shown, it is also extremely amusing. It brings out, as the moralists say, the worst that is in human nature, which is always the most charming. It reduces all men to one common level of ignominy, and so rids them of their customary false faces. They take on a new humanity. Ceasing to be guardians of the constitution, foes to the interests, apostles of economy, prophets of world peace, and suchlike banshees, they become ordinary men, like John Doe and Richard Roe. One beholds them sweating, not liquid idealism, but genuine sweat. They hope, fear, aspire, suffer. They are preyed upon, not by J. P. Morgan, but by designing cuties. They go to the White House, not to argue for the world court, but to hog patronage. From end to end of the chronicle there is absolutely no mention of the tariff, or of the farmer and his woes, or of the budget system, or of the far eastern question.

I marvel that more novelists have not gone to this lush and delightful material. The supply is endless, and lies wide open. Six months in Washington is enough to load an ambitious novelist for all eternity. (Think what George Moore has made of one love affair, 'way back in 1877!) The Washington correspondents, of course, look at it without seeing it, and so do all of the Washington novelists save Fergusson. But that is saying nothing. A Washington correspondent is one with a special talent for failing to see what is before his eyes. I have seen a whole herd of them sit through a national convention without once laughing.

IV

Fergusson, in *Capitol Hill*, keeps mainly to that end of Pennsylvania avenue which gives his book its name. I believe the makings of a far better novel of Washington life are to be found at the other end, to wit, in and about the alabaster cage which houses the heir of Washington, Lincoln, and Chester A. Arthur. Why, indeed, has no one ever put *kaiserliche Majestat* into fiction—save, of course, as a disembodied spirit, vaguely radiating idealism? The revelations in the Daugherty inquiry gave a hint of unworked riches—but there is enough dramatic and even melodramatic material without descending to scandal. A President is a man like the rest of us. He can laugh and he can groan. There are days when his breakfast agrees with him, and days when it doesn't. His eyes have the common optical properties: they can see a sweet one as far as they can see a member of the interstate commerce commission. All the funnels of intrigue are aimed at him. He is the common butt of every loud speaker. No other man in this sad vale has so many jobs to give out, or one-half so many. Try to imagine a day in his life, from dawn to midnight. Do it, and you will have the best Washington novel ever heard of.

(The Chicago Sunday Tribune, January 11, 1925)

On Literary Gents

On Literary Gents

Some time ago, discoursing in this place, I said that the chief subject of conversational remark among literary gents, at least in this great Republic, was the matter of their professional takings— that the common run of them seemed to be more interested in their honoraria than in anything else. There was, I fear, a certain exaggeration in the statement, and even a certain injustice. For there is one thing, in fact, the literary gents talk of even more than they talk of money. And that is the extremely painful character of the process whereby they get it.

Here, indeed, they all agree, and with great earnestness and eloquence. And the beautiful gals of the trade reinforce and ratify the plaint of the bucks. I know of no author, male or female, who does not believe and contend that writing is the most dreadful chore ever inflicted upon human beings. It is not only exhausting mentally; it is also extremely fatiguing physically. The writer leaves his desk, his day's work done, with his mind pumped dry of ideas and the muscles of his back and neck full of a crippling and painful stiffness. He has suffered horribly that the babies may be fed and beauty may not die.

The worst of it is that he must always suffer alone. If authors could work in large, well ventilated factories, like cigarmakers or garment workers, with plenty of their mates about and a flow of lively professional gossip to entertain them, their labor would be immensely lighter. But it is essential to their craft that they perform in tedious and vexatious operations *a capella,* and so the horrors of loneliness are added to its other unpleasantnesses. An author at work is continuously and inescapably in the presence of himself. There is nothing to divert and soothe him. So every time a vagrant regret or sorrow assails him it has him instantly by the ear, and every time a wandering ache runs down his leg it shakes him like the bite of a tiger.

*　*

I have yet to meet an author who was not a hypochondriac. Saving only physicians, who are always ill and in fear of death, the literati are perhaps the most lavish consumers of pills and philtres in this world, and the most-willing customers of surgeons. I can scarcely think of one, known to me personally, who is not constantly dosing himself with medicines, or regularly resorting to the knife. At the head of the craft stand men who are even more celebrated as invalids than they are as authors. I know one who—

But perhaps I had better avoid invading what, after all, may be private confidences, though they are certainly not imparted in confidential tones. The point is that an author, penned in a room during all his working hours with no company save his own, is bound to be more conscious than other men of the petty malaises that assail all of us. They tackle him, so to speak, in a vacuum; he can't seek diversion from them without at the same time suffering diversion from his work. And what they leave of him is tortured and demoralized by wayward and uncomfortable thoughts.

It must be obvious that other men, even among the intelligentsia, are not beset so cruelly. A judge on the bench, entertaining a ringing in the ears, can do his work almost as well as if he heard only the voluptuous rhetoric of the lawyers. A clergyman, carrying on his mummery, is not appreciably crippled by a sour stomach: what he says has been said before, and only scoundrels question it. And a surgeon, plying his exhilarating art and mystery, suffers no professional damage from the wild thought that the attending nurse is more slightly than his wife. But I defy any one to write a competent sonnet with a ringing in his ears, or to compose sound criticism with a sour stomach, or to do a plausible love scene in a novel with a head full of private amorous fancies. These things are sheer impossibilities. The poor literatus encounters them and their like every time he enters his workroom and spits on his hands. The moment the door bangs he begins a depressing losing struggle with his body and his mind.

* *

Why, then, do rational men and women engage in so barbarous and exhausting a vocation? What keeps them from deserting it for trades that are less onerous, and, in the public eye, more respectable? The answer, it seems to me, is as plain as mud. An author is simply a man in whom the normal vanity of all men is so vastly exaggerated that he finds it a sheer impossibility to hold it in. His overpowering impulse is to gyrate before his fellow men, flapping his wings and emitting defiant yells. This being forbidden by the *Polizei* of all civilized countries, he takes it out by putting his yells on paper. Such is the thing called self-expression.

In the confidences of the literati, of course, it is always depicted as something much more mellow and virtuous. Either they argue that they are moved by a yearning to spread the enlightenment and save the world, or they allege that what steams them and makes them leap is a passion for beauty. Both theories are quickly disposed of by an appeal to the facts. The stuff written by nine authors out of ten, it must be plain at a glance, has as little to do with spreading the enlightenment as the state papers of the late Dr. Warren Gamaliel Harding. And there is no more beauty in it, and no more sign of a feeling for beauty, than you will find in a hotel dining room or a college yell.

The impulse to create beauty, indeed, is rather rare in literary men, and almost completely absent from the younger ones. If it shows itself at all it comes as a sort of afterthought. My trade brings me into contact with a great many beginning authors, male and female. I think I may say truthfully that I have never encountered one, in the larval stage, who exhibited any passion for beauty, which is to say, any passion as what the world calls an artist. One and all, they were moved by a mere desire to make a noise. They yearned to be heard, read, attended to. They wanted their ideas to stagger humanity. Secondarily, most of them wanted to make money. Tertiarily, perhaps a few had an itch to manufacture loveliness. But not many.

* *

Some time ago I said here that most authors were dull fellows— that their conversation, taking one with another, was but little beyond that of so many Rotarians. There are, of course, brilliant exceptions. I know a few authors, and even a few successful ones —nay, even a few good ones—who are capital fellows, and full of that liveliness of mind and wide information which make conversation charming. But the majority have little to say that is worth hearing, and many have absolutely nothing. I can imagine no more horrible fate, indeed, than being penned up on a desert island with forty authors, especially if half of them were female.

What ails most of them, it seems to me, is precisely their defective feeling for beauty. It shows itself, commonly, in their almost incredible ignorance of the other arts. They seem to get very little pleasure out of beautiful things, and so their talk lacks imagination and enthusiasm—save for money. I'd have a hard job naming six American novelists who could be depended upon to recognize a fugue without prompting, or six poets who could give a rational account of the difference between a Gothic cathedral and a Standard Oil filling station. The thing goes even further. Most novelists, in my experience, know nothing of poetry, and very few poets have any feeling for the beauties of prose. As for the dramatists, three-fourths of them are unaware that such things as prose and poetry exist at all.

It pains me to set down such inconvenient and blushful facts. They will be seized upon, like my last confidences, by the evangelists of Kiwanis, and employed to support the doctrine that all authors are public enemies, and ought to be deported to Russia. I do not go so far. I simply say that many who pursue the literary life are less romantic and high toned than they might be—that communion with them is anything but the thrilling thing that provincial club ladies fancy. If the fact ought to be concealed, then blame my babbling upon scientific passion. That passion, today, happens to have me by the ear.

(*The Chicago Sunday Tribune, June 20, 1926*)

Mark Twain's Americanism

When Mark Twain died, in 1910, one of the magnificos who paid public tribute to him was William H. Taft, then President of the United States. "Mark Twain," said Dr. Taft, "gave real intellectual enjoyment to millions, and his works will continue to give such pleasure to millions yet to come. He never wrote a line that a father could not read to a daughter."

The usual polite flubdub and not to be exposed, perhaps, to critical analysis. But it was, in a sense, typical of the general view at that time, and so it deserves to be remembered for the fatuous inaccuracy of the judgment in it. For Mark Twain dead is beginning to show far different and more brilliant colors than those he seemed to wear during life, and the one thing no sane critic would say of him to-day is that he was the harmless fireside jester, the mellow chautauquan, the amiable old grandpa of letters that he was once so widely thought to be.

The truth is that Mark was almost exactly the reverse. Instead of being a mere entertainer of the mob, he was in fact a literary artist of the very highest skill and sophistication, and, in all save his superficial aspect, quite unintelligible to Dr. Taft's millions. And instead of being a sort of Dr. Frank Crane in cap and bells, laboriously devoted to the obvious and the uplifting, he was a destructive satirist of the utmost pungency and relentlessness, and the most bitter critic of American platitude and delusion, whether social, political or religious, that ever lived.

* *

Bit by bit, as his posthumous books appear, the true man emerges, and it needs but half an eye to see how little he resembles the Mark of national legend. Those books were written carefully and deliberately; Mark wrote them at the height of his fame; he put into them, without concealment, the fundamental ideas of his personal philosophy—the ideas which colored his whole view of the world. Then he laid the manuscripts away, safe in the knowledge that they would not see the light until he was under six feet of earth. We know, by his own confession, why he hesitated to print them while he lived; he knew that fame was sweet and he feared that they might blast it. But beneath that timorousness there was an intellectual honesty that forced him to set down the truth. It was really comfort he wanted, not fame. He hesitated, a lazy man, to disturb his remaining days with combat and acrimony. But in the long run he wanted to set himself straight.

Two of these books, *The Mysterious Stranger* and *What Is Man?* are now published, and more may be expected to follow at intervals. The latter, in fact, was put into type during Mark's lifetime and privately printed in a very limited edition. But it was never given to the public, and copies of the limited edition bring $40 or $50 at book auctions to-day. Even a pirated English edition brings a high premium. Now, however, the book is issued publicly by the Harpers, though without the preface in which Mark explained his reasons for so long withholding it.

* *

The ideas in it are very simple, and reduced to elementals, two in number. The first is that man, save for a trace of volition that grows smaller and smaller the more it is analyzed, is a living machine—that nine-tenths of his acts are purely reflex, and that moral responsibility, and with it religion, are thus mere delusions. The second is that the only genuine human motive, like the only genuine dog motive or fish motive or protoplasm motive is self interest—that altruism, for all its seeming potency in human concerns, is no more than a specious appearance—that the one unbroken effort of the organism is to promote its own comfort, welfare and survival.

Starting from this double basis, Mark undertakes an elaborate and extraordinarily penetrating examination of all the fine ideals and virtues that man boasts of, and reduces them, one after the other, to untenability and absurdity. There is no mere smartness in the thing. It is done, to be sure, with a sly and disarming humor, but at bottom it is done quite seriously and with the highest sort of argumentative skill. The parlor entertainer of Dr. Taft's eulogy completely disappears; in his place there arises a satirist with something of Rabelais's vast resourcefulness and dexterity in him, and all of Dean Swift's devastating ferocity. It is not only the most honest book that Mark ever did; it is, in some respects, the most artful and persuasive as a work of art. No wonder the pious critic of *The New York Times*, horrified by its doctrine, was forced to take refuge behind the theory that Mark intended it as a joke.

In *The Mysterious Stranger* there is a step further. *What Is Man?* analyzes the concept of man; *The Mysterious Stranger* boldly analyzes the concept of God. What, after all, is the actual character of this Being we are asked to reverence and obey? How is His mind revealed by His admitted acts? How does His observed conduct toward man square with those ideals of human conduct that He is said to prescribe, and whose violation He is said to punish with such appalling penalties?

* *

These are the questions that Mark sets for himself. His answers are, in brief, a complete rejection of the whole Christian theory—a rejection based upon a wholesale *reductio ad absurdum*. The thing is not mere mocking; it is not even irreverent; but the force of it is stupendous. I know of no agnostic document that shows a keener sense of essentials or a more deft hand for making use of the indubitable. A gigantic irony is in it. It glows with a profound conviction, almost a kind of passion. And the grotesque form of it—a child's story—only adds to the sardonic implacability of it.

As I say, there are more to come. Mark in his idle moments was forever at work upon some such riddling of the conventional philosophy, as he was forever railing at the conventional ethic in his private conversation. One of these pieces, highly characteristic, is described in Albert Bigelow Paine's biography. It is an elaborate history of the microbes inhabiting a man's veins. They divine a religion with the man as God; they perfect a dogma setting forth his desires as to their conduct; they engaged in a worship based upon the notion that he is immediately aware of their every act and jealous of their regard and enormously concerned about their welfare. In brief, a staggering satire upon the anthropocentric religion of man—a typical return to the favorite theme of man's egoism and imbecility.

All this sort of thing, to be sure, has its dangers for Mark's fame. Let his executors print a few more of his unpublished works—say, the microbe story and his sketch of life at the court of Elizabeth— and Dr. Taft, I dare say, will withdraw his pronunciamento that "he never wrote a line that a father could not read to his daughter." Already, indeed, the lady reviewers of the newspapers sound an alarm against him, and the old lavish praise of him begins to die down to whispers. In the end, perhaps, the Carnegie libraries will put him to the torture, and *The Innocents Abroad* will be sacrificed with *What Is Man?*

* *

But that effort to dispose of him is nothing now. Nor will it succeed. While he lived he was several times labeled and relabeled, and always inaccurately and vainly. At the start the national guardians of letters sought to dismiss him loftily as a hollow buffoon, a brother to Josh Billings and Petroleum V. Nasby. This enterprise failing, they made him a comic moralist, a sort of chautauquan in motley, a William Jennings Bryan armed with a slapstick. Foiled again, they promoted him to the rank of Thomas Bailey Aldrich and William Dean Howells, and issued an impertinent amnesty for the sins of his youth. Thus he passed from these scenes—ratified at last, but somewhat heavily patronized.

Now the professors must overhaul him again, and this time, I suppose, they will undertake to pull him down a peg. They will succeed as little as they succeeded when they tried to read him out of meeting in the early '80s. The more they tackle him, in fact, the more it will become evident that he was a literary artist of the very first rank, and incomparably the greatest ever hatched in these states.

One reads with something akin to astonishment of his superstitious reverence for Emerson—of how he stood silent and bareheaded before the great transcendentalist's house at Concord. One hears of him, with amazement, courting Whittier, Longfellow and Holmes. One is staggered by the news, reported by Traubel, that Walt Whitman thought "he mainly misses fire." The simple fact is that *Huckleberry Finn* is worth the whole work of Emerson with two-thirds of the work of Whitman thrown in for make-weight, and that one chapter of it is worth the whole work of Whittier, Longfellow and Holmes.

* *

Mark was not only a great artist; he was pre-eminently a great American artist. No other writer that we have produced has ever been more extravagantly national. Whitman dreamed of an America that never was and never will be; Poe was a foreigner in every line he wrote; even Emerson was no more than an American spigot for European, and especially German, ideas. But Mark was wholly of the soil. His humor was American. His incurable Philistinism was American. His very English was American. Above all, he was an American in his curious mixture of sentimentality and cynicism, his mingling of romanticist and iconoclast.

English Traits might have been written by any one of half a dozen Germans. The tales of Poe, printed as translations from the French, would have deceived even Frenchmen. And *Leaves of Grass* might have been written in London quite as well as in Brooklyn. But in *Huckleberry Finn*, in *A Connecticut Yankee* and in most of the short sketches there is a quality that is unmistakably and overwhelmingly national. They belong to our country and our time quite as obviously as the skyscraper or the quick lunch counter. They are as magnificently American as the Brooklyn Bridge or Tammany Hall.

Mark goes down the professorial gullet painfully. He has stuck more than once. He now seems fated to stick again. But these gaggings will not hurt him, nor even appreciably delay him. Soon or late the national mind will awake to the fact that a great man was among us—that in the midst of all our puerile rages for dubious foreigners we produced an artist who was head and shoulders above all of them.

(The New York Evening Mail, November 1, 1917)

Ambrose Bierce

The reputation of Ambrose Bierce, like that of Edgar Saltus, has always had something occult and artificial about it. He has been hymned in a passionate, voluptuous way by a small bank of disciples, and he has been passed over altogether by the great majority of American critics, and no less by the great majority of American readers. Certainly it would be absurd to say that he is generally read, even by the intelligentsia. Most of his books, in fact, are out of print and almost unobtainable, and there is little evidence that his massive collected works, printed in twelve volumes between 1909 and 1912, have gone into anything even remotely approaching a wide circulation.

I have a suspicion, indeed, that Bierce did a serious disservice to himself when he put those twelve volumes together. Already an old man at the time, he permitted his nostalgia for his lost youth to get the better of his critical faculty, never powerful at best, and the result was a depressing assemblage of wornout and fly-blown stuff, much of it quite unreadable. If he had boiled the collection down to four volumes, or even to six, it might have got him somewhere, but as it was his good work was lost in a maze of bad and indifferent work. I doubt that any one save the Bierce fanatics aforesaid has ever plowed through the whole twelve volumes. They are filled with epigrams against frauds long dead and forgotten, and echoes of old newspaper controversies, and experiments in fiction that belong to a dark and expired age.

In the midst of all this blather there are some pearls—more accurately, there are two of them. One consists of the series of epigrams called *The Devil's Dictionary*; the other consists of the war stories, commonly called *Tales of Soldiers and Civilians*. Among the latter are some of the best war stories ever written—things fully worthy to be ranged beside Zola's *L'Attaque du Moulin*, Kipling's *The Taking of Lungtungpen*, or Ludwig Thomas's *Handlergischer Soldat*. And among the former are some of the most gorgeous witticisms in the English language.

* *

Bierce, I believe, was the first writer of fiction ever to treat war realistically. He antedated even Zola. It is common to say that he came out of the civil war with a deep and abiding loathing of slaughter—that he wrote his war stories as a sort of pacifist. But this is certainly not believed by any one who knew him, as I did in his last years. What he got out of his service in the field was not a sentimental horror of it, but a cynical delight in it. It appeared to him as a sort of magnificent reductio ad absurdum of all romance. The world reviewed war as something heroic, glorious, idealistic. Very well, he would show how sordid and filthy it was—how stupid, savage, and degrading.

But to say this is not to say that he disapproved it. On the contrary, he vastly enjoyed the chance it gave him to set forth dramatically what he was always talking about and gloating over: the infinite imbecility of men. There was nothing of the milk of human kindness in old Ambrose; he did not get the nickname of Bitter Bierce for nothing. What delighted him most in this life was the spectacle of human cowardice and folly. He put man, intellectually, somewhere between the sheep and the horned cattle, and as a hero somewhere below the rats. His war stories, even when they deal with the heroic, do not depict soldiers as heroes; they depict them as bewildered fools, doing things without sense, submitting to torture and outrage without resistance, dying at last like hogs in Chicago, the literary capital of the United States.

So far in this life, indeed, I have encountered no more thoroughgoing cynic than Bierce. His disbelief in homo sapiens went even farther than Mark Twain's; he was quite unable to imagine the heroic in any ordinary sense. Nor, for that matter, the wise. Man, to him, was the most stupid and ignoble of animals. But at the same time the most amusing. Out of the spectacle of life about him he got an unflagging and Gargantuan joy. The obscene farce of politics delighted him. He was an almost amorous connoisseur of theology and theologians. He howled with mirth whenever he thought of a professor, a doctor, or a husband. His favorites among his contemporaries were such superb zanies as Bryan, Roosevelt, and Hearst.

* *

Another character that marked him, perhaps flowing out of this same cynicism, was his curious taste for the macabre. All of his stories show it. He delighted in hangings, autopsies, dissecting rooms. Death to him was not something repulsive, but a sort of low comedy—the last act of a squalid and rib rocking buffoonery. When, grown old and weary, he made his way to Mexico, marched into the revolution then going on, and had himself shot, there was certainly nothing in the transaction to surprise his acquaintances. The whole thing was typically Biercian. He died happy, one may be sure, if his executioners made a botch of dispatching him—if there was a flash of the grotesque at the end.

I once enjoyed the curious experience of going to a funeral with him. His conversation to and from the crematory was superb—a long series of gruesome but highly amusing witticisms. He had tales to tell of crematories that had caught fire and singed the mourners, of dead bibuli whose mortal remains had exploded, of widows guarding the fires all night to make sure that their dead husbands did not escape. The gentleman whose carcass we were burning had been a literary critic. Bierce suggested that his ashes be molded into bullets and shot at publishers, that they be presented to the library of the New York Lodge of Elks, that they be mailed anonymously to Ella Wheeler Wilcox. Later on, when he heard that they had been buried in Iowa, he exploded in colossal mirth. The last time I saw him he predicted that the peasants would dig them up and throw them over the state line. On his own writing desk, he once told me, he kept the ashes of a near relative. I suggested that the ceremental urn must be a formidable ornament.

"Urn, hell!" he exclaimed, "I keep them in a cigar box!"

* *

There is no adequate life of Bierce, and I doubt if any will ever be written. His daughter has forbidden the publication of his letters, and shows little hospitality, I am told, to volunteer biographers. One of his disciples, George Sterling, has written about him with great insight and affection, and another, Herman George Scheffauer, has greatly extended his fame abroad, especially in Germany. But neither seems disposed to do him in the grand manner, and I know of no one else competent to do so. He liked mystification, and there are whole stretches of his life that are unaccounted for. His end had mystery in it, too. It is assumed he was killed in Mexico, but no eye witness has ever come forward, and so the fact, if it is a fact, remains hanging in the air.

Bierce followed Poe in most of his short stories, but it is only a platitude to say that he wrote much better than Poe. His English was less tight and artificial; he had a far firmer grasp upon character; he was less literary and more observant. Unluckily, his stories seem destined to go the way of Poe's. Their influence upon the modern short story, at least on its higher levels, is almost nil. When they are imitated at all, it is by the lowly hacks who manufacture thrillers for the cheap magazines. Even his chief disciples Sterling and Scheffauer, do not follow him. Sterling is a poet whose glowing romanticism is at the opposite pole to Bierce's cold realism, and Scheffauer, interested passionately in experiment, has departed completely from the classicism of the master.

It is astonishing that his wit is so little remembered. In *The Devil's Dictionary* are some of the most devastating epigrams ever written. "Ah, that we could fall into women's arms without falling into their hands." It is hard to find a match for that in Oscar himself. I recall another: "Opportunity: a favorable occasion for grasping a disappointment." Another: "Once: enough." A third: "Husband, one who, having dined, is charged with the care of the plate." A fourth: "Our vocabulary is defective: we give the same name to woman's lack of temptation and man's lack of opportunity." A fifth: "Slang is the speech of him who robs the literary garbage cans on their way to the dump."

But I leave the rest to your own exploration.

(The Chicago Sunday Tribune, March 1, 1925)

Poe's Start in Life

For years it has been known that there existed in Richmond, Va., in the so-called Valentine museum, a packet of letters from Edgar Allan Poe to his foster-father, John Allan. A great mystery was made about them, for what reason I do not know, and few outsiders seem to have ever got a glimpse of them. But now they are all printed in a stately book, at $15 a copy, and so the whole world, or at all events the highly solvent minority, is free to read them at last. They are presented in transcript and in facsimile, and in front of each one there are useful explanations by an estimable Richmond lady, Mrs. Mary Newton Stanard.

As I say, I don't know why they were held back so long, for certainly there is nothing in them of a scandalous nature—that is, nothing save the news that Poe was once in danger of imprisonment for debt, a common hazard in his time, and his accusation in one letter that old Allan was "not very often sober," certainly nothing astonishing in the Richmond of 1830. After Allan's death, his surviving widow—not Poe's foster-mother, but a successor—gave the letters to her niece's husband, one Mayo, and in 1882 Mayo passed them on to Mann S. Valentine, a cousin of the first Mrs. Allan. This Valentine founded the Valentine museum, and there the letters gathered cobwebs, unread but much gabbled about, until a month ago.

There are twenty-seven letters from Poe to Allan, two from Allan to Poe, one from Mrs. Clemm to Allan, and one from Poe to Sergt. Samuel Graves of the regular army, a friend of Poe's soldiering days, from whom he borrowed money. Graves, evidently in despair of getting it back, sent the letter to Allan, and so the latter became privy to his foster-son's allegation that he was given to the bowl. There was no truce between Allan and Poe after that. The old man simply washed his hands of the young poet. Edgar was at last wholly on his own.

* *

The letters do little credit to either party to the long row. Poe alternates between whining and defiance. In one letter he protests that he is innocent of all the mysterious charges brought against him by his foster-father; in the next he begs maudlinly to be forgiven. Almost always he ends with a demand for money—often for a sum that, in those simple days, was enough to make even a well to do business man wince. Apparently it never occurred to Poe to go to work; a stout lad of 20, he was content to sponge upon Allan and upon his aged and poverty stricken grandmother, widow of Washington's quartermaster general, rather than get him a job. His enlistment in the army was mere melodrama. In a short while he was begging Allan to buy his discharge, and when the transaction was finally arranged he seems to have made an excellent profit on it.

As for Allan, he makes, in these tattered letters, a ridiculous and ignominious showing. Obviously, he was a Babbitt of purest ray serene: Poe's tendencies toward versifying not only failed to meet his encouragement, but aroused his violent opposition. He was apparently convinced that any young man who made rhymes was full of sin and doomed to the gallows. When *Tamerlane* came out, he got into a fearful sweat; when the Baltimore volume followed, he excommunicated his foster-son with bell and book. There is something downright pathetic, after all these years, in his tremors. He honestly believed that Poe, as a poet, would bring eternal dishonor upon the Allan house.

Worse, he was what has come to be called, in the language of modern America, a tightwad, and never yielded up a cent without a groan. He sent Poe to the University of Virginia with exactly $110 in hand. It was not enough, by two-thirds, for the first year's expenses. Poe had to pay $50 down for board and $60 for tuition fees, leaving him with nothing for room rent, furniture, and books. He sought to augment his funds by gambling, and was presently stone broke and in debt. Allan thereupon refused to pay his debts—some of them regarded by the Virginians of the time as debts of honor. In consequence, Poe had to leave the university.

* *

Most ambitious young men of today, so used by an unintelligent crab, would kiss him good-by and go to work. There were jobs in those days, as in these. But from some unknown source Poe had picked up the notion that a literary man needed what he called "a

liberal education," and so, instead of going on his own, he renewed his efforts to squeeze it out of the right thinking Allan.
Even his enlistment in the army as a common soldier was a device
to that end; he believed Allan would promptly buy his discharge
and return him to the university. When the scheme failed, he began his long effort to get into West Point.

It must be obvious, in retrospect, that this faith in "education"
was mistaken—that Poe would have escaped some of his worst
faults and so made his fame even more secure than it is if he had
never gone to college at all. The University of Virginia, in his
time, had just been started; its faculty was small and the courses it
offered were old fashioned and meager. It was nothing like the
great American universities of today; it was rather like the forlorn
one building "colleges" of the prairies. All it had to teach Poe was
a smattering of this and a smattering of that. It gave him the
delusion that he was an educated man without actually teaching
him anything worth knowing.

The fruits of that delusion appear in all that Poe wrote, and
especially in his criticism. He was a shrewd and able critic—perhaps the ablest America has ever produced—but his critical writings were so heavily burdened with pedantic affectations that they
had no influence in his day and have been forgotten since. He
could not write ten lines without trying to display his learning—
and most of it was bogus learning, schoolmasters' learning. Day
after day he dished up his stale scraps. He wanted people to admire him as a linguist, as a scientist, as a philosopher. And the
only result was that they failed to see his genuine worth as a critic.

* *

But the notion that Poe had to wait long for recognition and
that he had a hard time getting it is mainly sentimental. True
enough, he was never properly appreciated in his lifetime as a
critic, but all that belonged to the latter part of his life, long after
his celebrity as a poet and writer of stories was nationwide. His
poetry got notice almost instantly, and from competent men. His
first book was printed when he was but 18 years old; by the time he
was 22 he had three volumes behind him. And they were read and
praised.

One of the first to hail him was John Neal, editor of the Boston
Literary Gazette and perhaps the foremost American critic of the
era. Poe sent Neal some of his early poems and Neal gave them a

friendly notice in the *Literary Gazette*. Moreover, it was intelligent as well as friendly, for it pointed out Poe's tendency to put words above ideas. The things on his table, said Neal, were "rather exquisite nonsense"—but still nonsense. A profound criticism, and never bettered since. The best poems of Poe are lovely things, indeed, but they are as devoid of logical content as so many college yells.

Poe must have told Neal all his troubles, for the latter, in a subsequent issue of the *Literary Gazette*, gave him some excellent and much needed advice. It was to the general affect that a young poet's chief need in life is a "magnanimous determination to endure the present," letting the future take care of itself. The advice was wasted. Poe kept on hammering old Allan for money and posturing melodramatically as an ill used fellow. It became, in the end, his fixed character. He saw himself always as a pearl cast before swine. In the days, later on, when every American magazine was printing his stuff and the blue stockings of the time were flocking to hear him lecture—that is, whenever he was sober enough to perform—he indulged himself in maudlin debauches of self-pity and saw the whole world in conspiracy against him. A genius, and if not of the first rank, then at least near the top of the second—but a foolish, disingenuous, and often somewhat trashy man.

(*The Chicago Sunday Tribune, November 1, 1925*)

James Huneker

I

Two classes of men exist on this vast, lumbering, hideous, obscene ball of mud—the football of the devil. Those of the first class, probably 99.99998743%, labor horribly all their lives long that the rewards thereof may bring them a few moments of joy. Those of the other class, say .00001257%, get their joy out of their labor. To belong to this second class is to be one of the darlings of the gods—to enjoy daily such a huge good fortune that even the cherubim and seraphim, singing around the Throne, can scarcely be conceived as enjoying greater, save perhaps, on Sundays and legal holidays.

Well, the late James Huneker was one of these darlings. I have never known a man who had a better time of it in this world. Nor can I think of one that I have not known—not even Roosevelt, for Roosevelt was always gnawed by bounderish ambition and puerile vanities, and he died a disappointed and a bitter man. Huneker, of course, occasionally had to do without, too. Early in life, for example, he wanted to be a piano virtuoso—a romantic fellow with a shad-belly and long hair, eternally touring Europe, America, Asia, Africa and Oceania, the pet of flappers and aesthetic multiparae, the hero of love-affairs with harpists, countesses, Brünnhildes, and Marguerites de Gauthier. This noble aspiration, alas, came to naught. His thumbs, to the end, intruded gravel into the string of pearls. But the sharp edge of grief, if it was ever sharp at all, had been dulled long before I met him. By that time, having reached the middle years, he was content to play like a gentleman—Chopin as a steady diet, with Czerny to keep his knuckles oiled. Piano-playing was now mere play: work was criticism. And what a riotous time he had of it doing that work! What a stupendous gusto he put into it, and what a homeric joy he got out of it!

II

The first time I ever met Huneker was at Lüchow's famous tabernacle of beer in Fourteenth street, now a Herculaneum. Here he and Rafael Joseffy used to sit of an evening, and here he transacted most of his critical and personal business during the day. We sat down to *Rinderbrust mit Meerrettig* at one o'clock; at six, when I had to leave, Huneker had his tenth *Seidel* of Pilsner before him, and was launching into an intricate and enormously interesting account of the scandals at Bayreuth in 1886. What I carried away, at first flush, seemed no more than an impression of having read 20 volumes folio of a sort of international *Town Topics*—a meticulous and astounding chronicle of the drinking habits, love affairs, debts, private quarrels, warts, wens, blood pressures and tastes in victualry of every author, artist, composer, singer, conductor and actor in Europe, from Auber to Zola.

But that was only the first dizziness. Sorting out the loot the next day, I began to perceive that a sharp and searching criticism had leavened all this gossip—that when Huneker described the collars that Richard Strauss wore and the girl that Nietzsche fell in love with at Sils Maria, he was also, in his vivid and disarming way, delivering sound criticisms of "Ein Heldenleben" and "Jenseits von Gut und Böse." The better I got to know him, the more I understood this method, and the more I came to value it. For of all the things that he brought back with him from his early years in Paris, perhaps the best of all was the French critical doctrine that the work of art is inseparable from the artist—that what a man does is infinitely and inescapably conditioned by what he is. Huneker never had any doubt of it. Whenever he heard of a new man, his first curiosity was always about the man, the man's work could wait. It was by this route that he enriched his criticism with its innumerable small illuminations and got into it its extraordinary brilliancy and intimacy, its air of confidential revelation, its incomparable human interest. And it was thus that, in his own way, following his own sure instinct, he met the test for critics that Benedetto Croce sets up, following Goethe, Carlyle and all the royal line—the test that asks of criticism, not only a clear account of what the artist has done, but also a clear account of what he tried to do, and wherefore, and why.

III

This habit of studying the artist as a man was responsible, I believe, for most of Huneker's foreignness—a quality always urged against him in high dudgeon by the pedagogues who disliked him. He kept his eyes turned across the water because it was simply impossible for him to imagine a normal American being a great artist. Playing the fiddle is not a mere matter of irritating four wires of catgut and copper with a switch from a horse's tail: it is also a matter of inner attitudes, of private metaphysics, even of metabolism. One simply cannot image it done competently by a man who will leave the hall after it is over to be initiated into the Moose, or to attend a watch-night meeting in some forlorn chapel on a suburban dump, or to hear a lecture at the Harvard Club, or to sup on Uneeda biscuits and grapejuice.

So in all the other arts; so doubly on their creative sides. Huneker was the first American critic, after Poe, who was also an artist himself; all the rest were mere grammarians, theme-correctors, floggers of sophomores. Being an artist, he knew how cruelly unfavorable the national atmosphere was to the clan—how pitifully unlikely it was that Allentown, or Kansas City, or even New York would ever produce a Brahms. What he saw around him was simply a gigantically elaborated correctness—a system of taboos almost Polynesian in its scope—a race of people that had come even to exult and dream by a sort of goose-step. Where was there room for the gigantic eccentricity of the artist, his great disdain of Philistine conformity, his eager and iconoclastic curiosity, his rebellion against all the pruderies and holy joys of the greengrocer and the cheesemonger? "I am against tripe-sellers in the market-place," said Huneker in one of his last books. But here tripe-selling was respectable, honorable, almost a sacred rite. It was no wonder that he was forever sneaking aboard a *Doppel-schraubeuschnellpostdampfer* and seeking adventures for his soul in foreign parts. He could savor Wagner and Villiers de L'isle-Adam; he could even understand Maeterlinck and Yeats; but Henry van Dyke was incomprehensible to him, and the lady novelists simply maddened him.

IV

No man, of course, can stand quite clear of his country, its epistemology may sicken him, but he nevertheless breathes its air. Huneker had his moments when the Americano engulfed the artist. You will find the records of some of them in *Steeplejack*, a book of his decline, and full of doubts and hesitations. He was swept, in a weak mood, into the flaming orbit of Roosevelt, the incomparable mountebank. He parroted patriotic tosh. He tried to convince the pedagogues against all the evidence, that he was actually a sturdy supporter of the national letters. He allowed the *Saturday Evening Post* brethren to hang him with the ribbon of the National Institute of Arts and Letters—Beethoven elected to the Elks. He yielded to sentimentality, and praised frauds and dunderheads.

But not often. *Steeplejack* was written by diabetes, not by Huneker. Go back to his earlier books—*Iconoclasts, The Pathos of Distance, Melomaniacs, Visionaries,* above all, *Old Fogy.* Here is a body of criticism that is stupendously alive—criticism made into an art as brilliantly vivid as music. Here is stuff that is sound and important. The man who did it was no common man.

(The Baltimore Evening Sun, February 14, 1921)

Joseph Conrad

I

With Meredith gone and James gone, only Thomas Hardy remains to challenge the position of Joseph Conrad, the Pole, as the first living English novelists. He has been steadily growing in stature for a dozen years; he has of late taken his undisputed place in the front rank. A sombre spirit, still overwhelmingly Slavic, despite his long expatriation, he has brought into English fiction a note that sounds a deep bass beneath the prevailing chatter of lighter tones. There is no one like him; there is no one even remotely like him; he stands almost as solitary as Blake, or Richard Burton, or, to come nearer home, Ambrose Bierce. No wonder he refuses to fit into the shining generalities of the professors of literature! No wonder they deal with him gingerly and suspiciously! The man has done much more than open a new box of tricks. He has restored passion to the English novel. He has rescued it from mere clever craftsmanship, and put into it the sober beauty of a profound and moving art.

"Under all Conrad's stories," says Wilson Follet, in an excellent little study, "there ebbs and flows a kind of tempered melancholy, a sense of seeking and not finding." . . . The saying defines both the mood of the stories as works of the imagination and their burden and direction as criticisms of human life. Conrad, like Theodore Dreiser, is forever fascinated by "the immense indifference of things," the essential futility of all hope and striving, the meaninglessness of existence—fascinated, and left wondering. One looks in vain for any attempt at a solution of the riddle in the whole canon of his work. Dreiser, more than once, seems ready to take refuge in a vague sort of mysticism, but Conrad, from first to last, faces squarely the massive and intolerable fact.

II

His stories are not chronicles of heroes who conquer fate, nor even of heroes who hold out indomitably to the end, but of men who are themselves conquered and undone. Each protagonist is a new Prometheus; each goes down a Greek route to defeat and disaster, leaving nothing behind him save an unanswered question. I can scarcely recall an exception. Kurtz, Lord Jim, Razumov, Nostromo, old Captain Whalley, Yanko Goorall, Verloc, Heyst, Gaspar Ruis, Almayer: one and all they are destroyed by the blind, incomprehensible forces that beset them.

Even in *Youth* and *Typhoon,* superficially stories of the indomitable, that same vast melancholy, that same pressing sense of the irresistible and inexplicable, ebbs and flows beneath the surface. Captain MacWhirr gets the *Nan-Shan* to port at last; but it is a victory that stands quite outside the man himself; he is no more than a marker in the unfathomable game; the elemental forces, fighting one another, almost disregard him; the view of him that we get is one of disdain, almost one of contempt. So, too, in *Youth.* A tale of the spirit's triumph, of youth beating destiny? I do not see it so. To me its significance is all subjective; it is an aging man's hymn to the hope and high resolution that the years have blown away, a sentimental reminiscence of what the implacable gods have made a joke of, leaving only its gallant memory behind.

The whole Conradean system sums itself up in the title of *Victory,* an incomparable piece of irony. Imagine a better label for that tragic record of heroic and yet bootless effort, that incomparable picture, in microcosm, of the relentless, cruel revolutions in the macrocosm.

III

Mr. Follet, with too much critical facility, finds the cause of Conrad's unyielding pessimism in the circumstances of his own life—his double exile, first from Poland, and then from the sea. But this is surely stretching the facts to fit an hypothesis. Neither exile, it must be plain, was enforced, nor is either irrevocable. Conrad has been back to Poland, and he is free to return to the ships whenever the spirit moves him. I see no reason for looking in such directions for his view of the world, nor even in the direction of his nationality. We detect curious qualities in every Slav simply because he is more given than we are to revealing the qualities that are in all of us. Introspection is his habit; he carries the study of man and fate to a point that seems morbid to Westerners; but in the last analysis his verdicts are the immemorial and almost universal ones.

Surely his resignationism, so penetratingly described by William Lyon Phelps in the first of his essays on the Russian novelists, is not a Slavic copyright; all human philosophies and religions seem doomed to come to it at last. Once it takes shape as the concept of Nirvana, the desire for nothingness, the will to not-will. Again, it is fatalism in this form or that—Mohammedanism, Agnosticism . . . Presbyterianism! Yet, again, it is the "Out, out, brief candle!" of Shakespeare, the *Vanitas vanitatum; omnia vanitus!"* of the Preacher. Or, to make an end, it is millennialism, the theory that the world is going to blow up tomorrow, or the day after, or two weeks hence, and that all sweating and striving are thus useless. Search where you will, near or far, in ancient or modern times, and you will never find a race or an age that gave more than a passing bow to optimism!

Even Christianity, starting out as "glad tidings," has had to take on protective coloration to survive, and today its loudest professors moan and blubber like a prophet in a rain barrel. The sanctified are few and far between. The vast majority of us must suffer in hell, just as we suffer on earth. The divine grace, so omnipotent to save, is withheld from us. Why? There, alas, is your insoluble mystery, your riddle of the universe!

IV

This conviction that human life is a seeking without a finding, that its purpose is impenetrable, that joy and sorrow are alike meaningless, you will see written largely in the work of all great artists. It is obviously the final message, if any message is to be sought there at all, of the nine symphonies of Ludwig van Beethoven. It is the idea that broods over Wagner's Ring, as the divine wrath broods over the Old Testament. In Shakespeare, as Shaw has demonstrated, it amounts to a veritable obsession. What else is there in Turgenev, Dostoievski, Andrieff? Or in the Zola of *L'Assommoir, Germinal, La Débâcle,* the whole Rougon-Macquart series? (The Zola of *Les Quatres Evangiles,* and particularly of *Fécondité,*

turned uplifter and optimist, and became ludicrous.) Or in Haupt-
mann, or Hardy, or Sudermann? (I mean, of course, Sudermann
the novelist; Sudermann the dramatist is a mere mechani-
cian.) . . .

The younger men of today, in all countries, seem to cherish this
philosophy of impotence and surrender. Consider the last words
of *Riders to the Sea*. Or Gorky's *Nachtasyl*. Or Frank Norris'
McTeague. Or Dreiser's *Jennie Gerhardt*. Or George Moore's *Sister
Theresa*.

Conrad, more than any other of the men I have mentioned,
grounds his whole work upon a sense of this "immense indifference of things." The exact point of the story of Kurtz, in *Heart of
Darkness*, is that it is pointless, that Kurtz's death is as meaningless
as his life, that the moral of such a sordid tragedy is a wholesale
negation of all morals. And this, no less, is the point of the story of
Falk, and of that of Almayer, and of that of Jim. Mr. Follet (he
must be an American!) finds himself, in the end, unable to accept
so profound a pessimism unadulterated, and so he injects a gratu-
itous and mythical optimism into it, and hymns Conrad as "a comrade, one of a company, gathered under the ensign of hope for
common war on despair." With the highest respect, Pish! Conrad
makes war upon nothing; he is pre-eminently *not* a moralist. He
swings, indeed, as far from moralizing as is possible, for he does
not even criticize God. His undoubted comradeship, his plain
kindliness toward the souls he vivisects, is not the child of hope,
but of pity. Like Mark Twain, he might well say: "The more I see
of men, the more I laugh at them—and the more I pity them." He
is *simpatico* precisely because of his infinite commiseration. . . .

I have said that he does not criticize God; one may imagine him
even pitying God. . . .

V

As for Conrad the literary artist, opposing him for the moment
to Conrad the interpreter of human life, the quality that all who
write about him seem chiefly to mark in him is his deficient grasp
of form, his tendency to approach his story from two directions at
once, his frequent involvement in almost inextricable snarls of
narrative, sub-narrative and sub-sub-narrative.

Lord Jim starts out conventionally in the third person, presently
passes into an exhaustive psychological discussion by the mythical

Marlow, then goes into a brisk narrative at second (and sometimes third) hand, and finally comes to a halt on an unresolved dissonance, a half-heard chord of the ninth: "And that's the end. He passes away under a cloud inscrutable at heart, forgotten, unforgiven and excessively romantic." *Falk* is also a story within a story; this time the narrator is "one who had not spoken before, a man over 50." In *Amy Foster* the story is told by a country doctor; in *Under Western Eyes* by "a teacher of languages," endlessly lamenting his lack of the "high gifts of imagination and expression"; in *Youth* and *Heart of Darkness*, by Marlow; in *Romance (circa* 1900) the form is autobiographical; in *Chance* there are two separate stories, imperfectly welded together. Almost always there is heaviness in the getting under weigh. In *Heart of Darkness* we are on the twentieth page before we use the mouth of the great river, and in *Falk* we are on the twenty-fourth before we get a glimpse of Falk. *Chance* is nearly half done before the drift of the action is clearly apparent; in *Almayer's Folly* we are thrown into the middle of a story, and do not learn its beginning until we come to *An Outcast of the Islands,* a later book.

And in detail, as in structure, Conrad is full of hesitations and goings-back. He pauses to explain, to look about, to speculate. Whole chapters concern themselves with detailed discussions of motives, with exchanges of view, with generalizations. Even the author's own story. *A Personal Record* (in the English edition, *Some Reminiscences),* starts near the end, and then goes back, halting fortunately, to the beginning. . . .

VI

A fault? In the eyes of formalists, undoubtedly yes. To the reader accustomed, by incessant reading of the swift and superficial, to action, action, action, this method is loaded with weariness. And yet, in the end, I am inclined to see it as one of the chief causes, and perhaps the chiefest of them all, of that startling reality which Conrad invariably gets into his stories, even into the worst of them. They are, beyond everything, brilliant, convincing, vivid—and the origin of that vividness lies precisely in the dimness he so deliberately leaves there.

A paradox, of course, but I do not devise it for its own sake. What I mean to say is that Conrad always shows us a picture that is full of the little obscurities, the uncertainties of outline, the mysterious shadings-off, that we see in the real world around us. He does not pretend to the traditional omniscience of the novelist. He is not forever translating the unknowable in motive and act into ready formula; instead, he says frankly that he does not know, or, at best, "I believe," or "perhaps," or "Marlow thinks it possible."

A trick? To be sure. But also much more than a trick, for its constant repetition not only constitutes a manner but also indicates a state of mind. Conrad knows his characters too well to explain them too glibly. They are too real to him (and to us) to be made quite understandable. They keep to the end all of that fine mysteriousness which forever hangs about those who are most vividly before us. . . .

A man may profess to understand the President of the United States, but he seldom alleges, even to himself, that he understands his own wife.

(The Baltimore Evening Sun, June 20, 1916)

Peasant and Cockney

I

The extraordinary success of Sinclair Lewis' novel, *Main Street*, is hailed by many of the intelligentsia as proof of a new and highly gratifying interest in beautiful letters in America. It is actually nothing of the sort. *Main Street* is being vaselined by the newspaper Brander Mathewses and pawed by the women's clubs, not because it happens to be a very competent piece of writing, but simply and solely because it presents an extremely acidulous picture of human existence in a small American town, and thus caresses the vanity of all those who are able to thank God that they do not live in such a town, and are not as Dr. Lewis' folks are. In brief, its popularity rests upon malice far more than on anything properly describable as aesthetic appreciation. It is a big-city success, and so, since nine-tenths of all novel readers, live in big cities—the norm is a fattish and somewhat oxidized woman in a faded kimono, lying on a *chaise-lounge* on a rainy afternoon reading, smoking Camel cigarettes and dreaming of love—it is also a great financial success.

Here, of course, I do not sniff at Herr von Lewis' achievement. On the contrary, I seize the opportunity to say again, as I said a good while back, that *Main Street* is a very excellent piece of work, boldly imagined and often brilliantly executed. Some of its scenes —for example, the scene of the banquet of town boomers and that of the sermon by the Methodist dervish—combine a Dreiserian ruthlessness of observation with a Cabellian-Rabelaisian richness of humor—a truly amazing combination, goodness knows. But what I maintain is this—that the average reader of the book does not admire and enjoy this capital writing, he (or she) simply laughs at the monkey-shines of the Lewison poor fish and scuramouches, as a Presbyterian laughs at the Old Testament syntax of a Yiddish zanie in a vaudeville show.

II

This, alas, is not quite as it should be. There should be more aesthetic understanding in the land. Books as good as *Main Street* should be admired on a plane above mere prejudices, as the Parthenon and *Heart of Darkness* and Brahms' fourth symphony are admired. More, books that are better than *Main Street*—for example, Willa Cather's *My Ántonia* and Sherwood Anderson's *Winesburg, Ohio*—should be admired a great deal more, which is assuredly not the case. Again, the cockney should not be so ready to laugh at the poor yokel: he is quite as thumping an ass himself.

Consider our own imperial town, great Baltimore. Is its average citizen more civilized and intelligent than the average citizen of Gopher Prairie, as depicted by M. Lewis? I presume to doubt it. We have dervishes here who are fully as idiotic as the holy clerk in *Main Street;* we have had town boomers quite as noisy and hollow as Gopher Prairie's: we have women's clubbers, uplifters, bridge-players, neighborhood doctors, storekeepers and other such fauna who might be brothers and sisters to Lewis' poor mimes. Moreover, we have many more of them than Gopher Prairie has, and they are far more pretentious, and hence far more preposterous. There is nothing in his book so magnificently imbecile as the Merchants and Manufacturers' Association as it was in the palmy days of resoluting and honorary-pallbearing. He describes no intelligentsia so laughable as those who lately confessed that they had never heard of Lizette Woodworth Reese. He mentions no public building so inconceivably hideous as the Mulberry street home of the Enoch Pratt Library, or, for that matter, the bastile of the *Sunpaper*.

Two things surely lift this Dr. and Mrs. Kennicott far above the Baltimore level of mammalian life. One is that Dr. Kennicott, though a Philistine and a Knight of Pythias, is also a genuinely competent operative surgeon, with even a few glimmerings of pathology. The other is that Carol Kennicott, despite her reading of Maeterlinck, is really a very pretty and charming gal—one that any man might kiss behind the door without loss of self-respect. I invite you to contemplate the average Baltimore saw-bones—and the average Baltimore lady uplifter and yearner.

III

Alas, that no Baltimore novelist has ever put this town into a vast tome, as Lewis has put Gopher Prairie! Nyburg has nibbled around the edges of the subject, but he has never attempted it headlong, and with all arms. The tale would cover all other second-rate American cities, as *Main Street* covers all the Gopher Prairies between Salisbury and the Pacific Coast. They are all pretty much alike—huge, overblown villages run by lodge-joiners and green-grocers, some of them disguised as bankers, publicists and pedagogues. It is flattering to such folks to call them materialists, for a materialist is at least one who appreciates sauce Hollandaise. One grasps, perhaps, what is in their minds when one reflects that they are in favor of having a municipal symphony orchestra on the ground that it advertises the city. Imagine it! Beethoven as a sandwich man!

But the field remains strangely unworked. There are many American novels dealing with city life, and some of them tackle it on a large scale, but I can think of none that actually depicts the general life, the communal life; they all deal with some narrow circle, high or low, or with politics. The thing ought to be done in the manner of Arnold Bennett—which manner Lewis frankly borrowed for *Main Street*. Bennett sees everything, but he knows how to pick and choose; his story is never drowned in detail. Moreover, he knows that devastating satire is not enough; there must also be some feeling. Lewis gets that feeling into *Main Street*. His satire is uproarious, but it is never merely ill-natured. He is artist and humanist enough to see what Thackeray always forgot: that there is a man beneath the flunky's plush. One parts from Dr. Kennicott with something strangely resembling respect for him. He lies in the gutter with hogs, boomers, grand archons, poker-players and life-long Republicans, but his soul has caught a vision of the eternal stars.

IV

The idle reader, sweating through *Main Street* pleasantly, as through an agreeable game of tennis, will perhaps underrate it as a literary event. It is actually a phenomenon of the first order, and vastly more significant than a dozen books by Edith Wharton. What it represents is the first successful revolt of an inmate of the *Saturday Evening Post* seraglio. For years Lewis has been a popular and prosperous manufacturer of conventional fiction. He knows how to produce such stuff with an almost infallible art. He can concoct what looks to Gopher Prairie to be romance. He can arrest and enthrall the literary shoe-drummer in the Pullman smoking room. He has a fine talent for intriguing the melancholy housewife in her spotty kimono. His gift is one that is hugely rewarded in the republic. He gets more for one bad short story than Moses got for the whole Pentateuch.

Nevertheless, he gagged and revolted. Nevertheless, he felt the stirring of strange desires within him. Nevertheless, he turned his back upon all that easy money, spat homerically upon his hands, and set out to write a novel that should be genuinely good. Curiously enough, it is bringing him in more mazuma than even his shockers for shoe-drummers. For the first time, perhaps, in human history, virtue is actually its own reward.

(The Baltimore Evening Sun, January 3, 1921)

Sherwood Anderson

None of the new writers who have come into notice since the close of the Howells era in American letters seems to offer more difficulties to the academic critics than Sherwood Anderson. They alternately flirt with him and flee from him; it seems impossible for them to decide definitely either to embrace him, as they have embraced Sinclair Lewis and Hergesheimer, or to condemn him finally to their campus hell, as they have condemned Cabell and Dreiser.

The reason is not far to seek. Academic criticism is grounded firmly upon the doctrine that all literary values may be established scientifically and beyond cavil, as the values of hog fodders, say, may be established—in other words, that criticism is an exact science, like thermodynamics or urinalysis. It must thus view literature, the material it works with, as something complete, solid, definitive, static—something that begins from a premise and comes to a conclusion. Anderson throws that whole doctrine overboard. Literature, as he sees it and tries to produce it, is not a verdict but an inquiry. The agony of man in this world interests him immensely, but he doesn't know what causes it and he has no remedy for it. He describes it, he speculates about it, he feels the tragedy of it, but the riddle that is in it he doesn't undertake to solve.

This method leaves the learned professors dizzy and more than a little indignant. They like a more lucid and facile manner, a more elegant omniscience and tighter conclusions—conclusions that slip readily into pigeon-holes and may be fished out on occasion and inserted into the cerebral orifices of sophomores. A thing without a plain label, brilliantly printed in red, is something, to a pedagogue, that simply does not exist, or, at all events, that would not exist if the police were not so busy with bootlegging that they neglect all their duties to the human soul. Thus holding as a primary article of faith, the gentlemen of the birch are chilly to Anderson. Now and then—so artful is the fellow!—he wobbles them transiently, but always in the end they go back to the view that he is a quack and immoral, and sometimes they add the uneasy suspicion that he is spoofing them.

* *

But spoofing, I believe, is actually as far from Anderson's program as it is from Dreiser's or Mr. Coolidge's. He is, at bottom, a very serious fellow, and even his superficial humors have a tart and ferruginous flavor. What interests him most is not the show that life is, or the moral lesson, but the desperate struggle. Most of all, he is interested in that struggle on its lower levels, among poor, stupid and helpless folk. He sees it down there, not as some-thing trivial, but as something poignant and thrilling—a drama of commonplaces all compact, but deeply moving for all that. Thus, in his work, the idea of tragedy that prevailed among the Greeks is stood on its head. To the Greeks tragedy was a function of heroes, and of heroes only. No woes below those of an archbishop or a major-general of cavalry could move them. If a king lost an ear they shuddered and rolled their eyes; if a poor lime and cement dealer had both of his legs cut off they only complained of his yells.

The first news that there might be tragedy, too, among the plain people—that even a bookkeeper or a country schoolteacher might know what heartbreak was, and longing, and the slings and ar-rows of fate—came out of Russia, that sinful land. But Anderson did not borrow the notion from the Russians. He got it primarily by living among just such obscure and miserable people—by shar-ing their lonely lives with them in a remote Ohio country town. And when he came to write he got his method of dealing with them, I believe, from Dreiser, who had come by knowledge of them in the same way, and had already done two capital books about them.

He has stuck to them more faithfully than Dreiser, who was diverted, in *The Financier*, to higher and more familiar levels, and has never got back. Anderson's stories, from first to last, all deal with the simplest sort of simple folk—village storekeepers, coun-try town old maids, dreaming farm boys, humble servitors at the race tracks, miners and workmen, farm wives and hoboes. The most exalted character in his books that I can think of at the mo-ment is the protagonist in *Many Marriages*, a manufacturer of washing machines in a small way in a backwoods Wisconsin town. They are all people of the third rate and beyond. Their aspirations are puerile. They are stupid. They get nowhere. But Anderson feels with them and for them, and he knows how to make his readers feel with them and for them, too.

* *

His skill, indeed, is very great—greater, I believe, than even his admirers suspect. His uncertain, speculative, inquiring manner only too often leaves the impression that he doesn't know what he is about—that his story is too much for him. Now and then, per-haps, it actually is. But not often. Nine times out of ten his groping is no more than concealment of a highly deft and competent artistry. He turns his characters around slowly, inspecting them leisurely and from all sides. He pauses to wonder about them, to try to reconstruct their internal motives from their external acts. He frames hypotheses about them. In the end, instead of labeling them, he asks questions about them.

It is an unorthodox scheme, and, as I have said, it maddens the pedagogues, but its net effect is an extraordinary vividness—a truly brilliant realism. One suddenly remembers that this is precisely how one sees people in real life—that one does not look into their souls with the all-seeing eye of an old-time novelist, but must be content with the enigmatic outside of them, with the chance hints that flash along the surface—more often, indeed, lacking even hints, with mere surmises. No human being in this world ever knew another human being as completely as Thackeray professed to know Becky Sharp. A man's wife, save he be entirely unintelligent, remains a dark mystery to him to the end. Anderson deals in such dark mysteries. It is his business to show that they flourish under mail-order suits as well as under ermine—that man struggles with his destiny as bitterly in a village coal yard as on the steps of the throne.

His method, of course, is difficult. It is much easier to pretend to know it all, for that pretense, in the last analysis, always reduces itself to a confession that one knows, in reality, next to nothing. Anderson is far more searching, far more curious, far bolder. He tries to get through the skin. Sometimes he fails, as in *Many Marriages*. But more often he succeeds—almost always when he narrows his scene, and so avoids dispersing his effort. Some of his short stories are truly magnificent. They tell more in a few thousand words, and make it seem more important, more dramatic, more moving, than the orthodox novelist tells in a volume of 300 pages.

* *

His latest book, *A Story Teller's Story*, is not fiction, but a rambling record of his own life; nevertheless, he employs in its writing the same method that gives so luminous and vivid a quality to his stories. One of the characters in it, for example, is his father—a strange mixture of dreamer and vagrant, kind to his children but as improvident as a stray dog. How is he to be dealt with? The average writer, even the average skillful writer, would reduce him to a sort of catalogue of remembered facts, with interludes of more or less honest exposition. That catalogue, obviously, would not be complete—it would not be half complete, nor a hundredth part. Nor would the exposition be very illuminating, for there would have to be reticences in it, and hence great gaps.

Anderson is more original and very much more satisfying. He sketches in his father briefly, and then projects him into imaginary scenes. What we are shown is not what he did as a matter of historical fact, but what his son imagines he would have done under this or that set of circumstances. At once he begins to take on a striking reality. The hand of the artist is free: he is not hampered by discordant and fragmentary facts; he can get rid of his crude materials. But he still keeps all that is essential—all, indeed, that he has to work with—his fundamental memory of his father, his net impression of him. That impression he gets upon the printed page with extraordinary skill. It is a portrait study of the first quality. The man moves and breathes. He is not a mummy powdered and gilded for posterity, but a living creature.

The whole book repays study. It shows some of the best work, so far, of one of the most original talents America has ever produced. In spots Anderson is at his worst—confused, gummy and even sometimes a bit artificial. But elsewhere he is at his incomparable best.

(The Chicago Sunday Tribune, January 4, 1925)

Two Dreiser Novels

I

Of the five Dreiser novels so far published, the most popular, I believe, is *Sister Carrie*. After its suppression in 1900 it was half forgotten, but its republication in 1907 brought it into notice again, and since then it has made its way steadily. The causes of its relative popularity are not far to seek. It has, like *Jennie Gerhardt*, the capital advantage of having a young and appealing woman for its protagonist; and sentimentalists thus have a heroine to cry over and to put into a pigeonhole. And it is, at bottom, a tale of love—

the one theme of permanent interest to the average American novel reader, the chief stuffing of all our best-selling romances. But no more than a casual glance is needed to show that it is very much more than that—that its true place is not with the trashy novels of the hour, but with the enduring literature of the nation. No other story I know of gets closer to that blind, hopeful, unyielding struggle, that incessant battle against a hospitable and yet recalcitrant environment, which is the pre-eminent mark of American life; no other makes it more real, more poignant, more genuinely dramatic and moving; and no other evokes with greater skill the failure and heart-break that must be, for all the easy successes it shows, its normal and preponderous issue. Carrie Meeber is no mere individual; she is a type of the national character, almost the archetype of the muddled, aspiring, tragic, fate-flogged mass, and the scene in which she is set is brilliantly national too. The Chicago of those great days of feverish money-grabbing and crazy aspiration may well stand as an epitome of America. It is made clearer here than in any other American novel—clearer than in *The Pit* or *The Cliff Dwellers*—vastly clearer than in any book by an Easterner. Dreiser has not half so well with New York; the city is foreign to him, and its spirit seems to elude him; he cannot get down to its essential drama. And when he goes elsewhere he becomes the frank tourist, seeing only what is on the skin.

II

Sister Carrie is a truly astounding first book, and one marvels to hear that it was written lightly. Dreiser, in those days *(circa* 1899), had seven or eight years of newspaper work behind him, in Chicago, St. Louis, Toledo, Cleveland, Buffalo, Pittsburgh and New York, and was beginning to feel that reaction of disgust which attacks all newspaper men when the enthusiasm of youth wears out. He had been successful, but he saw how hollow that success was, and how little surety it held out for the future. The theatre was what chiefly lured him; he had written plays in his nonage, and he now proposed to do them on a large scale, and so get some of the easy dollars of Broadway. It was an old friend from Toledo, Arthur Henry, who turned him toward story-writing. The two had met while Henry was city editor of the *Blade*, and Dreiser a reporter looking for a job. (The episode is related in *A Hoosier Holiday.*) A firm friendship sprang up, and Henry conceived a high opinion of Dreiser's ability, and urged him to try a short story. Dreiser was distrustful of his own skill, but Henry kept at him, and finally, during a holiday the two spent together at Maumee, Ohio, he made the attempt. Henry had the manuscript typewritten and sent it to *Ainslee's Magazine.* A week or two later there came a cheque for $75.

This was in 1898. Dreiser wrote four more stories during the year following, and sold them all. Henry now urged him to write a novel, but again his distrust of himself held him back. Henry finally tried a rather unusual argument: he had a novel of his own on the stocks (*A Princess of Arcady,* published in 1900), and he represented that he was in difficulties of it and needed company. One day, in September, 1899, Dreiser took a sheet of yellow paper and wrote a title at random. That title was *Sister Carrie,* and with no more definite plan than the mere name offered, the book began. It went ahead steadily enough until the middle of October, and had come by then to the place where Carrie meets Hurstwood. At that point Dreiser gave it up in disgust. It seemed pitifully dull and inconsequential, and for two months he put the manuscript away. Then, under renewed urgings by Henry, he resumed the writing, and kept on to the place where Hurstwood steals the money. Here he went aground upon a comparatively simple problem: he couldn't devise a way to manage the robbery. Late in January he gave it up. But the faithful Henry kept at him, and in March he resumed work, and soon had the story finished. The latter part, despite many distractions, went quickly. Once the manuscript was complete, Henry suggested various cuts, and in all about 40,000 words came out. The fair copy went to the Harpers.

III

They refused it without ceremony, and soon afterward Dreiser carried the manuscript to Doubleday, Page & Co. He left it with Frank Doubleday, and before long there came a notice of its acceptance, and, what is more, a contract. But after the story was in type it fell into the hands of the wife of one of the members of the firm, and she conceived so strong a notion of its immorality that she soon convinced her husband and his associates. There followed a series of acrimonious negotiations, with Dreiser holding resolutely to the letter of his contract. It was at this point that Frank Norris entered the combat—bravely but in vain. The pious

Barabbases, confronted by their signature, found it impossible to throw up the book entirely, but there was no nomination in the bond regarding either the style of binding or the number of copies to be issued, so they evaded further dispute by bringing out the book in a very small edition and with modest unstamped covers. Copies of this edition are now eagerly sought by book collectors, and one in good condition fetched about $25 in the auction rooms. Even the second edition (1907), bearing the imprint of B. W. Dodge and Co., carries an increasing premium.

The passing years work strange farces. The Harpers, who had refused *Sister Carrie* with a spirit bordering upon indignation in 1900, took over the rights of publication from B. W. Dodge & Co. in 1912, and reissued the book in a new format, with a publisher's note containing smug quotations from the encomiums of the *Fortnightly Review,* the *Athenaeum,* the *Spectator,* the *Academy* and other London critical journals. More, they contrived humorously to push the date of their copyright back to 1900. But this new enthusiasm for artistic freedom did not last long. They had published *Jennie Gerhardt* in 1911 and they did *The Financier* in 1912, but when *The Titan* followed, in 1914, they were seized with qualms, and suppressed the book after it had gone into type. In this emergency the English firm of John Lane came to the rescue, and it has remained Dreiser's publisher ever since. . . . For his high service to American letters the active head of Doubleday, Page & Co., Walter H. Page, has been made Ambassador to England, where *Sister Carrie* is regarded (according to the Harpers) as "the best story, on the whole, that has yet come out of America." A curious series of episodes. Another proof, perhaps, of that cosmic imbecility upon which Dreiser himself is so fond of discoursing. . . .

IV

"The power to tell the same story in two forms," said George Moore not long ago, "is the sign of the true artist." You will think of this when you read *Jennie Gerhardt,* for in its objective plan, and even in the details of its scheme of subjective unfolding it suggested *Sister Carrie* at every turn. Reduce it to a hundred words, and those same words would also describe the earlier book. Jennie, like Carrie, is a rose grown from turnip-seed. Over each, at the start, hangs poverty, ignorance, the dumb helplessness of the Shudra, and yet in each there is that indescribable something, that element of essential gentleness, that innate inward beauty that levels all barriers of caste and makes Esther a fit queen for Ahasucrus. Some Frenchman has put it into a phrase: *"Une ame grande dans un petit destin"*—a great soul in a small destiny. Jennie has some touch of that greatness: Dreiser is forever calling her "a big woman"; it is a refrain almost as irritating as "the trig" of *The Titan*. Carrie, one feels, is of baser metal; her dignity never rises to anything approaching nobility. But the history of each is the history of the other. Jennie, like Carrie, escapes from the physical miseries of the struggle for existence only to taste the worse miseries of the struggle for happiness. Don't mistake me; we have here no maudlin tales of seduced maidens. Seduction, in truth, is far from tragedy for either Jennie or Carrie. The gain of each, until the actual event has been left behind and obliterated by experiences more salient and poignant, is greater than her loss, and that gain is to the soul as well as to the creature. With the rise from want to security, from fear to ease, comes an awakening of the finer perceptions, a widening of the sympathies, a gradual unfolding of the delicate flower called personality, an increased capacity for loving and living. But with all this, and as a part of it, there comes, too, an increased capacity for suffering—and so, in the end, when love slips away and the empty years stretch before, it is the awakened and supersentient woman that pays for the folly of the groping, bewildered girl. The tragedy of Carrie and Jennie, in brief, is not that they are degraded, but that they are lifted up, not that they go to the gutter, but that they escape the gutter and glimpse the stars.

V

But if the two stories are thus variations upon the same somber theme, if each starts from the same place and arrives at the same dark goal, if each shows a woman heartened by the same hopes and tortured by the same agonies, there is still a vast difference between them and that difference is the measure of the author's progress in his craft during the 11 years between 1900 and 1911. *Sister Carrie* is a first sketch, a rough piling-up of observations and impressions, disordered and often incoherent. In the midst of the story of Carrie, Dreiser pauses to tell the story of Hurstwood—an astonishingly vivid and tragic story, true enough, but still one that, considering form alone, breaks the back of the other. In *Jen-*

nie Gerhardt he falls into no such overelaboration of episode. His narrative goes forward steadily from beginning to end. Episodes there are, of course, but they keep their proper place, their proper bulk. It is always Jennie that holds the attention; it is Jennie's soul that every scene is ultimately played out.

I have spoken of reducing the story to a hundred words. The thing, I fancy, might be actually done. The machinery is not complex; there is no plot, as plots are understood; no puzzles madden the reader. Brander finds Jennie at her slavery's work, lightly seduces her and then discovers that, for some strange gentleness within her, he loves her. Lunacy—but he is willing to face it out. Death, however, steps in; Brander, stricken down without warning, leaves Jennie homeless and a mother. Now enters Lester Kane —not the villain of the books, but a normal, decent, cleanly American of the better class, well-to-do, level-headed, not too introspective, eager for the sweets of life. He and Jennie are drawn together; if love is not all of the spirit, then it is love that binds them. For half a dozen years the world lets them alone. A certain grave respectability settles over their relation; if they are not actually married, then it is only because marriage is a mere formality, to be put off until tomorrow. But bit by bit they are dragged into the light. Kane's father, dying with millions, gives him two years to put Jennie away. The penalty is poverty; the reward is wealth— and not only wealth itself, but all the pleasant and well-remembered things that will come with it; the lost friends of other days, a sense of dignity and importance, an end of apologies and evasions, good society, the comradeship of one decent woman. Kane hesitates, makes a brave defiance, thinks it over—and finally yields. Jennie does not flood him with tears. She has made progress in the world, has Jennie; the simple faith of the girl has given way to the pride and poise of the woman. Five years later Kane sends for her. He is dying. When it is over Jennie goes back to her lonely home, and there, like Carrie Meeber before her, she faces the long years with dry eyes and an empty heart. "Days and days in endless reiteration, and then"——

A moral tale? Not at all. It has no more moral than a string quartet or the first book of Euclid. But a philosophy of life is in it, and that philosophy is the same profound pessimism which gave a dark color to the best that we have from Conrad, Hardy, Moore, Zola and the Russians—the pessimism of disillusion—not the jejune, Byronic thing, not the green sickness of youth, but that pessimism which comes with the discovery that the riddle of life, despite all the fine solutions offered by the learned doctors, is essentially insoluble. And to me, at least, she is more tragic thus than Lear on his wild hearth or Prometheus on his rock. . . .

(The Baltimore Evening Sun, August 4, 1916)

Notice to Neglected Geniuses

Short Story Courses

How many schools of short story writing flourish in the federal union I don't know, but certainly there must be at least forty. Some are attached to colleges or universities, usually as appendages to journalism, and make a great show of academic dignity; others are run by private entrepreneurs and offer their services by correspondence and cut rates. It is my firm conviction, reached after long inquiry and due prayer, that all of these seminaries, great and small, are without discernible merit, and that their ministrations, taking one pupil with another, do far more harm than good.

I do not maintain, of course, that the art of the short story cannot be taught—within certain obvious limits. Within the same limits even the art of high jumping can be taught. All I maintain is that all the professors I have any knowledge of, to judge them by their advertisements, circulars, and occasional public remarks, appear to be unanimously incapable of teaching it—that is, as an art. What they actually teach, in so far as they teach anything at all, is the trade of manufacturing hack fiction for the cheap magazines. To this business, perhaps, they address themselves not unsuccessfully. The yearning show drummer or country schoolmarm is converted by an adept pedagogy into a favorite contributor to *Silly Stories* or *True Orgies*. But no aspirant of genuine talent, I believe, is ever helped in the slightest—and many a one is probably greatly damaged.

And no wonder! Suppose the teaching of music were taken over by hand organ players or greasers of phonographs, by trombone polishers or piano movers? The cases would be exactly parallel. I know of no professor of the short story in all this broad land who shows the least sign of knowing anything about the subject he professes. The critical standards exhibited by the whole faculty, male and female, are those of shop girls. The things they admire appear to be the things that the readers of tabloid newspapers admire. What they teach is a series of shallow and puerile tricks. Their chief aim, pedagoguelike, seems to be to reduce the whole mystery to a few childish rules. If you want to find out how little such rules are worth, simply read any of the short story master-pieces of Joseph Conrad.

* *

The technic of the short story, indeed, is so simple and transparent that not even a pedagogue, if he taught it honestly, could make it seem worth teaching. The whole of it flows easily and obviously out of the form; any intelligent child, essaying a story, discerns it instantly. First, there must be rigid economy of attention; the interest must be concentrated upon one conflict, one idea, or one character. Secondly, there must be a clear statement of the theme at the start; the short story writer, unlike the novelist, cannot waste time preparing his ground and spitting on his hands.

These principles, as I say, are obvious. Any person capable of writing a short story at all knows them almost by instinct, just as he knows that he must put ink on his pen. You will find them exemplified in every good short story ever written. Imagine them disregarded and you have imagined a bad short story—one plainly deficient in form and organization, a crippled and nonsensical thing.

But to teach them and have done, of course, is not enough for pedagogues, they must gild the job with the immemorial hocus-pocus of their order. That hocus-pocus takes the form of the child-ish rules of aforesaid. Mastering those rules burdens the cerebrum of the pupil, and so makes him believe that he is taking in knowl-edge. But all he is actually taking in is nonsense. All the pedagogi-cal rubbish about motivation, climax, and so on—all this is non-sense.

The net effect of such teaching is to concentrate the attention of aspirants upon trivial externals, and to make them forget the short story's interior substance. They manage after a time, perhaps, to turn out salable fodder for the news stand magazines, but they never get any nearer to writing self-respecting literature than they were when they began; only too often, indeed, they are completely diverted from that goal by their instructions. The result is gross damage to the American short story—an art form congenial to the American temperament, and one that we should intelligently cultivate. The popular magazines are filled every month with hundreds of stories, and not one in a thousand is worth reading.

* *

What is primarily needed, in order to write short stories of any dignity, is not a thimble rigging technic, but a capacity for accurate and original observation. The best short story writer, like the best novelist, is that one who observes the life about him with the greatest clarity and shrewdness, and sets it forth in the simplest and most understandable way. The materials of fiction are not to be got out of books, but out of life itself. Prose fiction, at its best, is always primarily representative; it is interpretative only as a sort of afterthought, and at its peril. The best short stories in the world teach nothing and preach nothing; they do not expostulate, and neither do they mourn; they simply set forth what has been seen and felt.

The good ones differ from the bad ones by the fact that they show an immensely superior plausibility—that the transactions they set forth appear to be real, and the emotions flowing out of them genuine. A capital example is afforded by Joseph Conrad's "Youth," perhaps the greatest short story in the English language. There is absolutely no trace in it of the rules laid down by the professors of short story writing. It cannot be analyzed by their formulae, just as many a ringing sentence cannot be parsed. But it embodies almost perfectly the basic principles that I have mentioned, for its theme is made plain in the first paragraph, and from that point until the end there is never any deviation from it.

The indomitability of youth—this is what Conrad is trying to set forth. Every incident is bent to his purpose, there is not a word that does not help. Nor is there a single instant when the illusion fails. The boy is absolutely and overwhelmingly real; he is the boy that every man has been; he is every boy. When he passes from the scene at last, he is as vividly real as if he had been sitting in the room, telling his story himself—more, he is almost as real as he must have been to those who helped him live it.

* *

Conrad did not prepare himself for writing fiction by sending $50 to some quack and then laboriously trying to learn to write like O. Henry. He prepared himself by stuffing his head with observations of this gaudy and inordinate world—by using his eyes sharply as he trafficked up and down its highways, by storing up memories of its higher fauna—above all, by seeing and remembering what escaped his fellow men. Many another sailor man traveled the same track and many another spun yarns afterward. But Conrad brought back a cargo of fresh and singular impressions, for he was a singular and extraordinary man. His superiority as a writer of stories was a function of his superiority as an observer of human beings. He said what was hidden from the general, and so he wrote what was new and fascinating to the general.

The mere business of writing, I believe, seldom gives much concern to first-rate writers. They know no more about the rules of style laid down by schoolmarms than they know about the rules of fiction laid down by other and worse schoolmarms. They are more interested in the thing they are describing than they are in the words with which they describe it, and so they write naturally, which is to say simply, which is to say well.

Conrad, when he began to write, felt himself so insecure in the English language that he actually thought of turning to French— like English, an acquired tongue. To the end of his days he did much of his thinking in his native Polish; there are Polish turns of phrase in all of his books. But he had all the English that was really necessary. He could make himself understood, and that was enough. The stories that he had to tell were so colossal that they would have carried him over far worse errors than he ever made— even over split infinitives, mixed cases, and all the horrors of the schoolmarm. For in such a story as "Youth" there is such profound observation, such a deep and moving understanding of the soul of man, that it would remain a great and beautiful thing even if it were told in the prattle of a child of 6 or the dreadful bombast of a professor of the short story.

(The Chicago Sunday Tribune, February 22, 1925)

The Trade of Letters

. . . Like most other editors, I receive a great many letters from them [young authors], and many of those letters ask for counsel. One question is in nearly all of them: Shall I throw up my job in the rolling mills and devote my whole time to poetry (or to short stories, or to criticism, or to the novel), or shall I hang on to my job and try to write in the scant leisure of my evenings, or on the Sabbath, when I should be engaged in religious exercises?

My answer is always the same: I advise them all to stick to their jobs. And for a plain reason: I do not believe it is possible for a man to write more in a day of 10 hours—that is, more of the best that is in him, more that is genuinely worth writing—than he writes in a day of three hours. The view to the contrary, so common among young authors, is a great delusion. It is grounded upon the error of assuming that creative work is a mere matter of time. It is, in fact, nothing of the sort; it is a matter purely of ideas. The more good ideas, the better the artist. I believe thoroughly that the world has never seen a poet or a novelist who had more good ideas than he could get upon paper in three hours' work a day. There have been plenty of men, of course, who write more, but what they wrote after the three hours were up was second-rate stuff—and sometimes third-rate, sixth- and tenth-rate stuff.

The danger that confronts the young author with nothing to do all day but write lies is the temptation to go on after the period of good work is up. The day lies before him. He still has paper on his table and ink in his well. He has notions of industry; it seems shameful to quit so soon; moreover, it is apt to cause talk in the family. So he plugs away gallantly and the result is a great mass of stuff that begins by being good, then proceeds to be indifferent and ends by being dreadful. But it is all precious to him. Contemplating it, he quickly loses his critical sense. In the end he is judged by his average, and his average tends to go lower and lower. I could name names, but refrain in Christian charity. The beaches of beautiful letters are strewn with the corpses of diligent men.

* *

There are few jobs in this golden age that do not give their holders three hours' leisure a day. These three hours achieved, I believe that the aspiring poet or novelist is the better off the farther his daily work lies from writing. His observations afield will be worth far more than his observations in his cell; moreover, the change in interests and surroundings will sharpen and mellow his mind. The trouble with most literary men is that they tend always to become too literary. The way to avoid the danger is to move in the world, and the best way to move in the world is to get a job in it.

On the precise nature of the job I have no advice to offer. It must be determined, obviously, by circumstances, even by mere luck. But, in general, it seems to me that the farther it lies afield the better it is for the writer who has it. Journalism is tempting for that very reason, and it is no wonder that so many authors have turned to it. It provides an easy living; it offers opportunities for useful observations; it has certain demure contacts with literature and yet is as far from literature proper as astronomy is from the pants business. The journalist is almost the exact opposite of a poet; he is even miles from a novelist. But there is nothing in his daily work to prevent him from turning to poetry when that work is done. It occupies the mind without exhausting it. It stores the memory with brilliant images of the fleeting world. It induces a pleasurable melancholy. What could be better preparation for poetry?

But I do not recommend journalism specifically; I only point out that it offers an agreeable living at small exertion. There may be far better berths for aspiring literati, for all I know, in railroad offices, door-knob factories and brokerage houses. There have been Wall Street poets before, and there will be more hereafter. Political jobs have kept many artists alive in the past: I recall Hawthorne and Herman Melville at once, not to mention Howells. Rich widows, the relics of wornout Babbitts, prowl the land. Love, as the poet hath it, finds a way. There is the patent medicine business. There is chiropractic. There is bootlegging. I know a sculptor who is a bootlegger. Why not a novelist?

As for the ladies of letters, my advice to them is always the same: Get married as soon as possible, and in your choice avoid artists as you would the pestilence. A husband without money is as bad as a husband with diabetes. Let your virgin fancy play upon a Babbitt, a sound Rotarian, a man with a good and growing business. Marry him as soon as possible, and then lay in a supply of typewriter paper and begin work on your masterpiece. If it pans out, he will be immensely proud of you. If it comes to naught, he will give thanks to God that you have abandoned your notions and come back to normalcy. Babbitts are best. Think of the wives of Shakespeare, Wagner and Ibsen!

(The Chicago Sunday Tribune, December 28, 1924)

Advice to Young Authors

The superstition that some sort of pull or drag is necessary in order to get into print in our great country—this superstition still flourishes east, west, north and south, despite the massive and obvious proofs of its unsoundness. In every mail I get letters from inspirants in the hinterland asking me to read their MSS. and recommend them to publishers. I can imagine no more unlikely way to crash the literary gates. The fact is that publishers are immensely suspicious of the recommendations of critics, and seldom follow them. My own publisher should certainly be well aware by this time that I am a highly sagacious fellow; nevertheless, of the last dozen MSS. that I have urged upon him, often with voluptuous eloquence, he has actually accepted but two.

The reason is not far to seek. Every publisher knows, by long and bitter experience, that the books which critics praise commonly lose him money. This, of course, is not because they are incompetent to distinguish sound literature from bad: as a matter of fact, the critics of the United States, taking one with another, show quite as much professional competence as the osteopaths, the psychical researchers, or the investment bankers. The trouble is that sound literature, or as such fanciers understand it, is not often very profitable—that a publisher who confined himself to it would quickly end in bankruptcy. In order to print enough of it to salve his conscience he must also do a great deal of less juicy and worthy stuff. This less juicy and worthy stuff is what he seeks and longs for. Of sound literature there is always plenty.

Thus publishers are somewhat wary of the advice of critics, who tend inevitably to forget printers' and advertising bills in their enthusiasm for new literary delicatessen. No sensible publisher ever hires a critic as his literary adviser. If he did so his list of publications would look like the table of contents of the Dial. No; he hires a Rotarian, and preferably one with experience in the automobile supplies business. Thus he becomes highly solvent and even rich, and is able when a Cabell or Hergesheimer comes along to take a chance.

* *

But it is one thing to say all this, and quite another thing to argue that the new author of genuine merit is barred out—that the gates of the publishers are closed to him. They are actually wide open—so long as he doesn't handicap himself by approaching them with letters from critics in his pocket. The publishers' readers are practical and horny-handed men, but there is a touch of wild romance in every one of them. It is the discovery of honest trade goods that pays their salaries and preserves their jobs, but it is the discovery of masterpieces that thrills them. They dream nightly of the pearl of great price. When one of them unearths such a pearl, news of it flies all over the publishing world in half an hour, as news of the arrival of a rum ship spreads among booticians.

Thus the young author need not fear that he will be neglected— so long, to repeat, as he does not raise up a prejudice against his masterpiece by engaging a critic to commend it. It will be examined with care, and if it shows any honest merit at all, it will be read to the end. If it is not, it will not be because publishers' readers are recreant to their trust, but simply because they have skill at their trade, and are quite able to detect a bad egg without eating all of it.

The signs of a bad MS., indeed, are almost as plain as those of a bad egg. There is something about its general appearance that instantly alarms the experienced reader—something hard to describe, but nevertheless quite real. So he reads the first page: it is, as he expected, flabby stuff. The second: it is worse. The last: it is horrible. He looks for corroborations, and they are always there. First, a florid letter from the author, detailing his triumphs at high school. Second, a letter from the city editor of the *Bingville Bugle*, certifying that he is the best reporter ever heard of between Cincinnati and Columbus. Third, the inevitable encomium from the critic of the *Jackass* [Miss.] *Daily News*, the *Tri-State Confectioner*, or the *Greenwich Village Libido*. The MS. goes back at once, charges collect.

* *

Magazine editors, like publishers' readers, are sorely beset by such communications and encomiums, and spend a great deal of time damning them. Here the main reason is that they greatly multiply the writing of polite but useless letters—an endless curse in every magazine office. An unaccompanied MS. from a stranger, if it turns out to be unavailable, may be returned with a rejection slip: a somewhat arctic politeness, but still enough. When, however, it comes in with a letter from some eminent critic, or from the editor of another magazine, or from one of the editor's private friends, it must have a personal letter—and writing such personal letters is extremely exhausting, not only to the intellect but also to the temper.

Naturally enough, no sane editor likes to write them, and so it is no wonder that every editor, when he encounters a MS. accompanied by encomiums, is instantly prejudiced against it. There is, indeed, no surer way for a young author to get his MS. rejected and himself disliked. If its normal chances of rejection are 100 to 1 —as they are in most magazine offices—then a letter from a critic, especially if it be long or handwritten, increases them to at least 1,000 to 1. In the course of many years spent in magazine offices, in fact, I have never heard of such a MS. getting into print. To expect it to be accepted is to ask far too much of human nature.

But the most fatal of all letters is one from another editor. Many editors write such letters in order to get rid of applicants otherwise hard to dispose of—relatives, say, of their wives, pastors, or bootleggers. "It lies outside the field of my own magazine," they say, "but Mr. Blank of the *Boil*, will undoubtedly be glad to have it." Such letters are sometimes written as practical jokes on friends in the craft; more often, perhaps, they are employed to pay off grudges. In either case the poor author is the goat. His MS. goes back to him at once, unread, and his name goes on the office blacklist, along with those of the lady authors who perfume their MSS.

* *

Well, then, how is a young author to reach editors? By the simplest of devices. Let him type his MS. on sound white paper, thick enough to conceal the page below, let him have a well inked ribbon on his typewriter, let him write his name and address plainly at the top of the first page, and then let him send his MS. to the editor he has chosen, without any accompanying letter of any sort, his own or another's. The editor is not wholly idiotic: he will know instantly why it was sent in. And he will read it diligently and at once, for whenever he confronts a pile of MSS. he always picks out for his first reading those that are shipshape and workmanlike, and will put the least burden upon his time, his temper and his eyes.

It is astounding how many MSS. that come into magazine offices—and into publishers' offices—are wholly unreadable, in the literal physical sense. Many are upon such thin paper that, attempting to read them, one sees the lines of two, three or even four pages at once. Many others are typed so faintly that it is ruinous to the eyes to try to make them out. Yet others are single spaced—an almost incredible fact, but still a fact. Is it any wonder that the editor concludes quickly that no one guilty of such imbecilities could conceivably write anything worth printing?

The prudent young author puts no such handicaps upon his merchandise. He avoids annoying any insulting editors with useless letters, and he avoids torturing them with illegible and unkempt MSS. His single aim, after he has composed his masterpiece, is to ease the job of the hard worked man who must read it —often on a long and busy day, and with Katzenjammer riding him, or his old war wounds troubling. This aim is easily achieved: it costs nothing save a little common sense. The author who achieves it has gone a long way toward success; even immortality is nearer to him than it was. More, he is laying up stores in heaven. For the editor, grateful to him, will not fail, at prayer, to bring his virtues to the attention of the celestial secretariat.

(The Chicago Sunday Tribune, June 12, 1927)

The Book Trade

The Avalanche of Books

The other day there came to me a package of books from a well-known American publishing house. It was one of six or eight that arrived that day, but by chance I opened it first, presently I was examining its contents: five new novels, all of them by authors unknown to me. Being in a lazy mood, and disinclined to literary composition, I spent the whole afternoon looking through them. What I found, not to put too fine a point upon it, was simply bilge. In the whole quintet there was not the slightest sign of anything even remotely describable as literary skill or passion. The five authors were only lucky bunglers who had somehow managed to get their drivel printed.

Why are such books published? On what theory do reputable publishers go to all the elaborate trouble of getting them set up, printing them, binding them, encasing them in gaudy slipcovers, advertising them voluptuously, and burdening the book stores with them? Who reads them? Who, having ordinary sanity and taste, *could* read them? I often wonder. For they come out in an endless stream, hailed, whooped up, and then suddenly forgotten. Six months after publication they have disappeared completely. Who stands the loss? And why?

* *

It is commonly believed that the authors pay for their publication, but that, I am convinced, is true very seldom. Not many American publishers of any dignity ever print books on that basis. A few third-raters do it—they are known in the trade as lemon squeezers—but they do not seem to prosper: it is too easy to get books published by reputable publishers, and at their expense. The firm that issued the five novels was of that character. It has many books of great importance on its list. It publishes authors of international celebrity. And yet it also published that depressing rubbish!

If this firm were singular, its hospitality to such rubbish might be set down to an aberration of its constituent Barabbases, but the fact is that practically all of the leading American publishers show the same weakness. Their lists are crowded with second- and third-rate books and they advertise some of them in a way almost worthy of a new cure for halitosis. There seems to be a race among them to find out which can publish the most books, and every contestant appears to be willing to call anything within covers a book in order to win. An author of honest purposes and dignified achievement finds himself cheek by jowl on his publisher's list with bogus geniuses just out of high school and all sorts of dull hacks and cheap jacks. Every imprint known to American readers during the last dozen years has appreciably diminished in value, and some have diminished so much that they are now of scarcely any value at all.

* *

I assume that the general prosperity of the book trade is partly to blame. The business of publishing since the war has been very good. Americans are reading far more books than they ever did before and paying higher prices for them. More, they are reading over wider fields. There was a time, and it was not long ago, when the only American best sellers were novels, but now it is not at all uncommon for a book of history or biography, or even a treatise on psychology or philosophy, to reach a huge sale. And, as sales have increased, book stores have multiplied, so that there are now a dozen where there used to be only one.

Thus it is easy for the publishers' drummers to take orders—far easier than it was before the war. If each book store in the country takes only five copies of a new book—and if it is sufficiently advertised they will certainly average more than five—there is already a good sale. If the book has a good press some of them will reorder instantly—and thereafter it is a pretty gamble. Every American publisher playing that game has rolled up now and then heavy winnings. So all of them keep on playing.

But there are too many players sitting in and too many chips on the table. With such immense numbers of new books coming out not one in ten can have a genuinely successful sale—that is, a sale profitable alike to the publisher, to the author, and to the book seller. Only too often the first orders are never repeated—and never worked off upon the public. Every book seller in the country has his shelves crowded with such failures. He contemplates them gloomily for a while, and then, with more and more new books crowding upon him, he tries to force the publisher to take them back. If he succeeds, the publisher faces a heavy loss. If he fails, he himself faces a heavy loss.

Such losses of late have been so numerous that a great many American publishers find their profits cut very seriously and a great many American book sellers are close to bankruptcy. Some time ago, indeed, a distinguished American publisher told me that he knew of not more than a score of book stores in the whole country, excluding department stores, that were indubitably solvent. The rest are hanging on by their eyebrows, accumulating more and more formidable inventories and demanding heavier and heavier discounts on new books. They are drowned in unsalable stock. They had to lay it in in order to show a wide assortment to their customers and meet the competition of their rivals. And now it drags them down.

* *

It is the sheer multiplicity of new books that is mainly to blame. So many come out every month that a book seller who pretends to carry a comprehensive stock must buy far more than he can sell. He has no means of determining in advance which of the newcomers will be successes and which will be flops. So in order to have all of the former in hand when the demand comes he buys great stacks of the latter—and presently he finds his shelves overloaded and his takings insufficient to meet his incoming bills. Hence the dreadfully long credits that he demands. And hence his endless struggle for larger and larger discounts.

Most American publishers of any standing have made money during the last few years, but not many, I suspect, have made as much as they ought to have made on their turnover. As fast as their returns come in they are invested in more books—which means that they are put into cold storage and remain unproductive for from six months to two years. Thus publishing begins to require more working capital than any other comparable business, and one really bad season would be sufficient to put more than one very prosperous house into difficulties.

* *

The way out, it seems to me, is for the publishers to abandon their present wild yearning to fatten their lists and go back to publishing only books that have a sound reason for being and are reasonably certain to have profitable sales. The current gambling is ruining the book sellers by loading them down with unsalable stock and imperiling the publishers themselves by tying up their capital. Who gains by it? The reading public? The reading public gains only the unhappy knowledge that honorable imprints are no longer worth as much as they used to be. The only real gainers are the bad authors. They get very little money, but their vanity is satisfied, and so the number of them tends to increase steadily.

The question whether a given manuscript is of sound merit and worth publishing is seldom hard to answer. Publishers' readers do not make many mistakes in that direction; the tales of rejected masterpieces that go 'round are tales only. A dozen years ago I offered free of charge to find a publisher for any genuinely good manuscript that was sent to me. About five hundred came in, but only one of them was good: I found a publisher for it within twenty-four hours. The present swamping of the book stores is caused by gambling in half good, quarter good, and no good ones. A piece of rubbish is printed with a great hullabaloo because it somehow resembles, or is thought to resemble, a book that made a success last season. The book sellers buy it, put it on their shelves —and then begin to contemplate the unpleasant business of getting enough money to pay for it. The publishers could save them by refusing to print such stuff. Unless they do so, and very shortly, they will get the whole trade into trouble.

(The Chicago Sunday Tribune, December 25, 1927)

Critics and Their Ways

The Critic and His Job

The assumption that it may be scientific is the worst curse that lies upon criticism. It is responsible for all the dull, blowsy, "definite" stuff that literary pedagogues write, and it is responsible, too, for the heavy posturing that so often goes on among critics less learned. Both groups proceed upon the theory that there are exact facts to be ascertained, and that it is their business to ascertain and proclaim them. That theory is nonsense. There is, in truth, no such thing as an exact fact in the realm of the beautiful arts. What is true therein today may be false tomorrow, or vice versa, and only too often the shift is brought about by something that, properly speaking, is not an aesthetic consideration at all.

The case of Whitman comes to mind at once. Orthodox criticism, in his own time, was almost unanimously against him. At his first appearance, true enough, a few critics were a bit dazzled by him, notably Emerson, but they quickly got control of their faculties and took to cover. Down to the time of his death the prevailing doctrine was that he was a third-rate poet and a dirty fellow. Any young professor who, in the seventies or even the early eighties, had presumed to whoop for him in class would have been cashiered at once as both incompetent and immoral. If there was anything "definitely" established in those days, it was that old Walt was below the salt.

Today he is taught to sophomores everywhere, perhaps even in Tennessee, and one of the most unctuously respectable of American publishing houses brings out *Leaves of Grass* unexpurgated, and everyone agrees that he is one of the glories of the national letters. Has that change been brought about by a purely critical process? Does it represent a triumph of criticism over darkness? It does not. It represents rather, a triumph of external forces over criticism. Whitman's first partisans were not interested in poetry; they were interested in sex. They were presently reinforced by persons interested in politics. They were finally converted into a majority by a tatterdemalion horde of persons interested mainly, and perhaps only, in making a noise.

* *

Literary criticism, properly so called, had little if anything to do with this transformation. No critic of any recognized authority had a hand in it. What started it off, after the first furtive, gingery snuffling over *A Woman Waits for Me* and the "Calamus" cycle, was the rise of political radicalism in the early eighties, in reaction against the swinish materialism that had followed the Civil War. I am tempted to say that Terence V. Powderly had more to do with the rehabilitation of Whitman than any American critic, or, indeed, than any American poet. And if you object to Powderly, then I offer you Karl Marx, with William Jennings Bryan—no less!—peeping out of his coat pocket.

The radicals made heavy weather of it at the start. To the average respectable citizen they seemed to be mere criminals. Like the Bolsheviki of a later era, they were represented by their opponents as the enemies of all mankind. What they needed, obviously, was some means of stilling the popular fear of them—some way of tapping the national sentimentality. There stood Whitman, conveniently to hand. In his sonorous strophes to an imaginary democracy there was an eloquent statement of their own vague yearnings, and, what is more, a certificate to their virtue as sound Americans. So they adopted him with loud hosannas, and presently he was both their poet and their philosopher. Long before any professor at Harvard dared to mention him (save, perhaps, with lascivious winks), he was being read to tatters by thousands of lonely Socialists in the mining towns.

As radicalism froze into liberalism, and so began to influence the intelligentsia, his vogue rose, and by the end of the century even school teachers had begun to hear of him. There followed the free verse poets, *i.e.*, a vast herd of emerging barbarians, with an itch to make an uproar in the world, and no capacity for mastering the orthodox rules of prosody. Thus Whitman came to Valhalla, pushed by political propagandists and pulled by literary mountebanks. The native Taines and Matthew Arnolds made a gallant defense, but in vain. In the remoter denominational colleges some of them still hold out. But Whitman is now just as respectable at Yale as Martin Tupper or Edmund Clarence Stedman.

* *

The point is that his new respectability is quite as insecure as his old infamy—that he may be heaved out on some bright tomorrow just as he was heaved in, and by a similar combination of purely non-literary forces. Already I hear rumors of a plan to make Dr. Coolidge king. If his conscience stays him, then the throne may go to William Wrigley, Jr., or Judge Elbert H. Gary, LL.D. Democracy, indeed, begins to sicken among us. The doctors at its bedside dose it out of a black bottle and make sinister signals to the coroner. If it dies, then Whitman will probably die with it.

Criticism, of course, will labor desperately to save him, but such struggles are nearly always futile. The most they ever accomplish is to convert the author defended into a sort of fossil, preserved in a showcase to plague and puzzle schoolboys. The orthodox literature books, used in all schools, are simply such showcases. They represent the final effort of pedants to capture zephyrs and change torrents. They are monuments to the delusion that criticism may be "definitive"—that appeals to the emotions, which shift and change with every wind, may be appraised and sorted out by appeals to the mind, whose processes are theoretically unchangeable.

Certainly every reflective student of any of the fine arts should know that this is not so. There is no such thing as a literary immortality. We remember Homer, but we forget the poets that the Greeks, too, forgot. You may be sure that there were Shakespeares in Carthage, and more of them at the court of Amenophis IV, but their very names are lost. Our own Shakespeare, as year chases year, may go the same way; in fact, his going the same way is quite as certain as anything we can imagine. A thousand years hence, even five hundred years hence, he may be, like Beowulf, only a name in a literature book, to be remembered against examination day and then forgotten.

* *

Criticism is thus anything but scientific, for it cannot reach judgments that are surely and permanently valid. The most it can do, at its best, is to pronounce verdicts that are valid here and now, in the light of living knowledge and prejudice. As the background shifts the verdict changes. The best critic is not that fool who tries to resist the process—by setting up artificial standards, by prattling of laws and principles that do not exist, by going into the dead past for *criteria* of the present—but that more prudent fellow who submits himself frankly to the flow of his time and rejoices in its aliveness. Charles Augustin Sainte-Beuve was a good critic, for he saw everything as a Frenchman of the Second Empire, and if his judgments must be revised today it still remains true that they were honest and intelligent when he formulated them. Professor Balderdash is a bad critic, for he judges what is done in the American empire of 1925 in the light of what was held to be gospel in the pastoral republic of a century ago.

For the rest, the critic survives, when he survives at all, mainly as artist. His judgments, in the long run, become archaic and may be disregarded. But if, in stating them, he has incidentally produced a work of art on his own account, then he is read long after they are rejected, and it may be plausibly argued that he has contributed something to the glory of letters. No one takes much stock in Macaulay's notions today. He is, in fact, fair game for any college tutor who has majored in what is called history. He fell into many gross errors, and sometimes, it is probable, he fell into them more or less deliberately. But his criticism is still read—that is, as much as any criticism is read. It holds all its old charm and address. For Macaulay, when he sat himself down to be critical, did not try fatuously to produce a scientific treatise. What he tried to do was to produce a work of art.

(The Chicago Sunday Tribune, July 5, 1925)

A Glance at Pedagogics

The Golden Age of Pedagogy

I

Just how many graduates the massed colleges of the United States are turning out this June I don't know, but certainly the number must run to tens of thousands. In some of the State universities, romantically so called, of the No-More-Scrub-Bulls Belt it is not unusual to discharge a thousand at a clip—four or five hundred bucks and five or six hundred fluttering fair ones. They are, in the overwhelming main, as much alike as peas in a pod. Not one-half of one percent of them are ever heard of afterward, save as members of clubs, associations, sodalities, unions, parties. They go into the world as standardized as so many Fords or Uneeda biscuits: the sole visible proof that they are educated, as the term is understood in the Republic, is that they are covered with rubber stamps. Some of them, returning to their wallows, proceed to iron out and standardize the generation following them. But not many from the minority that is intelligent.

The stray student of genuine intelligence, indeed, must find life in such great rolling-mills of learning very unpleasant, and I suppose that he seldom stays until the end of his course. He must see very quickly that the learning on tap in them is mainly formal and bogus—that it consists almost wholly of feeble nonsense out of textbooks, put together by men who are unable either to write or to think. And he must discover anon that its embellishment by the faculty is almost as bad—that very few college instructors, as he encounters them in practice, actually know anything worth knowing about the subjects they presume to teach. Has the college its stars—great whales of learning, eminent in the land? Well, it is not often that an undergraduate so much as sees those whales, and seldom indeed that he has any communion with them. The teaching is done almost exclusively by understrappers, and the distinguishing mark of those understrappers is that they are primarily pedagogues, not scholars. The fact that one of them teaches English instead of mathematics and another mathematics instead of English is trivial and largely accidental. Of a thousand head of such dull drudges not ten, with their doctors' dissertations behind them, ever contribute so much as a flyspeck to the sum of human knowledge.

II

Here, of course, I speak of the common run of colleges and the common run of pedagogues. The list of such colleges, in the *World Almanac,* runs to six pages of very fine print. They are scattered all over the land, but they are especially thick in the Cow States, where the peasants have long cherished a superstitious veneration for education, and credit it with powers almost equal to those of a United Brethren bishop or Lydia Pinkham's Vegetable Compound. The theory is that a plow hand, taught the binomial theorem and forced to read Washington Irving, a crib to Caesar's "De Bello Gallico," and some obscure Ph.D.'s summary of *The Wealth of Nations,* with idiotic review questions, becomes the peer of Aristotle, Abraham Lincoln, Andy Mellon, and B. J. Palmer, the Mr. Eddy of chiropractic. It is, I fear, a false theory: he becomes simply a bad plow hand—perhaps with overtones, if Mendel is kind to him, of a good Rotarian.

In the more pretentious vats of learning, I suppose there is an atmosphere more favorable to human husbandry, but even there it is probably far less favorable than popular legend makes it out. I can't imagine a genuinely intelligent boy getting much out of college, even out of a good college, save it be a cynical habit of mind. For even the good ones are manned chiefly by third-rate men, and any boy of sharp wits is sure to penetrate to their inferiority almost instantly. Men can fool other men, but they can seldom fool boys. The campus view of professors is notoriously highly critical, and even cruel. Well, this view is formulated by the whole body of students—the normal, half-simian majority as well as the intelligent minority. What must the really bright boys think!

Such bright boys, I believe, get little out of college, aside from the salubrious cynicism that I have mentioned. If they learn anything there, it is not by the aid of their instructors, but in spite of them. They read. They weight ideas. They come into contact, perhaps, with two or three genuinely learned men. They react sharply against the general imbecility of their fellows. Such is the process of education.

III

The half-wits get even less, but what they get is obviously more valuable to them. Though they emerge with their heads quite empty of anything rationally describable as knowledge, they have at least gained something in prestige: the hinds back at home, still chained to the plow, admire and envy them. So they go into politics and begin the weary trudge to Congress, or they enter upon one of the learned professions and help to raise it to the level of the realtor's art and mystery, or they become mortgage sharks, or perhaps they proceed to the lofty rank and dignity of *Artium Magister* or *Doctor Philosophiae*, and consecrate themselves to ironing out the rabble following after them.

In addition to the prestige, they carry home certain cultural (as opposed to intellectual) gains. They have learned the rules of basket-ball, football, high-jumping, pole-vaulting and maybe lawn tennis. They have become privy to the facts that a dress coat is not worn in the morning or with plus-fours, that an Episcopalian has something on a Baptist and even on a Presbyterian, that smoking cigarettes is not immediately followed by general paralysis, and that a girl may both believe in the literal accuracy of Genesis, and neck. They have become, in a sense, house-broken, and learned how to trip over a rug gracefully, without upsetting the piano. They have read *Mlle. de Maupin, Night Life in Chicago*, and the complete files of *Hot Dog*. They have tasted gin.

Above all, they have acquired heroes: the aurochs who broke the Ohio Wesleyan line, the swellest dresser on the campus, the master politician, the cheer leader, the senior who eloped with the ingénue of the No. 8 *Two Orphans* company, the junior caught in the raid on the road house, the sophomore who made $8,000 letting out *Ulysses* at $1 a crack, the baseball captain, the champion shot-putter, the winner of the intercollegiate golf tourney. In other words, they have become normal, healthy-minded Americanos, potential Prominent Citizens, the larvae of sound Coolidge men: they have learned how to meanly admire mean things.

IV

If I had a son and he seemed middling dull, I'd send him to Harvard, for Harvard is obviously the best of all American universities. It not only inculcates the sublime principles of Americanism as well as any other; it also inoculates all its customers with a superior air, and that superior air, in a democratic country, is a possession of the utmost value, socially and economically. The great masses of men never question it: they accept it at once, as they accept a loud voice. These masses of men are uneasy in their theoretical equality: their quest is ever for superiors to defer to and venerate. Such superiors are provided for them by Harvard. Its graduates have a haughty manner.

Moreover, they are entitled to it, for Harvard is plainly the first among American universities, and not only historically. I believe that a bright boy, sent to its halls, is damaged less than he would be damaged anywhere else, and that a dull boy enjoys immensely greater benefits. Its very professors show a swagger; there is about them nothing of the hang-dog look that characterizes their colleagues nearly everywhere else. The tradition of the place is independent and contumacious. It was the first American university to throw out the theologians. It encourages odd fish. It cares nothing for public opinion. But all the while it insists upon plausible table manners, and has no truck with orators.

A Harvard man feels at ease in Zion, and with sound reason. A Yale man, however he may snort and roar, can never get rid of the scarlet fact that, while he was being fattened for the investment securities business, he was herded into chapel every morning. It rides him through life like a Freudian suppression: he recalls it in the forlorn blackness of the night as a Y.M.C.A. secretary recalls a wicked glass of beer, or the smooth, demoralizing, horrible whiteness of a charwoman's neck. A Princeton man remembers the Fundamentalists at commencement—flies in amber, spectres at memory's feast. In all the other great universities there are co-eds. In the lesser colleges there are rules against smoking, beadles, courses in Americanization, praying bands. The Harvard man, looking back, sees only a pink glow. His college has not turned out a wowser in 150 years. His accent and necktie are correct. His classmates continue to be worth knowing. No wonder he regards the Republic as his oyster.

(The Baltimore Evening Sun, June 6, 1927)

The Scopes Trial

John Thomas Scopes, science teacher and athletic coach of Rhea County High School, had been arrested for teaching Darwin's theory of evolution, which stressed the scientific basis for man's existence (as opposed to the divine creation of man as taught in the Bible), thus violating the antievolution law which had been passed by the Tennessee legislature the previous March. Mencken helped enlist Clarence Darrow and Dudley Field Malone, perhaps the most outstanding lawyers of their day, as leaders of the team of defense attorneys for Scopes. William Jennings Bryan, presidential candidate and a Fundamentalist who believed that the antievolution code must be written into the Federal Constitution itself, volunteered to join the prosecution.

When Mencken arrived in Dayton, Tennessee, he found the town decked out as though for a carnival. The road leading into Chattanooga had been lined with signs that read, "Sweethearts, Come to Jesus," "You Need God in Your Business," and "Prepare to Meet Thy God." Across Main Street were strung colorful banners. Newly constructed hot dog, lemonade and sandwich stands lined the sidewalks. There were comic posters depicting monkeys and coconuts; a circus man brought two chimpanzees to testify for the prosecution and set them up as a sideshow. Many of the local populace had thought the trial would provide favorable publicity, and were greatly incensed when it turned against them. Notwithstanding this carnival atmosphere, Mencken found much to admire in Dayton: "The town, I confess, greatly surprised me," he wrote. ". . . What I found was a country town full of charm and even beauty—" But as the trial progressed, Mencken found a seamier underbelly to the town.

During that hot July, some 225 newspapermen representing the world press descended upon Dayton, among them some of the most distinguished reporters outside the national conventions. Inside of the freshly painted courtroom (in a glazed finish the same color as the glaring sun outside), reporters and newsreel operators stood on a table in the corner of a room, observing the trial. Mencken was among them, surveying his surroundings with an expression of delighted incredulity. The heat was intense; there were no electric fans in the courtroom, except the one provided for Judge Raulston. The crowd tried to keep cool; William Jennings Bryan fanned himself with an enormous palm-leaf fan, fighting off the assaults of flies which kept landing on his bald head and arms.

During the days of the trial, Mencken was to send back to Baltimore some of the most brilliant dispatches in the history of journalism, occasionally rousing one of the young telegraphers at two o'clock in the morning to immediately send out an idea. (Back at the Sunpapers, *Mencken's report about a camp-meeting revival was tacked on to the* Evening Sun's *bulletin board with the comment, "That's reporting.") He warned his readers not to look upon the Scopes Trial as merely "a trivial farce," saying it had more far-reaching implications that could affect every American for years to come. So did Clarence Darrow, who argued that the statute against evolution violated the principles of freedom guaranteed by the Constitution of the state of Tennessee, concluding:*

"If today you can take a thing like Evolution and make it a crime to teach it in the public schools, tomorrow you can make it a crime to teach it in the private schools, and the next year you can make it a crime to teach it in the hustings or in the churches. At the next session you may ban it in books and in newspapers. Soon you may set Catholic against Protestant and Protestant against Protestant, and try to foist your own religion upon the minds of men. If you can do one you can do the other. Ignorance and fanaticism are ever busy and need feeding. Always they are feeding and gloating for more. Today it is the public school teachers, tomorrow the private. The next day the preachers and lecturers, the magazines, the books, the newspapers. After a while, your Honor, it is the setting of man against man and creed against creed, until with flying banners and beating drums we are marching backward to the glorious ages of the sixteenth century when bigots lighted fagots to burn the men who dared to bring any intelligence and enlightenment and culture to the human mind."

Five days after the trial ended, on July 26, William Jennings Bryan died of a stroke while taking a nap. Judge Raulston denounced Scopes' crime as a "high misdemeanor," fining him $100. The Baltimore Evening Sun *paid the fine for John Scopes, and in 1927 the Tennessee Supreme Court* *reversed Judge Raulston's decision on the technicality that he, not the jury, had fixed the amount of the fine. The* Evening Sun's *money was returned, and Scopes was cleared, but it was not until May 16, 1967, that the antievolution law was repealed in the state of Tennessee. Today, on the wooded hill overlooking Dayton and the valleys of East Tennessee, stands the William Jennings Bryan College.*

Homo Neanderthalensis

I

Such obscenities as the forthcoming trial of the Tennessee evolutionist, if they serve no other purpose, at least call attention dramatically to the fact that enlightenment, among mankind, is very narrowly dispersed. It is common to assume that human progress affects everyone—that even the dullest man, in these bright days, knows more than any man of, say, the Eighteenth Century, and is far more civilized. This assumption is quite erroneous. The men of the educated minority, no doubt, know more than their predecessors, and of some of them, perhaps, it may be said that they are more civilized—though I should not like to be put to giving names —but the great masses of men, even in this inspired republic, are precisely where the mob was at the dawn of history. They are ignorant, they are dishonest, they are cowardly, they are ignoble. They know little if anything that is worth knowing, and there is not the slightest sign of a natural desire among them to increase their knowledge.

Such immortal vermin, true enough, get their share of the fruits of human progress, and so they may be said, in a way, to have their part in it. The most ignorant man, when he is ill, may enjoy whatever boons and usufructs modern medicine may offer—that is, provided he is too poor to choose his own doctor. He is free, if he wants to, to take a bath. The literature of the world is at his disposal in public libraries. He may look at works of art. He may hear good music. He has at hand a thousand devices for making life less wearisome and more tolerable: the telephone, railroads, bichloride tablets, newspapers, sewers, correspondence schools, delicatessen. But he had no more to do with bringing these things into the world than the horned cattle in the fields, and he does no more to increase them today then the birds of the air.

On the contrary, he is generally against them, and sometimes with immense violence. Every step in human progress, from the first feeble stirrings in the abyss of time, has been opposed by the great majority of men. Every valuable thing that has been added to the store of man's possessions has been derided by them when it was new, and destroyed by them when they had the power. They have fought every new truth ever heard of, and they have killed every truth-seeker who got into their hands.

II

The so-called religious organizations which now lead the war against the teaching of evolution are nothing more, at bottom, than conspiracies of the inferior man against his betters. They mirror very accurately his congenital hatred of knowledge, his bitter enmity to the man who knows more than he does, and so gets more out of life. Certainly it cannot have gone unnoticed that their membership is recruited, in the overwhelming main, from the lower orders—that no man of any education or other human dignity belongs to them. What they propose to do, at bottom and in brief, is to make the superior man infamous—by mere abuse if it is sufficient, and if it is not, then by law.

Such organizations, of course, must have leaders; there must be men in them whose ignorance and imbecility are measurably less abject than the ignorance and imbecility of the average. These super-Chandala often attain to a considerable power, especially in democratic states. Their followers trust them and look up to them; sometimes, when the pack is on the loose, it is necessary to conciliate them. But their puissance cannot conceal their incurable inferiority. They belong to the mob as surely as their dupes, and the thing that animates them is precisely the mob's hatred of superiority. Whatever lies above the level of their comprehension is of the devil. A glass of wine delights civilized men; they themselves, drinking it, would get drunk. *Ergo,* wine must be prohibited. The hypothesis of evolution is credited by all men of education; they themselves can't understand it. *Ergo,* its teaching must be put down.

This simple fact explains such phenomena as the Tennessee buffoonery. Nothing else can. We must think of human progress, not as of something going on in the race in general, but as of something going on in a small minority, perpetually beleaguered in a few walled towns. Now and then the horde of barbarians outside breaks through, and we have an armed effort to halt the process. That is, we have a Reformation, a French Revolution, a war for democracy, a Great Awakening. The minority is decimated and driven to cover. But a few survive—and a few are enough to carry on.

III

The inferior man's reasons for hating knowledge are not hard to discern. He hates it because it is complex—because it puts an unbearable burden upon his meager capacity for taking in ideas. Thus his search is always for short cuts. All superstitions are such short cuts. Their aim is to make the unintelligible simple, and even obvious. So on what seem to be higher levels. No man who has not had a long and arduous education can understand even the most elementary concepts of modern pathology. But even a hind at the plow can grasp the theory of chiropractic in two lessons. Hence the vast popularity of chiropractic among the submerged—and of osteopathy, Christian Science and other such quackeries with it. They are idiotic, but they are simple—and every man prefers what he can understand to what puzzles and dismays him.

The popularity of Fundamentalism among the inferior orders of men is explicable in exactly the same way. The cosmogonies that educated men toy with are all inordinately complex. To comprehend their veriest outlines requires an immense stock of knowledge, and a habit of thought. It would be as vain to try to teach to peasants or to the city proletariat as it would be to try to teach them to streptococci. But the cosmogony of Genesis is so simple that even a yokel can grasp it. It is set forth in a few phrases. It offers, to an ignorant man, the irresistible reasonableness of the nonsensical. So he accepts it with loud hosannas, and has one more excuse for hating his betters.

Politics and the fine arts repeat the story. The issues that the former throw up are often so complex that, in the present state of human knowledge, they must remain impenetrable, even to the most enlightened men. How much easier to follow a mountebank with a shibboleth—a Coolidge, a Wilson or a Roosevelt! The arts, like the sciences, demand special training, often very difficult. But in jazz there are simple rhythms, comprehensible even to savages.

IV

What all this amounts to is that the human race is divided into two sharply differentiated and mutually antagonistic classes, almost two genera—a small minority that plays with ideas and is capable of taking them in, and a vast majority that finds them painful, and is thus arrayed against them, and against all who have traffic with them. The intellectual heritage of the race belongs to the minority, and to the minority only. The majority has no more to do with it than it has to do with ecclesiastic politics on Mars. In so far as that heritage is apprehended, it is viewed with enmity. But in the main it is not apprehended at all.

That is why Beethoven survives. Of the 110,000,000 so-called human beings who now live in the United States, flogged and crazed by Coolidge, Rotary, the Ku Klux and the newspapers, it is probable that at least 108,000,000 have never heard of him at all. To these immortals, made in God's image, one of the greatest artists the human race has ever produced is not even a name. So far as they are concerned he might as well have died at birth. The gorgeous and incomparable beauties that he created are nothing to them. They get no value out of the fact that he existed. They are completely unaware of what he did in the world, and would not be interested if they were told.

The fact saves good Ludwig's bacon. His music survives because it lies outside the plane of the popular apprehension, like the colors beyond violet or the concept of honor. If it could be brought within range, it would at once arouse hostility. Its complexity would challenge; its lace of moral purpose would affright. Soon there would be a movement to put it down, and Baptist clergymen would range the land denouncing it, and in the end some poor musician, taken in the un-American act of playing it, would be put on trial before jury of Ku Kluxers, and railroaded to the calaboose.

(*The Baltimore Evening Sun, June 29, 1925*)

Mencken Finds Daytonians
Full of Sickening Doubts
About Value of Publicity

Dayton, Tenn., July 9.—On the eve of the great contest Dayton is full of sickening surges and tremors of doubt. Five or six weeks ago, when the infidel Scopes was first laid by the heels, there was no uncertainty in all this smiling valley. The town boomers leaped to the assault as one man. Here was an unexampled, almost a miraculous chance to get Dayton upon the front pages, to make it talked about, to put it upon the map. But how now?

Today, with the curtain barely rung up and the worst buffooneries to come, it is obvious to even town boomers that getting upon the map, like patriotism, is not enough. The getting there must be managed discreetly, adroitly, with careful regard to psychological niceties. The boomers of Dayton, alas, had no skill at such things, and the experts they called in were all quacks. The result now turns the communal liver to water. Two months ago the town was obscure and happy. Today it is a universal joke.

I have been attending the permanent town meeting that goes on in Robinson's drug store, trying to find out what the town optimists have saved from the wreck. All I can find is a sort of mystical confidence that God will somehow come to the rescue to reward His old and faithful partisans as they deserve—that good will flow eventually out of what now seems to be heavily evil. More specifically, it is believed that settlers will be attracted to the town as to some refuge from the atheism of the great urban Sodoms and Gomorrahs.

But will these refugees bring any money with them? Will they buy lots and build houses? Will they light the fires of the cold and silent blast furnace down the railroad tracks? On these points, I regret to report, optimism has to call in theology to aid it. Prayer can accomplish a lot. It can cure diabetes, find lost pocketbooks and restrain husbands from beating their wives. But is prayer made any more efficacious by giving a circus first? Coming to this thought, Dayton begins to sweat.

The town, I confess, greatly surprised me. I expected to find a squalid Southern village, with darkies snoozing on the horse-blocks, pigs rooting under the houses and the inhabitants full of hookworm and malaria. What I found was a country town full of charm and even beauty—a somewhat smallish but nevertheless very attractive Westminster or Belair.

The houses are surrounded by pretty gardens, with cool green lawns and stately trees. The two chief streets are paved from curb to curb. The stores carry good stocks and have a metropolitan air, especially the drug, book, magazine, sporting goods and soda-water emporium of the estimable Robinson. A few of the town ancients still affect galluses and string ties, but the younger bucks are very nattily turned out. Scopes himself, even in his shirt sleeves, would fit into any college campus in America save that of Harvard alone.

Nor is there any evidence in the town of that poisonous spirit which usually shows itself when Christian men gather to defend the great doctrine of their faith. I have heard absolutely no whisper that Scopes is in the pay of the Jesuits, or that the whisky trust is backing him, or that he is egged on by the Jews who manufacture lascivious moving pictures. On the contrary, the Evolutionists and the Anti-Evolutionists seem to be on the best of terms, and it is hard in a group to distinguish one from another.

The basic issues of the case, indeed, seem to be very little discussed at Dayton. What interests everyone is its mere strategy. By what device, precisely, will Bryan trim old Clarence Darrow? Will he do it gently and with every delicacy of forensics, or will he wade in on high gear and make a swift butchery of it? For no one here seems to doubt that Bryan will win—that is, if the bout goes to a finish. What worries the town is the fear that some diabolical higher power will intervene on Darrow's side—that is, before Bryan heaves him through the ropes.

The lack of Christian heat that I have mentioned is probably due in part to the fact that the fundamentalists are in overwhelming majority as far as the eye can reach—according to most local statisticians, in a majority of at least nine-tenths. There are, in fact, only two downright infidels in all Rhea county, and one of them is charitably assumed to be a bit balmy. The other, a yokel roosting far back in the hills, is probably simply a poet got into the wrong pew. The town account of him is to the effect that he professes to regard death as a beautiful adventure.

When the local ecclesiastics begin alarming the peasantry with word pictures of the last sad scene, and sulphurous fumes begin to choke even Unitarians, this skeptical rustic comes forward with his argument that it is foolish to be afraid of what one knows so little about—that, after all, there is no more genuine evidence that anyone will ever go to hell than there is that the Volstead act will ever be enforced.

Such blasphemous ideas naturally cause talk in a Baptist community, but both of the infidels are unmolested. Rhea county, in fact, is proud of its tolerance, and apparently with good reason. The klan has never got a foothold here, though it rages everywhere else in Tennessee. When the first kleagles came in they got the cold shoulder, and pretty soon they gave up the county as hopeless. It is run today not by anonymous daredevils in white nightshirts, but by well-heeled Free-masons in decorous white aprons. In Dayton alone there are sixty thirty-second-degree Masons—an immense quota for so small a town. They believe in keeping the peace, and so even the stray Catholics of the town are treated politely, though everyone naturally regrets they are required to report to the Pope once a week.

It is probably this unusual tolerance, and not any extraordinary passion for the integrity of Genesis, that has made Dayton the scene of a celebrated case, and got its name upon the front pages, and caused its forward-looking men to begin to wonder uneasily if all advertising is really good advertising. The trial of Scopes is possible here simply because it can be carried on here without heat—because no one will lose any sleep even if the devil comes to the aid of Darrow and Malone, and Bryan gets a mauling. The local intelligentsia venerate Bryan as a Christian, but it was not as a Christian that they called him in, but as one adept at attracting the newspaper boys—in brief, as a showman. As I have said, they now begin to mistrust the show, but they still believe that he will make a good one, win or lose.

Elsewhere, North or South, the combat would become bitter. Here it retains the lofty qualities of the *duello*. I gather the notion, indeed, that the gentlemen who are most active in promoting it are precisely the most lacking in hot conviction—that it is, in its local aspects, rather a joust between neutrals than a battle between passionate believers. Is it a mere coincidence that the town clergy have been very carefully kept out of it? There are several Baptist brothers here of such powerful gifts that when they begin belaboring sinners the very rats of the alleys flee to the hills. They preach dreadfully. But they are not heard from today. By some process to me unknown they have been induced to shut up—a far harder business, I venture, than knocking out a lion with a sandbag. But the sixty thirty-second degree Masons of Dayton have somehow achieved it.

Thus the battle joins and the good red sun shines down. Dayton lies in a fat and luxuriant valley. The bottoms are green with corn, pumpkins and young orchards and the hills are full of reliable moonshiners, all save one of them Christian men. We are not in the South here, but hanging on to the North. Very little cotton is grown in the valley. The people in politics are Republicans and put Coolidge next to Lincoln and John Wesley. The fences are in good repair. The roads are smooth and hard. The scene is set for a high-toned and even somewhat swagger combat. When it is over all the participants save Bryan will shake hands.

(The Baltimore Evening Sun, July 9, 1925)

Impossibility of Obtaining Fair Jury Insures Scopes' Conviction, Says Mencken

Dayton, Tenn., July 10.—The trial of the infidel Scopes, beginning here this hot, lovely morning, will greatly resemble, I suspect, the trial of a prohibition agent accused of mayhem in Union Hill, N.J. That is to say, it will be conducted with the most austere regard for the highest principles of jurisprudence. Judge and jury will go to extreme lengths to assure the prisoner the last and least of his rights. He will be protected in his person and feelings by the full military and naval power of the State of Tennessee. No one will be permitted to pull his nose, to pray publicly for his condemnation or even to make a face at him. But all the same he will be bumped off inevitably when the time comes, and to the applause of all right-thinking men.

The real trial, in truth, will not begin until Scopes is convicted and ordered to the hulks. Then the prisoner will be the Legislature of Tennessee, and the jury will be that great fair, unimpassioned body of enlightened men which has already decided that a horse hair put into a bottle will turn into a snake and that the Kaiser started the late war. What goes on here is simply a sort of preliminary hearing, with music by the village choir. For it will be no more possible in this Christian valley to get a jury unprejudiced against Scopes than would be possible in Wall Street to get a jury unprejudiced against a Bolshevik.

I speak of prejudice in its purely philosophical sense. As I wrote yesterday, there is an almost complete absence, in these pious hills, of the ordinary and familiar malignancy of Christian men. If the Rev. Dr. Crabbe ever spoke of bootleggers as humanely and affectionately as the town theologians speak of Scopes, and even Darrow and Malone, his employers would pelt him with their spyglasses and sit on him until the ambulance came from Mount Hope. There is absolutely no bitterness on tap. But neither is there any doubt. It has been decided by acclamation, with only a few infidels dissenting, that the hypothesis of evolution is profane, inhumane and against God, and all that remains is to translate that almost unanimous decision into the jargon of the law and so have done.

The town boomers have banqueted Darrow as well as Bryan, but there is no mistaking which of the two has the crowd, which means the venire of tried and true men. Bryan has been oozing around the country since his first day here, addressing this organization and that, presenting the indubitable Word of God in his caressing, ingratiating way, and so making unanimity doubly unanimous. From the defense yesterday came hints that this was making hay before the sun had legally begun to shine—even that it was a sort of contempt of court. But no Daytonian believes anything of the sort. What Bryan says doesn't seem to these congenial Baptists and Methodists to be argument; it seems to be a mere graceful statement of the obvious.

Meanwhile, reinforcements continue to come in, some of them from unexpected sources. I had the honor of being present yesterday when Col. Patrick Callahan, of Louisville, marched up at the head of his cohort of 250,000,000 Catholic fundamentalists. The

two colonels embraced, exchanged a few military and legal pleasantries and then retired up a steep stairway to the office of the
Hicks brothers to discuss strategy. Colonel Callahan's followers
were present, of course, only by a legal fiction; the town of Dayton would not hold so large an army. In the actual flesh there were
only the colonel himself and his aide-de-camp. Nevertheless, the
250,000,000 were put down as present and recorded as voting.

Later on I had the misfortune to fall into a dispute with Colonel
Callahan on a point of canon law. It was my contention that the
position of the Roman Church, on matters of doctrine, is not ordinarily stated by laymen—that such matters are usually left to high
ecclesiastical authorities, headed by the Bishop of Rome. I also
contended, perhaps somewhat fatuously, that there seemed to be a
considerable difference of opinion regarding organic evolution
among these authorities—that it was possible to find in their writings both ingenious arguments for it and violent protests against
it. All these objections Colonel Callahan waived away with a genial gesture. He was here, he said, to do what he could for the
authority of the Sacred Scriptures and the aiding and comforting
of his old friend, Bryan, and it was all one to him whether atheists
yelled or not. Then he began to talk about prohibition, which he
favors, and the germ theory of diseases, which he regards as bilge.

A somewhat more plausible volunteer has turned up in the person of Pastor T. T. Martin, of Blue Mountain, Miss. He has hired
a room and stocked it with pamphlets bearing such titles as
"Evolution a Menace," "Hell and the High Schools" and "God or
Gorilla," and addresses connoisseurs of scientific fallacy every
night on a lot behind the Courthouse. Pastor Martin, a handsome
and amiable old gentleman with a great mop of snow-white hair,
was a professor of science in a Baptist college for years, and has
given profound study to the biological sections of the Old Testament.

He told me today that he regarded the food regulations in Levit-
icus as so sagacious that their framing must have been a sort of
feat even for divinity. The flesh of the domestic hog, he said, is a
rank poison as ordinarily prepared for the table, though it is probably harmless when smoked and salted, as in bacon. He said that
his investigations had shown that seven and a half out of every
thirteen cows are quite free of tuberculosis, but that twelve out of
every thirteen hogs have it in an advanced and highly communica-
ble form. The Jews, protected by their piety against devouring

pork, are immune to the disease. In all history, he said, there is authentic record of but one Jew who died of tuberculosis.

The presence of Pastor Martin and Colonel Callahan has given renewed confidence to the prosecution. The former offers proof that men of science are, after all, not unanimously atheists, and the latter that there is no division between Christians in the face of the common enemy. But though such encouragements help, they are certainly not necessary. All they really supply is another layer of icing on the cake. Dayton will give Scopes a rigidly fair and impartial trial. All his Constitutional rights will be jealously safeguarded. The question whether he voted for or against Coolidge will not be permitted to intrude itself into the deliberations of the jury, or the gallant effort of Colonel Bryan to get at and establish the truth. He will be treated very politely. Dayton, indeed, is proud of him, as Sauk Center, Minn., is proud of Sinclair Lewis and Whittingham, Vt., of Brigham Young. But it is lucky for Scopes that sticking pins into Genesis is still only a misdemeanor in Tennessee, punishable by a simple fine, with no alternative of the knout, the stone pile or exile to the Dry Tortugas.

(The Baltimore Evening Sun, July 10, 1925)

Mencken Likens Trial to a Religious Orgy, with Defendant a Beelzebub

Chattanooga, Tenn., July 11.—Life down here in the Cumberland mountains realizes almost perfectly the ideal of those righteous and devoted men, Dr. Howard A. Kelly, the Rev. Dr. W. W. Davis, the Hon. Richard H. Edmonds and the Hon. Henry S. Dulaney. That is to say, evangelical Christianity is one hundred per cent triumphant. There is, of course, a certain subterranean heresy, but it is so cowed that it is almost inarticulate, and at its worst it would pass for the strictest orthodoxy in such Sodoms of infidelity as Baltimore. It may seem fabulous, but it is a sober fact that a sound Episcopalian or even a Northern Methodist would be regarded as virtually an atheist in Dayton. Here the only genuine conflict is between true believers. Of a given text in Holy Writ one faction may say this thing and another that, but both agree unreservedly that the text itself is impeccable, and neither in the midst of the most violent disputation would venture to accuse the other of doubt.

To call a man a doubter in these parts is equal to accusing him of cannibalism. Even the infidel Scopes himself is not charged with any such infamy. What they say of him, at worst, is that he permitted himself to be used as a cat's paw by scoundrels eager to destroy the anti-evolution law for their own dark and hellish ends. There is, it appears, a conspiracy of scientists afoot. Their purpose is to break down religion, propagate immorality, and so reduce mankind to the level of the brutes. They are the sworn and sinister agents of Beelzebub, who yearns to conquer the world, and has his eye especially upon Tennessee. Scopes is thus an agent of Beelzebub once removed, but that is as far as any fair man goes in condemning him. He is young and yet full of folly. When the secular arm has done execution upon him, the pastors will tackle him and he will be saved.

The selection of a jury to try him, which went on all yesterday afternoon in the atmosphere of a blast furnace, showed to what extreme lengths the salvation of the local primates has been pushed. It was obvious after a few rounds that the jury would be unanimously hot for Genesis. The most that Mr. Darrow could hope for was to sneak in a few men bold enough to declare publicly that they would have to hear the evidence against Scopes before condemning him. The slightest sign of anything further brought forth a peremptory challenge from the State. Once a man was challenged without examination for simply admitting that he did not belong formally to any church. Another time a panel man who confessed that he was prejudiced against evolution got a hearty round of applause from the crowd.

The whole process quickly took on an air of strange unreality, at least to a stranger from heathen parts. The desire of the judge to be fair to the defense, and even polite and helpful, was obvious enough—in fact, he more than once stretched the local rules of procedure in order to give Darrow a hand. But it was equally obvious that the whole thing was resolving itself into the trial of a man by his sworn enemies. A local pastor led off with a prayer calling on God to put down heresy; the judge himself charged the

grand jury to protect the schools against subversive ideas. And
when the candidates for the petit jury came up Darrow had to
pass fundamentalist after fundamentalist into the box—some of
them glaring at him as if they expected him to go off with a sulphurous bang every time he mopped his bald head.

In brief this is a strictly Christian community, and such is its
notion of fairness, justice and due process of law. Try to picture a
town made up wholly of Dr. Crabbes and Dr. Kellys, and you will
have a reasonably accurate image of it. Its people are simply unable to imagine a man who rejects the literal authority of the Bible. The most they can conjure up, straining until they are red in
the face, is a man who is in error about the meaning of this or that
text. Thus one accused of heresy among them is like one accused
of boiling his grandmother to make soap in Maryland. He must
resign himself to being tried by a jury wholly innocent of any
suspicion of the crime he is charged with and unanimously convinced that it is infamous. Such a jury, in the legal sense, may be
fair. That is, it may be willing to hear the evidence against him
before bumping him off. But it would certainly be spitting into
the eye of reason to call it impartial.

The trial, indeed, takes on, for all its legal forms, something of
the air of a religious orgy. The applause of the crowd I have already mentioned. Judge Raulston rapped it down and threatened
to clear the room if it was repeated, but he was quite unable to still
its echoes under his very windows. The courthouse is surrounded
by a large lawn, and it is peppered day and night with evangelists.
One and all they are fundamentalists and their yells and bawlings
fill the air with orthodoxy. I have listened to twenty of them and
had private discourse with a dozen, and I have yet to find one who
doubted so much as the typographical errors in Holy Writ. They
dispute raucously and far into the night, but they begin and end
on the common ground of complete faith. One of these holy men
wears a sign on his back announcing that he is the Bible champion
of the world. He told me today that he had studied the Bible four
hours a day for thirty-three years, and that he had devised a plan
of salvation that would save the worst sinner ever heard of, even a
scientist, a theater actor or a pirate on the high seas, in forty days.
This gentleman denounced the hard-shell Baptists as swindlers.
He admitted freely that their sorcerers were powerful preachers
and could save any ordinary man from sin, but he said that they
were impotent against iniquity. The distinction is unknown to

city theologians, but is as real down here as that between sanctification and salvation. The local experts, in fact, debate it daily. The Bible champion, just as I left him, was challenged by one such professor, and the two were still hard at it an hour later.

Most of the participants in such recondite combats, of course, are yokels from the hills, where no sound is heard after sundown save the roar of the catamount and the wailing of departed spirits, and a man thus has time to ponder the divine mysteries. But it is an amazing thing that the more polished classes also participate actively. The professor who challenged the Bible champion was indistinguishable, to the eye, from a bond salesman or city bootlegger. He had on a natty palm beach suit and a fashionable soft collar and he used excellent English. Obviously, he was one who had been through the local high school and perhaps a country college. Yet he was so far uncontaminated by infidelity that he stood in the hot sun for a whole hour debating a point that even bishops might be excused for dodging, winter as well as summer.

The Bible champion is matched and rivaled by whole herds of other metaphysicians, and all of them attract good houses and have to defend themselves against constant attack. The Seventh Day Adventists, the Campbellites, the Holy Rollers and a dozen other occult sects have field agents on the ground. They follow the traveling judges through all this country. Everywhere they go, I am told, they find the natives ready to hear them and dispute with them. They find highly accomplished theologians in every village, but even in the county towns they never encounter a genuine skeptic. If a man has doubts in this immensely pious country, he keeps them to himself.

Dr. Kelly should come down here and see his dreams made real. He will find a people who not only accept the Bible as an infallible handbook of history, geology, biology and celestial physics, but who also practice its moral precepts—at all events, up to the limit of human capacity. It would be hard to imagine a more moral town than Dayton. If it has any bootleggers, no visitor has heard of them. Ten minutes after I arrived a leading citizen offered me a drink made up half of white mule and half of coca cola, but he seems to have been simply indulging himself in a naughty gesture. No fancy woman has been seen in the town since the end of the McKinley administration. There is no gambling. There is no place to dance. The relatively wicked, when they would indulge themselves, go to Robinson's drug store and debate theology.

In a word, the new Jerusalem, the ideal of all soul savers and sin exterminators. Nine churches are scarcely enough for the 1,800 inhabitants: many of them go into the hills to shout and roll. A clergyman has the rank and authority of a major-general of artillery. A Sunday-school superintendent is believed to have the gift of prophecy. But what of life here? Is it more agreeable than in Babylon? I regret that I must have to report that it is not. The incessant clashing of theologians grows monotonous in a day and intolerable the day following. One longs for a merry laugh, a burst of happy music, the gurgle of a decent jug. Try a meal in the hotel; it is tasteless and swims in grease. Go to the drug store and call for refreshment: the boy will hand you almost automatically a beaker of coca cola. Look at the magazine counter: a pile of *Saturday Evening Post*s two feet high. Examine the books: melodrama and cheap amour. Talk to a town magnifico; he knows nothing that is not in Genesis.

I propose that Dr. Kelly be sent here for sixty days, preferably in the heat of summer. He will return to Baltimore yelling for a carboy of pilsner and eager to master the saxophone. His soul perhaps will be lost, but he will be a merry and a happy man.

(The Baltimore Evening Sun, July 11, 1925)

Yearning Mountaineers' Souls
Need Reconversion Nightly,
Mencken Finds

Dayton, Tenn., July 13.—There is a Unitarian clergyman here from New York, trying desperately to horn into the trial and execution of the infidel Scopes. He will fail. If Darrow ventured to put him on the stand the whole audience, led by the jury, would leap out of the courthouse windows, and take to the hills. Darrow himself, indeed, is as much as they can bear. The whisper that he is an atheist has been stilled by the bucolic make-up and by the public report that he has the gift of prophecy and can reconcile Genesis and evolution. Even so, there is ample space about him when he navigates the streets. The other day a newspaper woman was warned by her landlady to keep out of the courtroom when he was on his legs. All the local sorcerers predict that a bolt from heaven will fetch him in the end. The night he arrived there was a violent storm, the town water turned brown, and horned cattle in the lowlands were afloat for hours. A woman back in the mountains gave birth to a child with hair four inches long, curiously bobbed in scallops.

The Book of Revelation has all the authority, in these theological uplands, of military orders in time of war. The people turn to it for light upon all their problems, spiritual and secular. If a text were found in it denouncing the Anti-Evolution law, then the Anti-Evolution law would become infamous overnight. But so far the exegetes who roar and snuffle in the town have found no such text. Instead they have found only blazing ratifications and reinforcements of Genesis. Darwin is the devil with seven tails and nine horns. Scopes, though he is disguised by flannel pantaloons and a Beta Theta Pi haircut, is the harlot of Babylon. Darrow is Beelzebub in person and Malone is the Crown Prince Friedrich Wilhelm.

I have hitherto hinted an Episcopalian down here in the coca-cola belt is regarded as an atheist. It sounds like one of the lies that journalists tell, but it is really an understatement of the facts. Even a Methodist, by Rhea county standards, is one a bit debauched by pride of intellect. It is the four Methodists on the jury who are expected to hold out for giving Scopes Christian burial after he is hanged. They all made it plain, when they were examined, that they were free-thinking and independent men, and not to be run amuck by the superstitions of the lowly. One actually confessed that he seldom read the Bible, though he hastened to add that he was familiar with its principles. The fellow had on a boiled shirt and a polka dot necktie. He sits somewhat apart. When Darrow withers to a cinder under the celestial blowpipe, this dubious Wesleyan, too, will lose a few hairs.

Even the Baptists no longer brew a medicine that is strong enough for the mountaineers. The sacrament of baptism by total immersion is over too quickly for them, and what follows offers nothing that they can get their teeth into. What they crave is a continuous experience of the divine power, an endless series of evidence that the true believer is a marked man, ever under the eye of God. It is not enough to go to a revival once a year or twice a year; there must be a revival every night. And it is not enough to accept the truth as a mere statement of indisputable and awful fact: it must be embraced ecstatically and orgiastically, to the accompaniment of loud shouts, dreadful heavings and gurglings, and dancing with arms and legs.

This craving is satisfied brilliantly by the gaudy practices of the Holy Rollers, and so the mountaineers are gradually gravitating toward the Holy Roller communion, or, as they prefer to call it, the Church of God. Gradually, perhaps, is not the word. They are actually going in by whole villages and townships. At the last count of noses there were 20,000 Holy Rollers in these hills. The next census, I have no doubt, will show many more. The cities of the lowlands, of course, still resist, and so do most of the county towns, including even Dayton, but once one steps off the State roads the howl of holiness is heard in the woods, and the yokels carry on an almost continuous orgy.

A foreigner in store clothes going out from Dayton must approach the sacred grove somewhat discreetly. It is not that the Holy Rollers, discovering him, would harm him; it is simply that they would shut down their boiling of the devil and flee into the forests. We left Dayton an hour after nightfall and parked our car in a wood a mile or so beyond the little hill village of Morgantown. Far off in a glade a flickering light was visible and out of the silence came a faint rumble of exhortation. We could scarcely distinguish the figure of the preacher; it was like looking down the tube of a dark field microscope. We got out of the car and sneaked along the edge of a mountain cornfield.

Presently we were near enough to see what was going on. From the great limb of a mighty oak hung a couple of crude torches of the sort that car inspectors thrust under Pullman cars when a train pulls in at night. In their light was a preacher, and for a while we could see no one else. He was an immensely tall and thin mountaineer in blue jeans, his collarless shirt open at the neck and his hair a tousled mop. As he preached he paced up and down under the smoking flambeaux and at each turn he thrust his arms into the air and yelled, "Glory to God!" We crept nearer in the shadow of the cornfield and began to hear more of his discourse. He was preaching on the day of judgment. The high kings of the earth, he roared, would all fall down and die; only the sanctified would stand up to receive the Lord God of Hosts. One of these kings he mentioned by name—the king of what he called Greece-y. The King of Greece-y, he said, was doomed to hell.

We went forward a few more yards and began to see the audience. It was seated on benches ranged round the preacher in a circle. Behind him sat a row of elders, men and women. In front were the younger folk. We kept on cautiously, and individuals rose out of the ghostly gloom. A young mother sat suckling her baby, rocking as the preacher paced up and down. Two scared little girls hugged each other, their pigtails down their backs. An immensely huge mountain woman, in a gingham dress cut in one piece, rolled on her heels at every "Glory to God." To one side, but half visible, was what appeared to be a bed. We found out afterward that two babies were asleep upon it.

The preacher stopped at last and there arose out of the darkness a woman with her hair pulled back into a little tight knot. She began so quietly that we couldn't hear what she said, but soon her voice rose resonantly and we could follow her. She was denouncing the reading of books. Some wandering book agent, it appeared, had come to her cabin and tried to sell her a specimen of his wares. She refused to touch it. Why, indeed, read a book? If what was in it was true then everything in it was already in the Bible. If it was false then reading it would imperil the soul. Her syllogism complete, she sat down.

There followed a hymn, led by a somewhat fat brother wearing silver-rimmed country spectacles. It droned on for half a dozen stanzas, and then the first speaker resumed the floor. He argued that the gift of tongues was real and that education was a snare. Once his children could read the Bible, he said, they had enough. Beyond lay only infidelity and damnation. Sin stalked the cities. Dayton itself was a Sodom. Even Morgantown had begun to forget God. He sat down, and the female aurochs in gingham got up.

She began quietly, but was soon leaping and roaring, and it was hard to follow her. Under cover of the turmoil we sneaked a bit closer. A couple of other discourses followed, and there were two or three hymns. Suddenly a change of mood began to make itself felt. The last hymn ran longer than the others and dropped gradually into a monotonous, unintelligible chant. The leader beat time with his book. The faithful broke out with exultations. When the singing ended there was a brief palaver that we could not hear and two of the men moved a bench into the circle of light directly under the flambeaux. Then a half-grown girl emerged from the darkness and threw herself upon it. We noticed with astonishment that she had bobbed hair. "This sister," said the leader, "has asked for prayers." We moved a bit closer. We could now see faces plainly and hear every word.

What followed quickly reached such heights of barbaric grotesquerie that it was hard to believe it real. At a signal all the faithful crowded up the bench and began to pray—not in unison but each for himself. At another they all fell on their knees, their arms over the penitent. The leader kneeled, facing us, his head alternately thrown back dramatically or buried in his hands. Words spouted from his lips like bullets from a machine gun— appeals to God to pull the penitent back out of hell, defiances of the powers and principalities of the air, a vast impassioned jargon of apocalyptic texts. Suddenly he rose to his feet, threw back his head and began to speak in tongues—blub-blub-blub, gurgle-gurgle-gurgle. His voice rose to a higher register. The climax was a shrill, inarticulate squawk, like that of a man throttled. He fell headlong across the pyramid of supplicants.

A comic scene? Somehow, no. The poor half wits were too horribly in earnest. It was like peeping through a knothole at the writhings of a people in pain. From the squirming and jabbering mass a young woman gradually detached herself—a woman not uncomely, with a pathetic home-made cap on her head. Her head jerked back, the veins of her neck swelled, and her fists went to her throat as if she were fighting for breath. She bent backward until she was like half of a hoop. Then she suddenly snapped forward. We caught a flash of the whites of her eyes. Presently her whole body began to be convulsed—great convulsions that began at the shoulders and ended at the hips. She would leap to her feet, thrust her arms in air and then hurl herself upon the heap. Her praying flattened out into a mere delirious caterwauling, like that of a tomcat on a petting party.

I describe the thing as a strict behaviorist. The lady's subjective sensations I leave to infidel pathologists. Whatever they were they were obviously contagious, for soon another damsel joined her, and then another and then a fourth. The last one had an extraordinary bad attack. She began with mild enough jerks of the head, but in a moment she was bounding all over the place, exactly like a chicken with its head cut off. Every time her head came up a stream of yells and barkings would issue out of it. Once she collided with a dark, undersized brother, hitherto silent and stolid.

Contact with her set him off as if he had been kicked by a mule. He leaped into the air, threw back his head and began to gargle as if with a mouthful of BB shot. Then he loosened one tremendous stentorian sentence in the tongues and collapsed.

By this time the performers were quite oblivious to the profane universe. We left our hiding and came up to the little circle of light. We slipped into the vacant seats on one of the rickety benches. The heap of mourners was directly before us. They bounced into us as they cavorted. The smell that they radiated, sweating there in that obscene heap, half suffocated us. Not all of them, of course, did the thing in the grand manner. Some merely moaned and rolled their eyes. The female ox in gingham flung her great bulk on the ground and jabbered an unintelligible prayer. One of the men, in the intervals between fits, put on spectacles and read his Bible.

Beside me on the bench sat the young mother and her baby. She suckled it through the whole orgy, obviously fascinated by what was going on, but never venturing to take any hand in it. On the bed just outside the light two other babies slept peacefully. In the shadows, suddenly appearing and as suddenly going away, were vague figures, whether believers or of scoffers I do not know. They seemed to come and go in couples. Now and then a couple at the ringside would step back and then vanish into the black night. After a while some came back. There was whispering outside the circle of vision. A couple of Fords lurched up in the wood road, cutting holes in the darkness with their lights. Once some one out of sight loosed a bray of laughter.

All this went on for an hour or so. The original penitent, by this time, was buried three deep beneath the heap. One caught a glimpse, now and then, of her yellow bobbed hair, but then she would vanish again. How she breathed down there I don't know; it was hard enough ten feet away, with a strong five-cent cigar to help. When the praying brothers would rise up for a bout with the tongues their faces were streaming with perspiration. The fat harridan in gingham sweated like a longshoreman. Her hair got loose and fell down over her face. She fanned herself with her skirt. A powerful old gal she was, equal in her day to obstetrics and a week's washing on the same morning, but this was worse than a week's washing. Finally, she fell into a heap, breathing in great, convulsive gasps.

We tired of it after a while and groped our way back to our

automobile. When we got to Dayton, after 11 o'clock—an immensely late hour in these parts—the whole town was still gathered on the courthouse lawn, hanging upon the disputes of theologians. The Bible champion of the world had a crowd. The Seventh Day Adventist missionaries had a crowd. A volunteer from faraway Portland, Ore., made up exactly like Andy Gump, had another and larger crowd. Dayton was enjoying itself. All the usual rules were suspended and the curfew bell was locked up. The prophet Bryan, exhausted by his day's work for Revelation, was snoring in his bed up the road, but enough volunteers were still on watch to keep the battlements manned.

Such is human existence among the fundamentalists, where children are brought up on Genesis and sin is unknown. If I have made the tale too long, then blame the spirit of garrulity that is in the local air. Even newspaper reporters, down here, get some echo of the call. Divine inspiration is as common as the hookworm. I have done my best to show you what the great heritage of mankind comes to in regions where the Bible is the beginning and end of wisdom, and the mountebank Bryan, parading the streets in his seersucker coat, is pointed out to sucklings as the greatest man since Abraham.

(The Baltimore Evening Sun, July 13, 1925)

Darrow's Eloquent Appeal Wasted on Ears That Heed Only Bryan, Says Mencken

Dayton, Tenn., July 14.—The net effect of Clarence Darrow's great speech yesterday seems to be precisely the same as if he had bawled it up a rainspout in the interior of Afghanistan. That is, locally, upon the process against the infidel Scopes, upon the so-called minds of these fundamentalists of upland Tennessee. You have but a dim notion of it who have only read it. It was not designed for reading, but for hearing. The clanging of it was as important as the logic. It rose like a wind and ended like a flourish of bugles. The very judge on the bench, toward the end of it, began to look uneasy. But the morons in the audience, when it was over, simply hissed it.

During the whole time of its delivery the old mountebank, Bryan, sat tight-lipped and unmoved. There is, of course, no reason why it should have shaken him. He has those hill billies locked up in his pen and he knows it. His brand is on them. He is at home among them. Since his earliest days, indeed, his chief strength has been among the folk of remote hills and forlorn and lonely farms. Now with his political aspirations all gone to pot, he turns to them for religious consolations. They understand his peculiar imbecilities. His nonsense is their ideal of sense. When he deluges them with his theological bilge they rejoice like pilgrims disporting in the river Jordan.

The town whisper is that the local attorney-general, Stewart, is not a fundamentalist, and hence has no stomach for his job. It seems not improbable. He is a man of evident education, and his argument yesterday was confined very strictly to the constitutional points—the argument of a competent and conscientious lawyer, and to me, at least very persuasive.

But Stewart, after all, is a foreigner here, almost as much so as Darrow or Hays or Malone. He is doing his job and that is all. The real animus of the prosecution centers in Bryan. He is the plaintiff and prosecutor. The local lawyers are simply bottle-holders for him. He will win the case, not by academic appeals to law and precedent, but by direct and powerful appeals to the immemorial fears and superstitions of man. It is no wonder that he is hot against Scopes. Five years of Scopes and even these mountaineers would begin to laugh at Bryan. Ten years and they would ride him out of town on a rail, with one Baptist parson in front of him and another behind.

But there will be no ten years of Scopes, nor five years, nor even one year.

Such brash young fellows, debauched by the enlightenment, must be disposed of before they become dangerous, and Bryan is here, with his tight lips and hard eyes, to see that this one is disposed of. The talk of the lawyers, even the magnificent talk of Darrow, is so much idle wind music. The case will not be decided by logic, nor even by eloquence. It will be decided by counting noses—and for every nose in these hills that has ever thrust itself into any book save the Bible there are a hundred adorned with the brass ring of Bryan. These are his people. They understand him when he speaks in tongues. The same dark face that is in his own eyes is in theirs, too. They feel with him, and they relish him.

I sincerely hope that the nobility and gentry of the lowlands will not make the colossal mistake of viewing this trial of Scopes as a trivial farce. Full of rustic japes and in bad taste, it is, to be sure, somewhat comic on the surface. One laughs to see lawyers sweat. The jury, marched down Broadway, would set New York by the ears. But all of that is only skin deep.

Deeper down there are the beginnings of a struggle that may go on to melodrama of the first caliber, and when the curtain falls at least all the laughter may be coming from the yokels. You probably laughed at the prohibitionists, say, back in 1914. Well, don't make the same error twice.

As I have said, Bryan understands these peasants, and they understand him. He is a bit mangey and flea-bitten, but no means ready for his harp. He may last five years, ten years or even longer. What he may accomplish in that time, seen here at close range, looms up immensely larger than it appears to a city man five hundred miles away. The fellow is full of such bitter, implacable hatreds that they radiate from him like heat from a stove. He hates the learning that he cannot grasp. He hates those who sneer at him. He hates, in general, all who stand apart from his own pathetic commonness. And the yokels hate with him, some of them almost as bitterly as he does himself. They are willing and eager to follow him—and he has already given them a taste of blood.

Darrow's peroration yesterday was interrupted by Judge Raulston, but the force of it got into the air nevertheless. This year it is a misdemeanor for a country school teacher to flout the archaic nonsense of Genesis. Next year it will be a felony. The year after the net will be spread wider. Pedagogues, after all, are small game; there are larger birds to snare—larger and juicier. Bryan has his fishy eye on them. He will fetch them if his mind lasts, and the lamp holds out to burn. No man with a mouth like that ever lets go. Nor ever lacks followers.

Tennessee is bearing the brunt of the first attack simply because the civilized minority, down here, is extraordinarily pusillanimous.

I have met no educated man who is not ashamed of the ridicule that has fallen upon the State, and I have met none, save only

Judge Neal, who had the courage to speak out while it was yet time. No Tennessee counsel of any importance came into the case until yesterday and then they came in stepping very softly as if taking a brief for sense were a dangerous matter. When Bryan did his first rampaging here all these men were silent.

They had known for years what was going on in the hills. They knew what the country preachers were preaching—what degraded nonsense was being rammed and hammered into yokel skulls. But they were afraid to go out against the imposture while it was in the making, and when any outsider denounced it they fell upon him violently as an enemy of Tennessee.

Now Tennessee is paying for that poltroonery. The State is smiling and beautiful, and of late it has begun to be rich. I know of no American city that is set in more lovely scenery than Chattanooga, or that has more charming homes. The civilized minority is as large here, I believe, as anywhere else.

It has made a city of splendid material comforts and kept it in order. But it has neglected in the past the unpleasant business of following what was going on in the cross roads Little Bethels.

The Baptist preachers ranted unchallenged.

Their buffooneries were mistaken for humor. Now the clowns turn out to be armed, and have begun to shoot.

In his argument yesterday Judge Neal had to admit pathetically that it was hopeless to fight for a repeal of the anti-evolution law. The Legislature of Tennessee, like the Legislature of every other American state, is made up of cheap job-seekers and ignoramuses.

The Governor of the State is a politician ten times cheaper and trashier. It is vain to look for relief from such men. If the State is to be saved at all, it must be saved by the courts. For one, I have little hope of relief in that direction, despite Hays' logic and Darrow's eloquence. Constitutions, in America, no longer mean what they say. To mention the Bill of Rights is to be damned as a Red.

The rabble is in the saddle, and down here it makes its first campaign under a general beside whom Wat Tylor seems like a wart beside the Matterhorn.

(The Baltimore Evening Sun, July 14, 1925)

Law and Freedom, Mencken Discovers,
Yield Place to Holy Writ
in Rhea County

Dayton, Tenn., July 15.—The cops have come up from Chattanooga to help save Dayton from the devil. Darrow, Malone and
Hays, of course, are immune to constabulary process, despite their
obscene attack upon prayer. But all other atheists and anarchists
now have public notice they must shut up forthwith and stay shut
so long as they pollute this bright, shining, buckle of the Bible belt
with their presence. Only one avowed infidel has ventured to
make a public address. The Chattanooga police nabbed him instantly, and he is now under surveillance in a hotel. Let him but
drop one of his impious tracts from his window and he will be
transferred to the town hoose-gow.

The Constitution of Tennessee, as everyone knows, puts free
speech among the most sacred rights of the citizen. More, I am
informed by eminent Chattanooga counsel, that there is no State
law denying it—that is, for persons not pedagogues. But the cops
of Chattanooga, like their brethren elsewhere, do not let constitutions stand in the way of their exercise of their lawful duty. The
captain in charge of the squad now on watch told me frankly
yesterday that he was not going to let any infidels discharge their
damnable nonsense upon the town. I asked him what charge he
would lay against them if they flouted him. He said he would jail
them for disturbing the peace.

"But suppose," I asked him, "a prisoner is actually not disturbing the peace. Suppose he is simply saying his say in a quiet
and orderly manner."

"I'll arrest him anyhow," said the cop.

"Even if no one complains of him?"

"I'll complain myself."

"Under what law precisely?"

"We don't need no law for them kind of people."

It sounded like New York in the old days, before Mayor Gaynor took the constitution out of cold storage and began to belabor the gendarmerie with it. The captain admitted freely that speaking in the streets was not disturbing the peace so long as the speaker stuck to orthodox Christian doctrine as it is understood by the local exegetes.

A preacher of any sect that admits the literal authenticity of Genesis is free to gather a crowd at any time and talk all he wants. More, he may engage in a disputation with any other expert. I have heard at least a hundred such discussions, and some of them have been very acrimonious. But the instant a speaker utters a word against divine revelation he begins to disturb the peace and is liable to immediate arrest and confinement in the calaboose beside the railroad tracks.

Such is criminal law in Rhea county as interpreted by the uniformed and freely sweating agents. As I have said, there are legal authorities in Chattanooga who dissent sharply, and even argue that the cops are a set of numbskulls and ought to be locked up as public nuisances. But one need not live a long, incandescent week in the Bible belt to know that jurisprudence becomes a new science as one crosses the border. Here the ordinary statutes are reinforced by Holy Writ, and whenever there is a conflict Holy Writ takes precedence.

Judge Raulston himself has decided, in effect, that in a trial for heresy it is perfectly fair and proper to begin proceedings with a prayer for the confutation and salvation of the defendant. On lower levels, and especially in the depths where policemen do their thinking, the doctrine is even more frankly stated. Before laying Christians by the heels the cops must formulate definite charges against them. They must be accused of something specifically unlawful and there must be witnesses to the act. But infidels are *fera naturae*, and any cop is free to bag at sight and to hold them in durance at his pleasure.

To the same category, it appears, belong political and economic radicals. News came the other day to Pastor T. T. Martin, who is holding a continuous anti-evolution convention in the town, that a party of I.W.W.'s, their pockets full of Russian gold, had started out from Cincinnati to assassinate him. A bit later came word they would bump off Bryan after they had finished Martin, and then set fire to the town churches. Martin first warned Bryan and then complained to the police. The latter were instantly agog. Guards were posted at strategic centers and a watch was kept upon all strangers of a sinister appearance. But the I.W.W.'s were not caught. Yesterday Pastor Martin told me that he had news that they had gone back to Cincinnati to perfect the plot. He posts audiences at every meeting. If the Reds return they will be scotched.

Arthur Garfield Hays, who is not only one of the counsel for the infidel Scopes but also agent and attorney of the notorious American Civil Liberties Union in New York, is planning to hold a free speech meeting on the Courthouse lawn and so make a test of the law against disturbing the peace as it is interpreted by the *polizei*. Hays will be well advertised if he carries out this subversive intention. It is hot enough in the courtroom in the glare of a thousand fundamentalist eyes; in the town jail he would sweat to death.

Rhea county is very hospitable and, judged by Bible belt standards, very tolerant. The Dayton Babbitts gave a banquet to Darrow, despite the danger from lightning, meteors and earthquakes. Even Malone is treated politely, though the very horned cattle in the fields know that he is a Catholic and in constant communication with the Pope. But liberty is one thing and license is quite another. Within the bounds of Genesis the utmost play of opinion is permitted and even encouraged. An evangelist with a new scheme for getting into Heaven can get a crowd in two minutes. But once a speaker admits a doubt, however cautiously, he is handed over to the secular arm.

Two Unitarian clergymen are prowling around the town looking for a chance to discharge their "hellish heresies." One of them is Potter, of New York; the other is Birckhead, of Kansas City. So far they have not made any progress. Potter induced one of the local methodist parsons to give him a hearing, but the congregation protested and the next day the parson had to resign his charge. The Methodists, as I have previously reported, are regarded almost as infidels in Rhea county. Their doctrines, which seem somewhat severe in Baltimore, especially to persons who love a merry life, are here viewed as loose to the point of indecency. The four Methodists on the jury are suspected of being against hanging Scopes, at least without a fair trial. The State tried to get rid of one of them even after he had been passed; his neighbors had come in from his village with news that he had a banjo concealed in his house and was known to read the *Literary Digest*.

The other Unitarian clergyman, Dr. Birckhead, is not actually domiciled in the town, but is encamped, with his wife and child, on the road outside. He is on an automobile tour and stopped off here to see if a chance offered to spread his "poisons." So far he has found none.

Yesterday afternoon a Jewish rabbi from Nashville also showed up, Marks by name. He offered to read and expound Genesis in Hebrew, but found no takers. The Holy Rollers hereabout, when they are seized by the gift of tongues, avoid Hebrew, apparently as a result of Ku Klux influence. Their favorite among all the sacred dialects is Hittite. It sounds to the infidel like a series of college yells.

Judge Raulston's decision yesterday afternoon in the matter of Hays' motion was a masterpiece of unconscious humor. The press stand, in fact, thought he was trying to be jocose deliberately and let off a guffaw that might have gone far if the roar of applause had not choked it off. Hays presented a petition in the name of the two Unitarians, the rabbi and several other theological "reds," praying that in selecting clergymen to open the court with prayer hereafter he choose fundamentalists and anti-fundamentalists alternately. The petition was couched in terms that greatly shocked and enraged the prosecution. When the judge announced that he would leave the nomination of chaplains to the Pastors' Association of the town there was the gust of mirth aforesaid, followed by howls of approval. The Pastors' Association of Dayton is composed of fundamentalists so powerfully orthodox that beside them such a fellow as Dr. John Roach Straton would seem an Ingersoll.

The witnesses of the defense, all of them heretics, began to reach town yesterday and are all quartered at what is called the Mansion, an ancient and empty house outside the town limits, now crudely furnished with iron cots, spittoons, playing cards and the other camp equipment of scientists. Few, if any, of these witnesses will ever get a chance to outrage the jury with their blasphemies, but they are of much interest to the townspeople. The common belief is that they will be blown up with one mighty blast when the verdict of the twelve men, tried and true, is brought in, and Darrow, Malone, Hays and Neal with them. The country people avoid the Mansion. It is foolish to take unnecessary chances. Going into the courtroom, with Darrow standing there shamelessly and openly challenging the wrath of God, is risk enough.

The case promises to drag into next week. The prosecution is fighting desperately and taking every advantage of its superior knowledge of the quirks of local procedure. The defense is heating up and there are few exchanges of courtroom amenities. There will be a lot of oratory before it is all over and some loud and raucous bawling otherwise, and maybe more than one challenge to step outside. The cards seem to be stacked against poor Scopes, but there may be a joker in the pack. Four of the jurymen, as everyone knows, are Methodists, and a Methodist down here belongs to the extreme wing of liberals. Beyond him lie only the justly and incurably damned.

What if one of those Methodists, sweating under the dreadful pressure of fundamentalist influence, jumps into the air, cracks his heels together and gives a defiant yell? What if the jury is hung? It will be a good joke on the fundamentalists if it happens, and an even better joke on the defense.

(The Baltimore Evening Sun, July 15, 1925)

Mencken Declares Strictly Fair Trial Is Beyond Ken of Tennessee Fundamentalists

Dayton, Tenn., July 16.—Two things ought to be understood clearly by heathen Northerners who follow the great cause of the State of Tennessee against the infidel Scopes. One is that the old mountebank, Bryan, is no longer thought of as a mere politician and jobseeker in these Godly regions, but has become converted into a great sacerdotal figure, half man and half archangel—in brief, a sort of fundamentalist pope. The other is that the fundamentalist mind, running in a single rut for fifty years, is now quite unable to comprehend dissent from its basic superstitions, or to grant any common honesty, or even any decency, to those who reject them.

The latter fact explains some of the most astonishing singularities of the present trial—that is, singularities to one accustomed to more austere procedures. In the average Northern jurisdiction much of what is going on here would be almost unthinkable. Try to imagine a trial going on in a town in which anyone is free to denounce the defendant's case publicly and no one is free to argue for it in the same way—a trial in a courthouse placarded with handbills set up by his opponents—a trial before a jury of men who have been roweled and hammered by those opponents for years, and have never heard a clear and fair statement of his answer.

But this is not all. It seems impossible, but it is nevertheless a fact that public opinion in Dayton sees no impropriety in the fact that the case was opened with prayer by a clergyman known by everyone to be against Scopes and by no means shy about making the fact clear. Nor by the fact that Bryan, the actual complainant, has been preparing the ground for the prosecution for months. Nor by the fact that, though he is one of the attorneys of record in the case, he is also present in the character of a public evangelist and that throngs go to hear him whenever he speaks, including even the sitting judge.

I do not allege here that there is any disposition to resort to lynch law. On the contrary, I believe that there is every intent to give Scopes a fair trial, as a fair trial is understood among fundamentalists. All I desire to show is that all the primary assumptions are immovably against him—that it is a sheer impossibility for nine-tenths of those he faces to see any merit whatever in his position. He is not simply one who has committed a misdemeanor against the peace and dignity of the State, he is also the agent of a heresy almost too hellish to be stated by reputable men. Such reputable men recognize their lawful duty to treat him humanely and even politely, but they also recognize their superior duty to make it plain that they are against his heresy and believe absolutely in the wisdom and virtue of his prosecutors.

In view of the fact that everyone here looks for the jury to bring in a verdict of guilty, it might be expected that the prosecution would show a considerable amiability and allow the defense a rather free plan. Instead, it is contesting every point very vigorously and taking every advantage of its greatly superior familiarity with local procedure. There is, in fact, a considerable heat in the trial. Bryan and the local lawyers for the State sit glaring at the defense all day and even the Attorney General, A. T. Stewart, who is supposed to have secret doubts about fundamentalism, has shown such pugnacity that it has already brought him to forced apologies.

The high point of yesterday's proceedings was reached with the appearance of Dr. Maynard M. Metcalfe, of the Johns Hopkins. The doctor is a somewhat chubby man of bland mien, and during the first part of his testimony, with the jury present, the prosecution apparently viewed him with great equanimity. But the instant he was asked a question bearing directly upon the case at bar there was a flurry in the Bryan pen and Stewart was on his feet with protests. Another question followed, with more and hotter protests. The judge then excluded the jury and the show began.

What ensued was, on the surface, a harmless enough dialogue between Dr. Metcalfe and Darrow, but underneath there was very tense drama. At the first question Bryan came out from behind the State's table and planted himself directly in front of Dr. Metcalfe, and not ten feet away. The two McKenzies followed, with young Sue Hicks at their heels.

Then began one of the clearest, most succinct and withal most eloquent presentations of the case for the evolutionists that I have ever heard. The doctor was never at a loss for a word, and his ideas flowed freely and smoothly. Darrow steered him magnificently. A word or two and he was howling down the wind. Another and he hauled up to discharge a broadside. There was no cocksureness in him. Instead he was rather cautious and deprecatory and sometimes he halted and confessed his ignorance. But what he got over before he finished was a superb counterblast to the fundamentalist buncombe. The jury, at least, in theory heard nothing of it, but it went whooping into the radio and it went banging into the face of Bryan.

Bryan sat silent throughout the whole scene, his gaze fixed immovably on the witness. Now and then his face darkened and his eyes flashed, but he never uttered a sound. It was, to him, a string of blasphemies out of the devil's mass—a dreadful series of assaults upon the only true religion. The old gladiator faced his real enemy at last. Here was a sworn agent and attorney of the science he hates and fears—a well-fed, well-mannered spokesman of the knowledge he abominates. Somehow he reminded me pathetically of the old Holy Roller I heard last week—the mountain pastor who damned education as a mocking and a corruption. Bryan, too, is afraid of it, for wherever it spreads his trade begins to fall off, and wherever it flourishes he is only a poor clown.

But not to these fundamentalists of the hills. Not to yokels he now turns to for consolation in his old age, with the scars of defeat and disaster all over him. To these simple folk, as I have said, he is a prophet of the imperial line—a lineal successor to Moses and Abraham. The barbaric cosmogony that he believes in seems as reasonable to them as it does to him. They share his peasant-like suspicion of all book learning that a plow hand cannot grasp. They believe with him that men who know too much should be seized by the secular arm and put down by force. They dream as he does of a world unanimously sure of Heaven and unanimously idiotic on this earth.

This old buzzard, having failed to raise the mob against its rulers, now prepares to raise it against its teachers. He can never be the peasants' President, but there is still a chance to be the peasants' Pope. He leads a new crusade, his bald head glistening, his face streaming with sweat, his chest heaving beneath his rumpled alpaca coat. One somehow pities him, despite his so palpable imbecilities. It is a tragedy, indeed, to begin life as a hero and to end it as a buffoon. But let no one, laughing at him, underestimate the magic that lies in his black, malignant eye, his frayed but still eloquent voice. He can shake and inflame these poor ignoramuses as no other man among us can shake and inflame them, and he is desperately eager to order the charge.

In Tennessee he is drilling his army. The big battles, he believes, will be fought elsewhere.

(The Baltimore Evening Sun, July 16, 1924)

Malone the Victor, Even Though Court Sides with Opponents, Says Mencken

Dayton, Tenn., July 17.—Though the court decided against him this morning, and the testimony of the experts summoned for the defense will be banned out of the trial of the infidel Scopes, it was Dudley Field Malone who won yesterday's great battle of rhetoricians. When he got upon his legs it was the universal assumption in the courtroom that Judge Raulston's mind was already made up, and that nothing that any lawyer for the defense could say would shake him. But Malone unquestionably shook him. He was, at the end, in plain doubt, and he showed it by his questions. It took a night's repose to restore him to normalcy. The prosecution won, but it came within an inch of losing.

Malone was put up to follow and dispose of Bryan, and he achieved the business magnificently. I doubt that any louder speech has ever been heard in a court of law since the days of Gog and Magog. It roared out of the open windows like the sound of artillery practice, and alarmed the moonshiners and catamounts on distant peaks. Trains thundering by on the nearby railroad sounded faint and far away and when, toward the end, a table covered with standing and gaping journalists gave way with a crash, the noise seemed, by contrast, to be no more than a pizzicato chord upon a viola da gamba. The yokels outside stuffed their Bibles into the loud-speaker horns and yielded themselves joyously to the impact of the original. In brief, Malone was in good voice. It was a great day for Ireland. And for the defense. For Malone not only out-yelled Bryan, he also plainly out-generaled and out-argued him. His speech, indeed, was one of the best presentations of the case against the fundamentalist rubbish that I have ever heard.

It was simple in structure, it was clear in reasoning, and at its high points it was overwhelmingly eloquent. It was not long, but it covered the whole ground and it let off many a gaudy skyrocket, and so it conquered even the fundamentalists. At its end they gave it a tremendous cheer—a cheer at least four times as hearty as that given to Bryan. For these rustics delight in speechifying, and know when it is good. The devil's logic cannot fetch them, but they are not above taking a voluptuous pleasure in his lascivious phrases.

The whole speech was addressed to Bryan, and he sat through it in his usual posture, with his palm-leaf fan flapping energetically and his hard, cruel mouth shut tight. The old boy grows more and more pathetic. He has aged greatly during the past few years and begins to look elderly and enfeebled. All that remains of his old fire is now in his black eyes. They glitter like dark gems, and in their glitter there is immense and yet futile malignancy. That is all that is left of the Peerless Leader of thirty years ago. Once he had one leg in the White House and the nation trembled under his roars. Now he is a tinpot pope in the coca-cola belt and a brother to the forlorn pastors who belabor half-wits in galvanized iron tabernacles behind the railroad yards. His own speech was a gro-

tesque performance and downright touching in its imbecility. Its
climax came when he launched into a furious denunciation of the
doctrine that man is a mammal. It seemed a sheer impossibility
that any literate man should stand up in public and discharge any
such nonsense. Yet the poor old fellow did it. Darrow stared incredulous. Malone sat with his mouth wide open. Hays indulged
himself one of his sardonic chuckles. Stewart and Bryan *fils* looked
extremely uneasy, but the old mountebank ranted on. To call a
man a mammal, it appeared, was to flout the revelation of God.
The certain effect of the doctrine would be to destroy morality
and promote infidelity. The defense let it pass. The lily needed no
gilding.

There followed some ranting about the Leopold-Loeb case, culminating in the argument that learning was corrupting—that the
colleges by setting science above Genesis were turning their students into murderers. Bryan alleged that Darrow had admitted
the fact in his closing speech at the Leopold-Loeb trial, and
stopped to search for the passage in a printed copy of the speech.
Darrow denied making any such statement, and presently began
reading what he actually had said on the subject. Bryan then proceeded to denounce Nietzsche, whom he described as an admirer
and follower of Darwin. Darrow challenged the fact and offered to
expound what Nietzsche really taught. Bryan waved him off.

The effect of the whole harangue was extremely depressing. It
quickly ceased to be an argument addressed to the court—Bryan,
in fact, constantly said "My friends" instead of "Your Honor"—
and became a sermon at the camp-meeting. All the familiar contentions of the Dayton divines appeared in it—that learning is
dangerous, that nothing is true that is not in the Bible, that a yokel
who goes to church regularly knows more than any scientist ever
heard of. The thing went to fantastic lengths. It became a farrago
of puerilities without coherence or sense. I don't think the old
man did himself justice. He was in poor voice and his mind
seemed to wander. There was far too much hatred in him for him
to be persuasive.

The crowd, of course, was with him. It has been fed upon just
such balderdash for years. Its pastors assault it twice a week with
precisely the same nonsense. It is chronically in the position of a
populace protected by an espionage act in time of war. That is to
say, it is forbidden to laugh at the arguments of one side and
forbidden to hear the case of the other side. Bryan has been roving

around in the tall grass for years and he knows the bucolic mind. He knows how to reach and inflame its basic delusions and superstitions. He has taken them into his own stock and adorned them with fresh absurdities. Today he may well stand as the archetype of the American rustic. His theology is simply the elemental magic that is preached in a hundred thousand rural churches fifty-two times a year.

These Tennessee mountaineers are not more stupid than the city proletariat; they are only less informed. If Darrow, Malone and Hays could make a month's stumping tour in Rhea county I believe that fully a fourth of the population would repudiate fundamentalism, and that not a few of the clergy now in practice would be restored to their old jobs on the railroad. Malone's speech yesterday probably shook a great many true believers; another like it would fetch more than one of them. But the chances are heavily against them ever hearing a second. Once this trial is over, the darkness will close in again, and it will take long years of diligent and thankless effort to dispel it—if, indeed, it is ever dispelled at all.

With a few brilliant exceptions—Dr. Neal is an example—the more civilized Tennesseeans show few signs of being equal to the job. I suspect that politics is what keeps them silent and makes their State ridiculous. Most of them seem to be candidates for office, and a candidate for office, if he would get the votes of fundamentalists, must bawl for Genesis before he begins to bawl for anything else. A typical Tennessee politician is the Governor, Austin Peay. He signed the anti-evolution bill with loud hosannas, and he is now making every effort to turn the excitement of the Scopes trial to his private political uses. The local papers print a telegram that he has sent to Attorney-General A. T. Stewart whooping for prayer. In the North a Governor who indulged in such monkey shines would be rebuked for trying to influence the conduct of a case in court. And he would be derided as a cheap mountebank. But not here.

I described Stewart the other day as a man of apparent education and sense and palpably superior to the village lawyers who sit with him at the trial table. I still believe that I described him accurately. Yet even Stewart toward the close of yesterday's session gave an exhibition that would be almost unimaginable in the North. He began his reply to Malone with an intelligent and forceful legal argument, with plenty of evidence of hard study in it. But presently he slid into a violent theological harangue, full of extravagant nonsense. He described the case as a combat between light and darkness and almost descended to the depths of Bryan. Hays challenged him with a question. Didn't he admit, after all, that the defense had a tolerable case; that it ought to be given a chance to present its evidence? I transcribe his reply literally:

"That which strikes at the very foundations of Christianity is not entitled to a chance."

Hays, plainly astounded by this bald statement of the fundamentalist view of due process, pressed the point. Assuming that the defense would present, not opinion but only unadorned fact, would Stewart still object to its admission? He replied.

"Personally, yes."

"But as a lawyer and Attorney-General?" insisted Hays.

"As a lawyer and Attorney-General," said Stewart, "I am the same man."

Such is justice where Genesis is the first and greatest of law books and heresy is still a crime.

(*The Baltimore Evening Sun, July 17, 1925*)

Battle Now Over, Mencken Sees; Genesis Triumphant and Ready for New Jousts

Dayton, Tenn., July 18.—All that remains of the great cause of the State of Tennessee against the infidel Scopes is the formal business of bumping off the defendant. There may be some legal jousting on Monday and some gaudy oratory on Tuesday, but the main battle is over, with Genesis completely triumphant. Judge Raulston finished the benign business yesterday morning by leaping with soft judicial hosannas into the arms of the prosecution. The sole commentary of the sardonic Darrow consisted of bringing down a metaphorical custard pie upon the occiput of the learned jurist.

"I hope," said the latter nervously, "that counsel intends no reflection upon this court."

Darrow hunched his shoulders and looked out of the window dreamily.

"Your honor," he said, "is, of course, entitled to hope."

No doubt the case will be long and fondly remembered by connoisseurs of judicial delicatessen—that is, as the performances of Weber and Fields are remembered by students of dramatic science. In immediate retrospect, it grows more fantastic and exhilarating. Scopes has had precisely the same fair trial that the Hon. John Philip Hill, accused of bootlegging on the oath of Howard A. Kelly, would have before the Rev. Dr. George W. Crabbe. He is a fellow not without humor; I find him full of smiles today. On some near tomorrow the Sheriff will collect a month's wages from him, but he has certainly had a lot of fun.

More interesting than the hollow buffoonery that remains will be the effect upon the people of Tennessee, the actual prisoners at the bar. That the more civilized of them are in a highly feverish condition of mind must be patent to every visitor. The guffaws that roll in from all sides give them great pain. They are full of bitter protests and valiant projects. They prepare, it appears, to organize, hoist the black flag and offer the fundamentalists of the dung-hills a battle to the death. They will not cease until the last Baptist preacher is in flight over the mountains, and the ordinary intellectual decencies of Christendom are triumphantly restored.

With the best will in the world I find it impossible to accept this tall talk with anything resembling confidence. The intelligentsia of Tennessee had their chance and let it get away from them. When the old mountebank, Bryan, first invaded the State with his balderdash they were unanimously silent. When he began to round up converts in the back country they offered him no challenge. When the Legislature passed the anti-evolution bill and the Governor signed it, they contented themselves with murmuring pianissimo. And when the battle was joined at last and the time came for rough stuff only one Tennesseean of any consequence volunteered.

That lone volunteer was Dr. John Neal, now of counsel for the defense, a good lawyer and an honest man. His services to Darrow, Malone and Hays have been very valuable and they come out of the case with high respect for him. But how does Tennessee regard him? My impression is that Tennessee vastly underestimates him. I hear trivial and absurd criticism of him on all sides and scarcely a word of praise for his courage and public spirit. The test of the State is to be found in its attitude toward such men. It will come out of the night of fundamentalism when they are properly appreciated and honored, and not before. When that time comes I'll begin to believe that the educated minority here is genuinely ashamed of the Bryan obscenity and that it is prepared to combat other such disgraces hereafter resolutely in the open and regardless of the bellowing of the mob.

The Scopes trial, from the start, has been carried on in a manner exactly fitted to the anti-evolution law and the simian imbecility under it. There hasn't been the slightest pretense to decorum. The rustic judge, a candidate for re-election, has postured before the yokels like a clown in a ten-cent side show, and almost every word he has uttered has been an undisguised appeal to their prejudices and superstitions. The chief prosecuting attorney, beginning like a competent lawyer and a man of self-respect, ended like a convert at a Billy Sunday revival. It fell to him, finally, to make a clear and astounding statement of theory of justice prevailing under fundamentalism. What he said, in brief, was that a man accused of infidelity had no rights whatever under Tennessee law.

This is probably not true yet, but it will become true inevitably if the Bryan murrain is not arrested. The Bryan of today is not to be mistaken for the political rabble rouser of two decades ago. That earlier Bryan may have been grossly in error, but he at least kept his errors within the bounds of reason: it was still possible to follow him without yielding up all intelligence. The Bryan of today, old, disappointed and embittered, is a far different bird. He realizes at last the glories of this world are not for him, and he takes refuge, peasant-like, in religious hallucinations. They depart from sense altogether. They are not merely silly; they are downright idiotic. And, being idiotic, they appeal with irresistible force to the poor half-wits upon whom the old charlatan now preys.

When I heard him, in open court, denounce the notion that man is a mammal I was genuinely staggered and so was every other stranger in the courtroom. People looked at one another in blank amazement. But the native fundamentalists, it quickly appeared, saw nothing absurd in his words. The attorneys for the prosecution smiled approval, the crowd applauded, the very judge on the bench beamed his acquiescence. And the same thing happened when he denounced all education as corrupting and began arguing incredibly that a farmer who read the Bible knew more than any scientist in the world. Such dreadful bilge, heard of far away, may seem only ridiculous. But it takes on a different smack, I assure you, when one hears it discharged formally in a court of law and sees it accepted as wisdom by judge and jury.

Darrow has lost this case. It was lost long before he came to Dayton. But it seems to me that he has nevertheless performed a great public service by fighting it to a finish and in a perfectly serious way. Let no one mistake it for comedy, farcical though it may be in all its details. It serves notice on the country that Neanderthal man is organizing in these forlorn backwaters of the land, led by a fanatic, rid sense and devoid of conscience. Tennessee, challenging him too timorously and too late, now sees its courts converted into camp meetings and its Bill of Rights made a mock of by its sworn officers of the law. There are other States that had better look to their arsenals before the Hun is at their gates.

(*The Baltimore Evening Sun, July 18, 1925*)

Tennessee in the Frying Pan

I

That the rising town of Dayton, when it put the infidel Scopes on trial, bit off far more than it has been able to chew—this melancholy fact must now be evident to everyone. The village Aristides Sophocles Goldsboroughs believed that the trial would bring in a lot of money, and produce a vast mass of free and profitable advertising. They were wrong on both counts, as boomers usually are. Very little money was actually spent by the visitors: the adjacent yokels brought their own lunches and went home to sleep, and the city men from afar rushed down to Chattanooga whenever there was a lull. As for the advertising that went out over the leased wires, I greatly fear that it has quite ruined the town. Then people recall it hereafter they will think of it as they think of Herrin, Ill., and Homestead, Pa. It will be a joke town at best, and infamous at worst.

The natives reacted to this advertising very badly. The preliminary publicity, I believe, had somehow disarmed and deceived them. It was mainly amiable spoofing; they took it philosophically, assured by the local Aristideses that it was good for trade. But when the main guard of Eastern and Northern journalists swarmed down, and their dispatches began to show the country and the world exactly how the obscene buffoonery appeared to realistic city men, then the yokels began to sweat coldly, and in a few days they were full of terror and indignation. Some of the bolder spirits, indeed, talked gaudily of direct action against the authors of the "libels." But the history of the Ku Klux and the American Legion offers overwhelmingly evidence that 100 per cent Americans never fight when the enemy is in strength, and able to make a defense, so the visitors suffered nothing worse than black, black looks. When the last of them departs Daytonians will disinfect the town with sulphur candles, and the local pastors will exorcise the devils that they left behind them.

II

Dayton, of course, is only a ninth-rate country town, and so its agonies are of relatively little interest to the world. Its pastors, I daresay, will be able to console it, and if they fail there is always the old mountebank, Bryan, to give a hand. Faith cannot only move mountains; it can also soothe the distressed spirits of mountaineers. The Daytonians, unshaken by Darrow's ribaldries, still believe. They believe that they are not mammals. They believe, on Bryan's word, that they know more than all the men of science of Christendom. They believe, on the authority of Genesis, that the earth is flat and that witches still infest it. They believe, finally and especially, that all who doubt these great facts of revelation will go to hell. So they are consoled.

But what of the rest of the people of Tennessee? I greatly fear that they will not attain to consolation so easily. They are an extremely agreeable folk, and many of them are highly intelligent. I met men and women—particularly women—in Chattanooga who showed every sign of the highest culture. They led civilized lives, despite Prohibition, and they were interested in civilized ideas, despite the fog of Fundamentalism in which they moved. I met members of the State judiciary who were as heartily ashamed of the bucolic ass, Raulston, as an Osler would be of a chiropractor. I add the educated clergy: Episcopalians, Unitarians, Jews and so on

—enlightened men, tossing pathetically under the imbecilities of their evangelical colleagues. Chattanooga, as I found it, was charming, but immensely unhappy.

What its people ask for—many of them in plain terms—is suspended judgment, sympathy, Christian charity, and I believe that they deserve all these things. Dayton may be typical of Tennessee, but it is surely not *all* of Tennessee. The civilized minority in the State is probably as large as in any other Southern State. What ails it is simply the fact it has been, in the past, too cautious and politic —that it has been too reluctant to offend the Fundamentalist majority. To that reluctance something else has been added: an uncritical and somewhat childish local patriotism. The Tennesseeans have tolerated their imbeciles for fear that attacking them would bring down the derision of the rest of the country. Now they have the derision, and to excess—and the attack is ten times as difficult as it ever was before.

III

How they are to fight their way out of their wallow I do not know. They begin the battle with the enemy in command of every height and every gun; worse, there is a great deal of irresolution in their own ranks. The newspapers of the State, with few exceptions, are very feeble. One of the best of them, the Chattanooga *News*, set up an eloquent whooping for Bryan the moment he got to Dayton. Before that it had been against the antievolution law. But with the actual battle joined, it began to wobble, and presently it was printing articles arguing that Fundamentalism, after all, made men happy—that a Tennesseean gained something valuable by being an ignoramus—in other words, that a hog in a barnyard was to be envied by an Aristotle. The *News* was far better than most: it gave space, too, to the other side, and at considerable risk. But its weight, for two weeks, was thrown heavily to Bryan and his balderdash.

The pusillanimous attitude of the bar of the State I described in my dispatches from Dayton. It was not until the trial was two days old that any Tennessee lawyers of influence and dignity went to the aid of Dr. John R. Neal—and even then all of the volunteers enlisted only on condition that their names be kept out of the newspapers. I should except one T. B. McElwee. He sat at the trial table and rendered valuable services. The rest lurked in the background. It was an astounding situation to a Marylander, but it seemed to be regarded as quite natural in Tennessee.

The prevailing attitude toward Neal himself was also very amazing. He is an able lawyer and a man of repute, and in any Northern State his courage would get the praise it deserves. But in Tennessee even the intelligentsia seem to feel that he has done something discreditable by sitting at the trial table with Darrow, Hays and Malone. The State buzzes with trivial, idiotic gossip about him—that he dresses shabbily, that he has political aspirations, and so on. What if he does and has? He has carried himself, in this case, in a way that does higher credit to his native State. But his native State, instead of being proud of him, simply snarls at him behind his back.

IV

So with every other man concerned with the defense—most of them, slackaday, foreigners. For example, Rappelyea, the Dayton engineer who was first to go to the aid of Scopes. I was told solemnly in Dayton, not once but twenty times, that Rappelyea was (a) a Bowery boy from New York, and (b) an incompetent and ignorant engineer. I went to some trouble to unearth the facts. They were (a) that he was actually a member of one of the oldest Huguenot families in America, and (b) that his professional skill and general culture were such that the visiting scientists sought him out and found pleasure in his company.

Such is the punishment that falls upon a civilized man cast among fundamentalists. As I have said, the worst of it is that even the native intelligentsia help to pull the rope. In consequence all the brighter young men of the State—and it produces plenty of them—tend to leave it. If they remain, they must be prepared to succumb to the prevailing blather or resign themselves to being more or less infamous. With the anti-evolution law enforced, the State university will rapidly go to pot; no intelligent youth will waste his time upon its courses if he can help it. And so, with the young men lost, the struggle against darkness will become almost hopeless.

As I have said, the State still produces plenty of likely young bucks—if only it could hold them! There is good blood everywhere, even in the mountains. During the dreadful buffooneries of Bryan and Raulston last week two typical specimens sat at the press table. One was Paul Y. Anderson, correspondent of the St. Louis *Post-Dispatch*, and the other was Joseph Wood Krutch, one of the editors of the *Nation*. I am very familiar with the work of both of them, and it is my professional judgment that it is of the first caliber. Anderson is one of the best newspaper reporters in America and Krutch is one of the best editorial writers.

Well, both were there as foreigners. Both were working for papers that could not exist in Tennessee. Both were viewed by their fellow Tennesseeans not with pride, as credits to the State, but as traitors to the Tennessee *Kultur* and public enemies. Their crime was that they were intelligent men, doing their jobs intelligently.

(The Baltimore Evening Sun, July 20, 1925)

Bryan

I

It was plain to everyone, when Bryan came to Dayton, that his great days were behind him—that he was now definitely an old man, and headed at last for silence. There was a vague, unpleasant manginess about his appearance; he somehow seemed dirty, though a close glance showed him carefully shaved, and clad in immaculate linen. All the hair was gone from the dome of his head, and it had begun to fall out, too, behind his ears, like that of the late Samuel Gompers. The old resonance had departed from his voice: what was once a bugle blast had become reedy and quavering. Who knows that, like Demosthenes, he had a lisp? In his prime, under the magic of his eloquence, no one noticed it. But when he spoke at Dayton it was always audible.

When I first encountered him, on the sidewalk in front of the Hicks brothers law office, the trial was yet to begin, and so he was still expansive and amiable. I had printed in the *Nation*, a week or so before, an article arguing that the anti-evolution law, whatever its unwisdom, was at least constitutional—that policing school teachers was certainly not putting down free speech. The old boy professed to be delighted with the argument, and gave the gaping bystanders to understand that I was a talented publicist. In turn I admired the curious shirt he wore—sleeveless and with the neck cut very low. We parted in the manner of two Spanish ambassadors.

But that was the last touch of affability that I was destined to see in Bryan. The next day the battle joined and his face became hard. By the end of the first week he was simply a walking malignancy. Hour by hour he grew more bitter. What the Christian Scientists call malicious animal magnetism seemed to radiate from him like heat from a stove. From my place in the court-room, standing upon a table, I looked directly down upon him, sweating horribly and pumping his palm-leaf fan. His eyes fascinated me: I watched them all day long. They were blazing points of hatred. They glittered like occult and sinister gems. Now and then they wandered to me, and I got my share. It was like coming under fire.

II

What was behind that consuming hatred? At first I thought that it was mere evangelical passion. Evangelical Christianity, as everyone knows, is founded upon hate, as the Christianity of Christ was founded upon love. But even evangelical Christians occasionally loose their belts and belch amicably; I have known some who, off duty, were very benignant. In that very courtroom, indeed, were some of them—for example, old Ben McKenzie, Nestor of the Dayton bar, who sat beside Bryan. Ben was full of good humor. He made jokes with Darrow. But Bryan only glared.

One day it dawned on me that Bryan, after all, was an evangelical Christian only by sort of afterthought—that his career in this world, and the glories thereof, had actually come to an end before he ever began whooping for Genesis. So I came to this conclusion: that what really moved him was a lust for revenge. The men of the cities had destroyed him and made a mock of him; now he would lead the yokels against them. Various facts clicked into the theory, and I hold it still. The hatred in the old man's burning eyes was not for the enemies of God; it was for the enemies of Bryan.

Thus he fought his last fight, eager only for blood. It quickly became frenzied and preposterous, and after that pathetic. All sense departed from him. He bit right and left, like a dog with rabies. He descended to demagogy so dreadful that his very associates blushed. His one yearning was to keep his yokels heated up —to lead his forlorn mob against the foe. That foe, alas, refused to be alarmed. It insisted upon seeing the battle as a comedy. Even Darrow, who knew better, occasionally yielded to the prevailing spirit. Finally, he lured poor Bryan into a folly almost incredible.

I allude to his astounding argument against the notion that man is a mammal. I am glad I heard it, for otherwise I'd never believe it. There stood the man who had been thrice a candidate for the Presidency of the Republic—and once, I believe, elected—there he stood in the glare of the world, uttering stuff that a boy of eight would laugh at! The artful Darrow led him on: he repeated it, ranted for it, bellowed it in his cracked voice. A tragedy, indeed! He came into life a hero, a Galahad, in bright and shining armor. Now he was passing out a pathetic fool.

III

Worse, I believe that he somehow sensed the fact—that he realized his personal failure, whatever the success of the grotesque cause he spoke for. I had left Dayton before Darrow's cross-examination brought him to his final absurdity, but I heard his long speech against the admission of expert testimony, and I saw how it fell flat and how Bryan himself was conscious of the fact. When he sat down he was done for, and he knew it. The old magic had failed to work; there was applause but there was no exultant shouts. When, half an hour later, Dudley Field Malone delivered his terrific philippic, the very yokels gave him five times the clapper-clawing that they had given to Bryan.

This combat was the old leader's last, and it symbolized in more than one way his passing. Two women sat through it, the one old and crippled, the other young and in the full flush of beauty. The first was Mrs. Bryan; the second was Mrs. Malone. When Malone finished his speech the crowd stormed his wife with felicitations, and she glowed as only a woman can who has seen her man fight a hard fight and win gloriously. But no one congratulated Mrs. Bryan. She sat hunched in her chair near the judge, apparently very uneasy. I thought then that she was ill—she has been making the round of sanitariums for years, and was lately in the hands of a faith-healer—but now I think that some appalling prescience was upon her, and that she saw in Bryan's eyes a hint of the collapse that was so near.

He sank into his seat a wreck, and was presently forgotten in the blast of Malone's titanic rhetoric. His speech had been maundering, feeble and often downright idiotic. Presumably, he was speaking to a point of law, but it was quickly apparent that he knew no more law than the bailiff at the door. So he launched into mere violet garulity. He dragged in snatches of ancient chautauqua addresses; he wandered up hill and down dale. Finally, Darrow lured him into that fabulous imbecility about man as a mammal. He sat down one of the most tragic asses in American history.

IV

It is the national custom to sentimentalize the dead, as it is to sentimentalize men about to be hanged. Perhaps I fall into that weakness here. The Bryan I shall remember is the Bryan of his last weeks on earth—broken, furious, and infinitely pathetic. It was impossible to meet his hatred with hatred to match it. He was winning a battle that would make him forever infamous wherever enlightened men remembered it and him. Even his old enemy, Darrow, was gentle with him at the end. That cross-examination might have been ten times as devastating. It was plain to everyone that the old Berseker Bryan was gone—that all that remained of him was a pair of glaring and horrible eyes.

But what of his life? Did he accomplish any useful thing? Was he, in his day, of any dignity as a man, and of any value to his fellow-men? I doubt it. Bryan, at his best, was simply a magnificent job-seeker. The issues that he bawled about usually meant nothing to him. He was ready to abandon them whenever he could make votes by doing so, and to take up new ones at a moment's notice. For years he evaded Prohibition as dangerous; then he embraced it as profitable. At the Democratic National Convention last year he was on both sides, and distrusted by both. In his last great battle there was only a baleful and ridiculous malignancy. If he was pathetic, he was also disgusting.

Bryan was a vulgar and common man, a cad undiluted. He was ignorant, bigoted, self-seeking, blatant and dishonest. His career brought him into contact with the first men of his time; he preferred the company of rustic ignoramuses. It was hard to believe, watching him at Dayton, that he had traveled, that he had been received in civilized societies, that he had been a high officer of state. He seemed only a poor clod like those around him, deluded by a childish theology, full of an almost pathological hatred of all learning, all human dignity, all beauty, all fine and noble things. He was a peasant come home to the dung-pile. Imagine a gentleman, and you have imagined everything that he was not.

The job before democracy is to get rid of such canaille. If it fails, they will devour it.

(The Baltimore Evening Sun, July 27, 1925)

Aftermath

I

The Liberals, in their continuing discussion of the late trial of the infidel Scopes at Dayton, Tenn., run true to form. That is to say, they show all their habitual lack of humor and all their customary furtive weakness for the delusions of *Homo neanderthalensis.* I point to two of their most enlightened organs: the eminent New York *World* and the gifted *New Republic.* The *World* is displeased with Mr. Darrow because, in his appalling cross-examination of the mountebank Bryan, he did some violence to the theological superstitions that millions of Americans cherish. The *New Republic* denounces him because he addressed himself, not to "the people of Tennessee" but to the whole country, and because he should have permitted "local lawyers" to assume "the most conspicuous position in the trial."

Once more, alas, I find myself unable to follow the best Liberal thought. What the *World*'s contention amounts to, at bottom, is simply the doctrine that a man engaged in combat with superstition should be very polite to superstition. This, I fear, is nonsense. The way to deal with superstition is not to be polite to it, but to tackle it with all arms, and so rout it, cripple it, and make it forever infamous and ridiculous. Is it, perchance, cherished by persons who should know better? Then their folly should be brought out into the light of day, and exhibited there in all its hideousness until they flee from it, hiding their heads in shame.

True enough, even a superstitious man has certain inalienable rights. He has a right to harbor and indulge his imbecilities as long as he pleases, provided only he does not try to inflict them upon other men by force. He has a right to argue for them as eloquently as he can, in season and out of season. He has a right to teach them to his children. But certainly he has no right to be protected against the free criticism of those who do not hold them. He has no right to demand that they be treated as sacred. He has no right to preach them without challenge. Did Darrow, in the course of his dreadful bombardment of Bryan, drop a few shells, incidentally, into measurably cleaner camps? Then let the garrisons of those camps look to their defenses. They are free to shoot back. But they can't disarm their enemy.

II

The meaning of religious freedom, I fear, is sometimes greatly misapprehended. It is taken to be a sort of immunity, not merely from governmental control but also from public opinion. A dunderhead gets himself a long-tailed coat, rises behind the sacred desk, and emits such bilge as would gag a Hottentot. Is it to pass unchallenged? If so, then what we have is not religious freedom at all, but the most intolerable and outrageous variety of religious despotism. Any fool, once he is admitted to holy orders, becomes infallible. Any half-wit, by the simple device of ascribing his delusions to revelation, takes on an authority that is denied to all the rest of us.

I do not know how many Americans entertain the ideas defended so ineptly by poor Bryan, but probably the number is very large. They are preached once a week in at least a hundred thousand rural churches, and they are heard too in the meaner quarters of the great cities. Nevertheless, though they are thus held to be sound by millions, these ideas remain mere rubbish. Not only are they not supported by the known facts; they are in direct contravention of the known facts. No man whose information is sound and whose mind functions normally can conceivably credit them. They are the products of ignorance and stupidity, either or both.

What should be a civilized man's attitude toward such superstitions? It seems to me that the only attitude possible to him is one of contempt. If he admits that they have any intellectual dignity whatever, he admits that he himself has none. If he pretends to a respect for those who believe in them, he pretends falsely, and sinks almost to their level. When he is challenged he must answer honestly, regardless of tender feelings. That is what Darrow did at

Dayton, and the issue plainly justified the act. Bryan went there in a hero's shining armor, bent deliberately upon a gross crime against sense. He came out a wrecked and preposterous charlatan, his tail between his legs. Few Americans have ever done so much for their country in a whole lifetime as Darrow did in two hours.

III

The caveat of the *New Republic* is so absurd that it scarcely deserves an answer. It is based upon a complete misunderstanding of the situation that the Scopes trial revealed. What good would it have done to have addressed an appeal to the people of Tennessee? They had already, by their lawful representatives, adopted the anti-evolution statute by an immense majority, and they were plainly determined to uphold it. The newspapers of the State, with one or two exceptions, were violently in favor of the prosecution, and applauded every effort of the rustic judge and district attorney to deprive the defense of its most elemental rights.

True enough, there was a minority of Tennesseeans on the other side—men and women who felt keenly the disgrace of their State, and were eager to put an end to it. But their time had passed; they had missed their chance. They should have stepped forward at the very beginning, long before Darrow got into the case. Instead, they hung back timorously, and so Bryan and the Baptist pastors ran amok. There was a brilliant exception: John R. Neal. There was another: T. R. Elwell. Both lawyers. But the rest of the lawyers of the State, when the issue was joined at last, actually helped the prosecution. Their bar associations kept up a continuous fusillade. They tried their best to prod the backwoods Dogberry, Raulston, into putting Darrow into jail.

There was but one way to meet this situation and Darrow adopted it. He appealed directly to the country and to the world. He had at these recreant Tennesseeans by exhibiting their shame to all men, near and far. He showed them cringing before the rustic theologians, and afraid of Bryan. He turned the State inside out, and showed what civilization can come to under Fundamentalism. The effects of that cruel exposure are now visible. Tennessee is still spluttering—and blushing. The uproar staggered its people. And they are doing some very painful thinking. Will they cling to Fundamentalism or will they restore civilization? I suspect that the quick decision of their neighbor, Georgia, will help them to choose. Darrow did more for them, in two weeks, than all their pastors and politicians had done since the Civil War.

IV

His conduct of the case, in fact, was adept and intelligent from beginning to end. It is hard, in retrospect, to imagine him improving it. He faced immense technical difficulties. In order to get out of the clutches of the village Dogberry and before judges of greater intelligence he had to work deliberately for the conviction of his client. In order to evade the puerile question of that client's guilt or innocence and so bring the underlying issues before the country, he had to set up a sham battle on the side lines. And in order to expose the gross ignorance and superstition of the real prosecutor, Bryan, he had to lure the old imposter upon the stand.

It seems to me that he accomplished all of these things with great skill. Scopes was duly convicted, and the constitutional questions involved in the law will now be heard by competent judges and decided without resort to prayer and moving pictures. The whole world has been made familiar with the issues, and the nature of the menace that Fundamentalism offers to civilization is now familiar to every schoolboy. And Bryan was duly scotched, and, if he had lived, would be standing before the country today as a comic figure, tattered and preposterous.

All this was accomplished, in infernal weather, by a man of sixty-eight, with the scars of battles all over him. He had, to be sure, highly competent help. At his table sat lawyers whose peculiar talents, in combination, were of the highest potency—the brilliant Hays, the eloquent Malone, the daring and patriotic Tennesseean, Neal. But it was Darrow who carried the main burden, and Darrow who shaped the final result. When he confronted Bryan at last, the whole combat came to its climax. On the one side was bigotry, ignorance, hatred, superstition, every sort of blackness that the human mind is capable of. On the other side was sense. And sense achieved a great victory.

(*The Baltimore Evening Sun, September 14, 1925*)

The·Believing Mind

A Neglected Anniversary

On December 20 there flitted past us, absolutely without public notice, one of the most important profane anniversaries in American history—to wit: the seventy-fifth anniversary of the introduction of the bathtub into these states. Not a plumber fired a salute or hung out a flag. Not a governor proclaimed a day of prayer. Not a newspaper called attention to the day.

True enough, it was not entirely forgotten. Eight or nine months ago one of the younger surgeons connected with the Public Health Service in Washington happened upon the facts while looking into the early history of public hygiene, and at his suggestion a committee was formed to celebrate the anniversary with a banquet. But before the plan was perfected Washington went dry, and so the banquet had to be abandoned. As it was, the day passed wholly unmarked, even in the capital of the nation.

Bathtubs are so common today that it is almost impossible to imagine a world without them. They are familiar to nearly every one in all incorporated towns; in most of the large cities it is unlawful to build a dwelling house without putting them in; even on the farm they have begun to come into use. And yet the first American bathtub was installed and dedicated so recently as December 20, 1842, and, for all I know to the contrary, it may be still in existence and in use.

Curiously enough, the scene of its setting up was Cincinnati, then a squalid frontier town, and even today surely no leader in culture. But Cincinnati, in those days as in these, contained many enterprising merchants, and one of them was a man named Adam Thompson, a dealer in cotton and grain. Thompson shipped his merchandise by steamboat down the Ohio and Mississippi to New Orleans, and from there sent it to England in sailing vessels. This trade frequently took him to England, and in that country, during the 30s, he acquired the habit of bathing.

* *

The bathtub was then still a novelty in England. It had been introduced in 1828 by Lord John Russell and its use was yet confined to a small class of enthusiasts. Moreover, the English bathtub, then as now, was a puny and inconvenient contrivance—little more, in fact, than a glorified dishpan—and filling and emptying it required the attendance of a servant. Taking a bath, indeed, was a rather heavy ceremony, and Lord John in 1835 was said to be the only man in England who had yet come to doing it every day.

Thompson, who was of inventive fancy—he later devised the machine that is still used for bagging hams and bacon—conceived the notion that the English bathtub would be much improved if it were made large enough to admit the whole body of an adult man, and if its supply of water, instead of being hauled to the scene by a maid, were admitted by pipes from a central reservoir and run off by the same means. Accordingly, early in 1842 he set about building the first modern bathroom in his Cincinnati home—a large house with Doric pillars, standing near what is now the corner of Monastery and Oregon streets.

There was then, of course, no city water supply, at least in that part of the city, but Thompson had a large well in his garden and he installed a pump to lift its water to his house. This pump, which was operated by six Negroes, much like an old-time fire engine, was connected by a pipe with a cypress tank in the garret of the house and here the water was stored until needed. From the tank two other pipes ran to the bathroom. One, carrying cold water, was a direct line. The other, designed to provide warm water, ran down the great chimney of the kitchen and was coiled inside it like a giant spring.

* *

The tub itself was of new design and became the grandfather of all the bathtubs of today. Thompson had it made by James Guiness, the leading Cincinnati cabinet maker of those days, and its material was Nicaragua mahogany. It was nearly seven feet long and fully four feet wide. To make it water tight the interior was lined with sheet lead, carefully soldered at the joints. The whole contraption weighed about 1,750 pounds, and the floor of the room in which it was placed had to be reinforced to support it. The exterior was elaborately polished.

In this luxurious tub Thompson took two baths on December 20, 1842—a cold one at 8 A.M. and a warm one some time during the afternoon. The warm water, heated by the kitchen fire, reached a temperature of 105 degrees. On Christmas day, having a party of gentlemen to dinner, he exhibited the new marvel to them and gave an exhibition of its use, and four of them, including a French visitor, Col. Duchanel, risked plunges into it. The next day all Cincinnati—then a town of about 100,000 people—had heard of it, and the local newspapers described it at length and opened their columns to violent discussions of it.

The thing, in fact, became a public matter, and before long there was bitter and double-headed opposition to the new invention, which had been promptly imitated by several other wealthy Cincinnatians. On the one hand it was denounced as an epicurean and obnoxious toy from England, designed to corrupt the democratic simplicity of the republic, and on the other hand it was attacked by the medical facility as dangerous to health and a certain inviter of "phthisic, rheumatic fevers, inflammation of the lungs, and the whole category of zymotic diseases." (I quote from the *Western Medical Repository* of April 23, 1843.)

* *

The noise of the controversy soon reached other cities, and in more than one place medical opposition reached such strength that it was reflected in legislation. Late in 1843, for example, the Philadelphia common council considered an ordinance prohibiting bathing between November 1 and March 15, and it failed of passage by but two votes. During the same year the legislature of Virginia laid a tax of $30 a year on all bathtubs that might be set up, and in Hartford, Providence, Charleston, and Wilmington, Del., special and very heavy water rates were levied upon those who had them. Boston early in 1845 made bathing unlawful except upon medical advice, but the ordinance was never enforced and in 1862 it was repealed.

This legislation, I suspect, had some class feeling in it, for the Thompson bathtub was plainly too expensive to be owned by any save the wealthy. Indeed, the common price for installing one in New York in 1845 was $500. Thus the low caste politicians of the time made capital by fulminating against it, and there is even some suspicion of political bias in many of the early medical denunciations. But the invention of the common pine bathtub, lined with zinc, in 1847, cut off this line of attack, and thereafter the bathtub made steady progress.

The zinc tub was devised by John F. Simpson, a Brooklyn plumber, and his efforts to protect it by a patent occupied the courts until 1855. But the decisions were steadily against him, and after 1848 all the plumbers of New York were equipped for putting in bathtubs. According to a writer in the *Christian Register* for July 17, 1857, the first one in New York was opened for traffic on September 12, 1847, and by the beginning of 1850 there were already nearly 1,000 in use in the big town.

* *

After this medical opposition began to collapse, and among other eminent physicians Dr. Oliver Wendell Holmes declared for the bathtub, and vigorously opposed the lingering movement against it in Boston. The American Medical Association held its annual meeting in Boston in 1859, and a poll of the members in attendance showed that nearly 55 percent of them now regarded bathing as harmless, and that more than 20 percent advocated it as beneficial. At its meeting in 1850 a resolution was formally passed giving the imprimatur of the faculty to the bathtub. The homeopaths followed with a like resolution in 1853.

But it was the example of President Millard Fillmore that, even more than grudging medical approval, gave the bathtub recognition and respectability in the United States. While he was still Vice President, in March, 1850, he visited Cincinnati on a stumping tour, and inspected the original Thompson tub. Thompson himself was now dead, but the bathroom was preserved by the gentleman who had bought his house from his estate. Fillmore was entertained in this house, and according to Chamberlain, his biographer, took a bath in the tub. Experiencing no ill effects, he became an ardent advocate of the new invention, and on succeeding to the presidency at Taylor's death, July 9, 1850, he instructed his secretary of war, Gen. Charles M. Conrad, to invite tenders for the construction of a bathtub in the White House.

* *

This action, for a moment, revived the old controversy, and its opponents made much of the fact that there was no bathtub at Mount Vernon or Monticello, and that all the Presidents and other magnificoes of the past had got along without any such monarchical luxuries. The elder Bennett, in the *New York Herald,* charged that Fillmore aspired to buy and install in the White House a porphyry and alabaster bath that had been used by Louis Philippe at Versailles. But Conrad, disregarding all this clamor, duly called for bids, and the contract was presently awarded to Harper & Gillespie, a firm of Philadelphia engineers, who proposed to furnish a tub of cast iron, capable of floating the largest man.

This was installed early in 1851 and remained in service in the White House until the first Cleveland administration, when the present enameled tub was substituted. The example of the President soon broke down all that remained of the old opposition, and by 1860, according to the newspaper advertisements of the time, every hotel in New York had a bathtub, and some had two and even three. In 1862 bathing was introduced into the army by Gen. McClellan, and in 1870 the first prison bathtub was set up at Moyamensing prison in Philadelphia.

So much for the history of the bathtub in America. One is astonished, on looking into it, to find that so little of it has been recorded. The literature, in fact, is almost nil. But perhaps this brief sketch will encourage other inquirers and so lay the foundation for an adequate celebration of the centennial in 1942.

(The New York Evening Mail, December 28, 1917)

Hymn to the Truth

On May 23 last, writing in this place, I told the strange, sad story of an article that I printed in the New York *Evening Mail,* a paper now happily extinct, on December 28, 1917. The article, thrown off as a relief from the patriotic libido of war time, was, in substance, a burlesque history of the bathtub. I may confess that, when it was done, I fancied it no little. It was artfully devised, and it contained some buffooneries of considerable juiciness. I had confidence that the customers of the *Evening Mail* would like it.

Alas, they liked it only too well. That is to say, they swallowed it as gospel, gravely and horribly. Worse, they began sending clippings of it to friends east, west, north, and south, and so it spread to other papers, and then to the magazines and weeklies of opinion, and then to the scientific press, and finally to the reference books. To this day it is in circulation, and, as I say, has broken into the reference books, and is there embalmed for the instruction and edification of posterity.

On May 23, writing here, I exposed it at length. I pointed out some of the obvious absurdities in it. I confessed categorically that it was all buncombe. I called upon the historians of the land to take it out of their books. This confession and appeal was reprinted simultaneously in nearly thirty great American newspapers. One of them was the eminent Boston *Herald,* organ of the New England illuminati. The *Herald* printed my article on page 7 of its editorial section, under a four column head, and with a two column cartoon labelled satirically, "The American public will swallow anything." And then on June 13, three weeks later, in the same editorial section but promoted to page 1, this same *Herald* reprinted my 10 year old fake—soberly and as a piece of news!

* *

Do not misunderstand me: I am not seeking to cast a stone at the *Herald* or its talented and patriotic editors. It is, I believe, one of the glories of American journalism. It labors unceasingly for virtue and the flag. If it were suppressed by the Watch and Ward society tomorrow New England would revert instantly to savagery, wolves and catamounts would roam in Boylston street, and the Harvard Law school would be engulfed by bolshevism. Little does the public reck what great sums such journals expend to establish and disseminate the truth. It may cost $10,000 and a reporter's leg to get a full and accurate list of the guests at a Roxbury wake, with their injuries.

My point is that, despite all this extravagant frenzy for the truth, there is something in the human mind that turns instinctively to fiction, and that even journalists succumb to it. A German philosopher, Dr. Hans Vaihinger, has put the thing into a formal theory, and you will find it expounded at length in his book, *The Philosophy of As If.* It is a sheer impossibility, says Dr. Vaihinger, for human beings to think exclusively in terms of the truth. For one thing, the stock of indubitable truths is too scanty. For another thing, there is the instinctive aversion to them that I have mentioned. All of our thinking, according to Vaihinger, is in terms of assumptions, many of them plainly not true. Into our most solemn and serious reflections fictions enter—and three times out of four they quickly crowd out all the facts.

That this is true needs no argument. Every man, thinking of his wife, has to assume that she is beautiful and amiable, else despair will seize him and he will be unable to think at all. Every American, contemplating Dr. Coolidge, is physically bound to admire him: the alternative is anarchy. Every Christian, viewing the clergy, is forced into a bold theorizing to save himself from Darwinism. And all of us, taking stock of ourselves, must resort to hypothesis to escape the river.

* *

What ails the truth is that it is mainly uncomfortable, and often dull. The human mind seeks something more amusing, and more caressing. What the actual history of the bathtub may be I don't know: digging it out would be a dreadful job, and the result, after all that labor, would probably be a string of banalities. The fiction I concocted back in 1917 was at least better than that. It lacked sense, but it was certainly not without a certain charm. There were heroes in it, and villains. It revealed a conflict, with virtue winning. So it was embraced by mankind, precisely as the story of George Washington and the cherry tree was embraced, and it will live, I daresay, until it is displaced by something worse—and hence better.

In other words, it was poetry. And what is poetry? Poetry is simply a mellifluous statement of the obviously untrue. The two elements are both important, and perhaps equally. It is not sufficient that the thing said be untrue: it must also be said with a certain grace—it must soothe the ear while it debauches the mind. And it is not sufficient that it be voluptuous: it must also offer a rock and a refuge from the harsh facts of every day. All poetry embodies a lie. It may be an objective lie, as in "God's in His heaven; all's well with the world." Or it may be a subjective lie, as in "I am the master of my fate." But it must be a lie—and preferably a thumping one.

Poets, in general, protest against this doctrine. They argue that they actually deal in the truth, and that their brand of truth is of a peculiarly profound and esoteric quality—in other words, that their compositions add to the sum of human wisdom. It is sufficient answer to them to say that chiropractors make precisely the same claim, and with exactly the same plausibility. Both actually deal in fictions. Those fictions are not truth; they are not even truths in decay. They are simply better than truths. They make life more comfortable and happy. They turn and dull the sharp edge of reality.

*　*

It is commonly held that the vast majority of men are anesthetic to poetry, as they are alleged to be anesthetic to other forms of beauty, but this is a fiction, devised by poets to dignify their trade, and make it seem high toned and mysterious. The fact is that the love of poetry is one of the most primitive human traits, and that it appears in children almost as soon as they learn to speak. I do not refer here to the love of verbal jingles, but to the love of poetry properly so-called—that is, to the love of the agreeably not so. A little girl who nurses a rag doll is a poet, and so is a boy who plays at soldiers with a box of clothes pins. Their ma is another poet when she brags about them to the neighbors, and their pa when he praises the cooking of their ma.

The more simple minded the individual, indeed, the greater his need of poetry, and hence the more steady his demand for it. No poet approved by the intelligentsia ever had so many customers as Edgar A. Guest. Guest's dithyrambs are laughed at by the intelligentsia, not because the things they say are not so, but because the fiction in them is of a kind not satisfying to sniffish and snooty men. It is fiction suitable to persons of a less critical habit. It preaches the joys open to the humble. It glorifies their dire necessities. It cries down their lacks. It promises them happiness, and if not happiness, then at least contentment. No wonder it is popular! No wonder it is intoned every time Kiwanians get together and the reassuring slapping of backs begins. It is itself a sort of back slapping.

And so is all other poetry. The strophes of Robert Browning elude all the Kiwanians, but they are full of soothing for the young college professor, for they tell him that it is a marvelous and exhilarating thing to be as intellectual as he is. This, of course, is not true—which is the chief reason why it is pleasant. No normal human being wants to hear the truth. It is the passion of a small and aberrant minority of men, most of them pathological. They are hated for telling it while they live, and when they die they are swiftly forgotten. What remains to the world, in the field of wisdom, is a series of long tested and solidly agreeable lies.

(The Chicago Sunday Tribune, July 25, 1926)

Reflections on War

Reflections on War

I

The pacifists who now rant in the open forums and suffragette magazines all seem to ground their case on the thesis that the people of the United States naturally abhor war and shrink from its horrors as an I. W. W. shrinks from soap. The notion, it seems to me, has a flavor of applesauce. It would be far more accurate, though plainly not the whole truth, to say that they delight in war and enjoy its gaudy uproar as a country boy enjoys circus day. Were they unhappy during the late heroic crusade for democracy? Then so is a Methodist unhappy at a revival.

There was, to be sure, a minority of Americans who found war unpleasant, but they never ran to as much as one per cent, of the population, and most of them have learned to enjoy it vastly in retrospect, however much it may have fevered them while it was going on. I allude, obviously, to the young gentlemen who were assisted into the trenches by the draft. The records show, I believe, that fully seventy-five percent, of them tried, by one dodge or another, to avoid service. But that is not saying that they disliked war, once they had got into it. On the contrary, a great many of them enjoyed it immensely, and are among the most ardent warlocks now in practice among us.

To a young man, indeed, war is far more pleasant than unpleasant, especially if he be of simple mind—which is to say, especially if he be the normal infant of his species. The highly sophisticated youth, accustomed to ease and civilized society, finds it gross and filthy, but certainly those objections to it do not rest heavily upon the mind of a yokel from the cow belt or a youngster from a city slum. As poor men go in this world, soldiers are well fed and well clothed, and have very little work to do. Is the discipline irksome? Then certainly it is not half so irksome as the discipline of the rolling mill, the tannery, the flivver factory or the run-down farm. Is it even as irksome as the discipline of the office? I doubt it.

II

During the war I had occasion to make a journey in Western Pennsylvania, in the coal region. At the bottoms of the naked, frowning hills, alongside the railroad track, ran the straggling villages of the miners. The houses, on a winter day, looking extraordinarily forlorn and forbidding. Most of them stood up from the cinders on absurd stilts, and all of them were without paint. Wretched children played about their doors, waving their hands as the train rushed by. Slatternly women gaped from the windows. Sometimes there was a senile cow in a grassless yard. Every such house, absolutely without exception, flew a service flag. The draft got all the miners' boys.

But did it work any oppression upon them? Plainly it did not. It took them out of filth and introduced them to the bracing, highly agreeable feeling of being clean. It made them acquainted with clean food, decently cooked. It converted them into travelers, grandly seeing the world. It taught them the elements of decent manners. In brief, it civilized them—and if, in the course of that business, it civilized some of them to death, then surely the gain was worth the loss. The dead are remembered as heroes. The living have glorious memories, some of them authentic, and are at least a shade less degraded and miserable than they were.

The effect of war upon such young men, in fact, is mainly excellent, though their employers, when they get back, probably don't think so. They may be doomed to slavery, but they have at all events got some spirit of revolt in their blood. Some of them, perhaps, unable to return to the brutal routine of their fathers, take to the high road and engage the *Polizei;* many more go in for bootlegging, or some other such spacious, stimulating science. Moralists deplore the change, but moralists are seldom as wise as they look. Try to imagine a race so broken to the yoke that it no longer produced highwaymen! God help the United States if it ever comes to that.

III

But it is the general population, not the soldiers, that gets the most fun out of war. Who will forget the way the gals of this imperial republic, and especially the fat and faded ones, reacted to the late crusade? I can see them yet, prancing around in their pretty costumes, hobnobbing legally with the handsome con- scripts, and keeping their weather eyes upon the even handsomer lieutenants, captains, majors, colonels—yes, and generals. The war got many such a gal a husband, and even those who missed hus- bands at least enjoyed the thrills of an open and hearty chase, with all the usual rules suspended.

The Babbitts of the land got even more out of it than the fair. The years between 1916 and 1920, in fact, were their golden age, and they will never see another such until there is another war. Men of mark were made overnight, and hundreds of thousands of them survive, in all the far-flung towns of the realm, as men of vision. Congress is full of such fiery stay-at-homes today, and some of them are in places still higher. The demand for patriotic speak- ers in the movie parlors was insatiable, and every novice who got through his four minutes without fainting was practically sure of fame—at least, locally.

Moreover, the business paid. A few stimulating yells, to the applause of the commonalty—and the rest of the day was free for enlightened self-interest. I used to travel a good deal in those days, and so had to listen to the gabble of these idealists in the Pullman smokers. Their air was that of men who had struck it rich. They talked in large figures and smoked large cigars. They were crusad- ers shinning up the walls of a new and glittering Jerusalem, and every ten seconds they were showered with gold. Some of them, later on, went to jail, and many more went broke. But the major- ity hung on to their just and righteous rewards. They constitute the backbone of the right thinking, conservative *bloc* today, and are unanimously in favor of another war, if necessary, to put down Bolshevism.

IV

It is hard, indeed, to recall a class of Americans to whom the late war was unpleasant. There were, of course, others at home who watched and waited and feared and hoped, and some of them, alas! hoped in vain, but they were fewer than the soldiers and nothing much was heard from them. If they had made any protest, there would have been four minute men to caution them sharply and teach them the high privileges of patriotism. No other class showed any sign of discontent. The jobholders were safe, busy and happy. The honest workingman saw his wages multiply like magic and bought himself a phonograph, a still and a tin lizzie. The banker prepared for a killing in Liberty bonds. The publicist had an audience at last, rounded up to hear him, and forbidden to escape.

It is thus nonsense, and perhaps even libel, to say that the American people detest war. If they detest it, then they are idiots. Life was never so pleasant in America as it was during those three years. There was a gaudy show going on all the time, and parts in it for everyone. Even the pacifists themselves, going grandly to jail, enjoyed themselves immensely. It was not the publicity that delighted and soothed them but the inward thrill. For the first time in a generation they were able to do something dramatic and satisfying for the Holy Cause. No prohibitionist was ever happier, spying through a knothole at his neighbor.

My belief is that the next war will be just as merry. The United States is now so populous and so powerful that no enemy nation, or combination of enemy nations, could hope to tackle it head on. Our next ten or twelve wars will all be fought on foreign soil and in a safe and sanitary manner. No despot's heel will ever mark these virtuous shores in our time. War, to the soldiers told off to fight it, will be a junket, a picnic, a free foreign excursion—and to the heroes nominated to keep the home fires burning it will be a thrilling and magnificent show, with the spectators well paid for their applause. I believe that these facts are obvious to most Americans. And so believing, I am convinced that it is a gross slander upon their common sense to argue that they are pacifists at heart. But are they stayed by God's command, issued through His agents, the rev. clergy? Well, go read again what the rev. clergy had to say in 1917.

(The Chicago Sunday Tribune, September 26, 1926)

Reminiscence

I

When I read of the bombardments and slaughter in the Basque country the picture simply refuses to register. It seems as outlandish and impossible as a camp meeting in the gardens of the Vatican, or a Bach festival in Mississippi. For my only memory of that lovely region is a memory of the profoundest imaginable peace, to wit, peace after war. I came into it on a smiling day in early spring, *anno* 1917, after two months of a wartime journey that had taken me as far north as the Orkney Islands and as far east as the River Dvina, and had left me covered with frostbites and full of woe.

The frostbites were acquired in what is now Lithuania, along the German front running above a little town called Novo Alexandrovsk. This, at the beginning of 1917, was the spearhead of the great German *Vormarsch* into Russia, and the show it offered was certainly exciting enough to a novice. The outfit I was a part of included two other newspaper reporters—a Swiss and a Hollander—and two officers of the German General Staff. The job of these officers was to take us over the works, and they pursued it with great industry. All day we tramped the trenches, and every evening we were put up at some officers' mess.

There were *Polizeistünde* for all ordinary officers, including even generals: they had to shut down their meager revels at 10 P.M. But the young flying officers were allowed to carry on as late as they pleased, for it was understood that all of them would soon be dead anyhow, and everyone wanted to be nice to them. We pilgrims proceeded to their quarters at 10 o'clock, and there helped them to get down their evening ration of half French champagne and half English porter—both stolen goods, and hence extra sweet.

The General Staff brethren were under orders to bring their

charges back alive if practicable, but their colleagues at the front, after more than two years in the field, were somewhat inured to flying missiles, and in consequence there were occasions when we were conducted to seats that, to me at least, seemed rather too near the stage. I recall, for example, having dinner one evening with a division commander whose quarters were within point-blank range of the Russian artillery. He was an amiable old *Junker,* and he entertained us by propounding banal riddles out of some German almanac. I enjoyed them in a pallid, sneaky way, but there were undoubtedly moments when my mind wandered from them, speculating as to the probable effects if a shell landed in the middle of the dinner table.

II

But all this is now fading, and I no longer shiver when I think of it. Wars, indeed, are soon forgotten, else there would not be so many of them. The thing I remember most clearly of those brief days is not the risk of colliding with hog-wild metal, but the appalling and incomparable cold. It was far beyond anything in my previous experience, and even beyond anything I could imagine. It seemed to have almost a solid quality, like a downpour of gravel, and at the same time it was as penetrating as X-rays.

I had been warned about it in Berlin, and got to the front dressed almost like an Arctic explorer, but after the first day I began to lay on more and more furs. When the wind blew, which was often, there was simply no getting warm—that is, in the open. The quarters behind the line, mainly log houses built by Russian prisoners, were cozy enough, but in the field one froze and despaired. The precise temperature I never found out. Some said it was 30 below zero, and some said 40, 50, 100, 500, 1,000. The more impossible the guess, the more probable it seemed.

I got back to Berlin one dismal winter night, determined to hole in at the Adlon Hotel for a week, with four feather pillows under me and six or eight on top. But the first news I heard when I reached the hotel was of the Zimmerman U-boat note, and thus my week of rest blew up, and I was on the go day and night. The cold of Lithuania seemed to have followed me. Horrible blasts roared down Unter den Linden. The Friedrichstrasse was an icehouse. I swelled in all directions, and my hide turned a dark purple. I was stiff in every joint, and began to wheeze and choke up.

When Ambassador Gerard was recalled he went to Switzerland, and I went along. Zürich was deep in snow. Basel was buried in a dense white fog, as clammy as grave-clothes. On to Paris! A night on an unheated train, curled up on the floor. Paris was dark, damp and dismal. No lights in the streets. None in the hotels save one blue lamp to a floor. My teeth kept on chattering.

III

All ocean traffic was blockaded north of Spanish waters, so I decided to go to Madrid. It turned out to be surprisingly easy. A $20 American gold note, discreetly planted, got me a bootleg berth on a train leaving for the south that very night, and I turned in as soon as the gates opened. The car was like a refrigerator, and there was but one thin blanket. I began to believe that a new Ice Age had dawned. But somehow I fell asleep—and when I awoke in the morning it was to gape at the beautiful Bay of Biscay, with a row of palms along the shore and the good red sun beating down.

Where this was I don't know precisely—probably somewhere near St. Jean de Luz. All I recall is the immense, the almost unbearable joy of seeing the sun again. I had not had a clear look at it for at least six weeks. When the train stopped somewhere I rushed out to wallow in it. It seemed so big that it half filled the sky, and it glared down with all the hospitable ferocity of the gates of Hell. When I got back on the train I threw up my window and leaned out. It was infinitely warm and comfortable and soothing. It was like opium after pain.

We got to Hendaye on the border before noon, and were presently at Irun and on Spanish soil, with the war far behind and already half forgotten. Irun, I believe, is now a wreck—battered to pieces in one of the earlier battles of the Spanish revolution. But I can think of it only as it was that balmy winter day—a charming toy town, seemingly made of cardboard, with some of the houses painted red, and some blue, but most of them yellow, and the whole bathed in golden sunlight. The sun seemed to be shining on both sides of the streets. There were no shadows. It was a world all light, and warmth—and peace.

IV

I had lunch somewhere in the town—outdoors, of course—and afterward took a stroll. I recall the Basques sitting quietly before their Christmas-garden houses, snoozing away the lazy afternoon. Compared to the armed men I had been living with for weeks, they looked as harmless as so many tabby cats. Here and there a couple of children played somberly in a gutter. Now and then a housewife ambled along, burdened with marketing. I recall encountering a bookshop. The window was full of Spanish translations of the works of Orison Swett Marden and Upton Sinclair. Another war had been forgotten.

Toward the end of the afternoon the train for Madrid set out, and by dusk we were at San Sebastien. As the evening cool came down I was astonished to find that I liked it. The day before I had believed that I'd never be happy again save in front of a blast furnace. As I thawed out my chilblains began to abate, and I returned to my normal contours. It was a placid, dreamy, almost boozy feeling. Joint after joint lost its stiffness and began to function.

At San Sebastien there was a longish wait, and a good deal of pother on the platform. I went out to see what was up, and found that the private car of King Alfonso XIII was being attached to the train. We started up through the high, romantic Basque country in the late twilight, and as the darkness gathered I observed that there were armed sentries all along the track, with a corporal and his guard at every bridge.

Some time before this the anarchists of Barcelona had tried to bomb Alfonso, and the show of troops was to let him sleep. Another war was casting its shadows as before. But I didn't know it. The Basque country that I saw was as peaceful as a bankrupt church, soldiers or no soldiers. I find it almost impossible to think of it as shot to pieces.

(*The Baltimore Evening Sun, June 21, 1937*)

Conference Notes

I

Our old friend, American idealism, seems to be struggling to its feet again. Last week in this place, perhaps crowding the mourners, I ventured the view that it was down with paludal anemia and would be heard of no more. But now there is renewed burble about it in the public prints, including the estimable *Sunpaper*. I exclude the ironical allusions of the *Sunpaper*'s English and Japanese collaborators, and confine myself to two essays by Americans —both, in fact, Baltimoreans. The one is Hon. John W. Owens, staff correspondent at the actual Conference; the other is Prof. Dr. John H. Latane, head of the department of history in the Johns Hopkins University and professor of American history in the same great chautauqua. I quote the headline put upon Mr. Owens' treatise by an intelligent copy-reader:

> U.S. DELEGATES LAY STRESS UPON
> MORAL VALUES INVOLVED

And then, from the article itself:

> What stands out most clearly, after one week's work of the Conference on Limitation of Armament, is Secretary Hughes' . . . insistence upon the moral values involved . . .
> The next manifestation of this insistence upon moral values came when. . . .

The Disarmament Conference, held in Washington, D.C., November 12, 1921–February 6, 1922. The genesis of the conference lay in the widespread fear of an arms race between the victorious powers of World War I. Particularly acute was the fear of unrestrained competition in the naval armaments among Great Britain, the United States, and Japan. Britain was alarmed lest the United States seize control of the seas. Japan feared an overwhelming sea power that would threaten its independence in the Far East. At the outset, Secretary of State Charles Evans Hughes, the chairman of the conference, created a public sensation by his proposal for each country to scrap a certain ratio of its particular warships and limit construction of new ones. Baron Takaakira Kato, the most influential representative of the Japanese delegation, objected to the ratios, which were eventually modified and accepted. At the conclusion of the conference, China's position was theoretically improved by a treaty signed by all nine powers represented, recognizing its administrative independence.

Another manifestation of this insistence upon moral values came when Admiral Baron Kato submitted the Japanese proposal for "a slight increase" in the tonnage allowed Japan under the Hughes proposal.

Here is John Owens, a man grown bald in the trenches of journalism, a hard-boiled fellow if there ever was one—and yet he sits down in cold blood, writes such thumping tosh, and then deliberately signs his name to it! It is enough to make one give up the human race for lost, retire to some remote fastness, and there sicken and die. As a matter of sober and simple fact, there has been no more sign of moral intent or moral aim in the maneuvers of Dr. Hughes and his colleagues than there has been in the contrary writhings and squirming of the Japs. The Americans have tried to hamstring the Japs; the Japs have tried to upset the Americanos. The aim of the one gang and the aim of the other have been precisely the same: each has sought to get advantages for its own country at the expense of the other. No other actual purpose is in the Conference, save as an afterthought, a selling-point, a piece of cheese to bait the trap for boobs. In particular, no other purpose is visible in the American position. If Dr. Hughes' plan is carried out, then the United States will get its whack at Northern Asia without the preliminary trouble and expense of murdering the Japs. If it fails, then war will have to come first and the advance of Christian *Kultur* second.

II

Why pretend otherwise? Who, in fact, is deceived—that is, beyond the continental limits of this vast republic of buncombophagi? Are the Japs? Are the English, with their resolute and undisguised pursuit of the main chance? Are the French? Are the Russians? Are the Cubans, Puerto Ricans, Haitians, Dominicans—all the other Latin-Americans? Are the Chinese, most recent of victims of American shysterism? Are the neutrals in the late war? Are the people of the Central Powers? Are the Filipinos? Yet here is Dr. Latane printing over his sign manual a piece depicting the United States as a sort of international Pollyanna and visiting nurse—here is my learned and virtuous brother filling the *Sunpaper* with all the old tosh about American "unselfishness and disinterestedness"! Worse, here he actually lists Cuba and Haiti among the beneficiaries hereof!

If Dr. Latane is really under any illusions about Cuba, let him give his boys a holiday and go down there for a week or two of investigation. The first thing he will discover, if he is fortunate enough to come into contact with any genuine Cubans and has the art of winning their confidence, is that they are practically unanimously of the opinion that the United States is dishonest—that not one in 10 of them believes in any of the soaring purposes he speaks of—that they regard everything American and every American with suspicion and distaste. And the second thing he will discover is the reason therefore—a reason conveniently divided into two parts: (a) that the delivery of the Cubans from political slavery to the Spaniards has simply converted them into economic slaves to Americans, and (b) that American interference in Cuban politics, the last time in 1917, has invariably taken the form of help for capitalism, *i.e.*, for American hegemony. In brief, the Cubans are anti-American because American "unselfishness and disinterestedness," in the 23 years since 1898, have transferred a very large proportion of their sugar plantations, docks, railways and other property to American ownership, and because the American sabre rattles menacingly every time that ownership is imperiled.

It is quite nonsensical to attempt to estimate the American profit from the 1898 enterprise by confining one's inspection to imports, exports and balances of trade, as is usually done by statisticians. Of enormously greater importance to American capitalism than any balance of Cuban trade in our favor, or any development of Cuban markets for our phonograph records, chewing gum, Peruna, jig-saw puzzles, oleomargarine and other such cultural products, is the direct income that comes from Cuba investments, *i.e.*, from the labor of the Cuban people. I myself, for example, derive a part of my living from such investments, though I sell nothing in Cuba and seldom buy anything of Cuban manufacture save a pound of sugar or a bottle of smuggled rum. But I paid for my Cuban securities, you may object. The Cubans got something for my present vested right to their labor. True enough. I admit it. But is such a transaction to be described as "unselfish and disinterested"? Does Dr. Latane so lightly esteem me that he thinks I am fool enough to lay out my hard-earned money for what Mr. Owens calls "moral values"? If so, then I denounce him publicly as a slanderer, and instruct my solicitor to begin an action against him for a deliberate attempt to degrade and incriminate me.

III

Nay; there is no "unselfishness and disinterestedness" in such matter: there is only *Geschäft*. Any pretension to the contrary is easily disposed of by a moment's analysis. When Dr. Latane mentions Haiti he at once descends to the preposterous. Did the United States actually seize Haiti in order to prevent it lapsing into barbarism, as he hints? Then barbarism may be very simply defined as the failure to pay the interest upon one's debts—in particular, upon such of one's debts as were incurred by public thieves, without one's authority and without any appreciable benefit to one's personal fortunes. There is not the slightest evidence that the Haitians, for all their turmoils, ever menaced the person of any American; all they ever menaced was the property of Americans—and nine-tenths of it was property owned, not by Americans resident in Haiti, but by usurers living safely in New York. In order to protect this property—that is, in order to extort an unfair and excessive income from it—American marines were landed in Haiti, and several thousand Haitians, most of them poor yokels who had never heard of the debt, were murdered in cold blood, many with revolting tortures.

Such is American "unselfishness and disinterestedness" in Haiti —a bald fraud, as it is everywhere else. Ask the Filipinos what they think of it. Or the Colombians. Or the Puerto Ricans. Or even the Panamans, its latest beneficiaries. Or the Chinese. The Chinese in Washington know precisely what the American profession of altruism in Washington is worth. In answer to it, instead of tearful thanks, they offer an agreement which provides that, once the Japanese thieves are ousted from China, there shall be no looting by American and English thieves. This agreement has been put upon the shelf, where it will remain. I suggest that Dr. Latane read it—it is in the form of a brief statement of principles—every time the impulse arises in him to discuss American "unselfishness and disinterestedness," and, in particular, every time he feels himself slipping into the superstition that its beneficiaries believe in it.

(The Baltimore Evening Sun, November 24, 1921)

Etiquette Makes Rapid Progress Impossible at London, Mencken Says

London, Jan. 31.—No doubt connoisseurs at a distance marvel at the slowness with which the naval conference proceeds, but close by the wonder is that it makes any progress at all. The etiquette which governs the deliberations of such bodies antedates all secular diplomacy and goes back to the interminable councils of the medieval church. If there has been any change lately it is in the direction of increased ponderosity. Metternich and his friends, meeting behind closed doors, could occasionally take a short cut, but now that everything is done under the glare of spotlights every subtlety of decorum must be observed.

Consider the business translated into everyday terms. Suppose it were the rule that the drummer going out to sell his goods had to take along ten secretaries in plug hats, five admirals in full uniform, eight or ten head lawyers, and suppose the consumer prepared for him by assembling the same gaudy guard. Now, suppose the drummer had to prepare an opening speech two days in advance, have it translated into French and supply copies to all newspapers. And now suppose the customer, having heard it, had to reply by inviting the whole gang to a banquet followed by

The world's five major naval powers—Great Britain, the United States, France, Japan, and Italy—met in London on January 21 until April 22, 1930, to discuss the limitation on naval armaments. The London Naval Arms Conference (a sequel to the Disarmament Conference held in Washington, D.C., in 1921) led to an agreement on the regulation of submarine warfare and a five-year hiatus for capital ships construction. From the outset, there were suspicions on the French and Japanese sides that the two English-speaking powers had entered into an agreement to protect their fleets at the expense of other powers. "Only by divine intervention can the delegates solve the problem before them," Mencken reported. ". . . It may be done, but angels could do it better than politicians." France and Italy refused to agree to specific terms of the treaty, so the naval limitations applied only to Great Britain, the United States, and Japan. In a speech broadcast by radio from London to New York, Secretary of State Henry L. Stimson said the conference had given "me more confidence in my belief that the peaceful methods of diplomacy can eventually take the place of war." Eleven years later, all the countries of the conference would be involved in World War II.

speeches in English, French and Italian, with radio mikes every three feet and the gallery full of movie cameras.

Let us now leap forward a week. Two high contracting parties have been meeting twice daily and dining together every night and each has become aware of the intentions of the other. The drummer has made it clear that he wants to sell something and the customer admits he is willing to buy if he can get a close price. But before the drummer may make an actual offer of his goods, he must draw up a document setting forth in detail what he proposes to sell and why he wants to sell it, and this document must be submitted for approval to a committee consisting of two rival drummers and two competitors of the customer.

There ensues what is called a plenary session. That is to say, all parties at interest, accompanied by secretaries, admirals, lawyers, with 400 newspapermen ranged along the wall, meet in a public hall and proceed to deafen and demoralize one another with oratory. Some speak English, some French, some Italian. Interpreters interpret, bands play, soldiers march around the hall clanking guns, movie cameras click. All say the same thing, viz.: that they are ready and eager to do business. Secretaries take it down. It goes out by radio. It is cabled to Australia and Japan.

So far there is no mention of actual goods. It is too soon to speak of them. Before that stage is reached a steering committee must be appointed to draw up a protocol showing precisely what they are and setting rules to prevent the drummer from trying to sell more than so much. This committee will need a day to organize, a day to eat a banquet, a day to get over it, five days to exchange ideas, a week to draw up a report. Every day correspondents print false forecasts of that report and they have to be denied. The drummer gets hot telegrams from his home office. The customer is denounced as a jackass by his partners. He accuses his competitors of the main committee of trying to hornswoggle him. The drummer's rivals spread the report that he is on a drunk.

A million letters of complaint and protests come from radio fans. The band goes on strike, the soldiers bayonet a lawyer. There is a dense fog and the whole steering committee is lost.

Weeks pass. Half the correspondents have gone home. The radio has broken down. The admirals are all in sanitoria. Finally the steering committee completes its report and brings it in. It is translated into French, Italian and Japanese. Some one finds an error in the Japanese translation and a day is wasted hunting a dictionary.

But one day there is an end. The report is ratified at a plenary session, the drummer gets out his samples, the customer examines them and it is announced officially that actual haggling may begin.

I exaggerate very little. Precisely by such preposterous devices the new diplomacy carries on business. No party to negotiations ever dares say plainly what is in his mind. He always must remember the radio, the newspapers, the folk back home—above all the archaic and insane etiquette of his grotesque art. To let fall a frank word would be as grave indecorum as to come to the meeting without spats.

If the American and English delegates could meet as businessmen, they could settle the whole thing in two days and leave the French and Italians to find out from the newspapers. As it is, they will be here at least two months and in the end all really important matters they have met to discuss will be left for another time.

(The Baltimore Evening Sun, January 31, 1930)

Help for the Jews

It is to be hoped that the poor Jews now being robbed and mauled in Germany will not take too seriously the plans of various foreign politicos to rescue them. Those plans, in all cases, smell pungently of national politics, and in not a few cases they are obviously fraudulent. The last is especially true of the English scheme to plant the victims in such forlorn and uninhabitable places as British Guiana, and of the American scheme to help them by goading and inflaming the Nazi Ku Kluxers, while at the same time refusing to take any substantial number into the United States, or to relax the drastic immigration laws which now bar out virtually all the really helpless.

It may be that some of the so-called *Ostjuden,* or Eastern Jews, could survive in British Guiana, for they are a tough people and used to hard scrabbling, but certainly it would be next door to murder to send any German Jews there, for most of them are more or less educated folk, and long accustomed to the ways and comforts of civilization. Try to imagine condemning a German-Jewish lawyer, or insurance man, or merchant, or schoolmaster to a place where the climate is that of a Turkish bath, and there are no roads, no towns, no food supply, and hardly any inhabitants save snakes and mosquitoes!

Tanganyika is almost as bad. As readers of Marius Fortie's recent and excellent book, *Black and Beautiful,* must know, it has gone downhill ever since the English philanthropists took over the mandate. The unfortunate natives are so cruelly taxed that many of them are now quite destitute, and every effort to plant English settlers on the land has failed. The best that may be said of Tanganyika is that it is as good as the worst parts of Mexico. If a Jewish colony is planted there it will take at least a generation to make it self-sustaining, and the cost of supporting it meanwhile will make the millions poured out in Palestine seem puny.

* *

There is plenty of room for refugees in other and better British possessions. Canada could absorb 100,000, or even 200,000 with ease, and they would be useful acquisitions, especially in the western prairie provinces, which are dominated today by a low grade of farmers, without any adequate counter-balance of a competent middle class. Australia, now almost as exclusive as Sing Sing, which it somewhat resembles in population, could use quite as many, for more than a third of its population is crowded into two cities, and immense areas of good country behind the seacoast are undeveloped. As for New Zealand, it has less than the population of Maryland in an area ten times as large.

In all three of these Dominions the climate is at least as bearable as that of Northern Germany, and the beginnings of civilization are already visible. But in Tanganyika there is nothing but such bare land as the American pioneers saw when they crossed the Mississippi. An investment of billions would be needed to develop it even up to the point reached by, say, Venezuela or Haiti. Moreover, it would still remain a poor country, for its arable areas are remote from the world markets, and it lacks coal, oil and other essential minerals.

British Guiana is yet worse; indeed, it is so bad that nothing comparable to it can be found short of the Congo. The towns along its coast are malarious and miserable villages, the plowed area is less than 1/320 of the total territory, and all save a small

strip fronting the sea is such a howling wilderness that even prisoners escaping from Devil's Island keep out of it. To transport the
German Jews to such a hell hole would be even worse than condemning them to Devil's Island itself.

* *

The American plan for helping the refugees is less openly brutal than the English plan, but almost as insulting to them, and
even more futile. It confines itself, so far, to making bellicose
speeches, passing inflammatory resolutions, collecting money to
defend and glorify the assassin of the German attaché, and otherwise provoking Hitler to reprisals. In the same breath in which
the Hon. Mr. Roosevelt declared that he "could scarcely believe
that such things could occur in a Twentieth Century civilization,"
he assured the newspaper correspondents that he had no intention
of proposing a relaxation of the immigration laws. In other words,
he is sorry for the Jews, but unwilling to do anything about it that
might cause him political inconvenience at home.

Such gross and disgusting peck-sniffery is precisely what one
might expect from the right hon. gentleman, and I only hope the
American Jews who have swallowed so much of his other buncombe will not be fetched by it. The American newspapers with
their usual credulity, applauded it gravely—but not so the Negro
papers. The dark comrades point out that Roosevelt has never
been as solicitous about outrages on Negroes in this country. Says
George S. Schuyler, perhaps the best of all the Aframerican journalists, in the Pittsburgh *Courier:*

Imagine Roosevelt saying he "could scarcely believe" such atrocities could
take place in this day and time when white people had just got through
burning a schoolhouse and running Negroes out of Smyrna, Ga., and had just
finished jabbing red-hot pokers into a Negro youth in Ruston, La.!

* *

There is only one way to help the fugitives, and that is to find
places for them in a country in which they can really live. Why
shouldn't the United States take in a couple of hundred thousand
of them, or even all of them? I have heard, so far, but two objections to inviting them. The first is to the effect that there is far too
much unemployment here now, and that a fresh immigration,
even of so small a number, would only accentuate it. The second is

that bringing them in would arouse the native Ku Kluxers, and perhaps launch a formidable anti-Semitic movement.

Both objections seem to me to be very feeble. The first is based on the theory that all the refugees would either join the unemployed themselves, or increase the roll to their own number by displacing Americans now at work. Neither effect is even remotely probable. The Jews will find work very quickly, and whatever they produce will be more than balanced by what they consume. They will not compete on the low level of the present dolebirds; they will compete on higher levels, and the chances are at least even that they will soon be adding more to the national income than they take away.

The Ku Klux fear is equally without ground. If they were planted in Mississippi, Arkansas or some other such jumping-off place, the local Ku Kluxers would undoubtedly protest, but not many Jews are likely to go to Mississippi or Arkansas. Instead they will stay in the larger cities—and there the number of their people is already so large that a few more will hardly be noticed. The present Jewish population of New York city is 1,765,000— more than four times the Jewish population of Palestine. It is absurd to argue that an increase of five or six per cent would set the patriotic Aryans to burning and slaying.

* *

I am here speaking, of course, of German Jews, and of German Jews only. They constitute an undoubtedly superior group. Even their occasional rascals, so I was once told by a German police official, are far above the felonious common run. The question of the Eastern Jews remains, and it should be faced candidly. Many German Jews dislike them, and were trying to get them out of Germany before the present universal disasters came down. There is a faction of them that tends to be troublesome wherever they settle, and there is apparently ground for the general belief that in this country they incline toward the more infantile kinds of radicalism.

Fortunately, they are not numerous in German Jewry. The really large accumulations of them are in Poland and Rumania. It would be obviously impossible, even if it were prudent, for the United States to take them all in. But there is still plenty of room for them, and in a land where there is no prejudice against them, and their opportunities are immensely better than in Tanganyika or Guiana, or even Palestine. That land is Russia.

(The Baltimore Sun, November 27, 1938)

A Word for the Japs

The Japanese, judged by Western eyes, are an extremely homely people, and no doubt the fact has a good deal to do with their general unpopularity. In their aspect there is something both sinister and ludicrous. They look, taking one with another, like Boy Scouts with buck teeth, wearing horn-rimmed spectacles. Every normal adult, on encountering such a Scout, feels suddenly uncomfortable, and has to throttle an impulse to yell "Scat!" So with the constituents of H.I.M. Hirohito, himself a shining example of the species. I have never met a Caucasian who professed any affection for the Japs, though there are not a few white fans for the scenery, color printing, native booze and/or public stews of their picturesque country.

Nevertheless, they are a people of very considerable talents, and will have to be reckoned with in the future history of the human race. They have long since got past the stage of sitting respectfully at the feet of the West. For a generation past they have been squarely on their own, and making swift progress. In all the fields of human endeavor save theology, politics and swine justice they are showing the way to their ofay mentors. They have made important and durable contributions to knowledge in each and every one of the exact sciences, and they have taken such a lead in trade and industry that the only way left to beat them is to murder them.

This device has been advocated earnestly by the baffled entrepreneurs of other countries, and especially by those of England, but unfortunately the execution would probably be difficult, for in addition to all their other gifts the Japs show a considerable knack for war. This knack was not borrowed from the West; it goes back to the remotest days of Japanese history. But it has been cultivated by contact with the West, and is now manifested in namely Western terms. The Japs have a navy that surpasses all other navies save those of England and the United States, and an army that in active strength and trained reserves is outnumbered only by the army of Russia.

* *

The achievements of that army in China during the past two years have been generally cried down by the American newspapers, but that is only saying that the foreign news appearing in American newspapers is seldom accurate and not always honest. In large part it is written by bitter partisans, and not a few of them seem to be wholly unable to distinguish between agreeable fantasies and objective facts. Inasmuch as nearly all white men dislike the Japs and like the Chinese, the former have naturally got the worst of this wishful thinking. Their imminent collapse and defeat has been announced over and over again, and every time they have given the poor Chinese another wallop elaborate efforts have been made to prove that the only permanent damage it had done has been to the Japs themselves.

It may well be that the majority of the Americans swallow this nonsense, and look confidently for the ultimate triumph of the Hon. Chiang Kai-shek, but if so they are doomed to a disappointment almost as tragic as the one that apparently awaits them in Europe. The plain fact is that the Japs, under enormous difficulties, have performed a military feat almost unparalleled in modern times, and at a cost in men and materials that seems, by European standards, to be hardly more than trivial. With an army that, at most, can't have run beyond 1,000,000 men they have taken all the principal cities of China, driven its government into the far interior, seized all its main lines of communication, cut off nearly all its supplies, and seized at least nine-tenths of its trade and industry.

The argument that there are still armed Chinese in this colossal conquered territory is of very little appositeness. There were armed Indians roving the American West until the middle 90's, and not infrequently they tackled and defeated small parties of Federal troops, but no rational person maintained that they still held the country. They were doomed from the moment the army seized their principal strongholds and began to harass their lines of communication. They went on bushwhacking for almost a generation, but they were never able to wage anything properly describable as organized war, and their ultimate doom was always certain. So with the Chinese. They may fight gallantly and for a long while, but they can never win.

* *

Part of the propaganda against the Japs consists in spreading the legend that they fell upon an unarmed and unorganized enemy with overwhelming strength, and so engaged in a series of brutal massacres rather than in formal war. Nothing could be further from the truth. The Chinese, at the start of the uproar, had a very large and well-equipped army, and it had been in the field for ten years. Many of its units had been trained by European professionals, principally Germans and Russians, and they gave the Japs plenty to think about in the first fighting at Shanghai and thereabout.

Moreover, this army had ample sources of supply. There were arsenals in most of the big cities, and an enormous mass of material was sent in by the Russians. The French also helped, and the English were not far behind. Such things as food, clothing and labor-power were present in virtually unlimited amounts. The Japs, on their side, had to bring everything from men to rice across the water, and nearly all their landings were made in the face of violent resistance. Once they landed, they faced an extremely difficult terrain, and that must have been a rare battle in which they encountered odds of less than four to one.

Despite all this, they beat the Chinese nine times out of ten, and not only beat them, but routed them. Very few of the retreats of the Chinese army were orderly. Much more often it fled helter-skelter, with all its will to fight oozed out of it. In the early days of the war American newspaper readers were entertained with daily accounts of the stupendous feats of the Chinese air force, most of it provided and manned by Russians. But its superiority turned out to be as mythical as that of the Russian air force in Spain. In a little while the Japs had it on the run, and in all of China proper they are now in complete command of the air. Over and over again they have sent fleets of bombers all the way to Chungking, a good thousand miles from the coast, and brought them back with only the most trifling damage.

That the Russians have been doing any better along the Mongolian border is to be doubted. In war both sides tend to overestimate the losses of the enemy, but certainly the Japanese reports are likely to be more reliable than any emanating from

Moscow. The Japs lie now and then, but the Russians lie all the time, and the fact remains brilliantly plain that the Japs are still on the border, and still menacing the Russian communications from the West.

* *

It is well to give an occasional thought to facts of this sort in such mad, glad times as these. The Japs had a bad press to begin with, because of the general unpopularity that I have mentioned, and in recent months they have brought down on themselves a double dose of moral indignation by presuming to threaten the lucrative Chinese trade of England. The United States, as usual, has succumbed to English influence in the matter, both officially and journalistically. The State Department denounces the Japs for interfering with foreign rights in the war area, though it condones and even applauds the total destruction of foreign rights in Mexico, which is presumably at peace. And the newspapers belabor them virtuously for their wicked aggressions in China and elsewhere, though remaining charitably silent about the Russian aggressions in Outer Mongolia and Chinese Turkestan, not to mention China itself.

The Japs, in truth, had as sound a mandate to clean up China as the United States has had to clean up Cuba. Wracked by constant civil wars, and afflicted by a long succession of tin-pot Hitlers of the Chiang Kai-shek species, the poor Chinese were in a state of chaos, and constituted the sort of nuisance that no neighbor of any spirit could endure. They appear to be quite unable to govern themselves. For centuries they have escaped from one foreign hoof only to come under another. There is no evidence that the Japs will govern them less competently than the Manchus; indeed, all the probabilities run the other way. In any case, there seems to be no way to stop the process. Whatever altruistic power tries to do so, whether it be Russia, or England, or the United States, will come out very painfully convinced that it has been in a war.

(*The Baltimore Sun, August 13, 1939*)

Across the Border

England Revisited

I

No one can come back to England in these days without seeing at once that the country lies under an agony of spirit. The cockiness that followed the war has oozed away, and in place of it there is a feeling of doubt and insecurity, visible at a glance. One faction urges various heroic measures of reform and rehabilitation, mainly in gross contempt of such economic laws as yet retain any countenance. Another argues gloomily that it is too late to do anything—that a spookish, malarious *Gotterdämmerung* has already set in, and the Empire is fast going to the dogs.

A good deal of this, it seems to me, is sheer hypochondria, perhaps even neurasthenia. The English, inhabiting a damp, soggy land, with inadequate stoves to heat them, are greatly given to despair, especially in winter. The common American concept of them as bluff, hearty fellows, bursting with hormones, belongs to romance: their typical mood is really one of depression. They nurse difficulties and grievances with steadfast devotion, and are never so happy as when they face a sea of troubles, real or imaginary.

In the present case, it must be admitted, they have plenty to chew on. Business is bad, and growing worse. Unemployment is bad, and growing worse. The contumacy of the colonies and Dominions is bad, and growing worse. The international situation is bad, and growing worse. But when all this is put down the fact remains that the Empire, as an Empire, is still making a very good living, and that England itself is far, far from anything plausibly describable as disaster. Two-thirds of the problems which now upset everyone are no more than manifestations of the post-war *Katzenjammer,* and may be expected to solve themselves as it passes off. The rest are plainly more serious, but even the worst of them shows none of the horrible insolubility which marks the capital problems of such countries as Austria, Hungary and Poland, to say nothing of Italy, Spain and Japan. All that is needed, to get them moving toward solution, is a fresh attack and a new and firmer resolution.

II

Unluckily, nothing of the sort shows itself in England at the moment. The Labor party, which was expected to work a miracle with unemployment, is so patently bankrupt of effective ideas that it is pathetic, and the Conservatives seem to have nothing to offer save a crazy scheme to build a high tariff wall around the whole Empire. What good this wall would do to England, which could not live on the Empire's trade alone and must get a large part of its food and raw materials from outside the bounds, does not appear. Nor is it apparent how some of the Dominions would benefit by it, especially Canada.

The Labor party seems to be equally bankrupt when it comes to what is here called rationalization, which is to say, the reorganization of the national industries in a modern and efficient manner. The only plan it offers publicly is to turn the poor manufacturers over to the banks. But this simply means taking their factories away from them, and inasmuch as they already resist jealously every effort to limit their old reckless freedom by putting them into combinations with their fellows, it seems improbable that they can be induced to give up everything and become mere slaves of the Shylocks.

In other directions the Labor party shows the same incompetence to deal effectively with the grave questions confronting it.

Its General Staff, now in control of the Government, is made up largely of professional orators, full of sound and fury, signifying nothing. A few weeks ago, when the realists of the House of Lords tried to put a curb upon one of their gaudy but dubious schemes, they resorted to demagogy and the Lords had to back down. But the scheme remains dubious for all that, and presently it will be blowing up like the rest. Many of these orators are labor leaders by trade. There is no appreciable difference between labor leaders in England and labor leaders in the United States.

III

That the English will wriggle out of their difficulties soon or late is very probable, but that it will take them a long while and cost them a lot of effort and agony seems to be certain. What holds them back is their truly astounding incapacity for taking in new ideas, even the most persuasive. It is surely not poverty that keeps them from reorganizing their basic industries in a rational manner, for on their own showing there is plenty of money in the City for the purpose; it is sheer hunkerousness. And that hunkerousness shows itself in every detail of their private lives.

At the moment there is a moderate cold snap in England, and the mercury is down to 30 degrees. So much cold would not be noticed in the United States, but here it is downright paralyzing. Half the people one meets are snuffling and watery-eyed, and the papers are full of warnings about bursting water pipes. All this is due to the fact that not one Englishman in a hundred has adequate heating arrangements in his house. Even among the rich coal grates are still in almost universal use. Only the more modern hotels and a few great mansions have central heating.

The English coal grate has a certain cheeriness, but beyond that it is completely preposterous. Why no one has ever thought to design something better I can't make out. The thing as it stands throws out so little heat that one shivers ten feet from it. The far corners of the room are as cold as outdoors, and seem far colder. Yet just such ludicrous contraptions are used to heat huge dining rooms, with the women bare back and front, and the men freezing in their light dinner coats.

IV

The other afternoon, invited to luncheon in an otherwise charming house, I found myself carrying on a chattering conversation with an elderly English-woman, obviously of the upper class. The talk naturally turned on the cold, and presently she was asking me how we managed such things in America. When I described for her the heating arrangements commonly prevailing in Baltimore—a steam-pipe or hot-water scheme, with an automatic gas heater in the cellar—she was plainly unable to believe it.

"Do you mean to tell me," she demanded, "that you have no coals in the house?"

I assured her that there were none.

"But who looks after the gas machine? Certainly you could scarcely trust it to a servant! It sounds very dangerous."

I told her that no one had to look after it—that it looked after itself.

"But how do you prevent it roasting you alive? I know you Americans like hot rooms, but how"——

I tried to explain the thermostat, but soon had to give it up. It was taking its place in her mind, I could see plainly enough, with the inventions of Baron Münchhausen. She not only couldn't believe in it; she didn't *want* to believe in it; there was something about it that seemed to offer an impertinent criticism of the immemorial English way of doing things—the only correct, decent, brave, honorable and Christian way.

Another day I had a palaver with another English lady, the wife of a Londoner in very easy circumstances. She is the mistress of a house that, at all events in size and cost, would do no discredit to Guilford. When she told me that there was no refrigerator in it I almost fainted.

It will be hard for such a people to learn the new ways of the post-war world. They will fight desperately and gallantly against every change, at whatever inconvenience, at whatever cost. Thousands will perish that what was good enough for their fathers—in trade, in manufacturing, in all the business of everyday life—may be preserved. Nevertheless, I believe it would be going too far to say that they are hopeless. They have, after long doubts, taken to the telephone, and in a few years they will begin to put in elevators. There may be even greater marvels just ahead.

(The Baltimore Evening Sun, February 24, 1930)

Erez Israel

I

JERUSALEM IN MARCH.

At the time of the World War there were actually more Christians than Jews in Palestine, and of Moslems there were probably seven or eight times as many. But these relations have been changing rapidly, especially since 1920. Well over 125,000 Jews have come in during the past fourteen years, including 2,500 or more from the United States, and they now make up at least 200,000 of the country's total population of 1,100,000 or nearly 20%. Their birthrate is still relatively low, for many of them, as in any group of pioneers, are unmarried men, but their deathrate is also low, and so their annual increase is gradually overhauling that of the Arabs, who breed like flies but die in the same way.

How long will it take the Jews to saturate the country, and how many of them will it hold in the end? It is not easy to answer. A good half of the total area is bare mountain or blistering desert, but there is plenty of room left in the arable lands. The Arabs who still occupy this arable land farm it in the manner of Abraham. They use a wooden homemade plow so light that when his day's work is done a farmer shoulders it and carries it home. They raise the same crops year after year and never fertilize the soil. Their draft animals look as starved and flea-bitten as they do themselves. Thus it takes a large tract to support a meagre Arab village, and famine is always around the corner.

The earliest Jewish colonist—they began to filter in so long ago as the 70's of the last century—were mainly pious fellows who aspired to live like Abraham too, and in consequence they got on

---

Traditionally translated from the Hebrew as "Eretz Israel," meaning "Land of Israel."

but little better than the Arabs. Most of them were on their own, and not many of them had any capital. Their successors are quite different. My eye is trained to detect excess of piety, but I can find none of it in them. On the contrary, they are realistic and enterprising fellows who look like Americans, even when they are Poles or Rumanians; and whether they farm communistically or as individuals they have good cattle, modern farm machinery, and decent houses. Their colonies, seen from a distance, are extraordinarily charming, what with their red-roofed houses, their prospering orchards, vineyards and wood-lots, and their wide green fields; and at close hand they turn out to be swarming with Leghorn chickens, glossy Holstein cows, and fat, well-dressed children.

II

Any Jew, of course, is free to come to Palestine and buy a farm for himself—if he can find an Arab willing to sell. If he has £1,000 in cash he may even come in without regard to the quota that the English overlords have set up for poorer folk. But as a practical matter most of the colonists need assistance, and it reaches them through two organizations—the Jewish Agency, which is a sort of general manager of all Jewish affairs in the country, and the Jewish National Fund, which buys land in large tracts and plants colonies on it. Most of these tracts are remote from Jerusalem, for the country hereabout is hilly and bare. They lie mainly along the coastal plain (the Sharon of the Bible) or in the wide valleys of the north.

The title to the land remains vested in the Fund: all the colonist gets is a leasehold for a long term, devisable by will. Whatever stock and equipment he needs he must pay for, but he is given 15 years or more to do so, and he needn't make his first payment until he has got on his legs. Inasmuch as a large part of the land is owned by rich *effendis,* safely resident in Beirut or Cairo, the Fund commonly deals with them, but sometimes it buys from Arab villagers who hold tracts in common. Not infrequently an Arab commune sells part of its land, hoping to buy modern stock and machinery with the money and so improve what remains, but apparently this scheme seldom works, for the Arab doesn't learn easily, and his Jewish neighbors soon leave him far behind.

Thus the Arabs are being gradually shoved out of the valleys and into the hills. But setting up a new Jewish colony does not always, or necessarily, involve dispossessing Arabs. Sometimes the Fund buys a tract of swampland and puts colonists to work draining it. In this way thousands of acres have been recovered in the Valley of Jezreel. At other times it undertakes large irrigation or reforestation works. Thus land that formerly supported only a few malarious or sunbaked Arabs is converted into fertile farms, and thousands of Jews find homes upon it.

III

Broadly speaking, there are two kinds of colonies. The *kvuza* is purely communistic: everything is held in common, and every member has an equal right to the usufructs. The *moshav* is more individualistic: each member has his own piece of land and works it himself. But even on a *moshav* all buying and selling is done cooperatively, and the more expensive kinds of farm machinery are owned in common. In neither type of colony is hired labor permitted. The early colonists used to employ Arabs to work for them, but that is prohibited on land owned by the Fund. A farmer on a *moshav* must work his own land—with such aid, of course, as he can get from his family and his neighbors.

A *moshav* looks pretty much like any other group of small farms. The one called Nahalal, established in 1921 near the ancient battlefield of Armageddon, is perhaps typical. It runs to nearly 2,000 acres and supports about 700 people. In the center are the community-houses, including a school for farm girls, and around them in a circle are the homes of the farmers. Behind each home are the barns, and behind the barns the orchards and vineyards, and thereafter the land of each farmer stretches out to the bounds of the colony, ever widening like a slice of pie.

In company with Mr. A. L. Fellman of the Jewish Agency I dropped in on one of the farmers. He was out in the fields at the time, but we were received politely by his young daughter. On a shelf in his living-room was a long row of technical books—on poultry, on grape-growing, on fertilizers, and so on—, most of them in English. He came in presently and showed us his Leghorn chickens, and pointed with pride to a scheme he had devised to make it easy to clean their yard. Then he showed us his pet cow —a prize milker in those parts. Then he took us to his orchard and his vineyard, and pointed to his fields beyond. This man was once a farmhand in New Jersey. His wife did not appear. It turned out that she was taking her siesta.

IV

A typical *kvuza* is Ein Harod—2,250 acres, 320 workers, 200 children, 300 cows, 5,000 eggs in the incubator, 15 acres in olive trees, 80 in grapefruit, 70 in grapevines, 25 in vegetables for the table, 30 in a eucalyptus wood-lot, a flour-mill, a planing-mill, a machine shop, 120,000 grafted grape-vines for sale by the nursery. It lies on the northern slope of the Valley of Jezreel. Behind it, on the hill-top, is a squalid Arab town. In front of it, all green now, its fields run down in a magnificent sweep to the mountain which bounds the valley on the south. Bisecting them is the railroad which runs eastward to Trans-Jordan, and then north and south to Damascus and Medina.

The Ein Harod brethren are communists of the highest voltage. They even raise their babies in common. When a child is born it is taken in hand by professional nurses, bossed by a young and very scientific-looking doctor, and lodged in a spick-and-span nursery, the largest and finest building on the grounds. When it arrives at the age of three it is transferred to a kindergarten across the street, with a dormitory upstairs, and there it labors under other professionals until it is six. Then it enters school, and begins to live with its parents. How does the scheme work? I can only report that the children all looked healthy, and showed excellent manners to strangers.

Ein Harod, of course, is no mere farm. Its mills bring in quite as much as its lands, and its nursery for trees and vines, managed by a very intelligent man, Mr. Aaron Friedmann, is famous throughout Palestine. It was founded in 1921, and is still in the full flush of its first success. Will it last? Probably not. As soon as its present kindergartners grow up they will begin to marry outside, and then there will be quarrels over shares, and it will no doubt go the way of Brook Farm, Amana and all its other predecessors. But if that happens the land will revert to the Jewish National Fund, and new colonists will be settled on it.

That is, if Erez Israel itself lasts so long. The chances that it will do so seem to be about even. On the one hand, it is being planted intelligently and shows every sign of developing in a healthy manner. But on the other hand there are the Arabs—and across the

Jordan is a vast reservoir of them, all hungry, all full of enlightened self-interest. Let some catastrophe in world politics take the British cops away, and the Jews who now fatten on so many lovely farms will have to fight desperately for their property and their lives.

(The Baltimore Evening Sun, April 9, 1934)

Below the Rio Grande

The Sixth Pan American Conference

The Sixth Pan American Conference of the American States took place in Havana, Cuba, on January 16 through February 20, 1928. Twenty-one nations were represented at the conference, which considered the codification of international law and approved conventions on the states of orders, asylum, consular agents, the rights and duties of states in the event of civil strife, and treaties.

But the conference is remembered mainly for two events: the attendance of President Calvin Coolidge and the split that developed between the United States and most of the Latin American countries over Washington's policy of intervening in the affairs of Caribbean and Central American nations. Despite Coolidge's participation in the conference, which was only the fourth time a sitting President had traveled abroad, the Latin American delegates came to Havana determined to show their displeasure with U.S. interventionist policies. The focal point of this anger was the presence of U.S. Marines in Nicaragua.

President Woodrow Wilson had first sent the Marines into Nicaragua in 1916 but they were withdrawn in 1925. They returned a year later, however, after the country was in danger of splitting apart in a civil war. Nicaragua's Conservative party, which had overthrown an unstable coalition government, held power in the capital, while the rival Liberal party had installed a provisional government on the Atlantic coast. The Marines were sent into this chaotic situation, an action that rapidly became unpopular at home. Writing in the New York World *late in 1926, Walter Lippmann stated Nicaragua was "not an independent republic," and "the direction of its domestic and foreign policy are* [sic] *not determined in Nicaragua but in Wall Street."*

The Liberal faction owed a great deal of its strength to a young commander named Augusto César Sandino. American commanders in Nicaragua were convinced that Sandino and the Liberals were receiving outside assistance: their men seemed well trained; they were wearing khaki uniforms and were equipped with better weapons. Trying to rally support for his Nicaraguan policy to the American public, President Coolidge declared the problem was "outside interference—the real culprits were the Soviet Union and Mexico." Secretary of State Frank B. Kellogg alleged a Nicaraguan-Mexican-Soviet conspiracy to impose a "Mexican fostered Bolshevist hegemony" within striking distance of the Panama Canal. The U.S. Marines' role was to act as a shield for the Nicaraguan government.

As tensions mounted in 1927, Henry L. Stimson was sent to Nicaragua as a special envoy to resolve the conflict between the two factions. On May 4, 1927, they reached an understanding: in exchange for a U.S. supervised election the following year, and the creation of a supposedly nonpartisan National Guard, the Liberals would declare peace. Their negotiator was José María Moncada. Sandino, the only Liberal commander to reject the agreement, withdrew to wage a guerrilla campaign from a remote mountain stronghold. Meanwhile, discontent with the policy grew in the United States as Americans became aware of U.S. Marine casualties.

It was in this atmosphere that the Sixth Pan American Conference opened in Havana. Charles Evans Hughes, Secretary of State (1921–25) and now chairman of the U.S. delegation to Havana, succeeded in splitting the Latin American vote with his insistence that the United States had a perfect right ". . . I will not say to intervene, but to interpose a temporary manner to protect the lives and interests of its nationals." He received the complete support of Cuba (the host of the conference) and two factions within Nicaragua's Conservative party. General Gerardo Machado (commonly known in Cuba as "El Carnicero," or "the Butcher") announced that "the Monroe Doctrine is, and ought to remain, the common defensive policy for the territorial integrity of America." Hughes held up the United States' conduct in Cuba as proof that its actions in Nicaragua gave Latin Americans nothing to fear. But the Latin American nations, led by the delegate from El Salvador, later resolved at the conference that "No state has a right to intervene in the internal affairs of another." This declaration was the direct consequence of U.S. actions in Nicaragua and of earlier interventions in the Caribbean basin. The Marines eventually pulled out of Nicaragua in 1933, leaving behind a stalemate and Sandino in control of large stretches of country in the North.

Mencken had visited Cuba before. As a boy, his imagination soared as he smelled the fragrant tobacco leaves that came into his father's cigar factory from the exotic land far away, never dreaming that he would be on its shores in 1917, when he reported on the Cuban revolution for the Baltimore Evening Sun. *At that time, the country still housed many Americans, but now, in 1928, the American stronghold in Cuba was manifest. Golf courses, racetracks, country clubs—all were open to Americans; accommodations, transportation, and services were U.S. owned. During Prohibition, Cuba became a mecca for thirsty Americans—after a quick voyage by ship, its glittering bars provided unlimited quantities of what was forbidden back home.*

The Goosegreasers at Work

Havana, Jan. 19.—It is easy to denounce the diplomats assembled here for their laborious efforts to make the Sixth Pan-American Conference a glittering sham and futility, but the plain fact is that free speech, in international affairs, is a very dangerous privilege, and that its exercise at the current sessions would probably do vastly more harm than good. Nations get on with one another, not by telling the truth, but by lying gracefully. The truth, no matter which way it runs, is always unpleasant and often intolerable. Thus President Coolidge did a good job, politically speaking, when he drenched the welcoming Havanese with goosegrease, and the Havanese paid him back appropriately when they bombarded him with flowers.

Not one of the twenty-one nations here represented by bald and solemn men has a cause that will bear logical inspection. They are all dishonest, and some of them are so far gone in that direction that it would not be excessive to call them downright criminal. Compared to some of the others, the United States is actually relatively virtuous. Its butcheries in such places as Nicaragua and Haiti may be cruel, but they are surely not unprovoked. The alternative to them is not peace and plenty, but bloodshed ten times worse. Every Latin delegate to the Conference is quite well aware of this, and not a few of the more frank among them admit it, at least behind the arras.

A thing that should be remembered clearly is that agitation against the United States, in most Latin-American republics, is exactly on all fours with agitation against the Pope in the Hookworm Belt at home. That is, it is a device of local politicians to get themselves into jobs, and it is aimed chiefly at the lowest classes of the population. The so-called upper classes are everywhere more or less pro-American, for in their combats with proletarian rabble-rousers the United States commonly favors them, and in more than one country it is directly responsible for their hold upon public office and their enjoyment of the attendant usufructs. This is obviously true in Haiti and Nicaragua, and it is scarcely less true in Cuba. It would be, true, too, in Mexico if the aristocracy had sufficient energy to challenge the prevailing demagogues.

Politics in Latin America, as in the United States, is idealistic only in words. Fundamentally, it is simply a struggle for jobs, with the hindmost left to the Devil. Thus the understanding between the eminent American statesmen now engaged here and the distinguished spiggoty gentlemen with whom they do business is very intimate and tender, for the latter all represent the ins of their respective republics, and so their attitude of mind is almost precisely that of sound Coolidge men. To view then as patriots and heroes is very foolish. They may yank Uncle Sam's ear now and then for the sake of the effect at home, but down in their hearts they admire him unaffectedly, and all of them wish that they had his gallant marines at their disposal. If they had, the bombing would be continuous from the Rio Grande to the Orinoco.

So far as I can make out, no delegate at present in Havana argues seriously that intervention should be forbidden altogether, and for all purposes. The most any of them contends, in his most idealistic moments, is that it should not be employed for the collection of debts. But it must be obvious to even the least rational that, in most of the invaded countries, intervention is the only device that will ever collect debts at all—that if it were abandoned there would follow an intolerable debauch of graft and bankruptcy, with revolution as the second course. No reflective Latin-American of the well-fed class wants any such thing. He may not care much about the foreigner's money, but he has a very healthy regard for his own.

Moreover, he knows by bitter experience that revolution next door is almost as bad as revolution at home. So long as Haiti was running wild, life in Santo Domingo was full of hazards. If Sandino had not been chased by the Marines in Nicaragua he would have bulged over, soon or late, into Salvador. Such dangers are very disagreeable to gentlemen with vested interests. They love their money just as much in Ecuador or Costa Rica as they love it in Wall Street. And so they favor peace, even at the cost of a certain damage to national sovereignty. If there were Sandinos at large in New Jersey, and the Federal Government could not put them down, there would be no objection in Wall Street to intervention by England, or even by Italy, Portugal or the Irish Free State.

As everyone knows, the war to save democracy pretty well killed it north of the Palm Belt. We Americans now live in a *Polizeistaat*, and the rights for which the fathers bled and died are all in decay. The same thing has happened here in the South. The old democratic shibboleths have gone out of fashion, and the effort of all statesmen above the jungle level is to keep the masses in order and protect investments. The case of Cuba is typical. It started out as an independent nation to the tune of the most affecting yells for freedom ever heard, and the statues erected to its heroic liberators still stand in all its cities. But Cuba today is run exactly as Prussia used to be run—almost, indeed, as Pennsylvania and Colorado are run.

The Machado government rests squarely upon bayonets—and on them one easily detects the Yankee label. It has so manipulated the election laws that overthrowing it in a peaceable manner has become a practical impossibility—and the moment its opponents took to the brush the faithful Marines would take ship at Quantico. The two great parties on the island have become indistinguishable. Machado, in theory, is a Liberal—but so was the late Woodrow Wilson a Liberal, even while A. Mitchell Palmer and his merry men were filling the jails. The real Liberals are disorganized and impotent. They say that, at a fair test of strength, the overwhelming majority of Cubans would be with them. But no such fair test of strength will be permitted so long as Machado is satisfactory to the real rulers of the island, American and Cuban.

Havana is full of rumors of governmental oppressions. It is alleged that free assemblage is prohibited, that newspapers are suppressed, that the surviving press is bribed or dragooned into acquiescence, and even that persons venturing to oppose the Administration have been assassinated. I have met apparently reputable Cubans who showed me lists of such victims and offered to take me to see their sorrowing heirs and assigns. Certainly the Cuban police show a vast activity. Suspicious foreigners are treated almost as rudely as if they were in the United States. For any reason or no reason at all they are deported or clapped into jail.

But I see no evidence that the more opulent and influential sort of Cubans object to all this. On the contrary, they seem to be glad that the Government is strong, and that it has the good will of the United States. Upon that good will the security and prosperity of the island depend. It is hard up at the moment because the American tariff bears upon it harshly. Its statesmen hope to bring about an amelioration of that tariff. Apparently they believe that one way to do it is to play the American game at the Pan-American Conference. They began to do it from the start. And they celebrated the arrival of Mr. Secretary Kellogg at Havana by jailing two Bolsheviks. It was a delicate attention, and I believe it was appreciated.

The plain fact is that the United States is now too strong to be seriously challenged by the other twenty republics, either singly or altogether. They need it more than they need one another. Thus they face it without any resolution, and with little unanimity of purpose. A stray delegate or two, inflamed by ethyl alcohol, may make a scene before the Conference ends, and he may get a scattering of support, but it is highly improbable that there will be anything more. The United States will come out of the Conference as it went in—the undisputed boss of the Western World. What it gives to its opponents it will give by grace, and not by compulsion.

(The Baltimore Evening Sun, January 23, 1928)

Mr. Hughes Runs Things,
Though Not a Spaniard

Havana, Jan. 21.—Predictions as to the probable duration of the Sixth Pan-American Conference range from a scant four or five years to a century and a half. Its proceedings are being carried on in the rich and voluptuous Spanish language and its tempo is determined by Spanish notions of decorum. It could no more be speeded up to the pace of a convention of Rotary International than a grand council of Holy Church.

Not a few of its puissant and eminent members in their own unhappy countries are actually Rotarians, for American idealism is everywhere rampant in the Western tropics, but even Rotary, in these parts, slows down from the speed of electrocution to that of diabetes. Here in Havana the Rotarians do not refresh themselves after their spiritual exercises by blowing spitballs; they move pianos.

Not many plenary sessions will be held at the Conference. That is to say, there will not be many opportunities for rambunctious delegates to speak their minds on subjects of genuine interest and importance. All the work, romantically so-called, is being done by committees, or, as they are called in Spanish, commissions. The range of authority of each of these commissions is rigidly limited, and so it is easy to put down a heretic by discovering that what he proposes is *ultra vires,* and hence impossible. Even at a plenary mission he must obtain permission of two thirds of the delegates before he may disport himself outside the agenda.

Thus there is not much likelihood that the gentlemen who threaten to make trouble will actually make any. Moreover, most of the more ebullient ones are being further squelched by having high honors thrust upon them. Thus Dr. Gustavo Guerrero, of San Salvador, has been made president of the Commission on International Law and Frontier Police. As a simple delegate, he arrived in Havana full of fire. But as one of the official police of the

Conference, with an espantoon in his hand, he has become a far milder fellow.

The deliberations of the commission, as of the plenary council, are in Spanish and Spanish-speaking stenographers take them down. When Mr. Hughes or any other of the American delegates says anything in English, it is immediately translated into Spanish. So when the Haitian delegates say anything in French or the Brazilians speak Portuguese. But speeches in Spanish are not translated into these other languages. Thus Mr. Hughes, who speaks no Spanish and can understand only a few words of it, has to sit beside Ambassador Henry P. Fletcher, who is fluent in the language. Behind him there is another interpreter, to relieve Mr. Fletcher when he flags and help him out with the harder words. These two gentlemen whisper to Mr. Hughes from time to time. The day following a session, or two days following, he receives an official English translation of the proceedings, and every night he receives a brief summary, also in English.

The other American delegates, except Dr. Scott and Dr. Rowe, who understand Spanish, have to wait for these transcripts in order to find out what they have been listening to. During the actual sessions they drowse gently in their chairs.

But despite this clumsy machinery, Mr. Hughes easily dominates the Conference. No other delegate shows anything like his intellectual force and enterprise. Directly and indirectly he steadily pushes the American point of view upon his distinguished conferees. When he says anything they all listen very attentively, and when he is silent himself he is frequently heard through other delegates who enjoy his confidence, notably Dr. Crestes Ferrara, of Cuba. Dr. Ferrara, like all ornaments of the present Cuban administration, is extremely friendly to the United States. It was he who engineered the immolation of the peppery Dr. Guerrero, of Salvador. And his best work lies ahead of him.

Thus Havana opinion holds that there will be nothing at the Conference to raise the blood pressure.

It will get through an immense amount of routine work, some of it important. It will discuss sanitary matters, the shipment of automobiles, port charges, measures against anarchists, the white slave trade, meat inspection and frontier police. It will give ear to all sorts of discoveries of new cures for all the sorrows of the world. Its members will eat a long series of excellent banquets and get down many carboys of cocktails. They will wear out many plug hats and pairs of spats. They will play roulette at the Casino and go in swimming at the yacht club. Some of them, being under 70, will probably fall in love.

But it is not likely that they will get the marines out of Nicaragua or that they will prevent the marines going into Salvador or Guatemala later on.

(The Baltimore Evening Sun, January 24, 1928)

Gin Guzzling American Tourists Crowd Havana

Havana, Jan. 22 (By Mail).—The Paris Restaurant is the best eating-house in Havana. It lurks in the mysterious shadows of the O'Reilly, a street not more than ten feet wide. The main dining room, high-ceilinged and floored with ancient tiles, is exactly on the street level and gives upon the sidewalk through three French windows, always wide open. Across the narrow O'Reilly is the high, leprous wall of an old house. From the wall, perhaps twelve feet above the street, hangs a medieval lamp. Still higher, only half seen in the gloom, are a couple of windows with iron bars, and a wrought-iron balcony.

A charming scene of a balmy tropical night. And inside the restaurant, as I have said, the victuals are of a marked degree of virtue. A fish called the pargo is one of the specialties of the house. In life it resembles a pair of cymbals with a couple of long, thin tails. In death the chef of the Paris converts it, with the aid of thin-sliced potatoes and lemon juice, into something really distinguished. Another specialty is guinea-hen *en casserole* with mushrooms. The two are admirably aided in their progress through the little red door of the aesophagus by certain light Spanish wines, notably Castell del Remy.

Last night, in company with several colleagues of the press, I took a pew at the Paris and proceeded to play with these masterpieces of the establishment. We had a modest cocktail to begin with, and then some capital cold consommé. With the pargo came a bottle of white Castell del Remy. The meal was going very beautifully. All around us sat the loveliness and the chivalry of Latin-America, with a sprinkling of Americans. At the next table was one of the American delegates to the Pan-American Conference, a very learned and dignified man, with his charming wife. We observed the waiter coming in with the guinea hen, and decided to change from white Castell del Remy to red.

At that instant there was a yell in the O'Reilly and a huge touring car stopped at the door. The diners craned their necks and the head waiter, an elegant young Cuban, rushed forward. One second later he was bowled over, and a round dozen Americans leaped out of the touring car and into the room. Their leader was a handsome and well-dressed young man of the sort seen at country clubs, and hanging to his arm was a tall and very pretty girl. In two bounds he was in the middle of the floor. Then, pausing dramatically, he swept off his Panama hat, waved it in the air and howled "Hallelujah!"

There followed a shrill and inarticulate bawling. The six gentlemen of the party gave the signals and the six ladies responded. They fell over chairs. They ran into tables. They clapped diners on the back. Two pairs of them, halting in the middle of the floor, proceeded to neck. I caught only a few recognizable words: "Oh, look at Harold!" "Let go, you——— ——— ———!" "Whoopee!" The head-waiter and his aides, with great skill, closed in upon the party. Yelling and struggling, its members were herded to the back of the dining room, and then through a swinging door. Presently they were out in the alley behind, still bawling. The Latin-Americans, reassuring their women, resumed dinner.

Among the gentlemen with whom I was dining was one skilled in the art and mystery of the newspaper reporter. He was presently in possession of the news that the visitors were members of a large tourist party, in port for the day and night. Their ship, a magnificent floating palace, lay out in the harbor, hard by the place where the *Maine* went down. They were ashore for an evening of refined pleasure. Among them were several young married couples. All were of high social standing in the city of their residence. They came from—but perhaps I had better call it Zenith.

We finished dinner somewhat sadly. Around us the soft Spanish language made itself heard again. It seemed an inconvenient time to be speaking English, at all events with an American accent. Presently we abandoned our dinner and took a walk. At the corner of the street was a barroom, wide open to the sidewalk, as all barrooms are in the tropics. Two American women lolled against the bar, heavily gulping gin fizzes. We proceeded to another drinking place. Half a dozen Americans were there, including another woman. Two of the men were in Shriners' fezzes. A grand banquet to the Imperial Potentate of the order, just in from the United States on an official tour, was in progress at a nearby hotel.

We kept on, and eventually landed in Sloppy Joe's, a bar in the street running from the Plaza Hotel to the Biltmore-Seville—the Broadway of all visiting Americanos. The place was so crowded that the gang of customers bulged out upon the sidewalk. Four bartenders labored furiously, but to little force or effect. Over our shoulders, as we horned in, came a vast babble of orders. "Four Martinis! Say, there, what of those Scotches? How long have we got to wait for that beer?"

We began to observe the crowd more closely. It was unanimously American and obviously highly respectable. One finds its exact counterpart every Sunday afternoon on the veranda of every country club from Portland to Portland. There were half a dozen family parties—stout father, stouter mother and slim daughter or son. There were some obvious honeymooners. There were young couples plainly in the throes of love—sad victims of the excessive propinquity of tourist ships. There were unattached oldsters, male and female.

Finally, an elderly lady separated herself from the rest. Her hair was white, she had on clothes of good cut and material, and she was manifestly someone of importance in the place where she came from. Perhaps the boss of the local Friends of Art. Or the chief reliance of the rector of the Episcopal Church. Or maybe only grand empress of the Federation of Charities. One could not imagine her, at home, venturing beyond half a cocktail before dinner, and then only on gala occasions. But in Sloppy Joe's she was pouring down highball after highball, and with each she let a magnificent yell.

Nor was she alone. Her sisters ranged in age down to a scant 17, and in bulk from that of a captive balloon to that of a folded umbrella. But one and all they were awash. The slim Cuban waiters edged and wriggled through the crowd to serve them, but they never had enough. Some were guzzling Martinis; others fell upon whole fleets of highballs; yet others confined themselves discreetly to schooners of beer. They were in all the classical stages of alcoholic toxemia. Some of the younger gals stood up to it like police sergeants, but the old lady, as we left, was missing her face half the time and emptying her drinks down her facade.

One of the local papers observes today that the current crowd of Americans is even boozier than usual. A great many tourist ships have been coming in, and there is heavy travel southward by way of Key West. But in the nightly saturnalia, after all, there is nothing new. Some nights are worse than others, but not much worse. The difference at the moment is that Havana is filled with observers from all over Latin-America. By day they listen to Mr. Hughes and his colleagues expound the high idealism of the United States. By night they watch hordes of American women wallowing in the barrooms.

(The Baltimore Evening Sun, January 24, 1928)

Mencken Misses Pupils
at University of Havana

Havana, Jan. 23 (By Mail).—When the delegates to the Sixth Pan-American Conference and their attendant secretaries, spat-pressers, technical advisers and journalists arrived in Havana last week and saw the splendid quarters allotted to them in the fine new buildings of the University of Havana, the first question many of them asked was: "What has become of the professors and the students?" For not a sign of either was visible.

The classrooms were empty, the corridors were empty, and even the adjacent stadium, with its excellent baseball grounds, was empty. Now and then what appeared to be a student emerged from the medical school, clad in an operating-room skull-cap and long white gown; but it presently appeared that all these gentlemen were actually interns. The students, to stretch a legal term a bit, were unanimously *non est*.

It was hard to find out what had become of them. The attachés of the Cuban delegation were beautifully vague on the subject, and not much more, it appeared, was to be got from the rest of Cuban officialdom. There was nothing about the matter in the

Havana papers. Had the university been closed to make room for the Conference? If so, why had the whole place been shut down when a fourth of it or even an eighth of it would have sufficed to house the delegates? Any why were no students lurking about the grounds?

Finally, an answer began to circulate in the immense pressroom in the basement of the Engineering Building. President Machado had decided, it was said, that Cuba already had too many lawyers and quite enough engineers and philosophers. So he had declared a moratorium on the higher learning and sent both students and professors home.

This seemed somehow unreasonable, and patient inquiry developed the fact that it was also untrue. The university had not been shut down on any such flimsy grounds. It had been shut down for purely political reasons, and a long while ago, in fact, back in November. The students had been sent home for heresy, or, as the current phrase has it, for Bolshevism. They had dared to protest against President Machado's fine scheme to stretch his term from four years to six.

They have dared, further, to object to a tablet that he had set up on the university grounds, hailing himself as a great public benefactor and forward-looking patriot. And they had done both things in the violent, gaudy manner of Latin-American youth. So the police had closed in upon them, and that was all there was to it.

The whole episode throws an instructive light upon the current state of affairs in Cuba. Ostensibly, the island is a free democracy and the light and model of all the other Latin-American States. In fact, Dr. Coolidge was at great pains to hymn its free institutions during his historic visit last week. But actually it is run precisely like a house of correction. There is no free speech, there is no free press and there is no possibility of an organized opposition. Dr. Machado, despite his benignant air of a mellow Rotarian, is Pope and King veiled into one.

Not even the Du Ponts in Delaware or the grand goblins of the Klan in Indiana are more complete despots. Whatever he says goes. The moment a sound of dissent is heard, that moment the army and the gendarmerie come into action. The heretic, if he has friends to warn him, departs quietly for New York or comes down with some lingering but not fatal disease. If not, he goes to jail.

At the moment *El Presidente* (who is in private life a gas and electric light magnate, and hence highly satisfactory to the American and Cuban bankers who run the island) is throwing all his energies into his scheme to lengthen his term. A constitutional convention has been called to arrange the business, and the election laws have been so manipulated that only delegates in favor of it can be elected.

All the party hacks, whether they call themselves Liberals or Conservatives, are with the President, for their terms also as Congressmen, as Governors of provinces, even as city councilmen in the towns, will be lengthened with his. Denied a place on the ballot for the technical reason that they have no legal existence as a party, the opponents of the "reform" (so it is called by Dr. Machado) must content themselves with writing the names of their candidates in blank spaces on the ballots. And not a fifth of their supporters can read or write.

There is plenty of enlightened sentiment in Cuba in favor of lengthening the term of the President, but the strong-armed way in which the "reform" is to be put over has naturally aroused a great deal of discontent.

This discontent first showed itself in overt acts at the university. The students there, like their brethren everywhere else in Latin America, are ardent politicians, and so long ago as last spring they began bawling against the Machado program. They paraded on the campus, they harangued one another and they began invoking the sacred names of such constitutional heroes as Marti the Liberator. At the start nothing much happened. A few ringleaders, brought to trial before the university tribunal, were sentenced to lose their right to attend classes, some for as much as ten years, but most for only a short while.

But then Dr. Machado added insult to injury by ordering the erection of that tablet on the university grounds. Its inscription spoke of him in very complimentary terms. By building the long steps which now sweep up to the halls of learning he has caused, it appeared, the undying gratitude of posterity. He was, further, a great educator, a great administrator and a great patriot. The students, when they saw this tablet, were furious. They demanded loudly that it be taken down. More, they refused to attend any classes until it was gone.

This contumacy naturally caused a great deal of gabble in Havana, though the local papers reported it very vaguely and cautiously. Dr. Averhoff, the rector of the university, advised the rebellious boys (and girls) to forget their grievance and resume their studies. He pointed out that the Pan-American Conference was approaching, and that it would not do to greet it with a family quarrel. The other professors, or most of them, joined in this advice, and after long negotiations a peace was patched up. The students agreed, for the sake of the national dignity, to withdraw their protest and draw up a formal apology to the university authorities. But first they demanded a chance to consult with the venerable Dr. Enrique José Varona.

This Dr. Varona is the most learned man in the whole of Latin America and a great hero to the students. He used to be professor of moral philosophy at the university and was once also Secretary of Public Instruction and then Vice-President of the Republic. He organized the Cuban educational system. He is the author of books that every enlightened Latin American has read. He is, moreover, a man of advanced years and great dignity. Thus the students wanted to hear him before committing themselves, and to that end appointed delegates to wait upon him.

But no sooner had the delegates got into his house than the police arrived. The doors were broken open, the cops rushed and seized the delegation, and even Dr. Varona himself, according to some accounts, was roughly handled. He protested bitterly. It was unconstitutional and unheard of, he maintained, to break into his house and assault his peaceable guests. It was an outrage against the public peace and the higher learning. It would disgrace Cuba from the Rio Grande to Cape Horn.

But the cops hauled the boys away and left Dr. Varona to his indignation. Next day the rumor went 'round that he was to be jailed. It was not done—but enough had been done to raise the temperature of the students to at least 180 degrees Fahrenheit.

After that, there was no containing them. They threatened to remove the offending tablet by force and throw it into the sea. Dr. Machado responded by reminding them of what had happened to eleven students back in 1871, who desecrated the grave of a Spanish oppressor: they were shot at sunrise. The poor professors, meanwhile, had a dreadful time of it. If they supported the students they would probably land in jail. And if they supported the Government the students might be expected to roughhouse their classes. So they took to the woods, followed by Rector Averhoff, and the university fell into the hands of the police.

Next day it was shut down, and it remains shut down to this

day. Save for the few rooms that echo the hollow croakings of the assembled diplomats, it is given over to the bat and the owl. One may walk through its endless halls for half an hour without encountering a soul.

What the end of the business will be no one knows. Dr. Machado is plainly somewhat uneasy about its effects upon the visiting statesman. Not many of them, of course, are Liberals, but a good many of them are university men, and so they are likely to sympathize with the boys. On the other hand, it would not do to surrender, for if there is any yielding the boys will undoubtedly rouse fresh uproars. Some of them, back home, have already done so. In Santiago, I hear, twenty are in jail.

So the battle remains a sort of draw, with the higher learning completely adjourned in Cuba. No other law school exists; hence no Cuban is now studying law. So with medicine, engineering, metaphysical and philology. Some are planning to go abroad. But the majority are waiting for Dr. Machado to weaken.

They take some hope from the fact that he had begun to be a bit cautious in other directions. Six or eight months ago, he was jailing labor leaders by the hundred; now he operates more delicately. Not so many papers are being suppressed. Not so many soapboxers are disappearing between days. But what he will do after he puts through his "reform," and the ground is solid under him until 1931? There is a great deal of uneasy speculation in Havana about that.

(The Baltimore Evening Sun, January 25, 1928)

The Spanish Main

I

In the shed of the Customs House at Key West, Fla., set up at intervals of ten or fifteen feet, are copies of the following notice:

> Avoid Trouble: Before examination starts, tell the inspector of ALL liquor you have.

These melancholy words greet the returning Americano as he enters from the Havana boat. They do not surprise him: he has heard of them in Havana. More, he has heard that they mean precisely what they say, and so, save for a few pints and half-pints on his hip, he commonly comes down the gangplank quite innocent of contraband. A week or so ago I saw 450 such Americanos return thus to the hag-ridden native land. Not one of them was caught with a jug in his baggage.

But to the latter-day jobholder, of course, every citizen is a criminal, and so these sad homecomers are subjected to furious and meticulous search. I have never seen anything worse in Europe, even in wartime. The snouters in uniform not only demand that every piece of baggage, however small, be opened: they also thrust their paws into it, and upset it magnificently. I saw one of them divert himself for a full twenty minutes with the handbags of a lady who, in the end, turned out to have nothing worse in her possession than a jar of guava jelly. Her husband fared almost as evilly. The smeller, after first feeling of his golf-bag all along its length, finally made him empty it. It contained only golf-sticks.

I had to wait at least an hour before my own time came, and by then the booze-ferrets were tired out, and my bags got only the cursory examination that is customary at New York. My turn to suffer for democracy had come some time before, while I was still on the boat. For rather more than an hour I was penned in the dining-saloon along with a hundred or more other native-born white Americans while another set of inspectors examined our papers. The only question that I was asked was "Where were you born?" Inasmuch as my declaration that I was born in Maryland lay before the inspector, plainly written with a pen, the question seemed supererogatory. But I answered it politely, and was passed with a nod. I asked various persons, including officers of the ship, what the inspection was for. None of them knew.

II

The Cubans themselves, who carefully imitate whatever is worst in American practice, now have a formidable inspection of their own. Eleven years ago, coming into Havana from Spain, I was passed with courteous bows, but this time, coming from the United States, I had to wait in the line nearly an hour. A doctor wearing a heavy frown glared at me when he came to me, thus making sure, I suppose, that I was free from smallpox and leprosy. Another functionary gave me a ticket permitting me to leave Cuba whenever I wanted to go home. A third examined my baggage. For what? I say he examined it. In truth, he simply forced me to open it. Once it was open, he passed it without looking at it.

This aping of the abominable Yanqui is now visible everywhere in Havana. The changes of eleven years forced themselves upon me on all sides, and mainly, I must confess, unpleasantly. Havana now has traffic cops, numbered and lettered streets, realtors, Rotarians, press agents, a golf club, and all the other ineffable flowers of American *Kultur*. The Rotary Club, which is active in all good works, has an executive secretary, and his sign hung in plain sight of my window at the Plaza Hotel. At the University of Havana, now emptied of students by presidential fiat, there is a baseball diamond. In all the saloons are portraits of Coolidge, Lindbergh, Tom Mix, Tunney and the rest of the Yanqui hierarchy. Doug Fairbanks packs the largest theaters. Camel cigarettes are crowding out the native brands, though they cost, with the Cuban duty, 70 or 80 cents a package.

But it is in the bars that Americanization goes furthest. Eleven years ago they still carried a Spanish air. They were cafés rather than saloons, with little round white-topped tables, and patrons who drank vermouth from little glasses and laboriously read the papers. But now, save for the fact that they open upon the sidewalk, they are almost exactly like the old-time saloons of the

United States. There are the same brass rails, the same gaudy ranks of bottles behind the bar, and the same free lunches of olives, pickled onions, crackers and rat-trap cheese. Some of them even have Irish bartenders.

III

It is these bars that seem to attract most of the Americans who go to Havana, with the horse-racing at Oriental Park and the gambling at the Casino following after. Whenever a ship comes in there is a rush for them, and in half an hour the majority of their customers are roaring drunk and making a great clatter. One can hear the bawling in Sloppy Joe's place, apparently the most popular bar of the town, a block away. It keeps up until ungodly hours: there would seem to be no *Polizeistunde* in Havana, though there are surely plenty of *Polizei*. And among the hearty guzzlers who thus seek forgetfulness of the Volstead act there are quite as many ladies as gentlemen.

Cuban ladies, of course, do not drink at public bars. It is not common, indeed, for them to eat at public restaurants. But the visiting Americanos of the refined sex seem to enjoy it, and even to glory in it. I got the impression, watching them putting down round after round of cocktails, that they were mainly afraid that no one would see them. At all events, they were excessively amiable to strangers, and joined with loud hosannas in the drinks which their husbands insisted upon setting up for all comers. I speak here, remember, of well-dressed and apparently decent women. I saw no obvious drabs in the saloons, save once. All the rest of the gals, even when they were awash, looked highly respectable. And their husbands were covered with the insignia of all the more eminent fraternal orders.

I leave this curious spectacle to philosophers. Why should American women, going to Havana, indulge themselves in such gargantuan lushing? Can it be that they are shut off from stimulants at home—that there are parts of the United States which are actually dry? It seems incredible. I have traveled a great deal at home during the eight years of Prohibition—twice to the Pacific Coast, and many times in other regions—and I have yet to find or hear of an American town, however small, that was not copiously served by bootleggers. Maybe it is because the ladies believe the Havana booze is better—or safer. But is it? I doubt it. I found nothing there that I can't get in New York, and most of it I can get in Baltimore.

IV

My life-long aversion to horse-lovers kept me from going to the races at Oriental Park, but I spent a couple of evenings at the Casino, and on one of them I came very near the borderline of intoxication. The drinks there, indeed, are very good, and the food is certainly not bad. In the gambling hell I risked a modest $5 on a dice game, and lost it in two minutes. This was my first gambling since the year 1908, when I plunged at Monte Carlo, and lost $10— in modern money, almost $25.

The Casino is well turned out, but it would be absurd to compare it to Monte Carlo. One misses, first of all, the Russian grand dukes, and one misses, secondly, the glittering *heiarae*. The crowd at Havana looks highly respectable. Family parties gather at roulette, as they gather around the radio at home. No woman winked at me all evening, though I was in full evening dress and wore all my orders. Worse, I was not tempted to wink at any of the women, despite the fact, as I have hinted, that I was moderately inflamed by wine. The night ended with a long ride back to Havana, along the glorious sea. The driver of the car demanded $5—about twice the fair honorarium.

Such profiteering, I regret to have to report, is very common in that great city. There are no taxicabs, but all the automobiles for hire are licensed, and the legal fee for any drive within the city limits is 20 cents. The drivers almost invariably demand more. If there is a policeman with a white helmet in sight, there is escape for the victim, for the white helmet indicates that its wearer speaks English. Appealed to, he orders the driver to take the legal fee, and then turns wearily away. There are no hard feelings about it. The Yanqui is there to be looted—but the law is the law.

Well, I don't blame the Havanese. Their season is very short. They seldom see an American before Thanksgiving Day, and by March 1 the last one has departed. They are not as prosperous as they ought to be. Havana, with the flags flying, looks very gay, but the price of sugar is down below the cost of production, and Cuba as a whole is suffering from very hard times. Some Cuban friends of a Bolshevistic kidney offered to take me out to some of the nearby villages and show me how the poor were living. But I had an engagement to meet a Sunday-school superintendent and his wife at Sloppy Joe's.

(The Baltimore Evening Sun, January 30, 1928)

Manifest Destiny

I

Superficially, the United States is keeping hands off in Mexico; the fact, indeed, is cited as proof that American imperialism is no more than a phantasm of libelous Liberals. With the opportunity lying wide open, no army was sent in to grab the country. But is that quite true? I doubt it. An army was actually sent in, though there were no Americans in it. It consisted, and consists today, of Mexican Federals armed with American weapons. Without those weapons in its hands, it would have found fighting the rebels a formidable task, and might have succumbed to them. But with Uncle Sam serving it as *Kriegslieferant* it seems likely to win.

Thus Mexico moves toward the position of Cuba. It becomes a client state, a vassal state. The government is maintained in power by American bayonets, though no American troops are on Mexican soil. In order to hold on hereafter it must pay heed to every hint emanating from Washington. So long as it is in good odor there it will be safe, but the moment the news gets about that it has lost standing it will have a revolution on its hands, and its doom will be as good as sealed. If that is independence, then an Anti-Saloon Congressman is also independent.

This is a cheaper way to keep the dark brethren docile than sending in Marines to butcher them, but it will probably work quite as well in the long run. It is grounded on the sound theory that a politician cares nothing for his country, but will do anything to hold his job. The United States has simply gone on a hunt for Latin-American politicians who are willing to be good according to the American pattern, and guaranteed them the honors and usufructs of office. The thing has been done in Nicaragua, in Haiti, in Santo Domingo, in Panama and in Cuba, and now it is being done in Mexico. When the present uproar is over, there will be no need for an American ambassador there, and Dr. Morrow, his work accomplished, can come home. Dr. Gil, the so-called president of the country, will serve very acceptably in his place. And if Dr. Gil proves rambunctious, then some one will succeed him who is more tractable.

II

I was in Cuba, pursuing the gloomy duties of a newspaper reporter, at the time of the last uprising against the government. That was in 1917. The President then was one Menocal, who in private life was a manager of sugar estates for American investors. He had already served one term and had been a candidate for re-election early in the year. It was the universal belief in Havana that the other fellow, José Miguel Gomez, had won. In fact, he had won by an enormous majority, for nearly all patriotic Cubans, regarding Menocal as little more than an American agent, were against him. But he was counted in.

José Miguel then took to the bush, and a revolution was on. News came that a great battle was to be fought somewhere east of Havana, and along with the other reporters present I prepared to go out and see it. But before we could get under way news reached us that the revolution was off. That news came from American quarters. It took the form of a threat from the late Dr. Lansing, then Secretary of State, that if José Miguel did not give up his evil courses at once American Marines would come in and deal with him. So he surrendered and was locked up in the Morro, and Menocal began a second term. José Miguel had won in the election, but Menocal was preferred at Washington.

He postured as a conservative; his current successor, Machado, calls himself a liberal. But it is all one; Machado, like Menocal, works for *los blofistas*—the damned but irresistible Yankees. He is, in private life, manager of the Havana electric works. Last spring, like Menocal before him, he came up for re-election. He won by familiar Latin-American devices. The politicians of the opposition were brought to order by promising them security in their jobs; the patriots were dealt with by knocking them about. There was vast indignation in Havana—I happened to be there again, and had it poured into my ears—and wild talk of resistance by force. But it came to nothing, for Washington favored Machado, and the Marines stood ready to keep him in office. The Cuban patriots are romantic, but they are not so romantic that they believe they could beat the United States.

III

The thing goes further. Such clients of the State Department are not only docile; they are also diligent. Whenever a useful job is to be done they stand ready to do it. At the time of the Pan-American Conference in Havana last winter Machado did far more valuable work for the United States than any American delegate, save only the slippery Dr. Hughes. He was the host of the conference, and he stage-managed it in the Yankee interest. His retainers were busy everywhere, preaching brotherly love, shutting off killjoys, and playing all sorts of artful political tricks. He actually went to the length of barring contumacious delegates from Cuba. In Havana he closed the university and chased the students away, that their patriotic and anti-American ribaldries might not be heard.

He was earnestly supported by the delegates from Nicaragua, Haiti, Panama and Santo Domingo, all of them representing governments maintained in office by American bayonets. In Haiti and Nicaragua wars against the Yankees were going on, but nothing was heard of the fact at Havana. The delegates from those countries were all for Mr. Hughes, no matter what he said or demanded. With the American, Cuban, Dominican and Panaman delegations they constituted a solid and highly reliable *bloc*, and it was sufficiently strong, in the face of the natural differences of opinion between the other delegations, to get Mr. Hughes exactly what he wanted. True enough, there was murmuring, and the head of the Argentine delegation was so disgusted that he resigned and went home, but that was as far as opposition went.

The Mexicans, at Havana, rather stood aside. They were against American imperialism in the West Indies and Central America, but they felt themselves too weak to do anything about it. The Yankee pistol was at their heads. They remembered Vera Cruz and the Pershing invasion. The next time they will be members of the lodge, for Washington and the Mexican politicians have not come to terms. The Mexican Government will be stable hereafter—so long as it plays the game. A few jobholders may be assassinated now and then, but they will be safe otherwise, as Machado is safe in Cuba, Arosemena in Panama, Moncada in Nicaragua, and Borno in Haiti.

IV

I describe the business without heat. It seems atrocious to Latin-American patriots, but one need not share their indignation. Perhaps the fact that it works is sufficient excuse for viewing it with complacency. Cuba, if it ever got from under the Yankee hoof, would probably go to ruin. I have met, in my time, many Cuban patriots, and some of them I know pretty well. They are charming fellows, but highly impracticable. They seem to be unable to grasp the fundamental fact that all governments are bad. Whenever they observe that their own government is incompetent and corrupt, which is every two or three days, they yearn to overthrow it—by the ballot, if possible, but if not, then by force. It is hard to convince them that any government they set up in place of it would be quite as rotten.

I remember a curious palaver with a group of them a year ago. They described all sorts of atrocities—polling places raided by the military, opposition candidates beaten and put to flight, patriots jailed, deported or butchered. When I offered to match every story they had to tell with ten worse ones from the United States they were genuinely astonished. They had never heard of the doings in the Pennsylvania mining regions. Or of the Mooney case. Or of government by Methodist bishops. Or anything about the Ku Klux Klan save its name. They were certainly not friendly to the United States, but I could see that they doubted most of my tales. It seemed increaible to them that any people, without rising in arms against it, could endure such vile government as prevails in this great Christian republic. I kept off the Department of Justice; they would have laughed at me as a romancer.

Maybe they are luckier than they think. Washington governs them far better than they could govern themselves, and quite as well as the United States is governed. True enough, they see all sorts of rubbishy politicians put over them, but what other kind of politicians exist? Do they suffer humiliation as patriots? Then let them give patriotism a rest.

(The Baltimore Evening Sun, April 15, 1929)

Below the Rio Grande

The newspapers give so much space to the great crusade to rescue England that they have little left for events in other quarters. Thus there is not much in them these days about the doings of the Jap infidels in the Far East, though there is good reason to suspect that something unpleasant is afoot there. The most one hears is that the Siamese have taken to the warpath—for what reason, nobody knows—or that the New Deal philanthropists have lent another $100,000,000 to the poor Chinese. In the same way, little of a specific and illuminating character comes out of Latin America. One reads vaguely that the New Dealers are planning to spend $500,000,000 there in an effort to line up the politicians for "religion and morality," but that is about all. Even Mexico seldom makes the front pages any more.

Yet plenty of instructive stories are in process south of the Rio Grande, and some of them filter in by devious routes. I have just encountered one, for example, in the Panama *American* of December 15, sent to me by a customer traveling in those latitudes. It has to do with the plebiscite holden the same day in the little Republic which hugs the Canal Zone. The business before the electorate was the adoption or rejection of a new constitution, and it was adopted by an overwhelming vote. So much the public prints in the Colossus of the North reported the next day. But none of them, so far as I know, gave any attention to the way in which the plebiscite was carried.

According to the Panama *American*, the *modus operandi* was borrowed, not from the great democracies that now sweat for survival, but from the abhorrent Totalitarian Powers, and in particular from the example of fiendish Hitler. In brief, the Panamanians who went to the polls in Panama City—and they were all compelled to go—were confronted by a single ballot, already imprinted with the word *Si*, the exact equivalent of the Hitlerian *Ja*. There were no *No* ballots, just as there are no *Nein* ballots when Hitler takes the sense of his lieges. In consequence, the new constitution got the overwhelming approval before mentioned, and the contrary votes that were reported must have been thrown in by the judges of election in sheer ebullience of amiability, just as Tammany used to give the Republicans a few thousand votes in every election precinct in New York.

* *

The *American* says that there was some murmuring against this simple but ingenious procedure, and that a few rash voters went to the length of striking out the *Si* on the ballots and writing in *No*. Their reward was instant arrest on the charge of "defacing and mutilating an official document." "Many citizens telephoned the *American* asking where they might obtain negative ballots, but the newspaper was unable to tell them, or to find such ballots."

Nor was this voting scheme the only device borrowed from the wicked Adolf. The goons of President Arnulfo Arias, not content with stuffing the ballot box, embroidered their patriotic effort with a gaudy imitation of Nazi rabble-rousing. They howled on the radio, they hung all the towns of the Republic with fiery banners, and they scurried about in high-powered cars with loud-speakers vomiting forth the "Acción Comunál," the Horst Wessel song of the Arias party. Altogether, they staged a demonstration of "spontaneous enthusiasm" that must have made spiggoty history. "But none of this enthusiasm," says the *American*, "was evidenced in the streets or at points where the clustered loud-speakers were blaring."

So much for the election. Its aims and effects may be noted briefly. They were, as the Associated Press reported on January 2, to "denationalize about one-eighth of the total Panamanian population of 650,000." All persons born after November 3, 1903, whose parents were not Spanish-speaking by birth, were deprived of their citizenship by the new constitution, and also all persons whose parents were Asiatics. In other words, two distinct categories of Panamanians were set up, in precise imitation of the Hitler plan. Those of Class A were confirmed in all the rights of free citizens of a free state, including especially the right to vote *Si* on election day; those of Class B were reduced to the lowly status of blackamoors in Mississippi.

Most of the latter, in fact, are actually of the Negro race, and the rest are Mongols. The former are chiefly immigrants from Jamaica —a notoriously sassy subspecies of *Procyon sapiens*. Something had to be done about their constant contumacies to the Panamanian

New Deal and its inspired prophets, and that something was done on December 15.

* *

The new president, Hon. Arnulfo Arias, M.D., who took office last October, is spoken of by evil persons, according to the Associated Press, as "dictatorial, Nazi-inclined and opportunist," but we have his own solemn word for it that he is "a thorough believer in democratic processes," and he adds brightly that he hopes for and counts on the sympathetic understanding of the Roosevelt Administration. His assurance in the first case is supported by the election just described, and his hopes in the second will no doubt be borne out in the near future, for there is already talk of inviting him to Washington, as the humanity-loving Col. Fulgencio Batista of Cuba was invited last year.

A third great fan for "democratic processes," the Hon. Getulio Vargas of Brazil, is already in receipt of an invitation, and he intimates that he will accept as soon as he has finished some pressing business at home, to wit, the liquidation of certain rascals who talk foolishly against him. Some time ago he made the slip of speaking of the dictators in very flattering terms, but when his attention was called to it he protested that he was only spoofing. To keep his seat warm, and in the apparent hope of shutting off the murmuring of the *New Republic*, he is sending on a Brazilian novelist of pinkish inclinations, Senator Erico Verissimo.

Vargas was defeated for the Presidency of Brazil in 1929 by a conspiracy of fifth columnists, but struck back at the scoundrels by seizing the office by force on October 3, 1930. He is now operating under a constitution, written by himself, that embodies some novel democratic features. Its principal organ of legislation is a Council of National Economy, made up of representatives of the banks, the landowners, the transportation interests, and so on. This council has complete control over labor, and may suggest to suspicious minds the Grand Council of Mussolini. But Vargas says that it is thoroughly democratic, and the New Deal idealists believe him. He keeps a private concentration camp on the rocky, barren island of Fernando de Noronha, off the Brazilian coast, and there he is gradually accumulating all the evil characters who venture to incommode his struggles for democracy.

* *

One of the denizens of that island, until a short while ago, was an Argentine gentleman of the name of Señor Rodolfo Ghioldi, a preacher of New Deals since the great eruption of hope following the last war to save democracy. His own Government heaved him out in 1935, and he headed for points north, but seems to have lingered imprudently in Brazil, where Vargas's goons not only collared and jugged him, but also gave him what passes along the equator for the third degree. He languished on Fernando de Noronha for nearly three years, but was lately released as no longer a menace to democracy, and sent back to the Argentine.

What remained of him got a rousing reception there from the surviving Communists, but when he stepped off the ship they were somewhat shocked by his appearance, for he had lost four or five stone in weight, his face was drawn and haggard, he could barely walk, and all of his upper teeth were missing. He reported that life on Fernando de Noronha differed a great deal from life in a night club. The heat was considerable, and the more recalcitrant prisoners were subjected to frequent workouts by Vargas's agents. Ghioldi said that he mourned his lost upper teeth, but was glad these friends of democracy has spared his lower ones. Indeed; he was glad to be alive at all, for some of his fellow prisoners, including an American named Victor Barron, had been massaged so vigorously that they failed to recover, and had to be buried.

His teeth are now in the police refrigerator at Rio de Janeiro, and the Hon. Mr. Vargas will no doubt bring a handful of them along as souvenirs for the principal friends of democracy in Washington. It will be interesting to see what La Eleanor makes of his visit of state in "My Day."

(The Baltimore Sun, January 19, 1941)

From the Note-Book
of an American

<hr>

Off the Grand Banks

I

Come Saturday I shall be forty-five—older than my father was
when he died, almost up to the average span of the Menckenii for
three hundred years. We are, I suspect, a somewhat feverish race,
launching out into life prematurely and wearing out before most
are full grown. My grandfather was married at nineteen; my father had a business of his own at twenty-one; I was the city editor
of a daily newspaper at twenty-three. Exigent enterprises, and
mine, perhaps, the most exigent of the three. I have known what
hard work is. At the time of the Baltimore fire I worked continuously from eleven o'clock Sunday morning until the dawn of
Wednesday. Another time, for six months running, I ran an average of 5,000 words of news copy a day, getting the news myself
and writing it myself. The reporters of today lead lordly, voluptuous lives. There were no taxicabs in my time, and the telephone
was a toy. One man did the work of two, three, four. If it was a
boozy day in the office, and he was young and eager, of five, six,
seven.

Theoretically, I suppose, I am in the *Landsturm,* and even ready
to pass out of it. But where are the subjective symptoms? I search
for them a bit fearfully, and rejoice that they are not to be found.

Now and then it seems to me that I tire more easily than I used to, that my capacity for work is diminishing. The next day I do twelve hours straight. Moreover, didn't I tire back in 1902? God knows I did. There were nights when I reached bed scarcely able to put out the gas. It was a gaudy life, but it was killing. It taught me, perforce, a useful and perhaps life-saving trick: that of snatching a nap between rounds. If the pressure is heavy, I stretch out half an hour before dinner and depart to nothingness like a man hit with an ax. If there is more time, an hour or two of heavy exercise goes before—not your diabetic golfing, but work with hammer, saw and shovel, fit for a longshoreman. In the evening, after that, I am full of notions, and in excellent humor.

II

What keeps me going at my trade, I suppose, is my continuous curiosity, my endless interest in the stupendous farce of human existence. It is the principal and perhaps only stock of a journalist; when it begins to slip from him he is fit only for the knacker's yard. To be short of ideas is an experience that I have yet to suffer; it is, indeed, almost incomprehensible to me. Short of ideas in the Republic of today? As well try to imagine a Prohibition enforcement officer short of money! They dart and bang about one's ears like electrons in a molecule. A thousand new ones are born every day.

The hard job is to choose from among them, to get some coherence into them, to weave them into more or less orderly chains. In other words, the hard job is to reduce them to plausible and ingratiating words, to make them charming, to turn them into works of art. After thirty years of incessant endeavor in that direction I come to two conclusions about it: skill at it is never (or only miraculously) inborn, and it cannot be taught. How, then, is it to be acquired? By one method only; by hard work. By trial and error. By endless experiment. Is what was done today better than what was done last year? Does it move more gracefully? Is it better organized? Then keep on. But is it still clumsy, still stiff, still dull? Then back to the office stool!

Fortunately, the quest is without end. Of the other languages I know little, but of English I have learned something. Its charm is its infinite complexity, its impenetrable mystery. Do not suspect me of rhetoric when I say that it seems to change from year to year. Or maybe those of us who write it change. We hear new melodies, sometimes far below the staff. We are tripped by strange, occult surprises. A new and rich color appears. There is here something magnificently fascinating. The lesson is never quite learned.

Schoolmarms, of course, profess to teach it. To the lions with them! I am no pedagogue myself, assuredly, but at forty-five a man naturally yearns to wave his beard at the apprentices to his trade. My advice, brethren, if you would do honor to our incomparable tongue, is that you pay little heed to books, even the best. Listen to it on the street. It is there that it is alive.

III

In a moral Republic, a man engaged in controversy is naturally assumed to seek moral ends. That is, he is assumed to be a reformer. If he is palpably innocent of all the orthodox reforms, inspired by the angels, then he is guilty of sinister reforms of a downward trend, inspired by the devil. The first passion of a good Americano is to make his fellow-primates do something that they don't want to do. His second is to convince them that doing it will improve the world and please God.

Here, I believe, I lie outside the stream, at ease upon the bank. I can't imagine a man with less public spirit in him. Every day I receive an invitation to join this movement or that, sometimes toward consummations most laudable, and every day the invitation goes into my waste-basket. If I had it in my power to put down Prohibition overnight, or to scotch the Fundamentalists, or to hang all Men of Vision, I'd not have to flee from the temptation, for there would be no temptation. The lust to improve the world is simply not in me.

This attitude, I find, is incomprehensible to most Americans, and so they assume that it is a mere cloak for a secret altruism. If I describe the Fundamentalists *con amore*, dwelling luxuriously upon their astounding imbecilities, their pathetic exploitation by mountebanks, I am set down at once as one full of indignation against them, and eager to drag them to the light. Indignation? Is one indignant at a monkey doing his tricks? Or at a dry Congressman down with delirium tremens? Such spectacles do not make me indignant; they simply interest me immensely, as a pathologist, say, is interested by a beautiful gastric ulcer. It is, perhaps, a strange taste —that is, in a country of reformers. But there it is.

No doubt it keeps me from understanding reformers, as they are unable to understand me. But what are the odds? I do not argue that they should be put down; I simply presume to be unconvinced by their reforms. They are free to go on, convincing others if they can. All I ask is equal freedom. When it is denied, as it always is, I take it anyhow.

IV

Quod est veritas? I know the answer no more than Pilate did. But this, at least, I have observed in forty-five years: that there are men who search for it, whatever it is, wherever it may lie, patiently, honestly, with due humility, and that there are other men who battle endlessly to put it down, even though they don't know what it is. To the first class belong the scientists, the experimenters, the men of curiosity. To the second belong politicians, bishops, professors, mullahs, tin-pot messiahs, frauds and exploiters of all sorts —in brief, the men of authority.

My inclination, I suspect, makes me lean heavily in favor of the former. I am, as the phrase is, prejudiced in their favor. They fall, now and then, into grievous errors, but in their fall there is still something creditable, something that takes away all shame. What fetches them is the common weakness of humanity, imperfectly made by a God whose humor has been greatly underestimated. They have, at least, the virtue of fairness. And that of courage. Unhorsed, they pick themselves up and try again. They do not call for the police.

In the other camp I find no such virtues. All I find there is a vast enmity to the free functioning of the spirit of man. There may be, for all I know, some truth there, but it is truth made into whips, rolled into bitter pills. It is truth that has somehow lost all dignity, all beauty, all eloquence and charm. More often, it is not truth at all, but simply folly horribly bedizened. Whatever it is, it is guarded by the common enemies of mankind: theologians, lawyers, policemen, men armed with books, guns, clubs, goads, ropes.

I find myself out of sympathy with such men. I shall keep on challenging them until the last galoot's ashore.

(The Baltimore Evening Sun, September 7, 1925)

Acknowledgments

My first debt goes to Dr. Daniel and Ruth Boorstin; while serving as Editor at Large with Doubleday, Dr. Boorstin brought this manuscript to the publisher's attention. Of equal importance is my indebtedness to Averil Kadis, Director of the Enoch Pratt Free Library's Department of Public Relations, the representative for all Mencken estate matters: it is she and the Trustees of the Enoch Pratt Free Library who preside over the papers of H. L. Mencken and placed them at my disposal for this volume.

My deepest thanks to my editor, Sallye Leventhal at Anchor/Doubleday, for her enthusiasm and expertise; to Gore Vidal, who warmly and graciously consented to write the Foreword to this book; to David Levine, whose caricature of Mencken captures the Sage's mischief and fire of his later years—and to Ray Shapiro of the *New York Review of Books* for making possible its appearance on the cover; and to John Parker and his staff of Artography Labs, Inc., Baltimore, for the reproductions in this book.

Many thanks, too, for the extraordinary patience of the many men and women I interviewed for this volume and whose generosity of material, insights and observations will be used in another book to follow; to Neil Jordahl, Director of Humanities at the Enoch Pratt Free Library, and Vincent Fitzpatrick, Assistant Curator of the H. L. Mencken Collection, for their help and for making the Mencken Room such a joy to work in. Of special mention, to my sister, Linda M. Rodgers, and my brother, William F. Rodgers, for taking time from their hectic schedules to provide me with helpful suggestions. Also, to my uncle, Leon Livingstone, Professor Emeritus of SUNY at Buffalo.

A team of typists was required to put this volume together. My indebtedness to Lynn Lang and especially to Fran Gallagher is great and my admiration heartfelt as, armed with magnifying glasses, they deciphered the old newsprint which looks like so many fleas on a page: my thanks for their expert work.

Finally, a special debt of thanks to Barry, who devoted entire weekends away from the Washington Redskins to read the manuscript of this book. Although Barry didn't start out as a Mencken fan, the essays assembled both infuriated and amused him, and in the end brought about a grudging respect for the Sage of Baltimore that even surpassed his admiration for the Redskins. I am glad of the conversion, and thank him.

Notes to the Introduction

References to the Enoch Pratt Free Library, Baltimore, Maryland, and the New York Public Library have been abbreviated as *(EPFL)* and *(NYPL)*, respectively. *AN 1925* refers to Mencken's "Autobiographical Notes—1925," a two-hundred-page typescript deposited at the Enoch Pratt Free Library, and *AN 1941* refers to "Autobiographical Notes, 1941," a collection of miscellaneous notes which Mencken composed chiefly from 1941 on, but which have no page numbers. It is also deposited at the Enoch Pratt Free Library.

1. *Menckeniana* (Spring 1970), p 3.
2. *AN 1941. (EPFL)*
3. Mencken, "On Banks," Baltimore *Evening Sun,* June 22, 1936.
4. Mencken, "Help for the Jews," Baltimore *Sun,* November 27, 1938.
5. Mencken, "Henry L. Mencken Calls *Times* His Professional 'Alma Mater,'" Ellicott City *Times,* March 17, 1941.
6. "Aug. Mencken & Bro. Salesmen's Commission Books 1887–1902," p. 240. *(EPFL)*
7. *AN 1925,* p. 81. *(EPFL)*
8. Mencken, "H. L. Mencken, Childhood & Schooldays 1880–1896," p. 81. *(EPFL)*
9. Mencken, "H. L. Mencken Earliest Attempts at Verse & Prose Manuscripts 1895–1901," p. 64. *(EPFL)*
10. *AN 1941. (EPFL)*
11. Mencken, "NEWSPAPER DAYS by H. L. Mencken. Additions, Corrections and Explanatory Notes," p. 1. *(EPFL)*
12. Mencken, *Newspaper Days 1899–1906* (New York: Alfred A. Knopf, 1943), p. ix.

13. Mencken, "Two Journalists," *American Mercury* (December 1924), pp. 505–6.
14. Harold A. Williams, *The Baltimore Sun 1837–1987* (Baltimore: Johns Hopkins University Press, 1987), pp. 165–66.
15. Mencken to Gordon R. Behrens, April 8, 1948. *(NYPL)*
16. Mencken, "For the Associated Press, Feb. 8, '36," in "H. L. Mencken, Miscellaneous Statements and Interviews 1924–1936," pp. 172–73. *(EPFL)*
17. Alfred A. Knopf to Betty Adler, July 19, 1971. *(EPFL)*
18. *The Reminiscences of August Mencken* (New York: Columbia University, 1958), p. 18.
19. Mencken, "Max Ways as H. L. Mencken Knew Him," Baltimore *Evening Sun,* June 5, 1923.
20. Maclean Patterson to Mencken, November 16, 1948; Mencken to Maclean Patterson, November 17, 1948. *(EPFL)*
21. Paul Patterson to Mencken, February 5, 1920. *(EPFL)*
22. Quotations from Mencken, "The Reporter at Work," *American Mercury,* (August 1924), p. 509.
23. Mencken, *A Book of Prefaces* (New York: Alfred A. Knopf, 1924), p. 85.
24. Mencken to Hamilton Owens, June 7, 1930. *(EPFL)*
25. Mencken to Eddie Murphy, August 31, 1938. *(EPFL)*
26. Mencken, "San Francisco: A Memory," Baltimore *Evening Sun,* July 21, 1920; "Appalachia," Baltimore *Evening Sun,* August 8, 1927; "Reconnaissance to the Northward," Baltimore *Evening Sun,* September 8, 1930.
27. Mencken, "Gamalielese," Baltimore *Evening Sun,* March 7, 1921.
28. *AN 1941. (EPFL)*
29. William Zinssner, "That Perleman of Great Price at 65," New York *Times Magazine,* January 26, 1969.
30. Mencken to Folger McKinsey, August 24, 1938. *(EPFL)*
31. Mencken to Hamilton Owens, August 24, 1938 *(EPFL);* Mencken to Maclean Patterson, September 22, 1938. *(EPFL)*
32. Mencken to Paul Patterson, November 19, 1935. *(EPFL)*
33. "Preface," *Style Book: The Sunpapers of Baltimore,* in "Miscellaneous Type-scripts, Carbons and Clippings 1941–1945 H. L. Mencken," p. 94. *(EPFL)*
34. Mencken to William Manchester, November 17, 1948; *AN 1925,* p. 200. *(EPFL)*
35. Mencken, "H. L. Mencken, Dispatches to the Baltimore Sun from the Republican and Democratic National Conventions, June 1936," p. 2. *(EPFL)*
36. Mencken to John Owens, August 19, 1940. *(EPFL)*
37. *London Spectator,* July 30, 1948.
38. Mencken to Samuel C. Blythe, November 7, 1942. *(NYPL);* "H. L. Mencken Speaking," (New York: Caedmon Records, 1957).
39. Charles A. Fecher, "Preface," *Mencken: A Study of His Thought* (New York: Alfred A. Knopf, 1978), p. xx.
40. "Mencken's Prejudices Didn't Reflect Baltimore," Letters Column, *New York Times,* December 31, 1989; interviews with the author.
41. Mencken, *Menckeniana: A Schimpflexikon* (New York: Alfred A. Knopf, 1928), p. 123; Walter Lippmann, *H. L. Mencken: Reprinted from the Saturday Review of*

Literature December 11, 1926 (New York: Alfred A. Knopf, 1926), p. 1; *Sherwood Anderson, Selected Letters,* Charles E. Modlin, editor (Knoxville: University of Tennessee Press, 1984), p. 72.

42. Gerald Johnson, "How Things Look from Bolton Street," Viewpoint-WAAM, Broadcast August 15, 1952. *(EPFL)*

43. *AN 1925,* p. 132 *(EPFL);* Mencken, "Books and Authors Luncheon at the Hotel Astor, New York, April 7, 1942"; "Miscellaneous Typescripts, Carbons, and Clippings 1941–1945, H. L. Mencken," pp. 8 –10 *(EPFL);* Mencken, "H. L. Mencken Articles Written for the Chicago *Tribune* and Its Associated Newspapers Carbons 1924 –1928, Vol. I" *(EPFL);* William Manchester, *Disturber of the Peace* (New York: Harper & Brothers Publishers, 1951), p. 105; Mencken, "Notes and Corrections to *Happy Days,*" p. 3. *(EPFL)*

44. *AN 1925,* p. 165.

45. *AN 1925,* p. 168.

46. *Los Angeles Negro Paper,* November 5, 1926.

47. Arthur Schlesinger, "Letters to the Editor," *New Republic* (December 16, 1957); "Mencken Assails Lynching in State," Baltimore *Sun,* February 15, 1935.

48. G. B. Murphy to Mencken, September 24, 1935. *(EPFL)*

49. Clarence Mitchell III to author, February 23, 1987.

50. Mencken to John Owens, July 12, 1939. *(EPFL)*

51. Mencken to Hamilton Owens, January 13, 1939: "Echoes of it reach me almost weekly. I am thoroughly convinced that the human race will go on believing it." It has. *(EPFL)*

52. *AN 1925,* p. 168. *(EPFL)*

53. "H. L. Mencken Rides Again," *Editor and Publisher* (September 10, 1938).

54. L. C. Quinn, Senior Publisher, Crisfield *Times* to the *Sunpapers,* December 9, 1931. *(EPFL);* Easton *Journal* to the *Sunpapers,* December 17, 1931. *(EPFL)*

55. Richard Delmar of Delaware to the *Sunpapers,* December 12, 1931. *(EPFL)*

56. Mencken, "Al in the Free State," Baltimore *Evening Sun,* October 29, 1928.

57. Malcolm Moos, "Mencken, Politics, and Politicians," *On Mencken,* John Dorsey, editor (New York: Alfred A. Knopf, 1980), p. 151.

58. Mencken to Hamilton Owens, February 18, 1925. *(EPFL)*

59. Mencken to Paul Patterson, May 9, 1935. *(EPFL)*

60. Alistair Cooke, "Mencken and the English Language," *On Mencken,* p. 110.

61. Mencken, "Mencken Says Grateful Hoover Ought to Make Vare Secretary of State," Baltimore *Evening Sun,* June 13, 1928; Mencken, "Air of Deceit and Fraud Pervades Whole GOP Meeting, Says Mencken," Baltimore *Evening Sun,* June 12, 1928.

62. Mencken, "Scene Set, Foes Arriving for Democracy's Usual Warfare, Says Mencken," Baltimore *Evening Sun,* June 23, 1928.

63. Doug Trussel to author, February 29, 1988.

64. Mencken, "Mencken Says Grateful Hoover . . . ," Baltimore *Evening Sun,* June 13, 1928.

65. "H. L. Mencken Speaking," Caedmon Records.

66. Mencken, "Drys Emerge in Defeat, Says Mencken; Plank a 'Hollow Compromise,'" Baltimore *Evening Sun*, June 29, 1928.
67. Mencken, "Drys Out in Cold in Platform, Mencken Declares," Baltimore *Evening Sun*, June 16, 1932.
68. Quotations from Washington *Times*, February 25, 1938; Charleston *Courier*, February 15, 1938; Chattanooga *News*, February 17, 1938.
69. Ronald Steel, *Walter Lippmann and the American Century* (Boston: Little, Brown & Company, 1980), p. 319.
70. Peter Kurth, *American Cassandra: The Life of Dorothy Thompson* (Boston: Little, Brown & Company, 1990), p. 224.
71. Mencken to August Mencken, undated, "Friday Night, Chicago, 1940." *(EPFL)*
72. Mencken, "The Days Ahead," Baltimore *Sun*, August 25, 1940.
73. Mencken, "Associated Press Luncheon, New York, April 20, 1936," "H. L. Mencken: Miscellaneous Speeches 1913–38," pp. 48–53. *(EPFL)*
74. William E. Leuchtenburg, "Why Candidates Still Use FDR as Their Measure," *American Heritage Magazine* (February 1988), pp. 36–37; "The First Media President," Washington *Post*, January 31, 1982.
75. Leuchtenburg, p. 37.
76. Mencken, "Speech, Society of Newspaper Editors, Washington, D.C., April 20, 1939"; "H. L. Mencken: Typescripts and Carbons of Miscellaneous Articles Vol. I, 1939," p. 135. *(EPFL)*
77. Mencken to Paul Patterson, undated, "January 1937." *(EPFL)*
78. Mencken, *H. L. Mencken Diary 1942*, October 1, 1942. *(EPFL)*
79. *Ibid.*
80. Mencken to J. Edwin Murphy, February 14, 1941. *(EPFL)*
81. Mencken to Donald Patterson, March 1, 1940. *(EPFL)*
82. *Editor and Publisher* (September 10, 1938).
83. *Ibid.*
84. Byron Price, Director of the Office of Censorship, Washington, D.C., to H. L. Mencken, June 26, 1944. *(NYPL)*
85. *AN 1941. (EPFL)*
86. Mencken, "H. L. Mencken Dispatches to the Baltimore Sun from the Republican and Democratic National Conventions, June 1936," p. 2. *(EPFL)*
87. Mencken, *H. L. Mencken Diary 1944–1945*, March 20, 1945. *(EPFL)*
88. Mencken to Gerald Johnson, March 5, 1945 *(EPFL)*; Mencken, *H. L. Mencken Diary 1944–1945*, August 23, 1945. *(EPFL)*
89. Mencken to Maclean Patterson, April 14, 1948. *(EPFL)*
90. Mencken to Joseph Hergesheimer, undated, 1948. *(EPFL)*
91. *AN 1925*, p. 97. *(EPFL)*
92. *Menckeniana* (Spring 1970), p. 4.

Throughout my brief introductions preceding Mencken's reports from the Republican and Democratic National Conventions, the Scopes Trial, and the Pan American Conference, I have drawn upon various sources, including: George Black, *The Good Neighbor* (New York: Pantheon Books, 1988); Paul F. Boller, *Presidential Campaigns* (New York: Oxford University Press, 1984); Joseph Nathan Kane, *Facts About the Presidents 4th ed.* (New York: H. W. Wilson Company, 1981); Stefan Lorant, *The Glorious Burden: The American Presidency* (New York: Harper & Row, 1968); H. L. Mencken, *The Diary of H. L. Mencken,* Charles A. Fecher, editor (New York: Alfred A. Knopf, 1989); *H. L. Mencken: A Carnival of Buncombe,* Malcolm Moos, editor (Baltimore: Johns Hopkins Press, 1956); *Mencken and Sara: A Life in Letters,* Marion Elizabeth Rodgers, editor (New York: McGraw-Hill, 1987); H. L. Mencken, *Heathen Days: 1890–1936* (New York: Alfred A. Knopf, 1943); H. L. Mencken, *Making a President: A Footnote to the Saga of Democracy* (New York: Alfred A. Knopf, 1932); *Time* magazine (April 17, 1933); Geoffrey C. Ward, *A First-Class Temperament: The Emergence of Franklin Roosevelt* (New York: Harper & Row, 1989); Mencken's dispatches to the *Sunpapers;* as well as various letters and notes written by and about H. L. Mencken and deposited at the Enoch Pratt Free Library, Baltimore.

Index